W9-BBM-102

SECOND EDITION

INTRODUCTION TO GOVERNMENTAL AND NOT-FOR-PROFIT ACCOUNTING

Joseph R. Razek
University of New Orleans

Gordon A. Hosch
University of New Orleans

PRENTICE HALL, Englewood Cliffs, NJ 07632

Library of Congress Cataloging-in-Publication Data

Razek, Joseph R.
    Introduction to governmental and not-for-profit acounting / Joseph
R. Razek, Gordon A. Hosch.
      p.   cm.
    Includes bibliographical references.
    ISBN 0-13-484718-0
    1. Fund acccounting.   2. Finance, Public--Accounting.
3. Corporations, Nonprofit--Accounting.   I. Horch, Gordon, A.,
1941-   . II. Title.
HF5681.F84R39   1990
657'.835--dc20   90-30455
                                                          CIP

To our families . . .

Cordelia, Erica, Margaret, and Eleanor Razek
Kathy, Paige, Keith, and Kyle Hosch

Material from Uniform CPA examination questions and unofficial answers, copyright © 1954, 1964, 1967, 1968, 1970, 1971, 1972, 1974, 1975, 1976, 1977, 1978, 1979, 1980, 1981, 1982, 1983, 1984, 1985, 1986, 1987, 1988 by the American Institute of Certified Public Accountants, Inc., is reprinted (or adapted) with permission.

This book contains material from various GASB pronouncements. Copyright © by Governmental Accounting Standards Board, 401 Merritt 7, P.O. Box 5116, Norwalk, CT 06856-5116, U.S.A. Reprinted with permission. Copies of complete documents are available from the FASB.

This book contains material from various FASB pronouncements. Copyright © by Financial Accounting Standards Board, 401 Merritt 7, P.O. Box 5116, Norwalk, CT 06856-5116, U.S.A. Reprinted with permission. Copies of complete documents are available from the FASB.

This book contains material copyright © 1949, 1955, 1970, 1973, 1974, 1978, 1980, 1981, 1985, 1987, 1988 by the American Institute of Certified Public Accountants.

Editorial/production supervision and interior design: Maureen Wilson
Cover design: Lundgren Graphics Ltd.
Manufacturing buyer: Peter Havens

 © 1990 by Prentice-Hall, Inc.
A Division of Simon & Schuster
Englewood Cliffs, New Jersey 07632

Printed in the United States of America
10 9 8 7 6 5 4 3 2

ISBN 0-13-484718-0

Prentice-Hall International (UK) Limited, *London*
Prentice-Hall of Australia Pty. Limited, *Sydney*
Prentice-Hall Canada Inc., *Toronto*
Prentice-Hall Hispanoamericana, S.A., *Mexico*
Prentice-Hall of India Private Limited, *New Delhi*
Prentice-Hall of Japan, Inc., *Tokyo*
Simon & Schuster Asia Pte. Ltd., *Singapore*
Editora Prentice-Hall do Brasil, Ltda., *Rio de Janeiro*

CONTENTS

2

3

THE USE OF FUNDS IN GOVERNMENTAL ACCOUNTING   51

4

4

THE GOVERNMENTAL FUND ACCOUNTING CYCLE:
General and Special Revenue Funds—An Introduction   105

5-**5**

THE GOVERNMENTAL FUND ACCOUNTING CYCLE:
General and Special Revenue Funds—Special Problems   141

6-**6**

THE GOVERNMENTAL FUND ACCOUNTING CYCLE:
Capital Projects Funds, Account Groups, and Debt Service Funds   193

8- **7**

THE GOVERNMENTAL FUND ACCOUNTING CYCLE:
Special Assessment-Type Funds and Some Fiduciary-Type Funds   236

7- **8**

THE GOVERNMENTAL FUND ACCOUNTING CYCLE:
Proprietary-Type Funds and Some Fiduciary-Type Funds   275

9- **9**

THE GOVERNMENTAL FUND ACCOUNTING CYCLE:
The Comprehensive Annual Financial Report and Current Issues   325

13
ACCOUNTING FOR HOSPITALS   488

14
ACCOUNTING FOR VOLUNTARY HEALTH AND WELFARE AND OTHER NOT-FOR-PROFIT ORGANIZATIONS   526

PREFACE

This is a basic-level textbook on fund accounting. While the emphasis is on governmental units, other not-for-profit organizations are covered in some depth.

The text is organized and structured in a manner that permits its use by a number of different types of readers. For example, people interested exclusively in governmental units can skip the chapters on universities, hospitals, and other not-for-profit organizations. Those interested only in accounting and reporting for hospitals can skip the chapters on governmental units and other not-for-profit organizations, etc. We have also included an independent chapter on the fundamentals of bookkeeping for the benefit of those who have had no previous training in the basic accounting cycle.

Consistent with the focus on flexibility, this text can be used by people who want to emphasize the accumulation and reporting of financial information; they can answer the questions and work the exercises and problems at the end of each chapter. Those who are interested in a more conceptual approach (e.g., people in public administration classes) can avoid the presentation of detailed journal entries and financial statements by concentrating on the questions and exercises.

To make this text even more flexible, we have divided most of the chapters into independent sections which can be covered as separate units. Thus a section or two may be assigned for a particular class meeting, while an entire chapter may be assigned for another meeting.

This text can be used by six major groups because of its built-in flexibility:

1. Nonaccounting majors (e.g., students in public administration programs) who want a basic understanding of fund accounting.

2. Accounting majors who wish to learn the fundamentals of fund accounting in less than a full semester.
3. Accounting majors who want a full semester or quarter course on fund accounting. This text provides an excellent basis for discussions which can be expanded by using the suggested references.
4. People employed by governmental and not-for-profit organizations.
5. People preparing for Civil Service Examinations.
6. People preparing for the Certified Public Accountant (CPA) Examination.

In order to facilitate the transition into interfund accounting we have included, in Chapter 3, a conceptual preview of the individual fund financial statements. This preview permits a full discussion, throughout the text, of transactions which affect several funds.

NEW FEATURES IN THIS EDITION

We have increased coverage of several key areas in this edition. Many new problems and exercises were added to increase the flexibility of the use of this text. Several of these new problems include CPA exam questions. In addition, each chapter now contains learning objectives that provide an outline of the major topics discussed.

Chapter 1 has been rewritten to include new developments since the first edition. Throughout the text, we have also added materials on the major new GASB pronouncements issued since publication of the first edition. Special assessment fund accounting has been updated in Chapters 3 and 7. For those who are interested, we have included the "old" special assessment accounting procedures in an appendix.

In Chapter 9, we have added a section on the accounting entity, together with case study-type exercises and problems. We have also included a discussion of the single audit in Chapter 9, together with an overview of the measurement focus/basis of the accounting issue and its possible effect on governmental accounting. Chapter 9 also includes a discussion of interim financial reporting for governmental units.

The Cash Flow Exposure Draft issued by GASB has been used as a basis for illustrations which involve proprietary-type reporting. In addition, several sections have been rewritten using additional information obtained from reviewers and students. Based on comments by users, we revised the sections involving budgetary accounts, using a more popular format, and coverage of the depreciation issue has been expanded and also includes the current position of the GASB.

The materials on budgeting were expanded to permit students to follow a complete set of illustrations to prepare a budget for a governmental unit. The problems in this chapter also form a case (Bacchus City), permitting students to prepare a complete budget using individual problem materials. These problems can easily be adapted for a computerized project with additional data and "what-ifs" available to adopters.

Finally, we have reorganized coverage of some materials to bring together Capital Projects Funds, Debt Service Funds, and the account groups.

As in the first edition, this text includes actual financial statements issued by governmental units. We have, however, changed the governmental units illustrated. The use of actual financial statements adds an element of "real world" applications to the text.

ACKNOWLEDGMENTS

We would like to express our most sincere appreciation to the many students, faculty members, and members of the professional community who have reviewed this text and offered suggestions for improvement. We would also like to offer special thanks to the following people for their contributions to this endeavor:

Professor Robert J. Freeman, Texas Tech University
Professor Jacob M. Fried, Jr., University of New Orleans
Mr. Jim Bourgeois, City of New Orleans, Louisiana
Mr. Hugh J. Dorrian, City of Columbus, Ohio
Mr. Martin Ives, Governmental Accounting Standards Board
Mr. William Hoffman, Peat, Marwick, Main
Mr. Anthony P. Lorino, Deloitte & Touche
Mr. Paul C. Mitchell, Jr., City of New Orleans, Louisiana
Mr. William Brown, City of Baltimore, Maryland

We would also like to express our gratitude to the people at Prentice Hall who contributed greatly to this project.

In addition, we want to thank our office personnel, Marilyn F. Schiro, Lee C. Brady, and Eddie Schiro, for assistance in the preparation of the text and Josephine M. Razek and Kathy L. Hosch for proofreading the text.

Finally, our thanks go to Mr. Bobby Major of New Orleans and Dr. Jewel L. Prestage of Southern University in Baton Rouge for their support of the training programs which provided the original impetus for this text.

1

INTRODUCTION TO ACCOUNTING FOR NONBUSINESS ORGANIZATIONS

The accounting and reporting of economic events have evolved from their earliest form, writing on cave walls, to the present state of maintaining complex financial records and preparing sophisticated financial reports. Over this period of time, some of the changes have been revolutionary. Most, however, can best be described as evolutionary. Until recently there was not much interest in the accounting and reporting procedures used by governmental or other not-for-profit organizations. However, with the financial "crunch" encountered by some major cities in recent years, governmental accounting and reporting have become extremely important. In the not-for-profit field, the emergence of third-party insurers in the health-care field in the 1940s and the rapidly increasing inflation of the 1970s have created a great deal of interest in and attention upon the accounting and reporting problems of these organizations.

Another reason for the greater interest in the accounting and reporting problems of governmental and not-for-profit organizations is the growing realization that the financial reports of these organizations are a means by which the parties interested in them can evaluate their performance. Financial reports are often an important communication vehicle between these organizations and their constituents.

To simplify the terminology found in this text, we will use the term **nonbusiness organizations** to refer to both governmental units and not-for-profit organizations. This term was first used by the Financial Accounting Standards Board (FASB)[1] and is prevalent in the accounting literature.

---

[1]The FASB is the accounting rule-setting body of business and not-for-profit organizations.

Nonbusiness organizations have the following distinguishing characteristics:

1. Receipts of significant amounts of resources from resource providers who do not expect to receive either repayment or economic benefits proportionate to resources provided
2. Operating purposes other than to provide goods or services at a profit or profit equivalent
3. Absence of defined ownership interests that can be sold, transferred, or redeemed, or that convey entitlement to a share of a residual distribution of resources in the event of liquidation of the organization.[2]

WHAT IS ACCOUNTING?

Accounting has been defined as "the art of recording, classifying, and summarizing, in a significant manner and in terms of money, transactions and events which are, in part at least, of a financial character, and interpreting the results thereof."[3] Note the use of the word "art." Accounting is an art in that, while it follows a specified set of rules, the final decisions as to what methods and procedures to use and how to present financial information are still up to the accountant. This, of course, is analogous to the artist who, while following specified rules of color and perspective, still dictates the final product.

Another approach to defining accounting is the **trained observer approach.**[4] Under this approach, the accountant is perceived as a trained observer who observes economic events (transactions) and reports on them. The receivers of the reports, the decision makers, then take actions that create new events—which are observed and reported on by the accountant, and so forth.

In short, accounting is a process of communicating financial information. To be effective, the accountant must communicate this information in a manner that is both *useful* and *understandable* to the user.

USERS OF ACCOUNTING INFORMATION

Generally speaking, users of the accounting information of nonbusiness organizations fall into one of two categories: external or internal. **External users** are those persons or organizations who are *not* directly involved in the operations of the reporting entity. Among these users are:

1. The *federal government*—to evaluate the use of the proceeds of grants and to gather statistical information

[2]*Statement of Financial Accounting Concepts No. 4—Objectives of Financial Reporting by Nonbusiness Organizations* (Stamford, Conn.: Financial Accounting Standards Board, 1980), para. 6.

[3]AICPA, *Accounting Terminology Bulletin No. 2.*

[4]For a more complete discussion of this approach, see Norton M. Bedford and Vahe Baladouni, "A Communication Theory Approach to Accountancy," *Accounting Review* (October 1962), pp. 650–59.

2. *Bond-rating services*—to evaluate the creditworthiness of organizations issuing debt
3. The *electorate*—to evaluate the performance of elected officials; information is communicated to these persons primarily through the news media
4. *State legislative committees*—to oversee the operations of the various political subdivisions within the state
5. *Potential investors*—to determine the stability of the tax base

Internal users are those persons or groups of persons who are *directly* involved in the operations of the reporting entity. Among these users are:

1. *Program monitors*—to evaluate the activities of the programs
2. The *chief administrative officer*—to evaluate the financial operations and the effectiveness of the operating personnel of the organization
3. *Department heads*—to evaluate the performance of subordinates
4. The *mayor* and the *city council*—to determine the financial condition of the city and the need for additional resources
5. *Internal auditors*—to evaluate the effectiveness of financial and operating controls

GENERALLY ACCEPTED ACCOUNTING PRINCIPLES (GAAP)

The term **generally accepted accounting principles (GAAP)** has been defined as

> . . . the consensus at a particular time as to which economic resources and obligations should be recorded as assets and liabilities by financial accounting, which changes in assets and liabilities should be recorded, when these changes should be recorded, how the assets and liabilities and changes in them should be measured, what information should be disclosed and how it should be disclosed, and which financial statements should be prepared.
> Generally accepted accounting principles encompass the conventions, rules, and procedures necessary to define accepted accounting practice at a particular time. The standard of "generally accepted accounting principles" includes not only broad guidelines of general application, but also detailed practices and procedures.[5]

Before embarking on a study of the methods and procedures used by accountants, certain basic underlying concepts should be considered.

THE ENTITY CONCEPT

The reporting unit is a specific, identifiable **entity**. In commercial (business) organizations the reporting unit is *one* entity, no matter how large. For example, General Motors is actually a series of separate, but related, companies (ac-

---

[5]*Statement No. 4*, "Basic Concepts and Accounting Principles Underlying Financial Statements of Business Enterprises" (New York: AICPA, 1970), paras. 137 and 138.

counting subentities) located throughout the world. For reporting purposes, however, it is one company. The parent company and its subsidiaries are consolidated into one reporting unit.

In nonbusiness organizations the organization as a whole is considered to be the *basic* reporting entity, just as in business enterprises. However, each fund (or fund type) is *separately* identified on the organization's financial statements.[6] The funds are not consolidated into one set of data. Thus, if a nonbusiness organization uses a dozen different funds, it is really a dozen different accounting and reporting subentities.

PLANNING AND CONTROL

Planning is the act of determining the amount of and type of resources to be received and expended by the organization during a given period. Another name for planning is *budgeting*. **Control** is the act of determining whether the resources received and expended are done so in accordance with the budget.

THE MATCHING CONCEPT

The term **matching concept** denotes the fact that revenues are matched or compared with expenses (or expenditures). Business firms match revenues with expenses in order to determine their income for a period of time. Nonbusiness organizations match revenues with expenditures (or expenses) in order to determine the changes that take place in their fund balances over a period of time. In addition, they compare their actual revenues and expenditures (or expenses) with their budgetary authorizations in order to determine compliance with the budget. Governmental accounting generally emphasizes the inflows, outflows, and balances of expendable resources rather than the determination of revenues, expenses, and income.

CONSISTENCY

The term **consistency** denotes the treatment of like transactions in the same manner during consecutive periods so that the financial statements will be comparable. Procedures, once adopted, should be followed from period to period by the reporting entity.

PERIODICITY

The term **periodicity** denotes the practice of preparing financial reports that cover a defined period of time rather than the life of the reporting entity. The

---

[6]A **fund**, by definition, is an independent fiscal and accounting entity.

period used is generally one year, although quarterly and monthly reports (and sometimes daily and hourly reports) are common in certain instances.

ESTABLISHING GENERALLY ACCEPTED ACCOUNTING PRINCIPLES

As previously mentioned, generally accepted accounting principles are a consensus of acceptable concepts, practices, and so forth, in effect at a certain point in time. The determination of the acceptability of these concepts, practices, and so forth, for governmental-type organizations is made by the Governmental Accounting Standards Board (GASB). The GASB is a five-member board established in 1984 ". . . to promulgate standards of financial accounting and reporting with respect to activities and transactions of state and local governmental entities. The GASB is the successor organization to the National Council on Governmental Accounting (NCGA)."[7] Members of the GASB are appointed by the Financial Accounting Foundation (FAF). The members of the FAF are appointed by the American Institute of Certified Public Accountants (AICPA) and other accounting-related organizations.

Determination of the acceptability of accounting principles for business organizations is determined by the Financial Accounting Standards Board (FASB). The FASB is a seven-member board appointed by the Board of Trustees of the FAF. Both the GASB and the FASB have an advisory council that provides guidance in the standards-setting process. The GASB-FASB structure is shown in Figure 1–1.

In 1984 a jurisdictional agreement was approved by both the GASB and the FASB. This agreement provides for a separation of jurisdiction that makes GASB responsible for all financial accounting and reporting for governmental and government-related organizations. The FASB, on the other hand, is responsible for all other organizations. In summary, this means that if a question arises with respect to an accounting or reporting problem, a governmental organization would first look toward the GASB for a pronouncement. In the absence of such a pronouncement, any relevant FASB pronouncement would be followed.

FIGURE 1–1   Relationship between the FASB, GASB, and FAF

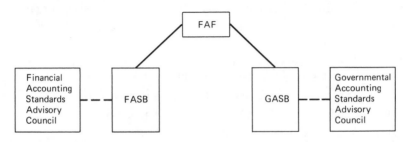

[7]GASB Codification, "Introduction," *Governmental Accounting and Financial Reporting Standards*, p. xi, as of June 15, 1987.

Not-for-profit organizations not related to a governmental unit would follow the same process, but in reverse. Such an organization would first look toward the FASB for a pronouncement on a financial accounting or reporting issue; in the absence of such a pronouncement, any relevant GASB pronouncement would be followed.

If we look closely at the GASB-FASB agreement, a serious "turf" question emerges. What would happen, for example, if the GASB developed a rule for government-owned universities and the FASB developed a different rule, for the same situation, for private universities?

This situation has actually developed. The FASB has recommended depreciation for plant and equipment-type assets, while the GASB has recommended that its constituents not adopt the FASB rule until the question can be studied in more depth. Other potential disagreements exist in the areas of pension accounting. At the time of this writing, efforts are being made to solve this jurisdictional dispute. Hopefully, by the time you read this chapter, an acceptable solution will have been found.

In addition, the GASB is currently undergoing a five-year "sunset" review. The FAF has established a task force to study the existence of two standard-setting bodies and the relationship between them. At the present time, the task force is gathering information. Hopefully, this issue will also have been resolved by the time you read this chapter.

Throughout this text references are made to various industry audit guides. These guides are issued by the AICPA. Although primarily designed for auditors, these publications discuss some of the accounting procedures that are applicable to specific nonbusiness organizations—e.g., governmental units, hospitals, colleges and universities, and so forth. The specific sources of GAAP for nonbusiness organizations that are not governmental units will be discussed in the chapters relating to these organizations.

REVIEW QUESTIONS

Q1–1   What does the term *accounting* mean?

Q1–2   Distinguish between a *commercial* and a *nonbusiness* organization.

Q1–3   What is the function of the Financial Accounting Standards Board (FASB)?

Q1–4   List six users of accounting information for nonbusiness organizations and describe the manner in which these people use this information.

Q1–5   What are *generally accepted accounting principles*?

Q1–6   What is the NCGA? The AICPA? The GASB?

Q1–7   What is the *entity concept*? The *matching concept*?

Q1–8   Distinguish between *planning* and *control*.

Q1–9   What do the terms *consistency* and *periodicity* mean to the accountant?

Q1–10   Briefly describe the standard-setting relationship that exists between the FASB and the GASB.

EXERCISES

E1–1   (Identifying basic accounting concepts)

Five basic accounting concepts were discussed in this chapter. Which concept is illustrated in each of the following situations?

1.   Although its jurisdiction is within the limits of a given city and it performs certain functions that are similar to those of the city (e.g., police patrols on certain streets), the Levee Board of this city maintains separate records and prepares an independent set of financial statements.

2.   Before the financial statements of an organization are prepared, the revenues of the period are compared with the expenditures of the period to determine if the organization's fund balance has increased or decreased.

3.   Before the start of a fiscal year, the city of Jewett prepares a budget. At the end of each month of the fiscal year, a report is prepared for each manager comparing the actual expenditures of his or her department with the budgeted expenditures of the period.

4.   Although several different methods of determining the value of its inventories are considered proper, Charity Hospital uses the same method year after year.

5.   Although it has been in existence for over two hundred years and will probably be in existence one hundred years from now, Episcopal Academy prepares financial reports every year.

E1–2   (Discussion of the need for a GASB)

Prior to the establishment of the GASB, the FASB wanted to have the authority to establish GAAP for governmental units. Do you think GAAP for governmental units should be established by the same body that is concerned with GAAP for nongovernmental organizations? Why?

E1–3   (Discussion of the GASB's operations with a local governmental official)

The establishment of the Governmental Accounting Standards Board is supposed to solve the major weaknesses of the National Council on Governmental Accounting in the standard-setting area. Contact a local governmental official familiar with the accounting standard-setting procedure and discuss the GASB's success or lack of success.

E1–4   (Opinion regarding the standard-setting process of the accounting profession)

As an individual with little or no practical accounting experience, what is *your* opinion of the standard-setting process used by the accounting profession?

2

FUNDAMENTALS
OF BOOKKEEPING

LEARNING OBJECTIVES

After completion of this chapter, you should be able to:

√ 1.   Define and distinguish between assets, liabilities, and capital
√ 2.   Explain the logic of the accounting equation
√ 3.   Explain the relationship between revenues and capital
√ 4.   Explain the relationship between expenses and capital
5.   State the rules of debit and credit for assets, liabilities, capital, revenues, and expenses
6.   Prepare an income statement, statement of changes in owner's capital, and a balance sheet
7.   Record transactions in a general journal
8.   Post transactions from a general journal to a general ledger
9.   Prepare adjusting and closing journal entries
10.   Identify and explain the steps in the accounting cycle

SECTION I—WORK SHEET ANALYSIS OF TRANSACTIONS

All organizations, whether they are designated as profit-oriented (business type) or non-profit-oriented (nonbusiness type), must keep records that reflect the acquisition and use of their resources. These resources, commonly called **assets**, represent items of value that are either owned or controlled by the organization. Common examples of assets are cash, buildings, and equipment. The operations of the organization are centered on the use of these resources for the purpose for which the organization was established.

These operations usually result in the incurrence of economic obligations called **liabilities**. An example of a typical liability is a note payable to a bank. Whenever a business borrows money, the owner or the manager usually signs a note specifying the interest rate, repayment schedule, and so forth. Another example of a liability is a debt that is owed to another organization for supplies or services that were received.

Every organization must have some form of equity or ownership interest. In a profit-oriented organization, if liabilities are claims against the organization's assets by *creditors*, the net assets (the excess of the assets over the liabilities) can be considered the *owner's* share of the assets. This equity interest of the owner is generally referred to as **capital**. Simply stated, capital refers to the assets that the owner contributes to the organization.

The Accounting Equation

The relationship between the three elements defined above can be expressed in an equation form. This equation is generally referred to as the **accounting equation** and is written

Assets = Liabilities + Capital

This equation states that the assets (resources) of the organization are equal to the sources of those assets: liabilities and capital. Since the statement is in the form of an equation, it *must always be in balance*. Therefore the dollar value of the assets must always equal the dollar value of the liabilities plus the dollar value of the capital.

✳ Recording Business Transactions

An organization encounters many different types of events in the course of its day-to-day operations. The basic accounting records are concerned only with economic events that will cause a change in one or more of the items included in the accounting equation: assets, liabilities, and capital. Therefore, when considering whether to record an event in the accounting records, it must first be determined if any of these items have changed.

While this textbook covers materials relevant to nonbusiness organizations, it is often easier to understand the basic accounting model by using a profit-oriented business as an illustrating tool. Therefore this chapter will deviate from the nonbusiness organization model in order to develop the basic recording and classifying system. This system will then be applied to nonbusiness organizations in the remainder of the text.

To establish an understanding of the items defined above, consider the operations of a computer education service that was started on January 2, 19X1, by Kyle Thomas. Mr. Thomas intends to operate his business by providing computer education classes for individuals who have purchased personal computers. Mr. Thomas will also provide these services to individuals who desire to learn more about computers.

On January 2, Mr. Thomas deposited $10,000 of his personal cash into a bank account. This cash will be used exclusively by the business. Remember that the entity concept requires that the operations of an organization be kept separate from the owner's personal financial records. Therefore we will consider only those transactions that affect the assets, liabilities, and capital of the business. This deposit causes an increase in the asset Cash. It also causes a corresponding increase in capital. This transaction is reflected in the accounting equation, as shown in Table 2–1.

TABLE 2–1

		ASSETS	=	LIABILITIES	+	CAPITAL
		Cash				K. Thomas, Capital
Owner invests cash in the business	+	$10,000 $10,000	= =	-0-	+ +	$10,000 $10,000

Two important observations about the transaction in Table 2–1 should be made:

1. The dollar amount of the items included in the transaction *must* balance in terms of the equation. That is, the net change in the assets must be equal to the net change in the liabilities plus (minus) the net change in capital.
2. The equation itself must balance after the transaction has been recorded.

On January 3, Mr. Thomas purchased ten computers. The computers cost him $30,000. He made a down payment of $3,000 and financed the remainder through the French Quarter Bank. The recording of this transaction will cause the accounting equation to expand, as shown in Table 2–2.

TABLE 2–2

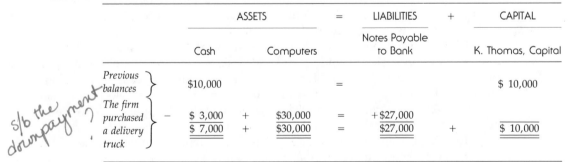

		ASSETS		=	LIABILITIES	+	CAPITAL
		Cash	Computers	=	Notes Payable to Bank		K. Thomas, Capital
Previous balances		$10,000		=			$ 10,000
The firm purchased a delivery truck	−	$ 3,000 $ 7,000	+ $30,000 + $30,000	= =	+ $27,000 $27,000	+	$ 10,000

s/b the down payment

Several observations should be made regarding this purchase:

1. The assets of the business increased by $27,000: Cash decreased by $3,000 and computers increased by $30,000.

2. The business now owes the bank $27,000. Thus a liability exists that must be reflected in the system.

3. The computers are recorded at their full cost, $30,000, even though Mr. Thomas borrowed $27,000 in order to purchase them.

In summary, the business now has assets totaling $37,000—that is, $27,000 contributed by creditors (the bank) and $10,000 contributed by the owner. Note that the acquisition of the computers did not affect the owner's capital, since he did not contribute any additional assets to the business as a result of this transaction.

A simple method of analyzing a transaction in terms of its effect on the accounting equation is to ask four questions:

1. Did any asset or assets increase or decrease?
2. Did any liability or liabilities increase or decrease?
3. Did the capital increase or decrease?
4. Does the transaction have a balanced effect on the equation?

For example, consider the acquisition of the computers:

1. The asset Cash decreased by $3,000 and the asset Computers increased by $30,000.
2. The liability Notes payable to bank increased by $27,000.
3. There was no change in capital.
4. The transaction increased assets by $27,000 and had a similar effect on total liabilities and capital. Therefore the accounting equation is still in balance.

While this type of analysis may seem cumbersome, it will be a great help when more complex transactions are encountered.

In order to have an office for the operation of the business, Mr. Thomas rented office space from the Mardi Gras Realty Company for $2,000 per month. Since the rental contract required payments at the beginning of each month, he immediately wrote a check for $2,000. Applying the four-step analysis, the transaction has the following effects on the accounting equation:

1. The asset Cash decreased by $2,000. Since the business now has "control" over the use of office space for the month of January, another asset has been acquired. This type of asset is usually called **Prepaid rent**, and it increased by $2,000. No other assets have changed as a result of this transaction.
2. Since the business does not owe any more or any less as a result of this transaction, no liabilities have changed.
3. Since the net effect of this transaction has been a decrease in one asset and an increase in another, the owner's share of the total assets did not change. Therefore there is no change in capital.
4. The transaction had a balanced effect on the accounting equation. The decrease in one asset was offset by an increase in another asset. Liabilities and capital were not affected by this transaction.

The result of the above analysis on the accounting equation is shown in Table 2–3. Note that the total of the assets ($37,000) is equal to the total of the liabilities plus the capital ($37,000).

TABLE 2–3

	ASSETS			=	LIABILITIES	+	CAPITAL
					Notes Payable to Bank		K. Thomas, Capital
	Cash	Computers	Prepaid Rent				
Previous balances	$7,000 +	$ 30,000		=	$ 27,000	+	$ 10,000
The firm paid the rent for the month	− $2,000 $5,000 +	$ 30,000	+ $2,000 + $2,000	= =	$ 27,000	+	$ 10,000

✓ At the end of January, Mr. Thomas sent bills to his students. Assume that the amount due him for services performed in January was $5,000. Applying the four-step analysis it can be determined that

1. The sending out of the bills is a formal recognition that Mr. Thomas's customers owe him $5,000 for services he rendered. As a result, he has a claim against each of them. These claims are assets because they give him the right to collect the amounts due. The title usually given to these assets is **Accounts receivable**. No other assets changed as a result of this transaction.
2. Since the business does not owe any more or any less as a result of this transaction, no liabilities have changed.
3. The result of the above analysis (steps 1 and 2) reflects an increase in assets of $5,000. Since each transaction must always have a balancing effect on the equation, and there were no changes in liabilities, there must have been an increase in capital of $5,000 (see discussion below).
4. The transaction had a balanced effect on the accounting equation: assets increased by $5,000, and liabilities + capital increased by $5,000.

The results of the above analysis on the accounting equation are shown in Table 2–4. Again note that the total of the assets ($42,000) is equal to the total of the liabilities plus the capital ($42,000).

In the above approach, we "backed into" the effect that assets generated through the profit-oriented operations of the business have on capital. The same results can be achieved by a direct analysis. A general rule can be made regarding this type of transaction.

> **Assets generated through the profit-oriented activities of a business always increase the owner's capital.**

Therefore, whenever a business increases its assets by carrying out the activities for which it was established, the owner's capital will always increase. This increase in capital is referred to as **revenue**.

TABLE 2–4

	ASSETS				=	LIABILITIES	+	CAPITAL
	Cash	Computers	Prepaid Rent	Accounts Receivable		Notes Payable to Bank		K. Thomas, Capital
Previous balances	$ 5,000 +	$ 30,000 +	$2,000		=	$ 27,000 +		$10,000
The firm billed customers				+ $ 5,000	=		+	$ 5,000
	$ 5,000 +	$ 30,000 +	$2,000 +	$ 5,000	=	$ 27,000 +		$15,000

✓

Next, assume that Mr. Thomas received a $300 utility bill for the month. Since the due date on the bill is February 10, it will not be paid until next month. The four-step analysis results in the following effects on the accounting equation:

1. Since the business does not have title to or control over any items of value that it did not have before this transaction, there are no changes in assets.
2. The business now owes money to an additional creditor. The receipt of the bill is a formal recognition of this fact. It necessitates the recording of a liability of $300. The title normally given to this account is **Accounts payable**.
3. The result of the above analysis (steps 1 and 2) reflects an increase in liabilities with no corresponding increase in assets. Since each transaction must have a balanced effect on the equation, there must have been a decrease in capital of $300 (see discussion below).
4. The transaction had a balanced effect on the accounting equation: assets did not change, and the net effect on liabilities + capital was zero ($300 - $300).

The result of the above analysis on the accounting equation is shown in Table 2–5. Again note that the total of the assets ($42,000) is equal to the total of the liabilities plus the capital ($42,000).

TABLE 2–5

	ASSETS				=	LIABILITIES		+	CAPITAL
	Cash	Computers	Prepaid Rent	Accounts Receivable		Notes Payable to Bank	Accounts Payable		K. Thomas, Capital
Previous balances	$5,000 +	$30,000 +	$2,000 +	$5,000	=	$27,000		+	$15,000
The firm received a bill for gas and oil					=		+ $300	–	$ 300
	$5,000 +	$30,000 +	$2,000 +	$5,000	=	$27,000 +	$300 +		$14,700

In the above approach, we backed into the effect that liabilities incurred in the profit-oriented operations of the business have on capital. The same results can be achieved by a direct analysis. A general rule can be made regarding this type of transaction.

Assets used in or liabilities incurred through the profit-oriented activities of a business always reduce the owner's capital.

This decrease in capital is referred to as an **expense**.

Although numerous other types of transactions could be illustrated for the operations of a business, those selected above should be sufficient to enable you to understand the process used for determining the effect of each transaction on the accounting equation.

SECTION I REVIEW EXERCISE

The following exercise should be completed by using the approach previously described. After completing a work sheet, compare it with the solution that follows so that you can determine how well you understand the concepts involved.

In this exercise, assume that Ms. Paige Keith is an independent tour guide who works for several large tour companies. Her income is determined by the number of individuals on each tour she hosts. To start the business, Ms. Keith incurred the following transactions:

19X1
JUNE

1   Ms. Keith placed $5,000 cash into a bank account to be used in the operations of her business, Kaki Tours.

2   Ms. Keith signed a contract with Tel-Ans, a telephone-answering service. The service cost $50 per month, payable at the beginning of each month. Ms. Keith paid Tel-Ans $50.

4   Ms. Keith paid Print Faster $55 for stationery and the various forms she needed.

5   Ms. Keith purchased office equipment for $250. She paid $25 down and will pay the remainder in 30 days.

7   Ms. Keith purchased additional office supplies costing $125. She paid cash for these supplies.

10   Ms. Keith billed several tour companies for tours she conducted during the month. The total billing was $300.

15   Ms. Keith received $250 from companies she billed earlier that month.

18   Ms. Keith hired an assistant and agreed to pay him 25 percent of her revenue from the tours that he helped to organize.

20   Ms. Keith deposited $130 in her bank account. This amount was collected from various walking tours she conducted.

25   Ms. Keith shared an office with someone and she paid $75 for her share of the June rent (including utilities).

30   Ms. Keith billed several tour companies for a total of $400 for tours she conducted during the month.

SOLUTION TO SECTION I REVIEW EXERCISE

The solution is to be found in Table 2–6.

TABLE 2–6

		ASSETS				=	LIABILITIES	+	CAPITAL
	Cash	Accounts Receivable	Prepaid Services	Office Supplies	Office Equipment		Accounts Payable		P. Keith, Capital
19X1									
June 1	+$5,000								+$5,000
2	−$ 50		+$50						
4	−$ 55			+$ 55					
5	−$ 25				+$250		+$225		
7	−$ 125			+$125					
10		+$300							+$ 300
15	+$ 250	−$250							
18	No transaction—no assets, liabilities, or capital have changed.								
	Nothing is owed to the assistant until he completes some work.								
20	+$ 130								+$ 130
25	−$ 75								−$ 75
30		+$400							+$ 400
	$5,050	$450	$50	$180	$250		$225		$5,755
		Total Assets* = $5,980					Total Liabilities + Capital* = $5,980		

*Cumulative totals after each transaction were omitted in order to conserve space.

SECTION II—USE OF ACCOUNTS: DEBIT AND CREDIT ANALYSIS

Use of Accounts

The analysis in Section I of this chapter will supply the data necessary to reflect the acquisition, use, and disposal of the resources of any small organization. However, as the organization expands, the use of a work sheet to analyze transactions becomes too cumbersome. Consider, for example, the size of the work sheet that would be necessary to record the transactions encountered by General Motors or Shell Oil. Companies of this size will encounter thousands of transactions and have many different kinds of assets, liabilities, and so forth. Therefore a more efficient system of analysis has been developed. This system is based on the accounting equation, as was the work sheet. However, it utilizes a different form of analysis.

Rather than use columns on a work sheet, an **account** is used to accumulate the increases and decreases in assets, liabilities, and capital. Since it is much easier to accumulate changes if like items are grouped, the increases are accumulated on one side of the account and the decreases on the other. Arbitrarily, the increases (+) in assets have been accumulated on the left and the decreases

$(-)$ on the right. As a result, it is much easier and faster to calculate the balance in an account at any point in time. This produces the following situation:

$$\frac{\text{ASSETS}}{+\;|\;-}$$

Since the system is based on the accounting equation, the following relationship develops:

$$\frac{\text{ASSETS}}{+\;|\;-} = \frac{\text{LIABILITIES}}{|} + \frac{\text{CAPITAL}}{|}$$

When the account form is transferred to the right side of the equation and is used to accumulate changes in liabilities and capital, the signs must change. The increases are accumulated on the right side and the decreases on the left side. This maintains the mathematical integrity of the transaction analysis and the system:

$$\frac{\text{ASSETS}}{+\;|\;-} = \frac{\text{LIABILITIES}}{-\;|\;+} + \frac{\text{CAPITAL}}{-\;|\;+}$$

Debit and Credit Analysis

In accounting terminology the left side of an account is referred to as the **debit side** and the right side is referred to as the **credit side**. Note that the terms *debit* and *credit* refer *only to position*. Without any association with a particular account, these terms *do not* mean plus or minus. Once a particular type of account has been considered, however, the terms do refer to plus or minus. For example, when assets are considered (see the illustration above), increases are accumulated on the left, or debit, side, while decreases are accumulated on the right, or credit, side. Liabilities and capital, however, are increased or decreased in the opposite manner: debits represent decreases, while credits represent increases. These rules are summarized in Table 2–7.

To complete the system, revenues and expenses must be analyzed in terms of their debit/credit effect. At the end of each period, it is important that management study the relative size of the individual revenues and expenses incurred in operating the organization. In the previous illustrations, revenues and expenses were recorded as direct increases or decreases in capital. To make such an analysis easier, however, we will begin to accumulate the changes in each revenue and expense in a separate account. This will avoid the rather cumbersome task of sorting out the revenues and expenses after they have been combined in the capital account.

TABLE 2–7

TYPE OF ACCOUNT	INCREASES	DECREASES
Assets	Debits	Credits
Liabilities	Credits	Debits
Capital	Credits	Debits

The debit/credit analysis of revenues and expenses is based on the relationship of each to capital. Remember that revenues and expenses were defined as directly affecting the capital of a firm. Since revenues cause capital to increase, they are recorded as credits. Any reductions of revenues are recorded as debits. This is shown in the following illustration:

REVENUES	
Debits	Credits
−	+

Note the *direct* relationship with capital. Capital is increased with credits. Since revenues increase capital, *revenues* are increased with *credits*. Capital is decreased with debits. Since decreases in revenue are decreases in capital, revenues are decreased with debits.

Expenses follow the same logic. The analysis, however, is a bit more complex. **Expenses** have been defined as those decreases in capital associated with the profit-oriented activities of the business. Therefore, as expenses increase, the amount of capital decreases. A decrease in capital is recorded as a debit (see Table 2–7). Continuing with this logic, then, an increase in an expense must be recorded with a debit. This procedure reflects the decrease in capital that is taking place.

This analysis can be extended to include a decrease in an expense, which results in a credit to the expense account and reflects the increase in capital that is taking place. This is shown in the following illustration:

EXPENSES	
Debits	Credits
+	−

Table 2–8 summarizes the debit/credit rules for the types of transactions covered so far. Owner withdrawals will be considered in a later section of this chapter.

TABLE 2–8

TYPE OF ACCOUNT	INCREASES	DECREASES
Assets	Debits	Credits
Liabilities	Credits	Debits
Capital	Credits	Debits
Revenues	Credits	Debits
Expenses	Debits	Credits

Note that this system is based on the mathematical integrity of the accounting equation. As a result, the equality mentioned in Section I still exists—i.e., the accounting equation must be balanced after the result of each transaction has been recorded. In terms of debit and credit, this equality can be stated as follows:

The total number of dollars of debits for any transaction must EQUAL the total number of dollars of credits.

This is an important rule to remember because it affects the integrity of the entire accounting system.

Transaction Analysis Using Debit and Credit

The effects of a transaction can now be measured in terms of debits and credits that reflect the increases or decreases in the accounts. Following are several examples taken from the Review Exercise in Section I.[1]

TRANSACTION	ANALYSIS
June 1 Ms. Keith invested $5,000 cash into a bank account to be used in the operation of her business, Kaki Tours.	*Debit:* Cash, $5,000—to reflect the increase in this asset. *Credit:* P. Keith, Capital, $5,000—to reflect the increase in capital.
June 2 Ms. Keith signed a contract with Tel-Ans, a telephone-answering service. The service cost $50 per month, payable at the beginning of each month. Ms. Keith paid Tel-Ans $50.	*Debit:* Prepaid services, $50—to reflect the increase in this asset. *Credit:* Cash, $50—to reflect the decrease in this asset.
June 4 Ms. Keith paid Print Faster $55 for stationery and various forms she needed.	*Debit:* Office supplies, $55—to reflect the increase in this asset. *Credit:* Cash, $55—to reflect the decrease in this asset.
June 5 Ms. Keith purchased office equipment for $250. She paid $25 down and will pay the remainder in 30 days	*Debit:* Office equipment, $250—to reflect the increase in this asset. *Credit:* Cash, $25—to reflect the decrease in this asset. *Credit:* Accounts payable, $225—to reflect the increase in this liability.

SECTION II REVIEW EXERCISE

Using the information presented below, prepare an analysis of the remaining transactions of Ms. Keith's tour business similar to that presented above. Compare your results with the solution that follows.

TRANSACTION

June 7   Ms. Keith purchased additional office supplies costing $125. She paid cash for these supplies.

[1]The effects of the transactions on the individual accounts are summarized in Table 2–9.

June 10 Ms. Keith billed several tour companies for tours she conducted during the month. The total billing was $300.

June 15 Ms. Keith received $250 from companies she billed earlier that month.

June 18 Ms. Keith hired an assistant and agreed to pay him 25 percent of her revenue from the tours that he helped to organize.

June 20 Ms. Keith deposited $130 in her bank account. This amount was collected from various walking tours she conducted.

June 25 Ms. Keith shared an office with someone and she paid $75 for her share of the June rent (including utilities).

June 30 Ms. Keith billed several tour companies for a total of $400 for tours she conducted during the month.

SOLUTION TO SECTION II REVIEW EXERCISE

June 7 *Debit:* Office supplies, $125—to reflect the increase in this asset.
Credit: Cash, $125—to reflect the decrease in this asset.

June 10 *Debit:* Accounts receivable, $300—to reflect the increase in this asset.
Credit: Tour revenue, $300—to reflect the increase in capital from profit-oriented activities.

June 15 *Debit:* Cash, $250—to reflect the increase in this asset.
Credit: Accounts receivable, $250—to reflect the decrease in this asset.

June 18 No transaction: no assets, liabilities, or capital have changed. Nothing is owed to the assistant until he completes some work.

June 20 *Debit:* Cash, $130—to reflect the increase in this asset.
Credit: Tour revenue, $130—to reflect the increase in capital from profit-oriented activities.

June 25 *Debit:* Office rent expense, $75—to reflect the decrease in capital from profit-oriented activities.
Credit: Cash, $75—to reflect the decrease in this asset.

June 30 *Debit:* Accounts receivable, $400—to reflect the increase in this asset.
Credit: Tour revenue, $400—to reflect the increase in capital from profit-oriented activities.

The results of the above transactions in accounts are summarized in Table 2–9.

COMPLETION OF SECTION II EXERCISE

Table 2–9 reflects each transaction in the exercise in Section I. In order to keep the exercise short, however, several transactions were omitted. These items will now be analyzed:

1. The assistant was not paid for the services he performed. Since this amount is owed at the end of the month, the amount earned must be recorded. This entry will record the liability owed and the effect on capital of the services performed by the assistant. Assuming this amount is $40, the following entry is necessary:

Debit: Salary expense, $40—to reflect the decrease in capital from profit-oriented activities.
Credit: Salary payable, $40—to reflect the increase in liabilities.

TABLE 2–9

CASH		ACCOUNTS RECEIVABLE		PREPAID SERVICES		OFFICE SUPPLIES	
5,000	50	300	250	50		55	
250	55	400				125	
130	25						
	125	700	250			180	
	75						
		450					
5,380	330						
5,050							

OFFICE EQUIPMENT		ACCOUNTS PAYABLE		P. KEITH, CAPITAL		TOUR REVENUE	
250			225		5,000		300
							130
							400
							830

OFFICE RENT EXPENSE	
75	

2. By the end of June, the services performed by Tel-Ans for the month were "used up" and no longer had any value. The following entry, therefore, is necessary:

Debit: Telephone-answering expense, $50—to reflect the decrease in capital from profit-oriented activities.
Credit: prepaid services, $50—to reflect the decrease in this asset.

Note: To save time, most companies record entries such as the payment for answering services directly in an expense account. This eliminates the need for a second entry like the one described above. If this procedure had been followed here, the June 2 entry would have required a debit to Telephone-answering expense and a credit to Cash for $50. Notice that the effect of these two procedures on the accounting equation is the same: assets decrease and capital decreases.

3. On June 4 office supplies totaling $55 were purchased. During the month some of these supplies were used. Assuming the cost of the supplies used was $30, the following entry is necessary:

Debit: Office supplies expense, $30—to reflect the decrease in capital from profit-oriented activities.
Credit: Office supplies, $30—to reflect the decrease in this asset.

4. The final item that must be considered is the office equipment. Whenever a business purchases an asset, it is really buying a "bundle of services." As

these services are used up, an expense is recorded. (This process is explained in the preceding entry for the asset Office supplies.) The using up of the services of an asset such as Office equipment is generally referred to as **depreciation**. Since this is the using up of an asset in the profit-oriented activities of the business, it is recognized as an expense. The following entry is, therefore, necessary (assume the amount is $5):

Debit: Depreciation expense—office equipment, $5—to record the decrease in capital from profit-oriented activities.

Credit: Accumulated depreciation—office equipment, $5—to reflect the decrease in the asset. Accumulated depreciation is credited instead of the asset itself because it is important to maintain the original cost in a separate account. The Accumulated depreciation account is treated as a negative, or contra, asset—the effect is the same as crediting the Office equipment account directly (see Table 2–13).

After these transactions have been entered into the system, the accounts will appear as shown in Table 2–10.

TABLE 2–10

CASH		ACCOUNTS RECEIVABLE		PREPAID SERVICES		OFFICE SUPPLIES	
5,000	50	300	250	50	50	55	30
250	55	400				125	
130	25			-0-			
	125	700	250			180	30
	75	450				150	
5,380	330						
5,050							

OFFICE EQUIPMENT		ACCUMULATED DEPRECIATION—OFFICE EQUIPMENT		ACCOUNTS PAYABLE	
250			5		225

SALARY PAYABLE		P. KEITH, CAPITAL		TOUR REVENUE		OFFICE RENT EXPENSE	
	40		5,000		300	75	
					130		
					400		
					830		

SALARY EXPENSE		TELEPHONE-ANSWERING EXPENSE		OFFICE SUPPLIES EXPENSE		DEPRECIATION EXPENSE—OFFICE EQUIPMENT	
40		50		30		5	

SECTION III—FINANCIAL STATEMENTS

The purpose of accounting is to provide information to decision makers. Such information helps reduce the uncertainty that exists relative to the future. Data presented in the form used in Table 2–10 are not as helpful as data that are grouped into meaningful statements. The statements commonly used are (1) an activity (income) statement, (2) a statement of changes in owner's capital, (3) a balance sheet, and (4) a statement of cash flows.

An activity statement compares the revenues earned with the expenses incurred in earning those revenues, and it reports the resulting net income or net loss. For a profit-oriented organization, this statement is called an **income statement**. An income statement for Ms. Keith's business—Kaki Tours—is shown in Table 2–11.

TABLE 2–11

Kaki Tours
Income Statement
For the Month Ended June 30, 19X1

Revenue		
Tour revenue		$830
Expenses		
Office rent expense	$75	
Salary expense	40	
Telephone-answering expense	50	
Office supplies expense	30	
Depreciation expense—office equipment	5	200
Net Income		$630

The **statement of changes in owner's capital** provides a reconciliation of the beginning and ending owner's capital balance. Items that increase owner's capital include the investments by the owner and net income for the period. Items that decrease the balance are owner's withdrawals and net losses. Owner's withdrawals are covered later in this chapter. A statement of changes in owner's capital is shown in Table 2–12.

TABLE 2–12

Kaki Tours
Statement of Changes in Owner's Capital
For the Month Ended June 30, 19X1

P. Keith, Capital, June 1, 19X1	$ -0-
Investment during June	5,000
Income for June	630
P. Keith, Capital, June 30, 19X1	$5,630

The final statement that will be illustrated is the **balance sheet**. This statement reflects the balances of the asset, liability, and capital accounts at the end of the period (see Table 2–13).

TABLE 2–13

Kaki Tours
Balance Sheet
June 30, 19X1

ASSETS

Cash		$5,050
Accounts receivable		450
Office supplies		150
Office equipment	$250	
Less: Accumulated depreciation	5	245
Total assets		$5,895

LIABILITIES AND CAPITAL

Liabilities		
Accounts payable	225	$225
Salary payable	40	40
Total liabilities		$ 265
Capital		
P. Keith, Capital		5,630
Total liabilities and capital		$5,895

An understanding of the accounting system requires an understanding of the relationship between the financial statements. Note how the net income for the period is taken from the income statement and is used to determine the ending balance in the owner's capital account. Note also how the ending balance in the owner's capital account is used to balance the balance sheet.

A **statement of cash flows** should also be prepared for a business, but a discussion of its preparation is beyond the scope of this text.

SECTION III REVIEW EXERCISE

Using the information presented below, prepare an income statement, a statement of changes in owner's capital, and a balance sheet for the Star Company. Compare your statements with the solution that follows. Assume that the business was started on August 1, 19X1, and that the account balances given are as of August 31, 19X1.

| | BALANCE | |
	Debit	Credit
Cash	$20,000	
Accounts receivable	8,000	
Office supplies	4,000	
Delivery equipment	20,000	
Accumulated depreciation—delivery equip ment		$ 400
Accounts payable		4,000
Notes payable to bank		19,600
Interest payable		1,000
F. T. Tillis, Capital		18,000
Service revenue		16,000
Oil and gas expense	4,000	
Salaries expense	1,500	
Interest expense	600	
Depreciation expense—delivery equipment	400	
Miscellaneous expenses	500	
	$59,000	$59,000

SOLUTION TO SECTION III REVIEW EXERCISE

Star Company
Income Statement
For the Month Ended August 31, 19X1

Revenue		
Service revenue		$16,000
Expenses		
Oil and gas expense	$4,000	
Salaries expense	1,500	
Interest expense	600	
Depreciation expense—delivery equipment	400	
Miscellaneous expenses	500	7,000
Net Income		$ 9,000

Star Company
Statement of Changes in Owner's Capital
For the Month Ended August 31, 19X1

F. T. Tillis, Capital, August 1, 19X1	$ -0-
Investment during August	18,000
Income for August	9,000
F. T. Tillis, Capital, August 31, 19X1	$27,000

Star Company
Balance Sheet
August 31, 19X1

ASSETS

Cash		$20,000
Accounts receivable		8,000
Office supplies		4,000
Delivery equipment	$20,000	
Less: Accumulated depreciation—delivery equipment	400	19,600
Total assets		$51,600

LIABILITIES AND CAPITAL

Liabilities

Accounts payable	$ 4,000
Notes payable to bank	19,600
Interest payable	1,000
Total liabilities	$24,600

Capital

F. T. Tillis, Capital	27,000
Total liabilities and capital	$51,600

SECTION IV—JOURNALS AND LEDGERS

The analysis in Section II provides sufficient data to prepare financial statements for any organization. It does, however, have two major shortcomings: (1) there is no system that cross-references the various data to the basic transactions, and (2) there is no formal recording format. These shortcomings are alleviated through the use of journals and ledgers.

The Journal

The **journal** is a book in which every transaction that affects the accounting equation is recorded in the *chronological* order incurred. Thus the journal is often referred to as the "book of original entry." As such, it is a permanent record of all the transactions of the business. The form used is shown in Exhibit 2–1.

EXHIBIT 2–1

GENERAL JOURNAL

Page 1

Date 19X1	Description	P.R.	Debit	Credit
Aug. 1	Cash	101	5000 —	
	P. Keith, Capital	301		5000 —
	Owner invested $5,000 in the business.			

Continuing the example used in Sections I and II, let us reconsider the first transaction illustrated. The following steps are used when entering information in the journal (follow each step by referring to the journal entry in Exhibit 2–1):

1. The year is written at the top of each page in the Date column.
2. The month of the transaction is entered. As additional transactions are entered, the month is usually not rewritten unless the same journal page is used for more than one month.
3. The third item of information is the date of the transaction. Since this helps separate transactions, the date for each transaction is usually entered—even if it is the same as that of the preceding transaction.
4. The debit account is entered next to the left-hand margin in the Description column. If there is more than one debit account in a transaction, all the debit items must be entered before any credit items are entered.
5. Each debit amount is entered in the Debit money column.
6. The credit account or accounts are entered and are *slightly indented* to the right.
7. The respective credit amount or amounts are placed in the Credit money column.
8. The final part of the entry is the explanation. Here a brief description of the transaction is entered. This helps to explain the event that has been recorded. It can be useful when attempting to analyze the events that caused a particular account to change.

The journal shown in Exhibit 2–1 is referred to as a **general journal**. Although other types of journals exist, a description of their use is beyond the scope of this text. The column titled P.R. (Posting Reference) will be explained later.

A line is usually skipped between journal entries in order to help separate the entries and to make the information included in the journal easier to read.

The Ledger and Posting

Changes in the accounting equation are accumulated in the journal by transaction. To provide more information to decision makers, these data must be summarized in useful categories. This is done in the **ledger**. Thus the ledger is a book with a separate page used to accumulate transaction data for *each account*. The traditional two-column ledger account is shown in Exhibit 2–2.

EXHIBIT 2–2

GENERAL LEDGER

Cash   Account No. 101

Date 19X1	Item	P.R.	Debit	Date	Item	P.R.	Credit
June 1		1	5000 –				

P. Keith, Capital   Account No. 301

Date	Item	P.R.	Debit	Date 19X1	Item	P.R.	Credit
				June 1		1	5000 —

Recording information in the ledger is referred to as **posting**. Posting is the process of transferring information from the journal to the ledger. The following steps are used when posting a debit entry to the ledger (follow each step by referring to the ledger in Exhibit 2–2):

1. The year is entered as the first item in the Date column on the debit side of the account. As in the journal, it is entered only once.
2. The next item of information is the month. It is placed beneath the year and is entered only once unless the same ledger page is used for more than one month.
3. The date of the transaction is the next piece of information placed in the ledger.
4. The amount of the transaction is then entered in the Debit money column.
5. Finally, the P.R. (Posting Reference) column is used to enter the page number where the transaction is recorded in the journal.
6. The account number (for Cash it is 101) is entered in the *journal* in the P.R. column (see Exhibit 2–1). Thus the cross-referencing system has been completed. The journal entry can be traced to the ledger, and the ledger entry can be traced back to the original transaction in the journal.

The above steps have followed the posting of a debit to the Cash account. The process is the same for each credit entry except that the recording is made on the credit side of the account. (See Exhibit 2–2 for the P. Keith, Capital, account, and follow the steps previously listed.)E

The ledger referred to in Exhibit 2–2 is a **general ledger**. Although other types of ledgers exist, a description of their use is beyond the scope of this text.

SECTION IV REVIEW EXERCISE

Record the entries for Kaki Tours, following the format in Exhibit 2–1; post the entries to the appropriate accounts, following the format in Exhibit 2–2. (The entries are described in Section III of this chapter. Don't forget the four entries used to "complete the exercise.") After performing these steps, compare your answer with the solution provided on pp. 28–31. You should begin by recording the first transaction—the deposit by Ms. Keith—in the journal.

SOLUTION TO SECTION IV REVIEW EXERCISE

GENERAL JOURNAL

Page 1

Date 19X1		Description	Ref.	Dr.	Cr.
June	1	Cash	101	5000 —	
		P. Keith, Capital	301		5000 —
		Owner invested $5,000 in the business.			
	2	Prepaid services	102	50 —	
		Cash	101		50 —
		Paid Tel-Ans for telephone answering services.			
	4	Office supplies	104	55 —	
		Cash	101		55 —
		Purchased stationery from Print Faster.			
	5	Office equipment	107	250 —	
		Cash	101		25 —
		Accounts payable	201		225 —
		Purchased office equipment.			
	7	Office supplies	104	125 —	
		Cash	101		125 —
		Purchased office supplies.			
	10	Accounts receivable	103	300 —	
		Tour revenue	401		300 —
		Billed tour companies for tours conducted.			
	15	Cash	101	250 —	
		Accounts receivable	103		250 —
		Collected accounts receivable.			
	20	Cash	101	130 —	
		Tour revenue	401		130 —
		Collected cash for tours conducted.			
	25	Office rent expense	501	75 —	
		Cash	101		75 —
		Paid rent on office.			
	30	Accounts receivable	103	400 —	
		Tour revenue	401		400 —
		Billed tour companies for tours conducted.			

GENERAL JOURNAL

Page 2

Date 19X1		Description	Ref.	Dr.	Cr.
June	30	Salary expense	502	40 –	
		Salary payable	202		40 –
		Recorded unpaid salary of assistant.			
	30	Telephone answering expense	503	50 –	
		Prepaid services	102		50 –
		Recorded telephone answering services used.			
	30	Office supplies expense	504	30 –	
		Office supplies	104		30 –
		Recorded office supplies used.			
	30	Depreciation expense – office equipment	505	5 –	
		Accumulated depreciation – office equipment	108		5 –
		Recorded depreciation for June.			

GENERAL LEDGER

Cash   101

Date 19X1		Item	P.R.	Debit	Date 19X1		Item	P.R.	Credit
June	1		1	5000 –	June	2		1	50 –
	15		1	250 –		4		1	55 –
	20		1	130 –		5		1	25 –
		(5,050.)		5380 –		7		1	125 –
						25		1	75 –
									330 –

Prepaid services   102

Date 19X1		Item	P.R.	Debit	Date 19X1		Item	P.R.	Credit
June	2	(Ø)	1	50 –	June	30		2	50 –

Accounts receivable   103

Date 19X1		Item	P.R.	Debit	Date 19X1		Item	P.R.	Credit
June	10		1	300 –	June	15		1	250 –
	30	(450)	1	400 –					
				700 –					

Office supplies   104

Date 19X1	Item	P.R.	Debit	Date 19X1	Item	P.R.	Credit
June 4		1	55 —	June 30		2	30 —
7		1	125 —				
	(150)		180 —				

Office equipment   107

Date 19X1	Item	P.R.	Debit	Date	Item	P.R.	Credit
June 5		1	250 —				

Accumulated depreciation — office equipment   108

Date	Item	P.R.	Debit	Date 19X1	Item	P.R.	Credit
				June 30		2	5 —

Accounts payable   201

Date	Item	P.R.	Debit	Date 19X1	Item	P.R.	Credit
				June 5		1	225 —

Salary payable   202

Date	Item	P.R.	Debit	Date 19X1	Item	P.R.	Credit
				June 30		2	40 —

P. Keith, Capital   301

Date	Item	P.R.	Debit	Date 19X1	Item	P.R.	Credit
				June 1		1	5000 —

Tour revenue   401

Date	Item	P.R.	Debit	Date 19X1	Item	P.R.	Credit
				June 10		1	300 –
				20		1	130 –
				30	(830.)	1	400 –
							830 –

Office rent expense   501

Date 19X1	Item	P.R.	Debit	Date	Item	P.R.	Credit
June 25		1	75 –				

Salary expense   502

Date 19X1	Item	P.R.	Debit	Date	Item	P.R.	Credit
June 30		2	40 –				

Telephone–answering expense   503

Date 19X1	Item	P.R.	Debit	Date	Item	P.R.	Credit
June 30		2	50 –				

Office supplies expense   504

Date 19X1	Item	P.R.	Debit	Date	Item	P.R.	Credit
June 30		2	30 –				

Depreciation expense — office equipment   505

Date 19X1	Item	P.R.	Debit	Date	Item	P.R.	Credit
June 30		2	5 –				

SECTION V—COMPLETION OF THE BOOKKEEPING PROCESS

The Trial Balance

In previous illustrations the financial statements were prepared directly from information recorded in the accounts. To help locate errors that may have been made in the recording or posting process, a **trial balance** is usually prepared. The trial balance is a columnar listing of each account, together with its balance. If both the debit and credit columns are equal, the system is in balance (see Table 2–14).

TABLE 2–14

Kaki Tours
Trial Balance
August 31, 19X1

	Debits	Credits
Cash	$5,050	
Accounts receivable	450	
Office supplies	150	
Office equipment	250	
Accumulated depreciation—office equipment		$ 5
Accounts payable		225
Salary payable		40
P. Keith, Capital		5,000
Tour revenue		830
Office rent expense	75	
Salary expense	40	
Telephone-answering expense	50	
Office supplies expense	30	
Depreciation expense—office equipment	5	
	$6,100	$ 6,100

Note that even if the totals of the debit and credit columns in the trial balance are equal, there can still be errors within the system. Examples of such errors include (1) entries that are not recorded, (2) amounts debited (credited) to incorrect accounts, and (3) complete entries recorded for incorrect amounts.

The financial statements are usually prepared directly from trial balance data. In some systems a formal adjusting process must be completed before the statements can be prepared. Such a process is discussed below.

Adjusting Entries

Adjusting entries are designed to bring the financial records up-to-date before the statements are prepared. In many instances the books are not maintained on a current basis in order to save time during the period. A prominent example in the Kaki Tours illustration is depreciation. Remember that depreciation was recorded in order to give recognition to the fact that the services of the asset (Office equipment) were being "used up."

Logic would indicate that the "using up" process is a gradual one that does not suddenly occur at the end of the period. If the books were to be maintained on a current basis, an entry for depreciation would frequently have to be made. Since financial statements are prepared only periodically, however, it is not necessary to have the books up-to-date until it is time to prepare the statements. Therefore adjusting entries are made at the end of each period before the financial statements are prepared.

In addition to depreciation in our illustration, another item that must be adjusted is Prepaid services. Although the services were used each day, it was not necessary to record the using up of the asset until the end of the period. (An exploration of all the types of adjustments is beyond the scope of this text; however, the reader should be alert to the need for these entries.)

Closing the Books

In this chapter the accounting equation was originally used to account for the acquisition and use of the resources of an organization. Table 2–1, which explained how transactions affect the equation, contained only three types of accounts: assets, liabilities, and capital. These are generally referred to as the **permanent** or **real accounts**. They are labeled *permanent* because they are carried from one period to another. Thus the ending balance of Cash of one period will be the beginning balance of Cash for the next period.

As the illustrations in this chapter became more complex, the changes in capital resulting from the operations of the business were accumulated in separate accounts called revenues and expenses. The purpose of these accounts was to identify the particular operating items causing capital to change. Thus these accounts became the source of the data that were presented on the activity (income) statement. These data were used to help decision makers evaluate the effectiveness of the use of the resources available to management.

Once such an evaluation has been made for the current period, however, the data lose their importance. The generation of revenue and the incurrence of expenses are relative to a certain period of time. It serves little purpose to know that a business that has been in operation for one hundred years has accumulated $500 million in revenue. Information on revenues and expenses is useful only for evaluating the operations of an organization on a period-by-period basis. As a result, the revenue and expense accounts are generally referred to as **temporary** or **nominal accounts**.

If temporary (revenue and expense) accounts are to be used to generate information relative to certain periods, they must be closed out (reduced to a zero balance) at the end of each period; and the balances in those accounts must be transferred to capital. The ledger in Table 2–10 shows a balance in the P. Keith, Capital, account, of $5,000, the initial contribution by Ms. Keith. Analysis of the balance sheet in Table 2–13, however, indicates a capital balance of $5,630. The reason for the difference between these two figures is that the former, the one found in the ledger, does not include the income for the period. Since the effects of operations have already been recorded in the asset and liability accounts,[2] they must also be reflected in the capital account so that the balance sheet will balance.

In summary, the trial balance figure for capital does not include the effect of operating the business. Therefore it must be updated. In addition, the revenue and expense accounts must be reduced to zero in order to begin accumulating data for the next period. The process of achieving these goals is referred to as **closing the books**. The closing entry for Kaki Tours at June 30, 19X1, is shown in Exhibit 2–3.

EXHIBIT 2–3

GENERAL JOURNAL

3

Date 19X1		Description	Ref.	Dr.	Cr.
June	30	Tour revenue	401	830 –	
		Office rent expense	501		75 –
		Salary expense	502		40 –
		Telephone-answering expense	503		50 –
		Office supplies expense	504		30 –
		Depreciation expense – office equipment	505		5 –
		P. Keith, Capital	301		630 –
		Record closing the revenue and expense accounts and transfer the net income to capital.			

The purpose of the closing process is to zero out the balances of the temporary accounts and transfer the net income for the period to the capital account. The steps involved in this process are as follows:

1. Debit each revenue account for the credit balance currently in the account.
2. Credit each expense account for the debit balance currently in the account.
3. Debit or credit the capital account for the amount needed to balance the journal entry—make the debits equal the credits. This is the amount of the net income or loss.

After posting these entries to the accounts, the general ledger will look like the one shown in Exhibit 2–4. (*Note:* The balance in each account that has more than one entry has been circled.)

Note that the revenue and expense accounts are the only accounts that have had their balances reduced to zero. The assets, the liabilities, and the capital accounts all have balances that will be carried into the next period as the beginning balances in those accounts. The zero balance in Prepaid services is due to the simplicity of the example, not the closing process.

---

[2]Revenues and expenses were defined earlier in this chapter in terms of their effect on assets and liabilities.

EXHIBIT 2—4

GENERAL LEDGER

Cash   101

Date 19X1	Item	P.R.	Debit	Date 19X1	Item	P.R.	Credit
June 1		1	5000 —	June 2		1	50 —
15		1	250 —	4		1	55 —
20		1	130 —	5		1	25 —
	(5,050)		5380 —	7		1	125 —
				25		1	75 —
							330 —
	Not Closed						

Prepaid services   102

Date 19X1	Item	P.R.	Debit	Date 19X1	Item	P.R.	Credit
June 2		1	50 —	June 30		2	50 —
	(∅.)						
	Not Closed						

Accounts receivable   103

Date 19X1	Item	P.R.	Debit	Date 19X1	Item	P.R.	Credit
June 10		1	300 —	June 15		1	250 —
30	(450)	1	400 —				
			700 —				
	Not Closed						

Office supplies   104

Date 19X1	Item	P.R.	Debit	Date 19X1	Item	P.R.	Credit
June 4		1	55 —	June 30		2	30 —
7	(150)	1	125 —				
			180 —				
	Not Closed						

Office equipment   107

Date 19X1	Item	P.R.	Debit	Date	Item	P.R.	Credit
June 5		1	250 —				
	Not Closed						

Accumulated depreciation — office equipment   108

Date	Item	P.R.	Debit	Date 19X1	Item	P.R.	Credit
				June 30		2	5 —
	Not Closed						

Accounts payable   201

Date	Item	P.R.	Debit	Date 19X1	Item	P.R.	Credit
				June 5		1	225 —
	Not Closed						

Salary payable   202

Date	Item	P.R.	Debit	Date 19X1	Item	P.R.	Credit
				June 30		2	40 —
	Not Closed						

P. Keith, Capital   301

Date	Item	P.R.	Debit	Date 19X1	Item	P.R.	Credit
				June 1		1	5000 —
				30		3	630 —
							5630 —
	Not Closed						

Tour revenue   401

Date 19X1	Item	P.R.	Debit	Date 19X1	Item	P.R.	Credit
June 30		3	830 —	June 10		1	300 —
				20		1	130 —
				30	(830)	1	400 —
			830 —				830 —

Office rent expense   501

Date 19X1	Item	P.R.	Debit	Date 19X1	Item	P.R.	Credit
June 25		1	75 —	June 30		3	75 —

Salary expense 502

Date 19X1	Item	P.R.	Debit	Date 19X1	Item	P.R.	Credit
June 30		2	40 –	June 30		3	40 –

Telephone-answering expense 503

Date 19X1	Item	P.R.	Debit	Date 19X1	Item	P.R.	Credit
June 30		2	50 –	June 30		3	50 –

Office supplies expense 504

Date 19X1	Item	P.R.	Debit	Date 19X1	Item	P.R.	Credit
June 30		2	30 –	June 30		3	30 –

Depreciation expense — office equipment 505

Date 19X1	Item	P.R.	Debit	Date 19X1	Item	P.R.	Credit
June 30		2	5 –	June 30		3	5 –

Withdrawals by the Owner

At this point it is important to discuss another type of transaction that can be recorded in the system. Withdrawals by the owner are not treated as an expense of the operations of the business. Therefore, had Ms. Keith taken any money or other assets from the business, the entry would have required a reduction of assets (credit) and a debit to an account called P. Keith, Withdrawals. This latter account would have been closed at the end of the period into Ms. Keith's capital. That is, the withdrawals account would have been credited and the capital account debited. This sequence of entries was omitted from the basic example because it has no counterpart in a nonbusiness system.

The Accounting Cycle

The process described in this chapter is normally referred to as the **accounting cycle**. It can be summarized in the following six steps:

1. Record entries in the journal.
2. Post the entries to the ledger.
3. Prepare a trial balance.

4. Adjust the accounts as necessary.
5. Prepare the financial statements.
6. Close the temporary accounts.

This cycle is repeated every accounting period. In specific cases it may be expanded or contracted to fit the particular circumstances facing the organization.

SECTION V REVIEW EXERCISE

Using the information in Table 2–15, prepare the necessary closing entry in the general journal and fill in the blanks that follow. Compare your results with the solution provided.

TABLE 2–15

ACCOUNT	BALANCE
Cash	$12,000
Accounts receivable	15,000
Prepaid rent	1,000
Office equipment	30,000
Accumulated depreciation—office equipment	14,000
Accounts payable	5,000
Notes payable to bank	10,000
Amy Norris, Capital	25,000
Service revenue	40,000
Depreciation expense—equipment	7,000
Rent expense	15,000
Salary expense	14,000

After posting the closing entry, indicate the balance of each of the accounts listed below:

Cash $_____

Accounts payable $_____

Amy Norris, Capital $_____

Service revenue $_____

Rent expense $_____

What was the net income for the period?_____

SOLUTION TO SECTION V REVIEW EXERCISE

GENERAL JOURNAL   Page 5

Date 19X1	Description	P.R.	Debit	Credit
Dec. 31	Service revenue		40000—	
	Depreciation expense--equipment			7000—
	Rent expense			15000—
	Salary expense			14000—
	Amy Norris, Capital			4000—
	To record the closing of the revenue and expense accounts and transfer the net income to capital.			

Cash $12,000
Accounts payable $5,000
Amy Norris, Capital $29,000 ($25,000 + $4,000)
Service revenue $-0- (closed)
Rent expense $-0- (closed)

The income for the period was $4,000 (the amount closed into capital).

CONCLUDING COMMENT

We have used a business organization as a vehicle for introducing the accounting cycle because most individuals can identify more easily with it than with a nonbusiness organization. The remaining chapters in this text will focus on the accounting and external reporting of financial information for nonbusiness organizations.

REVIEW QUESTIONS

Section 1

Q2–1 Define the following terms:
   a. Assets
   b. Liabilities
   c. Capital
   d. Revenue
   e. Expense
Q2–2 Write the accounting equation.
Q2–3 Must the accounting equation always balance? Why?

Section II

Q2–4 Explain the rules of debit and credit with respect to assets, liabilities, capital, revenues, and expenses.
Q2–5 A student of basic accounting made the following statement: "For each account debited, there must be another account credited for the same amount." Do you agree? Why or why not?
Q2–6 Why do credits increase the capital account?

Section III

Q2–7 What are the three basic financial statements illustrated in the text?
Q2–8 Describe the interrelationship between the three statements in Q2–7.
Q2–9 Why is it important to put the appropriate date or time period on a financial statement?

Section IV

Q2–10 What is a journal and how is it used in the accounting process?

Q2–11 What is a ledger and how is it used in the accounting process?

Q2–12 How are journals and ledgers interrelated in an accounting system?

Section V

Q2–13 What is the purpose of adjusting entries?

Q2–14 Which accounts are closed at the end of an accounting period? Why are these accounts closed?

Q2–15 If the columns of a trial balance total to the same amount, the information included in the accounts must be correct. Do you agree or disagree? Why?

EXERCISES

Section I

E2–1   (Preparing transactions)
For each of the following categories, compose a transaction that will cause that category to increase and one that will cause it to decrease:
a. Assets
b. Liabilities
c. Capital
d. Revenues
e. Expenses

E2–2   (Associating changes with specific accounts)
For each of the following transactions of the Kit-Kat Company, identify the accounts that would be increased and those that would be decreased:
a. The owner invested $25,000 in the business.
b. Rent for the month was paid to Jiffy Realty Company, $500.
c. A secretary was hired at a monthly salary of $550.
d. Customers were billed for services rendered, $700.
e. The utilities bill for the month was paid, $234.

E2–3   (Calculating the change in capital from balance sheet data)
The beginning and ending balances in certain account categories of the Release Company are listed below:

Account categories	Beginning balances	Ending balances
Assets	$306,000	$307,000
Liabilities	$107,000	$110,000

Based upon this information, what was the change in capital for the period?

Section II

E2–4   (Using debits and credits)

Identify the account(s) that would be debited and/or credited as a result of the following transactions:

a.   The owner invested $10,000 in the business.

b.   Supplies were purchased for cash, $800.

c.   Service revenue of $1,000 was received in cash.

d.   Customers were billed for services rendered, $500.

e.   Employees were paid their salaries totaling $800.

f.   Collections of accounts receivable totaled $300.

g.   Rent for the month was paid, $350.

h.   Salaries owed employees at the end of the month totaled $100.

i.   Supplies costing $300 were used.

E2–5   (Associating debits and credits with account categories)

Each of the account categories listed in Exercise 2–1 are increased with either a debit or credit. Indicate which is used to record an increase in each type of account and identify the usual balance in that account category.

E2–6   (Using debits and credits)

William T. Fudd III acts as a rental agent for several large apartment houses. Mr. Fudd's income is determined by a commission on the number of apartments he rents. During the month of January, Mr. Fudd incurred the following transactions. Identify the debits and credits to record each event.

19X1

JANUARY

2   Mr. Fudd placed $20,000 cash into a bank account to be used in the operation of his business, Apartment Locators.

2   Mr. Fudd hired a secretary and agreed to pay her $570 per month.

4   Mr. Fudd borrowed $10,000 from the Security Bank, signing a note for that amount.

5   Mr. Fudd purchased, for cash, office equipment that cost $3,000.

10   Mr. Fudd paid the rent for the month, $300.

14   Mr. Fudd received a check from one apartment owner for $3,000. This amount was his commission for renting apartments during the first two weeks of January.

17   Mr. Fudd paid his secretary half of the agreed-upon salary.

30   Mr. Fudd earned an additional $3,000 of commissions. He has not received these amounts; therefore, he sent bills to the owners.

31   Mr. Fudd collected $500 from one of the owners billed on January 30.

31   Mr. Fudd made a payment on his loan. The total payment was $1,200, of which $200 was interest. The remainder was a reduction of the amount of the loan.

Section III

E2–7   (Computation of balance sheet amounts)

Based upon the following information, compute total assets, total liabilities, and total capital; in addition, determine whether or not all of the accounts are listed:

Cash	$22,000
Accounts receivable	12,000
Accounts payable	15,000
Equipment	50,000
Rent expense	11,000
Service revenue	74,000
Notes payable	17,000
Accumulated depreciation	25,000
Depreciation expense	12,500
Office supplies	3,000
Office supplies expense	8,000
Salaries payable	4,000

E2–8   (Relating accounts and financial statements)
Identify the financial statement on which each of the following items would appear:
a. Bonds payable
b. Rent revenue
c. Owner's capital, beginning balance
d. Cash
e. Equipment
f. Supplies expense
g. Depreciation expense
h. Service revenue
i. Accounts receivable
j. Accounts payable
k. Owner's capital, ending balance
l. Rent expense
m. Accumulated depreciation
n. Net income
o. Salaries payable
p. Land
q. Supplies on hand

E2–9   (Fill-in-the-blanks—definitions)
Match the items on the left with those on the right by placing the appropriate letter in the space provided.

a. _____ Statement of changes in owner's capital

b. _____ Income statement

c. _____ Net income

d. _____ Additional investment by the owner

e. _____ Ending balance in owner's capital

f. _____ Balance sheet

1. A financial statement that presents the revenues and expenses of a business

2. A financial statement that presents a reconciliation of the beginning and ending owner's capital

3. An increase in owner's capital

4. A financial statement that presents the assets, liabilities,

and owner's capital of a
business
5. Can be found on a balance
sheet and a statement of
changes in owner's capital
6. An excess of revenues over
expenses

Section IV

E2–10   (Recording transactions in a general journal)
Record the following transactions in general journal form for the Control
Company, a private investigation service:

19X1
JAN.

2   Susan Bigger invested $10,000 in the business.
2   Ms. Bigger paid the rent on office space for January, $500.
4   Ms. Bigger purchased office supplies on credit for $200.
5   Ms. Bigger billed customers for $5,000 for services performed.
10   Ms. Bigger acquired an automobile for use in the business. The cost was $4,500. She
paid $1,000 as a down payment and signed a note for the remainder.
15   Customers paid Ms. Bigger $3,500 on their accounts.
20   Ms. Bigger billed customers for $2,000.
25   Ms. Bigger acquired the services of Answer Company, a telephone-answering service. She paid $10 for their services for the remainder of the month.
31   Depreciation of $100 was recorded on the automobile.
31   Office supplies used during the month totaled $100.
31   The utilities bills arrived in the mail; they totaled $800. Ms. Bigger will pay them in
February.
31   The cost of gasoline and oil for the automobile for the month was $134. Ms. Bigger
paid the service station that amount.

E2–11   (Posting to a general ledger)
Post the transactions in Exercise 2–10 to general ledger accounts.

E2–12   (Recording transactions in a general journal)
Using the data in Exercise 2–6, record the transactions in general journal
form.

Section V

E2–13   (Preparing a trial balance)
Using the following information, prepare a trial balance for the Forfeit
Company at June 30, 19X1.

Accumulated depreciation—equipment	$ 4,000
Taxes payable	200
Equipment	24,000
Cash	20,000
Utilities expense	1,000
Depreciation expense—equipment	600
Notes payable	24,000
Salaries expense	20,000
R. Key, Capital	15,800
Office supplies	2,000
Service revenue	32,000
Rent expense	8,600
Accounts payable	1,600
Office supplies expense	1,400

E2–14 (Preparing closing entries and determining the ending balance in capital)

Prepare the appropriate closing entry based on the information in Exercise 2–13 and determine the ending balance in R. Key, Capital.

E2–15 (Preparation of a trial balance)

Prepare a trial balance based upon the information in Exercises 2–10 and 2–11.

PROBLEMS

Section I

P2–1 (Analyzing transactions on a work sheet)

The following transactions relate to the Escape Travel Agency for March 19X1:

1 Mary Ann Ferrit invested $36,000 in a travel agency.
2 Mary Ann paid $700 rent on office space for the month.
3 Mary Ann purchased office equipment for $5,200, paying $200 as a down payment and signing a thirty day note for the remainder.
4 Printers, Inc., sold $1,000 of office supplies to Mary Ann. She will pay this amount in thirty days.
6 Mary Ann hired Lauralee as a secretary and agreed to pay her $450 per month.
10 The *Times* sent the agency a bill for $400 for advertising for the month. This amount was paid immediately.
15 Sales of tickets and tours for the first half of the month totaled $30,000. This amount was received in cash.
18 Mary Ann wrote checks totaling $22,000 to several airlines and national tour services for tickets.
20 Mary Ann sent out bills to clients totaling $15,000.
28 Clients paid $12,000 on their open accounts.
30 The utilities bills were received and paid. They totaled $800.
30 The agency received bills from various airlines and national tour services for $14,000. These will be paid in April.
30 The rent for April was paid.

31 Office supplies on hand at the end of the month totaled $500.

31 Lauralee was paid her monthly salary.

31 Mary Ann wrote a check for $280 for the March 30 payment on the office equipment. Included in this amount was $50 for interest.

REQUIRED: Analyze the above transactions on a work sheet similar to that illustrated in the text. You will need columns for Cash, Accounts receivable, Prepaid rent, Prepaid advertising, Office supplies, Office equipment, Accounts payable, Notes payable, and Mary Ann Ferrit, Capital.

P2–2   (Analyzing transactions on a work sheet)
The following transactions relate to Rosie's Auto Repair Shop. Record each on a work sheet similar to the one illustrated in the text.

19X1
SEPT.

1 Rose Gloro invested $10,000 in the business.

1 Ms. Gloro rented space adjacent to a large automobile parts store. The lease specified a monthly rental of $800. This amount was paid for September.

2 Ms. Gloro contracted with the Auto Parts Place to supply her with automobile parts at discount prices on credit. She will pay for them at the end of each month.

2 Ms. Gloro purchased a complete tool kit from the Auto Parts Place. The tools cost a total of $5,000. The entire amount was paid immediately. For simplicity, assume all of the tools are treated as a single asset for accounting purposes.

3 Ms. Gloro paid $400 in deposits for various utilities. Each of the deposits will be returned after five years or the closing of her business, whichever occurs first. These deposits included electricity, telephone, and water.

3 Ms. Gloro paid Pink-Pages $50 for an ad in the September issue of their monthly telephone directory.

4 Ms. Gloro charged customers $350 to repair their cars. The entire amount was collected in cash. While doing the repair work, she purchased parts costing $45.

9 Ms. Gloro purchased office supplies costing $130, cash.

12 Repairs for the week totaled $2,560; the entire amount was collected in cash. The cost of parts was $435.

15 Ms. Gloro paid her workers $500.

16 Ms. Gloro purchased office furniture for $200. She paid $50 down and will pay the remainder during the next thirty days.

18 Ms. Gloro "ran a special" on tune-ups. She advertised the special price in the *Daily News*. The cost of the ad, $100, was paid in cash.

19 Repairs for the week totaled $3,500. The cost of the parts was $1,000. A total of $2,500 was collected in cash; the remainder will be collected in the future.

30 Utility bills totaling $500 were received. Rose will pay these next month.

30 Ms. Gloro paid her workers $2,000.

30 Ms. Gloro recorded repairs for the last eleven days of the month. These totaled $4,500. The parts cost $2,000. She collected $4,000 from her customers; the remainder will be collected in the future.

30 Rose collected $500 from her customers on their accounts.

30 Rose paid the parts store the amount owed.

30 Office supplies costing $45 were used during the month.

REQUIRED: Analyze the above transactions on a work sheet similar to that illustrated in the text. You will need columns for Cash, Accounts receivable, Office supplies, Prepaid rent, Prepaid advertising, Office furniture, Tools, Utility deposits, Accounts payable, and Rose Gloro, Capital.

P2–3   (Analyzing transactions on a work sheet using inventory)
The following transactions related to the Trade-Mart Discount Store for
November 19X1:

1   Sherman Shasha contributed $100,000 to start a new business, the Trade-Mart Discount Store.

1   Sherman purchased land for $10,000 and a small building for $50,000. He paid $5,000 down and signed a mortgage for the remainder.

2   Sherman purchased $40,000 of goods to be sold in the store. He paid $10,000 down and put the rest on a charge account that is due at the end of the month. The merchandise was purchased from Regional Sales, Inc. (*Hint*: Use an asset account—Inventory.)

3   Equipment costing $2,000 was acquired; $400 was paid in cash and the remainder is due in sixty days.

4   Office supplies costing $500 were acquired for cash.

4   The business made utility deposits totaling $1,000. These amounts will be used to pay the final utility bill and the remainder will be returned.

5   Sherman contacted the local newspaper and purchased an advertisement. The cost of the ad was $450. The newspaper will send a bill for that amount.

7   Sales for the first week of operations totaled $25,000. Of this amount, $5,000 was cash and $20,000 was credit card sales. The VICCA credit card company charges the retailer a 2 percent fee for the use of the card. VICCA will pay the business twice a month for the sales using their card. The fee charged to the retailer is paid at the end of each month. (*Hint*: The credit card fee should be recorded as a separate expense.)

8   The bill for the newspaper ad arrived. Sherman decided to pay it later in the month.

15   Employees were paid their salaries, $5,000.

15   Sherman collected the amount due from VICCA.

18   Sales totaling $45,000 were recorded: $7,000 were cash sales; the remainder were VICCA card sales.

20   The newspaper bill was paid.

23   Sales totaling $25,000 were recorded: $4,000 were cash sales; the remainder were VICCA card sales.

24   Additional inventory was acquired from Regional Sales Company. The total amount was $50,000. Sherman paid $15,000 down, with the remainder due at the end of the month.

30   Sales totaling $30,000 were recorded; all were VICCA card sales.

30   Sherman paid Regional Sales the amount owed to that company.

30   Employee salaries of $7,000 were paid.

30   The utilities bills were received and paid. The total amount was $2,500.

30   A bill was received from the Ace Delivery Service for $800. Sherman signed a contract with Ace to deliver certain merchandise sold by the store. The bill will be paid next month.

30   Sherman collected the amount due from VICCA.

30   The first payment on the building mortgage was made. The total amount was $1,000, of which $600 was interest.

30   At the end of the month there was $4,000 of inventory in the store.

30   Sherman paid VICCA the amount owed.

30   Office supplies used during the month totaled $400.

REQUIRED: Analyze the above transactions on a work sheet similar to that illustrated in the text. You will need columns for Cash, Accounts receivable, Inventory, Office supplies, Prepaid advertising, Land, Building, Equipment,

Utility deposits, Accounts payable, Mortgage payable, and Sherman Shasha, Capital.

Section II

P2–4   (Debit and credit analysis of transactions)
Using the information given in Problem 2–1, indicate which account(s) would be debited and which account(s) would be credited for each transaction.

P2–5   (Debit and credit analysis of transactions)
Using the information given in Problem 2–2, indicate which account(s) would be debited and which account(s) would be credited for each transaction.

P2–6   (Debit and credit analysis of transactions)
Using the information given in Problem 2–3, indicate which account(s) would be debited and which account(s) would be credited for each transaction. (*Note*: The cost of inventory sold should be debited to "Cost of goods sold.")

Section III

P2–7   (Preparation of financial statements)
The following information was taken from the financial records of the Clear Company. The balances listed are as of the end of the accounting year, December 31, 19X1, the first year of operations.

	BALANCE	
	Debit	Credit
Cash	$10,000	
Accounts receivable	4,000	
Office supplies	2,000	
Delivery equipment	10,000	
Accumulated depreciation—delivery equipment		$ 200
Notes payable to bank		9,800
Interest payable		500
Accounts payable		2,000
W. T. Foxx, Capital		9,000
Delivery revenue		8,000
Expenses of operating delivery trucks	2,000	
Salary expense	1,000	
Interest expense	300	
Depreciation expense—delivery equipment	200	
	$29,500	$ 29,500

REQUIRED: Prepare the following financial statements:
1.   Income statement
2.   Statement of changes in owner's capital
3.   Balance sheet

P2–8   (Matching accounts and financial statements)

Following are several financial statement classifications and accounts:

Revenue	R
Expense	E
Asset	A
Liability	L
Owner's capital (balance sheet)	C
Statement of changes in owner's capital	SC

Caution: Some items may appear in more than one statement classification.

Example: ___A___ Cash

1. _____ Notes payable
2. _____ Additional investment by owner
3. _____ Automobile
4. _____ Depreciation expense—automobile
5. _____ Prepaid rent
6. _____ Utilities expense
7. _____ Consulting revenue
8. _____ Accounts payable
9. _____ Ending balance in owner's capital
10. _____ Office supplies
11. _____ Accumulated depreciation—automobile
12. _____ Salaries payable
13. _____ Office supplies expense
14. _____ Service revenue
15. _____ Interest expense
16. _____ Accounts receivable
17. _____ Loans made to other companies
18. _____ Deposit made with utility company. This amount will be repaid to the company for which we are keeping the records in five years.
19. _____ Cash held in a separate bank account from that mentioned above. This money will be used to buy a building in a few years.

REQUIRED: Identify the proper financial statement classification for each account by placing the appropriate key letter in the space provided.

P2–9   (Preparation of financial statements)

Following are the balances in the accounts of the V. Sera Company as of the year ended December 31, 19X2, unless otherwise noted:

Notes payable	$18,000
Cash	24,000
Consulting revenue	74,000
V. Sera, Capital	20,000
Office supplies expense	22,000
Accounts receivable	16,000
Rent expense	30,000

Office supplies	6,000
Service revenue	20,000
Accounts payable	2,000
Salary expense	2,000
Gasoline and oil expense	6,000
Prepaid rent (for 19X3)	6,000
Interest expense	2,000
Automobile	24,000
Depreciation expense—automobile	4,000
Accumulated depreciation—automobile	8,000

Note: The owner made an additional investment of $10,000 in the business on April 15, 19X2. This amount is included in the capital balance above.

REQUIRED: Prepare the following financial statements:
1. Income statement
2. Statement of changes in owner's capital
3. Balance sheet

P2–10   (Preparation of financial statements)

Following are the balances in the accounts of the Compost Company as of the year ended December 31, 19X2, unless otherwise noted:

Accounts payable	$ 1,000
Service revenue	15,000
Cash	22,000
Salary expense	5,000
Prepaid rent (for 19X3)	1,000
F. Willow, Capital (1/1/X2)	29,000
Utilities expense	4,000
Office equipment	20,000
Commission revenue	10,000
Rent expense	8,000
Depreciation expense—office equipment	1,000
Accumulated depreciation—office equipment	3,000

Note: The owner made an additional investment of $3,000 in the business on May 4, 1982. This amount is not included in the capital balance above.

REQUIRED: Prepare the following financial statements:
1. Income statement
2. Statement of changes in owner's capital
3. Balance sheet

Section IV

P2–11   (Recording and posting transactions)

Use the information given in Problem 2–1. In addition, assume that the depreciation on the office equipment is $100.

REQUIRED: 1.   Record the transactions in general journal form.
                 2.   Post the transactions to the appropriate general ledger accounts.

P2–12   (Recording and posting transactions)

Use the information given in Problem 2–2. In addition, assume that the depreciation on the tools is $150 and the depreciation on the office equipment is $5.

REQUIRED: 1.   Record the transactions in general journal form.
2.   Post the transactions to the appropriate general ledger accounts.

P2–13   (Recording and posting transactions)

Use the information given in Problem 2–3. In addition, assume that the depreciation on the building is $500 and the depreciation on the equipment is $5.

REQUIRED: 1.   Record the transactions in general journal form.
2.   Post the transactions to the appropriate general ledger accounts.

Section V

P2–14   (Preparing a trial balance and a closing entry)

REQUIRED: Based on the answers you obtained in Problem 2–11:
1.   Prepare a trial balance.
2.   Prepare a closing entry.
3.   Post the closing entry to the general ledger accounts.

P2–15   (Preparing a closing entry)

REQUIRED: Based on the answers you obtained in Problem 2–12:
1.   Prepare a trial balance.
2.   Prepare the closing entry.

P2–16   (Preparing a trial balance and a closing entry)

REQUIRED: Based on the answers you obtained in Problem 2–13:
1.   Prepare a trial balance.
2.   Prepare the closing entry.
3.   Post the closing entry to the general ledger accounts.

3

THE USE OF FUNDS
IN GOVERNMENTAL
ACCOUNTING*

LEARNING OBJECTIVES

After completion of this chapter, you should be able to:

1.   Identify the major fund categories currently used in governmental accounting
2.   Compare and contrast the main features of the cash basis, the accrual basis, and the modified accrual basis of accounting as used by governmental units
3.   Identify and describe the function of the funds used in governmental accounting
4.   Identify and describe the account groups used in governmental accounting
5.   Describe the relationship between the funds and account groups used in a governmental accounting system
6.   Describe the financial statements used by each fund and account group in a governmental accounting system

The Governmental Accounting Standards Board (GASB) has been very active in establishing accounting and reporting standards for governmental units. The centerpiece of their research is *Concepts Statement No.1: Objectives of Financial*

*This chapter contains a summary of the fund accounting system for governmental units. It therefore contains a great deal of factual information. You are not expected to remember all of the data included, but it should provide you with an overview of the system and its components and an excellent summary review as you complete each section of Chapters 4–8.

Reporting. In this statement, GASB assumes that all "state and local governmental financial reports . . . possess . . . certain basic characteristics: understandability, reliability, relevance, timeliness, consistency, and comparability."[1] Within the context of this background, GASB has established the following reporting objectives for state and local government units:

   a. Financial reporting should assist in fulfilling government's duty to be publicly accountable and should enable users to assess that accountability by:
     (1) Providing information to determine whether current-year revenues were sufficient to pay for current-year services.
     (2) Demonstrating whether resources were obtained and used in accordance with the entity's legally adopted budget, and demonstrating compliance with other finance-related legal or contractual requirements.
     (3) Providing information to assist users in assessing the service efforts, costs, and accomplishments of the governmental entity.

   b. Financial reporting should assist users in evaluating the operating results of the governmental entity for the year by:
     (1) Providing information about sources and uses of financial resources.
     (2) Providing information about how it financed its activities and met its cash requirements.
     (3) Providing information necessary to determine whether its financial position improved or deteriorated as a result of the year's operations.

   c. Financial reporting should assist users in assessing the level of services that can be provided by the governmental entity and its ability to meet its obligations as they become due by:
     (1) Providing information about its financial position and condition.
     (2) Providing information about its physical and other nonfinancial resources having useful lives that extend beyond the current year, including information that can be used to assess the service potential of those resources.
     (3) Disclosing legal or contractual restrictions on resources and the risk of potential loss of resources.[2]

In summary, governmental units are required to provide information that is *useful* in making decisions about the organization regarding its creditworthiness, its future cash flows, its resources and claims to those resources, and its ability to continue to provide services. These objectives do not differ significantly from the reporting objectives of business organizations. Both types of organizations provide information relating to the acquisition, use, and disposition of their resources.

The major difference between business and governmental organizations is that the users of commercial accounting data are interested in financial activities that are involved in measuring profit in order to ensure the continued existence of the organization. This is generally referred to as the **maintenance of capital** of the entity. The users of governmental accounting (as identified in Chapter 1),

---

[1]Governmental Accounting Standards Board, *Codification of Governmental Accounting and Financial Reporting Standards* (Norwalk, Conn., 1987), Sec. 100.162.
[2]GASB Cod. Sec. 100.177–79.

however, are interested in financial activities that are concerned with measuring the type and level of *services* provided by the organization *(spending activities) and,* in some instances, financial activities that are concerned with measuring the *maintenance of capital.*[3]

When we combine the necessity of separately measuring spending activities and of maintaining capital with the legal restrictions placed on certain operations of the governmental unit, the result is a need to maintain records for a series of separate entities *within* the government. These entities are call funds.

SECTION I—THE FRAMEWORK OF FUND ACCOUNTING

Fund accounting is based on the existence of entities within the organization that have characteristics that distinguish them from one another. The characteristics of these entities are the subject of this section.

The Fund

A **fund** is defined as

. . . a fiscal and accounting entity with a self-balancing set of accounts recording cash and other financial resources, together with all related liabilities and residual equities or balances, and changes therein, which are segregated for the purpose of carrying on specific activities or attaining certain objectives in accordance with special regulations, restrictions, or limitations.[4]

The term **fiscal entity** refers to the separate *budgetary* nature of a fund that has spendable resources, while the term **accounting entity** refers to the separate financial unit that is treated as an entity for *accounting* purposes. A commercial firm, whether it be General Motors or the corner grocery store, is *one* entity. A small city, however, can be made up of *several* entities, depending on the number of funds used. The exact number of entities (funds) is generally defined in the constitution, charter, statutes, and so forth, that regulate the governmental unit.

Since each fund is a separate accounting entity, each must have **self-balancing accounts**. That is, the total of the assets of a particular fund must equal the total of its liabilities and fund balance (or capital).[5] In addition, changes in these items must be reflected in the accounting records. Thus the accounting records for a particular fund must be designed to identify the assets, liabilities, and fund balance of that fund as distinguished from all other funds.

---

[3]Studies of the users of governmental accounting information have been made by several individuals. Some of these studies are listed as additional readings in Chapter 9.

[4]GASB Cod. Sec. 1300, Introduction.

[5]Fund balance will be defined in detail later in this text. At this point, however, it can be considered to be spendable resources.

Fund Categories

The funds used by a governmental unit are separated into three major categories. The first category includes the funds that focus on **spending activities (governmental-type)**. Within this category are the funds that primarily account for the receipt and disbursement of resources. Examples include those funds that account for the general operations of the governmental unit, the use of resources legally earmarked for a particular purpose, and the construction of major assets.

The second category includes the funds that focus on **capital maintenance (proprietary-type)**. These funds operate on a basis similar to that of a business in that they are usually self-supporting and involve the measurement of revenues and expenses. Examples include funds that account for the operations of a central motor pool and a government-owned electric utility.

The final category includes funds that involve an agency or trust relationship **(fiduciary-type)**. These funds focus on either the spending activities or the capital maintenance of the entity, depending on the nature of the activities involved. An example of a fiduciary-type fund that emphasizes spending activities is the fund used to record the disbursement of income from a trust. An example of a fiduciary-type fund that emphasizes capital maintenance is the fund used to record the operations of an employees' retirement system.

In summary, while a governmental unit may be composed of several different funds, these funds are separated into three major fund categories: governmental, proprietary, and fiduciary. These fund categories are discussed in greater depth later in this chapter.

Basis of Accounting

The term **basis of accounting** refers to the timing of the recognition (recording) of revenues and expenditures or expenses. Using the **cash basis** of accounting, these items are not recorded until cash changes hands. Receipts are not recognized until cash is received, and disbursements are not recognized until cash is paid out.

Cash basis systems are used primarily by individuals for tax purposes and by small businesses. Although a cash basis system is simple to install and use, it is seldom used to measure revenues and expenses. In reality, it is simply a measure of cash receipts and disbursements.

The **full accrual basis of accounting** does not require the movement of cash for accounting recognition. Instead, revenues are recognized in the period in which they are earned, and expenses are recognized in the period in which they are incurred in earning the revenue. If cash is not collected by the time the revenue is earned, a receivable is created. This receivable is removed from the accounts when the cash is collected. Expenses that are not paid for by the time they are incurred require the recognition of a liability in the accounts. When the liability is paid, it is removed from the accounts.

To illustrate the full accrual basis of accounting, assume that an organization renders a service to Sean Connerly on December 20, 19X1, for a fee of $200. Assume also that Mr. Connerly agreed to pay for the service in thirty days. The revenue is recorded as follows:

Accounts receivable	200	
Revenue		200

To record revenue for services performed for S. Connerly.

Collection of the receivable in January 19X2 should be recorded as follows:

Cash	200	
Accounts receivable		200

To record the collection of the S. Connerly account.

Notice that the $200 is recorded as revenue in the period earned (when the service is performed), (not) the period in which the cash is collected.

Using the cash basis of accounting, the only transaction recorded would be the receipt of cash in January as an **operating receipt**. This would be recorded as follows:

Cash	200	
Operating receipts		200

To record the collection of cash for services performed.

Furthermore, assume that the organization using the full accrual basis of accounting incurred a $100 expense on December 20, 19X1, but will not pay for it until January 20, 19X2. The following entry is made on December 20:

Expense	100	
Accounts payable		100

To record an expense.

Payment of the liability in January would require the following entry:

Accounts payable	100	
Cash		100

To record payment of a liability.

Notice that the $100 is recorded as an expense in the period incurred (when the benefit is received), *not* the period in which the cash is paid.

Using the cash basis of accounting, the only transaction recorded would be the payment of cash in January as an **operating disbursement**. This would be recorded as follows:

```
Operating disbursement                    100
    Cash                                          100
To record the payment for services received.
```

The cash basis and the accrual basis of accounting represent opposite ends of a spectrum. A compromise between these extremes, one used by most governmental units, is the **modified accrual basis**. When accounting systems use this basis of recognition, revenues are recorded in the period in which they are measurable and available. "Measurable" refers to the ability to state the amount of revenues in terms of dollars. " 'Available' means collectible within the current period or soon enough thereafter to be used to pay the liabilities of the current period."[6] In other words, revenues are recognized either when they are received in cash (licenses, fines, and so on) or when collection of the amount can be reasonably estimated to be received in the near future (such as property taxes).

Expenditures in a modified accrual system are *generally* recognized in the period in which goods or services are received or a liability is incurred. This, of course, is similar to the treatment such items would receive using the accrual basis of accounting. (Exceptions to the general rules of revenue and expenditure recognition are discussed in the chapters that follow.)

Notice that in the modified accrual basis of accounting the term *expenditures* is used in place of *expenses*. **Expenditures** include not only certain types of expenses incurred, in the commercial sense of the word, but also retirement of debt and capital outlays. In short, they represent any payment of cash or incurrence of a liability for the purpose of acquiring assets or services or settling losses. Expenditures are generally recorded when goods or services are received or a liability is incurred.

Table 3–1 summarizes the accounting procedures applicable to the funds used in governmental accounting. An overview of these procedures, together with the individual financial statements prepared for each fund, is presented in the remainder of this chapter. Chapters 4 through 9 focus on the activities usually found in each fund, together with the related accounting and reporting principles. In addition, Chapter 9 discusses financial reporting for the governmental unit as a whole.

[6]GASB Cod. Sec. 1600.106.

TABLE 3–1 Summary of Fund Accounting Procedures

Fund Type	Category	Accounting (Measurement) Focus	Basis of Accounting
General Fund	Governmental	Spending	Modified accrual
Special Revenue Funds	Governmental	Spending	Modified accrual
Debt Service Funds	Governmental	Spending	Modified accrual
Capital Projects Funds	Governmental	Spending	Modified accrual
Enterprise Funds	Proprietary	Capital maintenance	Full accrual
Internal Service Funds	Proprietary	Capital maintenance	Full accrual
Expendable Trust Funds	Fiduciary	Spending	Modified accrual
Nonexpendable Trust Funds	Fiduciary	Capital maintenance	Full accrual
Pension Trust Funds	Fiduciary	Capital maintenance	Full accrual
Agency Funds	Fiduciary	N/A*	Modified accrual

*Due to the nature of Agency Funds, there is no concept of measurement of operations.

Source: This table is a compilation of the data included in NCGA *Statement 1* and *Governmental Accounting, Auditing, and Financial Reporting (GAAFR)* (Chicago: Governmental Finance Officers Association of the United States and Canada, 1988).

SECTION II—GOVERNMENTAL-TYPE FUNDS AND ACCOUNT GROUPS

In Section I governmental-type funds are defined as those funds in which the accounting emphasis (measurement focus) is placed on spending activities. Within this group are the funds that primarily account for the receipt and disbursement of resources used to provide services. Specifically, the governmental-type funds are the General Fund, Special Revenue Funds, Debt Service Funds, and Capital Projects Funds. (Debt Service Funds are discussed on p. 70.)

The General Fund

While the specific number and type of funds utilized by a governmental unit are determined by the particular operations of that unit, every governmental body must at least have a **General Fund**. Technically, this fund is a residual fund—it is used to account for all governmental operations not accounted for in some other fund. In reality, however, the General Fund encompasses the overall operations of the governmental unit. Unless there is some legal, contractual, or managerial reason for separately accounting for an activity, it is recorded in the General Fund.

Included in the General Fund records are such activities as the police and fire departments, and the administrative operations of the government. The transactions recorded in the General Fund represent the collection of various sources of revenues and the disbursement of the resources for supplies, services, and so forth.

Assets usually found in the General Fund include cash, investments, receivables (usually property taxes), long-term advances to other funds, and receivables from other funds. In governmental accounting terminology, the receivables from other funds are referred to as **due from other funds**. If these receivables are not currently due, they are referred to as **advances to other funds**. Liabilities typicaly found in the General Fund include claims of various suppliers and payables to other funds. The latter items are referred to as **due to other funds**. As in the case of receivables, if these liabilities are not currently due they are referred to as **advances from other funds**.

Fund balance (equity) represents the excess of assets over liabilities (net resources that are available for spending). In those instances where an asset does not represent a resource available for current use, the fund balance must be restricted. In some instances this is accomplished by debiting the fund balance and crediting a reserve account. While this entry does not change the total fund balance, it does tell the reader that some of the assets are not currently available for spending.

To illustrate, assume that the long-term advances to other funds, mentioned above, total $20,000. The following entry is made at the end of the period:

Unreserved fund balance	20,000	
Fund balance reserved for		
advances to other funds		20,000
To adjust reserve account.		

The balance sheet would then show:

Fund Balance

Reserved for advances to other funds	$20,000
Unreserved fund balance	60,000 (assumed)
Total fund balance	$80,000

Note that the creation of the reserve in the manner described above *did not* change the total fund balance. While other reserves may be created in a different manner, all of them have the same effect: the disclosure of the fund balance that represents total spendable assets (unreserved fund balance) as opposed to the fund balance that does *not* represent spendable assets (various reserves).[7] The balance sheet for the General Fund in Table 3–2 indicates that one type of reserve is used by the city of Columbus—Reserve for encumbrances. Reserves are used to report assets that are not available for spending either because they are not in a spendable form (inventories, long-term receivables, and so on) or because they have previously been committed (encumbrances).[8]

[7]Designations of fund balance are discussed in Chapter 5.

[8]The concept of restricting fund balance is discussed in greater depth later in the text.

TABLE 3–2

City of Columbus, Ohio
General Fund
Balance Sheet
December 31, 19X1

ASSETS
Cash and investments with treasurer	$24,746,090	
Receivables (net of allowances for uncollectibles)	8,495,775	
Due from other funds	1,864,336	
Total assets		$35,106,201

LIABILITIES
Accounts payable	$ 1,531,789	
Due to other funds	566,006	
Accrued liabilities	10,837,232	
Total liabilities		$12,935,027

FUND BALANCE
Fund balance:		
Reserved for encumbrances	$ 6,769,580	
Unreserved, undesignated	15,401,594	
Total fund balance		22,171,174
Total liabilities and fund balance		$35,106,201

Note: Since the financial reporting process for governmental units does not emphasize the statements of individual funds, many governments do not prepare these statements for general issuance. Some of the statements of individual funds presented in this chapter were prepared from data included in various sections of the annual report of the governmental unit illustrated. Where these "other sources" were used, they are identified in the illustration with the notation "adapted from." If a separate source is not identified, that particular statement can be found in the annual financial report of the governmental unit illustrated. References to the notes to the financial statements have been omitted from these illustrations to avoid confusion. The concept of financial reporting, together with note disclosure, is discussed in Chapter 9.

Source: Adapted from the City of Columbus, Ohio, *Comprehensive Annual Financial Report,* December 31, 19X1, Combined Balance Sheet—All Fund Types and Account Groups.

Revenues usually available for use by the General Fund include taxes, licenses and permits, and fines and forfeitures. Expenditures are generally those associated with the services and supplies used in the various operating departments. An example of an operating statement combined with a statement of the changes in the fund balance (statement of revenues, expenditures, and changes in fund balance) is shown in Table 3–3.

Other financing sources (uses) are increases and decreases in fund balance that are not included in revenues and expenditures. They consist mainly of operating transfers (transfers of resources between funds) and, where applicable, proceeds from bond issues. **Operating transfers in** are transfers to the General Fund from other funds, whereas **operating transfers out** are transfers from the General Fund to other funds. A discussion of the technical aspects of

TABLE 3–3

City of Columbus, Ohio
General Fund
Statement of Revenues, Expenditures and Changes in Fund Balances
For the Year Ended December 31, 19X1

Revenues:		
Income taxes	$134,464,696	
Property taxes	13,416,233	
Grants and subsidies	177,381	
Investment earnings	6,234,829	
Licenses and permits	3,781,463	
Shared revenues	18,149,996	
Charges for services	4,015,310	
Fines and forfeits	8,035,698	
Miscellaneous	15,281,336	
Total revenues		$203,556,942
Expenditures:		
Current:		
General government	$ 35,583,610	
Public service	22,140,260	
Public safety	111,779,231	
Human services	1,581,875	
Development	4,943,998	
Health	98,047	
Recreation and parks	178,655	
Capital outlay	4,910,045	
Total expenditures		181,215,721
Excess of revenues over expenditures		$ 22,341,221
Other financing sources (uses):		
Operating transfers in	$ 5,316,544	
Operating transfers out	(23,310,773)	
Total other financing uses		(17,994,229)
Excess of revenues and other financing sources over expenditures and other financing uses		$ 4,346,992
Fund balance at beginning of year		17,824,182
Fund balance at end of year		$ 22,171,174

Source: Adapted from the City of Columbus, Ohio, *Comprehensive Annual Financial Report*, December 31, 19X1, Combined Statement of Revenues, Expenditures and Changes in Fund Balances—All Governmental Fund Types and Expendable Trust Funds.

transfers is included in Chapter 5. At this point it is only necessary for the reader to understand that many types of transfers take place in order to move resources from one fund to another.

Like all governmental-type funds, the accounting records of the General Fund are maintained on the modified accrual basis. A governmental unit may have only *one* General Fund.

Special Revenue Funds

Special Revenue Funds are used to account for the proceeds of revenue sources (other than expendable trusts, or those used for major capital projects) that must be spent for a particular purpose. The accounting treatment of these funds is identical to that of the General Fund. The primary difference between the two funds lies in the breadth of activities recorded in each.

Special Revenue Funds should be used only when required by law, charter, or other commitment. The main purpose of separating these types of activities from those of the General Fund is to maintain control over the collection and use of specific sources of revenue. For example, assume that a tax on gasoline is specifically dedicated to highway maintenance. Generally a Special Revenue Fund is required by the law establishing the tax. This makes it easy for the governmental unit to account for the dollars collected from the gasoline tax, as well as the expenditures for highway maintenance. If these funds were commingled with other revenues and expenditures, it would be much more difficult to account for the money collected and its use. Other examples of Special Revenue Funds include special income tax funds, hotel-motel tax funds, street construction and maintenance funds, and community development funds.

A governmental unit can have several Special Revenue Funds. Usually the law or commitment that requires the use of a Special Revenue Fund also requires that separate records be maintained for the activity. Each of these funds is treated as a separate accounting entity for record-keeping purposes.

The types of assets usually found in Special Revenue Funds include cash, investments, receivables (usually taxes), and amounts due from other funds. Liabilities common to these funds include the claims of various suppliers and payables to other funds. Since the accounting for Special Revenue Funds is identical to that of the General Fund, those comments made regarding the fund balance in our discussion of the General Fund are also relevant here. A balance sheet for a Special Revenue Fund is shown in Table 3–4.

Generally the sources of revenue for Special Revenue Funds are taxes, rents and royalties, and intergovernmental items (grants, shared revenues, and so forth). The expenditures made by these funds are usually for services and supplies specifically identified by the law establishing the particular fund (see Table 3–5).

The modified accrual basis of accounting is used for each Special Revenue Fund.

Capital Projects Funds

Capital Projects Funds account for the receipt and disbursement of resources used to acquire major capital facilities through purchase or construction. A Capital Projects Fund is not used to account for such assets acquired by an Enterprise Fund, an Internal Service Fund, a Trust Fund, or those assets that are purchased directly with current revenues of the General Fund or a Special Rev-

TABLE 3–4

City of New Orleans, Louisiana
Special Revenue Fund
Downtown Development District Fund
Balance Sheet
December 31, 19X1

ASSETS

Cash	$ 205,562	
Investments, at cost or amortized cost	3,797,293	
Accounts receivable (net of allowances for uncollectibles)	436,575	
Prepaid expenses and deposits	242	
Advances to other funds	176,126	
Total assets		$4,615,798

LIABILITIES AND FUND BALANCE

Liabilities:		
Accounts payable	$ 33,777	
Other payables and accruals	91,901	
Deferred revenues	27,996	
Total liabilities		$ 153,674

FUND BALANCE:

Reserved for long-term advances to other funds	176,126
Designated for subsequent years' expenditures	3,678,253
Unreserved, undesignated	607,745
Total liabilities and fund balance	$4,615,798

Source: Adapted from the City of New Orleans, Louisiana, *Comprehensive Annual Financial Report,* December 31, 19X1, Combining Balance Sheet—Special Revenue Funds.

enue Fund. However, it must be used where there is a legal requirement for such accounting or when the financing of a general governmental project involves the issuance of bonds, intergovernmental revenues, major private donations, or other restricted sources.[9]

Generally a separate Capital Projects Fund is used for each project. When a bond issue is involved in the financing, a separate fund is used for each bond issue. The use of a separate fund provides better control over the individual projects or the proceeds from a bond issue.

Projects usually accounted for in these funds include the construction of bridges, a new city hall, and the acquisition of assets that involve long-term financing. Examples of the types of acquisitions that usually do *not* require the

[9]*Governmental Accounting, Auditing and Financial Reporting (GAAFR)* (Chicago: Government Finance Officers Association of the United States and Canada, 1980), p.46.

TABLE 3–5

City of New Orleans, Louisiana
Special Revenue Fund
Downtown Development District Fund
Statement of Revenues, Expenditures and Changes in Fund Balance
For the Year Ended December 31, 19X1

Revenues:		
Taxes	$3,506,041	
Interest income	445,966	
Miscellaneous	10,157	
Total revenues		$3,962,164
Expenditures:		
General government	$ 764,577	
Public safety	669,169	
Public works	1,021,254	
Culture and recreation	99,760	
Total expenditures		2,554,760
Excess of revenues over expenditures		$1,407,404
Other financing uses:		
Operating transfers out		(1,726,903)
Excess of expenditures and other financing uses over revenues		$ (319,499)
Fund balance at beginning of year		4,781,623
Fund balance at end of year		$4,462,124

Source: Adapted from the City of New Orleans, Louisiana, *Comprehensive Annual Financial Report,* December 31, 19X1, Combining Statement of Revenues, Expenditures and Changes in Fund Balances—Special Revenue Funds.

use of a Capital Projects Fund are the purchase of automobiles, furniture, and minor equipment.

Assets normally found on the balance sheet of a Capital Projects Fund are shown in Table 3–6. These include cash, receivables, and amounts due from other funds or governments. Liabilities include accounts payable and amounts due to other funds or governments for services and materials associated with the construction projects (or to construction companies if the projects are completed by outside contractors).

A statement of revenues, expenditures, and changes in fund balance for a Capital Projects Fund is shown in Table 3–7. The normal sources of assets for these funds are federal and state grants, earnings on investments, issuance of debt securities, and possible transfers from other funds. Expenditures are usually limited to amounts related to the capital projects and include construction and engineering costs.

Since Capital Projects Funds are governmental-type funds, they follow the modified accrual basis of accounting.

TABLE 3–6

City of Columbus, Ohio
Capital Projects Fund
Street and Highway Improvement Fund
Balance Sheet
December 31, 19X1

ASSETS		
Cash and investments with treasurer	$571,416	
Due from other:		
Governments	169,325	
Funds	388,281	
Total assets		$1,129,022
LIABILITIES		
Accounts payable		$ 982
FUND BALANCE		
Reserved for encumbrances	$131,200	
Unreserved, undesignated	996,840	
Total fund balance		1,128,040
Total liabilities and fund balance		$1,129,022

Source: Adapted from the City of Columbus, Ohio, *Comprehensive Annual Financial Report*, December 31, 19X1, Combining Balance Sheet—All Capital Projects Funds.

TABLE 3–7

City of Columbus, Ohio
Capital Projects Fund
Street and Highway Improvement Fund
Statement of Revenues, Expenditures and Changes in Fund Balance
For the Year Ended December 31, 19X1

Revenues:	
Miscellaneous	$1,011,567
Expenditures:	
Capital outlay	398,437
Excess of revenue over expenditures	$ 613,130
Other financing sources:	
Operating transfers in	322,460
Excess of revenue and other financing sources over	
expenditures	$ 935,590
Fund balance at beginning of year	192,450
Fund balance at end of year	$1,128,040

Source: Adapted from the City of Columbus, Ohio, *Comprehensive Annual Financial Report*, December 31, 19X1, Combining Statement of Revenues, Expenditures and Changes in Fund Balance—All Capital Projects Funds.

ACCOUNT GROUPS

Certain types of assets and liabilities relate to the operations of the overall governmental unit rather than to those of a particular fund. These assets are not an appropriable resource, and the liabilities are not a current claim against the resources of a specific fund. They are, therefore, not reported on the financial statements of any fund. Instead, these assets and liabilities are recorded in **account groups**. An account group is not a fund because it is not an independent fiscal entity. Instead an account group is simply a self-balancing set of accounts used for *control* purposes. The two types of account groups used in governmental accounting are the General Fixed Assets Account Group and the General Long-Term Debt Account Group.

The General Fixed Assets Account Group (GFAAG)

The General Fixed Assets Account Group (GFAAG) is used to control the property, buildings, furniture, and equipment-type assets used by the governmental unit except for those found in proprietary-type funds and some Trust Funds. In general, the GFAAG is used to keep a record of the assets available for the overall operations of the governmental unit. Remember that the focus of the accounting system for the type of funds included (governmental-type funds and some Trust Funds) is on the spending of current resources. Since items of property and equipment are not available to be spent, they are not accounted for in those funds. In the balance sheets contained in previous tables in this chapter, the assets are generally limited to cash, receivables, investments, and amounts due from other governmental units—spendable resources or resources that will normally be converted into spendable resources.

Every governmental unit has a large amount of money invested in various types of property and equipment, and therefore some form of control is needed. This control is maintained by the accounting procedures followed in the GFAAG. Table 3–8 is a typical example of the financial reporting involved. While the statement is referred to as a "schedule" by the city of New Orleans, it is prepared in a balanced form similar to that of a balance sheet. The assets are listed first by major category: land, building(s), equipment, and construction in progress (partially completed assets). The balancing effect is achieved by listing the sources of the resources used to acquire the assets. In Table 3–8, these sources are debt, various types of grants, and resources obtained from specific funds. Note that the totals of the two categories balance. The total assets must *always* equal the total of the sources of the funds used to acquire the assets. Notice also that the city of New Orleans could not locate the sources of some of its assets acquired before January 1, 19XX. This situation is reasonably common in governmental reporting.

For control over individual assets, detailed subsidiary records must be maintained as to the type and location of each item, and the individual items

TABLE 3–8

City of New Orleans, Louisiana
General Fixed Assets
Schedule of General Fixed Assets—By Source
December 31, 19X1

General fixed assets:	
Land	$ 28,103,562
Buildings and improvements	141,694,594
Equipment	47,836,639
Construction in progress	41,820,947
	$259,455,742
Investment in general fixed assets from:	
Capital Projects Funds:	
General obligation bonds	$ 42,200,713
Federal grants	36,156,073
State grants	1,367,422
Miscellaneous capital funds	5,550,439
Gifts	3,880,079
Miscellaneous revenues	5,360,153
General Fund revenues	44,720,251
Unidentified sources*	120,220,612
	$259,455,742

*Purchases prior to January 1, 19XX, for which a funding source could not be identified.

Source: City of New Orleans, Louisiana, *Comprehensive Annual Financial Report*, December 31, 19X1, Schedule of General Fixed Assets—By Source.

must be physically identified. This is usually achieved by attaching a tag with a serial number to each asset and by keeping detailed information about each asset by serial number. Although this may be a monumental task, it is necessary to ensure that governmental assets are adequately protected. Such records also provide data needed to acquire adequate insurance coverage and to file claims when losses occur.

A schedule of changes in general fixed assets is shown in Table 3–9. While no activity statement is required for this reporting entity, the schedule of changes is required, either in statement form or in the notes to the financial statements, in order to conform to reporting requirements.

The General Long-Term Debt Account Group (GLTDAG)

Long-term debt is accounted for in the fund that has primary responsibility for the generation of the resources that will be used to retire the debt. For example, revenue bonds that will be retired from future revenue generated by

TABLE 3–9

City of New Orleans, Louisiana
General Fixed Assets
Schedule of Changes in General Fixed Assets—
By Function and Activity
For the Year Ended December 31, 19X1

Function and Activity	General Fixed Assets January 1, 19X1	Additions	Deductions	General Fixed Assets December 31, 19X1
General government:				
The Council	$ 257,937	58,414	48,009	268,342
The Mayor	3,310,323	352,159	128,466	3,534,016
Department of Law	64,797	—	—	64,797
Judicial and parochial	1,280,312	52,633	124,502	1,208,443
Department of Finance	1,705,071	9,318	77,829	1,636,560
Unattached boards and commissions	860,316	3,075	45,243	818,148
Department of Civil Service	88,380	18,706	10,121	96,965
General services	74,226	—	—	74,226
General government	75,579,980	100,000	—	75,679,980
Total general government	83,221,342	594,305	434,170	83,381,477
Public safety:				
Department of Police	25,148,685	67,419	1,367,704	23,848,400
Department of Fire	11,190,128	2,370	259,032	10,933,466
Department of Safety and Permits	371,858	625,152	14,684	982,326
Total public safety	36,710,671	694,941	1,641,420	35,764,192
Public works:				
Department of Streets	5,218,872	125,029	410,895	4,933,006
Department of Sanitation	14,447,053	3,035	1,490,990	12,959,098
Department of Property Management	586,619	353,453	40,315	899,757
Department of Utilities	37,506	2,370	—	39,876
Total public works	20,290,050	483,887	1,942,200	18,831,737
Health and welfare:				
Department of Health	6,178,491	20,181	61,431	6,137,241
Department of Welfare	3,135,122	14,740	59,352	3,090,510
Total health and welfare	9,313,613	34,921	120,783	9,227,751
Culture and recreation:				
Public Library	5,559,950	14,876	111,606	5,463,220
Cultural Commission	3,523,668	10,551	—	3,534,219
Department of Recreation	61,020,417	136,672	244,124	60,912,965
Total culture and recreation	70,104,035	162,099	355,730	69,910,404
Urban development and housing	459,653	16,255	7,857	468,051
Economic development and assistance	51,183	—	—	51,183
Construction in progress	28,047,377	15,331,439	1,557,869	41,820,947
Total general fixed assets	$248,197,924	17,317,847	6,060,029	259,455,742

Source: City of New Orleans, Louisiana, *Comprehensive Annual Financial Report*, December 31, 19X1, Schedule of Changes in General Fixed Assets—By Function and Activity.

an Enterprise Fund are reported as a long-term debt on the balance sheet of that fund.

By contrast, long-term debt that will be retired through the use of general resources available to the governmental unit is not generally reported on the balance sheet of any particular fund because of the current-spending focus of the accounting system. Instead, such debt (general obligation bonds) is reported in the General Long-Term Debt Account Group (GLTDAG) (see Table 3–10).

The format of the statement lists the resources that have been provided in a Debt Service Fund for the retirement of the debt (amount available in debt service funds) and the amount that has yet to be set aside for the retirement of the debt (amount to be provided). These latter amounts will be transferred to a Debt Service Fund in future years. The total of the resources provided and to be provided will be equal to the long-term debt outstanding.

Notice that all types of long-term debt are contained in the GLTDAG. While bonds have been used as examples in the above discussion, long-term leases, installment purchase contracts, and so forth, are also reported in this account group.

While no activity statement reporting the results of operations is required for an account group, the ending balance in the GLTDAG must be reconciled with the beginning balance. In other words, the changes in the general long-term debt must be reported either in the notes to the financial statements or in a separate statement. Since the statement approach was illustrated for the changes in the fixed assets, we will illustrate the reporting of the changes in long-term debt using the notes to the financial statements. Table 3–11 contains the note used by the city of Columbus.

TABLE 3–10

City of Columbus, Ohio
General Long-Term Debt Account Group
Schedule of General Long-Term Debt
December 31, 19X1

Amount available and to be provided for payment of long-term debt:	
Amount available in Debt Service Funds	$ 22,837,959
Amount to be provided for retirement of general long-term obligations	303,029,971
Total	$325,867,930
General long-term debt payable:	
Accrued liabilities	$ 44,563,328
Accrued vacation and sick leave	30,413,602
Bonds and loan payable	234,531,000
Obligations under capitalized leases	16,360,000
Total	$325,867,930

Source: Adapted from the City of Columbus, Ohio, *Comprehensive Annual Financial Report*, December 31, 19X1, Combined Balance Sheet—All Fund Types and Account Groups.

TABLE 3–11

City of Columbus, Ohio
General Long-Term Debt Account Group
Disclosure of Changes in General Long-Term Debt

Note G—Notes Payable and Long-Term Obligations*

A summary of notes payable and long-term obligation transactions for the year ended December 31, 19X1, follows:

Fund Type/Account Group	Balance December 31, 19X0	Additions	Deletions	Balance December 31, 19X1
		(in thousands)		
General Long-Term Obligations:				
Accrued liabilities—Note K	$ 44,840	—	277	44,563
Accrued vacation and sick leave	29,657	757	—	30,414
General obligation bonds	189,192	60,456	15,117	234,531
Obligations under capital leases—Note J	17,220	—	860	16,360
Total General Long-Term Obligations	280,909	61,213	16,254	325,868
Capital Projects—Notes payable	47,465	7,723	52,115	3,073
Enterprise:				
Water:				
General obligation bonds	123,610	—	6,421	117,189
Revenue bonds	142,800	—	600	142,200
Total Water	266,410	—	7,021	259,389
Sewer:				
Notes payable	15,000	35,000	50,000	—
General obligation bonds	128,560	2,914	7,750	123,724
Revenue bonds	—	209,000	—	209,000
OWDA loans	19,297	—	908	18,389
Total Sewer	162,857	246,914	58,658	351,113
Electricity:				
General obligation bonds	117,380	116,980	101,240	133,120
Revenue bonds	70,000	—	800	69,200
Total Electricity	187,380	116,980	102,040	202,320
Airport				
Notes payable	1,200	1,000	1,200	1,000
General obligation bonds	67,442	—	3,619	63,823
Total Airport	68,642	1,000	4,819	64,823
Total Enterprise	685,289	364,894	172,538	877,645
Internal Service:				
Notes payable	900	—	900	—
Computer notes payable	3,305	398	899	2,804
Total Internal Service	4,205	398	1,799	2,804
Total notes payable and long-term obligations	$1,017,868	434,228	242,706	1,209,390

*This table includes general obligation debt ($325,868) and all other notes and long-term obligations, which total to $1,209,390 (in thousands).

Source: The City of Columbus, Ohio, *Comprehensive Annual Financial Report*, December 31, 19X1, Notes to the General Purpose Financial Statements.

Debt Service Funds

Debt Service Funds account for the accumulation of resources that will be used to make the payments of principal and interest on general long-term debt.[10] This type of fund can also be used for the payment of long-term liabilities other than bonds, such as installment purchase contracts and lease-purchase agreements. (In most of the latter instances the payments are made directly from general revenues on an annual basis. Therefore they can be accounted for in the General Fund.) Unlike Special Revenue Funds, a single Debt Service Fund should be used for all general long-term debt whenever possible. In many instances, however, each debt issue may require the establishment of a separate Debt Service Fund.

The sources of the assets for Debt Service Funds include

1. Transfers from the General Fund (and/or other funds)
2. Income from the investment of the resources held by the Debt Service Funds
3. Taxes assessed to service the debt

The expenditures generally involve the payment of principal and interest on the debt. A statement of revenues, expenditures, and changes in fund balance for a Debt Service Fund is shown in Table 3–12.

As a result of the above types of transactions, the assets of Debt Service Funds usually consist of cash, investments, and possibly receivables. The liabilities are generally interest and principal *currently due*. The fund balance therefore represents the resources available to *service* (pay principal and interest on) the debt. The liability for the principal not currently due is reported in the General Long-Term Debt Account Group. A balance sheet for a Debt Service Fund is shown in Table 3–13.

Debt Service Funds follow the modified accrual basis of accounting.

Special Assessment Funds

Prior to the issuance of GASB *Statement No. 6*, "Accounting and Financial Reporting for Special Assessments," capital improvements and/or services financed by special assessments on properties were accounted for in **Special Assessment Funds**. Taxpayers who received these special benefits were assessed for their share of the cost of the project. Examples of such projects include paving of city streets, building of parking structures, and special police protection.

In *Statement No. 6*, the GASB separated these activities into two major groups: service assessments and capital improvements assessments. **Service assessments** generally include activities such as special police protection, storm

---

[10]Debt to be serviced by proprietary fund revenues is not serviced by these funds.

TABLE 3–12

City of Columbus, Ohio
Debt Service Fund
General Bond Retirement Fund
Statement of Revenues, Expenditures and Changes in Fund Balance
For the Year Ended December 31, 19X1

Revenues:		
Income taxes	$23,978,647	
Property taxes	545,889	
Investment earnings	949,589	
Special assessments	283,804	
Miscellaneous	240,532	
Total revenues		$25,998,461
Expenditures:		
Current:		
General government	$ 145,724	
Debt service:		
Principal retirement	12,377,048	
Interest and fiscal charges	16,852,044	
Total expenditures		29,374,816
Excess of expenditures over revenues		$(3,376,355)
Other financing sources (uses):		
Proceeds of refunding bonds	$ 4,256,000	
Operating transfers in	3,606,805	
Payment to refunded bond escrow agent	(4,256,000)	
Total other financing sources		3,606,805
Excess of revenues and other financing sources over expenditures and other financing uses		$ 230,450
Fund balance at beginning of year		3,014,446
Fund balance at end of year		$ 3,244,896

Source: Adapted from the City of Columbus, Ohio, *Comprehensive Annual Financial Report,* December 31, 19X1, Combining Statement of Revenues, Expenditures and Changes in Fund Balance.

sewer cleaning, and snow plowing. **Capital improvements assessments** generally include construction projects such as street improvements and sidewalks.

These types of activities were accounted for in a separate fund type prior to the issuance of *Statement No. 6.* The primary reasons for separating these projects from similar projects are related to the scope of benefit and the peculiar financing arrangements usually found with special assessments.

The scope of special assessment projects is very limited; generally, property owners in only a relatively small area benefit from the services. For example, the resurfacing of a neighborhood street does not benefit the citizenry as a whole, but it does benefit those who live in that neighborhood. In addition, these types of projects are often financed by a periodic fee that is assessed against the property holder or by special assessment debt that is secured by a lien on specific property. In many instances special assessment debt is not general obligation debt, but rather debt associated with a particular project.

TABLE 3–13

City of Columbus, Ohio
Debt Service Fund
General Bond Retirement Fund
Balance Sheet
December 31, 19X1

ASSETS		
Cash and investments with treasurer	$1,528,043	
Cash with fiscal and escrow agents	535,809	
Investments, at cost	4,592,063	
Receivables (net of allowance for uncollectibles)	1,006,280	
Total assets		$7,662,195
LIABILITIES		
Due to other funds	$3,069,366	
Deferred revenue	724,859	
Matured bonds payable	86,000	
Matured interest payable	537,074	
Total liabilities		$4,417,299
FUND BALANCE		
Fund balance:		
Unreserved, undesignated		3,244,896
Total liabilities and fund balance		$7,662,195

Source: Adapted from the City of Columbus, Ohio, *Comprehensive Annual Financial Report,* December 31, 19X1, Combining Balance Sheet—All Debt Service Funds.

Prior to the issuance of *Statement No. 6*, accounting for capital improvement-type special assessment projects created a major reporting problem. Since the debt was directly associated with the project, it was not reported in the General Long-Term Debt Account Group. Instead, it was reported as a liability of the particular Special Assessment Fund. Since most of these projects involved construction, a matching problem resulted. The construction costs were usually incurred early in the life of the project, often in the first few months, while the resources to pay for the expenditures, the special assessment fund revenues, were deferred over the life of the debt—often ten, fifteen or even twenty years. This problem was compounded by the fact that the debt was reported on the balance sheet as a fund liability and not on the operating statement as another financing source (see the discussion of Capital Projects Funds). Thus there were no financial resources to offset the expenditures on the project. As a result, these funds often reported large deficits until all of the special assessments were collected.

Deficits in a fund are very difficult to explain in governmental reports, especially those found in funds that are designed to be self-supporting. These situations caused concern among the members of the NCGA and, later, the GASB. Finally, the GASB issued *Statement No. 6* to resolve this problem.

Statement No. 6 provides for separating special assessment projects into the two basic types: service and capital improvements. **Service-type special assessments** are reported in the fund type that best reflects the nature of the transactions. Generally this involves the use of the General Fund, a Special Revenue Fund, or an Enterprise Fund (discussed later in this chapter). **Capital improvement-type special assessments** are generally reported as any other type of construction project: the construction activities are reported in a Capital Projects Fund, the related debt financing is reported in the General Long-Term Debt Account Group, and the debt servicing is reported in a Debt Service Fund. Additional information regarding the accounting and reporting of special assessment-type events is given in Chapter 7.

It is important to note that *Statement No. 6* does not eliminate Special Assessment Funds as an accounting entity. Many governmental units will have to comply with contractual and/or legal requirements for a separate accounting using these types of funds. Instead, the GASB simply stated that special assessment reporting was discontinued. In the remainder of this text all discussion and problems relating to special assessment-type activities will be presented in accordance with these provisions.

SECTION III—PROPRIETARY-TYPE FUNDS

Proprietary-type funds are those funds in which the accounting emphasis is placed on capital maintenance. Within this group are the funds that provide services that are paid for by user charges. The two types of funds found in this category are Enterprise Funds and Internal Service Funds.

Enterprise Funds

Enterprise Funds are used to account for products or services continuously provided by the governmental unit where (1) the users include the general public and (2) the costs of providing the products or services are financed mainly by user charges. They are also used when the management of a governmental unit feels that an accounting system similar to that of a commercial business is necessary for operational control over an activity. Types of operations normally found in Enterprise Funds include municipally owned utilities, airports, swimming pools, and golf courses. Generally a separate fund is established for each type of service provided.

The type of accounting used for Enterprise Funds is essentially the same as that used for commercial operations (full accrual accounting). Here the emphasis shifts from resources available for use (spending activities), as in governmental-type funds, to a capital maintenance approach. The reason for the shift is that a determination of the total cost of the services provided is needed either to develop user charges—similar to selling prices in a commercial enterprise—or to determine the amount of subsidy needed to support the activities, or some combination of these.

TABLE 3–14

City of New Orleans, Louisiana
Enterprise Fund
Sewerage and Water Board Fund
Balance Sheet
December 31, 19X1

ASSETS
Current assets:

Cash	$ 653,635	
Time certificates of deposit	56,675,000	
Investments	32,215,493	
Receivables (net of allowance for uncollectibles):		
Taxes	1,310,542	
Accounts	15,090,573	
Accrued interest	1,167,929	
Other	1,405,535	
Due from other funds	1,012,986	
Due from other governments	259,351	
Current portion of advance to other funds	330,347	
Inventory of supplies, at lower of cost or market	4,380,821	
Prepaid expenses and deposits	427,146	
Total current assets		$114,929,358
Advances to other funds		1,380,734
Restricted assets:		
Customer deposits	$ 4,390,740	
Construction account	47,786,807	
Current debt service account	1,454,013	
Future debt service account	17,606,506	
Escrow funds	27,755,646	
Other	212,000	
Total restricted assets		99,205,712
Property, plant, and equipment—at cost, less accumulated depreciation		498,773,017
Other assets		2,250,939
Total assets		$716,539,760

The balance sheet of an Enterprise Fund is shown in Table 3–14. Several major points regarding this financial statement should be noted. The first is the classified approach used by the Sewerage and Water Board Fund. A **classified balance sheet** presents the assets and liabilities grouped by major type. **Current assets** are those assets (including cash) that will be used up or collected within one year. **Current liabilities** are those debts that will be paid within one year, using current assets. **Long-term liabilities** are liabilities that will be paid later than one year in the future or will be paid from other than current assets. The general long-term debt payable represents general obligation debt that will be serviced by Sewerage and Water Board Fund assets.

The second major point that should be noted is the use of **restricted assets**. These assets represent resources that have been set aside for some particular use

TABLE 3–14 (cont.)

LIABILITIES AND FUND EQUITY

Current liabilities (payable from current assets):

Accounts payable	$ 8,697,349	
Retainages payable	888,108	
Other payables and accruals	11,342,107	
Due to other funds	1,959,992	
Deferred revenues	1,334,519	
Total current liabilities (payable from current assets)		$ 24,222,075
Current liabilities (payable from restricted assets):		
Retainages payable	$ 1,085,142	
Accrued interest	1,459,636	
Limited tax bonds	3,455,000	
Revenue bonds	5,765,000	
Deposits	4,390,740	
Other	46,794	
Total current liabilities (payable from restricted assets)		16,202,312
Total current liabilities		$ 40,424,387
Long-term liabilities:		
Limited tax bonds (net of current portion)	$ 91,215,000	
Revenue bonds (net of current portion)	50,805,000	
Total long-term liabilities		142,020,000
Total liabilities		$182,444,387
Fund equity:		
Contributed capital	$103,233,502	
Retained earnings:		
Reserved for revenue bond retirement	17,606,506	
Reserved for capital improvements	411,155,365	
Reserved for self-insurance	2,100,000	
Total fund equity		534,095,373
Total liabilities and fund equity		$716,539,760

Source: Adapted from the City of New Orleans, Louisiana, *Comprehensive Annual Financial Report*, December 31, 19X1, Combining Balance Sheet—Proprietary Fund Type—Enterprise Funds.

resulting from a legal, contractual, or regulatory restriction and are labeled "Restricted assets" on the balance sheet. The current liabilities that will be satisfied from such resources must also be segregated. Thus there are two sections of current liabilities on the statement.

Other asset categories used on the balance sheet include Advances to other funds; Property, plant, and equipment; and Other assets. The **Advances to other funds** section is used to report long-term receivables. The **Property, plant, and equipment** section includes the major assets that are used to provide the services for which the fund was established. The **Other assets** section is used as a catchall category. Any asset that does not fit into one of the specific categories is reported in the "other" category.

Finally, note that fund equity is divided into (1) capital contributed by the government, customers, and so forth, in the form of permanent contributions; and (2) retained earnings. The **retained earnings** represent the accumulate earnings (income) of the unit.

The balance sheet shown in Table 3–14 is in a form that is typical of commercial business—current assets and liabilities preceding noncurrent. It is not uncommon, however, to find the plant and the long-term debt first on utility balance sheets. This is because of the excessively larger percentage of the total assets or total equities these items represent for utilities, relative to other forms of business. The standard commercial form is followed quite often for governmental purposes because of the use of combined statements. (The "combined" aspect of governmental reporting is discussed in Chapter 9.) Unless there are legal restrictions involved, either is acceptable.

The operating revenues earned by an Enterprise Fund usually result from user charges (see Table 3–15). The expenses associated with the operations of the fund depend on the type of operations but usually include the cost of services, supplies used, utilities, depreciation, and so forth. Notice particularly the charge for depreciation. Since the Enterprise Funds use the full accrual method of accounting, depreciation must be included as an expense.

Notice also that operating expenses are deducted from operating revenues to calculate operating income or loss. The nonoperating items are then added or subtracted to determine the net income for the period. This figure is added, in the case of income, to the beginning balance in Retained earnings (or deducted in the case of a net loss) to determine the ending balance in that account.

Enterprise Funds are part of a governmental unit; therefore, operating transfers are often used to provide operating subsidies for the funds or to move resources from Enterprise Funds or other funds. These transfers should be reported after nonoperating revenues (expenses) and before extraordinary items. Extraordinary items are events that are not typical for such an organization and are incurred infrequently. In the instance of the loss on bond refunding, GAAP require this item to be reported as an extraordinary item.

Since the operations of an Enterprise Fund are essentially the same as those of a profit-oriented business, an additional statement must be prepared to be in accordance with GAAP. This statement is a **statement of cash flows**. Table 3–16 is an example of a statement of cash flows for the Sewerage and Water Board of the City of New Orleans. The purpose of this statement is to provide information regarding the sources and uses of cash by the fund for operating, investing, and financing activities.

Recently, the FASB has required the use of a cash flow statement. Prior to this change, organizations prepared a statement of changes in financial position. The statement of changes in financial position could be prepared using either cash or working capital (current assets – current liabilities) as a basis. The most recent FASB pronouncement requires cash (including cash equivalents) to be used as a basis for the statement and includes some format changes. At the time of this writing, the GASB is studying the cash flow

TABLE 3–15

City of New Orleans, Louisiana
Enterprise Fund
Sewerage and Water Board Fund
Statement of Revenues, Expenses, and Changes in Retained Earnings
For the Year Ended December 31, 19X1

Operating revenues:		
Charges for services	$89,837,147	
Other	173,957	
Total operating revenue		$ 90,011,104
Operating expenses:		
Personal services	$35,132,350	
Contractual services	15,551,344	
Materials and supplies	7,234,386	
Depreciation	11,293,854	
Other	3,845,566	
Total operating expenses		73,057,500
Operating income		$ 16,953,604
Nonoperating revenues (expenses):		
Taxes	$29,887,421	
Interest revenue	11,991,304	
Interest expense	(10,202,168)	
Other—net	849,524	
Total nonoperating revenues		32,526,081
Income before extraordinary items		$ 49,479,685
Extraordinary loss on bond refunding		(3,890,750)
Net income		$ 45,588,935
Retained earnings at beginning of year		385,272,936
Retained earnings at end of year		$430,861,871

Source: Adapted from the City of New Orleans, Louisiana, *Comprehensive Annual Financial Report*, December 31, 19X1, Combining Statement of Revenues, Expenditures, and Changes in Retained Earnings—Proprietary Fund Type—Enterprise Funds.

concept, and has issued an Exposure Draft requiring such a statement. As a result, we are using the GASB Exposure Draft as a basis for this illustration. The new statement has not been issued by any governmental unit. We have, therefore, adapted data included in the City of New Orleans 1986 *Comprehensive Annual Financial Report* to prepare the statement of cash flows illustrated in Table 3–16. Since the preparation of this statement is beyond the scope of this text, we have included Table 3–16 for illustrative purposes only.

Internal Service Funds

The second type of proprietary fund is the **Internal Service Fund**. This fund is used to account for the furnishing of goods or services within the governmental unit or to other governmental units on a user charge basis. The main

TABLE 3-16

City of New Orleans, Louisiana
Enterprise Fund
Sewerage and Water Board Fund
Statement of Cash Flows*
For the Year Ended December 31, 19X1

Cash flows from operating activities:		
Net operating income	$16,953,604	
Items not requiring cash currently:		
Depreciation	11,293,854	
Decrease in inventory of supplies	297,709	
Decrease in prepaid expenses and deposits	21,553	
Decrease in due from other governments	220,158	
Increase in other payables and accruals	1,926,378	
Increase in due to other funds	1,855,732	
Decrease in accounts payable	(265,938)	
Decrease in deferred revenue	(1,108,276)	
Increase in receivables	(2,609,066)	
Increase in due from other funds	(1,012,986)	
Net cash provided by operating activities		$27,572,722
Cash flows from noncapital financing activities:		
Advances to other funds		(1,711,081)
Cash flows from capital and related financing activities:		
Proceeds from sale of revenue and limited tax bonds	$80,910,000	
Taxes	29,887,421	
Interest revenue	11,991,304	
Contributions from capital grants	3,435,979	
Sale of investments	8,925,206	
Increase in retainages payable	482,398	
Other nonoperating revenues	849,524	
Refunding of bonds	(54,738,750)	
Retirement of long-term bonds	(7,205,000)	
Acquisition of property, plant, and equipment	(49,247,958)	
Interest expense	(10,202,168)	
Increase in other assets	(2,199,624)	
Increase in restricted assets	(11,442,775)	
Net reduction in current liabilities		
payable from restricted assets	(2,547,641)	
Net cash used for capital and related		
financing activities		(1,102,084)
Net increase in cash and cash equivalents		$24,759,557
Cash and cash equivalents at beginning of year		32,569,078
Cash and cash equivalents at end of year		$57,328,635

*Assuming the restricted assets do not contain cash or cash equivalents.

Source: Adapted from the City of New Orleans, Louisiana, Comprehensive Annual Financial Report, December 31, 19X1, Combining Statement of Changes in Financial Position—Proprietary Fund Type—Enterprise Funds.

reason for the establishment of such funds is to reduce the cost of obtaining goods or services and/or improve the distribution of these goods or services within the governmental unit. Typical Internal Service Funds include supplies distribution, motor pool operations, data processing, and so forth.

Since Internal Service Funds are classified as proprietary funds, the accounting system is designed to accumulate the total cost of the goods or services provided. Therefore the full accrual basis of accounting is used. The funds receiving the goods or services are billed by the Internal Service Fund, and this amount is treated as revenue for the Internal Service Fund and as an expenditure (or expense) for the other funds.

Since a major purpose of an Internal Service Fund is to recover the cost of providing goods or services, a separate fund is established for each identifiable unit.

The balance sheet for an Internal Service Fund is basically the same as that used by an Enterprise Fund. Therefore the comments made in the previous discussion are applicable here with two notable exceptions. The first exception deals with restricted assets. Due to the nature of the operations of an Internal Service Fund, there are usually no legal, contractual, or regulatory restrictions

TABLE 3–17

City of Columbus, Ohio
Internal Service Fund
Fleet Management Fund
Balance Sheet
December 31, 19X1

Assets		
Cash and investments with treasurer	$ 998,421	
Receivables (net of allowance for uncollectibles)	724	
Due from other funds	146,343	
Inventory	743,279	
Property, plant, and equipment—less accumulated depreciation	2,330,501	
Total assets		$4,219,268
Liabilities		
Accounts payable	$ 585,113	
Due to other funds	51,113	
Accrued liabilities	258,951	
Accrued vacation and sick leave	622,366	
Total liabilities		$1,517,543
Fund Equity		
Contributed capital	$1,750,788	
Unreserved retained earnings	950,937	
Total fund equity		2,701,725
Total liabilities and fund equity		$4,219,268

Source: Adapted from the City of Columbus, Ohio, *Comprehensive Annual Financial Report*, December 31, 19X1, Combining Balance Sheet—All Internal Service Funds.

placed on the use of certain assets. As a result, restricted assets seldom appear on the balance sheet. The second exception deals with the overall format of the balance sheet. The assets and liabilities of Internal Service Funds are seldom presented in other than the traditional current-noncurrent format.

The assets usually found in these funds include cash; amounts due from other funds; inventory (where applicable); and property, plant, and equipment. The liabilities generally include payables arising from the operations of the fund and possibly advances from the General Fund or other funds. Notice that in Table 3–17 a classified balance sheet is used (see Chapter 8). In addition, the fund equity is treated exactly like that of Enterprise Funds: contributed capital is segregated from retained earnings.

The operating statement (statement of revenues, expenses, and changes in retained earnings) of an Internal Service Fund is prepared in the same way as that of an Enterprise Fund (see Table 3–18). The difference between operating

TABLE 3–18

City of Columbus, Ohio
Internal Service Fund
Fleet Management Fund
Statement of Revenues, Expenses and Changes in Retained Earnings
Year Ended December 31, 19X1

Operating revenues:		
Charges for services	$10,412,024	
Other	48,604	
Total operating revenues		$10,460,628
Operating expenses:		
Personal services	$ 3,910,181	
Contractual services	1,586,484	
Materials and supplies	4,659,725	
Depreciation	291,804	
Other	31,565	
Total operating expenses		10,479,759
Operating loss		$ (19,131)
Nonoperating expenses:		
Interest expense		(46,000)
Loss before operating transfers		$ (65,131)
Operating transfer in		846,000
Net income		$ 780,869
Add depreciation on fixed assets acquired by contributed capital		259,389
		$ 1,040,258
Accumulated deficit at beginning of year		(89,321)
Retained earnings at end of year		$ 950,937

Source: Adapted from the City of Columbus, Ohio, *Comprehensive Annual Financial Report,* December 31, 19X1, Combining Statement of Revenues, Expenses and Changes in Retained Earnings (Accumulated Deficit)—All Internal Service Funds.

revenues and operating expenses is **net income** (operating income if other items are involved in the statement). This amount is added to the beginning balance of Retained earnings in order to calculate the Retained earnings at the end of the period. The exact items of revenue and expense will depend on the particular types of services performed. Those included in Table 3–18, however, are typical of Internal Service Funds. Notice particularly the charge for depreciation. Since these Internal Service Funds follow the full accrual basis of accounting, depreciation must be included as an expense.

Use of GAAP for these types of funds also requires a statement of cash flows similar to that presented for Enterprise Funds. Since the preparation of this statement is beyond the scope of this text, we have included Table 3–19 for illustrative purposes only.

TABLE 3–19

City of Columbus, Ohio
Internal Service Fund
Fleet Management Fund
Statement of Cash Flows*
Year Ended December 31, 19X1

Cash flows from operating activities:		
Operating loss	$ (19,131)	
Items not requiring cash currently:		
Depreciation	291,804	
Increase in receivables	(724)	
Increase in due from other funds	(28,785)	
Increase in inventory	(30,384)	
Decrease in accounts payable	(296,615)	
Decrease in due to other funds	(42,469)	
Decrease in accrued liabilities	(518)	
Decrease in accrued vacation and sick leave	(53,724)	
Net cash used by operating activities		$ (180,546)
Cash flows from noncapital financing activities:		
Operating transfers from other funds		846,000
Cash flows from capital and related financing activities:		
Acquisition of property, plant, and equipment	$ (44,408)	
Retirement of bonds	(800,000)	
Partial reduction in contributed capital	(175,778)	
Interest	(46,000)	
Net cash flows from capital and related financing activities		(1,066,186)
Net decrease in cash and cash equivalents		$ (400,732)
Cash and cash equivalents at January 1, 19X1		1,399,153
Cash and cash equivalents at December 31, 19X1		$ 998,421

*Assuming investments with treasurer are cash equivalents.

Source: Adapted from the City of Columbus, Ohio, *Comprehensive Annual Financial Report*, December 31, 19X1, Combining Statement of Changes in Financial Position—All Internal Service Funds.

SECTION IV—FIDUCIARY-TYPE FUNDS

Fiduciary-type funds are used to account for assets held by a government in an agency or trust capacity. In *Statement 1*, the NCGA further classified Trust and Agency Funds as Pension Trust, Nonexpendable Trust, Expendable Trust, and Agency Funds.[11]

The most widely used trust funds are **Pension Trust Funds**. They are used to account for the assets, liabilities, and so forth, of the public employee retirement systems (PERS) used by a governmental unit. **Nonexpendable Trust Funds** are those trust funds whose principal must be maintained. In most instances the governmental unit would be permitted to spend the income from the principal in some specified manner—e.g., to purchase library books. In this instance the principal would constitute a Nonexpendable Trust Fund and the earnings would be spent through an **Expendable Trust Fund**. Expendable Trust Funds are also used to account for those situations where the principal and income can be spent by the governmental unit.

An **Agency Fund** is used when a governmental unit is the *custodian* of resources that belong to some other organization. This type of fund is also used when a single fund is established to perform a central collection or distribution function for the resources of other funds of the governmental unit. Since the government does not have an equity interest in the assets, there is no fund balance for this type of fund. Rather, all the resources held are balanced against the liabilities that are to be paid from those resources, including the debt to the legal "owner" of the assets. Resources for which the governmental unit acts as an agent include withheld employees' Social Security and income taxes and taxes collected by a governmental unit for other governmental units (Tax Agency Funds). With respect to employees' Social Security and income tax withholdings, during the period of time in which these amounts are held by the governmental unit, they are properly accounted for in an Agency Fund. However, it is also acceptable to account for withholdings from employees' pay in the fund in which the gross pay is recorded.

It is possible to use one Agency Fund to account for several different agency relationships (assuming there are no legal restrictions). However, due to the legal problems that exist in situations involving trusts, a separate fund is generally used for each individual trust.

When accounting for Expendable Trust Funds, the focus is on the spending of the resources available; whereas Nonexpendable Trust Funds and Pension Trust Funds, by contrast, require a capital maintenance approach. Therefore the accrual basis is used for the latter two funds, while the Expendable Trust Funds follow the modified accrual basis of accounting. Since Agency Funds are strictly custodial in nature, the modified accrual basis of accounting is also used in these situations.

---

[11]NCGA, *Statement 1*, p. 6 [GASB Cod. Sec. 1300.104].

A balance sheet for each fiduciary-type fund is shown in Tables 3–20 through 3–23.[12] Assets usually found in these funds include cash, investments, receivables, and amounts due from other funds. The liabilities include the debts incurred in operating each fund and amounts due to other funds. The fund

TABLE 3–20

Name of Governmental Employee Retirement System
Illustrative Financial Statements
Balance Sheet
June 30, 19X1

ASSETS:		
Cash		$ 30,849
Accrued interest and dividends		4,822,076
Investments:		
Bonds, at amortized cost (market value $85,492,049)	$105,591,446	
Common stocks, at cost (market value $30,206,177)	27,199,702	
Commercial paper and repurchase agreements, at cost (market value $11,264,000)	11,215,833	
Total investments		144,006,981
Equipment and fixtures, net of accumulated depreciation of $24,673		19,585
Total assets		148,879,491
LIABILITIES:		
Accounts payable and accrued expenses		251,650
Net assets available for benefits		$148,627,841
FUND BALANCE:		
Actuarial present value of projected benefits payable to current retirants and beneficiaries		$ 32,240,515
Actuarial present value of projected benefits payable to terminated vested participants		3,610,310
Actuarial present value of credited projected benefits for active employees:		
Member contributions		38,786,483
Employer-financed portion		92,945,781
Total actuarial present value of credited projected benefits		167,583,089
Unfunded actuarial present value of credited projected benefits		(18,955,248)
Total fund balance		$148,627,841

Source: GASB Cod. Sec. Pe5.602.

[12]In June 1983, the NCGA issued *Statement 6*, "Pension Accounting and Financial Reporting: Public Employee Retirement Systems and State and Local Government Employers." Later the NCGA extended the effective date of *Statement 6* indefinitely because of differences of opinion regarding the proper accounting for pensions. In July 1984, the GASB issued *Statement 1*, "Authoritative Status of NCGA Pronouncements and AICPA Industry Audit Guide." The GASB *Statement 1* permits governmental units to follow one of several different pension accounting and reporting procedures until the issue is resolved. At the time of this writing, the GASB had not issued its "final" statement on this subject. NCGA *Statement 6* is used throughout this text because the authors feel it is the most informative of the alternatives. The topic of pensions is discussed in detail in Chapter 8.

TABLE 3–21

City of Baltimore, Maryland
Nonexpendable Trust Fund
Enoch Pratt Free Library Fund
Balance Sheet
June 30, 19X1

ASSETS		
Cash and cash equivalents	$ 225,000	
Investments	1,735,000	
Other assets	30,000	
Total assets		$1,990,000
FUND BALANCE		
Fund balance reserved for library services		$1,990,000

Source: Adapted from the City of Baltimore, Maryland, *Comprehensive Annual Financial Report,* June 30, 19X1, Combining Balance Sheet—Trust and Agency Funds.

TABLE 3–22

City of New Orleans
Expendable Trust Fund
Lafayette Cemetery No. 1 Under Will of Miss Lilly Violet Fund
Balance Sheet
December 31, 19X1

ASSETS		
Cash	$ 807	
Time certificates of deposit	1,200	
Total assets		$2,007
FUND BALANCE		
Unreserved, undesignated		$2,007

Source: Adapted from the City of New Orleans, Louisiana, *Comprehensive Annual Financial Report,* December 31, 19X1, Combining Balance Sheet—Expendable Trust Fund—Endowment Income Trust Funds.

TABLE 3–23

City of New Orleans, Louisiana
Agency Funds
Property Tax Fund
Balance Sheet
December 31, 19X1

ASSETS	
Property taxes receivable	$7,613,767
LIABILITIES	
Due to other governments	$7,613,767

Source: Adapted from the City of New Orleans, *Comprehensive Annual Financial Report,* December 31, 19X1, Agency Funds, Combining Schedule of Changes in Assets and Liabilities.

balance of each of those funds using a spending focus represents the spendable resources. In funds using the capital maintenance focus, the fund balance represents net assets of the fund. The reserves represent the "setting aside" of a portion of the fund balance for a particular purpose.

Tables 3–24 through 3–26 present the operating statements (including an analysis of changes in fund balance) of fiduciary funds. Since the Pension Trust Fund and the Nonexpendable Trust Fund follow a capital maintenance approach, the operating statements are similar in format to those of proprietary

TABLE 3–24

Name of Governmental Employee Retirement System
Illustrative Financial Statements
Statement of Revenues, Expenses, and Changes in Fund Balance
For the Fiscal Year Ended June 30, 19X1

Operating revenues:	
Member contributions	$ 8,009,400
Employer contributions	14,126,292
Investment income	14,262,845
Total operating revenues	36,398,537
Operating expenses:	
Annuity benefits	3,134,448
Disability benefits	287,590
Refunds to terminated employees	2,057,265
Administrative expenses	580,219
Total operating expenses	6,059,522
Net operating income	30,339,015
Fund balance, July 1, 19X0	118,288,826
Fund balance, June 30, 19X1	$148,627,841

Source: GASB Cod. Sec. Pe5.602.

TABLE 3–25

City of Baltimore, Maryland
Nonexpendable Trust Fund
Enoch Pratt Free Library Fund
Statement of Revenues, Expenses, and Changes in Fund Balance
For the Year Ended June 30, 19X1

Revenues:		
Interest and other investment income	$213,000	
Total revenues		$ 213,000
Expenses:		
Claims, awards, and benefits		168,000
Net income		$ 45,000
Fund balance, July 1, 19X0		1,945,000
Fund balance, June 30, 19X1		$1,990,000

Source: Adapted from the City of Baltimore, Maryland, *Comprehensive Annual Financial Report,* June 30, 19X1, Combining Statement of Revenues, Expenses, and Changes in Fund Balance.

funds, including a measure of net income. The types of revenues and expenses depend on the nature of the funds included. The shift in focus from capital maintenance to spending is highlighted by the fact that the operating statement for the Expendable Trust Funds contains revenues and *expenditures* (not expenses) (see Table 3–26). This difference is carried on to the measure of the excess of revenues over expenditures, which is referred to as "excess of revenues over expenditures," *not* net income. For each type of fund, however, the determination of the ending fund balance is the same.

Because of the peculiar relationship that Agency Funds have to the governmental unit, an operating statement is not used. Instead, a statement of changes in assets and liabilities is substituted (see Table 3–27). The purpose of

TABLE 3–26

City of New Orleans
Expendable Trust Fund
Lafayette Cemetery No. 1 Under Will of Miss Lilly Violet Fund
Statement of Revenues, Expenditures, and Changes in Fund Balance
For the Year Ended December 31, 19X1

Revenues:		
Interest income	$102	
Miscellaneous	46	
Total revenues		$ 148
Excess of revenues over expenditures		148
Fund balance at beginning of year		1,859
Fund balance at end of year		$2,007

Source: Adapted from the City of New Orleans, Louisiana, *Comprehensive Annual Financial Report*, December 31, 19X1, Combining Statements of Revenues, Expenditures, and Changes in Fund Balance—Expendable Trust Fund—Endowment Income Trust Funds.

TABLE 3–27

City of New Orleans, Louisiana
Agency Funds
Property Tax Fund
Statement of Changes in Assets and Liabilities
For the Year Ended December 31, 19X1

	Balance December 31, 19X0	Additions	Deductions	Balance December 31, 19X1
ASSETS				
Property taxes receivable	$6,032,837	$50,099,421	$48,518,491	$7,613,767
LIABILITIES				
Due to other governments	$6,032,837	$50,099,421	$48,518,491	$7,613,767

Source: Adapted from City of Columbus, Ohio, *Comprehensive Annual Financial Report*, December 31, 19X1, Agency Funds, Combining Schedule of Changes in Assets and Liabilities.

this statement is to relate to the reader changes in the various asset and liability accounts used by the funds. These changes are reflected as "additions" and "deductions" and account for the activity that has taken place within the fund during the reporting period.

Statement of Cash Flows

We have previously mentioned that those funds which follow commercial-type accounting procedures usually must prepare a statement of cash flows in addition to a balance sheet and an operating statement. Since the construction of this statement is beyond the scope of this text, we have only illustrated the appropriate statement. A statement of cash flows must be prepared for Nonexpendable Trust Funds (see Table 3–28). It is not required for Pension Trust Funds.

TABLE 3–28

City of Baltimore, Maryland
Nonexpendable Trust Fund
Enoch Pratt Free Library Fund
Statement of Cash Flows*
For the Year Ended June 30, 19X1

Cash flows from operating activities:	
Net income	$ 45,000
Items not requiring cash currently:	
Decrease in other assets	1,000
Net cash provided by operating activities	$ 46,000
Cash flows from investing activities:	
Decrease in investments	24,000
Net increase in cash	$ 70,000
Cash at beginning of year	155,000
Cash at end of year	$225,000

*Cash and cash equivalents.

Source: Adapted from the City of Baltimore, Maryland, *Comprehensive Annual Financial Report*, June 30, 19X1, Combining Statement of Changes in Financial Position—Nonexpendable Trust Funds.

REVIEW QUESTIONS

Section I

Q3–1   What are the reporting objectives of state and local governmental units as identified by the Governmental Accounting Standards Board?

Q3–2   Define *fund* as the term is used in governmental accounting.

Q3–3   How does the focus for governmental-type funds differ from that of proprietary-type funds?

Q3–4   How do the interests of the users of commercial accounting data differ from the interests of the users of governmental accounting data?

Q3–5   Compare the timing of revenue and expense or expenditure recognition in the full accrual basis with that in the modified accrual basis of accounting.

Q3–6   Why do governmental entities generally use the modified accrual basis of accounting?

Q3–7   Which funds use the modified accrual basis of accounting?

Q3–8   Which funds use the accrual basis of accounting?

Section II

Q3–9   List the governmental-type funds and briefly describe the use of each.

Q3–10 The controller for the city of Walla Walla recently made the following comment ". . . however, as a minimum, we could run city government with the use of only one fund." Do you agree with this statement? If so, why? If not, why?

Q3–11 Why is it important to restrict the fund balance for advances made to other funds?

Q3–12 Special Revenue Funds and the General Fund are identical in accounting treatment. When are Special Revenue Funds used instead of the General Fund, and what purpose do they serve?

Q3–13 Why are some fixed assets recorded in the General Fixed Assets Account Group?

Q3–14 What type of debt is recorded in the General Long-Term Debt Account Group?

Section III

- Q3–15 List the proprietary-type funds and briefly describe the use of each.
- Q3–16 Why do Enterprise Funds and Internal Service Funds use full accrual accounting?
- Q3–17 What are restricted assets?
- Q3–18 What is the difference between an Enterprise Fund and an Internal Service Fund?

Section IV

- Q3–19 List the fiduciary-type funds and briefly describe the use of each.
- Q3–20 Do Agency Funds have a fund balance? Why or why not?
- Q3–21 What type of activity statement is prepared for Agency Funds?

EXERCISES

Section I

E3–1 (Explanation of reporting objectives)
The Governmental Accounting Standards Board identified three major reporting objectives for state and local governmental units. Identify each of these objectives and explain how each might be achieved.

E3–2 (Fill-in-the-blanks—general terminology)
1. A _____ is a fiscal and accounting entity with a self-balancing set of accounts.
2. The spending measurement focus is used for _____ funds.
3. The basis of accounting refers to the _____ of the recognition of revenues and expenses (expenditures).
4. In 19X2 Water City collected revenue that was earned in 19X1. The entry to record the collection would include a credit to _____.
5. In 19X1 Review City recorded an expenditure that was incurred but would not be paid in cash until 19X2. The entry to record the expenditure in 19X1 would include a credit to _____.

E3–3   (Matching—general terminology)
Match the terms on the left with the descriptions on the right by placing the appropriate letter in the space provided (use each letter only once).

_____	1.	Basis of accounting
_____	2.	A fund is
_____	3.	Expenditure
_____	4.	To evaluate operating results
_____	5.	Fund categories
_____	6.	Spending activities
_____	7.	Capital maintenance
_____	8.	Recognition of revenue when the resources are available and measurable
_____	9.	Available
_____	10.	Governmental fund type

A. Focus for proprietary-type funds and some fiduciary-type funds

B. Type of fund that accounts for general governmental operations.

C. An objective of accounting for governmental units

D. A fiscal and accounting entity with a self-balancing set of accounts.

E. Governmental, proprietary, fiduciary.

F. Refers to the timing of the recognition of revenues and expenses or expenditures

G. Focus for governmental-type funds and some fiduciary-type funds

H. Modified accrual

I. Collectible within the current period or soon enough thereafter to be used to pay the liabilities of the current period.

J. Cash payment for services in a modified accrual accounting system

Section II

E3–4   (Fill-in-the-blanks—general terminology)
1. A _____ is used to identify a fund balance that is not available for current use.
2. A governmental unit may have _____ (one or more than one) General Fund.

3. Accounting for a _____ is the same as that of the General Fund.
4. _____ Funds are used to account for the receipt and disbursement of resources used to acquire major capital facilities.
5. The _____ is used to control property-type assets used by the general operations of the governmental unit.
6. Payments of principal and interest of general obligation governmental debt are generally recorded in a _____.
7. In *Statement No. 6,* the GASB separated special assessment activities into two major groups: _____ and _____.

E3–5   (Journal entries and their effect on financial statements)
The controller of the city of Watertite is currently making the final adjusting entries before the financial statements are prepared for the fiscal year ending June 30, 19X2. The balance in the Fund balance account of the General Fund is $507,000. During the year the General Fund advanced $100,000 to the Capital Projects Fund in order to begin the construction of a new city hall. This amount will be repaid in three years when the project has been completed.

REQUIRED: 1. Prepare any necessary entry or entries related to the above facts. Assume that the city had made no entries regarding this event.
2. If you did not make an entry for requirement 1, explain why. If you did make an entry for requirement 1, explain the effect on the financial statements of the General Fund.

E3–6   (Fund definitions through examples)
For each of the situations described below, indicate which fund and/or account group would be used to report the transaction.
1. A city paid $1 million to a contractor for the acquisition of land that will be used as a site for a new library. The payment was made from a fund that will be used to account for the acquisition of the land and the construction of the library.
2. The General Fund transferred resources to a fund that will be used to pay principal and interest on outstanding general obligation debt.
3. A truck is purchased by the General Fund.
4. Salaries are paid to employees of the mayor's office.
5. A special tax that is dedicated to providing textbooks for underprivileged children is collected.
6. The city paid rent separately on five trucks that are used by the streets department.
7. The city is building a new city hall. Payments are made to the contractor from a bond issue that was sold during the year.

Section III

E3–7   (Matching—use of funds)
Using the following codes, indicate which description best fits the funds listed by placing the code in the space provided.

General Fund	GF
Special Revenue Fund	SRF
Capital Projects Fund	CPF
Debt Service Fund	DSF
Enterprise Fund	EF
Internal Service Fund	ISF

1. _____ Services are provided to the general public and the costs of providing the services are financed by user charges.
2. _____ Resources are accumulated to pay principal and interest on general long-term debt.
3. _____ Accounting for the police department activities.
4. _____ Goods or services are furnished to other segments of the governmental unit on a user charge basis.
5. _____ Acquisition and use of resources provided by the U.S. government for a particular purpose.
6. _____ Expenditures are made by the city's streets department.
7. _____ A "net income" figure is computed each year.

E3–8   (Fund definitions through examples)
For each of the situations described below, indicate which fund and/or account group would be used to report the transaction.

1. A city-owned electric utility sent bills to the city and a separate school board.
2. The General Fund made a periodic payment to a city-owned electric utility as a subsidy of its rates.
3. The city issued property tax bills. These are expected to be collected within the accounting year.
4. The city purchased new police cars.
5. The city paid the principal and interest on a bond issue from resources that were accumulated for the purpose of making the payment.
6. A centralized purchasing facility billed the general city operations for part of the cost of the purchasing operations.
7. The city levied a special hotel tax. This tax is dedicated to paying interest on outstanding debt.

E3–9 (Journal entry to start up a fund)

On January 2, 19X1, the City of Starvey paid cash to a fund that would be used for a city motor pool. The amount of the payment was $1 million. The motor pool then purchased twenty-five vehicles for $10,000 each. Prepare the entries necessary to record the above transactions. (*Hint*: Debit Residual equity transfer on the books of the General Fund to make the payment.)

Section IV

E3–10 (Summary of general reporting)

For each of the following funds and accountgroups, check the items that would probably be appropriate regarding their financial statements.

Fund/Account Group	Expenditures	Net Income	Restricted Assets	Revenues	Statement of Changes in Assets and Liabilities
General Fund					
Special Revenue Fund					
Debt Service Fund					
Capital Projects Fund					
Enterprise Fund					
Internal Service Fund					
Pension Trust Fund					
Nonexpendable Trust Fund					
Expendable Trust Fund					
Agency Fund					
General Fixed Assets Account Group					
General Long-Term Debt Account Group					

E3–11   (Reporting for fiduciary-type funds)
Listed below are several types of fiduciary funds and several financial statement classifications used in those funds. Match the fund type with the financial statement classifications that would probably be found on the statements for that fund type:

Pension Trust Fund	PTF
Nonexpendable Trust Fund	NTF
Expendable Trust Fund	ETF
Agency Fund	AF

_____ 1. Net assets available for benefits
_____ 2. Amounts owed to contractors in a bid deposits fund
_____ 3. Investments whose principal must be maintained intact.
_____ 4. Annuity benefits
_____ 5. Actuarial present value of projected benefits payable to current retirants and beneficiaries
_____ 6. Fund balance
_____ 7. Member contributions

E3–12   (Fill-in-the-blanks—general terminology)
1. _____ are used to account for assets held by a government in an agency or trust capacity.
2. A _____ Fund is used when a governmental unit is the custodian of resources that belong to some other organization.
3. The measurement focus for Expendable Trust Funds is _____.
4. _____ Funds do not have a fund balance account.
5. _____ and _____ follow a capital maintenance measurement focus.
6. _____, _____, _____, and _____ are classified as fiduciary-type funds.
7. A statement of changes in assets and liabilities is required for each _____.

PROBLEMS

Section I

P3–1   (Journal entries—cash vs. accrual basis of accounting)
Record the following events assuming (1) a cash basis of accounting and (2) accrual basis of accounting. If no entry is required, write "None" next to the date.

1/2/X1   Performed services for $1,000. This amount was received in cash.
1/5/X1   Incurred expenses totaling $800. This amount was paid in cash.
1/10/X1 Performed services for $900. This amount will be paid to the organization on 2/10/X1.
1/15/X1 Incurred expenses totaling $500. This amount will be paid on 2/15/X1.

2/10/X1 Collected the amount due from the 1/10/X1 transaction.

2/15/X1 Paid the amount due from the 1/15/X1 transaction.

P3–2   (Identification of fund categories)
Identify and differentiate between the three types of fund categories used in governmental accounting. Include in your discussion factors such as use, measurement focus, and basis of accounting.

P3–3   (Differentiation between accrual and modified accrual accounting)
Explain what *basis of accounting* means and identify at least two differences between the accrual basis of accounting and the cash basis of accounting.

Section II

P3–4   (Statement preparation—General Fund)
Using the following data, prepare a statement of revenues, expenditures, and changes in fund balance for the General Fund of the City of Sertville for the calendar year ended December 31, 19X1.

Miscellaneous revenues	$ 180,000
Licenses and permits revenues	1,000,000
Expenditures for education	5,000,000
Expenditures for corrections	1,400,000
Operating transfers to other funds	2,000,000
Tax revenues	8,000,000
Expenditures for welfare	2,100,000
Federal grants	3,000,000
Expenditures for public safety	750,000
Expenditures for highways	900,000
Operating transfers from other funds	700,000
Fund balance at beginning of year	5,345,000

P3–5   (Identification of activities recorded in governmental-type funds)
Using *only* the governmental-type funds and account groups, indicate which would be used to record each of the following events.

General Fund	GF
Special Revenue Fund	SRF
Debt Service Fund	DSF
Special Assessment Fund	SAF
Capital Projects Fund	CPF
General Fixed Assets Account Group	GFAAG
General Long-Term Debt Account Group	GLTDAG

———— 1. Money is transferred from the General Fund to the Debt Service Fund.

———— 2. The city received its share of the state sales tax. The entire amount is legally required to be used to improve the library facilities.

_____ 3. General property taxes are levied by the city.

_____ 4. The city purchased a fire engine.

_____ 5. Property taxes were collected.

_____ 6. The city received a grant from the state to build an addition to the city hall.

_____ 7. The city issued general obligation bonds to finance the construction of new police stations.

_____ 8. The mayor was paid his monthly salary.

_____ 9. Expenses for the operation of the police department were recorded.

_____10. A new bridge across the Red River was constructed.

_____11. Tax monies were collected. These amounts were legally required to be used to maintain the city park system.

_____12. General governmental revenues were transferred to the fund that accumulates money to retire general long-term debt.

_____13. General governmental revenues were transferred to the City Hall Construction Fund.

_____14. A contractor received partial payment for the work done on the new city hall.

_____15. The city workers were paid their weekly salaries.

_____16. Outstanding bonds were retired, using monies accumulated for that purpose.

_____17. A federal grant was received to help pay for the cost of constructing the new city hall.

P3–6   (Transactions related to fund types)

For each of the following fund types and account groups, indicate three transactions that could be recorded in each fund or account group.

> *Fund types*
> General Fund
> Special Revenue Funds
> Capital Projects Funds
> Debt Service Funds
> *Account groups*
> General Fixed Assets Account Group
> General Long-Term Debt Account Group

Section III

P3–7   (Identification of activities recorded in governmental- and proprietary-type funds)

Using the governmental- and proprietary-type funds and the account groups, indicate which would be used to record each of the following events.

General Fund	GF
Special Revenue Fund	SRF
Debt Service Fund	DSF
Capital Projects Fund	CPF
Enterprise Fund	EF
Internal Service Fund	ISF
General Fixed Assets Account Group	GFAAG
General Long-Term Debt Account Group	GLTDAG

_____   1. The city electric utility retired bonds.

_____   2. Special assessments were levied to service the debt that was incurred to pay for a street-paving project.

_____   3. The General Fund made its annual contribution to the fund that pays principal and interest on outstanding debt.

_____   4. The city acquired land as part of a city hall expansion program. The resources used to acquire the land were provided by a general obligation bond issue.

_____   5. The Motor Pool Fund billed each department in the city for use of vehicles (assume all departments billed were accounted for in the General Fund).

_____   6. The police department salaries were paid.

_____   7. The city sold some of its excess properties (assume the revenue is accounted for in the General Fund).

_____   8. Revenue bonds were issued by the Electric Utility Fund to build a new plant.

_____   9. The Motor Pool Fund loaned $50,000 to the Central Purchasing Fund.

_____10. The Electric Utility Fund billed the General Fund for its share of the electricity cost.

_____11. The city charter required all hotel taxes to be accounted for in a separate fund. The collections for the period totaled $500,000.

_____12. The mayor was paid her salary.

_____13. Special assessment-type debt was issued to finance a street lighting project. (The city guaranteed this debt.)

_____14. Electric utility revenue bonds were retired.

_____15. General obligation city debt was retired, using resources previously accumulated for that purpose.

P3–8   (Comparison of financial statements)

Review the balance sheet and operating statement for the General Fund of Columbus (Tables 3–2 and 3–3) and the balance sheet and operating statement for the Sewerage and Water Board Fund of New Orleans (Tables 3–14 and 3–15). Identify the major similarities and differences between the two.

P3–9   (Correcting a trial balance)

The bookkeeper of New Found City has recently quit. The clerks working in the records department prepared the trial balance, based on the information in the accounts.

New Found City
Enterprise Fund
City Airport
Trial Balance
December 31, 19X1

Cash	$ 210,000	
Prepaid expenses	1,400	
Accounts receivable	303,164	
Supplies inventory	6,000	
Due from other funds	-0-	
Property, plant, and equipment	8,189,655	
Accumulated depreciation		$2,500,000
Accounts payable		681,786
Dut to other funds		74,000
Customer advanced for construction		-0-
Revenue bonds payable		396,000
Contributed capital		2,000,000
Retained earnings		3,121,048
Revenue		1,147,705
Operating expenses	748,120	
Administrative expenses	257,400	
Maintenance expenses	204,800	
	$9,920,539	$9,920,539

Your review of the financial records revealed the following:

1. Accounts payable included the following:

    Due to other funds $5,100

2. Depreciation was not recorded for 19X1. The proper amount was $250,000. Assume that the city treats depreciation as an operating expense.

3. The General Fund owes $10,000 for services rendered in 19X1. The previous bookkeeper only recorded revenue from the General Fund when cash was received; therefore the $10,000 has not been recorded.

4. Accounts receivable includes $650 that is actually a receivable from other governmental funds.

5. Advances to $2,000 received by customers for construction purposes were recorded as revenue.

6. Supplies of $250 purchased on credit and received on December 27, 19X1, were not recorded in the accounting records.

REQUIRED: Prepare an adjusted trial balance for the New Found City Airport.

Section IV

P3–10   (Multiple choice)
1. Which of the following funds of a governmental unit uses the General Fixed Assets Account Group to account for fixed assets?
    a. Internal Service
    b. Nonexpendable Trust
    c. Enterprise
    d. General Fund
2. Which of the following funds of a governmental unit uses the modified accrual basis of accounting?
    a. Internal Service
    b. Enterprise
    c. Nonexpendable Trust
    d. Debt Service
3. Under the modified accrual basis of accounting for a governmental unit, revenues should be recognized in the accounting period in which they
    a. become available and earned
    b. become available and measurable
    c. are earned and become measurable
    d. are collected
4. Which governmental fund would account for fixed assets in a manner similar to a for-profit organization?
    a. Enterprise
    b. Capital Projects
    c. General Fixed Assets Account Group
    d. General
5. The fixed assets of a central purchasing and stores department organized to serve all municipal departments should be recorded in
    a. An Enterprise Fund and the General Fixed Assets Account Group
    b. An Enterprise Fund
    c. The General Fixed Assets Account Group
    d. The General Fund
    e. None of the above
6. The monthly remittance to an insurance company of the lump sum of hospital-surgical insurance premiums collected as payroll deductions from employees should be recorded in
    a. The General Fund
    b. An Agency Fund
    c. A Special Revenue Fund
    d. An Internal Service Fund
    e. None of the above

7. The activities of a municipal employee retirement plan that is financed by equal employer and employee contributions should be accounted for in
    a. An Agency Fund
    b. An Internal Service Fund
    c. A Special Assessment Fund
    d. A Trust Fund
    e. None of the above

8. A city collects property taxes for the benefit of the local sanitary, park, and school districts and periodically remits collections to these units. This activity should be accounted for in
    a. An Agency Fund
    b. The General Fund
    c. An Internal Service Fund
    d. A Special Assessment Fund
    e. None of the above

9. A transaction in which a municipal electric utility issues bonds (to be repaid from its own operations) requires accounting recognition in
    a. The General Fund
    b. A Debt Service Fund
    c. Enterprise and Debt Service Funds
    d. An Enterprise Fund, a Debt Service Fund, and the General Long-Term Debt Account Group
    e. None of the above

10. The operations of a public library receiving most of its support from property taxes levied for that purpose should be accounted for in
    a. The General Fund
    b. A Special Revenue Fund
    c. An Enterprise Fund
    d. An Internal Service Fund
    e. None of the above

11. The liability for general obligation bonds issued for the benefit of a municipal electric company and serviced by its earnings should be recorded in
    a. An Enterprise Fund
    b. The General Fund
    c. An Enterprise Fund and the General Long-Term Debt Account Group
    d. An Enterprise Fund and disclosed in a footnote in the Statement of General Long-Term Debt
    e. None of the above.

12. The liability for special assessment bonds that carry a secondary pledge of a municipality's general credit should be recorded in
   a. An Enterprise Fund
   b. A Special Revenue Fund and the General Long-Term Debt Account Group
   c. A Special Assessment Fund and the General Long-Term Debit Account Group
   d. A Special Assessment Fund and disclosed in a footnote in the Statement of General Long-Term Debt
   e. None of the above

13. The proceeds of a federal grant made to assist in financing the future construction of an adult training center should be recorded in
   a. The General Fund
   b. A Special Revenue Fund
   c. A Capital Projects Fund
   d. A Special Assessment Fund
   e. None of the above

14. The receipts from a special tax levy to retire and pay interest on general obligation bonds issued to finance the construction of a new city hall should be recorded in
   a. A Debt Service Fund
   b. A Capital Projects Fund
   c. A Revolving Interest Fund
   d. A Special Revenue Fund
   e. None of the above

15. Several years ago, a city provided for the establishment of a Debt Service Fund to retire an issue of general obligation bonds. This year the city made a $50,000 contribution to the Debt Service Fund from general revenues and realized $15,000 in revenue from securities in the Debt Service Fund. The bonds due this year were retired. These transactions require accounting recognition in
   a. The General Fund
   b. A Debt Service Fund and the General Long-Term Debt Account Group
   c. A Debt Service Fund, the General Fund, and the General Long-Term Debt Account Group
   d. A Capital Projects Fund, a Debt Service Fund, the General Fund, and the General Long-Term Debt Account Group
   e. None of the above

16. The activities of a central motor pool that provides and services vehicles for the use of municipal employees on official business should be accounted for in
   a. An Agency Fund

    b. The General Fund

    c. An Internal Service Fund

    d. A Special Revenue Fund

    e. None of the above

17. A transaction in which a municipal electric utility paid $150,000 out of its earnings for new equipment requires accounting recognition in

    a. An Enterprise Fund

    b. The General Fund

    c. The General Fund and the General Fixed Assets Account Group

    d. An Enterprise Fund and the General Fixed Assets Account Group

    e. None of the above

18. To provide for the retirement of general obligation bonds, a city invests a portion of its general revenue receipts in marketable securities. This investment activity should be accounted for in

    a. A Trust Fund

    b. An Enterprise Fund

    c. A Special Assessment Fund

    d. A Special Revenue Fund

    e. None of the above

19. The operations of a municipal swimming pool receiving the majority of its support from charges to users should be accounted for in

    a. A Special Revenue Fund

    b. The General Fund

    c. An Internal Service Fund

    d. An Enterprise Fund

    e. None of the above

                                                      (AICPA adapted)

P3–11 (Financial statements used in governmental accounting)

Indicate which of the following financial statements generally would be used by each of the funds/account groups listed.

Balance sheet	BS
Operating statement	OS
Statement of cash flows	SCF
Schedule of general fixed assets	SGFA
Schedule of general long-term debt	SGLD
Schedule of changes in general fixed assets	SCGFA
Schedule of changes in general long-term debt	SCGLD
Statement of changes in assets and liabilities	SCAL

_____   General Fund

_____   Special Revenue Funds

_____ Debt Service Funds
_____ Capital Projects Funds
_____ Enterprise Funds
_____ Internal Service Funds
_____ Pension Trust Funds
_____ Nonexpendable Trust Funds
_____ Expendable Trust Funds
_____ Agency Funds
_____ General Fixed Assets Account Group
_____ General Long-Term Debt Account Group

P3–12 (Transactions involving all funds and account groups)
Indicate which fund(s) and/or account group(s) would be used to record each of the following events. Use the codes for the funds and account groups listed below:

General Fund	GF
Special Revenue Fund	SRF
Debt Service Fund	DSF
Capital Projects Fund	CPF
Enterprise Fund	EF
Internal Service Fund	ISF
Pension Trust Fund	PTF
Nonexpendable Trust Fund	NTF
Expendable Trust Fund	ETF
Agency Fund	AF
General Fixed Assets Account Group	GFAAG
General Long-Term Debt Account Group	GLTDAG

_____ 1. Bonds were issued to finance the construction of a new library.

_____ 2. The police department purchased ten police cars.

_____ 3. Sales taxes were collected.

_____ 4. The city sold some of its excess office equipment. The proceeds from the sale were to be used for general city operations.

_____ 5. General obligation bonds were retired, using monies accumulated in a fund.

_____ 6. The city-owned airport is accounted for as a separate fund. This fund issued bonds to finance airport improvements.

_____ 7. The city uses a separate fund to account for its central purchasing function. Supplies were purchased from this fund.

_____ 8. A wealthy citizen donated securities to the city. The principal amount donated must remain intact and the income must be spent to provide free food to the elderly.

_____ 9. The city made a contribution to the employees' retirement fund.

_____10. Taxes that are dedicated to street repairs were collected. The ordinance establishing the tax requires a separate accounting for these monies.

_____11. The contractors who were building a bridge were paid.

_____12. General governmental revenues were transferred to the fund that accumulates money to retire general long-term debt.

_____13. The salary of the chief of police was paid.

_____14. The central purchasing fund sent out bills for purchases to the police and fire departments and to the city airport.

_____15. The city received a gift from a citizen. The money must be used to provide concerts for local youth groups.

4

THE GOVERNMENTAL FUND ACCOUNTING CYCLE

General and Special Revenue Funds— An Introduction

LEARNING OBJECTIVES

When you finish studying this chapter, you should be able to:

1. Compare the objectives of fund accounting with those of commercial accounting
2. Contrast the accounting cycle of a governmental unit with that of a commercial organization
3. Explain why separate budgetary entries are used
4. Prepare operating entries for a governmental unit
5. Prepare closing entries for a governmental unit
6. Explain why revenues from property taxes are recorded when these taxes are levied, rather than when they are collected.
7. Describe how control and subsidiary accounts are used
8. Explain the use of encumbrances and how they should be recorded in the accounts

The most basic funds used by nonbusiness organizations are the General Fund and the Special Revenue Funds. The **General Fund** is used to record the overall operations of the organization and is a catchall for all revenues and expenditures not recorded in other funds. Activities accounted for in this fund include police and fire protection and other day-to-day operations of the governmental unit.

    Special Revenue Funds are used to account for the proceeds of revenue sources (other than special assessments, expendable trusts, and those used for major capital projects) that must be spent for particular purposes. Examples of Special Revenue Funds include funds used to account for the activities of libraries and parks and for federal and state grants. From an accounting standpoint, General and Special Revenue Funds are very similar.

Since General Funds are the most commonly used funds and the accounting for most other funds is very similar to that of General and Special Revenue Funds, these funds are discussed first. If you understand the entries used by these funds, you can easily learn those unique to the other funds.

As in commercial accounting, the objective of fund accounting is to convey to the reader of financial statements a picture of what happened in the past. From this information, the reader can make financially related decisions. Fund accounting, however, is also concerned with the future and with certain legal considerations. As a result, the fund accounting cycle is somewhat more complicated than the commercial accounting cycle—even though the end products are essentially the same. The two cycles are contrasted in Table 4–1.

TABLE 4–1   Fund Accounting vs. Commercial Accounting

FUND ACCOUNTING	COMMERCIAL ACCOUNTING
Objectives*	Objectives
• To show the financial condition of the organization	• To show the financial condition of the firm
• To show the results of operations of the organization	• To show the results of operations of the firm
• To show changes in the financial condition of the organization	• To show changes in the financial condition of the firm
• To show compliance with legal restrictions	
Accounting Cycle	Accounting Cycle
• Record the budget in the accounting records	
• Record transactions for the period	• Record transactions for the period
• Prepare closing entries	• Prepare closing entries
• Prepare financial statements	• Prepare financial statements
—Balance sheet	—Balance sheet
—Statement of revenues, expenditures, and changes in fund balance	—Income statement and statement of changes in retained earnings
—Statement of cash flows (only for proprietary funds and similar funds)	—Statement of cash flows
—Statement comparing budgeted and actual revenues and expenditures (of certain governmental-type funds)	

*For a more detailed listing of these objectives, see Chapter 3.

SECTION I—A BASIC FUND ACCOUNTING SYSTEM

The steps in the fund accounting cycle are shown in Table 4–1. Note that the cycle begins with the budget and that, unlike commercial accounting, the budget is formally recorded in the accounts.

The Budget

In fund accounting, the **budget** is usually a legal document. It is an estimate of the expenditures of a fiscal year and the means proposed to finance them. It is also the end product of a series of requests and proposals that originate with department heads and other managers and, after being screened and adjusted by the budget officer, are put into budgetary form. A typical budget is shown in Table 4–2.

The principal items in this budget are Estimated revenues, Appropriations, and Other financing sources. **Estimated revenues** are resources that have been, or are expected to be, made available to the organization. One such resource, unique to governmental units, is the right to levy taxes on real and personal property. In this budget, Estimated revenues are broken down into those obtained from ad valorem (property) taxes and other sources of income such as royalties, revenue sharing, and interest on investments.

Appropriations are allocations of the resources that will be used to carry out the activities of the organization (proposed expenditures). They represent the authority to spend money in accordance with the approved budget. This is not to imply, of course, that the money must be spent. Appropriations are made with the expectation of receiving a certain level of services. If such services should happen to be provided at less cost, the monies saved can be used to increase the fund balance or to provide additional services.

Appropriations are broken down by category or object and, in some cases, by department or function as well (e.g., Police—salaries). In this text, however, we will assume that appropriations are budgeted by object. This simplification makes it appear that each organization has only one department. In reality, of course, most organizations have many departments (or functions), with each department using its own set of operating accounts. Nevertheless, the entries illustrated in this chapter and Chapter 5 are applicable to nearly all nonbusiness organizations, the only difference being the level of detail involved.

Other financing sources are receipts of resources that are not revenues. Examples include the proceeds of an issue of notes and certain types of transfers from other funds, such as those from a trust fund to a Library (Special Revenue) Fund.

Other financing uses are disbursements of resources that are not expenditures. Examples include payments made by the General Fund to a Capital Projects Fund for the General Fund's share of the cost of constructing new facilities, and payments made by Special Revenue Funds to Debt Service Funds

TABLE 4–2

Orleans Levee Board
General Fund
Estimated Revenues, Appropriations, and Other Sources (Uses)
Fiscal Year July 1, 1987, to June 30, 1988

ESTIMATED REVENUES		
Ad valorem taxes	$6,720,232	
Royalties	1,000,000	
State revenue sharing	600,000	
New Orleans Lakefront Airport	1,086,361	
Orleans Marina	1,004,000	
Lake Vista Community Center	132,759	
Other locations	330,105	
Lakefront camps	15,450	
Interest on investments	785,000	
Miscellaneous	5,700	
Total estimated revenues		$11,679,607
APPROPRIATIONS		
Personal services	$6,305,764	
Travel	40,000	
Contractual services	2,670,040	
Materials and supplies	1,061,792	
Professional services	497,905	
Other charges	34,806	
Equipment	609,897	
Total appropriations		11,220,204
Excess of estimated revenues over appropriations		$ 459,403
OTHER FINANCING SOURCES (USES)		
Transfer from Special Levee Improvement Project Fund	$ 821,640	
Transfer to General Improvement Project Fund	(862,500)	
Transfer to Debt Service Fund	(70,878)	
Orleans Marina transfer to South Shore Harbor	(1,004,000)	
Contingent transfer from South Shore Harbor to Board	384,657	
Designations:		
Contingency—unemployment compensation payments	(9,500)	
Contingency—materials and supplies purchases	(5,000)	
Contingency—equipment purchases	(3,000)	
Contingency—A/C replacements	(25,000)	
Major heavy equipment replacement	(105,000)	
Amount provided for Capital Projects from prior-year project allocations	425,000	
Total other sources (uses)		(453,581)
Excess of estimated revenues and other financing sources over appropriations and other financing uses		$ 5,822

Source: Adapted from the *Annual Approved Budget for Fiscal Year July 1, 1987, to June 30, 1988,* of the Orleans Levee Board.

for the retirement of debt. Other financing sources (and uses) are broken down by type of transfer to and from the budgetary unit.

Opening Entries

At the beginning of the fiscal year, the approved budget is recorded in the accounts. Debits are made to the estimated revenue accounts and credits are made to the appropriation accounts. Any difference between Estimated revenues and Appropriations is debited or credited to Unreserved fund balance.

Fund balance is a residual account whose balance is equal to the difference between the assets and the liabilities of the organization. The account itself is "permanent" in nature—that is, its balance is carried forward into future periods. It is usually called **Unreserved fund balance**, the term *unreserved* indicating that part of the fund balance has not been set aside for any special purpose.

The difference (if any) between Estimated revenues and Appropriations represents the expected change in Unreserved fund balance during the year. If the actual revenues recorded during the year equal Estimated revenues and the expenditures incurred during the year equal Appropriations, no further adjustments to Unreserved fund balance will be necessary. The dollar amounts shown in the opening entry, which is known as a **budgetary entry**, should correspond to those found in the budget.

To illustrate the fund accounting cycle, assume that the city council of Simple City has just approved the budget shown in Table 4–3. At the beginning of the fiscal year, the following budgetary entry is made:

Estimated revenues	1,000,000	
Appropriations		990,000
Unreserved fund balance		10,000

To record the estimated revenues and appropriations for FY 19X1.

After this entry has been posted, the general ledger will appear as follows:

ASSETS	=	LIABILITIES	+	FUND BALANCE
Estimated revenues	=	Appropriations	+	Unreserved fund balance
$1,000,000	=	$990,000	+	$10,000

Estimated revenues and Appropriations are budgetary accounts. **Budgetary accounts**, by definition, are accounts used to enter the formally adopted annual budget into the general ledger. At the end of the period, all budgetary accounts are closed out (their balances are reduced to zero). Many nonbudgetary accounts, by contrast, are "permanent" in nature (e.g., the Unreserved fund balance); their balances are carried forward to the next accounting period.

TABLE 4–3

Simple City
General Fund Budget
Fiscal Year, 19X1

Estimated Revenues		
Property taxes	$900,000	
Fines, licenses, etc.	100,000	$1,000,000
Appropriations		
Salaries	$700,000	
Materials	200,000	
Other	90,000	990,000
Projected Increase in Fund Balance		$ 10,000

Recording Revenues and Expenditures

Revenue and expenditure accounting provides information for several purposes:

1. *To determine whether all revenues have been received.* Revenue accounting is the process of recording the amount of taxes, fees, and other revenues that have been received, as well as those still outstanding. Although the organization has the *right* to tax, it does not necessarily follow that the taxes have actually been collected.

2. *To determine whether expenditures were made in accordance with the budget.* Expenditure accounting is the process of recording the *actual* monies spent, on an item-by-item basis. It provides information on the relationship between budgeted and actual expenditures, as to both their nature and their size.

3. *To prepare various financial statements.* Revenue and expenditure accounting provide information for the balance sheet; for the statement of revenues, expenditures, and changes in the fund balance; and for any other financial statements that may be prepared.

4. *To assist in the preparation of future budgets.* The actual revenues collected are often used as a base in determining the size and composition of future tax levies and service charges. The actual expenditures determine the cost of services rendered. Both provide inputs into decisions as to what services should be made available in the future.

Revenue and expenditure accounts, like their commercial counterparts, are *nominal* accounts. They are not permanent in nature, as are assets and liabilities. Instead they are closed out (reduced to zero) at the end of each period.

The entries to record revenues are similar to those found in commercial accounting—debits to Cash or receivable accounts and credits to revenue accounts. To continue with the previous example, if all the revenues are collected at once and in cash, the entry is:

Cash	1,000,000	
Revenues		1,000,000

To record the collection of FY 19X1 revenues.

The entries to record expenditures are also similar to those used in commercial accounting: debits to expenditure accounts and credits to Cash or payable accounts. If all the monies appropriated for the period are spent (expended), the entry is:

Expenditures	990,000	
Cash		990,000

To record the incurrence of FY 19X1 expenditures.

Closing Entries

A **closing** usually takes place at year-end. Its purpose is to *close* (reduce to zero) the nominal (revenue and expenditure) and budgetary (estimated revenue and appropriation) accounts and, if necessary, to adjust the Unreserved fund balance to its "true" value.

In commercial accounting, revenues and expenses are "matched," and any difference is added to or deducted from capital or retained earnings. In not-for-profit accounting, a slightly different process is followed. Actual revenues are matched against estimated revenues, and expenditures are matched against appropriations. Any differences are added to or deducted from Unreserved fund balance. The net result of these entries is zero balances in the budgetary accounts and the revenue and expenditure accounts and, possibly, a revised end-of-year balance in Unreserved fund balance.

Continuing with our illustration, let us assume that revenues of $1 million are collected and that $990,000 is expended (paid out) during the year. The closing entries are

1.	Revenues	1,000,000	
	Estimated revenues		1,000,000

To close the Revenue and Estimated revenue accounts for FY 19X1.

2.	Appropriations	990,000	
	Expenditures		990,000

To close the Appropriation and Expenditure accounts for FY 19X1.

Each of the four accounts now has a zero balance. Since actual revenues equal estimated revenues and expenditures equal appropriations, there is no need to adjust the Unreserved fund balance. Its end-of-year balance ($10,000) will exceed its beginning-of-year balance ($0) by the amount recorded in the opening (budgetary) entry, $10,000.

An alternative approach to closing, preferred by some accountants, is to close the budgetary and nonbudgetary accounts separately. Thus, Estimated revenues are closed to Appropriations and Revenues are closed to Expenditures. Any differences between Estimated revenues and Appropriations and between Revenues and Expenditures are debited or credited to Unreserved fund balance.

Under this approach, the closing entries in our illustration would be:

1. Appropriations   990,000
    Unreserved fund balance   10,000
        Estimated revenues   1,000,000
    To close the budgetary accounts for FY 19X1.

2. Revenues   1,000,000
        Expenditures   990,000
        Unreserved fund balance   10,000
    To close the nonbudgetary accounts for FY
    19X1.

The net effect of these entries is the same as that of the entries previously illustrated—that is, zero balances in the Revenue, Estimated revenue, Expenditure, and Appropriation accounts and a $10,000 increase in the Unreserved fund balance. Although both approaches to closing are sound, we will follow the first approach because it is the one most commonly used.

After the closing entries have been posted, a postclosing trial balance is prepared, followed by financial statements. The postclosing trial balance for Simple City is shown in Table 4–4. The resulting financial statements are shown in Table 4–5.[1]

Table 4-5 is simplified and not very realistic. Nevertheless, all the elements of the fund accounting cycle are present. If you *understand* the example, you will easily master the refinements that are present in "real world" problems.

The example used in this section is summarized in Table 4-6. Before continuing, be certain that you understand *why* each entry was made and *what effect* it has on the accounting equation. The budget from which the opening entries are derived is on page 110. The statements are on page 113.

TABLE 4–4

Simple City
General Fund
Postclosing Trial Balance
December 31, 19X1

	DR	CR
Cash	$10,000	
Unreserved fund balance		$10,000
	$10,000	$10,000

[1]For the sake of brevity, it is assumed that the reader is able to make entries to the ledger. Chapter 2 discusses the mechanics of posting.

TABLE 4–5 Illustrative Financial Statements

Simple City
General Fund
Balance Sheet
December 31, 19X1

Assets		Liabilities and Fund Balance	
Cash	$10,000	Unreserved fund balance	$10,000

Simple City
General Fund
Statement of Revenues, Expenditures, and
Changes in Fund Balance
Fiscal Year 19X1

Revenues	$1,000,000
Expenditures	990,000
Increase in fund balance	$ 10,000
Fund balance, 1/1/X1	-0-
Fund balance, 12/31/X1	$ 10,000

TABLE 4–6 Summary of the Accounting Cycle of the General Fund of Simple City for Fiscal Year 19X1

The budgetary, or opening, entry is:

Estimated revenues	1,000,000	
Appropriations		990,000
Unreserved fund balance		10,000

To record the Estimated revenues and
Appropriations for 19X1.

The operating entries are:

Cash	1,000,000	
Revenues		1,000,000

To record the FY 19X1 revenues.

Expenditures	990,000	
Cash		990,000

To record the FY 19X1 expenditures.

The closing entries are:

Revenues	1,000,000	
Estimated revenues		1,000,000

To close the Revenue and Estimated revenue
accounts for FY 19X1.

Appropriations	990,000	
Expenditures		990,000

To close the Appropriation and Expenditure
accounts for FY 19X1.

SECTION II—A MORE-REFINED SYSTEM

The example in the preceding section, although theoretically correct, is over-simplified. Revenues are actually collected in uneven amounts throughout the year. In addition, many different revenue and expenditure accounts are used by most governmental units, and when certain goods or services are ordered monies are set aside (encumbered). In this section, three refinements will be made to the basic system previously illustrated: receivables, subsidiary accounts, and encumbrances.

Receivables

After the approved budget of a governmental unit has been recorded in the accounts, property taxes are levied. The governmental unit now has a claim against each taxpayer for his or her share of the property taxes due. To recognize this **receivable**, a debit is made to Property taxes receivable and a credit to a revenue account. When the taxes are collected, Cash is debited and Property taxes receivable is credited. The legal claim against the taxpayer or taxpayers has now been satisfied.

The above procedure differs from the one discussed in the preceding section in that revenues from property taxes are recorded when they are levied, rather than when they are collected. Under the modified accrual basis of accounting, which is used by governmental-type funds, such a procedure is required. This is because the amounts received from property taxes, unlike those received from other sources, are *available* and *measurable*, with a reasonable degree of accuracy, when the property taxes are levied.

In addition, the collection of revenues from property taxes is, in theory, fairly certain because the organization has a claim against specific tangible property. In the event of nonpayment of taxes, the governmental unit has the legal right to force the sale of the property and to deduct the taxes due from the proceeds.

To illustrate, assume that property taxes are budgeted at $900,000 and revenues from other sources at $100,000. The entry to recognize (record) the receivable is:

Property taxes receivable	900,000	
Revenues		900,000
To set up the receivable for FY 19X1 property taxes.		

When the property taxes are collected, the entry is:

Cash	900,000	
Property taxes receivable		900,000
To record the collection of property taxes.		

The above entry assumes, for illustrative purposes, that all taxes are collected at once. In reality, smaller amounts are collected each day. As a result, a *series* of entries, similar to the one shown above, is made, with the collections totaling $900,000.

Receivable accounts are generally used to record the assessment of property taxes. This is because property taxes are levied against a given base (the assessed value of the property within the governmental unit). Once the millage (tax rate) has been determined (usually when the budget is approved), the amount that should be received is known with a reasonable degree of certainty.

Income taxes, fees, fines, and other sources of revenue, however, are influenced by such variables as the level of employment, housing starts, and number of tourists. These revenues cannot be determined with certainty until they have been received. Therefore they are recognized when the cash is collected. This is done by means of a debit to Cash and a credit to a revenue account.

To illustrate, assume that the monies actually collected from "other" sources of revenue are $100,000 and that they are all received at once. The entry to recognize these revenues is:

Cash	100,000	
Revenues		100,00

To record the revenues from sources other than property taxes, FY 19X1.

Control and Subsidiary Accounts

In the preceding examples all revenues were combined into one account, as were all expenditures. This is not realistic or practical. Nonbusiness organizations, like their commercial counterparts, use control and subsidiary accounts. A **control account** is a summary account whose balance is equal to the total of the individual balances of its **subsidiary accounts**. The balances in the control accounts are changed when, and by the same amount that, changes are made in the subsidiary accounts. Examples of control accounts include Property taxes receivable (which are backed up by accounts for each taxpayer), Estimated revenues, Appropriations, and Expenditures (see Table 4–7).

An alternative to subsidiary and control accounts is the use of a large number of specialized accounts, similar in nature but different in detail. Many organizations do this on several levels. For example, appropriation and expenditure accounts are sometimes broken down by function or department (public safety, welfare, and so on) and then by object or category (salaries, supplies, and so on). Thus the account used to record the salaries of police officers would be Expenditures—Police Department—salaries. An account used to record revenues from licenses issued to owners of tour buses would be Revenues—license fees—tour buses.

Except for the following illustration, in which control and subsidiary accounts are used to record the collection of property taxes, a one-step breakdown is used throughout this text and control and subsidiary accounts are combined. This is done in order to keep the illustrative problems to a manageable size. Expanding the illustrations to include a two- or three-level breakdown or to include separate subsidiary and control accounts is fairly simple, requiring little more than time and a great deal of paper.

TABLE 4–7   Examples of Control and Subsidiary Accounts

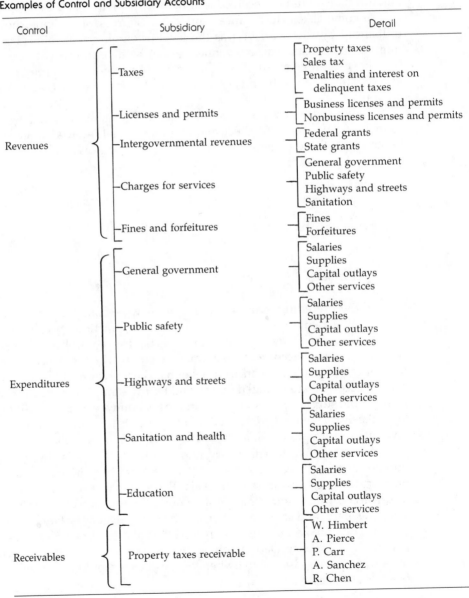

Control	Subsidiary	Detail
Revenues	Taxes	Property taxes Sales tax Penalties and interest on delinquent taxes
	Licenses and permits	Business licenses and permits Nonbusiness licenses and permits
	Intergovernmental revenues	Federal grants State grants
	Charges for services	General government Public safety Highways and streets Sanitation
	Fines and forfeitures	Fines Forfeitures
Expenditures	General government	Salaries Supplies Capital outlays Other services
	Public safety	Salaries Supplies Capital outlays Other services
	Highways and streets	Salaries Supplies Capital outlays Other services
	Sanitation and health	Salaries Supplies Capital outlays Other services
	Education	Salaries Supplies Capital outlays Other services
Receivables	Property taxes receivable	W. Himbert A. Pierce P. Carr A. Sanchez R. Chen

To illustrate the use of control and subsidiary accounts, as well as a number of different revenue and expenditure accounts, assume that a city has the following budgeted sources of revenue:

Property taxes	$ 900,000
License fees	50,000
Fines	40,000
Income taxes	10,000
Total	$1,000,000

Assume also that this city has five property owners, whose property taxes are levied as follows:

L. Armstrong	$500,000
P. Longhair	300,000
T. Monk	45,000
R. Whalen	30,000
O. Bryce	25,000
Total	$900,000

Finally, assume that the city has one department whose appropriations are as follows:

Salaries	$700,000
Supplies	200,000
Other	90,000
Total	$990,000

The budgetary, or opening, entry is:

Estimated revenues—property taxes	900,000	
Estimated revenues—license fees	50,000	
Estimated revenues—fines	40,000	
Estimated revenues—income taxes	10,000	
Appropriations—salaries		700,000
Appropriations—supplies		200,000
Appropriations—other		90,000
Unreserved fund balance		10,000

To record the Estimated revenues and Appropriations for FY 19X1.

If subsidiary and control accounts are used for property taxes, the entry to set up the receivable is

Property taxes receivable—control	900,000	
Revenues—property taxes		900,000

To set up the receivable for FY 19X1 property taxes.

Property Taxes Receivable—Subsidiary Ledger

	Debit
L. Armstrong	500,000
P. Longhair	300,000
T. Monk	45,000
R. Whalen	30,000
O. Bryce	25,000
Total	900,000

If these taxpayers pay their property tax bills in full during the period, the entry to record the payments is

Cash	900,000	
Property taxes receivable—control		900,000
To record the collectionof FY 19X1 property taxes.		

Property Taxes Receivable—Subsidiary Ledger

	Credit
L. Armstrong	500,000
P. Longhair	300,000
T. Monk	45,000
R. Whalen	30,000
O. Bryce	25,000
Total	900,000

Other revenues are recorded as they are collected. The entry to record these revenues is

Cash	100,000	
Revenues—license fees		50,000
Revenues—fines		40,000
Revenues—income taxes		10,000
To record the receipt of nonproperty tax revenues, FY 19X1.		

The entries to record the expenditures and their subsequent payment are

1.	Expenditures—salaries	700,000	
	Expenditures—supplies	200,000	
	Expenditures—other	90,000	
	Vouchers payable		990,000
	To record the FY 19X1 expenditures.		

| 2. | Vouchers payable | 990,000 | |
| | Cash | | 990,000 |

To record the payment of outstanding
FY 19X1 vouchers.

Finally, the closing entries are

1.	Revenues—property taxes	900,000	
	Revenues—license fees	50,000	
	Revenues—fines	40,000	
	Revenues—income taxes	10,000	
	Estimated revenues—property taxes		900,000
	Estimated revenues—license fees		50,000
	Estimated revenues—fines		40,000
	Estimated revenues—income taxes		10,000

To close the revenue and estimated revenue
accounts for FY 19X1.

2.	Appropriations—salaries	700,000	
	Appropriations—supplies	200,000	
	Appropriations—other	90,000	
	Expenditures—salaries		700,000
	Expenditures—supplies		200,000
	Expenditures—other		90,000

To close the appropriation and expenditure
accounts for FY 19X1.

Notice that these entries are very similar to those found in earlier illustrations. The only difference is that specific revenues and expenditures are now recorded in the accounts.

Vouchers

In the above example, the account Vouchers payable was used. A **voucher** is a written document that provides evidence that a transaction is proper. It also indicates the accounts in which the transaction is recorded.

The term *vouchers payable* is used in fund accounting in the same manner that the term *accounts payable* is used in business accounting—to represent the recording of a liability. The use of a voucher, however, indicates that payment has been approved by the appropriate authority and will definitely be made at a particular time. It also serves as a basis for classifying expenditures (i.e., putting them into various accounts).

Expenditure Control—Encumbrances

Before a nonbusiness organization makes an expenditure for materials or services, a **requisition** (a formal written order or request) is prepared. After this document has been approved, a *purchase order* is sent to the vendor. The organization now has an obligation to have sufficient funds available to pay the vendor within a reasonable length of time after the arrival of the materials or the performance of the services.

To meet this obligation, funds are set aside, or **encumbered**. The obligation itself is called an **encumbrance**. It represents resources that are now committed to a specific use and are no longer available for other expenditures. Since the materials or services have not yet been received, however, the organization has no legal financial obligation to the vendor. No liability (in the accounting sense) has been incurred, assets have not been increased, and the total fund balance has not been changed.

An encumbrance is recorded by means of a budgetary entry. Recording the encumbrance causes a portion of the appropriation to be set aside or "encumbered" until the materials are received or the services are performed. After the materials have been received or the services have been performed, the encumbrance is reversed out and a liability and an expenditure are recorded.

To determine the amount available for spending at any given point in time, both expenditures *and* encumbrances must be deducted from the appropriation or appropriations. To illustrate:

FY 19X1 appropriation	$990,000
Expenditures to date	500,000
Unexpended balance	$490,000
Outstanding encumbrances	200,000
Unencumbered (free) balance (available for spending)	$290,000

The above information tells us that the organization is "obligated" to spend $990,000 during the current fiscal year, of which $500,000 has already been spent and $200,000 is committed to specific purchases. Therefore the unit has $290,000 to spend for the remainder of the fiscal year.

When an encumbrance is recorded, a debit is made to an encumbrance account (e.g., Encumbrances—supplies) and a credit is made to an offsetting account called Reserve for encumbrances.

Reserves are used to set aside monies for specific purposes. They are also used to identify resources committed, but not expended, so that the unencumbered balance will reflect only monies that can still be spent.

The purpose of the Reserve for encumbrances account is to indicate that even though goods and services have not yet been received, an outstanding commitment exists for a given dollar amount. It also provides information on outstanding purchase orders. Like other reserves, the Reserve for encumbrances is a part of the fund balance.

To illustrate, assume that an order is placed for supplies costing, at the time of the order, $200,000. When the order is placed, an encumbrance is set up by means of the following entry:

Encumbrances—supplies	200,000	
Reserve for encumbrances		200,000
To record the encumbering of Purchase Order No. 1426		

Upon receipt of the supplies, the encumbrance is removed (reversed out) and an expenditure and a liability or a reduction of cash is recorded.

1.	Reserve for encumbrances	200,000	
	Encumbrances—supplies		200,000

To record the receipt of supplies ordered under Purchase Order No. 1426 and the removal of the encumbrance.

2.	Expenditures—supplies	200,000	
	Cash or Vouchers payable		200,000

To record the expenditure for the supplies purchased under Purchase Order No. 1426.

When an encumbrance is removed, the reversing entry is in the amount of the *purchase order*. The entry to record the expenditure, however, is in the amount of the *invoice*, the "actual" cost of the materials or services received. As long as these two dollar amounts are equal, there is no problem.

In many cases, however, the amount of the invoice differs from the amount of the purchase order. It is not unusual, for example, to have a price change between the time an order is placed and the time the materials or services ordered are received. In such a situation, the amount reversed out is the amount of the purchase order.

For example, if the actual invoice cost in the preceding illustration had been $210,000, the entry removing the encumbrance would still have been for the amount shown in the purchase order, $200,000. The original amount is *always* used, since the purpose of the reversing entry is to remove the purchase order and encumbrance from an outstanding status, not to record the expenditure. The expenditure, of course, would have been for $210,000.

If there is a difference between the amount of the purchase order and the invoice amount, the **unencumbered balance** of the appropriation is automatically adjusted because the outstanding encumbrance is replaced by an expenditure for the actual amount of the purchase.

To illustrate, assume that a city's appropriation for materials is for $100,000 and that a purchase order is issued for materials costing $34,000 (see Table 4–8). The balance of the appropriation, at the time the order is placed, is shown on the left. The effect of three different "actual" invoice amounts is shown on the right. Notice that

1. Regardless of the size of the invoice, the encumbered amount (the amount of the purchase order) is reversed out when the purchased materials arrive or the services ordered are provided.
2. If the amount of the invoice *equals* the amount of the purchase order (Case 1), recording the expenditure does *not* alter the unencumbered balance.
3. If the amount of the invoice is *smaller* than the amount of the purchase order (Case 2), the unencumbered balance is *increased* by the amount of the difference.

TABLE 4–8   Effect of Different Invoice Amounts on Unencumbered Balance

	When Purchase Order is sent to Vendor	CASE 1 Actual Invoice is $34,000	CASE 2 Actual Invoice is $33,000	CASE 3 Actual Invoice is $35,000
Appropriations—materials	$100,000	$100,000	$100,000	$100,000
Expenditures—materials	-0-	34,000	33,000	35,000
Unexpended balance	$100,000	$ 66,000	$ 67,000	$ 65,000
Amount encumbered for materials	34,000	-0-	-0-	-0-
Unencumbered ("free") balance—available for the purchase of additional material	$ 66,000	$ 66,000	$ 67,000	$ 65,000

4.   If the amount of the invoice is *greater* than the amount of the purchase order (Case 3), the unencumbered balance is *decreased* by the amount of the difference.

Budgetary and actual data are accumulated, for control purposes, in an **appropriation/expenditure ledger**. To illustrate, assume that the legislative body of a city approves the purchase of ten police cruisers for $80,000. On January 8, five cruisers are ordered. The vehicles are expected to cost $37,000. On March 18, the five cruisers arrive, along with an invoice for $36,000. On April 5, five more police cruisers are ordered, at an estimated cost of $43,000. On May 20, these cruisers arrive, along with an invoice for $44,000. Table 4–9 shows how this information would appear in an appropriation/expenditure ledger account.

Note how both the budgetary information and the actual information in Table 4–9 are used to control expenditures.

1.   The original budgetary appropriation is the *absolute* maximum that can legally be spent without further action by the legislative body.
2.   The placement of each order reduces the available balance, because of the effect of the encumbrance procedure.
3.   The receipt of each order causes the available balance to be increased or decreased. In this illustration, the actual cost of the first order of police cruisers was less than the amount encumbered. Therefore the available balance increased from $43,000 to $44,000. As a result, the city was able to order better-equipped vehicles after April 5. If the actual cost of the first order of vehicles had been greater than the amount encumbered, the available balance would have been reduced. As a result, it would have been necessary for the city to order either fewer vehicles or the same number of vehicles with less equipment.

Revenue Control

Revenues are controlled by means of a comparison of budgetary and actual data. This information is accumulated, by type of revenue, in a revenue ledger. An account from a revenue ledger is shown in Table 4–10.

TABLE 4–9   Appropriation/Expenditure Ledger (Police Vehicles)   FY 19X1

		APPROPRIATION	ENCUMBRANCES		EXPENDITURES	AVAILABLE BALANCE
Date	Item	CR	DR	CR	DR	CR
1/1	Budget	$80,000				$80,000
1/8	Order 5 vehicles		$37,000			43,000
3/18	5 vehicles arrive			$37,000		80,000
3/18	Record invoice				$36,000	44,000
4/5	Order 5 vehicles		43,000			1,000
5/20	5 vehicles arrive			43,000		44,000
5/20	Record invoice				44,000	-0-

TABLE 4–10   Revenue Ledger (Parking Meter Receipts)   FY 19X1

		Estimated Revenues DR	Actual Revenues CR	Difference DR (CR)
Date	Item			
1/1	Budget	$10,000		$10,000
1/31	Jan. collections		$1,000	9,000
2/28	Feb. collections		1,500	7,500

SUMMARY PROBLEM

This problem brings together the illustrations in this chapter. If you have any questions as you review the problem, turn back to the appropriate sections and reread the material.

On December 31, 19X0, the city council of Refined City approved the budget shown in Table 4–11. Refined City has five property owners, whose fiscal year (FY) 19X1 property taxes are as follows:

L. Armstrong	$500,000
P. Longhair	300,000
T. Monk	45,000
R. Whalen	30,000
O. Bryce	25,000
Total	$900,000

Among the accounting policies of Refined City are the following:

1. All purchases of supplies are encumbered.
2. Other expenditures do not require encumbrances.
3. Separate accounts (as opposed to control and subsidiary accounts) are maintained for each taxpayer.

TABLE 4–11

Refined City
General Fund Budget
For the Year Ended December 31, 19X1

Estimated Revenues		
Property taxes	$900,000	
License fees	50,000	
Fines	40,000	
Income taxes	10,000	$1,000,000
Appropriations		
Salaries	$700,000	
Supplies	200,000	
Other	90,000	990,000
Projected Increase in Fund Balance		$ 10,000

The opening, or budgetary, entry is

Estimated revenues—property taxes	900,000	
Estimated revenues—license fees	50,000	
Estimated revenues—fines	40,000	
Estimated revenues—income taxes	10,000	
Appropriations—salaries		700,000
Appropriations—supplies		200,000
Appropriations—other		90,000
Unreserved fund balance		10,000

To record the estimated revenues and appropriations for FY 19X1.

The operating entries are

1.	Property taxes receivable—Armstrong	500,000	
	Property taxes receivable—Longhair	300,000	
	Property taxes receivable—Monk	45,000	
	Property taxes receivable—Whalen	30,000	
	Property taxes receivable—Bryce	25,000	
	Revenues—property taxes		900,000

To set up the receivable for FY 19X1 property taxes.

2.	Encumbrances—supplies	200,000	
	Reserve for encumbrances		200,000

To record the encumbering of Purchase Order No. 1426.

3.	Cash	900,000	
	Property taxes receivable—Armstrong		500,000
	Property taxes receivable—Longhair		300,000
	Property taxes receivable—Monk		45,000
	Property taxes receivable—Whalen		30,000
	Property taxes receivable—Bryce		25,000

To record the collection of FY 19X1 property taxes.

| 4. | Reserve for encumbrances | 200,000 | |
| | Encumbrances—supplies | | 200,000 |

To record the receipt of supplies ordered under Purchase Order No. 1426 and the removal of the encumbrance.

| 5. | Expenditures—supplies | 200,000 | |
| | Vouchers payable | | 200,000 |

To record the expenditure for supplies purchased under Purchase Order No. 1426.

6.	Cash	100,000	
	Revenues—license fees		50,000
	Revenues—fines		40,000
	Revenues—income taxes		10,000

To record the collection of nonproperty tax revenues, FY 19X1.

| 7. | Vouchers payable | 200,000 | |
| | Cash | | 200,000 |

To record the payment for the supplies purchased under Purchase Order No. 1426.

8.	Expenditures—salaries	700,000	
	Expenditures—other	90,000	
	Vouchers payable		790,000

To record the expenditures for salaries and other items during FY 19X1.

| 9. | Vouchers payable | 790,000 | |
| | Cash | | 790,000 |

To record the payment of outstanding FY 19X1 vouchers.

The closing entries are

1.	Revenues—property taxes	900,000	
	Revenues—license fees	50,000	
	Revenues—fines	40,000	
	Revenues—income taxes	10,000	
	Estimated revenues—property taxes		900,000
	Estimated revenues—license fees		50,000
	Estimated revenues—fines		40,000
	Estimated revenues—income taxes		10,000

To close the revenue and estimated revenue accounts for FY 19X1.

2.	Appropriations—salaries	700,000	
	Appropriations—supplies	200,000	
	Appropriations—other	90,000	
	Expenditures—salaries		700,000
	Expenditures—supplies		200,000
	Expenditures—other		90,000

To close the appropriation and expenditure accounts for FY 19X1.

After the closing entries have been posted, the *postclosing trial balance* will appear as shown in Table 4–12.

TABLE 4–12

Refined City
General Fund
Postclosing Trial Balance
December 31, 19X1

	DR	CR
Cash	$10,000	
Unreserved fund balance		$10,000
	$10,000	$10,000

The resulting financial statements are shown in Table 4–13.

TABLE 4–13

Refined City
General Fund
Balance Sheet
December 31, 19X1

Assets		Liabilities and Fund Balance	
Cash	$10,000	Unreserved fund balance	$10,000

Refined City
General Fund
Statement of Revenues, Expenditures,
and Changes in Fund Balance
For the Fiscal Year Ended December 31, 19X1

Revenues		
Property taxes	$900,000	
License fees	50,000	
Fines	40,000	
Income taxes	10,000	$1,000,000
Expenditures		
Salaries	$700,000	
Supplies	200,000	
Other	90,000	990,000
Increase in Fund Balance		$ 10,000
Fund Balance, 1/1/X1		-0-
Fund Balance, 12/31/X1		$ 10,000

REVIEW QUESTIONS

Q4–1   How does the accounting cycle of a governmental unit compare with that of a business firm?

Q4–2   Define the term *budget*. What principal items are contained in a budget of a governmental unit?

Q4–3   Distinguish between *expenditures* and *expenses*.

Q4–4   What is an appropriation? How does it differ from an expenditure?

Q4–5   Why is the budget used by governmental units a "legal" document?

Q4–6   What are "budgetary" entries? When are they made?

Q4–7   Does the (nonbudgetary) fund balance account usually have a debit or a credit balance? What does the amount accumulated in the (nonbudgetary) fund balance account represent?

Q4–8   Why can a governmental unit record property tax revenues in the accounts before these revenues are actually received in cash? Why are other types of revenues, such as income taxes and license fees, recorded in the accounts after cash is received?

Q4–9   What is a *control account*? A *subsidiary account*?

Q4–10   What is a *voucher*? What purpose does it serve?

Q4–11   What is a *purchase order*? A *requisition*? An *invoice*?

Q4–12   How is a levy of property taxes recorded in the accounting records? How is the collection of the taxes recorded?

Q4–13   What is an *encumbrance*? When is it used? Is it used for all the expenditures of a governmental unit?

Q4–14   Why are city officials interested in the unencumbered balance of an appropriation?

Q4–15   What is the effect of encumbrances on the amount of an appropriation available for spending?

EXERCISES

E4–1   (Budgetary entries)
The city council of Alhambra approved the following budget:

Estimated Revenues		
Property taxes	$150,000	
Fines and fees	25,000	
Income taxes	15,000	
Licenses	10,000	$200,000
Appropriations		
Salaries	$100,000	
Materials and supplies	60,000	
Equipment	30,000	190,000
Projected Increase in Fund Balance		$ 10,000

REQUIRED: 1. Prepare the appropriate budgetary entry.
            2. Why can an increase in fund balance be put into the accounts at the *beginning* of the year?

E4–2   (Budgetary entries)
         The budget for the Graham Park Fund is as follows:

Estimated Revenues	
Property taxes	$2,400,000
Greens fees	600,000
Camping fees	400,000
Fines and permits	200,000
Appropriations	
Wage and salaries	$1,600,000
Grass seed	200,000
Animal food	200,000
Operating supplies	400,000
Outside services	600,000
Repave driveways	200,000
Move locomotive	50,000
Construct shelters	300,000

REQUIRED: 1. Prepare the entry to record the approved budget at the beginning of the year.
            2. If this is the park's first year of operation, how much should the fund balance contain at the end of the year if actual revenues and expenditures are as planned?

E4–3   (Budgetary and operating entries)
         The Board of Supervisors of Bluegrass County approved the following budget for FY 19X1:

Estimated Revenues		
Property taxes	$66,000	
Traffic fines	40,000	$106,000
Appropriations		
Salaries	$80,000	
Supplies	12,000	
Other	8,000	100,000
Projected Increase in Fund Balance		$ 6,000

The transactions for the year were as follows:
1. Collected property taxes of $66,000 in cash.
2. Purchased supplies for $12,000.
3. Paid salaries of $80,000.
4. Collected traffic fines of $40,000.
5. Purchased a membership in the Bluegrass Country Club for Col. H. P. (the "Fining Squire") Chicken, in recognition of his service to the county. The cost of the membership was $8,000.

REQUIRED: Prepare journal entries to set up the budgetary accounts and to record the above transactions.

E4–4   (Closing entries)

The ledger of the General Fund of the city of New Fargo shows the following balances at the end of the fiscal year:

Estimated revenues	$300,000
Appropriations	285,000
Unreserved fund balance	15,000
Revenues	300,000
Expenditures	285,000

REQUIRED: Prepare closing entries.

E4–5   (Complete budgetary cycle)

The Board of Supervisors of West Pitmann Township approved the following budget for FY 19X1:

Revenues		
Licenses	$10,000	
Fines	5,000	
Parking revenues	3,000	
Income taxes	20,000	
Gas royalties	2,000	$40,000
Appropriations		
Salaries	25,000	
Materials	10,000	
Equipment	3,000	38,000
Projected Increase in Fund Balance		$ 2,000

During the year, the actual revenues were

Licenses	$ 8,000
Fines	7,000
Parking revenues	3,000
Income taxes	16,000
Gas royalties	6,000

Actual expenditures were

Salaries	$25,000
Materials	8,000
Equipment	5,000

The township does *not* use encumbrances. All expenditures are paid in cash.

REQUIRED: 1. Prepare budgetary entries.
2. Prepare operating entries.
3. Prepare closing entries.

E4–6   (Receivables)
The city council of Great Knox has budgeted property tax revenues of $10,000 for fiscal year 19X1. The city has four property owners, whose property tax levies are as follows:

A. Able	$ 4,000
B. Baker	3,000
C. Charles	2,000
D. Delta	1,000
	$10,000

During the year, each of these property owners pays his taxes in full and on time. The city uses a one-step breakdown when recording revenues (e.g., Property taxes receivable—Baker   XXXX).

REQUIRED: Prepare journal entries recording
1. The setting up of the receivable for property taxes due.
2. The payment of the property taxes.

E4-7   (Encumbrances)
In February 19X1, the city of Golders Green ordered a fire engine, for which the manufacturer quoted a price of $120,000. The machine arrived the following month, along with an invoice for $120,000.

REQUIRED: 1. Make the appropriate journal entries to record
a. The setting up of the encumbrance
b. The removal of the encumbrance
c. The recording of the expenditure and the liability to the vendor
2. Assume that the actual cost of the fire engine was $125,000. Would your entries be the same as above? Why?

E4–8   (Encumbrances)
On January 10, the city of Wynnewood issued a purchase order to its stationery supplier for $50,000. On March 20, the stationery arrived, along with an invoice for $50,000, which was paid on April 15.

REQUIRED: Prepare the journal entries necessary to record
1. The setting up of the encumbrance
2. The arrival of the stationery on March 20
3. The payment for the stationery on April 15

E4–9   (Encumbrances)
On April 25, the city of Alden ordered supplies with a quoted price of $80,000. On May 15, one-half of the supplies arrived, along with an invoice for $40,000. On June 6, the other half of the order arrived, accompanied by an invoice for $42,000. Both invoices were paid at the end of the month of arrival.

REQUIRED: 1. Prepare entries to record
    a. The setting up of the encumbrance
    b. The arrival of the goods in May and June
    c. The payment for the goods
  2. What effect, if any, will the second invoice have on the balance of the appropriation?

E4–10   (Receivables)
The city council of Collegeville budgeted revenues of $100,000 from the following sources:

Property taxes	$ 60,000
Fines and penalties	30,000
Income taxes	10,000
	$100,000

The city has three property owners, whose tax bills are as follows:

U. Grant	$30,000
R. Lee	20,000
G. Patton	10,000
	$60,000

During the year, all property owners paid their taxes on time and in full. Collections from other sources of revenue were:

Fines and penalties	$30,000
Income taxes	10,000
	$40,000

Assume that appropriations amount to $100,000.

REQUIRED: Using a one-step breakdown (e.g., Revenues—income taxes), prepare the
  1. Budgetary entry
  2. Entry to set up receivable accounts for property taxes
  3. Entry or entries to record the collection of revenues
  4. Entry to close out the revenue accounts

E4–11   (Receivables—subsidiary and control accounts)
The city council of Small Rock estimated that revenues of $95,000 would be collected for the General Fund. The sources and amounts would be as follows:

Property taxes	$80,000
Parking meters	10,000
Fines and penalties	5,000

The city has four taxpayers, whose shares of the tax levy are as follows:

H. Tudor	$40,000
N. Bonapart	30,000
L. Nelson	6,000
D. Wellington	4,000

All of the taxpayers paid their property taxes on time and in full. Other collections throughout the year were as follows:

Parking meters	$6,000
Fines and penalties	8,000

REQUIRED: Prepare journal entries to record
1. The entry of the budgeted revenues into the accounts
2. The setting up of the receivable, using a control account for each taxpayer
3. The collection of the taxes
4. The collection of the other revenues

PROBLEMS

P4–1   (Discussion question on governmental accounting)
Governmental accounting gives substantial recognition to budgets, with those budgets being recorded in the accounts of the governmental unit.

REQUIRED: a. What is the purpose of a governmental accounting system and why is the budget recorded in the accounts of a governmental unit? Include in your discussion the purpose and significance of appropriations.
b. Describe when and how a governmental unit records its budget and closes it out.

(AICPA)

P4–2   (Complete set of entries and statements)
The following transactions apply to the fiscal year 19X1 operations of the Arid City Levee Board, a recently formed organization:
a. Revenues were estimated at $150,000. Appropriations of $145,000 were made.
b. Property taxes of $120,000 were collected during the year. Fines and penalties amounted to $30,000.
c. Supplies worth $35,000 were purchased during the year. Salaries paid amounted to $100,000.
d. Utilities for the year amounted to $10,000.

REQUIRED: 1. Prepare journal entries to record the transactions.
2. Post the entries made in requirement 1. (Use T-accounts.)
3. Prepare a preclosing trial balance.
4. Prepare closing entries.
5. Post the entries made in requirement 4.
6. Prepare a postclosing trial balance.
7. Prepare, in good form, a balance sheet and a statement of revenues, expenditures, and changes in fund balance for FY 19X1. Assume that the fund balance at the beginning of the year was zero.

P4–3   (Beginning balances; complete set of statements)
The ledger of the General Fund of the city of Bayou Cactus shows the following balances at the beginning of FY 19X1.

> Cash $38,000   Unreserved fund balance $38,000

The following transactions take place during the year:
a. The city council estimates General Fund revenues from all sources to be $600,000 and has approved a budget authorizing appropriations of $580,000.
b. Sales tax collections amount to $75,000 and fines total $25,000, all collected in cash.
c. Property owners pay $490,000 in taxes during the year in cash. Peter Smith has promised to pay his bill ($10,000) early in February of the *following* fiscal year, as soon as he receives his dividend check from a local utility. (*Hint*: Assume that this item is treated as a revenue of the current year and set up a receivable.)
d. Expenditures of $580,000 are incurred and are paid in cash during the year.

REQUIRED: 1. Prepare appropriate journal entries.
2. Post the above entries to the ledger. (Use T-accounts.)
3. Prepare a preclosing trial balance.
4. Prepare closing entries and post to the ledger.
5. Prepare a postclosing trial balance.
6. Prepare, in good form, a balance sheet and a statement of revenues, expenditures, and changes in fund balance for FY 19X1.

P4–4   (Beginning balances; complete set of statements)
The December 31, 19X1, postclosing trial balance of the General Fund of the city of Catfish was as follows:

	DR	CR
Cash	$500	
Accounts receivable	300	
Vouchers payable		$400
Unreserved fund balance		400
	$800	$800

a. The city council estimated revenues for FY 19X1 to be $1,500 and expenditures to be $1,450.
b. The city's outstanding voucher payable, due to a contractor for re-modelling city hall, was paid off in March.
c. Sales taxes of $1,000 were collected during the year.
d. The Provo Chemical Company paid the city $300 it owed for repairs to a fire hydrant because of damage done by a runaway delivery truck.

e. Speeding tickets, which resulted in fines of $500, were issued to tourists en route to Fun City. The fines were paid in cash.

f. Salaries of $1,000 were paid to the mayor and city clerk. Supplies costing $300 were purchased for cash.

g. A used traffic light was purchased from the city of Brownsville for $150, to be paid the following year.

REQUIRED: 1. Prepare journal entries to record the above transactions in the General Fund.
2. Post the above journal entries to the ledger. (Use T-accounts.)
3. Prepare a preclosing trial balance.
4. Prepare closing entries and post to the ledger.
5. Prepare a postclosing trial balance.
6. Prepare, in good form, a balance sheet and a statement of revenues, expenditures, and changes in fund balance.

P4-5   (Multiple choice)

1. The following proceeds were received by Kew City from specific revenue sources that are legally restricted to expenditures for specified purposes:

Gasoline taxes to finance road repairs	$400,000
Levies on affected property owners to finance sidewalk repairs	300,000

The amount that should be accounted for in Kew City's Special Revenue Fund is

a. $0
b. $300,000
c. $400,000
d. $700,000

2. The Estimated revenues control account of a governmental unit is debited when
a. The budget is closed at the end of the year
b. The budget is recorded
c. Actual revenues are recorded
d. Actual revenues are collected

3. Which of the following accounts of a governmental unit is debited when a purchase order is approved?
a. Encumbrances
b. Reserve for encumbrances
c. Vouchers payable
d. Appropriations

4. When a police car is received by a governmental unit, the entry on the books of the General Fund should include a debit to
a. Appropriations—police cars
b. Expenditures—police cars

    c. Encumbrances—police cars

    d. Unreserved fund balance

5. Which of the following terms refers to an actual cost, rather than an estimate?

    a. Expenditure

    b. Appropriation

    c. Budget

    d. Encumbrance

6. In approving the budget of the city of Troy, the city council appropriated an amount greater than expected revenues. This action will result in

    a. A cash overdraft during the fiscal year

    b. An increase in outstanding encumbrances by the end of the fiscal year

    c. A debit to Unreserved fund balance

    d. A necessity for compensatory offsetting action in the Debt Service Fund

7. If a credit was made to Unreserved fund balance when recording the budget, it can be assumed that

    a. Estimated expenditures exceed actual revenues

    b. Actual expenditures exceed estimated expenditures

    c. Estimated revenues exceed appropriations

    d. Appropriations exceed estimated revenues

8. Which of the following is a budgetary account?

    a. Expenditures—supplies

    b. Appropriations

    c. Revenues—property taxes

    d. Vouchers payable

9. Which of the following accounts of a governmental unit is credited when a purchase order is approved?

    a. Reserve for encumbrances

    b. Encumbrances

    c. Vouchers payable

    d. Appropriations

10. Entries similar to those for the General Fund may also appear on the books of a municipality's

    a. General Fixed Assets Account Group

    b. General Long-Term Debt Account Group

    c. Trust Fund

    d. Special Revenue Fund

11. What type of account is used to earmark a portion of the fund balance to liquidate the contingent obligation for goods ordered but not yet received?

    a. Appropriations

    b. Encumbrances

c. Obligations

d. Reserve for encumbrances

12. Authority granted by a legislative body to make expenditures and to incur obligations during a fiscal year is the definition of an

a. Appropriation

b. Authorization

c. Encumbrance

d. Expenditure

(AICPA adapted)

P4–6   (Complete set of entries; breakdown of revenue and expenditure accounts)

The city council of Ongar approved the following budget for its General Fund on December 31, 19X1:

Revenues	
Property taxes	$ 85,000
Income taxes	35,000
Parking meter revenues	15,000
Fines and penalties	10,000
Liquor licenses	5,000
Appropriations	
Salaries	$100,000
Supplies	20,000
Equipment	15,000
Motorcycles	10,000

The city has four property owners, whose tax assessments for fiscal year 19X1 are:

T. Calderon	$30,000
R. Freeman	25,000
M. Villere	20,000
E. Garcia	10,000

Fiscal year 19X1 is the first year of operation for this city. As a result, there are no balances in the accounts as of January 1, 19X1. During 19X1, the following transactions took place:

a. FY 19X1 tax bills were sent to the property owners.

b. Ordered supplies costing $20,000.

c. The supplies arrived, along with an invoice for $20,000; the invoice was paid immediately.

d. Paid salaries for the year—$100,000.

e. Ordered equipment costing $15,000.

f. Collected property taxes for the year, in full, from all property owners. Collections of income taxes were $35,000.

g. Four motorcycles were ordered from a local dealer, who had submitted a bid for $9,500.

h. Parking meter revenues for the year were $15,000, while receipts from the issue of liquor licenses amounted to $5,000.

i. Collections from fines and penalties were $10,000.

j. The equipment ordered arrived, along with an invoice for $15,000; the invoice was paid immediately.

k. The motorcycles arrived; because of an increase in their costs, the dealer asked the city to pay an additional $500 over the amount bid. Because of political considerations, the city agreed to do this and promptly issued a check for $10,000 to the dealer to cover the cost of the motorcycles.

REQUIRED: 1. Prepare appropriate journal entries to record the budget and these transactions.
2. Post the entries and prepare a preclosing trial balance.
3. Make closing entries and prepare a postclosing trial balance.
4. Prepare, in good form, a balance sheet and a statement of revenues, expenditures, and changes in fund balance.

P4–7   (Prior balances, encumbrances, complete cycle)

The city council of Prairieville approved the following budget for the General Fund for fiscal year 19X1:

Revenues		
Property taxes	$50,000	
License fees	10,000	
Fines and penalties	15,000	
Parking meter revenues	5,000	
Federal grants	20,000	$100,000
Appropriations		
Salaries	$60,000	
Materials	20,000	
Equipment	14,000	
Interest	1,000	95,000
Projected Increase in Fund Balance		$ 5,000

The postclosing trial balance for the fund, as of December 31, 19X0, was as follows:

	DR	CR
Cash	$ 5,000	
Due from federal government	10,000	
Vouchers payable		$ 8,000
Unreserved fund balance		7,000
	$15,000	$15,000

Transactions for FY 19X1 include the following:

a. FY 19X1 property tax bills were sent to the property owners.

b. Ordered two new police cars at an estimate total cost of $13,000.

c. Received a check from the federal government to cover 19X0 and 19X1 federal grants, $30,000.

d. Borrowed $15,000 from the Bank of Prairieville for six months.

e. Ordered materials costing $20,000.

f. Paid vouchers outstanding at the end of 19X0, $8,000.

g. License fees for 19X1 were $9,000; fines and penalties were $15,000.

h. The police cars arrived, along with an invoice for $14,000.

i. Parking meter revenues for 19X1 were $6,000.

j. Repaid loan to bank, along with accrued interest of $1,000.

k. The materials arrived, accompanied by an invoice for $18,000.

l. Paid the outstanding voucher for $14,000 to the vendor who supplied the police cars.

m. Salaries for the year were $62,000.

n. Property taxes received during the year were $50,000.

REQUIRED:　1. Prepare journal entries to record the budget and the above transactions.

2. Prepare a preclosing balance.

3. Prepare closing entries.

4. Prepare a postclosing trial balance.

5. Prepare a balance sheet and a statement of revenues, expenditures, and changes in fund balance for FY 19X1.

P4–8　(Comprehensive problem on fund accounting cycle)

The general ledger of the Greenview Park Fund shows the following balances as of December 31, 19X0:

	DR	CR
Cash	$10,000	
Accounts receivable—White	500	
Property taxes receivable—Johnson	1,500	
Due from General Fund	1,500	
Vouchers payable		$ 4,000
Notes payable		2,000
Due to Debt Service Fund		3,000
Unreserved fund balance		4,500
	$13,500	$13,500

The budget for FY 19X1 is as follows:

Revenues and Transfers

Property taxes	$8,000
Rentals	4,000
Concession fees	2,000
Transfer from General Fund	4,000

Appropriations

Salaries	$8,000
Outside services	4,000
Materials	3,000
Equipment	2,000
Interest	1,000

The Greenview Park Fund collects taxes directly from five property owners, whose land adjoins the park. The property owners and their fiscal year 19X1 assessments are:

R. Jordan	$3,000
E. Johnson	2,000
P. Ohl	1,000
E. Blank	1,200
G. Almstead	800

The Park Commission follows the policy of encumbering purchases of materials, equipment, and outside services. Since there has never been a problem of collections, no provision is made for uncollectible accounts.

Transactions for fiscal year 19X1 are as follows:

a. Bills for their FY 19X1 taxes were sent to the property owners.

b. R. Jordan and E. Blank paid their property taxes upon receipt of their tax bills.

c. G. Almstead paid one-half of his FY 19X1 property tax bill.

d. The commission paid the vouchers open (unpaid) as of the end of FY 19X0.

e. The commission issued tax anticipation notes of $10,000 on January 1, which bore interest at the rate of 12 percent per annum. (*Note:* These notes are recorded only in the Greenview Park Fund.)

f. E. Johnson paid his taxes for FY 19X0, $1,500; and for FY 19X1, $2,000.

g. Materials expected to cost $2,500 were ordered.

h. A contract was awarded to International Business Associates to conduct a series of training programs for park personnel. The contract price was $4,000.

i. A check was received from the General Fund for $5,500 to cover obligations from FY 19X0 and for FY 19X1. (*Hint:* Make a credit to Operating transfers from General Fund for $4,000.)

j. A new tractor was ordered; the price quoted by the dealer was $2,000.

k. The notes outstanding at the end of FY 19X0 were paid off, along with accrued interest of $100.

l. A check for $300 was received from the parents of Bob White, a local juvenile delinquent, to pay for damage he did to the park in FY 19X0.

m. Paid $3,000 (in cash) to the Debt Service Fund; this amount represented the final payment on a bond issue.

n. The materials ordered in (g) arrived, along with an invoice for $3,200, which the commissioners agreed to eventually pay.

o. Received a check for $1,500 from the operator of the park's concessions to cover her fee for the year.

p. Received a check for $1,000 from P. Ohl for payment of his property taxes.

q. The tractor arrived in December, along with an invoice for $1,800.

r. Paid the vendor for the materials, $3,200.

s. Repaid the tax anticipation notes, $10,000 *plus* accrued interest of $900.

t. Received rentals of $4,500 from people who camped in the park.

u. International Business Associates finished conducting the training programs and submitted a bill for $4,000, which was approved by the treasurer.

v. Paid salaries in cash, $8,000.

w. Paid voucher for payment to International Business Associates, $4,000.

REQUIRED: 1. Prepare appropriate budgetary and operating entries.
2. Prepare a preclosing trial balance.
3. Prepare closing entries.
4. Prepare a postclosing trial balance.
5. Prepare appropriate financial statements.

P4-9   (Relationship between encumbrances and free balance; appropriation/ expenditure ledger)

The city council made an appropriation to the police department of $100,000 for the purchase of supplies, equipment, and vehicles.

1. The department placed an order for ten police cars, estimated to cost $5,000 each.
2. The department placed an order with Owen Supply Company for crime prevention supplies; the estimated cost of the order was $30,000.
3. The police cars arrived in good condition, along with an invoice for $50,000.
4. An order was placed for radio equipment; estimated cost was $10,000.
5. The supplies ordered in number 2, arrived, along with an invoice for $32,000.
6. The radio equipment was received in acceptable condition; actual cost was $9,000.
7. The department purchased a new firearm for $75 cash, on an "emergency" basis, directly from a local dealer; no order had been placed.

REQUIRED: 1. Prepare an appropriation/expenditure ledger. Use columns for Appropriations, Encumbrances (Dr and Cr), Expenditures, and Available balance.
2. What was the free balance at the end of the period?

5

THE GOVERNMENTAL FUND ACCOUNTING CYCLE

General and Special Revenue Funds— Special Problems

LEARNING OBJECTIVES

After you complete this chapter, you should be able to:

1. Identify two methods of handling uncollectible property taxes
2. Explain the purpose of liens and how to account for them
3. Demonstrate how to handle encumbrances when partial orders are received
4. Explain the use of and accounting for allotments
5. Prepare the closing entries necessary when a surplus or deficit occurs
6. Explain two approaches to the handling of open encumbrances and the journal entries appropriate for each method
7. Identify five types of interfund transactions
8. Show how a budget revision is handled
9. Explain the accounting for fixed assets and prepaid expenses
10. Demonstrate two methods of accounting for inventories

Up to this point we have assumed that everything falls right into place. That is, all revenues that are budgeted are collected, only the amounts appropriated are spent, and all encumbrances are removed by the end of the fiscal year.

These assumptions, of course, are unrealistic. Taxpayers are sometimes unable or unwilling to pay their taxes, operating personnel seldom spend the exact amount appropriated, and in many instances some encumbrances are removed on a piecemeal basis while others are still outstanding at the end of the fiscal year. In addition, many transactions take place between the various funds of the governmental unit. The treatment of these and certain other problems will be discussed in this chapter.

UNCOLLECTIBLE RECEIVABLES

As was noted in Chapter 4, revenues from property taxes are recorded when these taxes are levied rather than when they are collected. This is because property taxes meet the "measurable" and "available" criteria at this point in time. While governmental units can, and sometimes do, jail people or seize their property for the nonpayment of taxes, such actions are not always expedient, especially in periods of high unemployment. Therefore, it is necessary to make some provision for uncollectible receivables.

There are two approaches to this problem: the direct write-off method and the allowance method.

Direct Write-off Method

Under the **direct write-off method**, uncollectible accounts are treated as reductions of revenue. When a debt is determined to be uncollectible, a revenue account is debited and a receivable account is credited.

To illustrate, assume that in March property taxes of $800 are levied against R. Grimm. In July, it is determined that Mr. Grimm will be unable to pay his tax bill and that it is not expedient to seize his property. As a result, city officials decide to write off the Grimm account as a total loss.

The appropriate entries are:

March 5	Property taxes receivable—all taxpayers	10,000	
	Revenues—property taxes		10,000
	To record the property tax revenues for FY 19X1, including the Grimm account.		
July 15	Revenues—property taxes	800	
	Property taxes receivable—Grimm		800
	To write off the Grimm account as uncollectible.		

If, at a later date (either in the current or in some later period), Mr. Grimm should pay his tax obligations, his payment will be treated as a revenue:

December 12	Cash	800	
	Revenues—property taxes		800
	To record the payment in full of the Grimm account, which was written off as uncollectible on July 15.		

It should be noted that the direct write-off method is *not* consistent with generally accepted accounting principles (GAAP). Therefore, its use is normally limited to those cases in which uncollectible accounts are few in number and relatively small.

Allowance Method

The second, and more commonly used, method of handling uncollectible accounts is the **allowance method**. This procedure contains a built-in assumption that a certain portion of the taxes levied will not be collected. Using past experience and predictions of future economic conditions, finance officials can estimate what percentage of the *total* taxes will be uncollectible. This can be done even though, at the time of the levy, it is not known which or whose particular taxes will not be collected.

When the taxes are levied, an **Allowance for uncollectibles** is recorded. This account has a credit balance and is a *contra asset*. Recording the Allowance has the effect of reducing the revenues of the period in which taxes are levied, rather than the period in which they are determined to be uncollectible, and provides a better measurement of revenues for each period. When it becomes known that a specific taxpayer's account is uncollectible, the Allowance for uncollectibles is debited (reduced) and the receivable in question is credited (also reduced).

To illustrate, assume that the property taxes levied in a given year amount to $1 million and that past experience has shown that 4 percent of the taxes levied are usually not collected. Therefore, an allowance of $40,000 is necessary. The entry to set up this allowance is:

Property taxes receivable—Morgan	525,000	
Property taxes receivable—Lohmann	350,000	
Property taxes receivable—Parker	35,000	
Property taxes receivable—Whalen	50,000	
Property taxes receivable—Olson	40,000	
Allowance for uncollectible property taxes		40,000
Revenues—property taxes		960,000

To set up the receivable for FY 19X1 property taxes, including an estimated 4 percent that is expected to remain uncollectible.

Assume further that in June it becomes apparent that Parker will be unable to pay his property taxes and it is not expedient to force a sale of his property. Thus, the account must be written off. The entry to do this is:

Allowance for uncollectible property taxes	35,000	
Property taxes receivable—Parker		35,000

To write off the Parker account for FY 19X1.

The entry to record the collection of the remaining property taxes is the same as the one previously illustrated:

Cash	965,000	
Property taxes receivable—Morgan		525,000
Property taxes receivable—Lohmann		350,000
Property taxes receivable—Whalen		50,000
Property taxes receivable—Olson		40,000
To record the collection of property taxes in FY 19X1.		

Notice that under this method the write-off of a bad debt does not effect revenues. The effect on revenues occurs when the Allowance is set up (i.e., when taxes are levied).

Adjustments to the Allowance for Uncollectibles

Sometimes the estimate of uncollectible property taxes is either too high or too low. When this happens an adjustment is made, either during or at the end of the year. If, for example, the allowance is too low and it has been decided to make an upward adjustment, the allowance account is credited (increased) and the revenue account is debited (decreased).

To illustrate, assume that in July city officials conclude that uncollectible property taxes will be $5,000 *higher* than anticipated. The adjusting entry is:

Revenues—property taxes	5,000	
Allowance for uncollectible property taxes		5,000
To adjust the revenue and allowance for uncollectible property tax accounts to reflect an increase in the estimate of uncollectible property taxes.		

If, on the other hand, city officials conclude that uncollectible property taxes will be $5,000 *lower* than anticipated, the reverse of the above entry is made:

Allowance for uncollectible property taxes	5,000	
Revenues—property taxes		5,000
To adjust the revenue and allowance for uncollectible property tax accounts to reflect a decrease in the estimate of uncollectible property taxes.		

At the end of the year, the balance in the Allowance for uncollectible property taxes account may not agree with taxes still outstanding. For example, the account may have a credit balance after all taxes have been collected or written off (the actual collections were higher than anticipated). In this case the remaining allowance must be reversed out. That is, the allowance must be reduced to zero and property tax revenues must be increased. This entry is necessary because when the original entry to record the tax levy was made, the amount that would prove uncollectible was overestimated and the revenues were underestimated.

To continue with the illustration on p. 143, assume that the original allowance is $40,000 and uncollectible accounts for the year amount to $35,000, leaving a credit balance of $5,000 in the Allowance for uncollectible property taxes account. The adjusting entry is:

Allowance for uncollectible property taxes	5,000	
Revenues—property taxes		5,000

To decrease the FY 19X1 allowance for uncollectible property taxes to reflect actual collections.

If, on the other hand, the allowance turns out to be inadequate and no adjustment has been made during the year (the Allowance for uncollectible property taxes account has a debit balance), an adjusting entry must be made to bring the balance in this account back to zero or to the remaining amount not expected to be colleced. This is done by crediting the allowance account for the shortfall and debiting (reducing) Property tax revenues for the same amount. To illustrate, assume that the original Allowance for uncollectible property taxes for 19X1 is $40,000, that FY 19X1 taxes of $35,000 have been written off so far, and that another $15,000 of taxes is not likely to be collected, resulting in a total of $50,000 of uncollectible, or potentially uncollectible, property taxes. The adjusting entry is:

Revenues—property taxes	10,000	
Allowance for uncollectible property taxes		10,000

To increase the FY 19X1 allowance for uncollectible property taxes to reflect actual collections.

DELINQUENT TAXES

Often a governmental unit will not write off a property tax receivable until officials are certain that the tax is uncollectible. Sometimes this is several years after the tax has been levied. Prudent management, however, necessitates keeping past due or delinquent taxes separate from those levied in the current year. To accomplish this, receivables are classified as *current* and *delinquent*. At some point in time (often the day they are due), outstanding current receivables are reclassified as delinquent. To illustrate, assume that on September 30, the due, or delinquent, date, taxpayers Whalen and Olsen owe $50,000 and $40,000, respectively, some of which the city reasonably expects to collect in the future. The adjusting entry is:

Property taxes receivable—		
delinquent—Whalen	50,000	
Property taxes receivable—delinquent—		
Olson	40,000	
Property taxes receivable—current—		
Whalen		50,000
Property taxes receivable—current—		
Olson		40,000

To reclassify FY 19X1 property taxes not collected by due date as delinquent.

In addition, the related Allowance for uncollectible property taxes must also be adjusted. Assume that this Allowance is equal to $15,000, which is the amount of the FY 19X1 property tax levy that city officials feel is unlikely to be collected. The entry to make this adjustment is:

Allowance for uncollectible property taxes—		
current	15,000	
Allowance for uncollectible property		
taxes—delinquent		15,000

To adjust the allowance for uncollectible property taxes—current for FY 19X1 property taxes that are no longer current.

Sometimes interest is charged on the delinquent taxes, or penalties are assessed against the taxpayer. When this happens, a debit is made to a receivable account in order to recognize this additional claim against the taxpayer. An offsetting credit to a revenue account is also made.

If penalties totaling $900 are assessed against Whalen and Olson, the entry is:

Interest and penalties receivable—Whalen	500	
Interest and penalties receivable—Olson	400	
Revenues—interest and penalties		900

To record the assessment of late-payment penalties.

If the receivables are eventually determined to be uncollectible, the previous entry will be reversed.

Sometimes an Allowance for uncollectible interest and penalties account is used. In most cases, however, the balance in the Interest and penalties receivable account is not large enough to warrant the extra effort involved in setting up an offsetting allowance.

When back taxes are owed, a governmental unit will sometimes place a lien against a piece of property. A **lien** is the legal right to hold or sell a piece of property in order to satisfy a claim against its owner. Such property cannot be sold or transferred by its owner until the lien is removed.

In extreme cases a governmental unit will exercise its right to seize the property and sell it to the highest bidder. After the taxes, penalties, and expenses of the sale have been deducted, the proceeds will be remitted to the former owner or owners of the property.

When a lien is placed against a piece of property, the existing receivable accounts are replaced by a new account called **Tax liens receivable**. To illustrate, assume that a lien is placed against the Whalen property. When this happens, the delinquent taxes, interest, and penalties are reclassified to reflect their new status:

Tax liens receivable—Whalen	50,500	
Property taxes receivable—		
delinquent—Whalen		50,000
Interest and penalties receivable—		
Whalen		500

To reclassify property taxes, interest, and penalties receivable to reflect the lien on the Whalen property.

If it costs $300 to process and advertise the lien, this cost will be added to the new receivable:

Tax liens receivable—Whalen	300	
Cash		300

To record the cost of processing and advertising the tax lien against the Whalen property.

If the Whalen property is sold for $120,000 and expenses related to the sale amount to $1,500, the following entries are used to record the sale and the amounts due to the auctioneer and to R. Whalen:

Cash	120,000	
Tax liens receivable-Whalen		50,800
Vouchers payable		69,200

To record the sale of the Whalen property, removal of the lien, and expenses related to the sale ($1,500).

Vouchers payable	69,200	
Cash		69,200

To record the payment of the expenses of the sale of the Whalen property and the amount due to R. Whalen.

OTHER ADJUSTMENTS

Even the best of systems is prone to error. Those used by governmental units are no exception. One source of error lies in the assessing of taxes. Taxpayers will often appeal their assessments, and as a result their tax bills will be adjusted. This, of course, increases or, more commonly, decreases the revenues of the governmental unit.

To adjust for an **overassessment**, the revenue account is debited (decreased) and the receivable account is credited (also decreased). If the taxpayer has already paid his or her entire tax bill, a cash refund is issued.

To illustrate, assume that the taxes originally levied on W. M. Lohmann's property are $350,000 and that when Mr. Lohmann appeals to his assessor, the taxes are lowered to $300,000. If Mr. Lohmann's tax reduction takes place *before* he pays his tax bill, the adjusting entry will be:

Revenues—property taxes	50,000	
Property taxes receivable—current—		
Lohmann		50,000
To adjust for an error on the FY 19X1 tax assessment of W. M. Lohmann.		

If, however, Mr. Lohmann pays the $350,000 when due and successfully appeals the assessment at a later date, the entry will be:

Revenues—property taxes	50,000	
Vouchers payable		50,000
To adjust for an error on the FY 19X1 tax assessment of W. M. Lohmann and to set up a liability for a refund		

In the case of **underassessments**, the receivable (and revenue) accounts are increased to cover the additional assessments. Assume, for example, that Mr. Lohmann not only loses his appeal but is assessed an additional $75,000. The adjusting entry is:

Property taxes receivable—current—		
Lohmann	75,000	
Revenues—property taxes		75,000
To adjust for an error on the FY 19X1 tax assessment of W. M. Lohmann.		

CLOSING WITH A SURPLUS OR DEFICIT

In the previous example it was assumed that actual revenues were equal to estimated revenues and that expenditures were equal to appropriations. This seldom happens in real life. In a more typical situation, actual revenues will be greater than or less than estimated revenues, and expenditures will not equal appropriations. When this happens, any differences must be added to or deducted from Unreserved fund balance. To illustrate, assume the following:

Estimated revenues from all sources	$1,000,000
Actual revenues from all sources	996,000
Appropriations of all types	990,000
Expenditures of all types	987,000

The entry to close the estimated and actual revenue accounts is:

Revenues—all sources	996,000	
Unreserved fund balance	4,000	
Estimated revenues—all sources		1,000,000

To close the estiamted and actual revenue accounts.

The entry to close the appropriation and expenditure accounts is:

Appropriations—all types	990,000	
Expenditures—all types		987,000
Unreserved fund balance		3,000

To close the appropriation and expenditure accounts.

These entries have the effect of decreasing the Unreserved fund balance from its planned end-of-the-year-balance (assumed to be $10,000) to its actual end-of-year-balance ($10,000 - $4,000 + $3,000 = $9,000).

Occasionally the Unreserved fund balance account becomes negative and has a debit balance. A negative fund balance is known as a **deficit**. This is a very unhealthy situation.

WARRANTS

Before a check can be "cut" (prepared) and payment made, a warrant is usually prepared. A **warrant** is an order, drawn by the appropriate authority, requesting the treasurer (or someone designated by that person) to pay a specified sum of money to a particular person or organization. Its purpose is to assist in the prevention of unauthorized payments. No journal entries are necessary when warrants are prepared.

PARTIAL ORDERS

In our previous discussion of encumbrances we emphasized that when an encumbrance is removed, the amount reversed out is the amount of the encumbrance. This is true even if the actual purchase cost is different. The amount shown as an expenditure, of course, always equals the amount *actually* paid.

The example used to illustrate the above points assumed that the *entire* order was received at one time. In many cases, however, orders of goods and services are received piecemeal throughout the year. A governmental unit will often place a **blanket order** for a quantity of goods or services, to be received gradually over a period of time (e.g., one-sixth of the order each month for six months). Payment for these goods or services is usually made shortly after the receipt of each shipment rather than at the end of the period covered by the order.

When this happens, a problem is created as to when the encumbrance should be removed. Although some accountants advocate waiting until the last item is received, most realize that this approach causes a loss of control over expenditures and defeats the purpose of the encumbrance. In addition, before all goods or services are received, the order may be canceled by operating personnel without informing the accounting department. This causes funds that could be used elsewhere to be tied up until year-end because accounting personnel are unaware that the funds will not be spent. As a result, they inadvertently turn down spending requests even though funds are actually available.

The alternative used by most organizations requires more paperwork but results in tighter control over expenditures. Under this approach, a portion of the encumbrance *equivalent to the portion of the goods or services that have been received* is removed when the voucher for payment is prepared. Thus, when one-fourth of an order arrives, one-fourth of the encumbrance is removed.

To illustrate, assume that one-fourth of the $200,000 of supplies ordered in the example in the previous chapter has been received, along with an invoice for $45,000. One-fourth of the encumbrance, $50,000, is removed while a voucher for the *actual* invoice amount is prepared:

Reserve for encumbrances	50,000	
Encumbrances—supplies		50,000
To record the receipt of one-fourth of the supplies ordered under P.O. No. 1426.		
Expenditures—supplies	45,000	
Vouchers payable		45,000
To record the liability for payment of one-fourth of the goods received under P.O. No. 1426.		

The first entry removes one-fourth of the original encumbrance. This reflects the fact that one-fourth of the goods were received. The second entry records the *actual* expenditure and liability.

This method gives managers a fairly accurate idea of how much of the order has arrived. It also prevents the tying up of large amounts of money until year-end, by which time the appropriation may have expired, and allows managers, if they desire, to adjust the encumbrances to correspond with actual prices at the end of the period.

OPEN ENCUMBRANCES

Until now it has been assumed that all materials and services ordered during a given period are received in that period. In reality, however, this is seldom the case. Deliveries are sometimes made after year-end. Materials that are ordered near the end of one year often arrive the following year. Finally, certain items have long lead times between order and delivery dates (e.g., fire engines). Since encumbrances are not removed until materials or services are received, a problem is created as to what to do with them at year-end. There are two approaches to the handling of this problem: (1) allow the encumbrances to lapse; or (2) keep the encumbrances "open" and remove them when the goods or services are received.

Encumbrances Lapse

The first approach is the one commonly used in practice (and is often the one legally required). When it is followed, all unexpended appropriations (encumbered and unencumbered) lapse at the end of the year, even if the governmental unit is committed to eventually accepting the goods and services. The expenditures relating to the items ordered, but not yet received, must be charged against the appropriations of the following year. To indicate that commitments are still outstanding, the balance in the Reserve for encumbrances is left intact.

To illustrate, assume that in fiscal year 19X1, the first year of operation of a governmental unit, appropriations of $750,000 are approved by the legislative body, all of which are encumbered. During the year goods and services, expected to cost $700,000, are received, along with invoices for $695,000. The purchase orders outstanding at the end of the year will be honored in fiscal year 19X2, even though the associated encumbrances have lapsed. The entry to set up the encumbrances for FY 19X1 is:

Encumbrances	750,000	
Reserve for encumbrances		750,000

To record the encumbering of FY 19X1 purchase orders.

The entries to record the receipt of goods and services are:

1.	Reserve for encumbrances	700,000	
	Encumbrances		700,000

To record the receipt of goods and services in FY 19X1 and the removal of outstanding encumbrances.

2.	Expenditures	695,000	
	Vouchers payable		695,000

To record the expenditures for goods and services received in FY 19X1.

At the end of the year, the remaining appropriation and expenditure accounts are closed out.

Appropriations	750,000	
Expenditures		695,000
Unreserved fund balance		55,000

To close the appropriation and expenditure accounts for FY 19X1.

The remaining encumbrances are also closed out. However, in order to keep the balance in Reserve for encumbrances intact, these encumbrances are closed to Unreserved Fund Balance.

Unreserved fund balance	50,000	
Encumbrances		50,000

To close the outstanding encumbrances for FY 19X1.

At the beginning of the following year, the above entry is reversed. This reversal has the effect of returning the Encumbrances and the Reserve for encumbrances accounts to their usual offsetting relationship. It also increases the Unreserved fund balance by a like amount, as it is no longer necessary to set aside this reserve for prior-year commitments.

Encumbrances	50,000	
Unreserved fund balance		50,000

To reestablish the encumbrances for goods and services ordered, but not received, in FY 19X1.

In 19X2, the legislative body should appropriate $50,000 to cover the expenditures for goods and services not received in 19X1, as well as an amount sufficient to cover the cost of goods and services expected to be purchased that year.

Some governmental units do not bother to keep their Reserve for encumbrances intact. They close their Encumbrances *and* their Reserve for encumbrances accounts at the end of the year. If they intend to honor prior-year commitments the following year, they set up appropriations, encumbrances, and a new Reserve for encumbrances for these purchase orders in the new year. Such commitments should be described in the notes to the financial statements.

Encumbrances Remain Open

Under the second approach encumbrances and their corresponding appropriations are kept "open" at year-end and are removed when goods and services are actually received. The journal entries used are similar to those used in the first approach. However, since Encumbrances and Appropriations are budgetary accounts, which are related only to the current period, they are closed at year-end. At the beginning of the following year, they are reopened and added to the "new" encumbrances and appropriations.

To illustrate, assume that at the end of 19X0 encumbrances amounting to $50,000 are still outstanding, and the governmental unit follows a policy of not allowing encumbrances to lapse. At the end of the year, the spent appropriations and the expenditure accounts are closed out.

Appropriations	700,000	
Expenditures		695,000
Unreserved fund balance		5,000

To close the spent appropriation and the expenditure accounts for FY 19X0.

The entry to close the remaining encumbrances and appropriations is:

Appropriations	50,000	
Encumbrances		50,000

To close the outstanding encumbrances and their corresponding appropriations for FY 19X0.

As with the previous approach, the Reserve for encumbrances remains intact, in order to indicate to readers of the financial statements that the governmental unit plans to honor those purchase orders still outstanding at the end of the year.

At the beginning of the next year, the following entry is made:

Encumbrances	50,000	
Appropriations		50,000

To restore the outstanding encumbrances and their corresponding appropriations.

This entry restores the outstanding encumbrances and their corresponding appropriations. It also indicates that these encumbrances represent prior-year commitments. The Reserve for encumbrances, of course, remains intact because it was never closed.

To continue with the example, assume that during 19X1 appropriations amounting to $200,000 (not counting the open encumbrances) are made and that this amount is encumbered. Assume also that all of the goods and services ordered the previous year (19X0) are received, at a cost of $48,000; that goods and services encumbered for $160,000 and actually costing $161,000 are received; and that the remaining goods and services ordered are expected to be received in 19X2. The entries to record the 19X1 activities are:

| 1. | Encumbrances | 200,000 | |
| | Reserve for encumbrances | | 200,000 |

To record the encumbering of FY 19X1 purchase orders.

| 2. | Reserve for encumbrances | 50,000 | |
| | Encumbrances | | 50,000 |

To record the receipt of goods and services ordered in FY 19X0 and the removal of outstanding encumbrances.

| 3. | Expenditures | 48,000 | |
| | Vouchers payable | | 48,000 |

To record the expenditures for goods and services ordered in FY 19X0 but received in FY 19X1.

| 4. | Reserve for encumbrances | 160,000 | |
| | Encumbrances | | 160,000 |

To record the receipt of goods and services ordered and received in FY 19X1 and the removal of the outstanding encumbrances.

| 5. | Expenditures | 161,000 | |
| | Vouchers payable | | 161,000 |

To record the expenditures for goods and services ordered and received in FY 19X1.

The closing entries for 19X1 are:

| 1. | Appropriations | 40,000 | |
| | Encumbrances | | 40,000 |

To close the outstanding encumbrances and their corresponding appropriations for FY 19X1 ($50,000 + $200,000 − $50,000 − $160,000 = $40,000).

2.	Appropriations	210,000	
	Expenditures		209,000
	Unreserved fund balance		1,000

To close the appropriation and expenditure accounts for FY 19X1 ($200,000 + $50,000 − $40,000 = $210,000).

At the beginning of 19X2, of course, encumbrances amounting to $40,000 are set up to cover the prior-year commitments.

| | Encumbrances | 40,000 | |
| | Appropriations | | 40,000 |

To restore the outstanding encumbrances and their corresponding appropriations.

ALLOTMENTS

To maintain closer control over expenditures, a governmental unit will sometimes divide appropriations into **allotments**. These pieces of the appropriation may be encumbered (obligated) or expended during the **allotment period**, which is usually a quarter-year or half-year.

If allotments had been used in the previous example, the **Unallotted appropriations account** would have replaced appropriations and the budgetary entry would have been:

Estimated revenues—various sources	1,000,000	
Unallotted appropriations		990,000
Unreserved fund balance		10,000
To record the estimated revenues and unallotted appropriations for FY 19X1.		

At the time formal allotments are made, the Unalloted appropriations account is reduced (debited) and an allotment account is set up by means of a credit to allotments. If, in the above illustration, the first period's allotment is $495,000, the following entry is appropriate:

Unallotted appropriations	495,000	
Allotments		495,000
To record the allotment for the first half of 19X1.		

If $485,000 is actually expended during the allotment period, the following entry is appropriate:

Expenditures (various)	485,000	
Vouchers payable		485,000
To record the expenditures incurred during the first half of 19X1.		

Under the more commonly used procedure, allotments are controlled by means of a three-column subsidiary ledger, which provides a running total of the balance available for spending. A subsidiary ledger is shown in Table 5-1.

At year-end Estimated revenues is closed out to Revenues, with any difference between these account balances being added to or deducted from Unreserved fund balance. Allotments is closed out to Expenditures, any difference between these account balances also being added to or deducted from Unreserved fund balance.

To illustrate, assume that in fiscal year 19X1, of the $990,000 allocated to an organization, $950,000 is actually spent. Assume also that this organization receives its funding in semiannual allotments of $495,000 and that the subsidiary ledger illustrated in Table 5-1 is maintained by this organization.

TABLE 5–1 Subsidiary Ledger for Allotments

Date	Allotment	Expenditures	Remaining Balance
1/1	$495,000		$495,000
1/8		$ 75,000	420,000
3/15		200,000	220,000
5/17		150,000	70,000
6/25		60,000	10,000
7/1	495,000		505,000
7/15		200,000	305,000
9/26		75,000	230,000
11/15		100,000	130,000
12/18		30,000	100,000
12/29		88,000	12,000
	$990,000	$978,000	$ 12,000

January 1	Estimated revenues—various sources	1,000,000		
	Unallotted appropriations		900,000	
	Unreserved fund balance		10,000	
	To record the estimated revenues, unallotted appropriations, and projected increase in fund balance for FY 19X1.			
January 1	Unallotted appropriations	495,000		
	Allotments		495,000	
	To set up the allotment for the first half of 19X1.			
January–June	Cash	500,000		
	Revenues—various sources		500,000	
	To record revenues for the first half of FY 19X1.			
	Expenditures—various	485,000		
	Vouchers—payable		485,000	
	To record expenditures for the first half of FY 19X1.			
July 1	Unallotted appropriations	495,000		
	Allotments		495,000	
	To set up the allotment for the second half of FY 19X1.			
July–December	Cash	500,000		
	Revenues—various sources		500,000	
	To record revenues for the second half of FY 19X1.			
	Expenditures—various	493,000		
	Vouchers payable		493,000	
	To record expenditures for the second half of FY 19X1.			

December	Revenues—various sources	1,000,000	
31	Estimated revenues—various sources		1,000,000

To close out the revenue and estimated revenue accounts for FY 19X1.

	Allotments	990,000	
	Expenditures—various		978,000
	Unreserved fund balance		12,000

To close out the allotment and expenditure accounts for FY 19X1.

INTERFUND TRANSACTIONS

Transactions between the individual funds of a governmental unit are called **interfund transactions**. Interfund transactions include (1) interfund loans or advances, (2) quasi-external transactions, (3) reimbursements, (4) residual equity transfers, and (5) operating transfers. Each of these is discussed below.

Interfund Loans or Advances

Interfund loans or advances arise when one fund lends money to another fund. The recipient fund recognizes a liability to the paying fund, and the paying fund recognizes a receivable from the recipient fund. When recording *short-term* receivables and payables (those due within one year), the terms "due from" and "due to" are used. When recording *long-term* receivables and payables (those due after one year), the terms "advances to" and "advances from" are used. The amounts shown on the financial statements as "due to" and "due from" and "advances to" and "advances from," for the governmental unit as a *whole*, should be equal at all times.

To inform readers of the financial statements that certain current financial resources are not available for spending, advances to other funds are generally reported as reservations of fund balance. The entries to record interfund loans or advances are (amounts assumed):

Entry in	Due from (advance to[1]) XX Fund	5,000	
the books	Cash		5,000
of the	To record loan to XX Fund.		
lending			
fund			

Entry in	Cash	5,000	
the books	Due to (advance from) YY		
of the	Fund		5,000
borrowing	To record loan from YY Fund.		
fund			

[1]This transaction requires a reservation of fund balance.

Quasi-external Transactions

Quasi-external transactions are interfund transactions that result in the recognition of revenues and expenditures (or expenses) to the funds involved. These transactions are unique in that they are the only ones, not involving parties external to the governmental unit, in which revenues and expenditures (or expenses) are recognized.

Quasi-external transactions occur when one fund performs services for another, one fund makes a payment to another in lieu of property taxes, and so forth. For example, a fund recognizes revenue when it provides services to an outside party. If, instead, it provides those same services to another fund, it is still appropriate for the fund to recognize revenue.

To continue with the analogy, if the fund receiving the services mentioned above contracts with an outside party for the same services, it will have an expenditure (or expense). The fact that the supplier of the services is another governmental unit will not change the recognition of the expenditure (or expense).

For example, assume that an Enterprise Fund (Water Utility Fund) provides water and sewerage services to the governmental unit. The billing from the Water Utility Fund to the General Fund will be recorded as follows (amounts assumed):

Entry in the books of the Enterprise Fund	Due from General Fund Sale of water and sewerage services To record the billing to the General Fund.	123,000	123,000
Entry in the books of the General Fund	Expenditures—water and sewerage services Due to Water Utility Fund To record the billing from the Water Utility Fund.	123,000	123,000

Since these transactions involve the recognition of revenues and expenditures (or expenses), they are reported on the statement of revenues, expenditures (or expenses), and changes in fund balance (or retained earnings).

Reimbursements

In some instances expediency may require that an expenditure (or expense) be paid by a fund other than the one properly chargeable for the transaction. For example, assume that the General Fund makes an expenditure of $25,000 for consulting services that benefit several different funds. If the General Fund initially pays the bill, with the allocation of the charges to be made at a later date, and if it is determined that the amount of the charge allocable to the Auditorium Fund, a Capital Projects Fund, is $5,000, the following entries will be made:

Entry in the books of the General Fund	Expenditures—consulting services	25,000	
	Cash		25,000
	To record the payment for consulting services that benefit several funds		

Entry in the books of the Auditorium Fund	Expenditures—consulting services	5,000	
	Cash		5,000
	To record the payment for consulting services		

Entry in the books of the General Fund	Cash	5,000	
	Expenditures—consulting services		5,000
	To record the reimbursement by the Auditorium Fund for consulting services paid for by the General Fund.		

The above entries "transfer" the expenditure from the books of the General Fund to the books of the Auditorium Fund. This ensures that the expenditure will not be recorded more than once, and that the fund receiving the benefit will recognize the expenditure.

Residual Equity Transfers

Transfers in general are defined as "all interfund transactions except loans or advances, quasi-external transactions, and reimbursements . . . ."[2] **Residual equity transfers** are further defined as "nonrecurring or nonroutine transfers of equity between funds . . . ."[3] Thus a contribution made by the General Fund to supply capital to an Electric Utility Fund (Enterprise Fund) is treated as a residual equity transfer. Likewise, the return of all or part of this contribution in a later period is treated as a residual equity transfer—assuming the return was not originally planned.

Other types of transactions that represent residual equity transfers include the transferring of the ending balance of a Capital Projects Fund to a Debt Service Fund and the transferring of any remaining fund balance of a Debt Service Fund to the General Fund, after the principal and interest have been paid.

A residual equity transfer of the remaining balance of a Debt Service Fund to the General Fund is recorded as follows (amounts assumed):

Entry in the books of the Debt Service Fund	Residual equity transfer to General Fund	32,000	
	Cash		32,000
	To record equity transfer of remaining fund balance to the General Fund.		

[2]GASB Cod. Sec. 1800.106.
[3]Ibid.

Entry in	Cash	32,000	
the books	Residual equity transfer from Debt		32,000
of the	Service Fund		
General	To record equity transfer of remaining fund		
Fund	balance from Debt Service Fund.		

Residual equity transfers should not be treated as revenues or expenditures (or expenses). Instead they should be treated as increases or decreases in the fund balances of governmental-type funds or as increases or decreases in the contributed capital of proprietary-type funds. In some instances these transfers should be treated as direct reductions of the retained earnings of proprietary-type funds.

Operating Transfers

All transfers that are not residual equity transfers are **operating transfers**. Thus the annual debt service payment made by the General Fund to a Debt Service Fund is classified as an operating transfer. Other examples of this type of shifting of resources include (1) an operating subsidy from the General Fund to an Electric Utility Fund (Enterprise Fund) and (2) a payment made by the General Fund for its share of the cost of constructing a civic auditorium.

Operating transfers should *not* be treated as revenues or expenditures (or expenses) by either fund involved in the transaction. Instead they should be reported as "Other Financing Sources (Uses)" for governmental-type funds and other funds that use a spending measurement focus in the statement of revenues, expenditures, and changes in fund balance. Proprietary-type funds and other funds that use the capital maintenance focus should report these transactions in the "Operating Transfers" section of the statement of revenues, expenses, and changes in retained earnings. The reporting of these transfers is illustrated in Chapters 3 and 9.

A typical operating transfer is a transfer from the General Fund to a Capital Projects Fund. The following entries are used to record this transfer (amounts assumed):

Entry in	Operating transfer to Capital Projects Fund	8,000	
the books	Cash		8,000
of the	To record a transfer to the Capital Projects		
General	Fund		
Fund			

Entry in	Cash	8,000	
the books	Operating transfer from General Fund		8,000
of the	To record a transfer from the General Fund.		
Capital			
Projects			
Fund			

OTHER PROBLEMS

Other problems faced by governmental units include the borrowing of money for short periods of time, budget revisions, the acquisition of assets with lives of more than one year, depreciation on long-lived assets, inventories, prepaid items, and reserves.

Borrowings

Governmental organizations sometimes make short-term (less than one year) borrowings. These are generally in the form of **notes**, which are often issued to banks and other financial institutions. A note is a written promise to pay a given amount of money at a particular point(s) in time. It can be secured by *collateral*, as in the case of a note signed by the purchaser of an automobile, or it can be *unsecured*. The latter type is more common in governmental units, as loans to these organizations are generally not very risky because these organizations (theoretically) have the power to raise taxes in the event of a need for more revenues.

Among the more commonly used types of notes are **tax anticipation notes**. These are used by governmental units to cover current financing obligations until the taxes are collected, which is often late in the year. The taxes collected are then used to retire the debt. Notes are also issued in anticipation of receiving funds from a bond issue. When the bonds are sold (issued), the proceeds are used to repay the notes.

The entries used to account for the issuance and repayment of notes are similar to those used by commercial enterprises. To illustrate, assume that a city borrows $100,000 from a bank, to be repaid (during the same fiscal year) from future tax revenues. The entry to record this transaction is:

Cash	100,000	
Tax anticipation notes payable		100,000
To record the issuance of tax anticipation notes.		

When the notes are repaid, the above entry will be reversed. This will result in a reduction of Cash and a reduction of the outstanding liability.

Budget Revisions

Sometimes budgets are revised during the year. Conditions such as disasters or severe unemployment can cause serious shortages of actual revenues. If this happens and a balanced budget is to be maintained, the appropriations must be reduced (many city charters and state constitutions require a balanced budget). Such adjustments are recorded by debiting *Appropriation* accounts, crediting *Estimated revenue* accounts, and reflecting any differences in the **Unreserved fund balance**.

Assume, for example, that a city begins fiscal year 19X1 with the following budget:

Estimated revenues	$1,000,000
Appropriations	990,000
Increase in fund balance	$ 10,000

Several months after the beginning of the year, the city council concludes that revenues for the year will be about 10 percent less than projected and votes to reduce the budget by the same percentage. The appropriate adjusting entry is:

Appropriations	99,000	
Unreserved fund balance	1,000	
Estimated revenues		100,000

To reflect the revisions to the FY 19X1 budget.

The governmental unit must now operate within the new budgetary constraints.

Assets with a Life of More Than One Year

Generally speaking, the purchase of assets with a life of more than one year is treated as an expenditure. That is, if a governmental unit acquires real estate or equipment, the *entire* outlay is charged against an appropriation of the year of *purchase*. This is different from commercial accounting, where a building or a piece of equipment expected to last for more than one year is recorded as an asset and "written off," as an expense, over its *useful life*.

For the purpose of control, most fixed assets of governmental units are listed in the General Fixed Assets Account Group, where debits are made to asset accounts (e.g., Equipment) and credits are made to accounts listing the sources of funding for the assets. The assets are *not* shown on the balance sheets of governmental-type funds. The are, however, shown as separate items on these organizations' schedules of general fixed assets. To illustrate assume that equipment costing $975,000 is purchased by a governmental unit:

Entry in the books of the General Fund

Expenditures—capital equipment	975,000	
Vouchers payable		975,000

To record the purchase of equipment in the General Fund and to recognize the liability to the vendor.

Entry in the General Fixed Assets Account Group

Equipment	975,000	
Investments in general fixed assets from General Fund revenues		975,000

To record the purchase of equipment in the General Fixed Assets Account Group

Sometimes it is necessary to dispose of property or equipment. This is done either because the asset is no longer needed by the governmental unit (surplus property) or because it has become obsolete or damaged. Such a transaction requires entries in the General Fund (or the fund that financed the purchase of the asset) and the General Fixed Assets Account Group. In the General Fund, Cash is debited and a revenue account is credited. In the General Fixed Assets Account Group, the entry recording the purchase of the asset is reversed. To illustrate, assume that a governmental unit disposes of a fire engine, which originally cost $50,000, for $10,000.

Entry in the books of the General Fund	Cash	10,000	
	Revenues—sale of general fixed assets		10,000
	To record the sale of one fire engine		
Entry in the General Fixed Assets Account Group	Investment in general fixed assets from General Fund revenues	50,000	
	Equipment		50,000
	To record the sale of one fire engine.		

This topic will be covered in greater depth in Chapter 6.

Depreciation

Except for the Internal Service, Enterprise, and certain Nonexpendable Trust Funds, no formal entries are made for depreciation. This means, of course, that only the original cost of most assets is shown in the accounting records. Depreciation is not recorded in most funds for three reasons:

1. Governmental units are concerned with matching actual revenues and expenditures with *estimated revenues* and *appropriations* rather than determining net income. Since depreciation is a "noncash" expense, it does not require an appropriation; and since there is no appropriation for depreciation, there is no need to recognize an expenditure. When an asset is replaced, an appropriation is made for the entire cost of the new asset.
2. Governmental units do not pay income taxes. Thus, there is no reason to account for the tax deduction that can be taken for depreciation.
3. No need exists for information on "return on investment," since governmental units are not expected to make a profit. Hence this measure of performance is superfluous.

Inventories

Governmental units normally record purchases of materials and supplies as expenditures when those purchases take place, even though the items purchased might be inventoried and not used until a later fiscal year. Under this procedure, called the **purchases method**, inventories are treated in the same manner as fixed assets. That is, they are "expensed" when purchased. However, since they are not recorded in the General Fixed Assets Account Group, there is no record of their existence on the date of the balance sheet.

When the purchases method is used, *spending* is defined as "the *acquisition* of assets." To meet the principle of full disclosure and to indicate that they are not "available spendable resources," the existence of these inventories is reported on the balance sheet by means of inventory accounts and a reserve account. To illustrate, assume that supplies costing $10,000 are still on hand at the end of a fiscal year and that this fact should be disclosed to readers of the financial statements. The appropriate entry is:

Supplies on hand	10,000	
Reserve for supplies on hand		10,000
To record the amount of supplies on hand at the end of FY 19X1.		

At the end of the following year, the inventory accounts and the reserve account should be adjusted to reflect the balance on hand at that point in time. For example, if the cost of the supplies on hand at the end of the second year is $14,000, the balance in the inventory and in the reserve account should be adjusted to this amount, as follows:

Supplies on hand	4,000	
Reserve for supplies on hand		4,000
To adjust the supplies and the reserve accounts so that they reflect the amount of supplies on hand at the end of FY 19X2.		

If the amount of supplies on hand had decreased rather than increased, the supplies account would have been credited and the reserve account would have been debited by the amount necessary to bring their balances down to the new level. Notice that only the *reserve* changes, not the Unreserved fund balance. This is because no change in available *spendable* resources has taken place.

Many governmental units, especially those with a large number of proprietary-type funds, follow the same practice as commercial organizations when recording inventoriable items. They record these items as assets when purchased, and as expenditures when "consumed." This method is known as the **consumption method**.

The logic behind the consumption method is that "spending" occurs when an asset is used. Therefore, the acquisition of an inventoriable item merely represents the exchange of one asset for another. To illustrate, assume that during the year purchases of supplies amount to $8,000 and that supplies costing $6,500 are used. The entry to record the purchases of supplies is:

Supplies on hand	8,000	
Vouchers payable		8,000
To record the purchase of supplies in FY 19X1.		

The entry to record the usage of supplies is:

Expenditures—supplies	6,500	
Supplies on hand		6,500
To record the usage of supplies in FY 19X1.		

Because inventories are *spendable* assets, reserves are required only in those instances when a certain minimum amount of inventory must be kept on hand and, therefore, is not considered to be a spendable asset.

Prepaid Items

Prepaid items (e.g., prepaid rent, prepaid insurance, etc.) are charged to expenditure accounts when the *payment* is made. Such items are not usually reported on the balance sheet, as they are in commercial accounting. If the governmental unit does decide to report prepaid items on the balance sheet, the purchases method is generally used.

Reserves and Designations

According to governmental GAAP, ". . . the use of the term 'reserve' should be limited to indicating that a portion of the Fund Balance [a] is not appropriable for expenditure or [b] is legally segregated for a specified future use."[4] An example of the first use of reserves (to indicate to the reader of the financial statements that a portion of the fund balance is not appropriable for future expenditures) is the Reserve for inventories, which is discussed above. An example of the second use of reserves (to indicate to the reader of the financial statements that a portion of the fund balance is legally segregated for a specific future use) is the Reserve for encumbrances. This reserve reflects the purchase orders that are outstanding as of the end of the fiscal year.

Sometimes a governmental unit will set aside or *designate* a portion of its fund balance in order to inform the readers of its financial statements of *tentative* or "informal" plans for the future use of financial resources, such as extra police protection for a special event or equipment replacement. These designations reflect *managerial* plans and have no formal legal basis. As a result, they should be clearly distinguished from formal reserves of fund balance. Unlike fund balance reserves, they are subject to change at the discretion of the management, rather than the legislative body, of the governmental unit. For example, the mayor of a city might decide that resources designated for extra police protection during Mardi Gras parades should be used to provide security for the Superbowl. Such a decision does not usually require the approval of the city council.

[4]GASB Cod. Sec. 1800.122.

SUMMARY PROBLEM

The city council of Realistic City approved the budget shown in Table 5–2 for that municipality's General Fund on December 31, 19X0.

TABLE 5–2

Realistic City
General Fund
Budget
For the Year Ended December 31, 19X1

Estimated Revenues and Proceeds of		
Issue of General Obligation Bonds		
Property taxes	$ 960,000	
License fees	45,000	
Interest and penalties	40,000	
Income taxes	55,000	
Proceeds from issue of bonds	900,000	$2,000,000
Appropriations and Transfers		
Salaries	$ 550,000	
Interest	100,000	
Supplies	250,000	
Transfer to Frazer Park Fund	20,000	
Capital equipment	1,070,000	1,990,000
Projected Increase in Fund Balance		$ 10,000

Realistic City currently has five property owners, whose fiscal 19X1 property taxes are as follows:

H. R. Morgan	$ 525,000
W. M. Lohmann	350,000
G. R. Parker	35,000
R. A. Whalen	50,000
P. R. Olson	40,000
Total	$1,000,000

One former property owner, L. J. Ahrens, still owes $500 of FY 19X0 property taxes. Past experience has shown that 4 percent of the property taxes levied are usually not collected.

Among the city's accounting policies are the following:

1. All purchases of supplies and capital equipment are encumbered.
2. Expenditures for salaries, interest, and transfers to other funds do not require encumbrances.
3. Encumbrances lapse at the end of the fiscal year; however, the Reserve for encumbrances is shown on the year-end balance sheet.
4. Separate accounts are maintained for each taxpayer.

The *postclosing* trial balance of the General Fund of Realistic City, as of December 31, 19X0, is as follows:

	DR	CR
Cash	$51,850	
Property taxes receivable—delinquent—Ahrens	500	
Allowance for uncollectible property taxes— delinquent		$ 400
Interest and penalties receivable—Ahrens	50	
Vouchers payable		8,000
Due to Frazer Park Fund		9,000
Reserve for encumbrances		20,000
Unreserved fund balance		15,000
	$52,400	$52,400

During fiscal year 19X1, the following transactions take place:

1. The purchase orders outstanding at the beginning of the year are encumbered. They are for supplies and amount to $20,000.
2. Individual accounts for Property taxes receivable are set up, along with an Allowance for uncollectible property taxes equal to 4 percent of the amount levied.
3. Property taxes are collected on time and in full from H. R. Morgan.
4. L. J. Ahrens is unable to pay her FY 19X0 property taxes in full. She pays the $50 penalty and $100 of these taxes. The remainder of her account is written off.
5. The city council decides, in late August, that the Allowance for uncollectible property taxes is too low and orders the city treasurer to increase it by $10,000.
6. The amount due to the Frazer Park Fund and the vouchers that were outstanding at the end of FY 19X0 are paid.
7. G. R. Parker is unable to pay his FY 19X1 property taxes. The city decides to write off the account without foreclosing on his property.
8. R. A. Whalen and P. R. Olson fail to pay their property taxes by the due date (September 30). The taxes are reclassified as delinquent, along with the Allowance for uncollectible property taxes.
9. Penalties of $500 and $400, respectively, are levied against Whalen and Olson.
10. A tax lien is placed against the Whalen property.
11. Costs of processing and advertising the lien amount to $300. They are paid immediately.
12. In November, the Whalen property is sold for $120,000. The auctioneer submits a bill for $1,500. Mr. Whalen and the auctioneer are paid in full.
13. W. M. Lohmann protests his tax bill. As a result, it is lowered to $300,000. Mr. Lohmann then pays his tax bill in full.
14. Supplies and equipment ordered the previous year arrive. Actual cost is $19,500. Payment is made the following week.
15. A cash payment of $15,000, representing part of the FY 19X1 contribution, is made to the Frazer Park Fund. A liability is set up for the remainder of the amount budgeted for this purpose.
16. Supplies costing $200,000 are ordered on P.O. No. 1426.

17. New fire engines, costing $950,000, are ordered on P.O. No. 1427.
18. One-fourth of the supplies ordered arrive, along with an invoice for $45,000. The invoice is paid the following week.
19. One-half of the supplies arrive, along with an invoice for $90,000. Payment is not made until the following year.
20. Salaries for the year amount to $580,000. These are paid in cash.
21. General obligation bonds, bearing an interest rate of 12 percent, are issued for $810,000 on March 1. In December, interest of $81,000 is recorded as an operating transfer. This amount will be paid to the Debt Service Fund the following year.
22. During the year, it becomes evident that the revenues and the proceeds from the bond issue are lower than planned. As a result, the city council reduces the budgeted appropriations and its estimate of the collections from all sources by 10 percent.
23. At the end of the year, it is determined that the balance in the Allowance for uncollectibles account is too low. The allowance is raised by $5,000.
24. The city disposes of one old fire engine for $10,000 (original cost was $50,000).
25. The fire engines arrive (actual cost is $975,000). The invoice is paid immediately.
26. Revenues from other sources, not already recorded, are:

License fees	$50,000
Interest and penalities	20,000
Income taxes	50,000

27. Supplies costing $10,000 are still on hand at the end of the year. It is felt that this fact should be disclosed in the financial statements.

REQUIRED FOR FY 19X1:
1. Prepare appropriate budgetary and operating entries in the General Fund.
2. Prepare a preclosing trial balance.
3. Prepare closing entries.
4. Prepare a postclosing trial balance.
5. Prepare appropriate financial statements.

The budgetary, or opening, entry is:

Estimated revenues—property taxes	960,000	
Estimated revenues—license fees	45,000	
Estimated revenues—interest and penalties	40,000	
Estimated revenues—income taxes	55,000	
Estimated proceeds from issue of bonds	900,000	
Appropriations—salaries		550,000
Appropriations—interest		100,000
Appropriations—supplies		250,000
Appropriations—transfers to other funds		20,000
Appropriations—capital equipment		1,070,000
Unreserved fund balance		10,000

To record the estimated revenues, estimated proceeds from the issue of bonds, appropriations, and projected increase in fund balance for FY 19X1.

The operating entries are:

1. Encumbrances—supplies   20,000
           Unreserved fund balance   20,000

    To reestablish the encumbrances for supplies
    ordered, but not received, in FY 19X0.

2. Property taxes receivable—current—Morgan   525,000
    Property taxes receivable—current—
           Lohmann   350,000
    Property taxes receivable—current—Parker   35,000
    Property taxes receivable—current—Whalen   50,000
    Property taxes receivable—current—Olson   40,000
           Allowance for uncollectible property
                taxes—current   40,000
           Revenues—property taxes   960,000

    To set up the receivable for the FY 19X1
    property taxes, along with an allowance for
    uncollectible property taxes of 4 percent.

3. Cash   525,000
           Property taxes receivable—current—
                Morgan   525,000

    To record the payment of property taxes by
    H. R. Morgan.

4. Cash   150
    Allowance for uncollectible property taxes—
           delinquent   400
                Interest and penalties receivable—
                     Ahrens   50
                Property taxes receivable—
                     delinquent—Ahrens   500

    To record the collection of the penalties and
    part of the FY 19X0 property taxes levied on
    L. J. Ahrens and to write off the remainder of
    the account.

5. Revenues—property taxes   10,000
           Allowance for uncollectible property
                taxes—current   10,000

    To increase the FY 19X1 allowance for uncol-
    lectible property taxes to reflect the actual
    collections

6. Due to Frazer Park Fund   9,000
    Vouchers payable   8,000
           Cash   17,000

    To record the payment of liabilities outstand-
    ing at the end of 19X0.

7. Allowance for uncollectible property taxes—
           current   35,000
           Property taxes receivable—current—
                Parker   35,000

    To write off the Parker account for FY 19X1.

8a.	Property taxes receivable—delinquent— Whalen	50,000	
	Property taxes receivable—delinquent— Olson	40,000	
	Property taxes receivable—current— Whalen		50,000
	Property taxes receivable—current— Olson		40,000
	To reclassify FY 19X1 property taxes not col- lected by due date as delinquent.		
8b.	Allowance for uncollectible property taxes— current	15,000	
	Allowance for uncollectible property taxes—delinquent		15,000
	To adjust the allowance for uncollectible prop- erty taxes—current for FY 19X1 property taxes that are no longer current.		
9.	Interest and penalties receivable—Whalen	500	
	Interest and penalties receivable—Olson	400	
	Revenues—interest and penalties		900
	To record the assessment of late-payment penalties.		
10.	Tax liens receivable—Whalen	50,500	
	Property taxes receivable— delinquent—Whalen		50,000
	Interest and penalties receivable— Whalen		500
	To reclassify property taxes, interest, and pen- alties receivable to reflect the lien on the Whalen property.		
11.	Tax liens receivable—Whalen	300	
	Cash		300
	To record the cost of processing and advertis- ing the tax lien against the Whalen property.		
12a.	Cash	120,000	
	Tax liens receivable—Whalen		50,800
	Vouchers payable		69,200
	To record the sale of the Whalen property, removal of the lien, and expenses related to the sale ($1,500).		
12b.	Vouchers payable	69,200	
	Cash		69,200
	To record payment to R. A. Whalen and of the expenses related to the sale of the Whalen property ($1,500).		
13a.	Revenues—property taxes	50,000	
	Property taxes receivable—current— Lohmann		50,000
	To adjust for an error in the FY 19X1 tax as- sessment of W. M. Lohmann.		

13b.	Cash	300,000	
	Property taxes receivable—current— Lohmann		300,000
	To record the payment of W. M. Lohmann's FY 19X1 property taxes.		
14a.	Reserve for encumbrances	20,000	
	Encumbrances—supplies		20,000
	To record the receipt of supplies ordered in FY 19X0.		
14b.	Expenditures—supplies	19,500	
	Vouchers payable		19,500
	To record the liability for payment of supplies ordered in FY 19X0.		
14c.	Vouchers payable	19,500	
	Cash		19,500
	To record payment of voucher.		
15.	Operating transfer to Frazer Park Fund	20,000	
	Due to Frazer Park Fund		5,000
	Cash		15,000
	To record the FY 19X1 contribution to the Frazer Park Fund.		
16.	Encumbrances—supplies	200,000	
	Reserve for encumbrances		200,000
	To record the placement of the order for FY 19X1 supplies, P.O. No. 1426.		
17.	Encumbrances—capital equipment	950,000	
	Reserve for encumbrances		950,000
	To record the placement of an order for new fire engines, P.O. No. 1427.		
18a.	Reserve for encumbrances	50,000	
	Encumbrances—supplies		50,000
	To record the receipt of one-fourth of the sup- plies ordered under P.O. No. 1426.		
18b.	Expenditures—supplies	45,000	
	Vouchers payable		45,000
	To record the liability for one-fourth of the supplies received under P.O. No. 1426.		
18c.	Vouchers payable	45,000	
	Cash		45,000
	To record payment of voucher.		
19a.	Reserve for encumbrances	100,000	
	Encumbrances—supplies		100,000
	To record the receipt of one-half of the sup- plies ordered under P.O. No. 1426.		
19b.	Expenditures—supplies	90,000	
	Vouchers payable		90,000
	To record the liability for payment of one-half of the supplies received under P.O. No. 1426.		

20.	Expenditures—salaries	580,000	
	Cash		580,000
	To record salaries paid during FY 19X1.		

21a.	Cash	810,000	
	Proceeds from issue of bonds		810,000
	To record the issue of general obligation bonds.		

21b.	Operating transfer to Debt Service Fund	81,000	
	Due to Debt Service Fund		81,000
	To record the liability for the FY 19X1 contribution toward the payment of interest on the bond issue.		

22.	Appropriations—salaries	55,000	
	Appropriations—interest	10,000	
	Appropriations—supplies	25,000	
	Appropriations—transfers to other funds	2,000	
	Appropriations—capital equipment	107,000	
	Unreserved fund balance	1,000	
	Estimated revenues—property taxes		96,000
	Estimated revenues—license fees		4,500
	Estimated revenues—interest and penalties		4,000
	Estimated revenues—income taxes		5,500
	Estimated proceeds from issue of bonds		90,000
	To reflect revisions to the FY 19X1 budget.		

23.	Revenues—property taxes	5,000	
	Allowance for uncollectible property taxes—delinquent		5,000
	To adjust property tax revenues for expected uncollectible amounts in excess of the adjusted FY 19X1 allowance. (*Note:* Since FY 19X1 property taxes outstanding are past due at this point, the "delinquent" allowance is increased).		

24.	Cash	10,000	
	Revenues—sale of general fixed assets		10,000
	To record the sale of one surplus fire engine.		

25a.	Reserve for encumbrances	950,000	
	Encumbrances—capital equipment		950,000
	To record the receipt of fire engines ordered under P.O. No. 1427.		

25b.	Expenditures—capital equipment	975,000	
	Vouchers payable		975,000
	To record the purchase of fire engines ordered under P.O. No. 1427 and to recognize the liability to the vendor.		

25c.	Vouchers payable	975,000	
	Cash		975,000
	To record the payment of voucher.		

26.	Cash	120,000	
	Revenues—license fees		50,000
	Revenues—interest and penalties		20,000
	Revenues—income taxes		50,000
	To record FY 19X1 revenues from various sources.		

27.	Supplies on hand	10,000	
	Reserve for supplies on hand		10,000
	To record the amount of supplies on hand at the end of FY 19X1.		

The closing entries are:

1.	Revenues—property taxes	895,000	
	Revenues—license fees	50,000	
	Revenues—income taxes	50,000	
	Revenues—interest and penalties	20,900	
	Revenues—sale of general fixed assets	10,000	
	Proceeds from issue of bonds	810,000	
	Estimated revenues—property taxes		864,000
	Estimated revenues—license fees		40,500
	Estimated revenues—income taxes		49,500
	Estimated revenues—interest and penalties		36,000
	Estimated proceeds from issue of bonds		810,000
	Unreserved fund balance		35,900
	To close the revenue and estimated revenue accounts for FY 19X1.		

2.	Appropriations—salaries	495,000	
	Appropriations—interest	90,000	
	Appropriations—supplies	225,000	
	Appropriations—capital equipment	963,000	
	Appropriations—transfers to other funds	18,000	
	Unreserved fund balance	19,500	
	Expenditures—salaries		580,000
	Expenditures—supplies		154,500
	Expenditures—capital equipment		975,000
	Operating transfer to Frazer Park Fund		20,000
	Operating transfer to Debt Service Fund		81,000
	To close the appropriation and expenditure accounts for FY 19X1.		

3.	Unreserved fund balance	50,000	
	Encumbrances—supplies		50,000
	To close the encumbrances still outstanding at the end of FY 19X1.		

TABLE 5–3

Realistic City
General Fund
Preclosing Trial Balance
December 31, 19X1

Cash	$ 216,000	
Property taxes receivable—delinquent—Olson	40,000	
Interest and penalties receivable—Olson	400	
Allowance for uncollectible property taxes—delinquent		$ 20,000
Supplies on hand	10,000	
Vouchers payable		90,000
Due to Frazer Park Fund		5,000
Due to Debt Service Fund		81,000
Encumbrances—supplies	50,000	
Reserve for supplies on hand		10,000
Reserve for encumbrances		50,000
Unreserved fund balance		44,000
Estimated revenues—property taxes	864,000	
Estimated revenues—license fees	40,500	
Estimated revenues—income taxes	49,500	
Estimated revenues—interest and penalties	36,000	
Estimated proceeds from issue of bonds	810,000	
Appropriations—salaries		495,000
Appropriations—interest		90,000
Appropriations—supplies		225,000
Appropriations—capital equipment		963,000
Appropriations—transfers to other funds		18,000
Revenues—property taxes		895,000
Revenues—license fees		50,000
Revenues—income taxes		50,000
Revenues—interest and penalties		20,900
Revenues—sale of general fixed assets		10,000
Proceeds from issue of bonds		810,000
Expenditures—salaries	580,000	
Expenditures—supplies	154,500	
Expenditures—capital equipment	975,000	
Operating transfers to Frazer Park Fund	20,000	
Operating transfers to Debt Service Fund	81,000	
	$3,926,900	$3,926,900

Realistic City
General Fund
General Ledger
Year Ended December 31, 19X1

Cash

Beg.	51,850	17,000	(6)
(3)	525,000	300	(11)
(4)	150	69,200	(12b)
(12a)	120,000	19,500	(14c)
(13b)	300,000	15,000	(15)
(21a)	810,000	45,000	(18c)
(24)	10,000	580,000	(20)
(26)	120,000	975,000	(25c)
	1,937,000	1,721,000	
	216,000		

Property Taxes Receivable —delinquent—Ahrens

Beg.	500	500	(4)

Allowance for Uncollectible Property Taxes—delinquent

(4)	400	400	Beg.
		15,000	(8b)
		5,000	(23)
	400	20,400	
		20,000	

Property Taxes Receivable —current—Morgan

(2)	525,000	525,000	(3)

Vouchers Payable

(6)	8,000	8,000	Beg
(12b)	69,200	69,200	(12a)
(14c)	19,500	19,500	(14b)
(18c)	45,000	45,000	(18b)
(25c)	975,000	90,000	(19b)
		975,000	(25b)
	1,116,700	1,206,700	
		90,000	

Reserve for Encumbrances

(14a)	20,000	20,000	Beg.
(18a)	50,000	200,000	(16)
(19a)	100,000	950,000	(17)
(25a)	950,000		
	1,120,000	1,170,000	
		50,000	

Interest and Penalties Receivable—Ahrens

Beg.	50	50	(4)

Allowance for Uncollectible Property Taxes—current

(7)	35,000	40,000	(2)
(8b)	15,000	10,000	(5)
	50,000	50,000	

Supplies on Hand

(27)	10,000	

Property Taxes Receivable —current—Lohmann

(2)	350,000	50,000	(13a)
		300,000	(13b)
	350,000	350,000	

Property Taxes Receivable —current—Parker

(2)	35,000	35,000	(7)

Property Taxes Receivable —current—Olson

(2)	40,000	40,000	(8a)

Property Taxes Receivable —delinquent—Whalen

(8a)	50,000	50,000	(10)

Interest and Penalties Receivable—Whalen

(9)	500	500	(10)

Property Taxes Receivable —current—Whalen

(2)	50,000	50,000	(8a)

Property Taxes Receivable —delinquent—Olson

(8a)	40,000	

Tax Liens Receivable—Whalen

(10)	50,500	50,800	(12a)
(11)	300		
	50,800	50,800	

Interest and Penalties Receivable—Olson

(9)	400	

Realistic City
General Fund
General Ledger
Year Ended December 31, 19X1

Unreserved Fund Balance

(22)	1,000	15,000	Beg.
		10,000	(B-1)
		20,000	(1)
	1,000	45,000	
(C-2)	19,500	44,000	
(C-3)	50,000	35,900	(C-1)
	69,500	79,900	
		10,400	

Due to Frazer Park Fund

(6)	9,000	9,000	Beg
		5,000	(15)
	9,000	14,000	
		5,000	

Due to Debt Service Fund

	81,000	(21b)

Encumbrances—supplies

(1)	20,000	20,000	(14a)
(16)	200,000	50,000	(18a)
		100,000	(19a)
	220,000	170,000	
	50,000	50,000	(C-3)

Encumbrances—capital equipment

(17)	950,000	950,000	(25a)

Reserve for Supplies on Hand

	10,000	(27)

Estimated Revenues—property taxes

(B-1)	960,000	96,000	(22)
	864,000	864,000	(C-1)

Estimated Revenues—license fees

(B-1)	45,000	4,500	(22)
	40,500	40,500	(C-1)

Estimated Revenues—income taxes

(B-1)	55,000	5,500	(22)
	49,500	49,500	(C-1)

Estimated Revenues—interest and penalties

(B-1)	40,000	4,000	(22)
	36,000	36,000	(C-1)

Estimated Proceeds from Issue of Bonds

(B-1)	900,000	90,000	(22)
	810,000	810,000	(C-1)

Appropriations—salaries

(22)	55,000	550,000	(B-1)
(C-2)	495,000	495,000	

Appropriations—interest

(22)	10,000	100,000	(B-1)
(C-2)	90,000	90,000	

Appropriations—supplies

(22)	25,000	250,000	(B-1)
(C-2)	225,000	225,000	

Appropriations—capital equipment

(22)	107,000	1,070,000	(B-1)
(C-2)	963,000	963,000	

Appropriations—transfers to other funds

(22)	2,000	20,000	(B-1)
(C-2)	18,000	18,000	

Revenues—property taxes

(5)	10,000	960,000	(2)
(13a)	50,000		
(23)	5,000		
	65,000	960,000	
(C-1)	895,000	895,000	

Revenues—license fees

(C-1)	50,000	50,000	(26)

Revenues—income taxes

(C-1)	50,000	50,000	(26)

Revenues—interest and penalties

		900	(9)
		20,000	(26)
(C-1)	20,900	20,900	

Revenues—sale of general fixed assets

(C-1)	10,000	10,000	(24)

Realistic City
General Fund
General Ledger
Year Ended December 31, 19X1

Proceeds from Issue of Bonds			Expenditures—salaries			Expenditures— capital equipment		
(C-1)	810,000	810,000 (21a)	(20) 580,000	580,000	(C-2)	(25b) 975,000	975,000	(C-2)

Expenditures—supplies			Operating Transfer to Frazer Park Fund			Operating Transfer to Debt Service Fund		
(14b)	19,500		(15) 20,000	20,000	(C-2)	(21b) 81,000	81,000	(C-2)
(18b)	45,000							
(19b)	90,000							
	154,500	154,500 (C-2)						

TABLE 5–4

Realistic City
General Fund
Postclosing Trial Balance
December 31, 19X1

Cash	$216,000	
Property taxes receivable—delinquent—Olson	40,000	
Interest and penalties receivable—Olson	400	
Allowance for uncollectible property taxes—delinquent		$ 20,000
Supplies on hand	10,000	
Vouchers payable		90,000
Due to Frazer Park Fund		5,000
Due to Debt Service Fund		81,000
Reserve for supplies on hand		10,000
Reserve for encumbrances		50,000
Unreserved fund balance		10,400
	$266,400	$266,400

TABLE 5–5

Realistic City
General Fund
Balance Sheet
December 31, 19X1

ASSETS

Cash		$216,000
Property taxes receivable—delinquent	$40,000	
Less: Allowance for uncollectible property taxes	(20,000)	20,000
Interest and penalties receivable		400
Supplies on hand		10,000
		$246,400

LIABILITIES AND FUND BALANCE

Vouchers payable	$ 90,000
Due to Frazer Park Fund	5,000
Due to Debt Service Fund	81,000
Reserve for supplies on hand	10,000
Reserve for encumbrances	50,000
Unreserved fund balance	10,400
	$246,400

TABLE 5–6

Realistic City
General Fund
Statement of Revenues, Expenditures,
and Changes in Fund Balance
Year Ended December 31, 19X1

Revenues

Property taxes	$895,000	
License fees	50,000	
Interest and penalties	20,900	
Income taxes	50,000	
Sale of general fixed assets	10,000	$1,025,900

Expenditures

Salaries	$580,000	
Supplies	154,500	
Capital equipment	975,000	1,709,500
Excess (deficiency) of revenues over expenditures		$ (683,600)

Other financing sources (uses)

Proceeds from issue of bonds	$810,000	
Operating transfers to Frazer Park Fund	(20,000)	
Operating transfers to Debt Service Fund	(81,000)	709,000

Excess (deficiency) of revenues and other sources over	
expenditures and other uses	$ 25,400
Reserves and unreserved fund balance at beginning of year	35,000
	$ 60,400
Increase in reserve for supplies on hand	10,000
Reserves and unreserved fund balance at end of year	$ 70,400

REVIEW QUESTIONS

Q5–1   What are the two methods of handling open encumbrances at year-end? What are the advantages and disadvantages of each method?

Q5–2   What is an allotment? Describe two methods of accounting for allotments. Describe the advantages of each.

Q5–3   Why is depreciation not always recorded by governmental units?

Q5–4   What are the two methods of handling uncollectible receivables? What are the advantages of each method?

Q5–5   Why aren't inventories of governmental units treated in the same manner as those of commercial enterprises? When it is necessary to record a change in the level of inventories at year-end, what entry is appropriate?

Q5–6   Why is a portion of an encumbrance removed from the accounting records when an order is only partially filled?

Q5–7   How are transfers between funds of the same organization recorded?

Q5–8   In the balance sheet of a commercial entity, assets are classified as short term or long term. Is this classification necessary for a governmental-type fund? Explain.

Q5–9   What does the term *lapse* mean when referring to encumbrances?

Q5–10   What events take place when a receivable becomes a lien and the property is subsequently seized and sold at auction? What are the appropriate entries?

Q5–11   What entries are appropriate to describe short-term borrowing by the General Fund? How does this differ from the treatment of long-term borrowing?

Q5–12   An Allowance for uncollectible taxes account is often set up when uncollectible taxes are not expected to be few in number and/or relatively small in amount. What advantage does this method offer over the direct write-off method?

Q5–13   What are interfund transactions?

Q5–14   Which type or types of interfund transactions result in the recognition of revenues and expenditures (expenses)?

EXERCISES

E5–1   (Uncollectible accounts—allowance method)
The City of Golder's Green levies property taxes of $150,000 in FY 19X1. Prior experience has shown that 10 percent of these taxes will not be collected.

REQUIRED: a. What is the appropriate entry to set up the receivable for FY 19X1 property taxes if the allowance method is used?

b. Taxpayer Holmes, whose tax levy is $2,000, is unable to pay her property taxes. The city decides to write off her account. Make the entry necessary to record this event.

c. If the Holmes account is not written off until FY 19X2, what effect will this have on the FY 19X2 revenues? Why?

E5–2   (Uncollectible accounts—direct write-off method)
The City of Erica uses the direct write-off method of treating uncollectible accounts. If Henry Tudor is unable to pay his tax levy of $200, what is the appropriate entry to write off his account?

E5–3   (Prior-year encumbrances that remain open)
The City of Eleanor follows a policy of allowing encumbrances to remain in force until the goods are delivered or the purchase orders are cancelled. At the end of FY 19X1, supplies costing $10,000 have not been delivered. In March 19X2, the supplies arrive, accompanied by an invoice for $12,000.

REQUIRED: a. What entry or entries should be made at the end of FY 19X1?
            b. What entry or entries should be made at the beginning of FY 19X2?
            c. What entry or entries should be made when the supplies arrive?

E5–4   (Prior-year encumbrances that lapse)
The City of Margaret follows a policy of allowing encumbrances to lapse at the end of the year if the goods are not received, the services are not performed or the purchase orders are not cancelled. At the end of FY 19X1, supplies expected to cost $50,000 have not been delivered.

REQUIRED: a. What entry or entries should be made at year-end, assuming the purchase orders will be honored in FY 19X2?
            b. What entry or entries should be made at the beginning of FY 19X2?
            c. The supplies arrive in FY 19X2, accompanied by an invoice for $49,500. What entry or entries should be made at this time?

E5–5   (Interfund transactions)
Identify the types of interfund transactions and briefly explain the purpose of each type.

E5–6   (Treatment of inventories—purchases method)
At the end of FY 19X1, the City of Kensington has a balance of $6,000 in its Reserve for supplies account. An inventory, taken at the end of 19X2, reveals that supplies valued at $7,000 are on hand. Kensington uses the purchases method to account for supplies.

REQUIRED: a. What entry should be made at the end of 19X2 to disclose this change in the amount of supplies on hand?
            b. Suppose the inventory shows that supplies valued at $4,000 are on hand. What entry should be made to disclose this fact?

E5–7   (Multiple choice—General and Special Revenue Funds)
1. The City of Brixton's General Fund budget for FY 19X1 shows esti-

mated revenues in excess of appropriations. The effect of this situation on the budgetary entries will be an increase in
a. Taxes receivable
b. Unreserved fund balance
c. Reserve for encumbrances
d. Encumbrances

2. The Reserve for encumbrances account is properly considered to be a
a. Current liability if payable within a year; otherwise a long-term debt
b. Fixed liability
c. Floating debt
d. Reservation of the fund's equity

3. Brocton City's water utility, an Enterprise Fund, submits a bill for $9,000 to the General Fund for water services supplied to city departments and agencies. Submission of this bill would result in
a. Creation of balances that will be eliminated on the city's combined balance sheet
b. Recognition of revenue by the Water Utility Fund and of an expenditure by the General Fund
c. Recognition of an encumbrance by both the Water Utility Fund and the General Fund
d. Creation of a balance that will be eliminated on the city's combined statement of changes in fund balance.

4. At the end of FY 19X1, Bond City has outstanding encumbrances amounting to $15,000. Although the city follows a policy of allowing outstanding encumbrances to lapse, it plans to honor the related purchase orders in FY 19X2. The management of the city wants the users of its financial statements to be aware of these outstanding purchase orders. Therefore, at year-end, the city's accountant should
a. Debit Reserve for encumbrances
b. Credit Appropriations
c. Debit Unreserved fund balance
d. Debit an expenditure account

5. Which of the following revenues of the General Fund are usually recorded before they are actually received?
a. Sales taxes
b. Property taxes
c. Fines and penalties
d. Parking meter receipts

6. If the City of Castletown sells an ambulance, which had been purchased by the General Fund several years earlier, to a local rock group, the entry to record this sale on the books of the General Fund should include

a. A credit to Revenues—sale of general fixed assets
b. A debit to Unreserved fund balance
c. A debit to Encumbrances—capital equipment
d. A credit to a fixed asset account

7. The town council of Bayou Brilleaux adopted a budget for FY 19X1 that indicated revenues of $750,000 and appropriations of $800,000. The entry to record this budget into the accounts is

	DR	CR
a. Estimated revenues	$750,000	
Reserve for deficits	50,000	
Appropriations		$800,000
b. Appropriations	$800,000	
Unreserved fund balance		$ 50,000
Estimated revenues		750,000
c. Estimated revenues	$750,000	
Unreserved fund balance	50,000	
Appropriations		$800,000

d. Only a memorandum entry is necessary

8. Which of the following will increase the fund balance of a governmental unit at the end of a fiscal year?
a. Appropriations are less than expenditures and reserve for encumbrances
b. Appropriations are less than expenditures and encumbrances
c. Appropriations are more then expenditures and encumbrances
d. Appropriations are more than estimated revenues

9. The Reserve for encumbrances—prior year account represents amounts recorded by a governmental unit for
a. Anticipated expenditures in the next year
b. Expenditures for which purchase orders were made in the prior year but disbursement will be in the current year
c. Excess expenditures in the prior year that will be offset against the current-year budgeted amounts
d. Unanticipated expenditures of the prior year that become evident in the current year

10. The following balances are included in the subsidiary records of Burwood Village's Parks and Recreation Department at June 30, 19X1.

Appropriations—supplies	$7,500
Expenditures—supplies	4,500
Encumbrances—supply orders	750

How much does the department have available for additional purchases of supplies?

a. $0
b. $2,250
c. $3,000
d. $6,750

11. Which of the following accounts of a governmental unit is (are) closed out at the end of the fiscal year?

	Estimated Revenues	Fund Balance
a.	No	No
b.	No	Yes
c.	Yes	Yes
d.	Yes	No

12. Which of the following is an appropriate basis of accounting for the General Fund of a governmental unit?

	Cash Basis	Modified Accrual Basis
a.	Yes	No
b.	Yes	Yes
c.	No	Yes
d.	No	No

(AICPA adapted)

PROBLEMS

P5–1   (Theory problem on the basis of accounting)
The accounting system of the Municipality of Kemp is organized and operated on a fund basis. Among the types of funds used are a General Fund, a Special Revenue Fund, and an Enterprise Fund.

REQUIRED: a. Explain the basic differences in revenue recognition between the accrual basis of accounting and the modified accrual basis of accounting as it relates to governmental accounting.
b. What basis of accounting should be used for each of the following funds?

● General Fund
● Special Revenue Fund
● Enterprise Fund

Why?
c. How should fixed assets and long-term liabilities related to the General Fund be accounted for?

(AICPA adapted)

P5–2   (Entries when actual and budgeted revenues and expenditures differ)
The members of the Finsbury Park Commission have approved the following budget:

Revenues

Property taxes	$300,000	
Concession rentals	100,000	
User charges	200,000	$600,000

Expenditures

Wages and salaries	$200,000	
Capital equipment	300,000	
Supplies	50,000	550,000
Projected increase in fund balance		$ 50,000

Actual revenues are:

Property taxes	$300,000
Concession rentals	120,000
User charges	185,000

Actual expenditures are:

Wages and salaries	$215,000
Capital equipment	290,000
Supplies	40,000

REQUIRED: 1. Prepare the budgetary entry.
2. Prepare the operating entries.
3. Prepare the closing entries.

P5–3   (Allowance for uncollectible property taxes—allowance method)
The City of Aldwich uses the allowance method of handling uncollectible property taxes. In FY 19X1, the following transactions took place:
1. At the end of FY 19X0, property taxes receivable were $10,000. The allowance for uncollectible property taxes was $3,000.
2. In FY 19X1, collections of FY 19X0 property taxes were as follows:

J. Bond	$5,000
J. Steed	3,000

J. Tebbe, who owed $2,000, was unable to pay his property taxes. The account was written off.
3. During FY 19X1, property taxes of $50,000 were levied. An Allowance for uncollectible property taxes of 6 percent was established for this particular tax levy. The property taxes were levied as follows:

J. Bond	$10,000
J. Steed	20,000
T. King	10,000
E. Peel	5,000
S. Templar	5,000
	$50,000

4. Bond and Steed paid their FY 19X1 property taxes in full and on time.

5. King refused to pay his FY 19X1 property taxes. As a result, a lien was placed against his property. Costs of processing the lien amounted to $200. Shortly thereafter, his property was seized and sold for $30,000. Costs of the sale were $2,000. After the appropriate deductions had been made, a check for the balance of the sale price of the property was sent to King.

6. E. Peel was unable to pay her taxes. Since her property was not saleable, the account was written off without any further legal action.

7. At the end of FY 19X1, S. Templar had not paid his property taxes. The Templar account was reclassified as delinquent.

8. In FY 19X2, the city established an allowance for uncollectible property taxes of $15,000. The FY 19X2 property taxes were levied as follows:

J. Bond	$10,000
J. Steed	25,000
E. Peel	10,000
S. Templar	5,000
J. Bergerac	10,000
	$60,000

9. J. Steed appealed his tax assessment and his levy was lowered to $20,000.

10. During the year, S. Templar paid his FY 19X1 property taxes. He was, however, unable to pay his FY 19X2 property taxes. Therefore, the account was written off.

11. Other collections during FY 19X2 were:

J. Bond	$10,000
J. Steed	20,000
E. Peel	10,000

12. J. Bergerac was unable to pay his property taxes. The account was written off because of Bergerac's adverse situation.

The city identifies receivables by year and by taxpayer (e.g., Property taxes receivable—FY 19X1—Bond, $10,000); and it identifies the allowance for uncollectible property taxes by year (e.g., Allowance for uncollectible property taxes—FY 19X1).

REQUIRED: Prepare entries to record (in chronological order):
1. The setting up of the FY 19X1 and the FY 19X2 receivable (and allowance for uncollectible property taxes)
2. The collection of property taxes in each year
3. The writing-off of uncollectible accounts

4. The treatment of the prior-year allowance for uncollectible property taxes in FY 19X1 and FY 19X2

5. The lien against, seizure, and sale of the King property

P5–4   (Allotments)

The City of Picadilly divides its appropriations into allotments, which are expended during the allotment period. In this city, allotments are made at the beginning of each quarter. In FY 19X1, estimated revenues are $500,000 and unallotted appropriations are $480,000. A $20,000 increase is projected for the fund balance. Actual revenues are $500,000. The allotments for the year are as follows:

1st quarter	$150,000
2nd quarter	100,000
3rd quarter	130,000
4th quarter	100,000

Expenditures for the year are as follows:

1/8	$20,000		7/28	$30,000
2/2	80,000		8/16	40,000
3/15	40,000		9/14	19,000
4/18	35,000		10/15	10,000
5/20	45,000		11/18	30,000
6/15	20,000		12/22	35,000
7/12	50,000		12/30	5,000

REQUIRED: 1. Prepare journal entries to record the allotments, expenditures, and unallotted appropriations for each period, including the year-end closing entries.

2. Prepare a subsidiary ledger for the allotments, using the following format:

Date	Allotments	Expenditures	Remaining Balance

P5-5   (Closing when actual revenues and expenditures are different from budget)

The city council of Notting Hill has approved the following budget for fiscal year 19X1 for that city's General Fund:

Estimated Revenues		
Property taxes	$85,000	
License fees	25,000	
Fines and penalties	35,000	
Parking meters	25,000	
Sale of surplus equipment	30,000	$200,000
Appropriations and Transfers		
Salaries	$80,000	
Supplies	40,000	
Capital equipment	50,000	
Transfers to other funds	20,000	190,000
Projected increase in fund balance		$ 10,000

The city uses the allowance method of handling past-due accounts. An allowance equal to 15 percent of the property taxes billed is recorded at the time the bills are sent. Its accounting policies include the following:
1. All purchases of supplies and capital equipment are encumbered.
2. Expenditures for salaries and transfers to other funds do not require encumbrances.
3. Outstanding encumbrances lapse at the end of each fiscal year. Outstanding purchase orders that will be honored the following year, however, are reported on its financial statements.
4. Separate accounts are maintained for each taxpayer.
5. At the end of each fiscal year, all outstanding property tax receivables are reclassified as delinquent.
6. The city uses the purchases method to record the purchase and use of supplies.

An inventory taken at the end of FY 19X0 revealed that supplies costing $5,000 were still on hand. At the beginning of FY 19X0, there were no supplies on hand.

The city has four property owners, whose taxes for FY 19X1 are:

R. Hood	$ 40,000
F. Tuck	10,000
M. Marian	20,000
A. Adale	30,000
	$100,000

The preclosing trial balance of Notting Hill, as of December 31, 19X0, was:

	DR	CR
Cash	$ 20,000	
Property taxes receivable—current—John	3,000	
Property taxes receivable—current—Adale	8,000	
Allowance for uncollectible property taxes—current		$ 3,000
Encumbrances—capital equipment	10,000	
Vouchers payable		8,000
Reserve for encumbrances		10,000
Unreserved fund balance		40,000
Estimated revenues—property taxes	80,000	
Estimated revenues—license fees	20,000	
Estimated revenues—fines and penalties	30,000	
Estimated revenues—parking meters	20,000	
Appropriations—salaries		70,000
Appropriations—supplies		30,000
Appropriations—capital equipment		40,000
Revenues—property taxes		80,000
Revenues—license fees		10,000
Revenues—fines and penalties		30,000
Revenues—parking meters		25,000
Expenditures—salaries	85,000	
Expenditures—supplies	40,000	
Expenditures—capital equipment	30,000	
	$346,000	$346,000

During FY 19X1, the following transactions occurred:

1. The FY 19X0 encumbrance for capital equipment was restored.
2. Tax bills amounting to $100,000 were sent to the FY 19X1 property taxpayers. Of the amount billed, $15,000 is not expected to be collected.
3. L. John left town suddenly. When he departed, his account was written off.
4. A. Adale paid his FY 19X0 property taxes in full, along with a late-payment penalty of $100.
5. R. Hood and M. Marian paid their property taxes on time and in full.
6. The capital equipment ordered in FY 19X0 arrived, along with an invoice for $10,000. The invoice was paid immediately.
7. Supplies costing $40,000 were ordered.
8. An operating transfer of $18,000 was made to the Hyde Park Fund. Of this amount, $10,000 was paid in cash; the remainder will be paid in the future.
9. All outstanding FY 19X0 vouchers were paid.
10. A surplus fire engine was sold for $25,000.
11. Salaries for the year were $80,000.
12. Five compact police cars, costing $8,000 each, were ordered.
13. One-half of the supplies arrived, along with an invoice for $25,000. The invoice was paid in October.
14. Three of the police cars arrived. The actual cost of $28,000 was paid immediately.
15. F. Tuck was unable to pay his property taxes. The account was written off.
16. A. Adale paid $25,000 of his property taxes. He hopes to pay the remainder next year.
17. Other FY 19X1 revenues were:

License fees	$25,000
Fines	40,000
Parking meter revenues	30,000

18. One-fourth of the supplies arrived, along with an invoice for $9,000.

REQUIRED: 1. Prepare closing entries and a postclosing trial balance for FY 19X0.
2. Prepare budgetary, operating, and closing entries for FY 19X1. Assume that outstanding purchase orders will be honored the following year and that supplies on hand at the end of FY 19X1 amount to $8,000.
3. Prepare preclosing and postclosing trial balances for FY 19X1.
4. Prepare a balance sheet and a statement of revenues, expenditures, and changes in fund balance for FY 19X1.

P5–6   (Journal entries and financial statement presentation—interfund transactions)

Following are several transactions for the city of Cricklewood:

1. The Water Purification Fund billed its customers for $124,000. Included in this amount was $12,000 to the General Fund (not encumbered by the General Fund) and $5,000 to the Electric Utility Fund. Both the Water Purification Fund and the Electric Utility Fund are Enterprise Funds.

2. A Special Revenue Fund lent a Capital Projects Fund $25,000, to be repaid in 9 months.

3. The General Fund made a permanent contribution of capital to the Civic Swimming Pool Fund, an Enterprise Fund. The amount of the contribution was $50,000.

4. The General Fund made its annual payment of $200,000 to a Debt Service Fund. Assume that $150,000 of the payment was for interest.

5. The General Fund paid $34,000 for consulting services. At the time the transaction was incurred, a debit for the entire amount was made to Expenditures—consulting services. Later a Capital Projects Fund paid the General Fund $9,000 for its share of the consulting costs.

REQUIRED: Prepare the journal entries necessary to record the above transactions and to identify the fund or funds used.

P5–7   (CPA Examination question on activities of a General Fund)
The General Fund trial balance of the City of Solna at December 31, 19X0, was as follows:

	DR	CR
Cash	$ 62,000	
Taxes receivable—delinquent	46,000	
Estimated uncollectible taxes—delinquent		$ 8,000
Stores inventory—program operations	18,000	
Vouchers payable		28,000
Fund balance reserved for stores inventory		18,000
Fund balance reserved for encumbrances		12,000
Unreserved, undesignated fund balance		60,000
	$126,000	$126,000

Collectible delinquent taxes are expected to be collected with 60 days after the end of the year. Solna uses the purchases method to account for stores inventory. The following data pertain to 19X1 General Fund operations:

1. Budget adopted:

Revenues and other financing sources	
Taxes	$220,000
Fines, forfeits, and penalties	80,000
Miscellaneous revenues	100,000
Share of bond issue proceeds	200,000
	$600,000

Expenditures and other financing uses

Program operations	$300,000
General administration	120,000
Stores—program operations	60,000
Capital outlay	80,000
Periodic transfer to special assessment fund	20,000
	$580,000

2. Taxes were assessed at an amount that would result in revenues of $220,800, after deduction of 4 percent of the tax levy as uncollectible.

3. Orders placed but not received:

Program operations	$176,000
General administration	80,000
Capital outlay	60,000
	$316,000

4. The city council designated $20,000 of the unreserved, undesignated fund balance for possible future appropriation for capital outlays.

5. Cash collections and transfer:

Delinquent taxes	$38,000
Current taxes	226,000
Refund of overpayment of invoice for purchase of equipment	4,000
Fines, forfeits, and penalties	88,000
Miscellaneous revenues	90,000
Share of bond issue proceeds	200,000
Transfer of remaining fund balance of a discontinued fund	18,000
	$664,000

6. Cancelled encumbrances:

	Estimated	Actual
Program operations	$156,000	$166,000
General administration	84,000	80,000
Capital outlay	62,000	62,000
	$302,000	$308,000

7. Additional vouchers:

Program operations	$188,000
General administration	38,000
Capital outlay	18,000
Transfer to special assessment fund	20,000
	$264,000

8. Albert, a taxpayer, overpaid his 19X1 taxes by $2,000. He applied for a $2,000 credit against 19X2 taxes. The city council granted his request.

9. Vouchers paid amounted to $580,000.

10. Stores inventory on December 31, 19X1, amounted to $12,000.

REQUIRED: Prepare journal entries to record the effects of the foregoing data. Omit explanations.

(AICPA adapted)

P5–8   (Adjusting and closing entries for a General Fund)

You have been engaged by the Town of Eego to examine its June 30, 19X1, balance sheet. You are the first CPA to be engaged by the town and find that acceptable methods of municipal accounting have not been employed. The town clerk stated that the books had not been closed and presented the following preclosing trial balance of the General Fund, as of June 30, 19X1:

	DR	CR
Cash	$150,000	
Taxes receivable—current year	59,200	
Estimated losses—current year taxes receivable		$ 18,000
Taxes receivable—prior year	8,000	
Estimated losses—prior year taxes receivable		10,200
Estimated revenues	310,000	
Appropriations		348,000
Donated land	27,000	
Expenditures—building addition constructed	50,000	
Expenditures—serial bonds paid	16,000	
Other expenditures	280,000	
Special assessment bonds payable		100,000
Revenues		354,000
Accounts payable		26,000
Unreserved fund balance		44,000
	$900,200	$900,200

Additional information

1. The estimated losses of $18,000 for current year taxes receivable were determined to be a reasonable estimate.

2. Included in the Revenues account is a credit of $27,000, representing the value of land donated by the state as a grant-in-aid for the construction of a municipal park.

3. The Expenditures—building addition constructed account balance is the cost of an addition to the town hall. This addition was constructed and completed in June 19X1. The General Fund recorded the payment as authorized.

4. The Serial bonds paid account reflects the annual retirement of general obligation bonds issued to finance the construction of the town hall. Interest payments of $7,000 for this bond issue are included in Expenditures—serial bonds paid account.
5. Operating supplies ordered in the prior fiscal year and chargeable to that year were received, recorded, and consumed in July 19X0. The outstanding purchase orders for these supplies—which were not recorded in the accounts at June 30, 19X0—amounted to $8,800. The vendors' invoices for these supplies totaled $9,400. Appropriations lapse one year after the end of the fiscal year for which they are made.
6. Outstanding purchase orders at June 30, 19X1, for operating supplies, totaled $2,100. These purchase orders were not recorded on the books.
7. The special assessments bonds were sold in June 19X1 to finance a street-paving project. No contracts have been signed for this project and no expenditures have been made.
8. The balance in the Revenues account includes credits for $20,000 for a note issued to a bank to obtain cash in anticipation of tax collections and for $1,000 for the sale of scrap iron from the town's water plant. The note was still outstanding at June 30, 19X1. The operations of the water plant are accounted for in the Water Fund.

REQUIRED: Prepare the formal adjusting and closing journal entries for the General Fund for the fiscal year ended June 30, 19X1.

(AICPA adapted)

6

THE GOVERNMENTAL FUND ACCOUNTING CYCLE

Capital Projects Funds, Account Groups, and Debt Service Funds

LEARNING OBJECTIVES

After completion of this chapter, you should be able to:

1. Explain why and how Capital Projects Funds are used in governmental accounting
2. Prepare the journal entries normally used in Capital Projects Funds
3. Prepare financial statements for Capital Projects Funds
4. Explain why and how the General Fixed Assets Account Group and the General Long-Term Debt Account Group are used in governmental accounting
5. Prepare the journal entries normally used in the account groups
6. Explain the relationship between the account groups and the governmental-type funds
7. Prepare financial statements for the account groups
8. Explain why and how Debt Service Funds are used in governmental accounting
9. Prepare the journal entries normally used in Debt Service Funds
10. Prepare financial statements for Debt Service Funds

The accounting procedures used for the General Fund and the Special Revenue Funds concentrate on the spending activities of the governmental unit. The accounting system used for these funds is designed to measure the dollars "received" and "spent" in accordance with legal or contractual restrictions. It does this by reporting the revenues and expenditures of each fund. Such a system provides the user of the financial statements with information about the number of dollars received from the various forms of financing used by the governmental unit and the number of dollars spent for each functional activity. When there is a legal requirement for separate accounting for an activity, a Special Revenue Fund must be used instead of the General Fund. Thus the **measurement focus** (what is being measured) of both the General and the Special Revenue Funds is *resources that are available for spending*. Generally accepted accounting principles require that all governmental-type funds (General, Special Revenue, Capital Projects, and Debt Service) follow this approach.

Emphasis on resources that are available for spending requires the measurement of the movement of dollars into and out of each fund. As a result, governmental-type funds generally do not include assets that cannot be "spent" in the coming period. Emphasis on resources that are available for spending also means that these types of funds generally do not include debt that will become due in periods beyond one year. Exceptions to these rules will be discussed in the present chapter and in Chapters 7, 8, and 9.

The timing of the recognition of the resources that are available for spending is referred to as the **basis of accounting.** This concept determines *when* the individual revenues and expenditures will be recorded (recognized). All governmental-type funds use the **modified accrual basis of accounting**. Using this approach, revenues are recorded when they are measurable and available. "Measurable" means that the accountant can place a monetary value on the amount of revenues. "Available" means that the revenues can be collected in time to pay the debts of the current period. For property taxes, this has been interpreted to mean due or past due and collectible during the current period or within sixty days after the end of the current period.[1] In general, application of the modified accrual basis of accounting results in the use of accrual accounting procedures for revenues, such as property taxes, where the amount and collectibility can reasonably be determined at the time the tax is levied.[2] Other items of revenue such as fines, forfeits, sales taxes, fees, parking meter receipts, and income taxes generally are recognized on the *cash* basis because they usually are not both measurable and available until received.

Using the modified accrual basis of accounting, expenditures generally are recognized on the accrual basis.[3] This means that the expenditures are recorded when the *liability* is incurred. The major exceptions to this general rule are:

---

[1]Additional discussion of the "available" criteria can be found in NCGA *Statement 1*, pp. 11–12; and NCGA *Interpretation No.3*, pp. 1–3. (GASB Cod. Sec. P70.101–108)

[2]If you are not familiar with accrual accounting concepts, you should review Chapter 2.

[3]See Chapter 2.

1. *Inventories of materials and supplies.* These may be recorded as expenditures as they are being acquired (purchase method) or used (consumption method). Due to the popularity and simplicity of the purchases method, we will use it in all the illustrations in this text.
2. *Prepaid expense items (such as insurance).* These can be recognized as expenditures when incurred.
3. *Interest on long-term debt.* This is generally recognized when it becomes legally payable during the period rather than as it accrues.
4. *Pensions, claims, and judgments.* The amount of these items recorded as an expenditure of the current period is that which would normally be liquidated with expendable available financial resources.

In summary, all governmental-type funds record revenues when they are measurable and available. They record expenditures under the accrual basis of accounting, with limited exceptions.

SECTION I—CAPITAL PROJECTS FUNDS

Description of Fund Activities

The acquisition or construction of major capital facilities, other than those financed by proprietary and trust funds, is accounted for in **Capital Projects Funds.** Capital Projects Funds must be used where they are legally required or where the projects are at least partially financed with restricted resources. Such projects generally include the construction of a new city hall, a new civic auditorium, a bridge, and so forth. The resources used to finance Capital Projects Funds usually come from general obligation debt, transfers from other funds, intergovernmental revenues, or private donations.

The acquisition of a capital asset of a relatively minor nature, such as a piece of furniture or an automobile, usually is financed through the General Fund or a Special Revenue Fund. For example, the purchase of a new police car or a desk for the mayor's office is recorded as an expenditure in the fund that made the acquisition (see Chapter 5).

Since generally accepted accounting principles require that the number of funds used be held to a minimum, related projects should be combined into a single Capital Projects Fund whenever possible. However, careful attention must be paid to any bond indenture provisions or restrictions placed on the use of certain types of resources. In many instances such restrictions will prevent the combination of different projects into the same fund.

The nature and order of events involving capital projects vary according to local ordinances and procedures, the relative size of the project, and the type of financing involved. However, these projects usually begin in the capital budget of the governmental unit. After approval, financing arrangements are made and contracts are let, if applicable. Although a Capital Projects Fund can be used to record the acquisition of assets, such funds are generally used for large construction projects.

To obtain financing for projects, governmental units usually issue general obligation bonds, solicit federal or state grants, and so forth. These funds are not always spent immediately upon receipt. In such cases the Capital Projects Fund will contain some investment activity.

As the construction work progresses, investments are liquidated and payments are made to the contractor until the project is completed and finally accepted. At this time, any assets remaining in the fund are transferred to another fund or returned to the donors.

Control of Fund Activities

The operations of a Capital Projects Fund are generally controlled through provisions of bond indentures, restrictive provisions of grant agreements, and so forth. Therefore, formal budgetary integration into the accounts, as used in the General and Special Revenue Funds, is not always necessary. For purposes of uniformity, however, we will assume that a budget is recorded and used for control purposes. Such accounting procedures are especially helpful if a single fund is being used to account for more than one project. Since the Capital Projects Funds are classified as governmental-type funds, the reporting of budget and actual data is only required in those instances where there is a legally adopted annual budget.

Encumbrance accounting is ordinarily used for these funds because of the extent of involvement with contracts, purchase orders, and so forth, and because of the need to control the related expenditures. Thus, in our example of a construction project, a regular encumbrance entry is made upon signing the contract. Expenditures on the contract are treated in the manner previously illustrated for encumbered purchase orders.

As with all governmental-type funds, the measurement focus of Capital Projects Funds is available spendable resources. Thus the accounting system is designed to provide information regarding the receipt and disbursement of resources. As a result, long-lived assets are not found in these types of funds, nor is there any long-term debt in the accounts. The "available spendable" criterion focuses on assets currently available and the current claims against those assets.

The modified accrual basis of accounting is used for Capital Projects Funds. Thus the timing of the recognition of revenues and expenditures is the same as that followed by the other governmental-type funds.

Accounting for Fund Activities

Operating entries

For illustrative purposes, assume that the city of Newville decides to build a new civic auditorium and includes the project in its 19X1 capital budget. Financing for the project consists of a general obligation bond issue for $20 million and an $8 million grant from the federal government. Since the federal grant is considered as revenue to the Capital Projects Fund and the proceeds from the bond issue are considered to be an "other financing source," the following entry is made to record the budget:

Estimated revenues	8,000,000	
Estimated other financing sources	20,000,000	
Appropriations		28,000,000
To record the budget.		

If the bonds are sold at par (face) value, the following entry is made:

Cash	20,000,000	
Proceeds from bond issue		20,000,000
To record the issuance of bonds.		

There are three reasons why the principal of the bonds is not recorded as a liability of the Capital Projects Fund: (1) Capital Projects Funds follow a spending measurement focus, therefore, they are used primarily to account for current items; (2) Capital Projects Funds are used to account only for acquisition or construction activities; and (3) Debt Service Funds are used to account for debt service activities (payment of principal and interest). Since the principal of the bonds is not recorded in a fund, control over general obligation long-term debt is maintained in the General Long-Term Debt Account Group. The entry to record the principal of the debt is:

Entry in the General Long-Term Debt Account Group

Amount to be provided in Debt	20,000,000	
Service Fund		
General obligation bonds payable		20,000,000
To record issuance of general obligation long-		
term debt.		

In the Debt Service Fund, the issuance of bonds may be accompanied by the recording of the budget (see discussion below). The entry to record the budget is:

Entry in the Debt Service Fund

Estimated revenues	2,500,000	
Estimated other financing sources	500,000	
Appropriations		500,000
Unreserved fund balance		2,500,000
To record the budget.		

This entry is discussed in detail in Section III of this chapter.

Thus the issuance of the bonds to finance the auditorium requires entries in two funds and an account group: a Capital Projects Fund, a Debt Service

Fund, and the General Long-Term Debt Account Group. The issuance of the bonds should be recorded in the Capital Projects Fund and the General Long-Term Debt Account Group when the bonds are sold. However, the entry to record the budget of the Debt Service Fund and the Capital Projects Fund should be made at the beginning of the year.

Federal grants are determined to be measurable and available, based upon the terms of the grant. We will assume that the terms of all such grants mentioned in our illustrations and problems make them measurable and available in the period they are received. As a result, the appropriate entry in the Capital Projects Fund is as follows:

Due from federal government	8,000,000	
Revenues—federal grant		8,000,000
To record federal grant.		

After the financing has been completed, the government will place the project in the hands of an architect, who has agreed to work on it for $400,000. Since this person is the "city architect," no public bids are necessary. At this time the contract with the architect is encumbered as follows:

Encumbrances	400,000	
Reserve for encumbrances		400,000
To record encumbrance of architect's fee.		

(For purposes of simplicity, a single encumbrance control account will be used in the remainder of this text.)

The contract with the architect requires the city to pay 90 percent of the fee when the plans are completed. Since the architect agreed to act as the adviser to the city for the project, the remainder of the fee will be paid upon completion of the auditorium. The following entries must be made when the plans for the auditorium are accepted:

Reserve for encumbrances	360,000	
Encumbrances		360,000
To reverse the part of the encumbrance earned by the architect.		
Expenditures—architect fees	360,000	
Vouchers payable		360,000
To record the liability for architect's fees.		
Vouchers payable	360,000	
Cash		360,000
To record payment of vouchers payable.		

After soliciting bids on the project, the city accepts the low bid of Fli-by-Nite Construction Company of $27.4 million. Upon signing the contract, the following entry is made:

Encumbrances	27,400,000	
Reserve for encumbrances		27,400,000
To record encumbrance of construction contract.		

Since the funds on hand are not needed immediately, the city invests $12.5 million in short-term securities:

Investments	12,500,000	
Cash		12,500,000
To record investment of idle cash.		

Several months later the contractor sends a progress billing report to the city requesting payment of $7 million on the project. The payment is approved, less the standard 10 percent **retained percentage**. The retained percentage will not be paid to the contractor until the project has been accepted and it has been determined that there are no outstanding liens relative to the contract. The following entries are made for the billing:

Reserve for encumbrances	7,000,000	
Encumbrances		7,000,000
To record removal of part of the encumbrance for the construction contract.		

Expenditures—construction costs	7,000,000	
Construction contracts payable		7,000,000
To record progress billing by contractor.		

The federal grant money is received from Washington and is recorded as follows:

Cash	8,000,000	
Due from federal government		8,000,000
To record collecton of federal grant.		

This money is then used to pay the contractor as follows:

Construction contracts payable	7,000,000	
Retained percentage on construction contracts		700,000
Vouchers payable		6,300,000
To record voucher for payment of contractor.		

Note the use of the Retained percentage on construction contracts account. Retaining a certain amount from each payment to a contractor enables the city to accumulate enough resources to "guarantee" that the contractor will complete the job satisfactorily or provide the monies to pay another contractor to complete the project. Since this amount is "owed" to the contractor, it is reported as a liability on the balance sheet of the appropriate fund—in this instance the Capital Projects Fund.

Vouchers payable	6,300,000	
Cash		6,300,000
To record payment of the voucher.		

Interest earned on the investments is $1,250,000. This amount is not received in cash but is accrued. Assume that the local laws permit Capital Projects Funds to use any interest earned through the investment of idle funds. The entry to record this interest is:

Interest receivable on investments	1,250,000	
Revenues—investments		1,250,000
To record interest earned on investments.		

Note that during the year, all costs incurred in the construction of the auditorium are charged (debited) to expenditures. At the end of the year, the Expenditures—construction costs account will be closed into the fund balance. As a result, there will be no permanent record of the asset acquired on the books of the Capital Projects Fund. This approach is consistent with the spending measurement focus used for governmental-type funds. To maintain a permanent record of the assets acquired through this fund, the following entry is made in the books of the General Fixed Assets Account Group:

Entry in the books of the General Fixed Assets Account Group

Construction in progress	7,360,000	
Investment in general fixed assets from federal government grants		7,000,000
Investment in general fixed assets from bond proceeds		360,000
To record the construction costs incurred during the year on the auditorium.		

In this illustration it was fairly easy to determine the source of the funds used to build the auditorium. In many cases, however, such identification during the project is impossible. When this happens, an arbitrary decision is made on an interim basis. When the project is completed, a final breakdown is determined. In addition, the Construction in progress account is closed and a building account is opened.

Although commercial accounting has specific rules regarding the inclusion of interest expense as part of the cost of assets constructed (capitalization of interest), the question is unanswered for governmental-type funds. In the gov-

TABLE 6–1

City of Newville
Capital Projects Fund
Civic Auditorium Fund
Trial Balance
December 31, 19X1

	DR	CR
Cash	$ 8,840,000	
Investments	12,500,000	
Interest receivable	1,250,000	
Retained percentage on construction contracts		$ 700,000
Revenues—federal grant		8,000,000
Revenues—investments		1,250,000
Proceeds from bond issue		20,000,000
Expenditures—architect's fees	360,000	
Expenditures—construction costs	7,000,000	
Estimated revenues	8,000,000	
Estimated other financing sources	20,000,000	
Appropriations		28,000,000
Encumbrances	20,440,000	
Reserve for encumbrances		20,440,000
	$78,390,000	$78,390,000

ernmental accounting literature, the only mention of interest capitalization is that "the accounting policy with respect to capitalization of interest costs incurred during construction should be disclosed and consistently applied."[4] Since application of this concept is beyond the scope of this text, we have *not* included interest as part of the cost of assets constructed.

Since all entries for the year have been recorded, a trial balance can be prepared (see Table 6–1).

Closing entries—19X1

At the end of the accounting period, December 31, 19X1, the following entries are necessary to close the books:

Revenues—federal grant	8,000,000	
Revenues—investments	1,250,000	
Estimated revenues		8,000,000
Unreserved fund balance		1,250,000

To close the revenues and estimated
revenues for 19X1.

Proceeds from bond issue	20,000,000	
Estimated other financing sources		20,000,000

To close the estimated other financing sources
and the proceeds from bond issue for 19X1.

[4]NCGA *Statement 1*, p. 10 (GASB Cod. Sec. 1400.111).

Appropriations	28,000,000	
Expenditures—architect's fees		360,000
Expenditures—construction costs		7,000,000
Encumbrances		20,440,000
Unreserved fund balance		200,000

To close the appropriations and expenditures
for 19X1.

One entry was used in the above example to close the Appropriations and
Expenditures accounts. In Chapter 5, two entries were used to close these accounts. The one-entry approach is used here and in Chapters 7 and 8 for purposes of simplicity. Both approaches accomplish the desired results: close the
nominal accounts and transfer any balance to the Fund balance account.

Continuation of the project—the following year

Although most governmental units use the fiscal year as their accounting
period, the authorization and control of capital projects relate to the projects'
entire lives. In our illustration, therefore, it is necessary to record the remainder
of the original budget, $20,640,000. This is the amount originally approved
($28,000,000) less the expenditures in 19X1 ($7,360,000). In addition, we must
record the budgeted revenues from investments in 19X2 of $1,500,000 and re-
establish the budgetary accounts for encumbrances ($20,440,000) at the begin-
ning of 19X2. The entries to record these are:

Estimated revenues	1,500,000	
Unreserved fund balance	19,140,000	
Appropriations		20,640,000

To record the remaining budget for the auditorium project for 19X2.

Encumbrances	20,440,000	
Unreserved fund balance		20,440,000

To reestablish encumbrances at the beginning
of the second year of the construction of the
auditorium.

When the project is completed, the contractor will submit a final bill for the
amount due, $20,400,000 (assume that only one billing is made in 19X2), and the
architect will submit a final bill for $40,000. Since the project has not yet been
examined and accepted, the city will withhold the 10 percent retainage percentage from the payment to the contractor. The entries to record these events will
be:

Reserve for encumbrances	20,440,000	
Encumbrances		20,440,000

To reverse the budgetary encumbrances for
the remaining cost of the contract.

Expenditures—architect's fees	40,000	
Vouchers payable		40,000
To record the amount owed the architect.		
Expenditures—construction costs	20,400,000	
Construction contracts payable		20,400,000
To record the final progress billing submitted		
by the contractor.		
Construction contracts payable	20,400,000	
Retained percentage on construction		
contracts		2,040,000
Vouchers payable		18,360,000
To record the amount owed to the contractor.		

In order to be able to pay the above amounts, the city will need to liquidate all the investments held by the Capital Projects Fund and record the related income. The entry to do this, assuming $15,250,000 has been received, is:

Cash	15,250,000	
Interest receivable on investments		1,250,000
Revenues—investments		1,500,000
Investments		12,500,000
To record the liquidation of investments and		
related revenues.		

Upon receipt of the proceeds of the sale of the investments, the contractors and the architect will be paid the amounts due:

Vouchers payable	18,400,000	
Cash		18,400,000
To record payment of vouchers to contractors		
and architect.		

At this time, the Retained percentage on construction contracts account will have a $2,740,000 balance. Assume that upon final inspection, the project manager finds several defects that need to be repaired before the project can be accepted. Since the construction company has already removed its equipment and employees, its owner authorizes the city to have the repairs made by another contractor. If this is done at a cost of $450,000, the following entry will be made:

Retained percentage on construction		
contracts	450,000	
Cash		450,000
To record payments to contractors to repair		
building defects.		

After the building has been accepted, the contractor will be paid the remaining amount under the contract, $2,290,000 ($2,740,000 − $450,000). This payment will be recorded as follows:

Retained percentage on construction contracts	2,290,000	
Cash		2,290,000

To record the final payment to the contractor on the auditorium.

Closing entries—19X2

Upon completion and acceptance of the project, the Civic Auditorium Fund must be closed. To do this, the following entries will be made:

Revenues—investments	1,500,000	
Estimated revenues		1,500,000

To close the revenue and estimated revenue for 19X2.

Appropriations	20,640,000	
Expenditures—architect's fees		40,000
Expenditures—construction costs		20,400,000
Unreserved fund balance		200,000

To close the appropriations and expenditures for 19X2.

When the above entries are made, the general fixed assets records will be updated to reflect the expenditures recorded in the current period as follows:

Entry in the books of the General Fixed Assets Account Group

Buildings	27,800,000	
Construction in progress		7,360,000
Investment in general fixed assets from federal grants		8,00,000
Investment in general fixed assets from bond proceeds		12,440,000

To record the construction costs incurred during the year and to establish the total cost of the auditorium.

Notice that the above entry only records the construction costs incurred in the second year. The costs incurred in the first year were previously recorded as Construction in progress. In addition, this entry closes the Construction in progress account and establishes the total cost of the auditorium in the Buildings account.

After completion of the project, the Capital Projects Fund has two account balances: Cash, $2,950,000; and Unreserved fund balance, $2,950,000. The use of these resources will depend on the provisions of the federal grant and the bond indenture. For illustrative purposes, assume that these amounts must be used to retire the bonds. This will result in the following entries:

Entry in the books of the Capital Projects Fund	Residual equity transfer to
	    Debt Service Fund
	        Cash
	To record the residual equity transfer to the
	Debt Service Fund.
		2,950,000	2,950,000

Entry in the books of the Capital Projects Fund	Fund balance
	        Residual equity transfer to Debt
	            Service Fund
	To close the residual equity transfer account.
		2,950,000	2,950,000

Entry in the books of the Debt Service Fund	Cash
	        Residual equity transfer from Capital
	            Projects Fund
	To record the residual equity transfer fromthe
	the Capital Fund.
		2,950,000	2,950,000

Entry in the books of the General Long-Term Debt Account Group	Amount provided in Debt Service Fund
	        Amount to be provided in Debt
	            Service Fund
	To record the increase in the resources avail-
	able to pay principal in the Debt Service
	Fund.
		2,950,000	2,950,000

The General Fixed Assets Account Group and the General Long-Term Debt Account Group are discussed in the next section; the Debt Service Fund is discussed in Section III.

Financial statements

The individual financial statements for the Capital Projects Funds are a balance sheet and an operating statement. These are illustrated in Tables 6–2 and 6–3 for the first year of the project. In addition, you should review the section on Capital Projects Funds in Chapter 3 and compare those financial statements (Tables 3–6 and 3–7) with the statements presented below. A budget-actual comparison will be required if the budget for the fund is a legally adopted annual budget. The overall reporting process is discussed in Chapter 9.

TABLE 6–2

City of Newville
Capital Projects Fund
Civic Auditorium Fund
Balance Sheet
December 31, 19X1

ASSETS		
Cash	$ 8,840,000	
Investments	12,500,000	
Interest receivable	1,250,000	
Total assets		$22,590,000
LIABILITIES AND FUND BALANCE		
Liabilities:		
Retained percentage on construction contracts		$ 700,000
Fund balance:		
Fund balance reserved for encumbrances	$20,440,000	
Unreserved fund balance	1,450,000	
Total fund balance		21,890,000
Total liabilities and fund balance		$22,590,000

TABLE 6–3

City of Newville
Capital Projects Fund
Civic Auditorium Fund
Statement of Revenues, Expenditures, and Changes in Fund Balance
For the Year Ended December 31, 19X1

Revenues:	
Federal grant	$ 8,000,000
Investments	1,250,000
Total revenues	$ 9,250,000
Expenditures:	
Capital outlay	7,360,000
Excess of revenues over expenditures	$ 1,890,000
Other financing sources:	
Bond proceeds	20,000,000
Excess of revenues and	
other financing sources over expenditures	$21,890,000
Fund balance at beginning of year	–0–
Fund balance at end of year	$21,890,000

SECTION II—ACCOUNT GROUPS: GENERAL FIXED ASSETS ACCOUNT GROUP

Description of Activities

In Chapters 4 and 5 and Section I of this chapter, the acquisition of fixed assets (land, buildings, equipment, and so on) is recorded as an expenditure. In other words, the assets are "written off" at the time they are acquired. This procedure results from the spending measurement focus that emphasizes assets which are spendable in nature. Under this approach, we concentrate on accounting for current assets and current liabilities. Since fixed assets cannot be spent, they have no place in the accounting records of governmental-type funds and some fiduciary-type funds. For effective control and management use, however, adequate records of such assets must be maintained. In addition, these records must serve as a basis for determining which assets are to be insured.

In Chapter 8 we will find that proprietary-type funds and those trust funds that use fixed assets to generate income are accounted for like businesses. Thus the land, equipment, and so forth, used by these funds are recorded as assets of the particular fund. The **General Fixed Assets Account Group** is used to account for the fixed assets that are acquired by the General Fund, Special Revenue Funds, Capital Projects Funds, and certain trust funds. It is not used to account for those fixed assets acquired by the proprietary-type funds and those trust funds that use such assets to generate income.

Certain fixed assets such as streets, lighting, and drainage are referred to as **infrastructure,** or **public domain, assets**. Since these have value only to the governmental unit, it is not considered mandatory to record them. However, it is important to maintain adequate control records for managerial purposes. The **summary of significant accounting policies** must fully disclose the procedures followed in accounting for these assets. The summary of significant accounting policies is generally the first note that follows the financial statements included in the annual report of a governmental unit and is discussed in greater detail in Chapter 9.

The fixed assets acquired by the funds using a spending measurement focus are maintained on the books of the account group until they are sold, traded in, or discarded. While it is permissible to record depreciation on these assets, most governmental units do not. If depreciation is recorded, it must *not* be included in the statement of revenues, expenditures, and changes in fund balance for the General Fund or any other governmental or similar fund. Thus the entry will be made only in the General Fixed Assets Account Group accounts.

Control of Activities

The General Fixed Assets Account Group does not have an operating budget. Instead, the acquisition and disposal of these assets are controlled through the operating budgets and capital budgets of the funds, using a spending measurement focus. The purpose of the General Fixed Assets Account Group is to provide accounting control over the physical assets themselves. Since it is not a fund, there is no concept of measurement focus or basis of accounting. Instead, the recording of these assets is determined by the recording rules for the funds that acquire and use them.

Accounting for Activities

Operating entries

The accounting procedures followed in the General Fixed Assets Account Group can be summarized as follows:

1. The acquisition of general fixed assets is recorded by debiting an appropriately entitled asset account and crediting an account called Investment in general fixed assets, followed by an identification of the source of the funds used.
2. When disposal of an asset takes place, the preceding entry is reversed. Note that the resources received from the sale or other disposition of the asset are recorded in the fund legally prescribed to receive them. If no such laws exist, the General Fund usually receives the resources.

Fixed assets are recorded at their cost. **Cost** is defined in governmental accounting as it is in commercial accounting: "the cash or cash equivalent price of the asset." In those instances where the asset has been donated to the governmental unit, the estimated fair market value should be used for recording purposes.

To illustrate, let us review the acquisition and disposal of equipment financed by the General Fund (see Chapter 5).

Entry in	Expenditures—capital equipment	975,000	
the books	Vouchers payable		975,000
of the	To record the purchase of equipment.		
General			
Fund			

Entry in	Equipment	975,000	
the books	Investment in general fixed assets from		
of the	General Fund revenues		975,000
General	To record the purchase of equipment.		
Fixed			
Assets			
Account			
Group			

The disposal of a piece of equipment would be recorded as follows:

Entry in	Cash	10,000	
the books	Revenue—sale of general fixed assets		10,000
of the	To record the sale of equipment.		
General			
Fund			

Entry in	Investment in general fixed assets from		
the books	General Fund Revenues	50,000	
of the	Equipment		50,000
General	To record the sale of equipment.		
Fixed			
Assets			
Account			
Group			

In the above entry note that the receipt of cash is the only entry made in the books of the General Fund and that the removal of the asset is the only entry made in the books of the General Fixed Assets Account Group.

In the Capital Projects section, we discussed the acquisition of assets through construction. If an outside contractor is used to build assets, the cost of the project will be determined by the contract price plus any incidental costs. If the governmental unit uses its own employees, materials, and so forth, to construct the asset, the recorded cost will be the total of the materials, labor, and overhead costs incurred.

The acquisition of the civic auditorium discussed earlier involved costs incurred over a two-year period for the construction of the asset. These costs were recorded in the Capital Projects Fund and the General Fixed Assets Account Group. The entries in the records of the Capital Projects Fund in 19X1 were in the following form:

Entry in	Expenditures—construction costs	7,000,000	
the books	Construction contracts payable		7,000,000
of the	To record progress billing by contractor.		
Capital			
Projects			
Fund			

The entry during each period to record expenditure was made only once, although there could have been several progress payments. Other costs that were debited to Expenditures during the first year totaled $360,000. Therefore the entry to record the asset in the books of the General Fixed Assets Account Group was:

Entry in	Construction in progress	7,360,000	
the books	Investment in general fixed assets from		
of the	federal government grants		7,000,000
General	Investmnent in general fixed assets		
Fixed	from bond proceeds		360,000
Assets	To record the construction costs incurred during		
Account	the year on the auditorium.		
Group			

The identification of the source of the funds is discussed in detail in the Capital Projects section of this chapter.

During the second and final year of the project, an additional $20,440,000 of costs was incurred. The entry to record the completion of the project was:

Entry in
the books
of the
General
Fixed
Assets
Account
Group

Buildings	27,800,000	
Construction in progress		7,360,000
Investment in general fixed		
assets from federal grants		8,000,000
Investment in general fixed		
assets from bond proceeds		12,440,000

To record the construction costs incurred during the year and to establish the total cost of the auditorium.

Although many other examples of the recording of general fixed assets could be given, those discussed above are representative and should enable you to understand the use of the General Fixed Assets Account Group.

Closing entries

Due to the continuous nature of the General Fixed Assets Account Group, there are no annual closing entries.

Financial statements

The General Fixed Assets Account Group does not use the traditional financial statements illustrated for the governmental-type funds. Instead a schedule of general fixed assets is presented (see Table 3–8). In addition, information regarding the changes in general fixed assets that took place during the reporting period must be disclosed either in a separate statement or in the notes to the financial statements. An example of separate statement disclosure of such changes is shown in Table 3–9.

Refer to the Schedule of General Fixed Assets by Source for New Orleans (Table 3–8). In addition to the identification as used in this text, the assets obtained through Capital Projects Funds were also grouped together. If we were to follow that format, the "source identification" for Capital Project Funds acquisitions would have to be modified to provide that information. Since this format is not required and is not used by all governmental units, we have used the simpler approach.

The overall reporting process is discussed in Chapter 9.

GENERAL LONG-TERM DEBT ACCOUNT GROUP

Description of Activities

Governmental-type funds do not report long-term debt on their balance sheets. Instead, the proceeds for the issuance of such debt are reported as an "other financing source" on the statement of revenues, expenditures, and changes in fund balance. This practice results from the emphasis placed on the spending activities of the fund and the focus on current assets and liabilities.

The difficulty with this procedure is that it results in no accounting for general long-term debt—i.e., debt secured by the "full faith and credit of the governmental unit. To solve this problem, governmental units use a **General Long-Term Debt Account Group** to fill this important void. This account group is used to record all the long-term debt that will be repaid from general governmental resources and the means by which such debt will be repaid.

Previous discussions have limited general long-term debt to bonds. However, any general obligation debt that will be paid in the future may be reported in the General Long-Term Debt Account Group. This includes debt arising from installment purchases, notes, pension contracts, and so forth. The key requirement for inclusion in this account group is that *general governmental resources* must be used to retire the debt. As a result, debt that will be retired with funds accumulated by proprietary-type funds or some trust funds is not included in this group.

It is also possible that general obligation debt will be serviced from the resources of an Enterprise Fund (a proprietary-type fund). In that case the debt should be reported on the balance sheet of that fund. Again, the *source* of the resources that will be used to retire the debt is the key for classification purposes.

The General Long-Term Debt Account Group is used to report only the *principal* amount of debt. Interest is not recorded in these accounts. Matured interest that has not been paid is included as a liability of the fund that is servicing the debt. In most instances a Debt Service Fund is used to account for the payment of principal and interest on general long-term debt.

General long-term debt is recorded when the debt is incurred—when the bonds are issued, when the installment purchase is made, and so forth. The debt remains in the account group until it becomes a liability that is payable by a specific fund. At that time, the fund servicing the debt will record an expenditure, and the related liability and the debt will be removed from the books of the General Long-Term Debt Account Group.

Control of Activities

The General Long-Term Debt Account Group is used to record the principal of the general obligation debt that is outstanding. It does not have operations as such. Instead, this account group is used to account for the outstanding general obligation debt. The issuance of new general obligation debt and the retirement of outstanding general obligation debt is controlled through the operating budgets of the governmental-type funds. Since the General Long-Term Debt Account Group is not a fund, there is no concept of measurement focus or basis of accounting. Instead the recording of these obligations is determined by the recording rules for the funds that issue, service, and retire them.

Accounting for Activities

Operating entries

Accounting for general obligation debt is a three-step process:

1. When the debt is incurred, a liability is recorded in the General Long-Term Debt Account Group. The offsetting debit is to an account entitled Amount to be provided in Debt Service Fund (or whatever fund will be used to service the debt.)
2. As amounts are accumulated to retire the debt, the amount to be provided is reduced (credited) and an account entitled Amount provided in Debt Service Fund (or whatever fund will be used to service the debt) is debited.
3. When the debt is recorded as a liability of the servicing fund, it is removed from the records of the General Long-Term Debt Account Group.

To illustrate, let us review the civic auditorium project discussed in Section I. The entries to record the issuance of the bonds were:

Entry in the books of the Capital Projects Fund	Cash	20,000,000	
	Proceeds from bond issue		20,000,000
	To record the issuance of bonds.		

Entry in the books of the General Long-Term Debt Account Group	Amount to be provided in Debt Service Fund	20,000,000	
	Serial bonds payable		20,000,000
	To record the issuance of general obligation serial bonds.		

At the end of the year, if $145,000 of the resources accumulated in the Debt Service Fund applied to the principal of the debt, the following entry would be made:

Entry in the books of the General Long-Term Debt Account Group	Amount provided in Debt Service Fund	145,000	
	Amount to be provided in Debt Service Fund		145,000
	To record the increase in resources available in Debt Service Fund.		

When debt is retired, the principal must be removed from the General Long-Term Debt Account Group. The entry to retire $1 million is as follows:

<table>
<tr><td>*Entry in*
the books
of the
General
Long-Term
Debt
Account
Group</td><td>Bonds payable
    Amount provided in Debt Service Fund
To record mature bond principal.</td><td>1,000,000</td><td>1,000,000</td></tr>
</table>

The entries related to these events that would be made in the Debt Service Fund are discussed in the next section.

Several observations can be made regarding the above entries:

1. Only the amount of the principal is recorded in the General Long-Term Debt Account Group.
2. When the liability is paid, it must be removed from the books of the General Long-Term Debt Account Group.
3. Usually the type of debt is identified in the accounts of the General Long-Term Debt Account Group (e.g., serial bonds, term bonds, and so on).

Many other examples of transactions recorded in the General Long-Term Debt Account Group could be presented. However, those discussed above and in the next section illustrate the types of events that affect these accounts and should be sufficient to enable you to understand the use of this account group.

Closing entries

Due to the continuous nature of the General Long-Term Debt Account Group, there are no annual closing entries.

Financial statements

The General Long-Term Debt Account Group does not use the traditional set of financial statements illustrated for governmental-type funds. Instead a schedule of general long-term debt is presented (see Table 3–10). In addition, information on the changes in general long-term debt that took place during the reporting period must be disclosed either in a separate statement or in the notes to the financial statements. An example of note disclosure of these changes is included in Table 3–11. The overall reporting process is discussed in Chapter 9.

SECTION III—DEBT SERVICE FUNDS

Description of Fund Activities

Almost every governmental issues **general obligation debt.** This debt is in the form of liabilities, usually bonds, that are secured by the "full faith and credit" of the governmental unit. The payment of principal and interest on a debt is called **servicing the debt.** Thus **Debt Service Funds** are used to accumulate resources that will be used to pay principal and interest on general obligation long-term debt. General obligation debt does not include debt that will be serviced from resources accumulated in Enterprise or similar funds.[5]

In many instances debt that becomes due in installments—e.g., **serial bonds**—can be serviced directly by the General Fund on an annual basis. However, if there is a legal requirement for a separate Debt Service Fund, such a fund must be established. In addition, a separate Debt Service Fund must be established if the governmental unit is accumulating resources now for the future servicing of bonds. Although this section will concentrate on bonds, it is important to remember that any form of long-term obligation, such as installment purchases or notes, may require the establishment of a Debt Service Fund.

While the exact events recorded in Debt Service Fund will vary according to the specific requirements of the bond indenture or the ordinance authorizing the bond issue, the following general summary of activity reflects the types of events normally incurred in Debt Service Fund operations. First, the resources are received by the fund. These are recorded as revenues or transfers from other funds—usually the General Fund. If the time period between the receipt of the resources and the payment of the principal and interest permits, the governmental unit will invest the assets. These investments are made in order to accumulate additional resources that can be used to service the debt, thus reducing the direct drain on existing assets. The investing activities are recorded in the Debt Service Fund. Finally, as the principal and interest come due, they are paid from the Debt Service Fund assets.

Control of Fund Activities

The operations of Debt Service Funds are generally controlled through the provisions of bond indentures and budgetary authorizations. Many governmental units do not actually record a budget for these funds. For purposes of uniformity, however, we will assume that a budget is recorded and used for control purposes. Even though the budget is recorded in the accounts, a governmental unit need not report comparisons of budget and actual data for Debt Service Funds unless there is a legally adopted annual budget.

Encumbrance accounting is seldom found in Debt Service Funds because of the lack of purchase orders, contracts, and so forth. The expenditures of these

---

[5]While it is possible to have general obligation debt that will be serviced by an Enterprise Fund, a discussion of such debt instruments is beyond the scope of this section.

funds primarily consist of payments of principal and interest. Since these types of expenditures are made according to the terms prescribed in the bond indenture, the addition of encumbrance accounting would not improve control over the use of resources.

As with all governmental-type funds, the measurement focus of Debt Service Funds is available spendable resources. This means that the accounting system centers on the accumulation of resources and the expenditure of those resources. As a result, long-lived (fixed) assets are not found in Debt Service Funds, nor is there any long-term debt in the accounts. The "available spendable" criterion focuses on assets currently available and the claims currently against those assets.

The timing of the recognition of revenues and expenditures is the same for Debt Service Funds as for all other governmental-type funds—modified accrual. Therefore the rules for recognition discussed at the beginning of this chapter are applicable to Debt Service Funds. In general, revenues are recorded when they are measurable and available, and expenditures are recorded when a liability is incurred.

When accounting for the operations of Debt Service Funds, it is important to remember that as few individual funds as possible should be used. In other words, individual Debt Service Funds should be combined into a single Debt Service Fund whenever such a combination is not prohibited by law or the individual debt instruments.

Accounting for Fund Activities

Operating entries

For illustrative purposes, assume that the city of Newville issues $20 million of serial bonds on January 1, 19X1, for the construction of the civic auditorium discussed in Section I. The bond indenture provides for semiannual interest payments of 5 percent (the annual percentage rate on the bonds is 10 percent) with $2 million of the principal to be repaid on January 1, 19X3, and every two years thereafter until the bonds mature on January 1, 19Z1. Further assume that the city desires to spread the burden of servicing the debt on the taxpayers evenly throughout the life of the bonds. To do this, a special addition to the local property tax for servicing the bonds is approved by the voters. This tax should provide $2.5 million of revenue in 19X1. In addition, it is agreed that the General Fund will transfer $500,000 to the Debt Service Fund on July 1, 19X1. (Entries involved in the actual issuance of the bonds are illustrated in Section I.)

The entry to record the legally adopted budget for the fund is as follows (amounts assumed):

Estimated revenues	2,500,000	
Estimated other financing sources	500,000	
Appropriations		1,010,000
Unreserved fund balance		1,990,000
To record the legally adopted budget.		

The account **Estimated other financing sources** is the budgetary account used to record the anticipated transfers from the General Fund.

Recording the tax accrual requires the following entry:

```
Taxes receivable—current                          2,512,000
        Estimated uncollectible current taxes                    12,000
        Revenues—taxes                                        2,500,000
    To record the tax levy.
```

The above entry assumes that $12,000 of the taxes will be uncollectible. Therefore the governmental unit will have to assess $2,512,000 in order to collect the needed $2,500,000.

The collection of $2,300,000 of the taxes results in the same entries as those illustrated for the General Fund and the Special Revenue Funds:

```
Cash                                              2,300,000
        Taxes receivable—current                             2,300,000
    To record collection of current taxes.
```

If $5,000 of uncollectible taxes are written off, the following entry is made:

```
Estimated uncollectible current taxes                 5,000
        Taxes receivable—current                                5,000
    To write off uncollectible accounts.
```

To generate assets in addition to those contributed by the taxpayers and the General Fund, the tax receipts are invested in marketable securities. If $2 million is invested, the following entry is made:

```
Investments                                       2,000,000
        Cash                                                 2,000,000
    To record the investment of excess cash.
```

When some of the investments mature, the following entry is made:

```
Cash                                              1,000,000
        Investments                                            900,000
        Revenues—investments                                   100,000
    To record investments liquidated and related
    income.
```

The interest due to the city's bondholders on July 1, 19X1, is recorded as follows:

```
Expenditures—interest                             1,000,000
        Matured interest payable                             1,000,000
    To record mature interest.
```

Sometimes a government will use a local bank or other financial institution as a **fiscal agent**. The fiscal agent will then make the payments of principal and interest to the individual bondholders. If that is done in this case, the city will have to transfer cash equal to the amount of the interest payment to the bank. The entry to record this is:

Cash with fiscal agent	1,000,000	
Cash		1,000,000
To record the payment of cash to the fiscal agent.		

Periodically the bank will report to the city regarding the amount of principal and interest paid. The entry to record this is (amount assumed):

Matured interest payable	900,000	
Cash with fiscal agent		900,000
To record payment of interest made by fiscal agent.		

The transfer of $500,000 from the General Fund is classified as an *operating transfer* and recorded as follows:

Entry in the books of the General Fund

Operating transfer to Debt Service Fund	500,000	
Cash		500,000
To record transfer to Debt Service Fund.		

Entry in the books of the Debt Service Fund

Cash	500,000	
Operating transfer from General Fund		500,000
To record transfer from General Fund.		

Note the difference between the accounting recognition given to the taxes, which are classified as revenues, and the accounting recognition given to operating transfers received by the Debt Service Fund.

When the fiscal agent submits a bill for $5,000 to the fund for servicing the debt, the following entry is made:

Expenditures—fiscal agent fees	5,000	
Cash		5,000
To record fiscal agent fees.		

The treatment of taxes receivable from the current stage through the delinquent and, finally, the lien stage in the Debt Service Fund is the same as in the General Fund. If you do not remember the sequence of entries, you should review Chapters 4 and 5.

One of the exceptions to the use of full accrual accounting for expenditures in a modified accrual system is interest on long-term debt. The general rule is that such interest is recorded as an expenditure in the period in which it becomes *legally due (matures)*. The reason for this rule is that most governmental units provide only enough resources to service principal and interest due each period. If interest payments are accrued or principal payments are recorded before due, it is possible that a debit balance (a *deficit*) will result in fund balance. This will give the reader of the financial statements an incorrect picture of the financial status of the fund. Rather than not being able to meet current debt interest or principal, the government has simply not yet provided the resources for the payments because they are not yet due. Even with extensive use of notes to the financial statements, it is difficult to explain a deficit in fund balance.

In those instances where resources are available for Debt Service Fund payments, governmental units have the option, under generally accepted accounting principles, of recording the liability and the associated expenditure at the end of the year before the payments are due. The appropriate entry is the same as that used when the interest matures except that an additional liability is established for the bond principal payable and the account titles do not include the word *mature*.

In contrast, an end-of-the-year entry is needed in order to record the interest earned but not received on the investments:

Interest receivable on investments	50,000	
Revenues—investments		50,000
To record the interest earned on investments.		

A trial balance for the city at the end of the year is shown in Table 6–4.

TABLE 6–4

City of Newville
Debt Service Fund
Civic Auditorium Bond Fund
Trial Balance
December 31, 19X1

Cash	$ 795,000	
Cash with fiscal agent	100,000	
Taxes receivable—current	207,000	
Estimated uncollectible taxes receivable—current		$ 7,000
Investments	1,100,000	
Interest receivable on investments	50,000	
Matured interest payable		100,000
Revenues—taxes		2,500,000
Revenues—investments		150,000
Operating transfer from General Fund		500,000
Expenditures—interest	1,000,000	
Expenditures—fiscal agent fees	5,000	
Estimated revenues	2,500,000	
Estimated other financing sources	500,000	
Appropriations		1,010,000
Unreserved fund balance		1,990,000
	$6,257,000	$6,257,000

Closing entries

At the end of the accounting period, December 31, 19X1, in our example, the following entries will be necessary to close the books:

Revenues—taxes	2,500,000	
Revenues—investments	150,000	
Estimated revenues		2,500,000
Unreserved fund balance		150,000

To close the revenues and estimated revenue account for 19X1.

Appropriations	1,010,000	
Expenditures—interest		1,000,000
Expenditures—fiscal agent fees		5,000
Unreserved fund balance		5,000

To close the appropriations and expenditures for 19X1.

Operating transfer from General Fund	500,000	
Estimated other financing source		500,000

To close the Operating transfer and Estimated other financing source accounts for 19X1.

The balance in the Fund balance account at the end of the year is $2,145,000. Since the interest for 19X2 will be paid before the retirement of principal, it is assumed that $2,000,000 will be applicable to interest and $145,000 to principal. Therefore an entry in the books of the General Long-Term Debt Account Group is necessary:

Entry in the books of the General Long-Term Debt Account Group

Amount provided in Debt Service Fund	145,000	
Amount to be provided in Debt Service Fund		145,000

To record the increase in the resources available in Debt Service Fund.

Selected entries for payment of principal

The entries in the General Long-Term Debt Account Group and the Debt Service Fund associated with the issuance of the civic auditorium bonds and the accumulation of resources to retire the principal are as follows:

Entry in the books of the General Long-Term Debt Account Group

Amount to be provided in Debt Service Fund	20,000,000	
Serial bonds payable		20,000,000

To record issuance of general obligations serial bonds.

Accumulation of resources to retire principal is recorded as follows (assuming the same amounts as recorded in the Debt Service Fund in 19X1):

Entry in the books of the General Long-Term Debt Account Group

Amount provided in Debt Service Fund	145,000	
Amount to be provided in Debt		
Service Fund		145,000
To record accumulation of resources.		

When all or a portion of the principal of the bond issue is paid, the liability must be "moved" from the General Long-Term Debt Account Group to the Debt Service Fund. The following entries are made for this purpose (assume we are recording the first principal payment in 19X3):

Entry in the books of the General Long-Term Debt Account Group

Serial bonds payable	2,000,000	
Amount provided in Debt		
Service Fund		2,000,000
To record the maturity of part of serial bond issue and the transfer of the liability to the Debt Service Fund.		

Entries in the books of the Debt Service Fund

Expenditures—bond principal	2,000,000	
Matured serial bonds payable		2,000,000
To record matured bond principal.		
Matured serial bonds payable	2,000,000	
Cash with fiscal agent		2,000,000
To record payment of matured principal.		

Financial statements

The individual financial statements for the Debt Service Funds are a balance sheet and an operating statement. These are illustrated for 19X1 in Tables 6–5 and 6–6. In addition, you should review the section on Debt Service Funds in Chapter 3 and compare those financial statements (Tables 3–12 and 3–13) with the statements presented. A budget-actual comparison will be required if the budget for the fund is a legally adopted annual budget. The overall reporting process is discussed in Chapter 9.

TABLE 6–5

City of Newville
Debt Service Fund
Civic Auditorium Bonds Fund
Balance Sheet
December 31, 19X1

Assets		
Cash		$ 795,000
Cash with fiscal agent		100,000
Taxes receivable—current	$207,000	
Less: Estimated uncollectible taxes—current	7,000	200,000
Interest receivable on inventments		50,000
Investments		1,100,000
Total assets		$2,245,000
Liabilities and Fund Balance		
Liabilities:		
Matured interest payable		$ 100,000
Fund balance:		
Unreserved fund balance		2,145,000
Total liabilities and fund balance		$2,245,000

TABLE 6–6

City of Newville
Debt Service Fund
Civic Auditorium Bonds Fund
Statement of Revenues, Expenditures, and Changes in Fund Balance
For the Year Ended December 31, 19X1

Revenues:		
Taxes	$2,500,000	
Investments	150,000	
Total revenues		$2,650,000
Expenditures:		
Interest	$1,000,000	
Fiscal agent fees	5,000	
Total expenditures		1,005,000
Excess of revenues over expenditures		$1,645,000
Other financing sources:		
Operating transfer in		500,000
Excess of revenues and other financing sources		
over expenditures		$2,145,000
Fund balance at beginning of year		-0-
Fund balance at end of year		$2,145,000

REVIEW QUESTIONS

Section I

Q6–1   Define the following terms:
a. Measurement focus
b. Basis of accounting
c. Modified accrual basis of accounting

Q6–2   How are Capital Projects Funds controlled?

Q6–3   Why is encumbrance accounting generally used for Capital Projects Funds?

Q6–4   Are fixed assets recorded in Capital Projects Funds? Why, or why not?

Section II

Q6–5   Are the account groups "funds" as the term is used in governmental accounting? Why, or why not?

Q6–6   When general obligation long-term debt is issued by a government, where is the principal of the obligation reported?

Q6–7   What is the purpose of the General Fixed Assets Account Group?

Q6–8   Would you recommend that a governmental unit use account groups? Why, or why not?

Section III

Q6–9   When is interest recorded as an expenditure in Debt Service Funds?

Q6–10   When is the principal of general long-term debt recorded in Debt Service Funds?

Q6–11   What information can a city oversight body obtain from a Debt Service Fund?

Q6–12   Explain the relationship among the Capital Projects Funds, the account groups, and the Debt Service Funds.

EXERCISES

Section I

E6–1   (Fill-in-the-blanks—general terminology)
1. Encumbrance accounting usually (is or is not) _____ used in Capital Projects Funds.
2. The entry to record the budget for a Capital Projects Fund would include a (debit or credit) _____ to Appropriations.
3. A contractor recently completed a bridge for the city of Paige. After the contractor removed his men and equipment, several deficiencies

were noticed. Another contractor was hired to repair these deficiencies. The cost of the repairs should be charged to _____.

4. A Capital Projects Fund must be used when fixed assets are _____ or _____ using restricted resources.

5. Long-term bonds issued by a Capital Projects Fund (are or are not) _____ reported as a liability of that fund.

6. During the year, a city acquired new furniture for the mayor's office, land for a parking garage, and a new fire truck. The furniture was financed from general city revenues; the land and part of the cost of the parking garage were financed primarily from bond proceeds; and the fire truck was financed from general tax revenues. Which of these projects would require the use of a Capital Projects Fund? _____.

E6–2   (Multiple choice)

1. The journal entry that is made in the Capital Projects Fund when a contract is signed and encumbrance accounting is used is

a. Encumbrances   XXXX
    Reserve for encumbrances   XXXX
b. Vouchers payable   XXXX
    Reserve for encumbrances   XXXX
c. Expenditures—construction costs   XXXX
    Vouchers payable   XXXX
d. Reserve for encumbrances   XXXX
    Fund balance   XXXX

2. The principal amount of bonds issued to finance the cost of a new city hall would be recorded as a liability in
a. The General Long-Term Debt Account Group
b. The General Fixed Assets Account Group
c. A Capital Projects Fund
d. A Debt Service Fund

3. Encumbrance accounting is usually used in Capital Projects Funds because
a. Long-term debt is not recorded in these funds
b. The budget must be recorded in these funds
c. It helps the government to control the expenditures
d. The modified accrual basis of accounting is used

4. The City of New Easton had a bridge constructed across the Lincoln Bayou. After completion of the project, the bridge should be recorded as an asset in
a. The General Fund
b. A Capital Projects Fund
c. The General Fixed Assets Account Group
d. b and c

5. The resources that may be used to finance Capital Projects Funds come from
   a. Private donations
   b. General obligation debt
   c. Intergovernmental revenues
   d. Transfers from other funds
   e. All of the above
6. The issuance of bonds to provide resources to construct a new court house should be recorded in a Capital Projects Fund by crediting
   a. Bonds payable
   b. Revenues—bonds
   c. Fund balance
   d. Proceeds from bond issue
7. When a construction project continues beyond the end of an accounting period, a special entry must be made at the beginning of the new period when encumbrance accounting is used. This entry includes
   a. A credit to Revenues
   b. A debit to Cash
   c. A debit to Expenditures
   d. A debit to Encumbrances.
8. Resources that remain in a Capital Projects Fund after the project is completed should be
   a. Transferred to the General Fixed Assets Account Group
   b. Transferred to the General Long-Term Debt Account Group
   c. Disbursed according to any restrictions in the agreement between the provider of the resources and the government
   d. Transferred to the General Fund

E6–3   (Closing journal entries)
The following are selected accounts from the trial balance of the Walker Tunnel Fund, a Capital Projects Fund as of June 30, 19X1 (the end of the fiscal year):

Appropriations	$3,711,000
Fund balance	78,000
Cash	245,000
Encumbrances	1,345,000
Revenues—grants	2,000,000
Estimated revenues	2,020,000
Expenditures—construction costs	2,356,000
Investments	75,000
Revenue—investments	19,000

REQUIRED: 1. Prepare the closing entry for 19X1.
2. Assuming no revenues are budgeted for fiscal 19X2, prepare the opening entries necessary for July 1, 19X1.

Section II

E6–4 (Journal entries)
Prepare the journal entries for each of the following transactions that would be recorded in an account group. In addition, identify the account group used.
1. A $5 million bond issue matured and was paid using resources previously accumulated for that purpose.
2. The chief of police acquired $3,000 of office furniture, using part of his general appropriation for the year.
3. The city sold the furniture used in the old Civil Court Building. The furniture originally cost $245,000. The proceeds from the sale totaled $10,000. There are no restrictions on the use of this money.
4. Interest of $234,000 on general obligation long-term debt matured and was paid.
5. A new computer was acquired at a cost of $1,000,000, using general tax revenues. The old computer was scrapped—it had no value; the original cost was $500,000.

E6–5 (Matching)
Identify which of the following situations would result in a journal entry in one of the account groups and identify the account group affected. Explain your answer in each case.
1. The city received a federal government grant and issued twenty-year general obligation bonds to purchase land and develop the land into a park.
2. The city issued six-month tax anticipation notes to obtain working capital until tax receipts are collected.
3. Revenue bonds were issued to finance the construction of an electric generating plant. The bonds will be serviced from the sale of electricity.
4. The current year's payment of principal and interest was made on general long-term debt.
5. The city paved several miles of streets.

E6–6 (Fill-in-the-blanks—general terminology)
1. Assets such as land, buildings, and equipment used by the city, in general, are recorded in the _____.
2. Assets such as lighting, drainage, and streets are called _____.
3. The cost of a fixed asset is defined as _____.
4. The General Long-Term Debt Account Group is used to account for the _____ amount of the outstanding debt.
5. The total of the Amount to be provided in the Debt Service Fund plus the Amount provided in the Debt Service Fund is equal to

_____.

6. The General Long-Term Debt Account Group (is or is not) _____ used to accumulate assets to retire general obligation debt.

Section III

E6–7   (Multiple choice)
1.   Several years ago a city provided for the establishment of a sinking fund to retire an issue of general obligation bonds. This year the city made a $50,000 contribution to the sinking fund from general revenues and realized $15,000 in revenue from securities in the sinking fund. The bonds due this year were retired. These transactions require accounting recognition in

a. The General Fund
b. A Debt Service Fund and the General Long-Term Debt Account Group
c. A Debt Service Fund, the General Fund, and the General Long-Term Debt Account Group
d. A Capital Projects Fund, a Debt Service Fund, the General Fund, and the General Long-Term Debt Account Group
e. None of the above.   (AICPA adapted)

2.   To provide for the retirement of general obligation bonds, a city invests a portion of its general revenue receipts in marketable securities. This investment activity should be accounted for in
a. A Trust Fund
b. An Enterprise Fund
c. A Special Assessment Fund
d. A Special Revenue Fund
e. None of the above   (AICPA adapted)

3.   In preparing the General Fund budget of Brockton City for the forthcoming fiscal year, the city council appropriated a sum greater than expected revenues. This action of the council will result in
a. A cash overdraft during the fiscal year
b. An increase in encumbrances by the end of that fiscal year
c. A debit to Fund balance
d. A necessity for compensatory offsetting action
                                                         (AICPA adapted)

4.   The operations of a public library receiving the majority of its support from property taxes levied for that purpose should be accounted for in
a. The General Fund
b. A Special Revenue Fund
c. An Enterprise Fund
d. An Internal Service Fund
e. None of the above   (AICPA adapted)

5.   A special tax was levied by Downtown City to retire and pay interest on general obligation bonds that were issued to finance the con-

struction of a new city hall. The receipts from the tax should be recorded in

a. A Capital Projects Fund
b. A Special Revenue Fund
c. A Debt Service Fund
d. The General Fund
e. None of the above

6. Which of the following funds used modified accrual accounting?
a. All governmental-type funds
b. The General Fund and Special Revenue Funds only
c. Only the General Fund
d. Only Debt Service Funds
e. None of the above

7. The term *spending measurement focus* refers to
a. The use of the modified accrual basis of accounting
b. The measurement of resources available for spending
c. The use of the full accrual basis of accounting
d. The timing of the recognition of revenues and expenditures
e. None of the above

8. In general, the modified accrual basis of accounting is similar to the accrual basis of accounting with respect to recognition of expenditures. Which of the following is an exception to this general rule?
a. Inventories
b. Prepaid expenses
c. Interest on long-term debt
d. All of the above
e. None of the above

E6–8 (Explanation of the financial reporting effects of the issuance and servicing of general obligation long-term debt)
When a city issues general obligation long-term debt, the accounting procedures are quite different from those found in profit-oriented organizations. Explain the financial reporting effects of the issuance and servicing of a general obligation long-term debt issue.

E6–9 (Journal entries for long-term debt)
Structure City issued $10 million of general obligation bonds to finance the construction of a new city hall. During the year, the Debt Service Fund levied $2,500,000 of taxes to service the bonds and collected $2,000,000 by year-end. Principal of $900,000 and interest of $500,000 matured and was paid during the year by Debt Service Fund.

REQUIRED: Prepare the journal entries to record the events described above and identify the fund(s) and/or account group(s) used.

PROBLEMS

Section I

P6–1   (Journal entries and financial statements—Capital Projects Fund)

7/1/X1 – 6/30/X2

1. The city of New Rouge approved the construction of a city hall complex for a total cost of $120 million. A few days later, a contract was signed with the Walker Construction Company for the complex. The buildings will be financed by a federal grant of $25 million and a general obligation bond issue of $100 million. During the current year, investment revenue of $4 million is budgeted. (Assume the budget is recorded in the accounts and encumbrance accounting is used.)

2. The bonds were issued for $90 million (the principal was $100 million). The difference between the actual cost and the bonds and the grant was expected to be generated by investing the excess cash during the construction period.

3. The city collected the grant from the government.

4. The city invested $90 million in certificates of deposit.

5. The contract signed with Walker stipulated that the contract price included architect fees. On this date, the architects were paid their fee of $45,000 by New Rouge. (Assume a vouchers payable account is used.)

6. Walker submitted a progress billing for $25 million.

7. Investments that cost $5 million were redeemed for a total of $5,020,000.

8. Investment income totaling $3,500,000 was received in cash.

9. The contractor was paid the amount billed in number 6, less a 5 percent retainage.

10. The contractor submitted another progress billing for $25 million.

11. Investments totaling $14,600,000 were redeemed, together with additional investment income of $1,400,000.

12. The contractor was paid the amount billed in number 10, less a 5 percent retainage.

13. Investment income of $250,000 was accrued.

14. Bond interest totaling $10 million was paid.

REQUIRED: 1. Prepare the journal entries necessary to record the above transactions in a Capital Projects Fund for the city of New Rouge. Assume the city operates on a fiscal year: July 1 to June 30.

2. Prepare a trial balance for the fund at June 30, 19X2, before closing.

3. Prepare any necessary closing entries at June 30, 19X2.

4. Prepare a balance sheet as of June 30, 19X2, and a statement of revenues, expenditures, and changes in fund balance for the year ended June 30, 19X2.

5. Prepare the journal entry (entries) necessary to record the remainder of the budget and to reestablish the budgetary accounts for encumbrances as of July 1, 19X2. Assume investment revenues of $2 million are expected in the 19X2 fiscal year.

P6–2   (Journal entries regarding a bond issue and an explanation of how a premium should be accounted for)

The City of Straights authorized a bond issue for a parking garage. The estimated cost was $4 million. The garage would be financed through a $3 million bond issue and a $1 million contribution from the General Fund. The General Fund made its contribution and the bonds were sold for $3,200,000.

REQUIRED: 1.   Prepare journal entries to record the budget for the parking garage, the payment and receipt of the General Fund's contribution, and the issuance of the bonds, assuming the premium remained in the Capital Projects Fund. Identify the fund(s) and account group(s) used to record the transactions.
2.   Discuss alternate methods of dealing with the bond premium.

P6–3   (Journal entries for several funds)

Following is a trial balance for the Old York Marina Capital Projects Fund and the transactions that relate to the 19X1–X2 fiscal year:

Old York
Capital Projects Fund
Boat Marina Fund
Trial Balance
July 1, 19X1

Cash	$ 30,000	
Investments	500,000	
Retained percentage on construction contracts		$ 10,000
Reserve for encumbrances		500,000
Unreserved fund balance		20,000
	$530,000	$530,000

19X1–X2

1. The budget for the marina project provided for a remaining appropriation of $500,000. Record the budget and reestablish the budgetary accounts for encumbrances. Assume $30,000 of investment income is budgeted.
2. The contractor, Sir Fixit, Inc., submitted a progress billing on the marina for $300,000.
3. Investments were redeemed for $320,000. This amount included $20,000 of investment income.
4. Sir Fixit was paid the amount billed, less a 10 percent retained percentage.
5. Investment income of $15,000 was received in cash.
6. The final billing was received from Sir Fixit for $200,000.

7. All remaining investments were redeemed for $205,000. This amount included $5,000 of investment income.
8. Sir Fixit was paid the amount billed, less a 10 percent retained percentage.
9. Before the project was formally approved, one of the piers fell into the lake. Since Sir Fixit had already removed its men and equipment, the city was authorized to have the repairs made by a local contractor at a cost not to exceed $40,000. The actual cost of the repairs totaled $32,000. The remainder of the retainage was sent to Sir Fixit.

   After the repairs, the project was formally approved and the accounting records were closed. The remaining cash should be transferred to the Debt Service Fund. The funds for this project came from a general obligation bond issue.

REQUIRED: 1. Prepare all the journal entries necessary to record the above transactions and close the Capital Projects Fund. In addition, identify the fund(s) and/or account group(s) used. A vouchers payable account is not used.
            2. Prepare a statement of revenues, expenditures, and changes in fund balance for the Marina Capital Projects Fund for the 19X1–X2 fiscal year.

Section II

P6–4   (Journal entries for the General Fixed Assets Account Group and the General Long-Term Debt Account Group)
Following are several transactions that relate to Clearview City:

1. The city acquired land for the expansion of the city hall. The cost was $1 million. The funds were obtained from a general obligation bond issue of $5 million.
2. A contract was signed with Oubre Brothers Construction Company to build the addition to the city hall at a total cost of $4.9 million.
3. The current installment of $10,000 on outstanding general obligation serial bonds was paid by the Debt Service Fund.
4. Miscellaneous office equipment used in the assessor's office was sold for scrap, and $100 was received. The original cost of $2,000 was paid from general tax revenues.
5. During the year, $2 million was spent on the city hall construction project. The building is approximately 40 percent completed.
6. A $4 million bond issue was redeemed through the use of resources accumulated in a Debt Service Fund.
7. A Street-Paving Fund paid a contractor $1 million to complete the paving of several miles of city streets. The project was started in 19X0 and $800,000 was paid to the contractor in that year. Assume that the city records all assets.

REQUIRED: Record the above transactions in the General Fixed Assets Account Group and the General Long-Term Debt Account Group and identify the account group used for each.

P6–5   (Journal entries and correcting entries for several funds and account groups)

The Township of Briner recently hired an inexperienced bookkeeper. Accounting records prior to January 1, 19X1, were maintained by the same individual who designed the accounting system and were audited each year. On January 2, 19X2, the bookkeeper accepted a job in another state and a new bookkeeper was hired. Below is a selection of transactions that occurred during 19X1 and a description of how each transaction was recorded.

1.   The township adopted a budget for the General Fund for 19X1 that included Estimated revenues of $900,000, Estimated other financing sources of $200,000, Appropriations of $800,000, and Estimated other financing uses of $150,000. The budget was not recorded in the books.

2.   The township purchased a fire truck in February. The bookkeeper made the following entry in the General Fund:

Fire truck	60,000	
Vouchers payable		60,000

Payment of the voucher was not recorded.

3.   A property tax levy was made in March. The total levy was $400,000. Approximately 2 percent was expected to be uncollectible. By the end of the year $390,000 had been collected and the remainder was delinquent. The only entries made during the year were for the collections as a debit to Cash and credit to Revenues—property taxes.

4.   Bonds were retired in June. The township had accumulated $505,000 in a Debt Service Fund by the end of 19X0. Part of these resources ($500,000) were used to retire the bonds. The remainder were available to be used by the township in any way it desired. The only entries recorded during the year were as follows (these entries were recorded in the General Fund, using Debt Service Fund resources):

Bonds payable	500,000	
Vouchers payable		500,000
Vouchers payable	500,000	
Cash		500,000

5.   Some surplus equipment was sold in September for $15,000 (there were no restrictions on the use of these resources). The equipment was originally purchased for $245,000 several years ago. The following entry was made in the General Fixed Assets Account Group:

Cash	15,000	
Loss on sale of equipment	230,000	
Equipment		245,000

6.   The General Fund made its annual contribution to a Debt Service Fund. These resources will be used to pay interest. The only entry made was in the General Fund:

Bonds payable	50,000	
Cash		50,000

7.   The interest paid during 19X1 on the debt mentioned in number 6 was recorded in the General Fund as follows:

Interest expense	50,000	
Cash		50,000

REQUIRED: Record the adjusting or correcting entries that are required from the above events. Also identify the fund(s) or account group(s) involved. Closing entries are not required. If no entry is required, write "None" next to the description number on your paper. The books for the current year have not been closed.

P6–6   (Journal entries for several funds)
Following are several transactions that relate to Lake Township:

19X2

1.   The city sold some of its street repair equipment. The equipment originally cost $50,000, but it was sold for $500.
2.   A $2 million bond issue was sold at par. The bonds were general obligation debt issued to finance the cost of an addition to the local court system building.
3.   Property taxes totaling $100,000 were collected.
4.   The construction of a bridge across the High Water River was completed at a total cost of $8 million. The bridge had been under construction since 19X0. Costs incurred in previous years totaled $7 million. With respect to the Capital Projects Fund, prepare only the closing entry for the expenditure. The cost of construction was entirely financed by a federal grant.
5.   A Debt Service Fund paid the interest on outstanding debt, $800,000.
6.   A Debt Service Fund retired bonds with a face value of $3 million.

7. The General Fund made its annual payment of $5 million to a Debt Service Fund. Of this amount, $4 million was for retirement of principal.
8. Old office equipment was discarded. The original cost of the equipment was $900.
9. A contract was signed with Legal, Inc., to construct an addition to the court building. The amount of the contract was $5 million.
10. The construction costs paid during the year on the court addition were $500,000. With respect to the Capital Projects Fund, record only the closing entry for the expenditure.
11. The fire department acquired a new fire engine. The vehicle was ordered earlier in the year. The order was encumbered for $140,000. The actual cost was $138,000.

REQUIRED: Record the above transactions in journal form. Also indicate the fund or account group in which each transaction is recorded.

Section III

P6–7   (Journal entries, trial balance, and financial statements for a Debt Service Fund)
Following is a trial balance for the City of Dolby and the transactions that relate to the Debt Service Fund:

City of Dolby
Debt Service Fund
Bridge Bonds Fund
Trial Balance
December 31, 19X0

	Debit	Credit
Cash	$60,000	
Investments	30,000	
Unreserved fund balance		90,000
	$90,000	$90,000

1. The city council of Dolby legally adopted the budget for the Debt Service Fund for 19X1. The estimated revenues totaled $1 million; the estimated other financing sources totaled $500,000; and the appropriations totaled $1,400,000.
2. The receivable from the General Fund for $500,000 was recorded.
3. To provide additional resources to service the bond issue, a tax was levied upon the citizens. The total levy was $1 million, of which $975,000 was expected to be collected. (Assume the allowance method is used.)

4. Taxes of $780,000 were collected.
5. Receivables of $5,000 were written off.
6. Income received in cash from investments totaled $5,000.
7. Taxes of $150,000 were collected.
8. The liability of $50,000 for interest was recorded, and that amount of cash was transferred to the fiscal agent.
9. The fiscal agent reported that $45,000 of interest had been paid.
10. The fiscal agent was paid a fee of $1,000.
11. Investment income of $3,000 was received in cash.
12. The liabilities for interest in the amount of $50,000 and principal in the amount of $100,000 were recorded and the total was transferred to the fiscal agent.
13. The fiscal agent reported that interest of $51,000 and principal of $95,000 had been paid.
14. Investment revenue of $1,000 was accrued.
15. Collected the amount due from the General Fund.
16. Purchased $1 million of investments.

REQUIRED: 1. Prepare all the journal entries necessary to record the above transactions on the books of the Debt Service Fund.
2. Prepare a trial balance for the Debt Service Fund as of December 31, 19X1.
3. Prepare a statement of revenues, expenditures, and changes in fund balance for 19X1 and a balance sheet as of December 31, 19X1, for the Debt Service Fund.
4. Prepare closing entries for the Debt Service Fund.

P6–8   (Journal entries for several funds)
Following are several transactions that relate to Sunshine City for the fiscal year 19X1 (assume a voucher system is not used):
1. The general operating budget was approved. It included Estimated revenues of $1 million, Estimated other financing sources of $300,000, Appropriations of $1,150,000, and Estimated other financing uses of $100,000.
2. The police department paid its salaries of $30,000.
3. The General Fund made its contribution to a Debt Service Fund of $100,000.
4. The city acquired new office furniture for $45,000. Old furniture that cost $23,000 was sold for $500. The proceeds could be used in any manner by the city.
5. The fire chief ordered $500 of supplies.
6. A billing of $600,000 was received from a contractor who was hired to build a bridge across the Savigon River. Payment was approved and made for 90 percent, with the remainder being withheld until the project is completed.
7. General obligation long-term debt principal matured and the final interest payment became due. These amounts were $75,000 and

$7,500, respectively. (Assume a Debt Service Fund and a fiscal agent are used.)

8. The appropriate amount of cash was sent to the fiscal agent to process the debt service payments described in number 7.

9. The supplies ordered in number 5 arrived. The actual cost was $490. A check was sent to the supplier.

10. The fiscal agent for the bonds notified the government that $70,000 of principal and $7,000 of interest had been paid.

11. The property tax for the year was levied by the General Fund. The total amount of the tax was $500,000. City officials estimated that 99 percent would be collected.

12. Collections of property taxes during the year totaled $490,000.

13. The remaining property taxes should be classified as delinquent after $2,000 were written off as uncollectible.

14. The General Fund received a $1,000 operating transfer from an Enterprise Fund (record only the General Fund portion).

REQUIRED: Prepare all the journal entries necessary to record the above transactions and identify the fund(s) and account group(s) used.

P6–9   (Journal entries)

Prepare journal entries for each of the following transactions. In addition, identify the fund in which each entry would be recorded.

1. Bonds were issued at face value to finance the construction of a city court complex. These bonds were twenty-year general obligation bonds; their face value was $4 million.

2. The General Fund made its annual contribution of $1,500,000 to the fund, which will pay $1 million principal and $500,000 interest on outstanding general obligation debt.

3. The city paid $1 million of principal and $500,000 of interest on outstanding general obligation bonds from resources previously accumulated.

4. A Debt Service Fund previously paid the total principal and interest on an outstanding bond issue. Currently there is $300,000 in the fund. These resources can be spent by the General Fund in any way the city manager feels is appropriate.

5. The police chief paid $300,000 for equipment. This equipment was ordered three months prior to delivery at an estimated cost of $295,000 (assume a voucher system is used).

6. The fiscal agent for the city was paid her annual $10,000 fee from resources accumulated in the only Debt Service Fund used by the city.

7

THE GOVERNMENTAL FUND ACCOUNTING CYCLE

Special Assessment-Type Funds and Some Fiduciary-Type Funds

LEARNING OBJECTIVES

After completion of this chapter, you should be able to:

1. Explain why and how special assessments are used in governmental accounting
2. Distinguish between service assessments and capital improvements assessments
3. Prepare the journal entries normally used for special assessments
4. Prepare financial statements for special assessment projects
5. Explain why and how Expendable Trust Funds are used in governmental accounting
6. Prepare the journal entries normally used in expendable Trust Funds
7. Prepare financial statements for Expendable Trust Funds
8. Explain why and how Agency Funds are used in governmental accounting
9. Prepare the journal entries normally used in Agency Funds
10. Prepare financial statements for Agency Funds

In this chapter we will discuss the present status of accounting for special assessments, Expendable Trust Funds, and Agency Funds. The rules for recognition of revenues, expenditures, and transfers for the funds previously discussed also apply to special assessment projects and Expendable Trust Funds. These rules can be summarized as follows:

1. **Revenues are recognized when they are measurable and available.**
2. **Expenditures are generally recognized when the associated liability has been incurred.**
3. **Transfers are recognized when the interfund receivable and payable arise.**

As discussed later in this chapter, Agency Funds do not report revenues and expenditures.

SECTION I—SPECIAL ASSESSMENT PROJECTS

Description of Project Activities

Special assessments are a means of financing services or capital improvements that benefit one group of citizens more than the general public. Taxpayers who receive the benefits of these activities are assessed for their share of the cost. Examples of these activities include projects such as special police protection, paving of city streets, and building parking structures. Prior to the issuance of GASB *Statement No. 6*, "Accounting and Financial Reporting for Special Assessments," these activities were accounted for and reported in a separate type of governmental fund: Special Assessments Funds. GASB *Statement No. 6* requires that Special Assessments Funds be discontinued as a reporting entity and that these activities be reported as any other service or capital improvement–type project.

Control of and Accounting for Project Activities

Service assessments

Service assessments generally include activities such as special police protection, storm sewer cleaning, and snow plowing. If these activities are financed by user charges in the form of special assessments, the reporting should be done in the General Fund, a Special Revenue Fund, or an Enterprise Fund—whichever best reflects the nature of the transactions.

Control over these activities is accomplished in the same manner as any other activity included in the particular fund type. In the governmental-type funds, control is accomplished through state and local laws and budgetary authorizations for the activities. When these funds are used, immediate control is achieved through a comparison of budget and actual data for revenues, expenditures, and other financing sources. This comparison must be presented in the annual report when an annual budget has been legally adopted. Use of encumbrance accounting is generally found in those instances where the General Fund or a Special Revenue Fund is used.

In those instances in which an Enterprise Fund is used, a flexible budget is the central control feature. In general, a flexible budget is prepared based upon the level of activity of the fund, and this is compared with the actual results of the period. This type of control is explained in more detail in Chapter 8.

The revenues and expenditures (expenses) are recognized according to the basis of accounting rules that are applicable to the particular fund type being used. Examples of this type of accounting and reporting can be found in Chapters 4 and 5 for the General Fund and Special Revenue Funds and Chapter 8 for Enterprise Funds.

To illustrate the use of the General Fund to account for service assessment activities, assume that the city of Newville levies a special assessment on the property holders in the Central Business District (CBD) to provide for special police protection. Assume further that these activities will be accounted for in the police department budget within the General Fund. The entries to levy the assessment and collect part of the receivables are as follows (amounts assumed):

Entry in the books of the General Fund	Special assessment receivables—current Revenues—special assessments To record levy of assessments for special police protection in the CBD.	200,000	200,000
Entry in the books of the General Fund	Cash Special assessment receivables—current To record collection of assessments for special police protection in the CBD.	190,000	190,000

If any of the receivables are not expected to be collected, a provision for uncollectible receivables should be established. If these receivables are not collected within a specific time period, they usually become delinquent and eventually are classified as a lien against the property in question. In these instances, the accounting would be the same as that illustrated in Chapter 5 for property taxes.

Any expenditures associated with these activities are recorded in the fund involved. Unless the ordinance establishing the assessment requires a separate accounting, these activities should not be segregated from the other activities of the police department.

Since the use of Enterprise Funds has not yet been described, we will not explore the use of this type of fund to account for service assessments. We will, however, discuss the use of these funds for service assessments in Chapter 8.

Capital improvements assessments

Capital improvements assessments generally include construction projects such as street improvements and sidewalks. If these activities are financed by a special assessment, and the governmental unit is "obligated in some manner," the reporting should be done in two funds and two account groups. The construction phase of the project is accounted for in a Capital Projects Fund, the debt service phase of the project is accounted for in a Debt Service Fund, the resulting asset is usually accounted for in the General Fixed Assets Account Group, and the debt is accounted for in the General Long-Term Debt Account Group. A governmental unit is "obligated in some manner" for the special assessment debt ". . . if (a) it is legally obligated to assume all or part of the debt in the event of default or (b) the government *may* take certain action to assume secondary liability for all or part of the debt—*and* the government takes, or has given indication that it will take, those actions."[1]

Accounting for capital improvements assessments in which the government is "obligated in some manner" is exactly like that previously illustrated in Chapter 6 for capital projects. If you are not familiar with those procedures, review that material before continuing.

In those instances in which the governmental unit is *not* obligated in any manner, the construction phase is still accounted for in a Capital Projects Fund and the fixed asset is accounted for in the General Fixed Assets Account Group (or an Enterprise Fund, as appropriate). The only significant difference is that the debt service phase of the project is reported in an Agency Fund ". . . to reflect the fact that the government's duties are limited to acting as an agent for the assessed property owners and the bondholders."[2] In addition, the proceeds from the issuance of the special assessment bonds is reported as "contribution from property owners" rather than "bond proceeds" in the Capital Projects Fund.

When special assessments are collected over a period of years, a problem arises as to the amount of revenue that should be recognized. Here we assume that applying the measurable and available concept results in recognition of revenue when the special assessment installments become current assets. Thus, if an assessment of $1 million is levied, of which $100,000 is current, the following entries are appropriate in the Debt Service Fund:

Entry in the books of the Debt Service Fund

Special assessment receivables—current	100,000	
Special assessment receivables—deferred	900,000	
Revenues—special assessments		100,000
Deferred revenues		900,000
To record the levy of special assessments.		

Collections of the assessments are recorded in the normal manner for receivables.

[1] GASB Cod. Sec. S40.116.
[2] GASB Cod. Sec. S40.119.

When the second payment becomes a current asset, a proportionate amount or revenue would be recognized (amounts assumed):

Entries in the books of the Debt Service Fund

Special assessment receivables—current	100,000	
Special assessments receivables—deferred		100,000

To record the current status of the second installment of the receivable.

Deferred revenues	100,000	
Revenues—special assessments		100,000

To record the revenue from current special assessments.

Financial statements

As mentioned above, reporting for special assessment activities can take one of several forms. Since the GASB conveniently aligned special assessment accounting with that of other types of funds, these activities are reported in the same manner as that described in previous chapters or in Chapter 8, if Enterprise Fund reporting is appropriate. As a result, separate statements are not provided in this section. You should review the financial statements for the General Fund (Tables 3–2 and 3–3), Special Revenue Funds (Tables 3–4 and 3–5), Capital Projects Funds (Tables 3–6 and 3–7), Debt Service Funds (Tables 3–12 and 3–13), the General Fixed Assets Account Group (Tables 3–8 and 3–9), and the General Long-Term Debt Account Group (Tables 3–10 and 3–11) at this time.

Application of *Statement No. 6* is required to be retroactive—i.e., the governmental unit must restate the funds as of the beginning of the period, assuming the new accounting procedures had been in effect. The city of Columbus, Ohio, for example, has complied with *Statement No. 6* and reclassified the accounts in Special Assessments Funds, Debt Service Funds, and the General Long-Term Debt Account Group, as required. Table 7–1 is the note explaining the net effects of the reclassification. You should examine this exhibit to make sure you understand the financial accounting implications of the reclassification. In effect, the Special Assessments Fund accounts previously used were closed and their balances were transferred to Debt Service Funds and the General Long-Term Debt Account Group.

Special concluding remarks

In Chapter 3 and the portion of this chapter that deals with special assessments, we discussed the possibility that special assessments may have to be accounted for and reported as separate entities under the rules in existence prior to the issuance of *Statement No. 6* by the GASB. Since these types of situations are not consistent with current GAAP, additional supplemental information must be disclosed by the governmental unit.

TABLE 7-1 Special Assessment Reconciliation Note

NOTES TO THE GENERAL PURPOSE FINANCIAL STATEMENTS (cont.)

NOTE B—FUND CLASSIFICATION CHANGES

Effective January 1, 19X1, the City eliminated the Special Assessment Fund Type for financial reporting purposes as required by GASB *Statement No. 6*, "Accounting and Financial Reporting for Special Assessments." All of the City's bonds identified in prior years as special assessment bonds are general obligation bonds for which the City is fully liable. Accordingly, beginning fund balances and the balance of general obligation bonds in the General Long-Term Obligations Account Group have been restated to reflect changes in fund classifications. The restatements are summarized as follows:

	Balances at December 31, 19X0, as Previously Reported	Reclassifications	Balances at December 31, 19X1, as Restated
Fund balance			
Debt Service	$ 18,475,818	176,591	18,652,409
Special Assessments (deficit)	(795,457)	795,457	—
General Long-Term Obligations			
General obligation bonds	188,220,000	972,048	189,192,048

Source: City of Columbus, Ohio, *Comprehensive Annual Financial Report*, December 31, 19X1, Notes to Financial Statements.

Despite the fact that, in many situations, the above accounting procedures can be followed and the special assessment data can be gleaned from the accounts, it is also possible to follow the "old" accounting procedures and reclassify the data in order to comply with current GAAP. Therefore, we have included an appendix to this chapter (Appendix 7A) outlining the accounting procedures previously followed for special assessment projects. Anyone interested in a further investigation of this topic may refer to the appendix.

SECTION II—SOME FIDUCIARY-TYPE FUNDS: EXPENDABLE TRUST FUNDS

In Chapter 3, fiduciary-type funds are subdivided into Pension Trust, Nonexpendable Trust, Expendable Trust, and Agency Funds. Expendable Trust Funds and Agency Funds are accounted for in a similar fashion; however, Pension Trust Funds and Nonexpendable Trust Funds follow a different set of rules. Since the accounting methods used for the first two funds mentioned are the same as those used for governmental-type funds, they will be discussed in this chapter. The accounting methods used for Pension Trust and Nonexpendable Trust Funds will be discussed in Chapter 8.

Description of Fund Activities

Expendable Trust Funds are generally used to account for resources the governmental unit can spend within the limits of a trust agreement. The source of these resources is usually (1) a trust that permits the governmental unit to spend both the principal and any income generated by the principal or (2) the income generated by a trust whose principal must be maintained intact. As the title indicates, the activities of these funds are governed by state and local trust laws. Since the assets of a trust can only be used in accordance with the trust agreement, a separate fund must be established for each individual trust.

Expendable Trust Funds should be established only when a legal trust agreement exists or when required by law. When legal or contractual agreements requiring the use of trusts are not present, the General Fund or a Special Revenue Fund should be used.

The operations of an Expandable Trust Fund are basically simple. The assets of the fund are recorded in the books when received from the **donor** (the individual establishing the trust) or from a Nonexpendable Trust Fund. These resources are then used within the guidelines established by the trust agreement. Often the most complex aspect of the operation of a trust fund is the determination of what activities can be funded through the assets accumulated. For this reason, a thorough understanding of the trust agreement is important.

Control of Fund Activities

The operations of all trust funds are controlled through the applicable state laws and the provisions of the individual trust agreements. Therefore the accounting system must be designed to provide the information and reports that permit a review of this stewardship role. Unless legally stipulated, formal integration of the budget into the accounting system is not usually required. In some instances, however, adequate control can only be maintained through the use of the budgetary procedures described for the General Fund. Likewise, the use of encumbrance accounting depends on applicable laws and the need for extensive spending control.

The recognition of revenues and expenditures is determined by the rules established for the governmental-type funds—spending measurement focus, which is consistent with the spendable nature of the assets. Like the governmental-type funds, Expendable Trust Funds also use the modified accrual basis of accounting for determining the timing of the recognition of the revenues and expenditures.

Accounting for Fund Activities

Operating entries

For illustrative purposes, assume that a prominent citizen establishes an educational trust fund for the governmental employees. The trust agreement provides for an initial contribution of $5 million. This amount will be invested and the income will be used to grant low-interest educational loans to employees. Assume also that the trust agreement provides that if an individual receives a degree, one-half of the loan principal will be canceled. In this situation the principal of $5 million is recorded in a Nonexpendable Trust Fund, and the income is transferred to an Expendable Trust Fund. Since we are discussing Expendable Trust Funds, we will only illustrate the entries relating to the income received from the investments. The nonexpendable portion of the trust will be discussed in Chapter 8.

In 19X1, the original investment and income from the investments will initially be recorded in the Nonexpendable Trust Fund. The investment income will be transferred to the Expendable Trust Fund at midyear and at the end of the year. The entry to record the amount receivable from the Nonexpendable Trust Fund at midyear will be as follows (amounts assumed):

Due from Educational Principal Trust Fund	250,000	
Operating transfer from Educational		
Principal Trust Fund		250,000

To record receivable from Educational Principal Trust Fund for the first six months of the year.

If the Nonexpendable Trust Fund actually transfers $200,000 in cash to the Expendable Trust Fund, the following entry will be made in the books of the Expendable Trust Fund:

Cash	200,000	
Due from Educational Principal Trust Fund		200,000

To record receipt of cash from Educational Principal Trust Fund.

If educational loans totaling $190,000 are made during 19X1, the following entry will be made:

Loans receivable	190,000	
Cash		190,000

To record loans made.

Loan repayments during the year amounted to $5,000. In addition, interest of $10,000 is earned, of which $5,000 is received in cash. These events are recorded in the following entry:

Cash	10,000	
Interest receivable	5,000	
Loans receivable		5,000
Revenues—interest		10,000

To record repayments of loans and interest earned during 19X1 on the loans outstanding.

If $240,000 of income is earned by the Educational Principal Trust Fund and $245,000 is transferred to the Educational Income Trust Fund in the second half of 19X1, the following entries will be made:

```
Due from Educational Principal Trust Fund      240,000
    Operating transfer from Educational
        Principal Trust Fund                                   240,000
To record receivable from Educational Princi-
pal Trust Fund for the second half of 19X1.

Cash                                           245,000
    Due from Educational Principal Trust Fund                  245,000
To record receipt of cash from Educational
Principal Trust Fund.
```

If three students graduate during the year, one-half of their loan balances will be canceled. Assuming this amount totaled $15,000, the following entry would be made:

```
Expenditures—loan reductions                    15,000
    Loans receivable                                            15,000
To record reduction in loan principal resulting
from graduation of individuals.
```

A trial balance for the fund at the end of the year is presented in Table 7–2. Notice that there are no operating expenses for the fund. It was assumed that the cost of operating the loan fund is nominal and not separately determinable, and, therefore, is included with the operating data of the General Fund.

In this illustration we did not use budgetary entries. Since Expendable Trust Funds are accounted for like governmental-type funds, budgets are often used to control their operations. In this illustration, however, the budget was

TABLE 7–2

City of Newville
Expendable Trust Fund
Educational Income Trust Fund
Trial Balance
December 31, 19X1

Cash	$265,000	
Due from Educational Principal Trust Fund	45,000	
Loans receivable	170,000	
Interest receivable	5,000	
Revenues—interest		$ 10,000
Expenditures—loan reductions	15,000	
Operating transfer from Educational Principal Trust Fund		490,000
	$500,000	$500,000

omitted because of the simplicity of the fund activities. In a more complex situation, a budget would have been recorded and used for control purposes.

Closing entry

At the end of the accounting period, December 31, 19X1, the following entry will be necessary to close the books:

Operating transfer from Educational		
Principal Trust Fund	490,000	
Revenues—interest	10,000	
Expenditures—loan reductions		15,000
Unreserved fund balance		485,000
To close the revenue, expenditure, and transfer accounts to fund balance.		

(*Note*: A single closing entry was used in this illustration because a budget was not recorded and there were only a few accounts involved. In more complex situations, the closing process illustrated for the General Fund would be followed.)

Financial statements

The financial statements for Expendable Trust Funds are a balance sheet and an operating statement. These are illustrated for the Educational Income Trust Fund in Tables 7–3 and 7–4. In addition, you should review the section on Expendable Trust Funds in Chapter 3 and compare those financial statements (Tables 3–22 and 3–26) with the statements presented below. The overall reporting process is discussed in Chapter 9.

TABLE 7–3

City of Newville
Expendable Trust Fund
Educational Income Trust Fund
Statement of Revenues, Expenditures, and Changes in Fund Balance
For the Year Ended December 31, 19X1

Revenues:	
Interest	$ 10,000
Expenditures:	
Loan reductions	15,000
Excess of expenditures over revenues	($ 5,000)
Other financing sources:	
Operating transfers in	490,000
Excess of revenues and operating transfers over expenditures	$485,000
Fund balance at beginning of year	-0-
Fund balance at end of year	$485,000

TABLE 7-4

City of Newville
Expendable Trust Fund
Educational Income Trust Fund
Balance Sheet
December 31, 19X1

ASSETS		
Cash	$265,000	
Due from Educational Principal Trust Fund	45,000	
Loans receivable	170,000	
Interest receivable	5,000	
Total assets		$485,000
FUND BALANCE		
Fund balance		$485,000

SECTION III—SOME FIDUCIARY-TYPE FUNDS: AGENCY FUNDS

Description of Fund Activities

An **Agency Fund** is used when a governmental unit is the *custodian* of resources that belong to some other organization. This type of fund is also used when a single fund is established to perform a central collection or distribution function for the resources of other funds of the governmental unit. Since the Agency Fund does not have title to nor control over these resources, there is no fund balance for this type of fund. Instead, all the resources held are balanced against the liabilities that are to be paid from those resources, including the debt to the legal "owner" of the assets.

A typical Agency Fund is one used to record the collection of property taxes. After the taxes have been collected at a central location, they are disbursed to the legally authorized recipients. It is also possible to use an Agency Fund to record FICA and other payroll deductions before these amounts are sent to the appropriate recipients. Agency Funds are also used for resources held in escrow, deposits from contractors doing business with the government, and unclaimed monies held by the government. A key factor in determining if an Agency Fund should be used is whether the government unit disburses the assets according to a previously agreed-upon formula, legal requirement, or instruction by the "owner." In other words, the government does not have discretionary use of the resources in these funds.

If the city of Newville establishes a Property Tax Collection Fund and the fund is used to account for the taxes collected, an Agency Fund would be created. (The actual levy would still be recorded in the General Fund, Special Revenue Fund, and so on.) In addition, this fund is used to record the distribution of the taxes to the legal recipients—e.g., school boards, levee districts, and so forth.

It should be noted that these activities are not unique to this particular fund; rather they are conducted by all Agency Funds—i.e., the collection and disbursement of resources.

If the resources received by an Agency Fund are not disbursed immediately, the governmental unit should invest them in marketable securities. Any income or expenses produced by these investments is usually distributed to the beneficiaries of the Agency Fund.

Control of Fund Activities

The primary element of control over an Agency Fund is the agreement between the governmental unit and the legal "owner" of the funds. As a result, there is usually no legally adopted budget, nor is there any need for encumbrance accounting. Since the governmental unit will disburse the assets of the fund only for the purposes indicated by the "owner" and only based on the request of the "owner," these controls are not needed.

While the modified accrual basis of accounting is used to determine the timing of the transactions recorded, there are no operations from the point of view of the governmental unit. Therefore there is no concept of measurement focus applicable to Agency Funds.

Depending on the legal or contractual problems involved, a separate Agency Fund may have to be established for each unique relationship. However, related situations can often be combined in a single fund.

Accounting for Fund Activities

Operating entries

For illustrative purposes, let us continue with the example of the Property Tax Collection Fund mentioned above. Assume that the city collects property taxes and distributes one-third of the collections to the local school board, a levee district, and the General Fund of the city, respectively. The levy of the tax is recorded by each governmental unit. To keep the example manageable, however, we will illustrate only the General Fund and the Agency Fund for the city of Newville. Entries similar to those for the General Fund are made by the other governmental units. The applicable entries are, assuming the amounts as given:

Entry in	Property tax receivable—current	5,000,000	
the books	Estimated uncollectible		
of the	property taxes—current		1,000
General	Revenues—property taxes		4,999,000
Fund	To record levy of 19X1 property tax.		
Entry in	Property tax receivable for the city and		
the books	other governmental units—current	15,000,000	
of the	Due to the city and other		
Agency	governmental units		15,000,000
Fund	To record levy of 19X1 property tax.		

Because of the services provided, the city charges the school board and the levee district a 2 percent fee. This amount is deducted from the amount owed to them when the taxes are collected. Any amounts earned by an Agency Fund are usually recorded as revenues of the General Fund.

If $9 million is collected, the school board and the levee district will each receive $2,940,000 ($3,000,000 x .98), and the General Fund will receive $3,120,000 ($3,000,000 + $60,000 + $60,000). The entries in the Agency Fund necessary to record the collection and the distribution are as follows:

Cash	9,000,000	
Property tax receivable for the city and		
other governmental units—current		9,000,000
To record the collection of part of the 19X1		
property tax.		
Due to the city and other		
governmental units	9,000,000	
Due to General Fund		3,120,000
Due to School Board		2,940,000
Due to Levee District		2,940,000
To record allocation of taxes collected.		
Due to General Fund	3,120,000	
Due to School Board	2,940,000	
Due to Levee District	2,940,000	
Cash		9,000,000
To record distribution of the collection of part		
of the 19X1 property tax net of collection		
fees.		

The entry in the books of the General Fund to record the receipt of its share of the property taxes and the collection fee is:

Entry in the books of the General Fund

Cash	3,120,000	
Property tax receivable—current		3,000,000
Revenues—miscellaneous		120,000
To record receipt of part of the 19X1 property		
tax plus a collection fee.		

The other governmental units will recognize the difference between the debit to Cash and the credit to Property tax receivable—current as a debit to an expenditure or an expense, as appropriate. To illustrate, the entry that would be recorded on the books of the Levee District (a Special Revenue Fund) is:

Entry in the books of the Special Revenue Fund

Cash	2,940,000	
Expenditure—fee for collection		
of property taxes	60,000	
Property tax receivable—current		3,000,000
To record receipt of part of the		
19X1 property tax and a collection		
fee owed to the General Fund.		

When the uncollectible accounts are written off, the appropriate entry in the books of the Agency Fund is:

Due to the city and other governmental units	300	
Property tax receivable for the city and other governmental units—current (delinquent or lien)		300

To record the write-off of uncollectible property taxes.

In addition, the appropriate entry, as discussed in Chapter 5, is made in the books of the General Fund and the Special Revenue Fund. Note that the activities described do not result in either a revenue or an expenditure to the Agency Fund.

A trial balance for the fund at the end of the year is presented in Table 7–5.

TABLE 7–5

City of Newville
Agency Fund
Tax Agency Fund
Trial Balance
December 31, 19X1

	Debit	Credit
Property tax receivable for the city and other governmental units—current	$5,999,700	
Due to the city and other governmental units		$ 5,999,700
	$5,999,700	$ 5,999,700

Closing entries

Since only balance sheet accounts are involved in the activities of an Agency Fund, no closing entries are needed.

Financial statements

The financial statements of the Agency Funds are a balance sheet and a statement of changes in assets and liabilities. These are illustrated for 19X1 in Tables 7–6 and 7–7. In addition, you should review the section on Agency Funds in Chapter 3 and compare those financial statements (Tables 3–23 and 3–27) with the statements presented. The fact that there is no fund balance for Agency Funds cannot be overemphasized. These funds do not have title to nor do they control any of their assets. A review of the Tax Agency Fund described in this chapter clearly illustrates this point. The overall reporting process is discussed in Chapter 9.

TABLE 7–6

City of Newville
Agency Fund
Tax Agency Fund
Statement of Changes in Assets and Liabilities
For the Year Ended December 31, 19X1

	Balance December 31, 19X0	Additions	Deductions	Balance December 31, 19X1
ASSETS				
Property taxes receivable	-0-	$15,000,000	$9,000,300	$5,999,700
LIABILITIES				
Due to the city and other governmental units	-0-	$15,000,000	$9,000,300	$5,999,700

TABLE 7–7

City of Newville
Agency Fund
Tax Agency Fund
Balance Sheet
December 31, 19X1

ASSETS	
Property taxes receivable for the city and other governmental units—current	$5,999,700
Total assets	$5,999,700
LIABILITIES	
Due to the city and other governmental units	$5,999,700
Total liabilities	$5,999,700

APPENDIX 7A—SPECIAL ASSESSMENT FUNDS
(Accounting and Reporting Prior to GASB *Statement No. 6*)

This discussion of Special Assessment Funds is provided for those governmental units that must follow the accounting rules that were in effect prior to GASB *Statement No. 6*. These procedures are *not* GAAP, but are provided for those governmental units that must provide this information for legal or contractual purposes. As noted in Section I of this chapter, this type of supplemental information may be gleaned from the accounts, using the accounting specified in GASB *Statement No. 6*. It is also possible, however, to keep the financial records, using the "old" procedures and reclassify the account balances for compliance with GASB *Statement No. 6.*

Definition of Activities

Improvements or services provided by a governmental unit will often benefit one group of citizens more than the general public. These activities are usually financed, at least partially, by assessments on the property in the area primarily receiving the benefit of the project. When these conditions are present, legal or contractual commitments may require use of a **Special Assessment Fund** for accounting purposes. Typical improvements financed through special assessments include street paving, installation of subsurface drainage, and street lighting.

While the use of special assessments to finance services is less prevalent, a governmental unit will occasionally provide such services as street cleaning or storm sewer cleaning financed in this manner. Since most Special Assessment Funds are used for capital improvements, we will limit our discussion in this chapter to a street-paving project.

Although the property owners who receive the benefit of projects must pay for them, there is often an overall benefit to the governmental unit from such improvements. Therefore, it is customary for the government to pay a portion of the cost of each project. In the case of such projects as street paving, one-half or more of the cost may be borne by the governmental unit.

In those instances in which a separate accounting for special assessments is mandated, the procedures discussed in this appendix are usually sufficient to meet these requirements. Due to the limited number of beneficiaries of these activities, it is important to establish a separate fund for each project. This separation is often required in the bond indentures of the special assessment bonds that provide the initial financing for the improvements.

The accounting for improvements such as street paving usually starts with the capital budget of the governmental unit. Contributions made by the government must be approved by the city council or the governing board.

In most instances the collection of the assessments against the property in the benefit area will extend over many years. Therefore the initial financing is usually achieved through the issuance of special assessment bonds. These bonds are serviced by means of special assessments upon the property holders and by general government contributions.

The accounting for the actual construction of the improvements is the same as that used for Capital Projects Funds. After the project has been completed, however, the Special Assessment Fund continues to be used until all the assessments from the property holders and the governmental contributions have been received and the bonds are retired. During this period, the collection of the receivables and the servicing of the debt are accounted for in the Special Assessment Fund. In summary, a Special Assessment Fund is actually a combination of a Capital Projects Fund, a Debt Service Fund, and the General Long-Term Debt Account Group.

Control of Activities

Control over Special Assessment Funds is achieved through state and local laws and budgetary authorizations for the projects. The budgetary authorization of a project usually follows a petition by the property owners, requesting the improvement. In many instances a formal budgetary entry is integrated into the accounts in a manner similar to that of the General Fund. When this happens, immediate control is achieved through a comparison of actual and budgetary revenues, other financing sources, and expenditures.

Since construction projects are often complicated, encumbrance accounting is generally used to control expenditures. The encumbrance procedures followed are the same as those used for Capital Projects Funds.

As with the governmental-type funds, the measurement focus of Special Assessment Funds is *available spendable* resources. Thus the accounting system used for these funds is designed to provide information on the receipt and disbursement of resources. As a result, we will not find long-lived (fixed) assets in these funds. However, Special Assessment Funds do account for the special assessment receivables and the long-term special assessment bonds payable. Therefore, although the available spendable criterion focuses on assets currently available and the claims currently against these assets, the unique financing of special assessment projects requires that long-term receivables and long-term debt appear in Special Assessment Funds.

The modified accrual basis of accounting is used for Special Assessment Funds. Thus the timing of the recognition of revenues and expenditures is the same as that followed by the governmental-type funds. The use of the modified accrual basis of accounting for Special Assessment Funds creates a problem in that their fund balances often are negative (have a debit balance). This condition arises when expenditures (e.g., construction costs) are incurred early in the life of the project, whereas revenues (e.g., assessments) are recognized throughout the life of the fund.

A complicating factor results from the fact that much of the financing for construction expenditures is achieved through the use of special assessment bonds. The proceeds of the sale of these bonds are a liability of the fund. Since they are not revenues or other financing sources, they cannot be used to offset expenditures. The result of these conditions is usually a negative fund balance.

Accounting for Fund Activities

Operating entries

For illustrative purposes, assume that the street commissioner of the city of Newville and a few neighborhood groups get together and propose the paving of several miles of city streets. After approval by the city council and the citizens, the project is included in the budget for 19X1. The financing of the construction is to be by means of ten-year special assessment bonds.

The cost of the project, as determined by contracts with Taylor Concrete, Inc., is $5 million. The agreement with the property owners stipulates that they will pay the total cost of the project over the ten-year period, plus interest. Special assessments of $500,000 per year will be used to retire the bonds. The interest paid by the property holders will be used to pay the interest on the outstanding bonds.

The entry to record the budget for the project is:

Estimated revenues	1,120,000	
Unreserved fund balance	3,940,000	
Appropriations		5,060,000

To record the budget for 19X1.

Note that the city projects a budgetary deficit of $3,940,000 for the current year. The current revenues will consist of $1,120,000—the payment that will be collected this period, $500,000; the next payment (which will be a current asset at the end of this year), $500,000; the estimated earnings from the investments, $60,000; and the interest on the special assessments, $60,000. In determining the amount of revenue to be recognized, we are assuming that the application of the measurable and available criteria will result in revenue recognition when the assessment installments become current assets. The appropriations include the cost of the project, $5 million, plus the current interest on the bonds that will be issued, $60,000.

The entry to record the levy of the special assessment is:

Special assessment receivables—current	500,000	
Special assessment receivables—deferred	4,500,000	
Revenues—special assessments		500,000
Deferred revenues		4,500,000

To record the levy of the special assessments.

Note that only the portion of the receivable that will be collected this year is classified as current. Therefore only that portion, $500,000, can be classified as a revenue at this time.

The entry to record the encumbrance of the paving contract with Taylor is:

Encumbrances	5,000,000	
Reserve for encumbrances		5,000,000

To record the signing of the paving contract.

The issuance of the bonds will actually provide the cash to pay the contractor for the project. Assuming that $5 million of bonds are sold at face value, the entry is:

Cash	5,000,000	
Special assessment serial bonds payable		5,000,000

To record the issuance of the special assessment serial bonds.

If the project manager invests the $5 million in short-term securities, the following entry will be made:

Investments	5,000,000	
Cash		5,000,000

To record the investment of idle cash.

When the contractor submits a bill for one-half of the total project cost and is paid, the following entries will be necessary:

Reserve for encumbrances	2,500,000	
Encumbrances		2,500,000

To record removal of part of the encumbrance for the construction contract.

Expenditures—construction costs	2,500,000	
Construction contracts payable		2,500,000

To record progress billing by contractor.

Cash	2,600,000	
Investments		2,500,000
Revenues—investments		100,000

To record the redemption of part of the investments plus interest to obtain the cash needed to pay the contractor.

Construction contracts payable	2,500,000	
Retained percentage on construction contracts		250,000
Cash		2,250,000

To record the payment made to Taylor Concrete, Inc., less a 10 percent retainage.

The collection of $500,000 of receivables plus $60,000 of interest is recorded as follows:

Cash	560,000	
Special assessment receivables—current		500,000
Revenues—interest on special assessments		60,000

To record the collection of the first installment on the special assessments, plus interest.

The payment of the first installment on the bonds, together with interest, is recorded as follows:

Serial bonds payable	500,000	
Expenditures—interest	60,000	
Cash		560,000

To record the payment of the first installment on the serial bonds, plus interest.

In Chapter 6 we indicated that under the modified accrual basis of accounting, expenditures are recognized when incurred. One exception to this rule is interest on outstanding bonds in the Special Assessment Fund. In addition, recognition of interest revenue on the outstanding special assessments receives special attention. "When interest expenditures on special assessment indebtedness are approximately offset by interest earnings on special assessment levies, both may be recorded when due rather than being accrued."[3]

Because of this rule, neither the interest expenditure nor the revenue in this example is accrued. Thus the only amounts recorded are those that are paid (or matured, but not paid).

When the paving of the streets is completed, the contractor will submit a final bill. If the project is accepted, and the entire amount due will be paid to Taylor, the appropriate entries will be:

Reserve for encumbrances	2,500,000	
Encumbrances		2,500,000
To record removal of part of the encumbrance for the construction contract.		
Expenditures—construction costs	2,500,000	
Construction contracts payable		2,500,000
To record final billing by contractor.		
Cash	2,700,000	
Investments		2,500,000
Revenues—investments		200,000
To record the redemption of investments for face value plus interest to obtain the cash needed to pay the contractor.		
Construction contracts payable	2,500,000	
Retained percentage on construction contracts	250,000	
Cash		2,750,000
To record final payment to the contractor upon acceptance of the job.		

At the end of the year, it will be necessary to reclassify the next installment of the special assessment receivables as current. The entry to record this will be:

Special assessment receivables—current	500,000	
Special assessment receivables—deferred		500,000
To reclassify the 19X2 installment on the special assessments as current.		

Let us also assume that the application of the measurable and available criteria for revenues requires the recognition of a similar amount of revenue in 19X1.

[3]NCGA, *Statement 1*, p. 12.

The entry to record this is:

Deferred revenues	500,000	
Revenues—special assessments		500,000

To record revenues on current special assessments.

A trial balance prepared at the end of 19X1 for this fund is shown in Table 7–8.

Closing entries

The closing process for special assessments is similar to that of the other governmental funds. This is done as follows:

Revenues—special assessments	1,000,000	
Revenues—investments	300,000	
Revenues—special assessment interest	60,000	
Estimated revenues		1,120,000
Unreserved fund balance		240,000

To close the estimated revenues and the revenue accounts.

Appropriations	5,060,000	
Expenditures—interest		60,000
Expenditures—construction costs		5,000,000

To close the appropriations and the expenditure accounts.

TABLE 7–8

City of Newville
Special Assessments Fund
Street-Paving Project
Trial Balance
December 31, 19X1

Cash	$ 300,000	
Special assessments receivable—current	500,000	
Special assessments receivable—deferred	4,000,000	
Special assessment serial bonds payable		$ 4,500,000
Deferred revenues		4,000,000
Revenues—special assessments		1,000,000
Revenues—investments		300,000
Revenues—special assessment interest		60,000
Expenditures—interest	60,000	
Expenditures—construction costs	5,000,000	
Estimated revenues	1,120,000	
Unreserved fund balance	3,940,000	
Appropriations		5,060,000
	$14,920,000	$14,920,000

Note the debit balance (deficit) of $3,700,000 ($3,940,000 − $240,000) in the fund balance account. This results primarily from the financing of the $5 million of construction expenditures from the proceeds of the bond issue. Since the bonds will be reported as a liability, they cannot be used as an "other financing source" to offset the expenditures of the current period. The deficit in the fund balance does *not* mean that the fund is in financial difficulty.

The resources to service the bonds will be provided by the collection of the special assessments (including interest). Thus future collections of the assessments will eventually provide the necessary revenues to eliminate the deficit in the fund balance. This situation can be very confusing to the average reader of the financial statements and would require the use of a note to the financial statements to explain the circumstances. This is the primary reason why the accounting for these projects has been changed (see Section I).

Continuation of the Project— The Following Years

In the example presented above, the construction company was able to complete the project before the end of the accounting period. If construction had continued into future periods, it would have been necessary to record the budget for the current year and to reestablish the encumbrances in the manner previously illustrated for Capital Projects Funds. However, the unique activities of Special Assessment Funds require their continuation until the assessments are collected and the bonds are retired. Thus the activities recorded in the fund illustrated will continue for another nine years. The collection of the assessments and the payment of principal and interest on the bonds will be recorded until the last assessment is paid or written off and the last bond is redeemed.

When closing entries are recorded on the books of the Special Assessment Fund, an entry to record the assets acquired will be made in the books of the General Fixed Assets Account Group:

Entry in the books of the General Fixed Assets Account Group

Improvements other than buildings	5,000,000	
Investment in general fixed assets from special assessments		5,000,000
To record the paving of city streets.		

Note that interest was not capitalized as part of the cost of the assets. The alternatives regarding interest capitalization were explained in our discussion of Capital Projects Funds.

Financial statements

Financial statements for special assessment projects accounted for as illustrated in this appendix probably would include a statement of revenues, expenditures, and changes in fund balance and a balance sheet. These are presented in Tables 7–9 and 7–10.

TABLE 7–9

City of Newville
Special Assessment Projects
Street-Paving Project
Statement of Revenues, Expenditures, and Changes in Fund Balance
For the Year Ended December 31, 19X1

Revenues:		
Special assessments	$1,000,000	
Investment revenue	300,000	
Special assessment interest	60,000	
Total revenues		$1,360,000
Expenditures:		
Construction costs	$5,000,000	
Interest	60,000	
Total expenditures		$5,060,000
Excess of expenditures over revenues		($3,700,000)
Fund balance at beginning of year		-0-
Fund balance at end of year (deficit)		($3,700,000)

TABLE 7–10

City of Newville
Special Assessment Projects
Street-Paving Project
Balance Sheet
December 31, 19X1

ASSETS		
Cash	$ 300,000	
Special assessments receivable—current	500,000	
Special assessments receivable—deferred	4,000,000	
Total assets		$4,800,000
LIABILITIES AND FUND BALANCE		
Liabilities:		
Special assessment serial bonds payable	$4,500,000	
Deferred revenues	4,000,000	
Total liabilities		$8,500,000
Fund balance:		
Deficit		($3,700,000)
Total liabilities and fund balance		$4,800,000

REVIEW QUESTIONS

Section I

Q7–1   The bookkeeper of the city of New Sharman recently made the following
statement: "A Capital Projects Fund should be used for all special assessment projects." Do you agree or disagree? Why?

Q7–2 Lakefront Township recently assessed property holders for the cost of removing snow from the streets in each subdivision. What type of accounting would you recommend for this activity?

Q7–3 Has the GASB eliminated the Special Assessment Fund as an accounting entity?

Q7–4 Explain how the financing of projects with special assessments differs from the use of general obligation bonds.

Section II

Q7–5 How does an expendable trust differ from a nonexpendable trust?

Q7–6 How are the operations of an Expendable Trust Fund controlled?

Q7–7 Jessie Razemink donated $500,000 to a city to provide for concerts for elderly citizens. Explain how you would account for this donation and its expenditure.

Q7–8 Does an Expendable Trust Fund have a fund balance? Why or why not?

Section III

Q7–9 Assume a freshman student approached you and asked you to define an agency relationship. How would you respond?

Q7–10 Is an operating statement prepared for an Agency Fund? Why or why not?

Q7–11 Does an Agency Fund have a fund balance? Why or why not?

Q7–12 If the activities of an Agency Fund produce revenues, where are these revenues usually accounted for?

EXERCISES

Section I

E7–1 (Fill-in-the blanks—general terminology)
1. When special assessment bonds are issued to finance the cost of paving streets, the principal usually is recorded as a liability in

   _____.
2. The project described in number 1 is called a _____ by the GASB.
3. If a city used a special assessment to finance the cost of storm sewer cleaning, the project would be called a _____ by the GASB.
4. The accounting procedures used to record the activities involved in installing street lighting in a neighborhood are the same as those used in a _____.
5. The activities involved in a "service assessment" should be accounted for in _____, _____, or _____ as appropriate.

6. If a governmental unit is not "obligated in some manner" for the debt resulting from a special assessment construction project, the debt service activities should be accounted for in a (an) _____.

7. In the situation described in number 6, the construction activities would be accounted for in a (an) _____.

E7–2   (Discussion of "obligated in some manner")
Explain the term *obligated in some manner* as it is used by the FASB, and indicate how it affects special assessment accounting.

E7–3   (Multiple choice)

1. The construction of a new criminal court building, using a federal grant for three-quarters of the cost, would be accounted for in
    a. The General Fund
    b. A Special Assessment Fund
    c. A Capital Projects Fund
    d. The General Fixed Assets Account Group
    e. Any of the above

2. The city of Milta financed the construction of a new street-lighting system through special assessments. The resulting asset (street lights) should be recorded in
    a. The General Fund
    b. The Street Light Fund (a Special Assessment Fund)
    c. The Street Light Fund (a Capital Projects Fund)
    d. The General Fixed Assets Account Group
    e. None of the above

3. A comparison of budgetary and actual data must be reported for Capital Projects Funds
    a. When the actual exceed the budgeted amounts
    b. When the budgeted amounts exceed the actual
    c. Whenever a Capital Projects Fund is used
    d. When there is a legally adopted annual budget for a Capital Projects Fund
    e. None of the above

4. A deficit in a fund
    a. Results when the revenues in the early years of the project exceed the expenditures
    b. May arise in the early years of a project because the expenditures are usually initially financed with the proceeds of a bond issue
    c. Always indicates that the fund is in serious financial difficulty
    d. Reflects poor management by the government
    e. None of the above

5. The Special assessments receivable—deferred account is used
    a. To record the amount of revenue recognized from special assessments in a particular period
    b. To offset any deficit arising from a special assessment project

   c. As a budgetary account

   d. To record the amount of assessments that will be collected in future periods

   e. None of the above

6. The Encumbrances account is reported

   a. On the balance sheet

   b. On the statement of revenues, expenditures, and changes in fund balance

   c. On either a or b

   d. On the statement comparing the budgeted and actual revenues for a Special Revenue Fund

   e. None of the above

7. The activities of the police department of the City of Brent are recorded in

   a. The General Fund

   b. A Capital Projects Fund

   c. A Special Assessments Fund

   d. A combination of b and c

   e. None of the above

8. The minimum number of funds a city may use for accounting purposes is

   a. One

   b. Two

   c. Three

   d. Four

   e. Eight

Section II

E7–4   (True or false)

Indicate whether the following statements are true or false. If any are false, indicate why each is false.

1. Expendable Trust Funds are classified as governmental-type funds.

2. Expendable Trust Funds follow accrual accounting procedures.

3. Expendable Trust Funds are controlled by state laws and the provisions of the individual trust agreement.

4. Funds classified as Expendable Trust Funds follow a spending measurement focus.

5. Resources received by an Expendable Trust Fund from a Nonexpendable Trust Fund are recorded as an operating transfer.

6. Expendable Trust Funds do not have revenues and expenditures.

7. A statement of revenues, expenses, and changes in fund balance is prepared for each Expendable Trust Fund.

8. Expendable Trust Funds do not have a fund balance.

9.   If a governmental unit uses an Expendable Trust Fund, it must also use a Nonexpendable Trust Fund for that activity.

10.   Budgets are never used to control Expendable Trust Funds.

E7–5   (Journal entries)

Record the following journal entries in the Library Book Fund, and Expendable Trust Fund:

1.   A wealthy citizen donated $250,000 to New Hope, a city in the northeastern United States. This money was to be used to acquire children's books for the local library.

2.   The city invested $200,000 in certificates of deposits.

3.   Books costing $45,000 were acquired.

4.   Income of $20,000 was received in cash from the investments.

5.   The books were closed for the year.

E7–6   (Multiple choice)

1.   Which of the following types of funds use the modified accrual basis of accounting?
   a. Capital Projects Funds
   b. Expendable Trust Funds
   c. General Fund
   d. Special Revenue Funds
   e. All of the above

2.   Which of the following funds can be used to account for the spendable income from a trust whose principal is nonexpendable?
   a. An Agency Fund
   b. The General Fund
   c. A Capital Projects Fund
   d. An Expendable Trust Fund
   e. None of the above

3.   Which of the following funds does not follow the spending measurement focus?
   a. Expendable Trust Funds
   b. The General Fund
   c. Special Revenue Fund
   d. Capital Projects Fund
   e. All of the above funds follow the spending measurement focus

4.   The use of assets accumulated in a trust fund must conform with the provisions of
   a. State and local laws
   b. The trust agreement
   c. Items a and b
   d. The modified accrual basis of accounting
   e. None of the above

5. A citizen donated $450,000 to a city upon her death. Her will provided that these resources be maintained in a trust and spent to provide free tickets to local concerts for school children. Accounting for these activities should be done in
   a. The General Fund
   b. A Special Revenue Fund
   c. An Expendable Trust Fund
   d. A Nonexpendable Trust Fund
   e. Both c and d

6. A city service financed through a special assessment should be accounted for in
   a. A Special Revenue Fund
   b. The General Fund
   c. An Enterprise Fund
   d. Either a, b, or c, as appropriate
   e. None of the above

Section III

E7-7   (Journal entries)
Prepare the following journal entries in the Bid Deposits Fund, an Agency Fund. This fund is used to record all deposits made by contractors doing work for the city. Any earnings of these resources are required to be paid to the depositing companies.
1. Deposits totaling $750,000 were received.
2. The amount received in number 1 was invested in local banks.
3. Income from the investments totaling $70,000 was received.
4. Deposits of $93,750 were returned to contractors upon successful completion of the projects on which they were working. In addition, these contractors received $8,750 of earnings on their deposits (their share of the earnings of the fund for the year). (*Hint*: Don't forget to liquidate some of the investments.)
5. The books were closed for the year.

E7-8   (True or false)
Indicate whether the following statements are true or false. If any are false, indicate why each is false.
1. The resources in an Agency Fund belong to the governmental unit.
2. A separate Agency Fund must be established for each agency relationship.
3. Revenues earned through an Agency Fund are usually recorded as revenue in the General Fund.
4. Uncollectible property taxes will result in an expense in a Property Tax Agency Fund.

5. Closing entries are not required in an Agency Fund.

6. Financial statements are not prepared for an Agency Fund.

7. Agency Funds are used to disburse earnings from a Nonexpendable Trust Fund.

8. An Agency Fund can be used in any situation in which a Special Revenue Fund can be used.

E7–9   (Multiple choice)

1. The fee for the collection of property taxes by an Agency Fund will result in revenue to
   a. The General Fund and the Agency Fund
   b. The Agency Fund
   c. A Capital Projects Fund
   d. A Special Revenue Fund and the Agency Fund
   e. None of the above

2. Blaken Township established an Agency Fund to account for the collection and distribution of a general sales tax. The tax is collected for the General Fund, a school district, and several drainage districts. The school district and the drainage districts are entities that are separate from the city. During the year, $500,000 was collected in sales tax. Entries to record the collection and distribution of the resources for the city should be made in
   a. The General Fund
   b. The Agency Fund
   c. The General Fund and the Agency Fund
   d. A Special Revenue Fund and the Agency Fund
   e. None of the above

3. Collection of resources that must be distributed to other funds should be recorded in an Agency Fund as a debit to Cash and a credit to
   a. Revenues
   b. Expenditures
   c. Other financing sources
   d. Other financing uses
   e. None of the above

4. Which of the following funds does not have a fund balance account?
   a. The General Fund
   b. A Special Revenue Fund
   c. A Capital Projects Fund
   d. An Expendable Trust Fund
   e. An Agency Fund

5. An Agency Fund is used to account for
   a. The revenue generated from a property tax levy
   b. The expenditures of the General Fund

    c. The debt service of a capital improvements project financed through special assessments, where the government is not obligated in any manner

    d. The debt service of general obligation bonds used to finance an addition to city hall

    e. None of the above

6. According to GAAP for Expendable Trust Funds, which of the following is true?

    a. Revenues must be transferred to a Nonexpendable Trust Fund

    b. Payments of resources are recorded as expenditures

    c. There is no fund balance

    d. All disbursements must be made to the General Fund

    e. None of the above

PROBLEMS

Section I

P7–1   (Journal entries and financial statements for a street-lighting project that was financed with a special assessment)

19X1–X2

1. The managing board of Vera Township approved the capital budget for the fiscal year July 1, 19X1– June 30, 19X2. Included in this budget was a drainage project that was to be funded through special assessments and a contribution from the township. Intermediate financing was furnished by a bond issue that would be repaid with collections of the special assessments. The managing board also approved the budget for the project. Included in the budget were estimated revenues of $200,000 for the current year and appropriations of $1,600,000 for the project. The township's share of the cost for this project was $40,000. Assume the township guaranteed payment of the special assessment bonds used to finance the project.

2. A construction contract with Jorge Construction Company was approved for $1,400,000.

3. Special assessments totaling $1,360,000 were levied against the property holders that would benefit from the project. Of this amount, $100,000 was considered to be current and recognized as revenue. This same amount will become current next year.

4. Collection from property holders totaled $90,000.

5. Special assessment bonds totaling $1,360,000 were issued for $1,360,000.

6. A progress billing was received from the contractor for $500,000.

7. The contractor was paid the amount of the billing, less a 10 percent retainage. (Assume the city does not use a voucher system.)

8. Short-term securities were purchased for $900,000, using Capital Projects Fund resources.

9. An additional billing was received from the contractor for $600,000.

10. Investments that cost $600,000 were redeemed for $620,000. The difference was investment revenue.

11. The contractor was paid, less the agreed-upon retainage.

12. Investments that cost $300,000 were redeemed for $330,000. The difference was investment revenue.

13. The contractor completed the project and submitted a final bill for $300,000. After an examination of the work, it was accepted by the city and the full amount of the billing plus all previously retained amounts were paid.

14. Interest of $140,000 was paid on the special assessment bonds.

15. The township's share of the project was paid to the fund where the construction was recorded.

REQUIRED:

1. Prepare the journal entries necessary to record the above events and indicate the fund(s) and account group(s) used. (Assume there is no interest on the assessments for 19X1.)

2. Prepare a trial balance for the fund where the construction accounting was recorded.

3. Prepare all necessary year-end entries and closing entries in the Capital Projects Fund. After the project has been completed, any fund balance should be transferred to the Debt Service Fund. Assume the township records all fixed assets. (*Hint*: Don't forget the status of the receivables in the Debt Service Fund at year end.) Omit year-end entries in the General Long–Term Debt Account Group.

4. Prepare a statement of revenues, expenditures, and changes in fund balance and a balance sheet for the fund where the construction was recorded.

P7–2   (Journal entries for several funds and account groups)

19X1

1. A street-lighting project was approved by the city managers of Wakefield City; the total cost was $750,000. Revenues of the Capital Projects Fund for the current year are estimated to be $50,000 and special assessment bonds will be used to finance the remainder. Interest on outstanding bonds payable is estimated to be $75,000 for the year. (Assume a budget is not recorded in the Debt Service Fund; however, a budget is recorded in the Capital Projects Fund.)

2. General governmental resources were used to acquire new equipment for the mayor's office. The total cost of the equipment was $3,000. This expenditure previously had been encumbered at $3,200.

3. A contract was signed for the construction of an addition to the city hall. The total cost was $900,000.

4. Special assessment bonds were issued for the street-lighting project. The bonds were issued for their face value of $700,000.

5. A contract was let with Old Iron Construction Company for the street-lighting project at a total cost of $750,000.

6. Interest of $95,000 was recorded and paid from a Debt Service Fund.

7. A special assessment of $750,000 was levied to pay for the cost of the street-lighting project. The current portion of the installment was $50,000. Revenue of $50,000 was recorded at that time.

8. Old Iron submitted a progress billing for $200,000.

9. Old Iron was paid $190,000; the remainder was retained until the completion of the project.

10. Construction cash from the street-lighting project totaling $500,000 was invested in marketable securities.

11. Bonds with a face value of $800,000 were issued for that amount. The proceeds were used to begin construction of an addition to the city office building complex. (*Hint*: Don't forget to record the bond liability.)

12. The General Fund transferred $75,000 to a Debt Service Fund to be used to retire outstanding bonds.

13. The Debt Service Fund mentioned above (number 12) retired $100,000 of outstanding bonds. Assume that all interest had previously been paid.

14. Special assessments totaling $50,000 were collected.

15. Interest of $75,000 was paid on the special assessment bonds outstanding.

16. The next installment of the special assessment was $50,000.

REQUIRED: Prepare all the journal entries necessary to record the above transactions. In addition, identify the fund(s) and account group(s) in which each entry is recorded. Where multiple types of the same fund are used, label them as 1, 2, and so on (e.g., CPF-1, CPF-2). The street-lighting project should be CPF-1 and DSF-1; the city office complex addition should be CPF-2; the Debt Service Fund in number 6 should be DSF-3 and the Debt Service Fund in number 12 should be DSF-2.

Section II

P7–3 (Journal entries for an Expendable Trust Fund)

1. The City of Newfonia received a gift of $2 million from the First Tire Company. The company required the city to maintain the principal of the gift and use any income to beautify the town square. A formal trust agreement was prepared and the appropriate legal acts were passed.

2. The city invested the entire gift in certificates of deposit.

3. Investment income of $100,000 was received in cash and $90,000 was transferred to the fund that will use these resources.

4. Since plans to beautify the town square were incomplete, the $90,000 was invested in short-term securities.

5. After beautification plans were completed, the city "cashed in" one-half of the $90,000 investments and received $54,000; the excess over principal was investment income.

6. The city purchased trees and shrubs from a local nursery for $35,000. In addition, the nursery charged the city $8,000 to prepare the ground and plant the trees and shrubs.

7. As part of a continuing campaign, the city received a $300,000 gift from the Second Tire Company. The same restrictions, as indicated in number 1, applied to this gift. In an attempt to make the accounting easier, both companies agreed that the income from the gifts could be combined as long as the principal of each gift was separately maintained. The proceeds of the Second Tire Company gift were immediately invested in short-term securities.

8. The First Tire Fund received $100,000 in income.

9. The Second Tire Fund received $12,000 in income.

10. Each of the principal funds transferred the amounts received in 8 and 9 to the income fund.

11. Additional beautification projects costing $97,000 were paid for.

REQUIRED: 1. Prepare the journal entries necessary to record the above events on the books of the fund that will spend the resources to beautify the town square.

2. Prepare a statement of revenues, expenditures, and changes in fund balance and a balance sheet for the fund that will spend the resources to beautify the town square. The accounting period ended December 31, 19X1.

3. Prepare closing entries for the fund.
   (Note: Problem 8–7 is a continuation of this problem; see p. 318.)

P7–4 (Journal entries for several funds)
Listed below are several transactions occurring during 19X1 that relate to Canal Vista, a city in the southwestern United States:

1. The general operating budget was approved. It included estimated revenues of $2,000,000 and appropriations of $1,950,000.

2. A general obligation bond issue of $10 million was sold to finance the construction of a new parking garage. The bonds were sold for

$10,400,000. The premium was transferred to the fund that will pay the principal and interest on the debt.

3. The city uses a Property Tax Fund (an Agency Fund) to collect property taxes. The tax levy was a total of $20 million. Of this amount, $10 million was for the General Fund, $5 million was for a Special Revenue Fund, and $5 million was for a Debt Service Fund. Each fund expected to collect 99 percent of the taxes.

4. A contract for the parking garage was signed with University Construction, Inc., for $9,500,000.

5. Property taxes were collected totaling $12 million, and amounts proportionate to the original levy were distributed to each participating fund. The Special Revenue Fund and the Debt Service Fund each paid .001 of the proceeds to have the collections made for them.

6. University Construction submitted a progress billing of $1 million.

7. Interest of $200,000 was paid from a Debt Service Fund.

8. University Construction was paid the amount owed after deducting a 5 percent retainage.

9. The salaries of the mayor and the other general governmental employees were paid. These totaled $145,000. Assume salaries are not encumbered.

10. Supplies costing $8,000 were ordered by the mayor's office.

11. Equipment costing $5,000 was acquired for cash by a department in the General Fund.

12. The supplies ordered in number 10 arrived and $8,200 was billed to the city. Assume the invoice was paid after the additional amount was approved.

REQUIRED: Prepare all the journal entries necessary to record the above transactions. In addition, identify the fund(s) and account group(s) in which each entry is recorded.

P7–5   (Financial statements and closing entries for an Expendable Trust Fund) The city of New Baton received a gift from a wealthy citizen several years past. The gift established a trust of $1,000,000 that must be maintained intact. The income from the trust must be used to maintain an old section of the city called the Vieux Carre. Since the citizen was an accountant, she insisted that an annual budget be prepared and that the fund use budgetary accounting, including the use of encumbrances. After several years of operation, the Expendable Trust Fund had the following account balances at the end of the fiscal year:

City of New Baton
Expendable Trust Fund
Kathy Paige Income Fund
Trial Balance
June 30, 19X1

	Debit	Credit
Cash	$ 2,000	
Investment	25,000	
Due from Kathy Paige Principal Fund	12,000	
Accounts payable		$ 4,000
Unreserved fund balance		39,000
Reserve for encumbrances		2,000
Encumbrances	2,000	
Estimated revenues	4,100	
Estimated other financing sources	45,000	
Revenues—investments		4,000
Operating transfer from Kathy Paige Principal Fund		40,000
Appropriations		49,100
Expenditures—capital outlay	14,000	
Expenditures—maintenance	34,000	
	$138,100	$138,100

REQUIRED: 1.   Prepare a statement of revenues, expenditures, and changes in fund balance and a balance sheet for the Kathy Paige Income Fund.
2.   Prepare any closing entries necessary at June 30, 19X1.

Section III

P7–6   (Journal entries and financial statements for an Agency Fund)
The city of New Tuckett recently hosted a state fair. The city levied a special 1 percent sales tax on all sales made at the fair, the proceeds of which will be used to help retire outstanding debt and finance improvements to the area after the fair closed. The improvements will be accounted for in a Special Revenue Fund. Money will be used by the Special Revenue Fund as needed, and any excess will be paid to a Debt Service Fund. The city used an Agency Fund to account for the collection of these tax monies. The dates of the fair spanned two fiscal periods. The following trial balance is available at the end of 19X1:

City of New Tuckett
Agency Fund
State Fair Sales Tax Fund
Trial Balance
December 31, 19X1

	Debit	Credit
Cash	$ 3,500	
Time certificates of deposit	46,600	
Due to other governmental funds		50,100
	$50,100	$50,100

The following transactions took place during 19X2:

1. Investments costing $15,000 were redeemed for a total of $18,000; the difference was investment revenue.
2. Contractors were paid $1,000 by the Special Revenue Fund after receiving the money from the Agency Fund.
3. The fund collected $800 in interest on investments.
4. Workers were paid $800 to begin dismantling the exhibits. City employees were used to begin the cleanup process.
5. The fair paid the fund the total amount due as a result of 19X2 sales, $134,000.
6. A contractor was hired at a cost of $125,000 to finish the cleanup.
7. The contractor was paid $35,000 on the contract.
8. The remaining investments were redeemed for $36,000.
9. The amount due the cleanup contractor was paid to the Special Revenue Fund.

REQUIRED:
1. Prepare the entries necessary to record the above entries on the books of the Agency Fund.
2. Prepare the financial statements for the Agency Fund for 19X2.

P7–7 (Journal entries and trial balance for several funds)
Following are several transactions that relate to the city of Pagedan.

1. The general operating budget was approved. It included estimated revenues for $800,000 and appropriations of $790,000.
2. A general obligation bond issue of $6 million was sold to finance the construction of a new bridge. The bonds were sold at their face amount.
3. The city uses a Property Tax Fund (an Agency Fund) to collect property taxes. The tax levy was a total of $7 million. Of this amount, $4 million was for the General Fund, $2 million for a Special Revenue Fund, and $1 million for a Debt Service Fund.
4. A contract for the bridge was signed with Wilt Construction Company for $5.9 million.
5. Property taxes totaling $6.3 million were collected and the appropriate amounts were distributed to each participating fund.
6. Interest of $100,000 was paid from the Debt Service Fund.
7. The bridge contractor submitted a progress billing of $1 million.
8. The bridge contractor was paid the amount of the billing, less a 10 percent retainage.
9. The city has a Housing Trust Fund (a Nonexpendable Trust Fund) established by gifts from several citizens. The income earned by the investment of this fund is spent through the Housing Authority Fund (an Expendable Trust). During the year, the Housing Authority Fund received $25,000 from the Housing Trust Fund. (Omit the entries for the Housing Trust Fund.)

10. The salaries of the mayor and the other general governmental employees were paid. Cash was distributed in the amount of $500,000. (Assume that salaries are not encumbered.)

11. Expenditures of $10,000 were made from Housing Authority funds for repairs to apartments.

12. The General Fund made its annual payment of $200,000 to the Debt Service Fund. Of this amount, $175,000 was for interest.

REQUIRED: Prepare all the journal entries necessary to record the above transactions and identify the fund in which each entry is recorded.

P7–8   (Correcting entries for several funds)

1. The city acquired land for an expansion of the main library. The entire project was financed through a bond issue. The following entry was made in the General Fund:

Expenditures—capital outlay	123,000	
Cash		123,000

The bond proceeds were used to acquire the land.

2. Interest on outstanding debt was paid from resources previously accumulated for that purpose. The only entry that was made was the following in a Debt Service Fund:

Expenditures—mature interest	50,000	
Cash		50,000

3. Bond principal was retired from resources previously accumulated for that purpose. The only entry that was made was the following in a Debt Service Fund:

Expenditures—mature bond principal	200,000	
Cash		200,000

4. Miscellaneous office equipment that originally cost $5,000 was sold for $800. The proceeds were recorded in a Special Revenue Fund because of the restrictions place upon the use of the money by the original grant that was used to buy the equipment. No other entries were made.

5. The city acquired several fire engines at a total cost of $500,000. The resources that were used were part of a federal grant to acquire various fire-fighting equipment and build two fire stations. The following entry was recorded in the General Fund:

Equipment	500,000	
Cash		500,000

6. The city entered into a contract with Crackel, Inc., a construction company, to build a bridge across the Bouga Bayou. The contract

cost was $1,750,000. The contract was signed on August 1, 19X0, and the appropriate entries were made during that year. An inexperienced bookkeeper did not make any entries for 19X1, the current year. After accumulating the appropriate papers, you have been able to determine the following information:

a. The costs incurred in 19X0 totaled $900,000.

b. The project was completed on June 15, 19X1, at a total cost of $1,750,000. The job was accepted on June 30, 19X1.

c. All entries for 19X0 were made correctly.

d. A progress payment of $400,000 was made on April 1, 19X1.

e. Instead of retaining some of each progress payment, the last payment to the contractor was not made until the project was completed and accepted.

f. The project was financed with a bond issue.

(*Hint*: Don't forget to make budgetary entries.)

7. An Agency Fund is used to collect property taxes. The taxes are then disbursed to various city departments and the local school board (not part of the city). The following entries were made to record the collection and disbursement of the taxes in the Agency Fund (no entries were made in the General Fund):

Cash	1,234,000	
Revenues—property taxes		1,234,000
Expenditures—property taxes—General		
Fund	234,000	
Expenditures—property taxes—school		
board	1,000,000	
Cash		1,234,000
Cash	10,000	
Revenues—property tax collection		
fee from school board		10,0000

REQUIRED: Prepare any correcting entries that are necessary as a result of the above information. Identify any fund(s) and account group(s) used.

Appendix 7A

P7–9   (Journal entries and financial statements for a Special Assessments Fund, based on accounting and reporting procedures in effect prior to the issuance of GASB *Statement No. 6*)

1. The managing board of Capital City approved the city's capital budget for 19X1. Included in this budget was a drainage project that was to be funded through special assessments and a contri-

bution from the city. On this date, the managing board also legally approved the budget for the drainage project. It included estimated revenues of $100,000 for the current year and appropriations of $770,000 for the project. The city's share of the cost is $20,000.

2. A construction contract with George, Inc., was approved for $700,000.

3. Special assessments totaling $500,000 were levied against the property holders that would benefit from the project. Of this amount, $50,000 was considered to be current each year and recognized as revenue.

4. Collections from property holders totaled $45,000.

5. Special assessment bonds totaling $700,000 were issued for $700,000.

6. A progress billing was received from the contractor for $250,000.

7. The contractor was paid the amount of the billing, less a 10 percent retainage.

8. Short–term securities were purchased for $450,000.

9. An additional billing was received from the contractor for $300,000.

10. Investments that cost $300,000 were redeemed for $310,000. The difference was investment revenue.

11. The contractor was paid, less the agreed-upon retainage.

12. Investments that cost $150,000 were redeemed for $165,000. The difference was investment revenue.

13. The contractor completed the project and submitted a final bill for $150,000. After an examination of the work, it was accepted by the city and the full amount of the billing plus all previous retained amounts were paid.

14. Interest of $70,000 was paid on the special assessment bonds.

15. The city's share of the project for 19X1 was paid to the Special Assessment Fund.

REQUIRED: 1. Prepare the journal entries necessary to record the above transactions in a Special Assessments Fund. (Assume that the city operates on a calendar year.)

2. Prepare a trial balance for the Special Assessments Fund at December 31, 19X1, before closing.

3. Prepare a balance sheet as of December 31, 19X1, and a statement of revenues, expenditures, and changes in fund balance for 19X1.

4. Prepare any necessary closing entries at December 31, 19X1.

8

THE GOVERNMENTAL FUND ACCOUNTING CYCLE

Proprietary-Type Funds and Some Fiduciary-Type Funds

LEARNING OBJECTIVES

After completion of this chapter, you should be able to:

1. Explain why and how Internal Service Funds are used in governmental accounting
2. Prepare the journal entries normally used in Internal Service Funds
3. Prepare financial statements for Internal Service Funds
4. Explain why and how Enterprise Funds are used in governmental accounting
5. Prepare the journal entries normally used in Enterprise Funds
6. Prepare financial statements for Enterprise Funds
7. Explain why and how Nonexpendable Trust Funds are used in governmental accounting
8. Prepare the journal entries normally used in Nonexpendable Trust Funds
9. Prepare financial statements for Nonexpendable Trust Funds
10. Explain why and how Pension Trust Funds are used in governmental accounting
11. Prepare the journal entries normally used in Pension Trust Funds
12. Prepare financial statements for Pension Trust Funds

Many governmental units conduct activities that are similar to those conducted by business enterprises. Examples of such activities include the operations of electric utilities, airports, golf courses, central motor pools, and central inventory supplies. The accounting for such activities takes place in *proprietary-type funds*.

The procedures used to account for governmental-type activities concentrate on the receipt and spending of resources. In most instances they are not appropriate for measuring business-type activities because the effective and efficient operation of business-type activities requires information on the *revenues* earned and the *expenses* incurred in providing goods or services. A "business" cannot operate properly with an accounting system that only reports on spending controls. It must also have information on the *matching* of revenues and expenses and the resulting profit or loss. The accounting system must also be able to provide information on the total cost of a service or product because the users are paying directly for it. A simple accumulation of the number of dollars spent during a given period of time is not sufficient to control the operations of such an activity. The accounting procedures used in proprietary-type funds provide this information.

The *revenues* and *expenditures* of governmental-type funds usually do not have the same *cause-and-effect* relationship that exists in a business organization. Instead the expenditures relate to the level of services provided for the citizens, and the revenues are an *independent* means of financing these services. Those who provide resources to a government usually do not receive services from the government in the same proportion. For example, those citizens on welfare receive more benefits from the government than they supply in taxes, and those who pay a large amount of taxes to the government seldom, if ever, receive benefits equal to the resources they have provided. Thus the appropriate measurement focus for governmental-type funds is spending. In the case of proprietary-type funds, however, the level of services provided is a direct function of the revenues provided by the users of the services. As a result, it is necessary to focus on the "profitability" of the fund, or the *maintenance of capital*.

In addition, the timing of the recognition of transactions is different for proprietary-type funds. Since the activities for which such funds are used are similar to those of business organizations, revenues and expenses must be recorded in the same fashion. Therefore a different basis of accounting must be used—*full accrual*. Data that can be used to compare the operations of governmental units with those of business organizations providing the same goods or services are thus available.

As we mentioned earlier, the types of funds used to record "business-type" activities are called *proprietary funds*. Within this group are Internal Service Funds and Enterprise Funds. The first two sections of this chapter will discuss each of these.

SECTION I—PROPRIETARY-TYPE FUNDS: INTERNAL SERVICE FUNDS

Description of Fund Activities

A governmental unit will often find that certain goods or services can be supplied by a department or agency to other departments or agencies at a lower cost than if the same function were to be supplied by an outside organization. It is also possible that an internal department or agency can supply these goods or services more conveniently or dependably than a private contractor. Thus the government will establish an **Internal Service Fund** to account for business-type activities of supplying goods or services to departments or agencies within the governmental unit or to other governmental units.

The result is that the government establishes a business operation. The accounting and management procedures followed should be similar to those followed by business organizations outside the governmental unit. Thus the users of these goods or services should be charged on a cost-reimbursed basis. The amount of the charge should be at least be enough to recover the costs incurred. Therefore it is necessary to measure the full cost of the goods or services.

Internal Service Funds are usually established to account for such activities as central data-processing services, central motor pools, and central inventory and supply functions. Since the purpose of this type of fund is to provide information for a businesslike evaluation of the operations, it is essential that each activity be accounted for by a separate fund.

Many different types of activities require the use of an Internal Service Fund. In this chapter we will limit our discussion to a central motor pool. The operations of this type of service are typical for governmental units and are illustrative of the general operations of Internal Service Funds.

The first step is to acquire capital from the General Fund or some other fund. This money is used to acquire automobiles, trucks, and so forth. As the vehicles are being used, each department is billed based on the miles driven. The revenue from the billing is used to pay the operating costs of the vehicles and, possibly, for their replacement.

Control of Fund Activities

The operations of Internal Service Funds are controlled indirectly by the operating budgets of the funds using the goods or services and directly by means of flexible budgets. Since other funds must pay for the goods or services supplied, the approval of their budgets acts as an indirect control device for the Internal Service Fund.

A **flexible budget** is a budget in which the level of budgeted expenses is related to the level of operations. Thus, in our example of a central motor pool, the allowable gasoline and oil costs will vary directly with the number of miles the vehicles are used. Governmental-type funds, by contrast, operate under a **fixed budget**. Thus, if a department head is given $4,000 for supplies for the year, that amount cannot be exceeded—regardless of the level of operations. In effect, the use of a fixed budget actually sets the limit on the level of operations of the governmental unit.

The difference in budgeting practices between governmental-type funds and Internal Service Funds results from the fact that the revenue generated by the latter will increase as the level of operations increases. Since there is a cause-and-effect relationship between the level of operations and the revenues earned and the expenses incurred, the flexible budget will allow higher levels of expenses at higher levels of operating activity. As previously explained, no such relationship usually exists between revenues and expenditures of governmental-type funds.

Because of the use of flexible operating budgets, we usually do not find the budget recorded in the accounts of Internal Service Funds, nor do we usually find the use of encumbrance accounting for these funds. Since there is no absolute spending limit, the use of encumbrance accounting would not serve any purpose. However, some state or local laws do require the use of encumbrances for Internal Service Funds. Since this is not the general case, we will assume that encumbrance accounting is not used.

The operations of an Internal Service Fund are similar to those of a private business. The users of goods or services are charged a fee based on what is provided. Therefore it is necessary to measure the full costs incurred in providing goods or services. This results in a capital maintenance measurement focus. The extent of the charges will depend on the management philosophy employed. It is possible to set the charges to simply cover the actual cash costs incurred. It is also possible to set the charges to permit the replacement of any fixed assets involved, or to allow for the future expansion of the fund activities.

The use of the capital maintenance approach results in the recording of *all* the costs incurred in providing the goods or services. These include depreciation on fixed assets, an item not found in the governmental-type funds or in the other funds that follow a spending measurement focus. In addition, fixed assets are included on the balance sheet of an Internal Service Fund. Thus the balance sheet and the income statement of an Internal Service Fund will be similar to those of a private business providing the same goods or services.

The **full accrual** basis of accounting is used for Internal Service Funds. Revenues are recognized when they are earned and expenses are recorded when they are incurred in earning the revenues. The use of the capital maintenance measurement focus, together with the full accrual basis of accounting, makes the accounting for Internal Service Funds very similar to that used for commercial enterprises.

Accounting for Fund Activities

Operating entries

For illustrative purposes, let us continue with the example of a central motor pool. Assume that in order to start up the fund, the General Fund makes an equity transfer of $405,000 to the Motor Pool Fund. The entries to record this transfer are:

Entry in the books of the General Fund	Residual equity transfer to Motor Pool Fund	405,000	
	Cash		405,000
	To record transfer to Internal Service Fund for start-up purposes.		
Entry in the books of the Internal Service Fund	Cash	405,000	
	Contributed capital from General Fund		405,000
	To record equity transfer from General Fund.		

Note that the treatment of a residual equity transfer for a propriety-type fund and for a governmental-type fund requires different accounts. Remember that the contributed capital account is part of the equity of the Internal Service Fund.

If the Internal Service Fund acquires a fleet of vehicles for $400,000, the following entry is made:

Automobiles	300,000	
Trucks	100,000	
Cash		400,000
To record the acquisition of vehicles.		

Billings of $60,000 to the various departments for use of the vehicles are recorded as follows:

Entry in the books of the Internal Service Fund	Due from departments	60,000	
	Revenues—vehicle charges		60,000
	To record charges to departments for use of vehicles.		
Entry in the books of a governmental-type fund using the vehicles	Expenditures—vehicle usage	8,000	
	Due to Motor Pool Fund		8,000
	To record the use of vehicles during the period.		

Payments of $58,500 from the departments are recorded as follows:

Entry in the books of the Internal Service Fund	Cash	58,500	
	Due from departments		58,500
	To record payments received from departments using vehicles.		
Entry in the books of a governmental-type fund using the vehicles	Due to Motor Pool Fund	8,000	
	Cash		8,000
	To record payment to Motor Pool Fund.		

The above illustration is used to show how the billings to the departments and the collections are recorded. Note that the entries regarding the departmental usage are limited, for illustrative purposes, to a single department and that the "due to" and "due from" account titles are still used for intergovernmental receivables and payables.

During the year, gasoline, oil, and maintenance expenses totaling $14,000 are incurred. These are recorded in the Internal Service Fund as follows:

Gasoline and oil expense	9,500	
Maintenance expense	4,500	
Cash		10,000
Accounts payable		4,000
To record the gasoline and oil and mainte-nance expense for the period.		

The payment of salaries of $10,000, ignoring withholdings and so forth, is recorded as follows:

Salaries expense	10,000	
Cash		10,000
To record salaries expense.		

If the motor pool rents warehouse space from the government for $3,000 per year, the entry to record the rental will be:

Rent expense	3,000	
Cash		3,000
To record the rent for the year.		

The General Fund will record the receipt of the rent as follows:

<table>
<tr><td>*Entry in*</td><td>Cash</td><td>3,000</td><td></td></tr>
<tr><td>*the books*</td><td>   Revenues—rental</td><td></td><td></td></tr>
<tr><td>*of the*</td><td>   of warehouse space</td><td></td><td>3,000</td></tr>
<tr><td>*General*</td><td>To record the receipt of the rent from the</td><td></td><td></td></tr>
<tr><td>*Fund*</td><td>motor pool.</td><td></td><td></td></tr>
</table>

As previously indicated, depreciation is an expense that is recognized in Internal Service Funds. Assuming the amounts given, the entry to record this for the year is:

Depreciation expense—automobiles	20,000	
Depreciation expense—trucks	10,000	
Accumulated depreciation—		
automobiles		20,000
Accumulated depreciation—trucks		10,000

To record depreciation for the year.

Although additional entries can be made, the above summary journal entries are sufficient to reflect the type of activities engaged in by Internal Service Funds and the recording of the related revenues and expenses.

A trial balance for the Motor Pool Fund at the end of the year is shown in Table 8–1.

TABLE 8–1

City of Newville
Internal Service Fund
Motor Pool Fund
Trial Balance
December 31, 19X1

Cash	$ 40,500	
Due from departments	1,500	
Automobiles	300,000	
Accumulated depreciation—automobiles		$ 20,000
Trucks	100,000	
Accumulated depreciation—trucks		10,000
Accounts payable		4,000
Contributed capital from General Fund		405,000
Revenues—vehicle charges		60,000
Gasoline and oil expense	9,500	
Maintenance expense	4,500	
Salaries expenses	10,000	
Rent expense	3,000	
Depreciation expense—automobiles	20,000	
Depreciation expense—trucks	10,000	
	$499,000	$499,000

Closing entry

The closing process for Internal Service Funds is similar to the one used for commercial enterprises. That is, each of the revenue, expense, and other temporary accounts is closed; and the net operating figure is recorded in Retained earnings. The following entry relates to our illustration:

Revenues—vehicle charges	60,000	
Gasoline and oil expense		9,500
Maintenance expense		4,500
Salaries expense		10,000
Rent expense		3,000
Depreciation expense—automobiles		20,000
Depreciation expense—trucks		10,000
Retained earnings		3,000

To close the revenue and expense accounts
for the period.

Financial statements

The individual financial statements for the Internal Service Funds are a balance sheet; a statement of revenues, expenses, and changes in retained earnings; and a statement of cash flows.[1] These are illustrated for 19X1 in Tables 8–2, 8–3, and 8–4. In addition, you should review the section on Internal Service

TABLE 8–2

City of Newville
Internal Service Fund
Motor Pool Fund
Statement of Revenues, Expenses, and Changes in Retained Earnings
For the Year Ended December 31, 19X1

Operating revenues:		
Vehicle charges		$60,000
Operating expenses:		
Gasoline and oil	$ 9,500	
Maintenance	4,500	
Salaries	10,000	
Rent	3,000	
Depreciation—automobiles	20,000	
Depreciation—trucks	10,000	
Total operating expenses		57,000
Net income		$ 3,000
Retained earnings at beginning of year		-0-
Retained earnings at end of year		$ 3,000

[1] At the time of this writing, the GASB had an *Exposure Draft* proposing a statement of cash flows to replace the previously required statement of changes in financial position. This *Exposure Draft* is the basis for the cash flow discussion in this chapter.

TABLE 8–3

City of Newville
Internal Service Fund
Motor Pool Fund
Balance Sheet
December 31, 19X1

ASSETS
Current assets

Cash	$ 40,500	
Due from departments	1,500	
Total current assets		$ 42,000

Fixed assets

Automobiles (net of accumulated depreciation of $20,000)	$280,000	
Trucks (net of accumulated depreciation of $10,000)	90,000	
Total fixed assets		370,000
Total assets		$412,000

LIABILITIES AND FUND EQUITY
Liabilities
Current liabilities

Accounts payable		$ 4,000

Fund Equity
Contributed capital

Capital contributed by municipality	$405,000	
Retained earnings	3,000	
Total fund equity		408,000
Total liabialities and fund equity		$412,000

Funds in Chapter 3 and compare those financial statements (Tables 3–17, 3–18, and 3–19) with the statements presented below. The overall reporting process is discussed in Chapter 9.

Note that in Table 3–18, depreciation on fixed assets acquired by contributed capital is added back to net income. The effect is that depreciation expense is closed to contributed capital rather than retained earnings. This is permissible (not required) when the assets being depreciated have been acquired though the use of externally restricted grants. Since the resources used to acquire the assets in our illustration came from the governmental unit, this option is not available.

Notice that a classified balance sheet was presented in Table 8–3 above, but not in Table 3–17. The city of Columbus does not use the classified format in its *Comprehensive Annual Financial Report*. This is probably because the classified format is not used for governmental-type funds, nor is it used in the Combined Balance Sheet—All Funds and Account Groups. As a result, the combining balance sheet ties in closer with the combined balance sheet. We have used the classified approach for the statement provided above because we feel it is more informative.

TABLE 8—4

City of Newville*
Internal Service Fund
Motor Pool Fund
Statement of Cash Flows
December 31, 19X1

Cash flows from operating activities:		
Net income	$ 3,000	
Items not requiring cash currently:		
Increase in receivables	(1,500)	
Depreciation	30,000	
Increase in payables	4,000	
Net cash provided by operating activities		$35,500
Cash flows from capital and related financing activities:		
Capital contributed by municipality	405,000	
Acquisition of automobiles and trucks	(400,000)	
Net cash provided by capital and related financing activities		5,000
Net increase in cash		$40,500
Cash at beginning of year		-0-
Cash at end of year		$40,500

*Based on GASB *Exposure Draft* (see Chapter 3).

SECTION II—PROPRIETARY-TYPE FUNDS: ENTERPRISE FUNDS

Description of Fund Activities

An **Enterprise Fund** is used when a governmental unit provides goods or services to consumers who are not part of a government. Although it is possible that other governmental departments, agencies, or other units will use these goods or services, the factor that separates the use of Enterprise Funds from the use of Internal Service Funds is the presence of consumers outside a governmental unit.

While these goods or services are usually financed through user charges, such charges are not mandatory. Enterprise Fund accounting can be used in any instance where the government feels that the calculation of net income can provide information for control of the activities.

The types of operations that normally require the use of an Enterprise Fund are those that perform services usually rendered by public utilities: electricity, natural gas, water, and so on. However, Enterprise Funds are also used for the operations of ports, airports, public swimming pools, golf courses, and so forth. In other words, an Enterprise Fund should be used any time a governmental unit supplies goods or services to outsiders, and the determination of the cost of the operations is relevant for the purpose of pricing or management.

The use of an Enterprise Fund is especially important in those instances where the governmental unit provides an operating subsidy for an activity. By computing the activity's full cost of operations, and comparing these costs with the revenues earned, the extent of the subsidy needed can easily be determined.

The operating cycle of an Enterprise Fund is similar to that of a business organization. That is, goods or services are provided to the consumers, who must pay for them. During the operating period, the fund acquires such assets as supplies, property, and equipment. The cost of using these assets is recorded along with other operating expenses. Revenues from user charges must also be recorded. Thus we have the cause-and-effect relationship mentioned earlier— i.e., the expenses are incurred in order to earn the revenues.

Control of Fund Activities

The operations of an Enterprise Fund are controlled by many different means. Since the functions of this type of activity are to supply goods or services to a general market, there is some control exercised by the consumer. The purchase or nonpurchase of a particular service is true "marketplace control." However, since many Enterprise Funds are public utilities, they have **monopoly operating rights**. In many cases, therefore, no competitive goods or services are available. Control must be achieved through the governing boards that determine the rates the utility can charge. These boards use outside consultants and operating data extensively to determine reasonable service charges. In these cases, accounting data are invaluable for measuring the results of operations.

Flexible budgets are used for the measurement and control of operations in Enterprise Funds in the same manner that they are used in Internal Service Funds. Thus we have an additional element of control. Since the use of flexible budgets precludes the recording of the budget in the accounts, the direct spending control we found in the General Fund is not present in Enterprise Funds. In addition, because of the lack of absolute spending control, encumbrance accounting is not generally used for Enterprise Funds.

Still another method of control lies in the budgets of those funds who use the goods or services provided by the fund. While this is an indirect method of control, it is still effective, especially for those funds that follow a spending measurement focus.

The *capital maintenance* measurement focus is used in Enterprise Fund accounting because of the need to determine the full cost of operations. Thus, as with Internal Service Funds, we have abandoned the spending measurement focus for a much more comprehensive approach. The capital maintenance focus results in the computation of expenses (including depreciation) and revenues, which are recorded under the *accrual* basis of accounting. Therefore we will record revenues when earned and expenses when incurred in the earning of the revenues. Because of the use of these procedures, the financial statements for Enterprise Funds include all the assets used in the operations of the funds: liquid assets (cash, receivables, inventory, and so on) and fixed assets (property, plant, and equipment). In addition, both current and long-term liabilities are carried on the balance sheet.

Accounting for Fund Activities

Operating entries

For illustrative purposes, assume the city of Newville owns and operates a yacht harbor. A trial balance for the yacht harbor is presented in Table 8–5.

If 19X1 billings to the boat owners for the use of the harbor and boating facilities totaled $750,000, and $5,000 of that amount is for services rendered to the city, the following entry would be made:

Accounts receivable	745,000	
Due from General Fund	5,000	
Revenue from habor and boating rentals		750,000

To record revenue for the year.

Collections during the year total $740,000, of which $5,000 is from the General Fund. These are recorded as follows:

Cash	740,000	
Accounts receivable		735,000
Due from General Fund		5,000

To record collections from customers.

TABLE 8–5

City of Newville
Enterprise Fund
Municipal Yacht Harbor Fund
Trial Balance
December 31, 19X0

	Debit	Credit
Cash	$ 24,000	
Accounts receivable	16,000	
Supplies	6,000	
Restricted assets	144,000	
Land	500,000	
Equipment	500,000	
Accumulated depreciation—equipment		$ 95,000
Buildings	1,500,000	
Accumulated depreciation—buildings		500,000
Accounts payable		18,000
Revenue bonds payable		1,000,000
Contributions from municipality		500,000
Retained earnings reserved for restricted assets		144,000
Unreserved retained earnings		433,000
	$2,690,000	$2,690,000

The appropriate entries in the books of the General Fund for these two events are:

Expenditures—boat facilities	5,000	
Due to Municipal Yacht Harbor Fund		5,000
To record cost of boat facilities for 19X1.		
Due to Municipal Yacht Harbor Fund	5,000	
Cash		5,000
To record payment made to Municipal Yacht Harbor Fund.		

Operating expenses (exclusive of depreciation) total $500,000. Of this amount, $50,000 is paid in cash and the remainder is on credit. The entry to record this information is:

General operating expenses	500,000	
Cash		50,000
Accounts payable		450,000
To record operating expenses for 19X1.		

The above expenses do not include depreciation. Since we are accumulating the full cost of operating the yacht harbor, depreciation must be recorded. Assuming the appropriate amounts are as indicated in the entry, the following is recorded:

Depreciation expense—equipment	15,000	
Depreciation expense—buildings	50,000	
Accumulated depreciation—equipment		15,000
Accumulated depreciation—buildings		50,000
To record depreciation for 19X1.		

Payments to creditors total $435,000 during the year. These payments are recorded as follows:

Accounts payable	435,000	
Cash		435,000
To record payments on accounts payable.		

The account generally used to record the long-term debt is called **Revenue bonds payable**. Revenue bonds are debt securities that are serviced by the revenues generated by the utility. The entry to record interest of $100,000 for the current year on the long-term debt is:

Interest expense	100,000	
Cash		100,000
To record bond interest for the year.		

Here it is assumed the bond interest is all paid in cash—i.e., $50,000 is payable on June 30 and December 31 of each year. If the interest is not due at the end of the year, a proportionate amount is still recorded as an expense. When this happens, however, Interest payable is credited. For simplicity's sake we have assumed the interest payments on the revenue bonds do not require the use of restricted assets.

Note the treatment of the accrued interest under the accrual basis as opposed to that followed by the modified accrual basis used in the Debt Service Funds. In most governmental-type funds, interest is not recorded until it legally matures and becomes payable.

Assume that during the year the harbor management begins a policy of requiring a $50 deposit from each customer. This policy is designed to reduce the losses suffered in prior years due to customers leaving the city and not paying their bills. Since these assets are owned by the customers, they must be recorded in a restricted asset account. The offsetting liability is Customers' deposits. If $20,000 is collected, the actual entry appears as follows:

Restricted assets	20,000	
Customers' deposits		20,000

To record amounts received for customers' deposits.

Also assume that in addition to requiring deposits, management establishes a provision for uncollectible accounts. The proper amount for 19X1 is $5,000. This is recorded as follows:

Uncollectible accounts expense	5,000	
Estimated uncollectible accounts		5,000

To record the estimated uncollectible accounts at December 31, 19X1.

The Estimated uncollectible accounts account is reported as a deduction from Accounts receivable on the balance sheet. The Uncollectible accounts expense is reported on the operating statement. Notice the treatment afforded uncollectible accounts for proprietary-type funds as opposed to that used for governmental-type funds. Remember that in governmental-type funds, the provision for uncollectible accounts is treated as a direct reduction from revenue rather than as an expenditure.

The Restricted assets account represents the amounts the utility is required to set aside each year according to regulatory requirements, bond indentures, customer deposit agreements, and so forth. Although these amounts should be identified in more detail (see Table 3–14), we will use one account for simplicity. In addition, with the exception of customers' deposits, we will assume that no special liabilities exist at the balance sheet date that will require the use of restricted assets.

Refer to the trial balance in Table 8–6. Notice that the total of the Restricted assets ($144,000) less the liabilities payable with restricted assets ($-0-) is equal to the Retained earnings reserved for restricted assets ($144,000). This equality must be maintained. At the end of each period, therefore, the reserve must be adjusted to the difference between any restricted assets and the liabilities payable from the restricted assets.

In this illustration we have assumed that the only restricted assets and related liabilities to change was the cutomers' deposits. Since that amount is offset by the liability account, there is no need to change the reserve amount.

In summary, Retained earnings is reserved to reflect the restricted use of the assets. In each case these simplifying assumptions are made to keep the illustration at an elementary level. Regulatory requirements often result in control over the number and type of accounts a utility can use. In addition, the method of accounting for particular events often differs from traditional commercial accounting procedures. We have eliminated these factors because of the introductory nature of this textbook.

The balance sheet illustrated in Chapter 3 for an Enterprise Fund in New Orleans (Table 3–14) includes Restricted assets of $99,205,712 from various sources. These consist of cash, investments, and accounts receivable. The Liabilities payable from these assets total $16,202,312. Thus a reserve of $83,003,400 is required. Notice that the reserves in the fund equity section of the balance sheet far exceed that amount. This means that the Sewer and Water Board has reserved retained earnings in excess of the amount required only for the restricted assets.

During the year the fund used $3,000 of supplies. The entry to record this is:

Supplies expense	3,000	
Supplies		3,000

To record supplies used during 19X1.

Although additional entries can be made, the above summary journal entries reflect the type of activities and the recording of revenues and expenses normally incurred by Enterprise Funds.

A trial balance for the Municipal Yacht Harbor Fund at December 31, 19X1, is presented in Table 8–6.

TABLE 8—6

City of Newville
Enterprise Fund
Municipal Yacht Harbor Fund
Trial Balance
December 31, 19X1

	Debit	Credit
Cash	$ 179,000	
Accounts receivable	26,000	
Estimated uncollectible accounts		$ 5,000
Supplies	3,000	
Restricted assets	164,000	
Land	500,000	
Equipment	500,000	
Accumulated depreciation—equipment		110,000
Buildings	1,500,000	
Accumulated depreciation—buildings		550,000
Accounts payable		33,000
Customers' deposits		20,000
Revenue bonds payable		1,000,000
Contributions from municipality		500,000
Retained earnings reserved for restricted assets		144,000
Unreserved retained earnings		433,000
Revenue from harbor and boating rentals		750,000
General operating expenses	500,000	
Depreciation expense—equipment	15,000	
Depreciation expense—buildings	50,00	
Interest expense	100,000	
Uncollectible accounts expense	5,000	
Supplies expense	3,000	
	$3,545,000	$3,545,000

Closing entry

The closing process for Enterprise Funds involves transferring the balances of the revenues, expenses, and other temporary accounts to Unreserved retained earnings. The appropriate entry, using the data given in the example, is:

Revenue from harbor and boating rentals	750,000	
General operating expenses		500,000
Depreciation expense—equipment		15,000
Depreciation expense—buildings		50,000
Interest expense		100,000
Uncollectible accounts expense		5,000
Supplies expense		3,000
Unreserved retained earnings		77,000

To close the revenue and expense accounts for the period.

Financial statements

The individual financial statements for Enterprise Funds are a balance sheet; a statement of revenues, expenses, and changes in retained earnings; and a cash flow statement. These are illustrated for 19X1 in Tables 8–7, 8–8, and 8–9. In addition, you should review the section on Enterprise Funds in Chapter 3 and compare those financial statements (Tables 3–14, 3–15, and 3–16) with the statements presented in Table 8–7, 8–8, and 8–9. The overall reporting process is discussed in Chapter 9.

TABLE 8–7

City of Newville
Enterprise Fund
Municipal Yacht Harbor Fund
Balance Sheet
December 31, 19X1

ASSETS		
Current Assets		
Cash	$179,000	
Accounts receivable (net of estimated		
uncollectible accounts of $5,000)	21,000	
Supplies	3,000	
Total current assets		$ 203,000
Restricted Assets		164,000
Fixed Assets		
Land	$500,000	
Equipment (net of accumulated		
depreciation of $110,000)	390,000	
Buildings (net of accumulated		
depreciation of $110,000)	950,000	
Total fixed assets		$1,840,000
Total assets		$2,207,000
LIABILITIES AND FUND EQUITY		
Liabilities		
Current liabilities		
Accounts payable		$ 33,000
Liabilities payable from restricted assets		
Customers' deposits		20,000
Long-term liabilities		
Revenue bonds payable		1,000,000
Total liabilities		$1,053,000
Fund Equity		
Contributed capital		
Contributions from municipality	$500,000	
Retained earnings		
Reserved for restricted assets	144,000	
Unreserved retained earnings	510,000	
Total fund equity		1,154,000
Total liabilities and fund equity		2,207,000

TABLE 8–8

City of Newville
Enterprise Fund
Municipal Yacht Harbor Fund
Statement of Revenues, Expenses, and Changes in Retained Earnings
For the Year Ended December 31, 19X1

Operating revenues:		
Harbor and boating rentals		$750,000
Operating expenses:		
General operating expenses	$500,000	
Depreciation expense—equipment	15,000	
Depreciation expense—buildings	50,000	
Uncollectible accounts expense	5,000	
Supplies expense	3,000	
Total operating expenses		573,000
Operating income		$177,000
Nonoperating expense:		
Interest expense		100,000
Net income		$ 77,000
Retained earnings at beginning of year		577,000
Retained earnings at end of year		$654,000

TABLE 8–9

City of Newville*
Enterprise Fund
Municipal Yacht Harbor Fund
Statement of Cash Flows
For the Year Ended December 31, 19X1

Cash flows from operating activities:		
Net income	$77,000	
Items not requiring cash currently:		
Increase in receivables	(5,000)	
Decrease in supplies	3,000	
Depreciation	65,000	
Increase in payables	15,000	
Net cash provided by operating activities		$155,000
Net increase in cash		$155,000
Cash at beginning of year		24,000
Cash at end of year		$179,000

*Based on GASB *Exposure Draft* (see Chapter 3).

Use of Special Assessments for Services

In Chapter 7 we discussed the accounting for special assessments for ser-vice-type activities where a General Fund or Special Revenue Fund was used. If the governmental unit wishes to charge a full-cost price for the services to determine the "true" subsidy provided to the citizens, an Enterprise Fund should be used to account for the service. This is because the accrual basis of accounting is used, including a calculation of a charge for depreciation.

The use of an Enterprise Fund for these types of service activities that are financed with special assessments results in entries similar to those previously presented in this chapter. The only major change is that the term *special assess-ment* is generally used to describe the receivable for the charge.

SECTION III—FIDUCIARY-TYPE FUNDS: NONEXPENDABLE TRUST FUNDS

Description of Fund Activities

A **Nonexpendable Trust Fund** is used to account for the portions of the resources held by a governmental unit, in a trustee capacity, that must be main-tained intact—i.e., cannot be spent. This is usually the principal amount of a trust. In Chapter 7 we discussed the use of an Expendable Trust Fund to account for the portion of the trust principal and income that can be spent by the governmental unit. We will now concentrate on the portion that is *not* spend-able.

The same laws that govern the expendable portion of a trust have provi-sions for the nonexpendable portion. Therefore we must look to the particular trust agreement, and to the applicable state and local laws, for guidance as to the definition of income and principal, permissible investment activity, and so forth.

The receipt of the principal from the donor provides resources (cash or investments) to the governmental unit. If not already in investment form, these amounts are invested according to the provisions of the *trust agreement*. As income is received, it is recorded in the Nonexpendable Trust Fund. If the government has the authority to spend it, the income is transferred to an Ex-pendable Trust Fund. The other type of activity usually found in a Nonexpend-able Trust Fund is the buying and selling of investments in order to earn an additional return on the principal.

In some instances a nonexpendable trust will receive rental or business property as a donation. The operations of such a business will be accounted for in the same manner as a commercial-type operation. In this section we will limit our discussion to those instances where the income earned is from investments.

Control of Fund Activities

The operations of all trust funds are controlled through applicable state laws and the provisions of individual trust agreements. Thus the accounting system must be designed to provide information and reports that permit a review of this stewardship role from an accounting and legal perspective. Unless legally required, the budget is not formally integrated into the accounting system.

The capital maintenance measurement focus is used for Nonexpendable Trust Funds. In addition, the full accrual basis of accounting is followed. Thus the basic accounting principles of Nonexpendable Trust Funds are similar to those of propriety-type funds.

General Accounting Procedures

Operating entries

To illustrate the activities of a Nonexpendable Trust Fund, let us continue the example used in Chapter 7 for Expendable Trust Funds. As you will recall, a prominent citizen gave $5 million to the governmental unit for the establishment of an Educational Principal Trust Fund, the earnings of which were to go to an Educational Income Trust Fund that would be used to provide educational assistance for governmental employees. The receipt of the funds is recorded in the Nonexpendable Trust Fund as follows:

Cash	5,000,000	
Fund balance		5,000,000
To record the receipt of cash for the establishment of an Educational Principal Trust Fund.		

To generate income, the money is invested in securities. This is recorded as follows:

Marketable securities	5,000,000	
Cash		5,000,000
To record the purchase of marketable securities.		

The entry to record $250,000 of investment earnings, of which $200,000 is received in cash during the first six months of the year, is as follows:

Cash	200,000	
Interest receivable	50,000	
Revenues—investments		250,000
To record the income earned during the first six months of the year		

The entries to record the amount owed to the operating fund and the actual transfer of $200,000 are as follows:

Operating transfers to Educational Income Trust Fund	250,000	
Due to Educational Income Trust Fund		250,000
To record the amount owed to the operating fund.		

| Due to Educational Income Trust Fund | 200,000 | |
| Cash | | 200,000 |

To record the payment of part of the amount
owed to the operating fund.

Since the effect of the transactions involving the operating fund (Educational Income Trust Fund) has already been illustrated, the transactions will not be reproduced in this chapter. For a review of the operating funds, see Chapter 7.

Assume that investments that cost $140,000 are sold at a gain of $15,000. The entry to record this is as follows:

Cash	155,000	
Marketable securities		140,000
Fund balance—gain on sale of		
investments		15,000

To record sale of investments.

Note how the sale is recorded. The total of the receipts is debited to Cash; the cost of the investments is credited to Marketable securities; and the difference, a credit, is recorded as Fund balance—gain on sale of investments. The treatment of gains (or losses) may vary under some circumstances. Whether gains or losses are treated as part of the income of the trust or part of the principal is dependent on the trust agreement. If no mention is made of how income is defined, the applicable local and state laws should be followed. In the above example, we assume that all gains become part of the principal, since this is the usual case. If the amount of the gain is *not* part of the principal, the gain would be recorded in a revenue account and the following entry is also recorded:

Operating transfers to Educational Income		
Trust Fund	15,000	
Due to Educational Income Trust Fund		15,000

To record amount owed to the operating
fund.

Assume that the total cash collected from investment earnings in the last half of the year is $250,000, of which $50,000 is earnings previously recorded but not received (see earlier entry). The entry to record this is as follows:

Cash	250,000	
Interest receivable		50,000
Revenues—investments		200,000

To record the collection of a portion of the
investment income earned in the second half
of the year and the investment income
earned but not received in the first half of the
year.

If additional investment earnings of $40,000 for the last half of the year are accrued, the entry will be:

| Interest receivable | 40,000 | |
| Revenues—investments | | 40,000 |

To record investment income earned but not
received in the last half of the year.

The entries necessary to record the amounts owed to the operating fund (Educational Income Trust Fund) and the actual transfer of $245,000 are:

| Operating transfers to Educational Income Trust Fund | 240,000 | |
| Due to Educational Income Trust Fund | | 240,000 |

To record the amount owed to the operating
fund.

| Due to Educational Income Trust Fund | 245,000 | |
| Cash | | 245,000 |

To record the amount transferred to the operating fund.

A trial balance for the fund at the end of the year is shown in Table 8–10.

TABLE 8–10

City of Newville
Nonexpendable Trust Fund
Educational Principal Trust Fund
Trial Balance
December 31, 19X1

	Debit	Credit
Cash	$ 160,000	
Marketable securities	4,860,000	
Interest receivable	40,000	
Due to Educational Income Trust Fund		$ 45,000
Fund balance		5,000,000
Revenues—investments		490,000
Fund balance—gain on sale of investments		15,000
Operating transfers to Educational Income Trust Fund	490,000	
	$5,550,000	$5,550,000

Closing entry

At the end of the accounting period, December 31, 19X1, the following entry will be necessary to close the books:

Revenues—investments	490,000	
Fund balance—gain on sale of investments	15,000	
Operating transfers to Educational Income Trust Fund		490,000
Fund balance		15,000

To close the revenue and transfer accounts to fund balance.

Financial statements

The individual financial statements for Nonexpendable Trust Funds are a balance sheet; a statement of revenues, expenses, and changes in fund balance; and a statement of cash flows. These are illustrated for 19X1 in Tables 8–11, 8–12, and 8–13. In addition, you should review the section on Nonexpendable Trust Funds in Chapter 3 and compare those financial statements (Tables 3–21, 3–25, and 3–28) with these statements. The overall reporting process is discussed in Chapter 9.

TABLE 8–11

City of Newville
Nonexpendable Trust Fund
Educational Principal Trust Fund
Statement of Revenues, Expenses, and Changes in Fund Balance
For the Year ended December 31, 19X1

Revenues:	
Investment revenue	$ 490,000
Operating income	$ 490,000
Operating transfer to Educational Income Trust Fund	490,000
Net income	$ -0-
Fund balance at beginning of year	-0-
Principal of gift received during year	5,000,000
Gain on sale of investments	15,000
Fund balance at end of year	$5,015,000

TABLE 8–12

City of Newville
Nonexpendable Trust Fund
Educational Principal Trust Fund
Balance Sheet
December 31, 19X1

ASSETS		
Cash	$ 160,000	
Interest receivable	40,000	
Marketable securities	4,860,000	
Total assets		$5,060,000
LIABILITIES AND FUND BALANCE		
Liabilities		
Due to Educational Income Trust Fund		$ 45,000
Fund balance		5,015,000
		$5,060,000

TABLE 8–13

City of Newville*
Nonexpendable Trust Fund
Educational Principal Trust Fund
Statement of Cash Flows
For the Year Ended December 31, 19X1

Cash flows from operating activities:			
Net income		$ -0-	
Items not requiring cash currently:			
Increase in payable		45,000	
Increase in receivable		(40,000)	
Net cash provided by operating activities			$ 5,000
Cash flows from noncapital financing activities:			
Gift received during the year			5,000,000
Cash flows from investing activities:			
Sale of investments		$ 155,000	
Purchase of investments		(5,000,000)	
Net cash used in investing activities			(4,845,000)
Net increase in cash			$ 160,000
Cash at beginning of year			-0-
Cash at end of year			$ 160,000

*Based upon GASB *Exposure Draft* (see Chapter 3).

SECTION IV—FIDUCIARY-TYPE FUNDS: PENSION TRUST FUNDS

Description of Fund Activities

Public Employee Retirement Systems (PERS) operated by governmental units are accounted for in **Pension Trust Funds.** These systems provide retirement benefits for governmental employees. The employee groups can be defined as narrowly as the employees of a particular governmental unit, or as broadly as the employees of an entire state. The expenditures (or expenses) associated with the contributions to the pension plans are recorded in the particular funds from which the employees are paid. Pension Trust Funds are used to account for the resources accumulated in the PERS and the payment of retirement benefits.

The normal activities of a PERS include the accumulation of direct contributions made by the governmental units or withholdings from the salaries of their employees or both. Some of the activities that were previously discussed for Nonexpendable Trust Funds are also performed by Pension Trust Funds. These activities include the investment of assets to generate a return in the form of interest or dividends or income from business activities. One unique activity is the making of periodic payments to those employees who have retired from the system.

Control of Fund Activities

Operating control of a PERS is achieved through the various laws of local, state, and federal governments. These laws cover the operations of retirement systems in general and PERS in particular. They vary in scope, ranging from laws that limit the types of investments that can be made with fund assets to laws that require specified periods of service before employees can qualify for pension benefits.

As a result of the extensive legal involvement with Pension Trust Funds, their accounting systems and financial reports must be designed to provide the information necessary to satisfy generally accepted accounting principles and to comply with the various legal requirements. In addition, the system must be designed to measure the capital maintenance aspects of the operations of the fund based on the full accrual basis of accounting. Encumbrance accounting generally is not used.

Accounting for Fund Activities

Operating entries[2]

For illustrative purposes, assume that the city of Newville has had a PERS in operation for several years. The PERS trial balance as of December 31, 19X0, is presented in Table 8–14.

TABLE 8–14

City of Newville
Pension Trust Fund
Public Employees Retirement System
Trial Balance
December 31, 19X0

	Debits	Credits
Cash	$ 132,000	
Interest receivable	55,000	
Investments	5,500,000	
Accounts payable		$ 75,000
Actuarial present value of projected benefits payable to current retirants and beneficiaries		987,000
Actuarial present value of projected benefits payable to terminated vested participants		269,000
Actuarial present value of credited projected benefits for active employees— member contributions		2,328,000
Actuarial present value of credit projected benefits for active employees—employer- financed portion		2,328,000
Unfunded actuarial present value of credited projected benefits	300,000	
	$5,987,000	$5,987,000

[2] For the current status of pension plan accounting, see footnote 12 in Chapter 3.

Note that Table 8–14 contains five new accounts. These accounts are used to accumulate data regarding the financial status of the fund, based upon the assets valued at cost (or amortized cost), and the liabilities that existed at a particular date. The first of these accounts, **Actuarial present value of projected benefits payable to current retirants and beneficiaries,** represents the present value of amounts payable in the future to individuals who have retired and their beneficiaries, based upon mortality tables and other actuarial and retirement plan assumptions. The second of these accounts, **Actuarial present value of projected benefits payable to terminated vested participants**, represents the present value of amounts payable in the future to individuals who are no longer in the employ of the governmental unit, but have earned pension benefits that are guaranteed to them.

The third and fourth of these accounts, **Actuarial present value of credited projected benefits for active employees** . . . , represents the present value of amounts payable in the future to individuals who are currently working for the government unit and earning additional pension benefits. Notice that this amount is presented in two parts: the amount financed through member (employee) contributions, and the amount financed through contributions of the governmental unit (employer-financed portion).

The final account in the fund equity section, **Unfunded actuarial present value of credited projected benefits**, represents the lack of sufficient net assets (assets — liabilities) in the plan, based upon the benefits prescribed in the plan that have been earned by the employees. If the net assets in the plan exceeded the actuarial present value calculations, the excess (a credit) would be **Net assets available for future benefit credits**.

Some additional key definitions that are important to an understanding of pension accounting are:

Actuarial present value. The value, as of a specified date, of an amount or series of amounts payable or receivable thereafter, with each amount adjusted to reflect (a) the time value of money (through discounts for interest) and (b) the probability of payment (by means of decrements for events such as death, disability, withdrawal, or retirement) between the specified date and the expected date of payment.

Pension benefit obligation. The actuarial present value of credited projected benefits, prorated on service, and discounted at a rate equal to the expected return on present and future plan assets.

Pension obligation. . . . [The] benefits attributable to (a) retirees, beneficiaries, and terminated employees entitled to benefits and (b) current covered employees, as a result of their credited service to date.

Projected benefit obligation. . . . [T]he actuarial present value as of a date of all benefits attributed by the pension benefit formula to employee service rendered prior to that date.

Vested benefits. Benefit rights are vested when employees may retain them, even if they withdraw from active service before normal retirement age.[3]

---

[3] GASB Cod. Sec. Pe6.530.

The definitions above clearly indicate that the computations of the contribution requirements and the balance in the actuarial present value accounts are very complex. They involve estimation of future benefits to be paid to retire employees, based upon salary increases, expected mortality rates, and so on. These amounts are then discounted by the expected earnings rate to determine their present value. Since the exact determination of these amounts is beyond the scope of this text, we will provide these figures in the illustrations and problems without further discussion. In addition, it is important to understand that the coverage of pension accounting and reporting presented in this section is merely an overview, at an introductory level. Coverage in more depth is beyond the scope of this textbook.

The PERS plan illustrated requires equal contributions by the employees and the governmental unit. When the amount of each contribution is determined, $155,000 in this case, the following entry is made:

Due from General Fund	310,000	
Revenues—pension contributions—		
members		155,000
Revenues—pension contributions—		
employer		155,000

To record the amount due from the General
Fund for pension contributions.

Note that the receivable is specifically identified as being from the General Fund. For simplicity, we will assume that the General Fund is the only fund that has employees who participate in the PERS. If any other funds become involved, a separate receivable will be established for each.

Collections from the General Fund of $310,000 are recorded as follows:

Cash	310,000	
Due from General Fund		310,000

To record payment received from the General
Fund.

The entries in the books of the General Fund are (amounts assumed):

Entries in the books of the General Fund

Expenditures—payroll	997,000	
Due to U.S. government		120,000
Due to PERS		155,000
Cash		722,000
To record payroll.		
Expenditures—retirement benefits	155,000	
Due to PERS		155,000
To record retirement contributions.		
Due to PERS	310,000	
Cash		310,000
To record payment to PERS.		

Assume that investment income of $500,000 is received in cash. This amount includes income accrued at the beginning of the year, $55,000. In addition, sales of investments result in a gain of $10,000. The amount collected from these sales is $50,000. These items of investment income are recorded as follows:

Cash	500,000	
Interest receivable		55,000
Revenues—investments		445,000

To record the receipt of income from investments.

Cash	50,000	
Investments		40,000
Revenues—gain on sale of investments		10,000

To record the sale of investments.

When employees retire, an entry is made to transfer the appropriate present value amount from the active employees accounts to the retired employees account. The amount of the transfer is computed in accordance with the pension plan regulations and should be the present value of the future benefits earned by the newly retired employees. Assuming the amount is $57,500, the entry to record this is:

Actuarial present value of credited projected benefits for active employees— member contributions	57,500	
Actuarial present value of credited projected benefits for active employees— employer-financed portion	57,500	
Actuarial present value of projected benefits payable to current retirants and beneficiaries		115,000

To record the retirement of employees.

When the payment of retirement annuities is made to the retired employees, an expense and a liability are recorded. Since both the expense and the liability are recorded on the accrual basis, the timing of the actual cash payment may differ. If they are the same, $230,000, the accounting recognition of these events results in the following entries:

Expenses—retirement annuities	230,000	
Retirement annuities payable		230,000

To record the retirement annuities.

Retirement annuities payable	230,000	
Cash		230,000

To record the payment of retirement annuities.

In some instances the operating costs of PERS are borne by the General Fund and no operating costs appear on the financial statements of the Pension Trust Fund. In our illustration, however, we will assume that the PERS must pay for its share of the accounting and investment management costs. If these costs amount to $20,000, the following entry is made:

Expenses—operating costs	20,000	
Due to General Fund		20,000

To record operating costs for the current year.

This information would be recorded in the General Fund as follows:

Entry in the books of the General Fund

Due from PERS	8,000	
Expenditures—operating costs		8,000

To record reimbursement of operating costs from PERS.

Since we are using full accrual accounting, investment income of $40,000 that has been earned but not received at the end of the year will be recorded as follows:

Interest receivable	40,000	
Revenues—investments		40,000

To record investment income earned but not received.

During the year, the Accounts payable balance was paid and additional operating costs of $15,000 were incurred and will be paid in 19X2. These activities result in the following journal entries:

Accounts payable	35,000	
Cash		35,000

To record payments of liabilities.

Expenses—operating costs	15,000	
Accrued expenses		15,000

To record operating costs.

Excess cash was invested. The total cost of the investments was $722,000. The entry to record this is:

Investments	722,000	
Cash		722,000

To record investments made during the year.

While additional journal entries can be made, the above summary entries are sufficient to reflect the type of activities and the recording of the revenues and expenses normally incurred by the typical PERS.

A trial balance for the fund at the end of the year is shown in Table 8–15.

Closing entries

At the end of the accounting period, several closing/adjusting entries must be made in order to complete the recording of the activities of a Pension Trust Fund. The first entry closes the contributions received during the period into the appropriate projected benefit obligation account:

```
Revenues—pension contributions—members   155,000
Revenues—pension contributions—employer  155,000
    Actuarial present value of credited
      projected benefits for active
      employees—member contributions                   155,000
    Actuarial present value of credited
      projected benefits for active
      employees—employer-financed
      portion                                          155,000
To close the contribution accounts into the ap-
propriate projected benefit obligation accounts.
```

The second entry reduces the pension obligation account by the benefits paid during the year:

```
Actuarial present value of projected
  benefits payable to current retirants
  and beneficiaries                       230,000
    Expenses—retirement annuities                      230,000
To reduce the pension obligation account
by the benefits paid during the year.
```

The third and fourth entries adjust the present value of the pension fund balance accounts (the pension benefit obligation accounts) by the amount of the earnings for the current year included in the present value calculations. The account that reflects the relationship between the net assets of the fund and the present value of the benefits is also adjusted by the difference between the actual earnings of the fund and the amount assumed in the present value calculations. Since the pension fund balance accounts represent the present value of the pension benefits, each must be updated to reflect the increase or decrease during the period. As explained earlier, this involves many complex calculations. For our purposes, the appropriate amounts are presented in the journal entry:

```
Revenues—investments                      485,000
Revenues—gain on sale of investments       10,000
    Expenses—operating costs                            35,000
    Excess of investment revenues over
      operating costs                                  460,000
To close the investing and operating accounts.
```

TABLE 8-15

City of Newville
Pension Trust Fund
Public Employees Retirement System
Trial Balance
December 31, 19X1

	Debits	Credits
Cash	$ 5,000	
Interest receivable	40,000	
Investments	6,182,000	
Due to General Fund		$ 60,000
Accrued expenses		15,000
Actuarial present value of projected benefits payable to current retirants and beneficiaries		1,102,000
Actuarial present value of projected benefits payable to terminated vested participants		269,000
Actuarial present value of credited projected benefits for active employees—member contributions		2,270,500
Actuarial present value of credited projected benefits for active employees—employer-financed portion		2,270,500
Unfunded actuarial present value of credited projected benefits	300,000	
Revenues—pension contributions—members		155,000
Revenues—pension contributions—employer		155,000
Revenues—investments		485,000
Revenues—gain on sale of investments		10,000
Expenses—retirement annuities	230,000	
Expenses—operating costs	35,000	
	$6,792,000	$6,792,000

Excess of investment revenues over operating costs	460,000	
Actuarial present value of projected benefits payable to current retirants and beneficiaries		83,481
Actuarial present value of credited projected benefits payable to terminated vested participants		14,481
Actuarial present value of credited projected benefits for active employees—member contributions		178,889
Actuarial present value of credited projected benefits for active employees—employer-financed portion		178,889
Unfunded actuarial present value of credited projected benefits		4,260

To record the distribution of the net investment earnings over the pension fund balance accounts.

In the above entry, notice that the investment earnings for the year were in excess of the amount needed to update the pension fund balance accounts for their theoretical growth. As a result, the portion of the fund that has not yet been funded had decreased from $300,000 to $295,740 ($300,000 − $4,260).

Financial statements

The individual financial statements for Pension Trust Funds are a balance sheet and a statement of revenues, expenses, and changes in fund balance. These are illustrated for 19X1 in Tables 8–16 and 8–17. In addition, you should review the section on Pension Trust Funds in Chapter 3 and compare those financial statements (Tables 3–20 and 3–24) with the statements presented below. The overall reporting process is discussed in Chapter 9.

TABLE 8–16

City of Newville
Pension Trust Fund
Public Employees Retirement System
Statement of Revenues, Expenses, and Changes in Fund Balance
December 31, 19X1

Operating revenues:		
Member contributions	$155,000	
Employer contribution	155,000	
Investment revenue	485,000	
Gain on sale of investments	10,000	
Total operating revenues		$805,000
Operating expenses:		
Retirement annuities	$230,000	
Operating costs	35,000	
Total operating expenses		265,000
Net income		$ 540,000
Fund balance at beginning of year*		5,612,000
Fund balance at end of year*		$6,152,000

* The composition of the beginning and ending fund balance is as follows:

	Ending Fund Balance	Beginning Fund Balance
Actuarial present value of projected benefits payable to current retirants and beneficiaries	$ 955,481	$ 987,000
Actuarial present value of projected benefits payable to terminated vested participants	283,481	269,000
Actuarial present value of credited projected benefits for active employees— member contributions	2,604,389	2,328,000
Actuarial present value of credited projected benefits for active employees— employer-financed portion	2,604,389	2,328,000
Unfunded actuarial present value of credited projected benefits	(295,740)	(300,000)
Total fund balance	$6,152,000	$5,612,000

TABLE 8–17

City of Newville
Pension Trust Fund
Public Employees Retirement System
Balance Sheet
December 31, 19X1

ASSETS		
Cash	$ 5,000	
Interest receivable	40,000	
Investments	6,182,000	
Total assets		$6,227,000
LIABILITIES		
Due to General Fund	$ 20,000	
Accrued expenses	55,000	
Total liabilities		75,000
Net assets available for benefits		$6,152,000
FUND BALANCE		
Actuarial present value of projected benefits payable to current retirants and beneficiaries	$ 955,481	
Actuarial present value of projected benefits payable to terminated vested participants	283,481	
Actuarial present value of credited projected benefits for active employees:		
Member contributions	2,604,389	
Employer-financed portion	2,604,389	
Total actuarial present value of credited projected benefits		$6,447,740
Unfunded actuarial present value of credited projected benefits		295,740
Total fund balance		$6,152,000

Concluding Comment

The actuarial information in Table 8–17 is required for the individual fund statements of Pension Trust Funds. When these funds are combined with the other funds in the annual report of a governmental unit, a single fund balance account entitled Fund balance reserved for employees' retirement system is used. This makes the reporting of the fund balance consistent among the funds. When this is done, the actuarial information is presented in the notes to the financial statements.[4] This process is described in greater detail in Chapter 9.

The above discussion of pension plan accounting is, by design, an overview. We have described the basic concepts involved in the area of accounting and financial reporting for Pension Trust Funds. Because of the complexities involved in pension plan accounting, the users of the financial statements must be supplied with extensive notes that fully disclose the provisions of the plan together with its actuarial status. These notes should include such information as a description of the plan, actuarial cost method and assumptions, and funding requirements. In addition, schedules are prepared to report such information as the net assets of the plan for the past ten years and the actuarial present value of credited projected benefits for the past ten years.[5]

REVIEW QUESTIONS

Section I

Q8–1   What is the cause-and-effect relationship between the revenues and expenses of a proprietary fund?

Q8–2   Why are the revenues and expenditures of governmental-type funds "independent"?

Q8–3   When should an Internal Service Fund be used?

Q8–4   What is a *flexible budget*?

Q8–5   How does the *fund equity* section of a balance sheet of an Internal Service Fund differ from that of a governmental-type fund?

Q8–6   Why is depreciation recorded as an expense in Internal Service Funds, but not as an expenditure in governmental-type funds?

Section II

Q8–7   What is the difference between an *Enterprise Fund* and an *Internal Service Fund*?

Q8–8   Is there a cause-and-effect relationship between the revenues and expenses of an Enterprise Fund? Explain your answer.

---

[4]NCGA *Statement 6*, p. 9 (GASB Cod. Sec. P20.109).
[5]*Ibid.*, pp. 7-8 (GASB Cod. Sec. Pe6.130-134).

Q8–9   Why is depreciation considered to be an expense for Enterprise Funds?

Q8–10   What are revenue bonds?

Section III

Q8–11   What is the difference between an *expendable trust* and a *nonexpendable trust*?

Q8–12   How are gains and losses on the sale of investments recorded in a Nonexpendable Trust Fund?

Q8–13   Comment on the following statement: "Nonexpendable Trust Funds can only be used by a governmental unit when someone contributes investment securities and the principal must be maintained intact."

Section IV

Q8–14   What is a PERS?

Q8–15   How are the operations of PERS controlled?

Q8–16   Explain the difference, if any, between the following actuarial present value computations:
1. Projected benefits payable to current retirants and beneficiaries
2. Projected benefits payable to terminated vested participants
3. Credited projected benefits for active employees
4. Unfunded actuarial present value of credited projected benefits

Q8–17   What types of financial reporting are usually done for PERS?

EXERCISES

Section I

E8–1   (True or false; if false, why?)
1. There is a direct cause-and-effect relationship between the revenues and expenses of an Internal Service Fund.
2. Internal Service Funds are used to account for activities that involve providing services and/or products to the general public.
3. Internal Service Funds use the modified accrual basis of accounting.
4. All capital received by an Internal Service Fund is credited to the Fund balance account.
5. A flexible budget is used to control Internal Service Funds.
6. The budget is not usually recorded for an Internal Service Fund.
7. Fixed assets used in an Internal Service Fund are reported in the General Fixed Assets Account Group.

8. Depreciation expense is recorded in an Internal Service Fund that uses fixed assets.

9. A net income figure is calculated for Internal Service Funds.

10. Contributed capital for an Internal Service Fund includes the accumulated earnings since the date of establishment of the fund.

E8–2   (Interpreting the operating statement for an Internal Service Fund)
The City of Newville has an operating policy that its Internal Service Funds will operate on a break-even basis—i.e., revenues will equal expenses. Did the Motor Pool Fund illustrated in this chapter operate at the break-even level during 19X1? Explain.

E8–3   (Explanation of the relationship of a fixed asset to depreciation)
Does the cost of the automobiles and trucks in the Motor Pool Fund illustrated in this chapter ever enter into the calculation of income? Explain.

Section II

E8–4   (Closing entries for an Enterprise Fund)
The Municipal Park Fund for the Directory Township had the following preclosing trial balance:

Directory Township
Enterprise Fund
Municipal Park Fund
Preclosing Trial Balance
June 30, 19X1

Cash	$ 500	
Membership dues receivable	200	
Land	10,000	
Equipment	1,000	
Accumulated depreciation—equipment		$ 400
Accounts payable		200
Contribution from municipality		10,000
Retained earnings		800
Revenues from fees		5,000
Salaries expense	4,000	
Depreciation expense—equipment	100	
Utilities expense	400	
Miscellaneous expense	200	
	$16,400	$16,400

REQUIRED: 1. Prepare the closing entry or entries necessary at June 30, 19X1.
2. Did the fund earn a profit during 19X1? How can you tell?

E8–5   (Comparison of accounting for long-term debt and acquisition of fixed assets, using governmental-type funds and an Enterprise Fund)

The town of West End acquired a police car for $9,700 through the General Fund and a truck for $15,000 through an Enterprise Fund. The town also issued $75,000 in long-term debt through a Capital Projects Fund and an Enterprise Fund.

REQUIRED: Prepare the entries necessary to record the above events and label the fund(s) and account group(s) used.

E8–6   (Billings and collections between an Enterprise Fund and the General Fund)
A city used an Enterprise Fund to provide services to the General Fund. A total of $3,000 was billed and collected thirty days later.

REQUIRED: Prepare the journal entries necessary to record the above information and label the fund(s) and account group(s) used.

Section III

E8–7   (True or false; if false, why?)
1. Nonexpendable Trust Funds use a capital maintenance measurement focus for recording events.
2. Nonexpendable Trust Funds use an accrual basis of accounting for recording events.
3. The transfer of income from a Nonexpendable Trust Fund to an Expendable Trust Fund is recorded as a residual equity transfer.
4. Nonexpendable Trust Funds have two fund equity accounts: Contributed capital and Retained earnings.
5. The receipt of a gift by a Nonexpendable Trust Fund is recorded as a direct entry into a contributed capital account.
6. A fixed budget is used to control a Nonexpendable Trust Fund.
7. The gain resulting from a sale of assets held in a Nonexpendable Trust Fund can be considered revenue or a part of fund balance.
8. A statement of cash flows is prepared for a Nonexpendable Trust Fund.
9. A net income figure is calculated for a Nonexpendable Trust Fund.
10. The activities of a Nonexpendable Trust Fund may encompass the operation of a business.

E8–8   (Discussion of alternatives for use of trusts)
You have recently been approached by a wealthy individual who would like to set up a trust for the education of children of deceased police officers. That person has asked you to explain the types of trusts available and make a recommendation. Prepare a written statement regarding your response.

E8–9   (Compare and contrast the accounting of an Expendable Trust Fund with that of a Nonexpendable Trust Fund)

Identify the major similarities and differences between accounting followed by Expendable Trust Funds and Nonexpendable Trust Funds.

Section IV

E8–10   (Definition of terms)
A. Define the following terms as they relate to Pension Trust Funds:
  1. Actuarial present value of projected benefits payable to current retirants and beneficiaries
  2. Actuarial present value of projected benefits payable to terminated vested participants
  3. Actuarial present value of credited projected benefits for active employees
  4. Unfunded actuarial present value of credited projected benefits
  5. Net assets available for future benefit credits
B. Redefine each term in your own words.

E8–11   (Description of net assets and fund balance)
Refer to the trial balance in Table 8–14. Calculate the fund balance and the net assets for the Public Employees Retirement System Fund. Are the two amounts equal. Why, or why not?

E8–12   (Financial reporting for a PERS)
Obtain a copy of a set of financial statements for a PERS and a governmental unit that reports the PERS as part of its Comprehensive Annual Financial Report (CAFR); compare the reporting with that described in the text.

PROBLEMS

Section I

P8–1   (Journal entries and financial statements for an Internal Service Fund)
The following entries and financial statements relate to Thomasville. (Assume a voucher system is used.)

19x1   1. The General Fund made a permanent contribution of capital to the Data Processing Fund (an Internal Service Fund). This fund will provide data processing services to all governmental units for a fee. The initial contribution was $2 million.
  2. The fund paid $1.9 million for a Z109 computer.
  3. Supplies costing $1,500 were purchased on credit.
  4. Bills totaling $650,000 were sent to the various city departments.
  5. Repairs to the computer were made at a cost of $400. A voucher was prepared for that amount.
  6. Collections from the departments for services were $629,000.
  7. Salaries of $180,000 were paid to the employees of the computer center.

8. Vouchers totaling $1,900 were paid.
9. As of the end of the period, $300 of supplies had not been used.
10. Depreciation on the computer was $250,000.
11. The city charged the computer center $2,000 for the rental of office space and $500 for the rental of office equipment for the year. This amount was not paid at the end of the year.
12. Miscellaneous expenses not paid by the end of the year totaled $700. These amounts were owed to businesses outside the governmental unit.

REQUIRED:
1. Prepare the journal entries necessary to record the above information in the Data Processing Fund.
2. Prepare a balance sheet as of December 31, 19X1, and a statement of revenues, expenses, and changes in retained earnings for the Data Processing Fund for 19X1.

P8–2   (Preparing a budget for an Internal Service Fund)
The city of Adolphusville established a Central Computer Service Fund (an Internal Service Fund) during 19X0. The trial balance for the fund after all nominal accounts were closed is presented below:

City of Adolphusville
Internal Service Fund
Central Computer Service Fund
Trial Balance
June 30, 19X1

	Debit	Credit
Cash	$ 7,000	
Due from other funds	38,000	
Supplies	23,000	
Office equipment	75,000	
Accumulated depreciation—office equipment		$ 7,500
Computer	1,385,500	
Accumulated depreciation—computer		76,000
Accounts payable		9,000
Accrued expenses		4,000
Due to Special Revenue Fund		32,000
Advance from Special Revenue Fund		400,000
Contributed capital from municipality		1,000,000
	$1,528,500	$1,528,500

Note: 1.   The advance is due in five annual payments of $80,000, beginning on December 31, 19X1. Simple interest at 8 percent is calculated and due on December 31 of each year. Payment was held up because of a cash shortage. The advance was made on July 1, 19X0. The fund must make both interest payments by June 30, 19X2. In addition, the principal payment due on December 31, 19X1, may be delayed until June 30, 19X2. The extension of terms was agreed to by the city management to allow the fund to get its operations started.
2.   The following operating statement is available for 19X0–X1:

City of Adolphusville
Internal Service Fund
Central Computer Service Fund
Statement of Revenues, Expenses, and Changes in Retained
Earnings
For the Year Ended June 30, 19X1

Operating revenues:		
Billings to departments	$592,300	
Miscellaneous	3,000	
Total revenues		$595,300
Operating expenses:		
Salaries	$350,000	
Supplies	78,000	
Utilities	65,000	
Interest	32,000	
Depreciation—office equipment	7,500	
Depreciation—computer	76,000	
Total expenses		608,500
Operating loss		($ 13,200)
Operating transfers:		
From General Fund		13,200
Net income		$ -0-
Fund balance at beginning of year		-0-
Fund balance at end of year		$ -0-

Additional information:

1. Management of the computer fund expects to bill the departments for 10,000 hours of operating time in fiscal year 19X1–X2.

2. Supplies and utilities will vary directly with the number of hours the computer is used (billed). The computer was used 8,000 hours in fiscal year 19X0–X1.

3. Salaries and depreciation are fixed—i.e., they will not change in fiscal 19X1–X2.

4. Miscellaneous revenues of $5,000 (all cash) are expected in fiscal 19X1–X2.

5. All receivables and payables as of June 30, 19X1, will be collected or paid during the year.

6. Ninety-five percent of the billings during fiscal 19X1 will be collected during that year.

7. The supplies inventory will remain the same dollar amount.

8. Accounts payable and accrued expenses at June 30, 19X2, will be $4,000 and $6,000, respectively.

9. Cash should be $11,000 at June 30, 19X2.

REQUIRED: 1.   Prepare a cash budget for the computer fund for fiscal 19X1–X2. Assume the General Fund will not provide any additional transfers, and all payments on the advance and the interest will be delayed until June 30, 19X2. (Round out all calculations to whole dollars.)

2.   What billing rate should the management of the computer fund charge for fiscal 19X1–X2. (Round your answer to cents.)

P8–3   (Journal entries for several funds and statements for an Internal Service Fund)

The following transactions relate to Pleasant Village for the fiscal year ended June 30, 19X2:

1.   The city established a Central Supplies Fund for the purpose of handling the acquisition and disbursement of supplies. The General Fund made a capital contribution of $60,000 to form the initial capital for the fund.

2.   The General Fund ordered equipment for the police department. The total cost was $34,000.

3.   The Central Supplies Fund purchased supplies for $25,000. This amount will be paid later.

4.   The Debt Service Fund paid $120,000 of interest that had not previously been recorded.

5.   Billings to departments totaled $30,000. These supplies cost $22,000. Record the cost of the supplies as an expense.

6.   A Capital Projects Fund paid a contractor $100,000. The contractor had previously submitted a progress billing for $110,000. The difference between the billing and the amount paid is the retained percentage. The billing was properly recorded when received by the fund.

7.   The Central Supplies Fund acquired office equipment for $2,000. A 90-day note was signed for that amount.

8.   Collections from the departments by the Central Supplies Fund totaled $28,000.

9.   Collections of current special assessments totaled $50,000.

10.   Salaries paid to Central Supplies Fund employees were $20,000.

11.   The police department equipment ordered in number 2 was delivered at a cost of $35,000. The invoice price will be paid later.

12.   Depreciation on the office equipment of the Central Supplies Fund was $400.

13.   Old office furniture used by the governmental unit was scrapped, with no cash received. The furniture originally cost $2,800.

14.   The Central Supplies Fund paid $25,000 to various creditors outside the governmental unit.

REQUIRED: 1.   Prepare all the journal entries necessary to record the above transactions and identify the fund(s) and account group(s) used.

2. Prepare a balance sheet as of June 30, 19X2, and a statement of revenues, expenses, and changes in retained earnings for the Central Supplies Fund for fiscal 19X1–X2.

Section II

P8–4   (Journal entries and financial statements for an Enterprise Fund)
The following transactions relate to New Louie City's Municipal Airport Fund for the fiscal year ended June 30, 19X1:

1. The General Fund made a permanent contribution of $3 million for working capital to start a municipal airport. The city used part of that money, together with the proceeds from a $25 million revenue bond issue, to purchase an airport from a private company. The fair market value of the assets and liabilities were as follows:

Accounts receivable	$ 8,000
Land	21,000,000
Buildings	5,000,000
Equipment	1,800,000
Accounts payable	12,000

The city purchased the airport for the fair market value of its net assets.

2. Airlines were billed $3,700,000 for rental rights to use ticket counters and landing and maintenance space. Of this amount, $3,690,000 is expected to be collectible.
3. Supplies totaling $1,500 were purchased on credit.
4. Collections from airlines totaled $3,680,000.
5. Salaries of $200,000 were paid to airport personnel.
6. Utility bills totaling $100,000 were paid.
7. Notice was received from the Last District Bankruptcy Court. Air Lussa was declared bankrupt. The airport collected only $1,000 on its bill of $5,000.
8. The airport collected $3 million of permanent contributions from the airlines to help finance the operations of the airport.
9. Interest of $2,125,000 was paid to the bondholders.
10. Supplies used during the year totaled $1,200.
11. The General Fund made an advance to the airport of $2 million. This amount must be repaid within five years. Currently, airport management plans to begin repaying the advance in 19X4.
12. A contract was signed with The Construction Company for the new facilities for a total price of $5 million.
13. The airport management invested $2 million in certificates of deposit.
14. The airport management received $315,000 upon redeeming $300,000 of the certificates of deposit mentioned in number 13.

15. The airport purchased additional equipment for $300,000 cash.

16. Interest expense of $500,000 was accrued at the end of the year.

17. Other accrued expenses totaled $50,000.

18. Depreciation was recorded as follows:

Buildings	$500,000
Equipment	180,000

19. Paid $13,000 of Accounts payable.

20. Received $150,000 of interest revenue.

21. Excess cash of $4.3 million was invested in certificates of deposit.

REQUIRED: 1. Prepare the journal entries necessary to record the above transactions in the Municipal Airport Fund.
2. Prepare a trial balance at June 30, 19X1.
3. Prepare a statement of revenues, expenses, and changes in retained earnings for the 19X0–X1 fiscal year and a balance sheet as of June 30, 19X1.

P8–5   (Journal entries for several funds and a statement of revenues, expenses, and changes in retained earnings for an Enterprise Fund)
Following are several transactions for Green Valley Village:

19x1   1. The Electric Fund, an Enterprise Fund that supplies electricity to the city, returned part of the original contribution made by the General Fund. The amount returned was $100,000. The General Fund transferred $500,000 to the Electric Fund ten years ago. At that time, the transfer was treated as a permanent contribution by both funds. No other such payments are planned in the future.

2. Police department salaries of $50,000 were paid. Assume that the salaries were previously encumbered.

3. A Special Revenue Fund collected $64,000 of taxes previously levied against property holders in the city.

4. The Electric Fund mailed bills of $400,000 to the residents.

5. Two years ago, the city began to construct several housing units. Currently the Iberville Street units are under construction. The contractor submitted a progress billing for $300,000. The total contract price was $3 million. Encumbrance accounting is used. Record the progress billing.

6. Salaries paid to Electric Fund employees totaled $130,000.

7. Collections of gas bills were $385,000.

8. The Electric Fund issued $1 million of 2-year notes.

9. To finance the paving of some of the city's streets, $3 million of special assessment bonds were issued.

10. To provide funds for the construction of new housing units on Fifth Street, $4.5 million of general obligation bonds were issued.

11. Operating expenses of the Electric Fund were $150,000. Of this amount, $130,000 was paid in cash.

12. The city was billed for $12,000 for electric service.

13. Depreciation on plant and equipment for the Electric Fund was $50,000.

14. Supplies previously ordered by the General Fund were received. The actual cost was $14,000. The order was encumbered for $15,000.

REQUIRED: 1. Prepare all the journal entries necessary to record the above transactions; identify the fund(s) and account group(s) involved.

2. Prepare a statement of revenues, expenses, and changes in retained earnings for the Electric Fund for 19X1. (Assume that the beginning balance in Retained earnings was $29,870.)

P8–6 (Explanation of basis of accounting and fixed assets for different funds) The accounting system of the municipality of Kemp is organized and operated on a fund basis. Among the types of funds used are a General Fund, a Special Revenue Fund, and an Enterprise Fund.

a. Explain the basic differences in revenue recognition between the accrual basis of accounting and the modified accrual basis of accounting as it relates to governmental accounting.

b. What basis of accounting should be used for each of the following funds?

• General Fund
• Special Revenue Funds
• Enterprise Funds

Why?

c. How should fixed assets and long-term liabilities related to the General Fund and to the Enterprise Fund be accounted for?

(AICPA adapted)

Section III

P8–7 (Journal entries for a Nonexpendable Trust Fund)

Note: This problem is continuation of P7–3 (see p. 268).

REQUIRED: 1. Refer to the transactions presented in P7–3 for the city of Newfonia. Prepare the journal entries necessary to record the transactions in the Nonexpendable Trust Funds. Identify each individual fund used.

2. Prepare a statement of revenues, expenses, and changes in retained earnings and a balance sheet for the First Tire Company Principal Trust Fund.

P8–8 (Journal entries and financial statements for Nonexpendable Trust Fund and an Expendable Trust Fund)

Following are several transactions incurred by Uno City for the George Ferret Memorial funds—a Nonexpendable Trust Fund for the principal of the gift and an Expendable Trust Fund to spend the income from the fund.

19x1
1. Mr. George Ferret gave the city ownership of a small service business that had assets of: Cash, $2,000; Accounts receivable, $5,000; and Furniture and fixtures, $15,000. All liabilities were paid before the gift was made. According to the trust document, the income from the business must be used to provide meals and medical care for the elderly and those without homes.
2. The business billed customers for $236,000.
3. Customer accounts totaling $232,000 were collected.
4. Salaries of business employees totaling $79,000 were paid.
5. Cash of $20,000 was given to the Expendable Trust Fund to provide meals during the Christmas season.
6. Utilities for the business were paid, $2,500.
7. The income fund paid $3,700 for holiday meals.
8. Medical bills were paid for those citizens who could not afford them, $7,500.
9. Materials used in the operation of the business were acquired and paid for, $4,500. These were used as they were acquired.
10. Depreciation on business assets was $3,000.
11. The books for the business were closed, and the amount due the income fund was paid.
12. The Expendable Trust Fund purchased $100,000 of investments.

REQUIRED:
1. Prepare the journal entries necessary to record the above information and identify the fund(s) and account group(s) used.
2. Prepare a statement of revenues, expenses, and changes in retained earnings and a balance sheet for the Nonexpendable Trust Fund.
3. Prepare a statement of revenues, expenditures, and changes in fund balance for the Expendable Trust Fund.

P8–9   (Journal entries for several funds)
Following are several transactions for the Village of Roux for 19X1:
1. A contract was signed with Signet Construction Company to build a bridge across the Green River. The amount of the contract was $10 million. The financing of the project was through a $5 million general obligation bond issue and a $5 million federal grant. Assume that the bonds were issued at face value and the grant was received. The laws of Roux require that the budget be recorded in the accounts.

2. A citizen of Roux donated $1 million of marketable securities to the city to be used as the principal of a nonexpendable trust—the Concert Principal Trust Fund. This fund would be used to generate income that would be spent through the Concert Operating Fund for free concerts for the youth of the city.

3. The Electric Utility Fund sent bills to its customers for $123,000. In addition, the General Fund was billed for $8,000 for the electricity used by the village.

4. Income of $50,000 was received in cash by the Concert Principal Trust Fund. This amount was transferred to the Concert Operating Fund.

5. The Concert Operating Fund spent $10,000 for a concert.

6. The bridge contractor submitted a progress billing of $200,000.

7. The contractor in number 6 was paid the amount billed, less a 10 percent retainage.

8. Investments held by the Concert Principal Trust Fund that cost $50,000 were sold for $60,000. (Assume that all gains become part of principal.)

9. Additional investments were purchased by the Concert Principal Trust Fund for $55,000.

10. The General Fund levied a property tax of $2,000,000. Of this amount, $1,990,000 is expected to be collected.

11. Current special assessments of $150,000 were collected. These assessments paid for street paving.

12. Salaries of $500,000 were paid to the general governmental employees. Omit withholdings and so on, and assume that all were employed by the General Fund. (Salaries are not encumbered.)

13. The electric utility paid its employees $100,000. Omit withholdings and so on.

14. A fire engine ordered earlier in the year was delivered at a total cost of $120,000. When the order was placed, $118,000 was encumbered.

REQUIRED: Prepare all the journal entries necessary to record the above transactions and identify the fund(s) and account group(s) used.

Section IV

P8–10 (Journal entries and statements for a Pension Trust Fund)
The city of Saintsville has had an employee pension fund for several years. The following is a trial balance for the fund at December 31, 19X0, and several transactions that occurred during 19X1:

City of Saintsville
Pension Trust Fund
Employees Retirement Fund
Trial Balance
December 31, 19X0

	Debits	Credits
Cash	$ 52,500	
Investment income receivable	210,000	
Investments	50,575,000	
Accrued expenses		$ 12,000
Actuarial present value of projected benefits payable to current retirants and beneficiaries		20,000,600
Actuarial present value of projected benefits payable to terminated vested participants		8,600,000
Actuarial present value of credited projected benefits for active employees—member contributions		7,850,000
Actuarial present value of credited projected benefits for active employees—employer-financed portion		14,896,600
Unfunded actuarial present value of credited projected benefits	521,700	
	$51,359,200	$51,359,200

19x1
1. Contributions from the General Fund totaled $750,000; included in this amount was $258,750 from the employees and $491,250 from the city.

2. Investments costing $500,000 were purchased.

3. Income earned from investments was $4,800,000. Of this amount, $4,500,000 was in cash. This included the investment income that was accrued at the end of 19X0.

4. Employee retirement benefits of $3,500,000 were paid.

5. Additional investments of $1,100,000 were acquired.

6. Several employees retired during 19X1. The amount that should be transferred to the current accounts—members and employer are $2,088,975 and $3,966,025, respectively.

7. Costs of operating the pension plan were $175,000; of this amount $150,000 was paid in cash and the remainder was accrued expenses. The accrued expenses at the beginning of the year were also paid.

8. Close the contribution revenue accounts to the appropriate fund balance accounts.

9. Close the retirement benefits expense to the appropriate fund balance account.

10. Close the other revenue and expense accounts to the "Excess of investment revenues over operating costs" account.

11. Close the Excess account established in number 10 to the fund balance accounts in the following percentages:

. . . current retirants and beneficiaries	38%
. . . vested participants	17%
. . . member contributions	15%
. . . employer financed portion	29%

Hint: Remember to watch for an adjustment in the "unfunded" account.

REQUIRED:

1. Prepare the journal entries necessary to record the above transaction in the pension fund.

2. Prepare a statement of revenues, expenses, and changes in retained earnings and a balance sheet for the fund.

3. Is this fund in good shape financially? Explain.

P8–11   (Journal entries for several funds)
Following are several transactions for the Village of Sol:

1981

1. Supplies of $15,000 were ordered by the General Fund.

2. Property taxes of $300,000 were assessed through a Special Revenue Fund. Of this amount, $290,000 is expected to be collected.

3. Contributions to the PERS from the General Fund were $150,000. An equal amount was deducted from the salaries of the city workers. Assume that the entire payroll was $1 million and that $200,000 was withheld and recorded as "Due to U.S. Government." The entire amount due was paid to the pension fund.

4. Collections of water bills by the Water Utility Fund were $1,325,000. Of this amount, $100,000 was from the General Fund. Assume that any revenue/expenditure had previously been recorded.

5. The General Fund made its annual payment to a Debt Service Fund, $250,000 of which $200,000 was for principal. Assume that this amount was not encumbered.

6. Interest of $100,000 and principal of $75,000 were paid by a Debt Service Fund. Assume that no previous entries were made for these amounts.

7. Interest of $50,000 was paid by the Electric Utility Fund on outstanding bank loans.

8. A contractor submitted a progress billing of $80,000 on a street-paving project that was financed with special assessments. Of this amount, $72,000 was paid. The remainder is being withheld until

the contract has been completed. Assume the village records all fixed assets.

9. New furniture was received for the mayor's office. The actual cost was $30,000. An encumbrance was set up for $30,000 when the order was placed.

10. Benefits paid to retired employees were $50,000.

11. Property tax receivables totaling $500 were written off as uncollectible in the Special Revenue Fund.

REQUIRED: Prepare all the journal entries necessary to record the above transactions and identify the fund(s) and account group(s) used.

P8–12   (Adjusting and correcting entries for several funds)

With the exception of the following events, the City of Lizabethville's books were maintained according to GAAP. Prepare any necessary adjusting or correcting entries based upon the information given and identify the fund(s) and account group(s) used. The current year is 19X1.

1. Interest of $149,000 had been earned by general obligation bondholders. This amount, together with $21,000 more, would be paid in February 19X2. No entries were made for these amounts.

2. The General Fund paid $200,000 in cash to the PERS for the governmental employees. The city contributed $165,000 of the total. The entry in the PERS to record the receipt was:

Cash	200,000	
Revenues—pension contribution		200,000

3. A general obligation bond issue was sold by a Capital Projects Fund for $3,050,000. The face value of the bonds is $3 million. Local laws permit the fund to use the premium for construction costs. The only entry made for the sale of the bonds was recorded in the Capital Projects Fund as follows:

Cash	3,050,000	
Bonds payable		3,000,000
Premium on bonds payable		50,000

4. The city purchased ten police cars for a total of $200,000. The only entry made for the purchase was recorded in the General Fund as follows:

Automobiles	200,000	
Cash		200,000

5. Revenue bonds with a face value of $8,000,000 were issued by the Municipal Electric Fund, an Enterprise Fund. The entries made for the issuance were recorded as follows:

EF	Cash	8,000,000	
	Proceeds from bond issue		8,000,000
GF	Bonds in Municipal Electric Fund	8,000,000	
	Bonds payable		8,000,000

6. The Last National Bank gave the city $500,000 to establish a trust fund that must be maintained intact. Any income generated by the fund can be spent only for employing college students on a part-time basis. During the year, the fund earned $3,000, of which $2,900 was spent to hire students. The entry for the gift was properly recorded. The remaining events were recorded as follows:

GF	Cash	3,000	
	Revenues from investments		3,000
GF	Expenditures for salaries	2,900	
	Cash		2,900

9

THE GOVERNMENTAL FUND ACCOUNTING CYCLE

The Comprehensive Annual Financial Report and Current Issues

LEARNING OBJECTIVES

After completion of this chapter, you should be able to:

1. Identify the basic components of a comprehensive annual financial report (CAFR)
2. List the combined financial statements included in the CAFR
3. Explain how a "combined" financial statement is constructed
4. Explain the relationships presented in the Financial Reporting Pyramid
5. Explain how notes are used for financial statement reporting
6. Explain the relationship between individual fund financial statements and combining and combined financial statements
7. Identify the statistical tables that are required in a CAFR
8. Explain how accountants define the "reporting entity"
9. Explain the importance of interim financial reporting
10. Explain the purpose of the Certificate of Achievement for Excellence in Financial Reporting
11. Discuss the purpose of single audits and how they differ from traditional audits

In previous chapters we have discussed the process of accumulating financial information for governmental units. This information is communicated to individuals and institutions outside the government, and to some extent inside, through the **Comprehensive Annual Financial Report (CAFR)**. The purpose of the CAFR has been summarized as follows:

> The CAFR is the governmental unit's official annual report and should contain introductory information, schedules necessary to demonstrate compliance with finance-related legal and contractual provisions, and statistical data.[1]

MAJOR COMPONENTS OF THE CAFR

In outline form, the CAFR contains the following major components:

I.   Introductory Section
II. Financial Section
     A. Auditor's Report
     B. General Purpose Financial Statements (Combined Statements—Overview)
     C. Combining and Individual Fund and Account Group Statements and Schedules
III. Statistical Tables

The CAFR begins with an introductory section that includes a table of contents, letters of transmittal, and any other data that the management of the governmental unit feels is important to the reader. The second section of the CAFR is the financial section—the auditor's report, the General Purpose Financial Statements (GPFS), and the combining and individual fund and account group statements and schedules.

The General Purpose Financial Statements consist of the following:

1. Combined balance sheet—all fund types and account groups
2. Combined statement of revenues, expenditures, and changes in fund balances—all governmental fund types
3. Combined statement of revenues, expenditures, and changes in fund balances—budget and actual—general and special revenue fund types (other funds may also be included)
4. Combined statement of revenues, expenses, and changes in retained earnings (or equity)—all proprietary fund types
5. Combined statement of changes in financial position—all proprietary fund types
6. Notes to the financial statements (*Note:* The treatment of trust funds is discussed later in this chapter.)

The preparation of the CAFR is basically an aggregation process, as shown in Exhibit 9–1. The transactions form the basis of the system and then, as the "pyramid" indicates, this information is aggregated into the individual fund financial statements. The individual statements are then aggregated into the combining statements, and those data are aggregated again into the combined

---

[1] NCGA, *Statement 1*, p. 19 (GASB Cod. Sec. 1900.109).

EXHIBIT 9-1   The Financial Reporting "Pyramid"

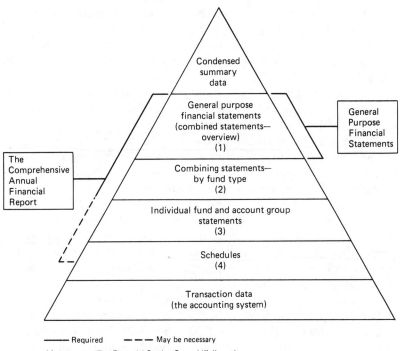

Condensed
summary
data

General purpose
financial statements
(combined statements—
overview)
(1)

General
Purpose
Financial
Statements

The
Comprehensive
Annual
Financial
Report

Combining statements—
by fund type
(2)

Individual fund and account group
statements
(3)

Schedules
(4)

Transaction data
(the accounting system)

———— Required   — — — May be necessary

( ) Refers to "The Financial Section Pyramid" discussion

Source: NCGA, *Statement 1*, p. 20 (GASB Cod. Sec. 1900.114).

financial statements. Since the combined financial statements form the main focus of attention in the CAFR, we will discuss the financial report beginning with these statements.

Previous exhibits in this text were of financial statements that were prepared for the *individual* funds. The issuance of NCGA *Statement 1* in 1979 changed the emphasis of financial reporting from individual fund statements to **combined financial statements**. A CAFR must treat these combined financial statements as the main focus of the report. A combined financial statement, by definition, is a single financial statement, such as a balance sheet, that has a separate column for each fund included (see Exhibit 9–2).

The combined balance sheet—all fund types and account groups for the city of Columbus is a typical combined balance sheet.[2] This statement provides an overview of the balance sheet accounts for the governmental unit. Note that only one column is used for each fund type. The accumulation of the data for each of the individual funds comprising each fund type will be discussed later.

[2]The statement titles used in this chapter are those suggested by the NCGA in *Statement 1*. A careful reading of some of the statements issued by Columbus will disclose slight wording differences from those used in the text. The reader should be aware that there are acceptable alternatives to the wording used in *Statement 1*.

The final column on the *combined balance sheet—all fund types and account groups* is labeled "Total (Memorandum Only)." This particular column is optional but, if included, must be labeled "Memorandum Only." It is the total of each of the balance sheet items for each fund listed. If any interfund transactions are eliminated, this fact must be clearly disclosed. The process of eliminating interfund transactions is not discussed here because it is beyond the scope of this text.

The second financial statement included in the CAFR is the *combined statement of revenues, expenditures, and changes in fund balances—all governmental fund types* (see Exhibit 9–3). Notice that a separate column is used for each fund that uses a spending measurement focus and the modified accrual basis of accounting. Although the city of Columbus combines its Expendable Trust Funds with its governmental-type funds for purposes of this statement, it is possible to report trust activities on a separate combined statement.

The third statement included in the CAFR is the *combined statement of revenues, expenditures, and changes in fund balances—budget and actual—budgetary general and special revenue fund types*. This statement compares the legally adopted budget with the actual data for the General Fund, Special Revenue Fund(s), and any other governmental-type funds that have a legally adopted annual budget. See Exhibit 9–4.

Notice that the total revenues for the General Fund in this statement ($201,365,005) do not agree with the total revenues reported in the previously described statement (Exhibit 9–3: $203,556,942). This is because the budget is prepared on a basis other than the modified accrual basis of accounting used for the *statement of revenues, expenditures, and changes in fund balances—all governmental fund types and expendable trust funds*. To make the budget and actual comparison meaningful, it is necessary to prepare this statement using the same measurement rules that were used to develop the budget. Thus when the budget is prepared on a basis other than that provided by generally accepted accounting principles (GAAP), the numbers will not be the same on both statements. Notice that the same observation is true with respect to the expenditures and other financing sources (uses). Another difference between Exhibits 9–3 and 9–4 is that encumbrances are reported as if they were expenditures on the budget and actual statement (Exhibit 9–4). This procedure is not permitted for the regular operating statement (Exhibit 9–3). However, the inclusion of encumbrances on the budget and actual statement provides a better comparison of these two sets of data.

When the budgetary basis differs from GAAP, it is necessary to disclose this fact in the report and to reconcile GAAP and budget data. Columbus does this in a note to the financial statements (see Exhibit 9–5). An alternative reporting presentation is to add a section to the bottom of the operating statement and include the reconciliation on the face of the statement. Notice that Exhibit 9–5 includes only the reconciliation for the General Fund. The statement in the CAFR prepared for Columbus also included Special Revenue Funds and Budgeted Debt Service Funds. These latter two funds are omitted from the exhibit to simplify the example and to more clearly illustrate the type of comparison that is being made.

EXHIBIT 9–2

Combined Balance Sheet
All Fund Types and Account Groups
City of Columbus, Ohio
December 31, 19X1

	GOVERNMENTAL FUND TYPES				PROPRIETARY FUND TYPES		FIDUCIARY FUND TYPES	ACCOUNT GROUPS		TOTALS (MEMORANDUM ONLY)	
	General	Special Revenue	Debt Service	Capital Projects	Enterprise (Note S)	Internal Service	Expendable Trust and Agency	General Fixed Assets	General Long-Term Obligations	19X1	19X0
ASSETS											
Cash and investments with treasurer—Note C	$24,746,090	14,354,636	16,279,122	63,154,159	78,412,516	2,025,607	21,454,364	—	—	220,426,494	205,863,705
Cash with fiscal and escrow agents—Note L	—	348,094	535,809	—	—	—	18,492,120	—	—	19,376,023	13,241,426
Investments, at cost	—	—	4,592,063	—	—	—	600,820	—	—	5,192,883	4,980,237
Receivables (net of allowances for uncollectibles)—Note D	8,495,775	30,490,903	3,670,501	—	20,639,823	54,955	—	—	—	63,351,957	52,416,738
Due from other: Governments	—	1,196,569	—	522,546	609,280	137,707	—	—	—	2,466,102	14,143,144
Funds—Note E	1,864,336	3,010,885	2,321,672	1,238,856	4,210,826	2,615,863	6,373	—	—	15,268,811	55,851,358
Inventory	—	—	—	—	8,397,658	790,774	—	—	—	9,188,432	7,932,483
Restricted assets: Cash with treasurer and trustee—Note G	—	—	—	—	297,014,517	—	—	—	—	297,014,517	157,690,192
Due from other funds—Note E	—	—	—	—	101,366	—	—	—	—	101,366	
Property, plant and equipment, less accumulated depreciation—Note F	—	—	—	—	791,196,273	5,842,797	144,724	255,555,524	—	1,052,739,318	1,006,531,089
Amount available in debt service funds	—	—	—	—	—	—	—	—	22,837,959	22,837,959	18,652,409
Amount to be provided for retirement of general long-term obligations	—	—	—	—	—	—	—	—	303,029,971	303,029,971	262,256,721
Total assets	$35,106,201	49,401,087	27,399,167	64,915,561	1,200,582,259	11,467,703	40,698,401	255,555,524	325,867,930	2,010,993,833	1,799,559,502

EXHIBIT 9–2 (cont.)

Combined Balance Sheet
All Fund Types and Account Groups
City of Columbus, Ohio

	GOVERNMENTAL FUND TYPES				PROPRIETARY FUND TYPES		FIDUCIARY FUND TYPES	ACCOUNT GROUPS		TOTALS (MEMORANDUM ONLY)	
	General	Special Revenue	Debt Service	Capital Projects	Enterprise (Note S)	Internal Service	Expendable Trust and Agency	General Fixed Assets	General Long-Term Obligations	19X1	19X0
LIABILITIES											
Accounts payable	$ 1,531,789	4,853,479	102	1,520,207	3,474,907	722,448	532	—	—	12,103,464	14,683,484
Customer deposits	—	—	—	—	2,113,164	1,887,952	—	—	—	4,001,116	3,640,241
Due to other:											
Governments	—	18,890,052	—	—	—	—	7,644,197	—	—	26,534,249	24,449,162
Funds—Note E	566,006	1,110,619	3,213,173	1,315,151	4,458,636	61,409	4,597,449	—	—	15,322,443	55,810,508
Other	—	—	—	—	—	—	26,419,398	—	—	26,419,398	19,464,841
Payable from restricted assets:											
Accounts payable	—	—	—	—	4,740,501	—	—	—	—	4,740,501	2,860,713
Due to other funds—Note E	—	—	—	—	47,734	—	—	—	—	47,734	40,850
Accrued interest payable	—	—	—	—	1,147,082	—	—	—	—	1,147,082	1,268,393
Bonds payable—Note G	—	—	—	—	48,300,000	—	—	—	—	48,300,000	48,300,000
Deferred revenue and capital contributions	—	684,006	724,859	—	613	—	—	—	—	1,409,478	2,188,276
Matured bonds payable	—	—	86,000	—	—	—	—	—	—	86,000	140,000
Matured interest payable	—	—	537,074	—	—	—	—	—	—	537,074	505,250
Accrued interest payable	—	—	—	—	10,000,651	—	—	—	—	10,000,651	10,718,964
Accrued liabilities—Note G	10,837,232	2,486,493	—	—	2,948,879	572,505	—	—	44,563,328	61,408,437	59,970,773
Accrued vacation and sick leave—Note G	—	—	—	—	6,518,046	1,540,247	—	—	30,413,602	38,471,895	37,637,550
Notes payable—Note G	—	—	—	3,073,000	1,000,000	2,804,214	—	—	—	6,877,214	67,869,958
Bonds and loan payable—Note G	—	—	—	—	828,345,504	—	—	—	234,531,000	1,062,876,504	809,980,939
Obligations under capitalized leases—Notes G and J	—	—	—	—	—	—	—	—	16,360,000	16,360,000	17,220,000
Total liabilities	12,935,027	28,024,649	4,561,208	5,908,358	913,095,717	7,588,775	38,661,576	—	325,867,930	1,336,643,240	1,176,749,902

EXHIBIT 9–2 (conc.)

Combined Balance Sheet
All Fund Types and Account Groups
City of Columbus, Ohio

	GOVERMENTAL FUND TYPES				PROPRIETARY FUND TYPES		FIDUCIARY FUND TYPES	ACCOUNT GROUPS		TOTALS (MEMORANDUM ONLY)	
	General	Special Revenue	Debt Service	Capital Projects	Enterprise (Note S)	Internal Service	Expendable Trust and Agency	General Fixed Assets	General Long-Term Obligations	19X1	19X0
FUND EQUITY											
Investment in general fixed assets	—	—	—	—	—	—	—	255,555,524	—	255,555,524	243,136,402
Contributed capital	—	—	—	—	119,704,376	2,062,597	—	—	—	121,766,973	119,599,349
Unreserved retained earnings	—	—	—	—	167,782,166	1,816,331	—	—	—	169,598,497	178,195,676
Fund balances (deficit):											
Reserved for encumbrances	6,769,580	30,359,049	1,082,204	12,865,871	—	—	—	—	—	51,076,704	44,814,199
Unreserved, undesignated	15,401,594	(8,982,611)	21,755,755	46,141,332	—	—	2,036,825	—	—	76,352,895	37,063,974
Total retained earnings/ fund balances	22,171,174	21,376,438	22,837,959	59,007,203	167,782,166	1,816,331	2,036,825	—	—	297,028,096	260,073,849
Total fund equity— Note O	22,171,174	21,376,438	22,837,959	59,007,203	287,486,542	3,878,928	2,036,825	255,555,524	—	674,350,593	622,809,600
Commitments and contingencies— Notes F, G, J and T	—	—	—	—	—	—	—	—	—	—	—
Total liabilities and fund equity	$35,106,201	49,401,087	27,399,167	64,915,561	1,200,582,259	11,467,703	40,698,401	255,555,524	325,867,930	2,010,993,833	1,799,559,502

See accompanying notes to the general purpose financial statements.*

*The notes are not included with illustrations. The references are put on the statements only for illustrative purposes.

Source: Adapted from the City of Columbus, Ohio , *Comprehensive Annual Financial Report,* December 31, 19X1.

EXHIBIT 9–3 Combined Statement of Revenues, Expenditures and Changes in Fund Balances
All Governmental Fund Types and Expendable Trust Funds
City of Columbus, Ohio
Year Ended December 31, 19X1

	GOVERNMENTAL FUND TYPES				FIDUCIARY FUND TYPES	TOTALS (MEMORANDUM ONLY)	
	General	Special Revenue	Debt Service	Capital Projects	Expendable Trust	19X1	19X0
Revenues:							
Income taxes—Note M	$134,464,696	—	44,747,650	—	—	179,212,346	165,590,910
Property taxes—Note N	13,416,233	3,306,368	545,889	—	—	17,268,490	16,281,132
Grants and subsidies	177,381	19,653,679	—	1,373,177	—	21,204,237	31,709,143
Investment earnings—Notes C and G	6,234,829	4,911,624	1,871,909	—	225,488	13,243,850	9,288,445
Special assessments	—	—	283,804	—	—	283,804	264,484
Licenses and permits	3,781,463	1,016,109	—	—	—	4,797,572	3,509,220
Shared revenues	18,149,996	12,320,278	—	—	—	30,470,274	28,685,535
Charges for services	4,015,310	10,851,394	—	—	—	14,866,704	12,835,441
Fines and forfeits	8,035,698	224,987	—	—	—	8,260,685	7,643,162
Miscellaneous—Note P	15,281,336	9,737,047	1,311,251	1,242,169	3,493,216	31,065,019	22,928,145
Total revenues	203,556,942	62,021,486	48,760,503	2,615,346	3,718,704	320,672,981	298,735,617
Expenditures:							
Current:							
General government	35,583,610	5,558,079	191,809	—	2,635,502	43,969,000	38,621,161
Public service	22,140,260	14,857,227	2,449,645	—	—	39,447,132	40,913,504
Public safety	111,779,231	221,054	—	—	—	112,000,285	106,580,409
Human services	1,581,875	10,918,839	—	—	—	12,500,714	10,526,206
Development	4,943,998	1,771,962	—	—	—	6,715,960	8,932,388
Health	98,047	15,842,878	—	—	—	15,940,925	14,912,821
Recreation and parks	178,655	21,776,735	—	—	24,265	21,979,655	21,599,691
Capital outlay	4,910,045	3,807,280	110,199	26,457,318	—	35,284,842	30,687,952
Debt service:							
Principal retirement and payment of obligations under capitalized leases	—	—	12,377,048	—	—	12,377,048	12,407,000
Interest and fiscal charges—Note G	—	—	16,852,044	2,672,656	—	19,524,700	13,533,544
Total expenditures	181,215,721	74,754,054	31,980,745	29,129,974	2,659,767	319,740,261	298,714,676
Excess (deficiency) of revenues over expenditures	22,341,221	(12,732,568)	16,779,758	(26,514,628)	1,058,937	932,720	20,941

EXHIBIT 9–3 (conc.)

Combined Statement of Revenues, Expenditures and Changes in Fund Balances
All Governmental Fund Types and Expendable Trust Funds
City of Columbus, Ohio

	GOVERNMENTAL FUND TYPES				FIDUCIARY FUND TYPES	TOTALS (MEMORANDUM ONLY)	
	General	Special Revenue	Debt Service	Capital Projects	Expendable Trust	19X1	19X0
Other financing sources (uses):							
Proceeds of general obligation bonds and notes	—	—	—	56,200,000	—	56,200,000	48,615,000
Proceeds of refunding bonds—Note G	—	—	4,256,000	—	—	4,256,000	—
Operating transfers in—Note Q	5,316,544	21,350,065	3,606,805	5,183,640	—	35,457,054	31,447,655
Operating transfers out—Note Q	(23,310,773)	(6,026,857)	(16,201,013)	(1,499,705)	—	(47,038,348)	(46,027,855)
Payment to refunded bond escrow agent—Note G	—	—	(4,256,000)	—	—	(4,256,000)	—
Total other financing sources (uses)	(17,994,229)	15,323,208	(12,594,208)	59,883,935	—	44,618,706	34,034,800
Excess of revenues and other financing sources over expenditures and other uses	4,346,992	2,590,640	4,185,550	33,369,307	1,058,937	45,551,426	34,055,741
Fund balances at beginning of year, as adjusted—Note B	17,824,182	18,785,798	18,652,409	25,637,896	977,888	81,878,173	47,421,008
Residual equity transfers							401,424
Fund balances at end of year	$22,171,174	21,376,438	22,837,959	59,007,203	2,036,825	127,429,599	81,878,173

See accompanying notes to the general purpose financial statements.*

* Notes not included.

Source: Adapted from the City of Columbus, Ohio, *Comprehensive Annual Financial Report*, December 31, 19X1.

EXHIBIT 9—4

Combined Statement of Revenues, Expenditures, and Changes in Fund Balances—
Budget and Actual—General, Special Revenue, and Budgeted Debt Service Funds—
Budget Basis—Note R
City of Columbus, Ohio
Year ended December 31, 19X1

	GENERAL FUND		
	Revised Budget	Actual	Variance-Favorable (Unfavorable)
Revenues:			
Income taxes	$131,200,000	133,061,273	1,861,273
Property taxes	13,302,800	13,415,070	112,270
Grants and subsidies	177,000	177,381	381
Investment earnings	6,210,000	6,234,829	24,829
Licenses and permits	3,536,000	3,780,593	244,593
Shared revenues	17,703,300	18,149,996	446,696
Charges for services	4,133,300	4,375,666	242,366
Fines and forefeits	7,914,000	8,035,698	121,698
Miscellaneous	14,825,000	14,134,499	(690,501)
Total revenues	199,001,400	201,365,005	2,363,605
Expenditures:			
Current:			
General government	35,659,695	34,658,869	1,000,826
Public service	26,690,590	24,972,403	1,718,187
Public safety	115,030,847	114,282,850	747,997
Human services	1,728,203	1,709,127	19,076
Development	5,371,911	5,047,986	323,925
Health	98,047	98,047	—
Recreation and parks	178,655	178,655	—
Expenditures paid through County Auditor	4,655,000	4,710,209	(55,209)
Total expenditures	189,412,948	185,658,146	3,754,802
Excess (deficiency) of revenues over expenditures	9,588,452	15,706,859	6,118,407
Other financing sources (uses):			
Operating transfers in—Note Q	5,145,000	5,332,190	187,190
Operating transfers out—Note Q	(20,889,112)	(20,751,027)	138,085
Total other (financing sources (uses)	(15,744,112)	(15,418,837)	325,275
Excess (deficiency) of revenues and other financing sources over expenditures and other uses	(6,155,660)	288,022	6,443,682
Fund balances at beginning of year	7,837,419	7,837,419	—
Lapsed encumbrances	1,215,456	1,215,456	—
Residual equity transfer	214,408	214,408	—
Fund balances (deficit) at end of year	$ 3,111,623	9,555,305	6,443,682

Source: Adapted from the City of Columbus, Ohio, *Comprehensive Annual Financial Report,*
December 31, 19X1.

EXHIBIT 9–5   *this note goes w/ Statement on page 334*

Note R—Budget Basis of Accounting

Adjustments necessary to convert the results of operations and fund balances at end of year on the GAAP basis to the budget basis as follows:

	EXCESS (DEFICIENCY) OF REVENUES OVER EXPENDITURES AND OTHER SOURCES (USES)			FUND BALANCES AT END OF YEAR		
	General	Special Revenue	Debt Service	General	Special Revenue	Debt Service
	(in thousands)					
GAAP basis	$ 4,347			22,171		
Increases (decreases):						
From revenues:						
Received in cash during year but already accrued as receivables (GAAP) at December 31, 19X0	8,471			—		
Accrued as receivables at December 31, 19X1, but not recognized in budget	(10,360)			(10,360)		
Deferred at December 31, 19X0, but not recognized in budget	—			—		
Deferred at December 31, 19X1, but recognized in budget	—			—		
From encumbrances:						
Expenditures of amounts encumbered during the year ended December 31, 19X0	10,152			—		
Recognized as expenditures in budget	(13,367)			(13,553)		
From expenditures:						
Accrued as liabilities at December 31, 19X0, recognized as expenditures (GAAP) but not in budget	(11,603)			—		
Accrued at liabilities at December 31, 19X1	12,935			12,935		
Funds not budgeted	—			—		
Other, net	(287)			(1,638)		
Budget basis	$ 288			9,555		

Source: Adapted from the City of Columbus, Ohio, *Comprehensive Annual Financial Report,* December 31, 19X1

The fourth statement included in the CAFR is the *combined statement of revenues, expenses, and changes in retained earnings (equity)—all proprietary fund types*. This is the combined operating statement for those funds using the accrual basis of accounting. As we found on the statements previously discussed, a separate column is used for each type of fund—i.e., Enterprise and Internal Service (see Exhibit 9–6). Notice that Columbus does not include Nonexpendable Trust Funds and Pension Trust Funds on this statement. This is because the city did not have these types of funds.

Whenever the full accrual basis of accounting is used, GAAP require a statement of cash flows.[3] The *combined statement of cash flows—all proprietary fund types* provides this information in the CAFR. If a city had Nonexpendable Trust Funds and Pension Trust Funds, they would be included on this statement. As we mentioned in Chapter 3, this statement provides information on the operating, financing, and investing activities of the funds. Since the preparation of this statement is beyond the scope of this text, we will only mention that it is one of the required statements in the *Comprehensive Annual Financial Report* (see Exhibit 9–7).

At the bottom of each of the financial statements is a notation "See accompanying notes to general purpose financial statements." The purpose of this notation is to remind the reader that important financial information is included in the notes to the statements. Exhibit 9–8 is a reproduction of three pages of the notes from the CAFR of the City of Columbus. The entire Notes section covers thirty-four pages in that city's 19X1 CAFR.

Exhibit 9–8 presents descriptive materials. Note A, "Summary of Significant Accounting Policies," contains a definition of the reporting entity, a description of each of the funds used by the city in its financial report, a definition of modified accrual accounting, and other items (only the first three pages of the note have been reproduced). In general, this note describes the methods and procedures used in the financial accounting system. Other notes provide detailed information on items such as fixed assets, long-term obligations, leases, and retirement plans. While some of this information could be included on the face of the financial statements, it would require so much detail that the major relationships between important items would be obscured.

Thus the notes provide additional information that should be used in analyzing the financial data of the governmental unit. The fact that such information is not included on the financial statements themselves does not mean that it is not useful. These data are an integral part of the financial reporting package, just like the data in the various statements.

Up to this point we have discussed six components of the financial section of the CAFR. These components plus the auditor's report form the General Purpose Financial Statements (GPFS). The GPFS are designed to permit the

---

[3]At the time of this writing, the GASB had an *Exposure Draft* proposing a statement of cash flows to replace the previously required statement of changes in financial position. This *Exposure Draft* is the basis for the cash flow material in this chapter.

EXHIBIT 9–6

Combined Statement of Revenues, Expenses, and
Changes in Retained Earnings—All Proprietary Fund Types
City of Columbus, Ohio
Year ended December 31, 19X1

	PROPRIETARY FUND TYPES		TOTALS (MEMORANDUM ONLY)	
	Enterprise —Note S	Internal Service	19X1	19X0
Operating revenues:				
Charges for services	$153,420,507	18,824,109	172,244,616	155,237,936
Other	654,314	53,498	707,812	1,024,088
Total operating revenues	154,074,821	18,877,607	172,952,428	156,262,024
Operating expenses:				
Personal services	41,245,305	8,321,461	49,566,766	45,704,463
Contractual services	32,149,355	3,325,782	35,475,137	31,859,639
Materials and supplies	10,075,226	5,384,652	15,459,878	23,458,476
Purchased power	3,078,975	—	3,078,975	1,470,146
Coal	3,542,488	—	3,542,488	—
Depreciation	25,633,620	1,712,028	27,345,648	25,786,835
Other	5,599,154	38,725	5,637,879	4,011,380
Total operating expenses	121,324,123	18,782,648	140,106,771	132,290,939
Operating income	32,750,698	94,959	32,845,657	23,971,085
Nonoperating revenues (expenses):				
Interest income	17,968,167	—	17,968,167	10,198,134
Interest expense	(54,842,757)	(337,101)	(55,179,858)	(43,767,469)
Total nonoperating revenues (expenses)	(36,874,590)	(337,101)	(37,211,691)	(33,569,335)
Loss before operating transfers	(4,123,892)	(242,142)	(4,366,034)	(9,598,250)
Operating transfers in— Note H	10,735,294	846,000	11,581,294	14,580,200
Income before extradordinary item	6,611,402	603,858	7,215,260	4,981,950
Extraordinary item Accounting loss on advance refunding—Note G	19,727,097	—	19,727,097	—
Net income (loss)	(13,115,695)	603,858	(12,511,837)	4,981,950
Add depreciation on fixed assets acquired by contributed capital	3,614,456	300,202	3,914,658	4,205,155
Increase (decrease) in retained earnings	(9,501,239)	904,060	(8,597,179)	9,187,105
Retained earnings at beginning of year	177,283,405	912,271	178,195,676	169,008,571
Retained earnings at end of year	$167,782,166	1,816,331	169,598,497	178,195,676

See accompanying notes to the general purpose financial statements.

Source: Adapted from the City of Columbus, Ohio, *Comprehensive Annual Financial Report,* December 31, 19X1.

EXHIBIT 9–7

Combined Statement of
Cash Flows—All Proprietary Fund Types
City of Columbus, Ohio
Year ended December 31, 19X1

	PROPRIETARY FUND TYPES		Total* (Memorandum Only)
	Enterprise —Note S	Internal Service	
Cash flows from operating activities:			
Income before extraordinary items	$ 6,611,402	$ 603,858	$ 7,215,260
Items not requiring cash currently:			
Depreciation	25,633,620	1,712,028	27,345,648
Increase in receivables	(2,041,201)	(5,350)	(2,046,551)
Decrease in due from other governments	1,894,534	387,116	2,281,650
Decrease (increase) in due from other funds	2,776,252	(436,314)	2,339,938
Increase in inventory	(1,227,560)	(28,389)	(1,255,949)
Decrease in accounts payable	(3,325,054)	(426,174)	(3,751,228)
Increase in deferred revenue	613	—	613
Increase in accrued liabilities	497,710	16,217	513,927
Increase (decrease) in accrued vacation and sick leave	154,820	(76,948)	77,872
Net cash provided by operating activities	30,975,136	1,746,044	32,721,180
Cash flows from noncapital financing activities:			
Increase (decrease) in customer deposits	(168,775)	529,650	360,875
Cash flows from capital and related financing activities:			
Net borrowings	364,894,000	398,000	365,292,000
Increase in contributed capital	5,985,245	97,037	6,082,282
Net increase in restricted assets	(125,310,295)	—	(125,310,295)
Acquisition of plant and equipment	(60,304,661)	(830,091)	(61,134,752)
Retirement of notes, bonds, and loans	(192,264,484)	(1,798,744)	(194,063,228)
Net increase in payables from restricted assets	1,765,361	—	1,765,361
Increase in due to other funds	2,531,669	(39,406)	2,492,263
Decrease in accrued interest payable	(718,313)	—	(718,313)
Net cash used for capital and related financing activities	(3,421,478)	(2,173,204)	(5,594,682)
Net increase in cash and cash equivalents	27,384,883	102,490	27,487,373
Cash and cash equivalents at beginning of year	51,027,633	1,923,117	52,950,750
Cash and cash equivalents at end of year	$ 78,412,516	$2,025,607	$ 80,438,123

*The comparative total column was omitted because it is not relevant to this illustration.

Source: Adapted from the City of Columbus, Ohio, Comprehensive Annual Financial Report, December 31, 19X1, Combined Balance Sheet—All Fund Types and Account Groups; and Combined Statement of Changes in Financial Position—All Proprietary Fund Types.

EXHIBIT 9–8

Notes to the General Purpose Financial Statements
City of Columbus, Ohio
December 31, 19X1

Note A—Summary of Significant Accounting Policies

The City of Columbus (the "City") was organized on March 3, 1834, and is a home-rule municipal corporation under the laws of the State of Ohio. The City operates under a Council-Mayor form of government and provides the following services as authorized by its charter: public safety, public services, human services, health, recreation and development.

The accompanying general purpose financial statements comply with the provisions of Governmental Accounting Standards Board (GASB) Codification Section 2100, in that the financial statements include all the organizations, activities, and functions in which the City (the reporting entity) exercises oversight responsibility. Determination of oversight responsibility included consideration of such factors as financial interdependency, selection of governing authority, designation of management, ability to significantly influence operations, and accountability for fiscal matters. Oversight responsibility implies that a governmental unit is dependent on the City and should therefore be reported as part of the City.

Education services are provided by the Columbus City School District (District). Low-rent housing facilities are provided by the Columbus Metropolitan Housing Authority (the "Authority"). Community action programs to prevent and alleviate poverty and its causes are provided, in part, by the Columbus Metropolitan Area Community Action Organization (CMACAO). The District, the Authority, and CMACAO are separate entities from the City with no financial interdependency. All have separately selected governing authorities and separate designations of management. In addition, the City has no ability to significantly influence operations and no accountability over the fiscal matters of these entities. As a result, the City has no oversight responsibility and the District's, the Authority's, and CMACAO's separate financial statements are not included herein.

The accounting policies and financial reporting practices of the City conform to generally accepted accounting principles as applicable to governmental units. The following is a summary of its significant accounting policies:

(a) Basis of Presentation—Fund Accounting

The accounts of the City are organized on the basis of funds or account groups, each of which is considered a separate accounting entity. The operations of each fund are accounted for with a separate set of self-balancing accounts that comprise its assets, liabilities, fund equity, revenues, and expenditures (expenses). The various funds are summarized by type in the general purpose financial statements. The following fund types and account groups are used by the City:

Governmental Funds

General Fund. The General Fund is the general operating fund of the City. It is used to account for all financial resources except those required to be accounted for in another fund.

Special Revenue Funds. Special Revenue Funds are used to account for revenues derived from specific taxes, grants, or other restricted revenue sources. The uses and limitations of each Special Revenue Fund are specified by City ordinances or Federal and State statutes.

EXHIBIT 9–8 (Continued)

Debt Service Funds. Debt Service Funds are used to account for the accumulation of resources for, and the payment of, general long-term debt principal, interest, and related costs.

Capital Project Funds. Capital Project Funds are used to account for financial resources used for the acquisition or construction of major capital facilities (other than those financed by proprietary or trust funds).

Proprietary Funds

Enterprise Funds. Enterprise Funds are used to account for operations that are financed and operated in a manner similar to private business enterprises—where the intent of the governing body is that the costs of providing goods or services to the general public on a continuing basis be financed or recovered primarily through user charges. The City has separate enterprise funds for its water, sewer, electricity, and airport services.

Internal Service Funds. Internal Service Funds are used to account for the financing of goods or services provided by one department or agency to other departments or agencies of the City, generally on a cost-reimbursement basis.

Fiduciary Funds

Trust and Agency Funds. Trust and Agency Funds are used to account for assets held by the City in a trustee capacity or as an agent for individuals, private organizations, other governments, and/or other funds. Assets held for other funds or governments include payroll taxes and other employee witholdings (which are combined into one agency fund for ease of payment) and income taxes and utility charges collected by the City on behalf of other municipalities in the surrounding area. Expendable Trust Funds are accounted for and reported similar to governmental funds. Agency Funds are custodial in nature (assets equal liabilities) and do not involve measurement of results of operations.

Account Groups

General Fixed Assets Account Group. This account group is established to account for fixed assets of the City, other than those accounted for in the proprietary and trust funds.

General Long-Term Obligations Account Group. This account group is established to account for all long-term debt of the City, except that accounted for in the proprietary funds.

(b) Basis of Accounting

The modified accrual basis of accounting is followed by the governmental funds and expendable trust and agency funds. Under the modified accrual basis of accounting, revenues are recorded when susceptible to accrual—i.e., both measurable and available. "Available" means collectible within the current period or soon enough thereafter to be used to pay liabilities of the current period. Expenditures, other than interest on long-term debt which is recorded when due, are recorded when the liability is incurred.

In applying the susceptible to accrual concept to intergovernmental revenues (grants, subsidies, and shared revenues), the legal and contractual requirements of the numerous individual programs are used as guidance. There are, however,

EXHIBIT 9–8 (Continued)

essentially two types of these revenues. In one, monies must be expended on the specific purpose or project before any amounts will be paid to the City; therefore, revenues are recognized based upon the expenditures recorded. In the other, monies are virtually unrestricted as to purpose of expenditure and nearly irrevocable, i.e., revocable only for failure to comply with prescribed compliance requirements, e.g., equal employment opportunity. These resources are reflected as revenues at the time of receipt or earlier if they meet the criterion of availability.

Licenses and permits, shared revenues (which represent a portion of Ohio state taxes and license fees which are returned to the City), fines and forfeits, and miscellaneous revenues are recorded as revenues when received in cash because they are generally not measurable until actually received. Investment earnings are recorded as earned since they are measurable and available. Property taxes levied for collection in 1986 and uncollected at December 31, 1986, are recorded as receivables, net of an allowance for uncollectibles. Property tax revenue is recognized to the extent cash is received during the year and within 60 days thereafter.

Source: Adapted from the City of Columbus, Ohio, *Comprehensive Annual Financial Report,* December 31, 19X1.

governmental unit to supply a complete set of financial statements that have been prepared in conformity with GAAP, without having to provide the user with a complete CAFR. In many instances this "summarized disclosure" is sufficient for certain types of users. Thus the use of GPFS enables the governmental unit to supply financial data that are prepared in compliance with GAAP without having to go to the expense of providing a complete annual report.

The "Combining Financial Statements" section of CAFR includes the **combining financial statements** and, if necessary, the **individual financial statements** for each fund. These statements are the basic support for the combined statements previously discussed. A typical combining balance sheet is shown in Exhibit 9–9. Notice that this is a combining balance sheet for Capital Projects Funds. Notice also that this exhibit is only a part of the entire statement. Since Columbus has forty Capital Projects Funds, the actual statement covers eleven pages in the city's 19X1 CAFR. On this statement, each type of Capital Projects Fund is shown in a separate column. To understand the relationship between the combined and the combining balance sheets, you should trace the amounts included in the Total column from this statement (page 342) to the respective amounts on the combined balance sheet in Exhibit 9–2 (page 329). For example, the total balance of the Cash accounts of all the Capital Projects Funds is $63,154,159 in Exhibit 9–9. Trace this figure to Exhibit 9–2.

A combining statement for each of the types of financial statements identified in the GPFS must be presented in the CAFR. Thus the reader will be able to identify the specific assets, liabilities, revenues, expenditures (or expenses), and so forth, for each fund used by the governmental unit. As a further example of this type of statement, a **partial** *combining statement of revenues and expenses and changes in equity—enterprise funds* is shown in Exhibit 9–10. Trace some of the items in the Total column from this statement (page 343) to Exhibit 9–3. (*Note:* To

EXHIBIT 9–9

City of Columbus, Ohio
Combining Balance Sheet
All Capital Projects Fund
December 31, 19X1

	Express St. & Traffic Control	Storm Sewer Sys. Improv. 75	St. Light & Power Plant	Street & Highway Improvement	Neighborhood Commercial Revitalization	Capitol South Utilities Relocation	Lands & Buildings Note 1-78	Street Lighting Note 1-72	Total
ASSETS									
Cash and investments with treasurer	$277,731	—	—	571,416	12,806	316,009	12,122	551	$63,154,159
Due from other:									
Governments	—	—	—	169,325	—	—	—	—	522,546
Funds	—	—	—	388,281	—	—	—	—	1,238,856
Total assets	$277,731	—	—	1,129,022	12,806	316,009	12,122	551	$64,915,561
LIABILITIES									
Accounts payable	—	—	—	982	—	—	—	—	1,520,207
Due to other funds	—	—	—	—	—	11,534	—	—	1,315,151
Notes payable	—	—	—	—	—	1,700,000	—	—	3,073,000
Total liabilities	—	—	—	982	—	1,711,534	—	—	5,908,358
FUND BALANCES									
Fund balances (deficit):									
Reserved for encumbrances	272,362	—	—	131,200	8,519	177,619	—	551	12,865,871
Unreserved, undesignated	5,369	—	—	996,840	4,287	(1,573,144)	12,122	—	46,141,332
Total fund balances (deficit)	277,731	—	—	1,128,040	12,806	(1,395,525)	12,122	551	59,007,203
Total liabilities and fund balances	$277,731	—	—	1,129,022	12,806	316,009	12,122	551	$64,915,561

Source: Adapted from the City of Columbus, Ohio, *Comprehensive Annual Financial Report*, December 31, 19X1.

EXHIBIT 9–10

City of Columbus, Ohio
Combining Statement of Revenues, Expenditures, and Changes in Fund Balances
All Capital Projects Funds
December 31, 19X1

	Express St. & Traffic Control	Storm Sewer Sys. Imprv. 75	St. Light & Power Plant	Street & Highway Improvement	Neighborhood Commercial Revitalization	Capitol South Utilities Relocation	Lands & Buildings Note1–78	Street Lighting Note 1–72	Total
Revenues:									
Grants and subsidies	$ —	—	—	—	—	—	—	—	$ 1,373,177
Miscellaneous	—	—	—	1,011,567	—	—	—	—	1,242,169
Total revenues	—	—	—	1,011,567	—	—	—	—	2,615,346
Expenditures:									
Capital outlay	—	340,336	148,324	398,437	—	1,475,621	—	88,440	26,457,318
Debt service:									
Interest and fiscal charges	—	—	—	—	28,750	—	—	—	2,672,656
Total expenditures	—	340,336	148,324	398,437	28,750	1,475,621	—	88,440	29,129,974
Excess (deficiency) of revenues over expenditures	—	(340,336)	(148,324)	613,130	(28,750)	(1,475,621)	—	(88,440)	(26,514,628)
Other financing sources (uses):									
Proceeds of general obligation bonds and notes	—	—	—	—	—	—	—	—	56,200,000
Operating transfers in	—	—	—	322,460	28,750	—	—	—	5,183,640
Operating transfers out	(362,722)	—	—	—	—	—	—	—	(1,499,705)
Total other financing sources (uses)	(362,722)	—	—	322,460	28,750	—	—	—	59,883,935
Excess (deficiency) of revenues and other financing sources over expenditures and other uses	(362,722)	(340,336)	(148,324)	935,590	—	(1,475,621)	—	(88,440)	33,369,307
Fund balances (deficit) at beginning of year	640,453	340,336	148,324	192,450	12,806	80,096	12,122	88,989	25,637,896
Fund balances (deficit) at end of year	$277,731	—	—	1,128,040	12,806	(1,395,525)	12,122	551	$59,007,203

Source: Adapted from the City of Columbus, Ohio, *Comprehensive Annual Financial Report, December 31, 19X1.*

provide additional information regarding the detailed operations of each type of fund, the combining statements may be presented in more detail than the combined statements.)

In those instances where it is deemed necessary for fair presentation of the financial data for the governmental unit, individual fund statements are used. These are similar to the statements in Chapter 3 of this text. When presented in the CAFR, these statements usually are presented in more detail than either the combined or the combining financial statements. This is consistent with the concept of expanding the detail of information disclosed as we descend the Financial Reporting Pyramid (see Exhibit 9–1).

A review of Table 3–7 will clearly indicate that the individual operating statement for the Street and Highway Improvement Fund and the information for that fund included in Exhibit 9–10 are on the same level of detail. This is because the city of Columbus did not provide individual fund financial statements in its 19X1 CAFR. Some of the individual fund statements used in this text were prepared from the data provided in the combining statements. The movement away from presenting individual fund financial statements in their annual reports is a trend that most governmental units are following in their financial reporting. This approach is based on the emphasis GAAP place on reporting of the combined financial statements to provide an "overview" of the financial operations and the financial condition of the governmental unit.

The extent to which a governmental unit reports detailed information for each fund—i.e., the extent to which it descends the reporting pyramid into the area marked with the broken line (see Exhibit 9–1)—will depend on the interpretation of **adequate disclosure** by the management of the governmental unit. The overall guideline is that each governmental unit must present enough financial information to reflect (1) the financial position and results of operations of each fund and account group, (2) compliance with legal and contractual requirements of a financial nature, and (3) sufficient disclosure of the financial activities of each fund.[4]

The final section of the Comprehensive Annual Financial Report consists of the **statistical tables**. Fifteen individual tables are recommended:

a. General Governmental Expenditures by Function—Last Ten Fiscal Years
b. General Revenues by Source—Last Ten Fiscal Years
c. Property Tax Levies and Collections—Last Ten Fiscal Years
d. Assessed and Estimated Actual Value of Taxable Property—Last Ten Fiscal Years
e. Property Tax Rates—All Overlapping Governments—Last Ten Fiscal Years
f. Special Assessment Billings and Collections—Last Ten Fiscal Years (if the government is obligated in some manner for related special assessment debt)
g. Ratio of Net General Bonded Debt to Assessed Value and Net Bonded Debt per Capita—Last Ten Fiscal Years
h. Computation of Legal Debt Margin, if not presented in the General Purpose Financial Statements (GPFS)
i. Computation of Overlapping Debt (if not presented in the GPFS)
j. Ratio of Annual Debt Service for General Bonded Debt to Total General Expenditures—Last Ten Fiscal Years

[4]GASB Cod. Sec. 1900.109.

   k. Revenue Bond Coverage—Last Ten Fiscal Years
   l. Demographic Statistics
  m. Property Value, Construction, and Bank Deposits—Last Ten Fiscal Years
  n. Principal Taxpayers
  o. Miscellaneous Statistics[5]

Exhibit 9–11 is an example of General Governmental Expenditures by Function—Last Ten Fiscal Years, and Exhibit 9–12 is an example of General Revenues by Source—Last Ten Fiscal Years reported by the city of Columbus. The purpose of the statistical section of the report is to provide the reader with additional financial, economic, and social information on the governmental unit. While specific tables are recommended, the governmental unit can, where applicable, add any information its management feels will be useful to the reader.

THE REPORTING ENTITY

One of the most significant questions that must be answered regarding governmental financial reporting is that of the scope of the basic reporting unit: the **reporting entity**. Governmental units usually have many commissions, special districts, authorities, and so forth, associated with their operations. For example, several of these subunits for the City of New Orleans are identified in Exhibit 9–13. Generally accepted accounting principles prescribe that all special districts, authorities, and so on over which the governmental unit has the ability to exercise **oversight responsibility** should be included in the financial statements as part of the reporting entity.

Oversight responsibility is determined by an analysis of the relationship between the governmental unit and each subunit. It ". . . implies that a governmental unit is dependent on another and the dependent unit should be reported as a part of the other."[6] To make such a rule operational, the GASB has identified several factors that must be considered for each subunit. (We will refer to these subunits with the generic term "agency.") These are:

1. Financial interdependency
2. Selection of governing authority
3. Designation of management
4. Ability to significantly influence operations
5. Accountability for fiscal matters

In addition to oversight responsibility, management must consider the **scope of public service** offered by an agency and the existence of any **special funding arrangements** with an agency when evaluating the agency for inclusion in the reporting entity. The management of the governmental unit must review these factors and then make a decision as to whether the preponderance of the evidence indicates the agency should or should not be included in the reporting entity.

[5]GASB Cod. Sec. 2800.103.
[6]GASB Cod. Sec. 2100.109.

EXHIBIT 9–11

City of Columbus, Ohio
General Governmental Expenditures by Function*
Last Ten Fiscal Years

Fiscal Year	General Government	Public Service	Public Safety	Human Services	Development	Health	Recreation and Parks	Debt Service†	Capital Outlay	Total
19W2	$18,364,557	$22,846,585	$53,393,727	$13,125,179	$8,138,841	$6,536,846	$11,669,632	$10,883,193	$4,855,011	$149,813,571
19W3	21,172,669	24,696,401	59,566,616	23,656,170	8,691,704	7,225,635	15,889,163	11,800,072	9,485,177	182,183,607
19W4	25,304,666	31,733,513	66,705,385	21,518,862	10,370,190	8,235,769	16,211,954	11,617,767	3,923,602	195,621,708
19W5	26,006,547	29,294,561	76,409,740	27,142,582	10,754,225	9,286,496	17,939,404	14,230,265	4,895,205	215,959,025
19W6	22,684,511	31,852,895	82,781,211	20,692,398	18,765,874	10,336,013	17,093,301	16,809,930	4,764,876	225,781,009
19W7	27,979,361	32,165,520	85,939,134	10,319,136	23,045,273	10,800,156	17,871,359	18,295,713	3,655,159	230,070,811
19W8	31,590,284	32,524,519	94,060,294	10,569,040	16,664,277	11,638,727	17,692,734	19,555,542	5,147,597	239,443,014
19W9	34,228,627	36,432,064	96,514,246	7,379,003	12,177,467	13,844,219	18,591,714	24,120,634	4,784,498	248,072,472
19X0	38,588,668	40,913,504	106,580,409	10,526,206	8,932,388	14,912,821	21,592,888	24,394,400	7,791,872	274,233,156
19X1	41,333,498	39,447,132	112,000,285	12,500,714	6,715,960	15,940,925	21,955,390	29,229,092	8,827,524	287,950,520

* Includes General, Special Revenue, and Debt Service Funds.
† Includes all general obligation debt service other than enterprise.

Source: City of Columbus, Ohio, City Auditor, and City of Columbus, Ohio, *Comprehensive Annual Financial Report*, December 31, 19X1.

EXHIBIT 9–12

City of Columbus, Ohio
General Revenues by Source*
Last Ten Fiscal Years

Fiscal Year	Income Taxes	Property Taxes	Grants and Subsidies	Investment Earnings	Special Assessments	Licenses and Permits	Shared Revenues	Changes for Services	Fines and Forfeits	Miscellaneous	Total
19W2	$62,407,599	$9,487,623	$36,309,204	$6,836,391	$294,293	$1,882,441	$19,923,368	$6,887,165	$5,042,771	$7,887,757	$156,958,612
19W3	69,303,039	10,012,808	52,254,987	8,287,013	396,642	2,125,702	16,738,219	7,643,992	5,110,932	10,877,511	182,750,845
19W4	77,834,255	11,242,571	46,262,482	16,996,884	344,292	2,239,772	19,968,934	11,159,570	5,170,658	13,567,071	204,786,489
19W5	85,018,472	11,946,642	50,348,621	21,284,719	301,564	1,950,391	20,968,716	11,652,872	5,720,832	11,781,512	220,974,341
19W6	89,621,214	12,780,188	49,433,451	23,553,300	355,675	1,967,623	23,056,962	10,645,726	6,149,139	21,634,459	239,197,737
19W7	95,167,647	14,056,811	38,246,341	18,364,265	390,891	2,233,970	23,344,673	11,215,331	6,772,787	14,830,346	224,623,062
19W8	120,303,375	14,435,536	36,202,362	9,500,941	400,866	2,817,120	24,677,573	11,677,797	7,251,374	14,855,314	242,122,258
19W9	150,606,421	15,443,550	28,097,100	13,627,409	415,412	3,122,097	26,961,924	12,430,146	7,369,341	14,948,243	273,021,643
19X0	165,590,910	16,281,132	28,228,303	9,288,445	357,239	3,509,220	28,685,535	12,835,441	7,643,162	21,020,688	293,440,075
19X1	179,212,346	17,268,490	19,831,060	13,018,362	283,804	4,797,572	30,470,274	14,866,704	8,260,685	26,329,634	314,338,931

*Includes General, Special Revenue, and Debt Service Funds.

Source: City of Columbus, Ohio, City Auditor, and City of Columbus, Ohio, *Comprehensive Annual Financial Report*, December 31, 19X1.

EXHIBIT 9–13

City of New Orleans, Louisiana
Notes to General Purpose Financial Statements
December 31, 19X1

(1) Summary of Significant Accounting Policies

The City of New Orleans, Louisiana (the City), was incorporated in 1805. The City's system of government was established by its Home Rule Charter, which became effective in 1954. The City operates under a Mayor-Council form of government. The City provides the following types of services as authorized by its charter: public safety, health, streets, sanitation, water and sewerage, planning and zoning, recreation, and general administrative services. Education and welfare are administered by other governmental entities.

The accounting policies of the City conform to generally accepted accounting principles as applicable to governmental units except for the accounting for certain claims and losses under its self-insurance programs (note 14(d)). The following is a summary of the more significant policies.

Reporting Entity

The general purpose financial statements of the City include all government activities, organizations, and functions for which the City exercises oversight responsibility. The criteria considered in determining governmental activities to be reported within the City's general purpose financial statements include the degree of oversight responsibility exercised by the City over a government organization, activity, or function, the City's accountability for the activity's fiscal matters, its scope of public service, and the nature of any special financing relationships which may exist between the City and a given government activity. Based upon the foregoing criteria, the financial statements of the following associated organizations are included in the accompanying general purpose financial statements.

Almonaster-Michoud Industrial District
Audubon Park Commission
Board of Liquidation, City Debt
Delgado-Albania Plantation Commission
Downtown Development District
French Market Corporation
New Orleans Aviation Board
New Orleans Municipal Yacht Harbor Management Corporation
Orleans Parish Communication District
Upper Pontalba Building Commission
Sewerage and Water Board of New Orleans
Vieux Carre' Commission

While the City includes the Sewerage and Water Board of New Orleans as a component unit according to the criteria set forth by the Government Accounting Standards Board (GASB), the Sewerage and Water Board of New Orleans has interpreted the criteria differently and does not consider itself a component unit of the City.

EXHIBIT 9–13 (Continued)

The following organizations, although associated with the City and engaged in rendering an activity within the City's boundaries for the benefit of the City and/or its residents, are excluded from the accompanying general purpose financial statements for the reasons stated below.

1. The following organizations are excluded because they are not within the oversight of the City, they are not included under the City Charter, they are not subject to the financial controls of the Finance Director or budgetary controls of the Mayor and City Council, the management is not appointed by or held accountable to the City, and there is minimal financial interdependency. These organizations are governed by an official or board elected by popular vote:

Board of Assessors	Criminal Sheriff's Office
Civil District Court	District Attorney's Office
Civil Sheriff's Office	First City Court
Clerk, Civil District Court	Juvenile Court
Clerk, Criminal District Court	Record of Mortgages
Constable, First City Court	Registrar of Conveyances
Constable, Second City Court	Second City Court
Criminal District Court	

In addition to the above criteria, the Orleans Parish School Board (School Board) is excluded because it receives no City funding, no manifestations of oversight responsibilities exist, and all School Board facilities are financed and owned by the School Board.

2. The following organizations are also excluded because of the criteria noted above. However, some or all of the members of the boards are appointed by the Mayor and/or City Council. These appointees are not held accountable to and do not maintain a significant continuing relationship with the City Council with respect to carrying out the organizations' functions.

Community Improvement Agency	New Orleans Citywide
Housing Authority of New Orleans	Development Corp.
New Orleans City Park Improvement	New Orleans Exhibition
Association	Hall Authority
New Orleans Home Mortgage	Public Belt Railroad
Association	Commission

Source: Adapted from the City of New Orleans, *Comprehensive Annual Financial Report,* December 31, 19X1.

Oversight Responsibility

The most significant factor for determining oversight responsibility is financial interdependency. **Financial interdependency** is the extent to which a separate agency has a financial effect on the reporting entity. This can be exhibited by responsibility for deficits, entitlement to surpluses, guarantees of debt, and so forth. If the reporting entity has such a financial relationship with an agency, this would be an indication that the agency should be part of the reporting entity; and therefore its financial data should be included in the government's CAFR.

Other factors that must be considered to evaluate oversight responsibility are who has the authority to select the members of the agency's governing body and who has the authority to select the operating managers. If the governmental unit has this authority, this would be an indication that an agency should be considered as part of the reporting entity. In addition, if the governmental unit has the authority to significantly influence operations through such controls as approval of budgets and budget adjustments, signing of contracts, and so on, this too, would be an indication that an agency should be part of the reporting entity.

Further evidence of oversight responsibility is the ability of the governmental unit to significantly influence the fiscal operations of an agency. If the governmental unit can significantly influence the fiscal operations of an agency, this would be an indication that the agency should be considered as part of the reporting entity. Influence over fiscal operations can be manifested by such situations as the right to require an audit and the authority to determine how surplus funds will be used.

Special Funding Relationships and Scope of Public Service

The previously mentioned factors are used to determine whether a governmental unit has oversight responsibility with regard to an agency. Where that oversight responsibility exists, the agency should become a component unit of the reporting entity. As a **component unit**, the agency is considered a part of the reporting entity. Other factors that must be considered are special funding relationships and the scope of public service.

Special funding relationships often exist between an agency and the reporting entity such that exclusion of that agency from the reporting entity would be misleading. An example of this type of situation is where the governmental unit owns property that is managed by an agency, as in the case of a housing authority.

Finally, to determine whether an agency should be included in the reporting entity, the scope of the services offered by the agency should be considered. If the agency offers services limited to the citizens of the governmental unit, this is an indication that the agency should be included in the reporting entity.

Financial reporting of component units

After all of the data described above have been accumulated for a specific agency, the management of the governmental unit must then make a professional judgment as to whether or not the agency should be part of the reporting entity. The weight given to each factor must be determined in relation to the facts and circumstances of each case.

The governmental unit must include a discussion of the scope of the reporting entity in its CAFR. This is done by means of a note to the financial statements in which the governmental unit explains why each agency is or is not included in the reporting entity. Exhibit 9–8 is an example of how this information was reported by the City of Columbus, and Exhibit 9–13 is part of the disclosure used by the City of New Orleans. (Only part of the note from the New Orleans CAFR has been reproduced; the entire description is three pages in length.)

When an agency is determined to be a component unit of the reporting entity, each fund of that agency is treated as a fund of the same type of the reporting entity. For example, a Capital Projects Fund of an agency that is determined to be a component unit would be included as a separate column in the combining statements of the reporting entity and, therefore, the assets, liabilities, revenues, and so on, would be included in the total for all Capital Projects Funds of the reporting entity.

Examine Exhibit 9–9. The assets, liabilities, and fund balance accounts of each of the Capital Projects Funds of a component unit would be included as a separate column on this statement. One exception to this form of reporting is the General Fund. Since there can be only one General Fund for a reporting entity, the General Fund of the oversight unit is considered to be the General Fund of the reporting entity. The General Funds of all component units are treated as Special Revenue Funds of the reporting entity.

INTERIM FINANCIAL REPORTING

To function properly, a governmental unit needs more information than that which is provided by the annual financial reports. The operations are so complex and dynamic that data for evaluation and control purposes must be available on a more frequent basis—usually monthly, but in some instances daily reports on items such as cash balances are necessary. These reports are generally prepared for internal use and are usually prepared on the budgetary basis. Often they contain year to date information in addition to the current data.

Interim reports prepared by some governmental units are as simple as a listing of the accounts under the control of a manager, together with the budgeted and actual balances. Other governmental units use the account format, but include a beginning balance, transactions that occurred during the period, and an ending balance. Some even include a complete set of financial statements.

GAAP for interim reporting is very broad and undefined. It can best be summed up with the following statement:

> The key criteria by which internal interim reports are evaluated are their relevance and usefulness for purposes of management control, which include planning future operations as well as evaluating current financial status and results to date. Continual efforts should be made to assure that accounting and related interim information properly serve management control needs. Because managerial styles and perceived information needs vary widely, however, appropriate internal interim reporting is largely a matter of professional judgment. . . .[7]

[7]GASB Cod. Sec. 2900.103.

One form of interim balance sheet used by some governmental units presents the assets and liabilities as of the interim date, and it includes the estimated effects of the budgetary accounts. This format is illustrated in Table 9–1.

Notice that the interim balance sheet illustrated below differs from the ending balance sheet in two major respects: (1) estimated revenues (net of revenues) are treated as assets; and (2) appropriations (net of expenditures) are treated as liabilities.

Concluding Comment on Financial Reporting

Notice the reporting of the fund balance for the Pension Trust Funds in Exhibit 9–14. As indicated in Chapter 8, this format of one Fund balance account for the combined balance sheet is different from that used for the individual

TABLE 9–1

City of Metairie
General Fund
Balance Sheet
For the Six Months ended June 30, 19X1

ASSETS AND ESTIMATED REVENUES

Cash		$ 10,000
Supplies		2,000
Property taxes receivable	$200,000	
Less: Allowance for uncollectible property taxes	10,000	190,000
Due from other funds		12,000
Estimated revenues	$800,000	
Less: Revenues	350,000	450,000
Total assets and estimated revenues		$664,000

LIABILITIES, APPROPROPRIATIONS, AND FUND BALANCE

Liabilities:		
Vouchers payable	$ 6,000	
Due to other funds	4,000	
Total liabilities		$ 10,000
Appropriations:		
Appropriations	$790,000	
Less: Expenditures	360,000	
Total appropriations		430,000
Fund balance:		
Reserved for encumbrances	$ 28,000	
Unreserved fund balance	196,000	
Total fund balance		224,000
Total liabilities, appropriations, and fund balance		$664,000

Pension Trust Fund balance sheet. Compare the reporting format for these funds in Table 3–20 with that followed in Exhibit 9–14. Remember that the actuarial present value information included in Table 3-20 should be reported in the notes to the GPFS.

Whether a PERS is considered to be part of the governmental reporting unit or a separate reporting entity, extensive note disclosure is required. In those instances where the PERS is considered to be part of the governmental unit, the financial statement disclosure is described above. The note disclosure includes (1) an identification of the plan and a description of its terms, (2) a description of the actuarial cost method used, (3) a brief summary of the accounting policies followed, and (4) statistical data covering the preceding ten-year period for items such as net assets available for benefits, the unfunded liability, and revenues by source.[8]

If a PERS is considered to be a separate reporting entity, a separate set of GPFS and a CAFR must be prepared for it. In such instances, extensive note disclosure is also required.

The Certificate of Excellence in Financial Reporting

By now it should be apparent that the financial reporting process for governmental units, although very complex, is essential for the dissemination of information on the financial activities of these organizations. In 1945, the Municipal Finance Officers Association (now the Government Finance Officers Association) acknowledged the need to recognize those governmental units that produce a good annual report. To reward the organizations that meet the high standards of reporting set by the GFOA, the Certificate of Conformance Program was established. When an annual report—now referred to as a Comprehensive Annual Financial Report (CAFR)—is deemed to meet the requirements of the GFOA, a **Certificate of Conformance**— now referred to as a **Certificate of Excellence in Financial Reporting**—is awarded to the organization issuing the report. Exhibit 9–15 contains a copy of the Certificate of Excellence earned by the City of Columbus for its 19X1 CAFR.

> To earn a Certificate of Conformance (Excellence), a CAFR must tell its financial story clearly, thoroughly and understandably. Certificates of Conformance (Excellence) reports are efficiently organized, employ certain standardized terminology and formatting conventions, minimize ambiguities and potentials for misleading inference, enhance understanding of current GAAP theory, and generally demonstrate a constructive "spirit of full disclosure."[9]

---

[8]An extended description of the note disclosures can be found in GASB Cod. Sec. Pe5 and Pe6.

[9]"Certificate of Conformance," Supplement to MFOA *Newsletter*, January 16, 1983, p. 1.

EXHIBIT 9–14

City of Baltimore
Combined Balance Sheet
All Fund Types and Account Groups
June 30, 19X1
(expressed in thousands)

| | GOVERNMENTAL FUND TYPES | | | | PROPRIETARY FUND TYPES | | FIDUCIARY FUND TYPES | ACCOUNT GROUPS | | | Total |
	General	Special Revenue	Debt Service	Capital Projects	Enterprise	Internal Service	Trust and Agency	General Fixed Assets	General Long-Term Obligations	Higher Education	(Memorandum Only)
ASSETS											
Cash and cash equivalents	$120,433	$ 6,165	$1,142	$ 1,447	$ 80,780	$32,330	$ 115,058			$ 1,343	$ 238,265
Investments		30,032	7,088	83,968	20,851	3,030	1,077,622				1,343,024
Property taxes receivable (net of allowance of $8,500,000)	8,930										8,930
Other accounts receivable, net	13,136	461	79	20,756	45,319	203				940	80,894
Due from other governments	27,762	48,103								940	76,805
Due from other funds	3,375			1,619	1,271					177	6,442
Inventories, at cost	6,214	2,034			2,475	174				208	11,105
Notes and mortgages receivable, net	54,720	10,559			182,028						247,307
Other assets	4,486	122			10,191	900	12,852			5	28,556
Restricted assets:											
Cash, investments, loans, and accounts receivable, net					89,514	264					89,778
Property, plant, and equipment, net					649,693	33,985		$1,417,491		28,702	2,129,871
Amount to be provided for the payment of vested compensated absences									$ 36,098		36,098
Amount available in debt service fund for retirement of general long-term debt									8,099		8,099
Resources to be provided in future years									562,116		562,116
Total assets	$239,056	$97,476	$8,309	$107,790	$1,082,122	$70,886	$1,205,532	$1,417,491	$606,313	$32,315	$4,867,290

Notes to financial statements not included.

353

EXHIBIT 9–14 (continued)

LIABILITIES AND FUND EQUITY
Liabilities:

| | GOVERNMENTAL FUND TYPES | | | | PROPRIETARY FUND TYPES | | FIDUCIARY FUND TYPES | ACCOUNT GROUPS | | | Total |
	General	Special Revenue	Debt Service	Capital Projects	Enterprise	Internal Service	Trust and Agency	General Fixed Assets	General Long-Term Obligations	Higher Education	(Memorandum Only)
Cash and cash equivalents—overdraft	$ 66,248										$ 66,248
Accounts payable and accrued liabilities	41,549	$13,444		$17,757	$ 15,648	$ 8,906	$ 2,360			$1,223	100,887
Retainages payable				8,235							8,235
Property taxes payable—State	183										183
Due to other governments					2,920						2,920
Due to other funds		4,994			1,271					177	6,442
Deposits subject to refund	3,291				247					28	3,566
Estimated liability for claims in process						13,690					13,690
Other liabilities					9,635	1,534	980			855	13,004
Liabilities payable from restricted assets:											
Accounts payable					9,268						9,268
Deferred revenue	72,062	24,503			3,806	86				143	100,600
Vested compensated absences									$ 36,098		36,098
Notes payable					1,901						1,901
Mortgage payable										448	448
Revenue bonds payable					284,560						284,560
Matured bonds—principal and interest payable			$210								210
Deferred compensation benefits							46,185				46,185
General long-term debt payable					56,063				455,671		511,724
Capital lease obligations									114,544		114,544
Total liabilities	183,333	42,941	210	25,992	385,309	24,216	49,525		606,313	2,874	1,320,713

EXHIBIT 9–14 (continued)

	GOVERNMENTAL FUND TYPES				PROPRIETARY FUND TYPES		FIDUCIARY FUND TYPES	ACCOUNT GROUPS			Total
	General	Special Revenue	Debt Service	Capital Projects	Enterprise	Internal Service	Trust and Agency	General Fixed Assets	General Long-Term Obligations	Higher Education	(Memorandum Only)
Commitments and contingencies											
Fund Equity:											
Contributed capital					630,898	23,399					654,297
Investment in general fixed assets								$1,417,491		28,356	1,445,847
Retained earnings:											
Reserved for:											
Revenue bond retirements					43,794						43,794
Future obligations					1,338						1,338
Self-insurance claims						11,763					11,763
Capital improvements						264					264
Unreserved					20,783	11,244					32,027
Fund balance:											
Reserved for:											
Encumbrances	21,424	4,838		147,134							173,396
Inventories	6,214	2,034									8,248
Other assets	1,162	122								234	1,518
Pension benefits							1,152,418				1,152,418
Library services							1,990				1,990
Scholarships, memorials and landmarks							1,599				1,599
Unreserved:											
Designated for:											
Debt service			8,099								8,099
Subsequent years' expenditures	26,122	8,817									
Undesignated (deficit)	801	38,724		(65,336)						2,096	37,035
										(1,245)	(27,056)
Total fund equity	55,723	54,535	8,099	81,798	696,813	46,670	1,156,007	1,417,491		29,441	3,546,577
Total liabilities and fund equity	$239,056	$97,476	$8,309	$107,790	$1,082,122	$70,886	$1,205,532	$1,417,491	$606,313	$32,315	$4,867,290

Notes to financial statements not included.

Source: Adapted from the City of Baltimore, Maryland, *Comprehensive Annual Financial Report,* June 30, 19X1.

EXHIBIT 9–15

Certificate of Achievement for Excellence in Financial Reporting

Presented to

City of Columbus, Ohio

For its Comprehensive Annual
Financial Report
for the Fiscal Year Ended
December 31, 19X1

A Certificate of Achievement for Excellence in Financial
Reporting is presented by the Government Finance Officers
Association of the United States and Canada to
governmental units and public employee retirement
systems whose comprehensive annual financial
reports (CAFR's) are judged to substantially
conform to program standards.

President

Executive Director

Source: City of Columbus, Ohio, *Comprehensive Annual Financial Report*, December 31, 19X1.

Participation by Other Organizations

A major bond-rating agency, Standard & Poor's Corporation, has taken an active role in governmental financial reporting by insisting that governmental units follow GAAP.[10] Standard & Poor's (S&P) has indicated that any problems that arise in the reporting format, timing of the issuance of the report, and so forth, will be taken into consideration when the government's bonds are rated. Since the effect of such ratings is felt immediately in the "pocketbook" of a governmental unit (bonds with low ratings must be issued with higher yields or rates of interest than those with high ratings), it is possible that the actions of S&P may have a greater impact on governmental financial reporting than the Certificate of Excellence Program.

Other financial institutions are also penalizing governmental units for substandard financial reporting. In a survey, many underwriters, bankers, and managers of other institutions providing financial services to governmental organizations indicated that they often require higher interest rates from those governmental units whose financial reports are not prepared in accordance with GAAP. In addition, they indicated that if poor financial reporting practices persist, future penalties may make it difficult for governmental units to issue debt securities of any kind.[11]

SINGLE AUDIT

One problem faced by governmental units in the past was the large number of audits to which they were subjected. It was not uncommon for a large governmental unit to have from twenty-five to fifty or more audits in a single year. Each of these audits was conducted by a different federal or state audit agency or independent public accountant and was centered on one particular facet of the organization's operations—e.g., revenue sharing, a research grant, or an entitlement program. The audits disrupted the operations of the governmental units and required a great deal of time and effort on the part of organizational personnel, not to mention the cost of the audits themselves.

To alleviate this problem, the U.S. Office of Management and Budget (OMB) proposed that "single audits" be performed on certain organizations. The premise of a **single audit** is that one carefully planned audit can perform the same function as many smaller audits, and can do so more efficiently and effectively. It can also greatly reduce the disruptions to the organization being audited. Essentially, a single audit is an expanded financial audit. However, it also includes certain elements of a compliance audit.

The authority for single audits comes from the Single Audit Act of 1984. In 1985, the OMB issued Circular A-128, *Audits of State and Local Governments*, to facilitate the implementation of the Single Audit Act. This document establishes

---

[10]For example, see *Standard & Poor's Perspective*, "Who's Watching the Books?" (1980), p. 6.

[11]Ibid., pp. 2-3.

specific audit requirements for state and local governmental units that receive financial assistance from the federal government and defines federal responsibilities for implementing and monitoring these requirements.

The requirements of the Single Audit Act and Circular A-128 apply to those state and local governmental organizations that receive federal financial assistance totaling $100,000 or more in any fiscal year. A governmental unit with federal financial assistance of $25,000 or more, but less than $100,000, in any fiscal year may elect to implement the requirements of the Single Audit Act in lieu of the specific compliance and financial audit requirements of the various programs for which they receive federal assistance. Governmental units receiving less than $25,000 in any fiscal year are exempt from the Single Audit Act and all other federal audit requirements. However, these organizations must maintain adequate accounting records and make them available to grantor federal agencies and the U. S. Comptroller General upon request.

Under the Single Audit Act, each governmental unit is assigned a **Cognizant Agency** by the OMB. This agency, which is usually the one providing the most federal funds to the governmental unit, represents the federal government in all matters pertaining to the audit. It is required, among other things, (1) to make certain that audits are performed in a timely manner and in accordance with the requirements of Circular A-128; (2) to coordinate, as far as is practicable, audits performed by or under contract to other federal agencies that are in addition to the single audit and to make certain that these audits build upon the single audit; (3) to make certain that the audit reports, plans for corrective action, and reports of illegal acts or irregularities are transmitted to the appropriate federal, state, and local officials; and (4) to make, or obtain, quality control reviews of the work of nonfederal audit organizations and, when appropriate, provide the results of these reviews to other organizations.

A single audit must include an audit of the governmental unit's general purpose financial statements (GPFS), additional tests of compliance with applicable legal requirements and reviews of the specific internal control systems of the various federal financial assistance programs. Each audit must be conducted in accordance with generally accepted *governmental* auditing standards, which are set forth in the U. S. General Accounting Office (GAO) publication *Standards for Audit of Governmental Organizations, Programs, Activities, and Functions* (commonly known as the "yellow book"). These standards are based on the AICPA *Statements on Auditing Standards* for fieldwork and reporting. However, they establish additional requirements for compliance and internal control reviews and reports. Single audits may be performed by state or local governmental auditors or by public accountants who meet the independence and qualification standards set forth by the GAO.

The Single Audit Act and Circular A-128 require that the auditor issue, for the *governmental unit*, reports on (1) its examination of the GPFS of the organization as a whole, or the agency, department, or establishment covered by the audit; (2) internal accounting control, based solely on a study and evaluation made as part of the audit of the entity; and (3) compliance with laws and regulations that might have a material (significant) effect on the entity's financial statements.

In addition, the auditor must include, with respect to the governmental unit's federal financial assistance programs, a supplementary schedule showing the total expenditures made for each program and reports on (1) the accounting and administrative controls used in administering these programs; (2) compliance with laws and regulations relating to the federal programs, identifying all findings of noncompliance and questioned costs; and (3) any fraud, abuse, or illegal acts or indications of such acts. When such acts are discovered, a separate written report must be issued.

Single audit reports must be transmitted, within thirty days, to the appropriate federal officials and made available by the governmental unit for public inspection. If any material internal control weaknesses or incidents of noncompliance with applicable laws and regulations are found, the governmental unit must submit a plan of corrective action or a statement explaining why corrective action is not necessary.

CURRENT ISSUES

Measurement Focus/Basis of Accounting Project

The most far-reaching development contemplated by the Government Accounting Standards Board is the proposed change in the measurement focus and basis of accounting used by governmental-type funds, as well as Expendable Trust Funds, Agency Funds, and account groups. The measurement focus, you will recall, measures *what* is being reported. The basis of accounting refers to *when* transactions or events should be recorded.

The basic premise of this proposal is that the measurement focus used by affected funds would be the **flow of financial resources**. Under this measurement focus, operating results would show the extent to which the financial resources obtained during a period were sufficient to cover the claims incurred in that period. The financial position (balance sheet), under this method, will reflect net financial resources available for future periods. The flow of financial resources measurement focus is accomplished by measuring the increases or decreases in Fund balance and the claims against financial resources by means of what amounts to, for all practical purposes, the *accrual* basis of accounting (see Exhibit 9–16). One major difference between the proposed method and the accrual method is that the proposed method does not include depreciation.

The justification for this change in measurement focus is the perception of many professionals of a need to carefully match revenues and expenditures. While this is done, to a certain extent, through the budgetary process, this proposal brings the matching process one step closer to reality. The general feeling of persons advocating this change is that although specific revenues and specific services of governmental-type activities bear no direct relationship to each other, they both can be related directly to specific time periods and, in the aggregate, can be related to each other. A measurement focus that measures the relationship between aggregate revenues and aggregate services within a comparable time period, therefore, is appropriate for measuring **interperiod equity** (the measure of whether current-year revenues are sufficient to pay for current-year services). The relationship of revenues and services to a specific time period can best be expressed by using the accrual basis of accounting because this basis recognizes the effects of transactions or events on the fund balance of an entity when they take place (a specific time period), regardless of when cash is received or paid.

The specifics of this proposal are shown in Exhibit 9–16. Notice that revenues are categorized as those from **nonexchange transactions** and those from **exchange transactions**. The former are revenues for which nothing specific is "provided" to the payer (e.g., income taxes), while the latter are revenues for which something "specific" (e.g., a privilege or the use of specified resources) is provided.

Notice also that general long-term debt will have two components: capital-related debt and noncapital-related (operating) debt, and that the fund balance, which is to be called the "GAAP fund balance," will contain three components: budgetary fund balance, unbudgeted funds, and budget to GAAP differences. Finally, notice that the proposed statement will also require separate classification of current and noncurrent assets and liabilities.

As was mentioned earlier, the GASB is also working on projects concerned with pensions, other postemployment benefits, risk retention, and insurance. Since these projects interrelate and, in most cases, will require a large adjustment to the financial statements of governmental entities, the GASB is planning for all of these projects to become effective at the same time (the "big bang"). However, because of the magnitude of the changes required and the considerable opposition that has been voiced to certain aspects of the proposals, there may be a lengthy phase-in period if, in fact, the proposals ever do take effect. As of this writing these proposals were still under discussion.

EXHIBIT 9–16

SUMMARY OF MEASUREMENT FOCUS/BASIS OF ACCOUNTING PROJECT (as of December 1987)

REVENUES AND OTHER FINANCING SOURCES

Nonexchange Transactions: Revenues are recognized when the transactions take place, regardless of when cash is received.
Exchange Transactions: Revenues are recognized when earned, regardless of when cash is received.

Source of Revenue	WHEN RECOGNIZED	
	Proposed	Current
Nonexchange Revenue		
Taxes based upon a particular transaction (e.g., sales taxes)	When transaction takes place	When measurable and available to finance expenditures of the fiscal period

EXHIBIT 9–16 (Continued)

Source of Revenue	WHEN RECOGNIZED	
	Proposed	Current
Taxes based upon events over a time period (e.g., income taxes and property taxes)	Period in which events occur or in the period for which levied	When measurable and available to finance expenditures of the fiscal period
Other taxes	When transaction takes place or period in which events occur, as appropriate	When measurable and available to finance expenditures of the fiscal period
Traffic fines	When violation is observed	When measurable and available to finance expenditures of the fiscal period
Other fines	When fine is imposed	When measurable and available to finance expenditures of the fiscal period
Fees for particular transactions	When entity has a legal claim	When measurable and available to finance expenditures of the fiscal period
Fees for services or priviledges	Rateably over period covered	Rateably over period covered
Donations	When assets are received	When assets are received
Exchange Transactions		
User fees	When services are performed	When serviced are performed
Investment gains and losses	When investment sold	When investment sold
Investment income	When earned	When earned
Leases of capital assets	Inception of lease term	When made available to the governmental unit to pay debts in the current period
Sale of capital assets	When title passes	When title passes

EXPENDITURES AND OTHER FINANCING USES

Expenditures should generally be recognized when transactions take place, regardless of when cash is paid.

Type of Expenditure	WHEN RECOGNIZED	
	Proposed	Current
Operating (e.g., salaries)	When transaction takes place	When transaction takes place
Inventories (e.g., supplies)	When purchased or consumed	When purchased or consumed
Depreciation	Not recognized	Not recognized
Prepaid items	When received/consumed	When purchased or received/consumed
Compensated absences	When earned by employees	Amount accrued during the year that will be liquidated with available expendable financial resources
Capital	Time of acquisition or construction	Time of acquisition or construction
Debt issuance costs	When debt is issued or liability is incurred	When debt is incurred or liability is incurred

EXHIBIT 9-16 (Continued)

GENERAL LONG-TERM DEBT

Proposed	Current
Will report two categories:	
A. General long-term *capital* debt will be reported in the General Long-Term Debt Account Group.	All general long-term debt
B. Governmental fund (operating) debt will be recorded as a liability equal to the face amount of the debt, when issued, by the governmental-type fund receiving the proceeds. Interest on this debt will be accrued.	

FUND BALANCE

Proposed		Current	
Will be called *GAAP Fund Balance* and will have three components:		Fund balance has three components:	
1. Budgetary fund balance	Fund balance measured on the basis used in the budget	1. Reserved	Resources not available for appropriation or expenditures because of legal or contractual restrictions
2. Budget to GAAP	Basis, timing, and perspective differences	2. Designated	Resources "set aside" by management of the governmental unit
3. Unbudgeted funds	Fund balance of any governmental-type fund for which budgets are not prepared	3. Unreserved, undesignated	Fund balance available for future appropriations or expenditures

BALANCE SHEET CLASSIFICATION

	Proposed	Current
Assets	Current/Noncurrent	Assets are not classified
Liabilities	Current/Noncurrent	Liabilities are not classified

Summary of GASB Activities

At the time of this writing, the Governmental Accounting Standards Board (GASB) is fully operational. Based on information currently available, the GASB is studying topics such as:

1. Basis of accounting as it relates to the individual funds (see previous discussion)

2. Financial reporting, with emphasis on the entity concept and the degree of aggregation found in the financial statements
3. Pension accounting
4. Reporting of cash flows
5. Capital reporting
6. Other postemployment benefits
7. Fixed assets
8. Self-insurance

We have included these brief comments on issues that are on the agenda of the GASB to indicate that financial accounting and reporting for governmental units is in a constantly evolving state. As a result, many changes may have taken place by the time you read this text. The role of the governmental accountant is partially devoted to maintaining a current knowledge of the field and an ability to interpret the pronouncements of the rule-making body or bodies.

SELECTED REFERENCES

AMERICAN INSTITUTE OF CERTIFIED PUBLIC ACCOUNTANTS. *Audits of State and Local Governmental Units.* Rev. ed. New York, 1986.

ANTHONY, ROBERT. *Financial Accounting in Nonbusiness Organizations.* Stamford, Conn.: Financial Accounting Standards Board, 1978.

_____. "Making Sense of Nonbusiness Accounting," *Harvard Business Review* (May–June 1980), pp. 83-93.

COMPTROLLER GENERAL OF THE UNITED STATES. *Standards for Audit of Governmental Organizations, Programs, Activities, and Functions.* Rev. ed. Washington, D.C.: U.S. General Accounting Office, 1988.

COPELAND, RONALD, AND ROBERT INGRAM. *Municipal Financial Reporting and Disclosure Quality.* Reading, Mass.: Addison-Wesley, 1983.

DREBIN, ALLAN, JAMES CHAN, AND LORNA FERGUSON. *Objectives of Accounting and Financial Reporting for Governmental Units: A Research Study.* Vols. 1 and 2. Chicago: National Council on Governmental Accounting, 1981.

ERNST & WHINNEY (Certified Public Accountants). *How Cities Can Improve Their Financial Reporting.* Cleveland: Ernst & Whinney, 1979.

_____. *How Your Government Can Apply GAAP.* Cleveland: Ernst & Whinney, 1982.

MUNICIPAL FINANCE OFFICERS ASSOCIATION. *Governmental Accounting, Auditing, and Financial Reporting.* Chicago: Municipal Finance Officers Association of the United States and Canada, 1988.

GOVERNMENTAL ACCOUNTING STANDARDS BOARD. *Governmental Accounting and Financial Reporting Standards (as of June 15, 1987).* 2nd ed. Stamford, Conn.

HAMILTON, CHUCK. "SIS10: The Uniform Single Financial Audit Bill," *Government Accountants' Journal*, 32(3) (1983):1.

OFFICE OF MANAGEMENT AND BUDGET. *Audits of State and Local Governments.* Circular No. A-128. Washington, D.C.: U.S. Government Printing Office, 1985.

REVIEW QUESTIONS

Q9–1   What is a CAFR?

Q9–2   What is a *combined* financial statement?

Q9–3   What are *notes* to the financial statements?

Q9–4   What is a *combining* financial statement?

Q9–5   Define the term *reporting entity.*

Q9–6   Management must decide which agencies to include in its CAFR. If you were the manager of a governmental unit, how would you make such a decision?

Q9–7   What are *interim financial statements*?

Q9–8   Are PERS reported on a combined balance sheet?

Q9–9   What is a *Certificate of Excellence*?

Q9–10 How have financial institutions tried to enforce good financial reporting of governmental units?

Q9–11 What are the effects of a lower bond rating when bonds are issued?

Q9–12 What is a *single audit*? *A cognizant agency*?

Q9–13 Name two sources of authority and guidance for single audits.

Q9–14 What is the *yellow book*?

EXERCISES

E9–1   (Organization of the CAFR)
Assume that you have been asked to explain the organization of the Comprehensive Annual Financial Report, as specified in NCGA *Statement 1*, to a group of city controllers. Outline your talk.

E9–2   (Certificate of Excellence)
Obtain a copy of a CAFR from a governmental unit. Determine whether it has received a Certificate of Excellence. How can you determine this? Explain what the "certificate" means.

E9–3   (Entity note)
Explain the purpose of the financial statement note describing the reporting entity. Using one of the agencies included in either the Columbus or New Orleans entity note, write part of the note as if the agency were included in the reporting entity, and write another note as if the agency were not included.

E9–4   (Analysis of a CAFR)
Obtain a CAFR from a governmental unit and examine the notes section. Write a brief report summarizing each note. In addition, compare the CAFR you have to the statements illustrated in this chapter. Explain any significant differences.

E9–5   (Analysis of a situation involving the reporting entity)
Below is a description of a school system and its relationship to the city in which it exists:

A school system is separately chartered from the city in which it exists. The school system was established by an act of the state legislature that designated a school board as the governing authority. Members of the school board are elected by the public. The school board has control over hiring and firing employees, and the power to contract for schools, purchase equipment, eminent domain, and so forth. The school board is required by an act of the state legislature to submit an annual budget to the city council for approval and is prohibited from spending or obligating funds in excess of the maximum amount approved by the city council. Taxes are levied by the city council and are collected by the city and distributed to the school system. The school system also receives funds from the state and county. The school board does not have the authority to borrow funds or issue bonded indebtedness, but the city council may and does borrow funds and issues bonds for the school system.   (GASB Cod. Sec. 2100.603)

REQUIRED: Review the above facts and determine whether the school system should be included in the reporting entity of the city. Explain your answer.

E9–6   (Description of the Financial Reporting Pyramid)
         Describe the Financial Reporting Pyramid as set forth in NCGA *Statement 1*. Be sure to explain the relationship between the various levels of the pyramid and the amount of detail that must be included in the CAFR.

E9–7   (Multiple choice)
         Select the correct answer to each of the following:
   1.   The "yellow book" contains
         a. A list of procedures to use when performing audits
         b. Generally accepted auditing standards
         c. Generally accepted governmental auditing standards
         d. Generally accepted accounting principles for governmental units
         e. Sample audit reports for different types of governmental units

   2.   A single audit is required for a governmental unit when amounts received by the government from federal financial assistance exceed
         a. $100,000
         b. $250,000
         c. $500,000
         d. $1,000,000
         e. A single audit is always required

   3.   Specific guidance for conducting single audits is provided by the Single Audit Act and
         a. NCGA *Statement 1*
         b. OMB Circular A-128
         c. The "yellow book"
         d. GAAFR
         e. AICPA SOP 80-2
         f. b and c

PROBLEMS

P9-1   (Review of an actual CAFR)
         Obtain a CAFR from a governmental unit and write a report identifying

the statements included and your impression of the strengths and weaknesses of the reporting format used.

P9–2   (Reporting entity)

Below are descriptions of three agencies and their relationship to the city in which each exists:

A. A public benefit corporation was created by a city to provide subsidized public housing in accordance with federal legislation. The mayor appoints members of the governing board for staggered terms; they, in turn, elect a chairman. The governing board employs executives; authorizes contracts of subsidy with the U.S. Department of Housing and Urban Development pursuant to the latter agency's regulations and statutory authorizations; and causes the corporation to construct, own, and operate public housing facilities within the boundaries of the city. The financial liability of the housing agency is essentially supported by the operating and debt service subsidies received under contract from the federal government, although services or cash subsidies may be, and from time to time are, received from the city as well.   (GASB Cod. Sec. 2100.604)

B. A city holds title to the land on which a museum is constructed. The museum is operated by a nonprofit corporation that is supported principally through citizen contributions and endowments. The city levies an annual tax, however, for the purpose of partially deferring the cost of maintenance of the museum building and grounds. The proceeds of this tax are remitted to the nonprofit corporation and expended by it. The nonprofit corporation operates under the governance of a board of directors elected by contributing members and leases the property from the city for $1 per year. Facilities of the museum are free to contributing members and open to the public for a minimum fee on weekends and no fee on other days.   (GASB Cod. Sec. 2100.605)

C. A public benefit corporation was created by a state to provide mass transit (subways and buses) activities within the geographical boundaries of a city. Of the 15-member board of directors, 11 are appointed by the governor and 4 by the mayor of the city. The city owns all of the transit facilities and provides capital construction funds for new facilities. Operating subsidies are provided by the city, state, and federal governments.   (GASB Cod. Sec. 2100.610)

REQUIRED: Examine the facts of each situation and determine whether or not each agency should be included in the reporting entity of the city. Explain your reasons for inclusion or exclusion.

P9-3   (Multiple choice)

1. The Comprehensive Annual Financial Report (CAFR) of a governmental unit should contain a combined statement of cash flows for

	Governmental Fund	Account Groups
a.	Yes	No
b.	Yes	Yes
c.	No	Yes
d.	No	No

(AICPA adapted)

2. The Comprehensive Annual Financial Report (CAFR) of a government unit should contain a combined statement of revenues, expenses, and changes in retained earnings for

	Governmental Funds	Proprietary Funds
a.	No	Yes
b.	No	No
c.	Yes	No
d.	Yes	Yes

(AICPA)

3. Which of the following is an appropriate basis of accounting for a proprietary fund of a governmental unit?

	Cash basis	Modified accrual basis
a.	Yes	Yes
b.	Yes	No
c.	No	No
d.	No	Yes

(AICPA)

4. Fixed assets used by a governmental unit should be accounted for in the

	Capital Projects Fund	General Fund
a.	No	Yes
b.	No	No
c.	Yes	No
d.	Yes	Yes

(AICPA)

5. Fixed assets of an Enterprise Fund should be accounted for in the
   a. General Fixed Assets Account Group, but no depreciation on the fixed assets should be recorded
   b. General Fixed Assets Account Group, and depreciation on the fixed assets should be recorded
   c. Enterprise Fund, but no depreciation on the fixed assets should be recorded
   d. Enterprise Fund, and depreciation on the fixed assets should be recorded

(AICPA adapted)

6. Which of the following funds of a governmental unit would include contributed capital in its balance sheet?
   a. Expendable Trust Fund
   b. Special Revenue Fund
   c. Capital Projects Fund
   d. Internal Service Fund

(AICPA adapted)

7. The Amount available in Debt Service is an account of a governmental unit that would be included in the
a. Liability section of the Debt Service Fund
b. Liability section of the General Long-Term Debt Account Group
c. Asset section of the Debt Service Fund
d. Asset section of the General Long-Term Debt Account Group

(AICPA)

8. The Comprehensive Annual Financial Report (CAFR) of a governmental unit should contain a combined statement of revenues,
expenditures, and changes in fund balances for

	Governmental funds	Account groups
a.	Yes	Yes
b.	Yes	No
c.	No	No
d.	No	Yes

(AICPA)

9. Fixed assets should be accounted for in the General Fixed Assets
Account Group for the

	Capital Projects Funds	Internal Service Funds
a.	Yes	Yes
b.	Yes	No
c.	No	No
d.	No	Yes

(AICPA)

10. The Comprehensive Annual Financial Report (CAFR) of a governmental unit should contain a combined balance sheet for

	Governmental Funds	Proprietary funds	Account groups
a.	Yes	Yes	No
b.	Yes	Yes	Yes
c.	Yes	No	Yes
d.	No	Yes	No

(AICPA)

P9–4   (Multiple choice)

1. The combined statement of revenues, expenditures, and changes
in fund balances—budget and actual—general and special revenue
fund types is prepared using
a. A GAAP basis
b. The budgetary basis
c. A cash receipts and disbursements basis

    d. The modified accrual basis

    e. None of the above

2. The revenues and expenditures (expenses) of governmental-type and proprietary-type funds are

    a. Reported on different statements

    b. Reported on the same statements

    c. Not both reported for the same governmental unit

    d. Not required in the CAFR

    e. None of the above

3. The Summary of Significant Accounting Policies

    a. Is not required in the CAFR

    b. Describes the methods used in the financial accounting system

    c. Is a summary of the financial results of the operations of the governmental unit

    d. Is usually the last note found in the CAFR

    e. Items b and d are correct

4. Individual fund financial statements are

    a. Never required in the CAFR

    b. Always required in the CAFR

    c. Required in the CAFR if necessary to present the financial information fairly

    d. The major components of the CAFR

    e. None of the above

5. The Financial Reporting Pyramid

    a. Is the CAFR for the city of Pyramid

    b. Depicts the relationship between the various elements of the financial accounting system

    c. Is a listing of the individual parts of a CAFR

    d. Is a listing of the various statistical tables required in the CAFR

    e. None of the above

6. The financial reporting emphasis in NCGA *Statement 1* is

    a. The financial statements of the individual funds

    b. The combined financial statements

    c. The monthly financial reports issued for internal governmental use

    d. Detailed written discussions of the results of operating the government over the past year

    e. None of the above

7. A combined financial statement

    a. Includes assets, liabilities, revenues, and expenses

    b. Must be prepared using the full accrual basis of accounting

    c. Has a separate column for each fund type

    d. Contains individual fund financial statements

    e. None of the above

8. Which of the following is not a required financial statement in the CAFR?
   a. Combined statement of revenues, expenditures, and changes in fund balance—all governmental-type funds
   b. Combining statement of proprietary fund revenues, expenses, and changes in retained earnings (or equity) by fund type
   c. Combined statement of revenues, expenses, and changes in retained earnings (or equity)—all proprietary fund types
   d. Combined balance sheet—all fund types and account groups
   e. None of the above—i.e., all of the above are required statements in the CAFR

9. The term *CAFR* refers to the
   a. Capital Assessments Fund Report
   b. Cumulative Annual Fund Review
   c. City Annual Fund Review
   d. Comprehensive Annual Financial Report
   e. None of the above

10. Which of the following is not a major component of the CAFR?
    a. Statistical tables
    b. Introductory data
    c. Financial statements and related data
    d. All of the above
    e. None of the above—i.e., all of the above are major components of the CAFR

P9–5   (Discussion related to a single audit)

The City of New Mexizona receives federal financial assistance in excess of $10 million per year from several different federal agencies. As a result, it must have a single audit.
1. What is a single audit and how does it differ from a "traditional" audit?
2. Who is likely to be New Mexizona's cognizant agency?
3. What reports must be provided by the single audit? When are they due?

SUMMARY PROBLEMS FOR CHAPTERS 4–9

I.   (Adjusting and correcting journal entries for several funds and a General Fund balance sheet)

You have been engaged to examine the financial statements of the City of Rego for the year ended December 31, 19X1. Your examination disclosed that, due to the inexperience of the town's new bookkeeper, all transactions for the year 19X1 were recorded in the General Fund. The following General Fund trial balance as of December 31, 19X1, was furnished to you.

City of Rego
General Fund
Trial Balance
December 31, 19X1

Cash	$ 20,800	
Short-term investments	180,000	
Accounts receivable	11,500	
Taxes receivable—current	30,000	
Tax anticipation notes payable		$ 58,000
Appropriations		927,000
Expenditures	795,200	
Estimated Revenues	927,000	
Revenues		750,000
General city property	98,500	
General obligation bonds payable	52,000	
Unreserved fund balance		380,000
	$2,115,000	$2,115,000

Note: 1. Single control accounts were used for items such as Appropriations and Expenditures.
2. The budget is only recorded for the General Fund.

Your audit disclosed the following additional information:

1. During the year, equipment with a book value of $9,000 was removed from service and sold for $6,400. In addition, new equipment costing $104,900 was purchased. These transactions were recorded in the General city property account. No other amounts were recorded relative to these events.

2. During the year, one hundred acres of land were donated to the town for use as an industrial park. The land had a value of $125,000. No recording of this donation had been made.

3. To service other municipal departments the town, at the beginning of the year, authorized the establishment of a central supplies warehouse (an Internal Service Fund). During the year, supplies totaling $90,000 were purchased and charged to Expenditures in the General Fund. A physical inventory of supplies on hand at December 31, 19X1, was taken; and this count disclosed that supplies totaling $84,000 had been used. Other records indicate that departments using the supplies were billed $92,400. No entries were made for the billings. The General Fund acquired and used all the supplies mentioned above.

4. Outstanding purchase orders at December 31, 19X1, not recorded in the accounts, amounted to $22,000. While encumbrance accounting is required by city charter, it was not used during the year.

5. On December 31, 19X1, the State Revenue Department informed the town that its share of a state-collected, locally shared tax would be $58,500. No entry was made for this information.

6. The Accounts receivable of $11,500 includes $2,000 due from Rego's electric utility for the sale of old equipment on behalf of the town. Accounts for the municipal electric utility operated by the town are maintained in a separate fund. The scrap was sold to K.R., Inc., which will pay for it in July. The old equipment originally cost $15,000. The entry made on the books of the General Fund to record the sale was:

Accounts receivable	2,000	
Revenues		2,000

No entries were made on the books of the utility for this transaction.

7. The balance in Taxes receivable—current is now considered delinquent, and the town estimates that $4,000 will be uncollectible.

8. On December 31, 19X1, the town retired, at face value, 6 percent general obligation serial bonds totaling $40,000. The bonds were issued on January 1, 19X0, at a face value of $200,000. Interest of $12,000 was paid during 19X1 and debited to General obligation bonds payable. A Debt Service Fund was established in 19X0.

REQUIRED: 1. Prepare all the entries necessary to correct the town's records. Identify the funds and account groups used.
2. Prepare a revised trial balance for the General Fund.
3. Prepare the closing entries for the General Fund after the corrections have been made.

Hint: If an item is recorded in an incorrect fund, it will require an entry to remove it from that fund and a separate entry to record it in the proper fund.

(AICPA adapted)

II. (Journal entries for several funds and a balance sheet for a Capital Projects Fund)

The City of Westgate's fiscal year ends on June 30. During the fiscal year ended June 30, 19X2, the City authorized the construction of a new library and sale of general obligation term bonds to finance the construction of the library. The authorization imposed the following restrictions: Construction cost was not to exceed $5,000,000; annual interest rate was not to exceed 8 1/2 percent.

The City records project authorizations, and other budgetary accounts are also maintained in the General Fund and Capital Projects Funds. The following transactions relating to the financing and constructing of the library and other events occurred during the fiscal year ended June 30, 19X2:

1. On July 1, 19X1, the City issued $5 million of 30-year, 8 percent general obligation bonds for $5,100,000. The semiannual interest dates are December 31 and June 30. The premium of $100,000 was transferred to the Library Debt Service Fund.

2. On July 3, 19X1, the Library Capital Projects Fund invested $4,900,000 in short-term commercial paper. These purchases were at face value with no accrued interest. Interest on cash invested by the Library Capital Projects Fund must be transferred to the Library Debt Service Fund during the fiscal year ended June 30, 19X1; estimated interest to be earned is $140,000.

3. On July 5, 19X1, the City signed a contract with F & A Construction Company to build the library for $4,980,000.

4. The General Fund made one-half of its annual payment to the Library Debt Service Fund, $200,000. The other half will be made later in the year.

5. The Library Debt Service Fund made a semiannual interest payment.

6. On January 15, 19X2, the Library Capital Projects Fund received $3,040,000 from the maturity of short-term notes purchased on July 3. The cost of these notes was $3,000,000. The interest of $40,000 was transferred to the Library Debt Service Fund.

7. On January 20, 19X2, F & A Construction Company properly billed the City $3,000,000 for work performed on the new library. The contract calls for a 10 percent retention until final inspection and acceptance of the building. The Library Capital Projects Fund paid F & A the appropriate amount.

8. The General Fund made another debt service payment to the Library Debt Service Fund.

9. On June 30, 19X2, the Library Debt Service Fund made the appropriate interest payment.

10. On June 30, 19X2, the Library Capital Projects Fund made the proper adjusting entries (including accrued interest receivable of $103,000) and closing entries. Closing entries are not required for any other fund.

REQUIRED:

1. Prepare in good form journal entries to record the above information and identify each fund(s) or account group(s) used. (Except for the issuance of bonds, assume the General Fixed Assets Account Group and the General Long-Term Debt Account Group are updated for changes during the period in which closing entries are prepared.)

2. Prepare in good form a balance sheet for the City of Westgate—Library Capital Projects Fund as of June 30, 19X2.

(AICPA adapted)

III. (Journal entries for several funds)

Following are several transactions that relate to Weaverstown for 19X1:

1. The general operating budget was approved as follows:

Appropriations	$5,200,000
Estimated revenues	5,000,000
Estimated other financing sources	300,000

2. Plans for a new criminal courts building were approved. General obligation bonds with a face value of $7 million were issued for $7,200,000. Local laws stipulate that any premium must be transferred to the appropriate Debt Service Fund. In addition, a federal grant of $8 million was received.

3. The fire department ordered new equipment to replace outdated equipment. The new equipment cost $35,000. The old equipment cost $23,000 but was sold for $750.

4. The city received $400,000 from the state. This amount represents the city's share of the state gasoline tax. This money can only be spent to repair streets, and a separate accounting is required by the state.

5. General obligation bonds of $5 million were retired by a Debt Service Fund. At this time, interest of $150,000 was also paid to the bondholders.

6. The 19X1 property tax was levied by the city. The total amount was $3,000,000, of which $2,990,000 was expected to be collected.

7. Salaries of governmental employees were paid, totaling $800,000. Of this amount, $50,000 was withheld and included in an account called "Due to federal government" as income tax payments. In addition, the city paid its share of retirement benefits, $100,000, and the employees' share, $50,000, to the city's PERS. Assume that all employees were paid through the General Fund. (Salaries and related costs are encumbered.)

8. The Central Supplies Fund, an Internal Service Fund, billed the General Fund $10,000 and the Gas Service Fund, an Enterprise Fund, $5,000 for supplies. Assume that the General Fund previously encumbered $11,000 for supplies.

9. The Gas Service Fund billed the General Fund for $2,500, the Central Supplies Fund for $1,000, and the remainder of its customers for $2,500,000. The General Fund had encumbered $2,600 for this expenditure.

10. The General Fund made its annual contribution of $200,000 to the Debt Service Fund. Assume that $150,000 was for interest.

11. The contract for the new court building was signed with Excell Construction Company for $14,500,000.

12. The fire equipment ordered in number 3 arrived. The total cost was $36,000. The city paid the bill upon delivery. (Assume the excess expenditure was approved.)

13. Excell Construction Company sent a progress billing for $1,500,000.

14. Property taxes of $2,800,000 were collected and $5,000 was written off as uncollectible. The remainder became delinquent.

15. Suzanne Night gave the city $500,000 of marketable securities. The securities were to be used as the principal of a trust that must be maintained intact. The income earned from these investments can only be used for purchasing library books.

16. A property tax bill from 19X0 for $200 was written off as uncollectible. At this time the receivable was in a delinquent state.

17. Special assessment bonds with a face value of $345,000 were issued for a drainage project. The total assessment was $345,000. Of this amount, $30,000 was considered to be current and to be revenue of 19X1. (Assume the city guaranteed the bonds.)

18. Income of $14,000 was received by the Night Principal Trust Fund (see number 15). This amount was immediately transferred to the Night Operating Trust Fund and $12,600 was used to purchase library books.

REQUIRED: Prepare the journal entries necessary to record the above transactions and indicate the fund(s) or account group(s) used.

10

THE BUDGETARY PROCESS

LEARNING OBJECTIVES

After completion of this chapter, you should be able to:

1. Discuss three types of budgets
2. Contrast four approaches to budgeting
3. List the steps involved in preparing a budget
4. Prepare a revenue forecast
5. Use a trend analysis to predict future revenues
6. Discuss the contents of a budget document
7. Calculate the millage rate used by a governmental unit
8. Prepare a budget for a small governmental unit

In previous chapters we have discussed the *collecting* and *reporting* of financial information. Such information, however, is of limited utility if the reader (1) has no "standard" with which to compare it and (2) is unable to use it to make judgments on and improvements in the efficiency and effectiveness of the operations of the organization. A device that can be used to enhance the usefulness of financial information is the budget.

A **budget** is a formal estimate of the resources that an organization *plans* to expend for a given purpose or over a given period, and the proposed means of acquiring these resources. It informs the reader of what activities the organization plans to undertake and how the organization expects to finance these activities; and thus it acts as a standard against which efficiency and effectiveness can be measured. It also acts as a representation of public policy in that its adoption implies that certain objectives, as well as the means of accomplishing these objectives, have been determined by the legislative body.

In addition to serving as a framework for operations, the budget often acts as a legal document for certain types of organizations, principally governmental units, as it forms the basis for the appropriations made by the legislative bodies of these organizations. As was mentioned earlier, resources cannot be expended by governmental units unless they are appropriated.

Even if not required by law, the use of a budget is strongly recommended. The GASB, for example, expresses the need for budgets in the following principles:

a. An annual budget(s) should be adopted by every governmental unit.
b. The accounting system should provide the basis for appropriate budgetary control.
c. Budgetary comparisons should be included in the appropriate financial statements and schedules for governmental funds for which an annual budget has been adopted.[1]

In this chapter we will discuss some types of budgets and approaches to budgeting, as well as the process of preparing a budget.

TYPES OF BUDGETS

Nonbusiness organizations use many different types of budgets. They use short- and long-term operating budgets, capital budgets, and, in many cases, cash budgets.

Operating Budgets

Operating budgets (also known as current budgets) are general-purpose budgets used by organizations to formalize their activities of a given period, usually a fiscal year. They include estimates of the resources expected to be available during the year and projections of how these resources will be expended. Since operating budgets are the primary means by which most activities of organizations are controlled, they serve as the basis for the budgetary entries discussed in previous chapters.

For many organizations, the use of an operating budget is required by law. Many cities and states also require that by the beginning of each fiscal year, a *balanced* budget (one in which the total of the estimated funds available from the projected revenues and fund balance must be sufficient to meet the anticipated expenditures) be approved by their legislative bodies (e.g., city councils or boards of trustees). Even if not required by law, however, every organization should adopt an annual operating budget in order to control its expenditures. Preparing the budget in conformity with generally accepted accounting principles (GAAP) will ensure that the accounting records are also prepared in this manner and will make it easier for the organization to prepare monthly and annual budgetary control reports.

Operating budgets are generally prepared for each fund used, as well as for the organization as a whole. Revenues are broken down by source; and expenditures are broken down by type and by department, program, or other

---

[1]GASB Cod. Sec. 1100.109.

operating unit. Actual revenues and expenditures are generally shown for one or two prior years and, if possible, the current year. In addition, the estimated revenues and proposed expenditures of the budget year are shown.

A budget can provide information on the specific purpose of and services performed by each operating unit. It can also provide information on (1) personnel and salaries, (2) proposed bond issues, (3) proposed methods of reducing costs, and (4) the cost of operating specific facilities and providing specific services. Since the budget is often a widely read legal document, great care should go into its preparation. The organization should use it, along with an annual report, as a means of presenting its "story" to the public.

Capital Budgets

Capital budgets (also known as capital programs) are the plans of expenditures, and the means of financing these expenditures, expected to be made for long-lived or "capital" assets, such as land, buildings, and equipment. They usually cover a four- to six-year period. Many organizations maintain a "running" or "continuous" capital budget, adding a future year and dropping the past year when annual revisions are made. Such budgets are very helpful when an organization is attempting to determine when and if it will be necessary to incur debt.

Cash Budgets

Cash budgets are plans of the actual monies expected to be received and expended during a particular period. Since most governmental units use the modified accrual basis of accounting, their operating budgets often do not reflect the actual inflows and outflows of cash. In addition, many governmental units receive a large percentage of their revenues in the latter part of the fiscal year. Since their expenditures are generally spread out evenly over the year, cash shortages often result. Organizations that use cash budgets can anticipate cash shortages and surpluses before they occur. As a result, these organizations are able to obtain more favorable interest rates than organizations that borrow or invest on a "crash" basis. A cash budget is shown in Table 10–1.

APPROACHES TO BUDGETING

The uses of budgets are many and varied. Budgets can serve as contracts (legal documents), control mechanisms, means of communication, planning tools, and bases for the creation of short- and long-term policies. Depending on their intended usage, they can be prepared under one of several approaches: object-of-expenditure, performance, program and planning-programming-budgeting (PPB), or zero-based. Budgets prepared under each approach differ as to what type of information is presented and as to how expenditures are aggregated.

TABLE 10–1   Sample Cash Budget

City of Light
General Fund
Cash Budget
Second Quarter, 1990

	April	May	June	Quarter
Beg. cash balance	$ 12,000	$ 10,500	$ 16,350	$ 12,000
Cash receipts:				
Property taxes	$ 83,000	$ 90,000	$ 98,500	$271,500
Sales taxes	95,000	98,000	96,000	289,000
Fixed asset sales	500	—	3,000	3,500
Fines and penalties	15,000	15,000	18,000	48,000
License fees	5,500	3,000	1,600	10,100
Total cash receipts	$199,000	$206,000	$217,100	$622,100
Cash available*	$211,000	$216,500	$233,450	$634,100
Cash disbursements:				
Personal services	$ 56,000	$ 58,000	$ 57,500	$171,500
Travel	2,500	6,000	9,000	17,500
Operating expenses	32,000	36,000	35,500	103,500
Equipment	10,000	40,000	15,000	65,000
Transfers to Capital				
Projects Funds	200,000	—	12,000	212,000
Transfers to Debt				
Service Funds	—	50,000	—	50,000
Total disbursements	$300,500	$190,000	$129,000	$619,500
Minimum cash balance	10,000	10,000	10,000	10,000
Total cash required	$310,000	$200,000	$139,000	$629,500
Excess (deficiency) of cash available over cash required	$ (99,500)	$ 16,500	$ 94,450	$ 4,600
Financing:				
Tax anticipation notes	$100,000	—	—	$100,000
Repayments of notes	—	$ (10,000)	$ (90,000)	(100,000)
Interest	—	(150)	(800)	(950)
Net financing	$100,000	$ (10,150)	$ (90,800)	$ (950)
Ending cash balance	$ 10,500	$ 16,350	$ 13,650	$ 13,650

*Before financing.

The Object-of-Expenditure Approach

The **object-of-expenditure approach** (also known as the traditional or line-item approach) is the most popular approach to budgeting. Under this approach, the budgets that are prepared show, as **line items**, every category of expenditure to be made during the year. For example, the budget of a state-run university might show each faculty and administrative position by salary, by title, and, in many cases, by the name of the person holding that position, as a line item. Supplies used by a particular department, however, would be shown in their entirety, even though several purchases (and expenditures) might be made during the year.

After review and revision by the chief executive officer (CEO) of the organization, the budget is submitted to the organization's legislative body (e.g., city council, state legislature, board of trustees, and so forth). This body reviews and sometimes revises the budget. After it approves the budget, the legislative body makes line-item appropriations, which are incorporated into the organization's accounts.

Performance or program data may be included with an object-of-expenditure-type budget. Such data, however, are used only to support or supplement the various requests for funding. A portion of an object-of-expenditure budget is shown in Table 10–2.

Among the advantages of the object-of-expenditure approach to budgeting are the following:

1. The budgets are uncomplicated and can easily be prepared.
2. Not only the preparers but also the users can understand the budgets.
3. Information presented in this type of budget can easily be incorporated into the accounting system.
4. Detailed comparisons between budgeted and actual revenues and expenditures can easily be made.

Critics of this approach, however, cite the following points:

1. It provides data useful primarily in the short run. As a result, the long-run goals of the organization may be jeopardized.
2. It is oriented more toward providing a framework for sets of financial records that comply with legal requirements than with providing useful management-type information.
3. It encourages, rather than discourages, spending. Managers are led to believe that an important objective is to spend exactly the amount budgeted and that if this amount is not spent, the following year's appropriation will be cut. As a result, there is little incentive for them to economize.
4. Legislative bodies are given more detail than they can handle. Therefore, they tend to focus on individual items (such as the amount of supplies consumed) rather than on the overall goals and programs of the organization.

In spite of these deficiencies, the object-of-expenditure approach to budgeting is the one most commonly used by nonbusiness organizations. Because of its popularity, it will be discussed in greater detail later in this chapter.

TABLE 10–2 Sample Object-of-Expenditure Budget

Orleans Levee Board
FY 89 Budget Presentation
Airport Safety

Acct #	Account Name	Previous Actual FY 87	Approved Budget FY 88	Proposed FY 89
5410	Office supplies	345	1,572	500
5411	Copier supplies	0	0	0
5412	Computer supplies	0	0	0
5431	Janitorial supplies	130	562	262
5432	Medical supplies	0	750	50
5433	Safety apparel and supplies	5,158	0	5,295
5434	Clothing supplies	8,129	10,875	10,000
5435	Police supplies	1,227	5,050	2,000
5436	Fire fighting supplies	4,507	9,980	6,000
5437	Sodding/herbicides/fertilizer	0	0	0
5440	Improvements—other than buildings	0	0	0
5441	Hardware supplies	210	1,044	300
5442	Mounted patrol	0	0	0
5443	Dive team supplies	0	0	0
5451	Boat/motor/trailer—GOS	0	0	0
5452	Autos/trucks—GOS	8,447	7,706	9,000
5453	Tractors and grass cutters	120	0	0
5461	Buildings	36	0	0
5471	Airfield/runways/taxiway	0	0	0
5472	Bridges/floodgate/floodwall	0	0	0
5473	Grounds	0	0	0
5474	Levees	0	0	0
5475	Emergency supplies	0	0	0
5476	Fountain and pool supplies	0	0	0
5477	Piers, catwalks, bulkheads	0	0	0
5478	Roads, streets, parking lots	0	0	0
5481	Miscellaneous equipment	0	0	0
5482	Autos (parts)	1,809	1,808	1,900
5483	Boats, motors, trailers	49	0	0
5484	Heavy construction equipment	0	0	0
5485	Office equipment—furniture	0	0	0
5486	Police	0	0	0
5487	Radio communications	194	0	0
5488	Recreational	0	0	0
5489	Tractors and grass cutters	0	0	0
5490	Trucks and trailers	0	0	0
5491	Hand tools and minor equipment	273	0	0
	Total material and supplies	30,634	39,347	35,307

Source: Orleans Levee Board.

The Performance Approach

Budgets prepared under the **performance approach** emphasize output and efficiency. **Output** is measured in terms of the amount of goods or services produced, the number of cases handled, the number of persons impacted, and so forth. **Efficiency** is usually measured in terms of cost per unit (e.g., persons trained). The main focus of the performance approach to budgeting is the **evaluation of performance**.

The information presented in a performance budget centers on **activities** and **tasks**, rather than on organizational subunits and objects-of-expenditure. Thus, it is possible to include costs incurred by several different departments within one expenditure category. For example, if several persons from different departments work part time on a particular activity, the portions of their salaries allocable to the activity can be combined and treated as an expenditure of the activity, rather than as expenditures of their individual departments. Under the object-of-expenditure approach, this grouping is more difficult, since expenditures are recorded by department (or other subunit) and by object-of-expenditure.

Among the advantages of the performance approach to budgeting are the following:

1. Since the budget includes a narrative description of each project, the CEO and the members of the legislative body are well informed as to the goals of and the services provided by the organization.
2. Both input *and* output are measured. The results of each activity are formally monitored, as are the costs incurred in obtaining these results.
3. Emphasis is placed on carrying out the activities of the organization, as well as on controlling costs. As a result, each manager can be evaluated on how well he or she meets certain stated objectives, as well as on how well he or she controls costs.
4. Because of the emphasis on the activities of each subunit and the narrative description of these activities provided in the budget, decision makers can readily see the "big picture." That is, they can see how each activity interrelates with other activities and can easily spot those activities that duplicate or conflict with other activities.
5. Each subunit of the organization is forced to think through its objectives. The managers of the various subunits are forced to take a close look at each activity and to determine whether it is justified and whether it fits into the overall goals of the organization.

In spite of its many advantages, performance budgeting is not as widely used as object-of-expenditure budgeting. This is because performance budgets are more difficult to prepare and to understand than object-of-expenditure budgets. To use performance budgets effectively requires a staff of accountants and budget analysts. Few nonbusiness organizations can afford such a staff. In addition, many objectives of such organizations are not measurable in quantitative terms (e.g., fire protection). Thus the practical applications of this method of budgeting are somewhat limited.

The Program and Planning-Programming-Budgeting (PPB) Approaches

The **program** approach to budgeting is a *planning-oriented* one which emphasizes programs, activities and functions rather than evaluation and control. It takes several forms, the best known of which is the *planning-programming-budgeting system* (PPB or PPBS). Under this system information is presented in the form of budgetary requests and reports on broad programs, rather than in the form of detailed listings of activities and line items.

Before a program budget can be prepared, the fundamental objectives of the organization must be identified. All activities must then be related to these objectives, and the future implications and costs of each activity must be identified. Finally, an analysis of the various alternatives must be performed, and the alternatives that will enable the organization to meet its goals in the most efficient manner, using available resources, must be selected. These alternatives then become the programs that make up the budget.

The PPB approach offers a number of advantages over other approaches to budgeting. It forces its users to practice long-range planning on a routine basis and to review and update programs and objectives frequently. It also forces the various subunits of the organization to coordinate their efforts and resources, since PPB budgets are organized by programs rather than by administrative units. It permits flexibility in the management of the organization, since appropriations are by "lump sum" rather than by line item. And, finally, it permits an analysis of changes in existing programs, in terms of marginal (additional) costs and benefits. Other approaches to budgeting tend to focus on total or average expenditures.

While PPB has many attractive features, certain realities have limited its acceptance. First, it is difficult to formulate a set of goals that will be acceptable to all the parties involved. (Business organizations, of course, have the primary goal of maximizing profits.) This problem is compounded by the existence of elected officials who are often reluctant to commit themselves to long-run policies. In addition, a great deal of time and money, as well as analytical ability on the part of both preparers *and* users, is required if a sound PPB-type budget is to be prepared and properly used. Finally, PPB-type budgets require many long-run estimates of costs and benefits. The use of such estimates makes the objective measurement of performance very difficult.

The PPB approach to budgeting was developed by the federal government in the 1950s. It proved unworkable in practice, however, and was discontinued by the Nixon administration. The approach was somewhat more successful when used by certain state and local governmental units, especially after these organizations had modified it to make it more compatible with object-of-expenditure budgeting. Today PPB-type budgets are used by a limited number of organizations to supplement object-of-expenditure-type budgets.

The Zero-Based-Budgeting Approach

The **zero-based-budgeting (ZBB) approach** is one that forces managers to assess the value of and to justify the continuation of each activity under their supervision. Since every activity must be justified each year, the managers, in a sense, start from scratch or "zero"—hence the name "zero-based budgeting."

Zero-based budgeting is a combination of thought and action processes. After a top-to-bottom review, a series of **budget units** is developed. Each unit consists of a description of (1) the project or activity, (2) the expected level of accomplishment, (3) the advantages of retaining the activity, and (4) the consequences of eliminating it, as well as dollar estimates of alternative ways of performing it.

An important aspect of zero-based budgeting is the consideration given to each level of "accomplishment" that is likely to result from an activity. In presenting safety messages, for example, the activity might be the reaching of a television audience. Relevant questions might deal with the demographics of the audience—i.e., what type of person is most likely to benefit from the message.

Questions might also be raised as to what effect increasing or decreasing the amount of funding provided to the activity by various increments (e.g., 10 percent, 20 percent, and so on) would have on the level of accomplishment. This step—the dividing of budget units into different levels of accomplishment—results in basic decision units called **decision packages**.

The final step in the process is to rank the decision packages. Management lists these packages in order of decreasing benefit to the organization, identifies the benefits likely to be derived from various overall levels of spending, and studies the consequences of not approving those decision packages ranked below any given level of spending.

Because of the forced-thought process inherent in ZBB, managers must view their areas of responsibility more completely and more objectively than under other approaches to budgeting. Other benefits of ZBB include (1) the identification of identical services and activities being performed within a given unit, (2) the emergence of a systematic priority of services, and (3) the matching of costs and benefits at the lowest spending levels.

Benefits, however, do not accrue without costs. Among the disadvantages of ZBB are (1) the large amount of effort and paperwork required to implement and update them, (2) resistance, on the part of managers and other decision makers, to the abandonment of other forms of budgeting, and (3) the inability of many managers to accept the idea of a reduction in the scope of their activities.

Zero-based budgeting is an idea whose time appears to have come and gone. Under the Carter administration, it was instituted in the federal government with much fanfare. It met with a great deal of resistance, however. The idea of curtailing certain governmental activities was unthinkable to many persons inside and outside the government. In addition, it was felt that the benefits resulting from the use of ZBB did not justify the effort and disruption of routine activities involved in the preparation and ranking of decision packages. Finally, popular sentiment at this time was moving toward fewer, rather than more, governmental activities. The public was not in the mood for innovations that created more bureaucracy. When the Reagan administration assumed power, ZBB on the federal level became a thing of the past. Its use on the state and local levels also seems to have diminished.

Conclusion

In this section we have discussed the major types of budgets used by non-business organizations—operational, capital, and cash. We have also discussed the four approaches to budgeting most commonly used by these organizations—object-of-expenditure, performance, planning-programming-budgeting (PPB), and zero-based (ZBB). Table 10–3 compares the four approaches to budgeting. Note that each approach is appropriate for a given purpose. Because most nonbusiness organizations are primarily concerned with control and communication, the object-of-expenditure approach is the one most commonly used. We will focus on this approach in the next section.

PREPARING THE BUDGET

The preparation of the budget, although difficult at first, becomes easier with practice. After a while it just becomes a matter of "doing it." It can, however, be very time consuming.

The budgetary process can be broken down into the following steps, the order of which may vary between organizations:

1. Prepare budgetary policy guidelines
2. Prepare a budget calendar
3. Prepare and distribute budget instructions
4. Prepare revenue estimates
5. Prepare departmental (or program) expenditure requests[2]
   a. Personal services work sheet
   b. Travel work sheet
   c. Operating expense work sheet
   d. Equipment work sheet
   e. Capital outlay request summary
6. Prepare nondepartmental expenditure requests
7. Consolidate departmental expenditure requests, nondepartmental expenditure requests, and revenue estimates. Submit to the CEO for review and revision
8. Prepare the budget document

---

[2]The same procedures are used for both departmental and program expenditure requests. To facilitate this presentation, we will discuss departmental expenditure requests. However, everything said for departmental expenditure requests also applies to expenditure requests prepared for programs.

9. Present the budget document to the legislative body
10. Record the approved budget in the accounts
11. Determine the property tax (millage) rate

TABLE 10–3

Approaches to Budgeting

Budgetary Purposes	Budget Format	Focuses Mainly On These Program Measures
Control *Communication* —tells how many and how much resources will be utilized	Line item/ object-of- expenditure	*Input*
Contract —lets citizens know what products they will receive and the relative efficiency of their government *Management* —provides information that allows managers to assess efficiency of their agency *Communication* —shows basis of estimation —provides information as to what is being produced	Performance	*Efficiency* *Output* —workload —product —program size
Planning —shows the goals and objectives to be achieved *Policy* —allows choice between different policy goals and between alternative means of reaching these goals *Communication* —shows the purpose of expenditures, the policies and priorities of the government *Contract* —lets citizens see what objectives are achieved	PPB(S) (Program)	*Impact* —measure of effectiveness
Policy —allows choices between different levels of output associated with each funding level	Zero-based	*Output* —product *Input* —costs Perhaps impact

Source: Blue Wooldridge, "Towards the Development of an Integrated Financial Management System," *Government Accountants' Journal*, 31, No. 3 (1982): 39.

Budgetary Policy Guidelines

Before considering the various segments involved in the budgetary process, the CEO, the budget officer, or both should discuss, with the members of the legislative body, what policies will be followed when preparing the budget. During these discussions, the fiscal conditions of the current year should be reviewed, along with the prospects for the following year. In addition, the following points should be considered:

1. The level of revenues collected, to date, during the current year, and the level of revenues likely to be collected during the remainder of the year
2. Possible increases or decreases in current taxes and fees, and ideas for new taxes and fees
3. Current and future economic conditions, as well as any possible developments that might affect the revenues or expenditures of the following year (e.g., a plant closing or the loss of federal funds)
4. Items that fall due the following fiscal year and might require an unusually large expenditure, such as the repayment of a bond issue
5. The status of the current year's expenditures and the possibility of a surplus (or deficit)

An analysis of the above issues will provide insight into the financial problems likely to be faced by the organization during the following year. From the discussions of these issues, budgetary policies satisfactory to the legislative body, the CEO, and other affected parties should emerge. These policies should cover, at a minimum

1. Permissible merit salary increases
2. Permissible cost-of-living adjustments
3. Inflationary adjustments to be used
4. Permissible increases or decreases in taxes and fees
5. Changes in capital spending
6. Types of programs and services to be emphasized and de-emphasized

The budgetary policies should be disseminated, in the form of **budgetary policy guidelines**, to all persons responsible for preparing and reviewing the various segments of the budget.

The Budget Calendar

In order for the budgetary process to proceed in an organized manner, certain deadlines must be met. If each person involved in this process is aware of when his or her part is due and if the time allotted to each task is reasonable, the process should take place smoothly with misunderstandings kept to a minimum. One way to ensure that each person knows when his or her (and everyone else's) part of the budgetary process is due is to prepare a **budget calendar**.

A budget calendar formalizes all key dates in the budgetary process. The calendar itself can be a simple listing of dates or it can be in the form of a complex flow chart. At a minimum, it should list the steps of the budgetary process and the dates on which each of the various steps should be finished. More elaborate calendars often list who is responsible for each step and what data must be provided by whom and to whom. A sample budget calendar is shown in Table 10–4.

Budget Instructions

To disseminate the budgetary policy guidelines and to assist the various subunits in the preparation of their expenditure requests, a set of **budget instructions** should be prepared and sent to each person responsible for a segment of the budget. These instructions should be distributed early enough to provide these persons sufficient time to prepare their budget requests in a thoughtful, orderly manner.

In addition to copies of the forms and work sheets to be used, the budget instructions should contain

1. A budget calendar
2. A copy of the budgetary policy guidelines
3. A statement summarizing the organization's anticipated fiscal condition for the following year
4. A statement of specific policies to be followed when preparing expenditure requests
5. A set of inflationary guidelines to be used in estimating the future costs of equipment, supplies, and so on.
6. Specific instructions on how each form and work sheet should be completed
7. Instructions on where to seek help and clarification of any ambiguities that might arise.

TABLE 10–4   Typical Budget Calendar

July 6	Departments receive instructions for the preparation of the budget.
August 15	Departmental expenditure requests are returned to the budget officer.
September 6–21	Departmental hearings are held with the mayor.
October 1–8	Review and preliminary presentation is made to the city council.
October 9–31	Budget is reviewed and finalized by the mayor.
November 5–18	Budget printing and production take place.
November 20	Mayor formally presents the budget to the city council.
November 21– December 15	City council conducts public hearings.
December 18	City council formally votes on the budget.
December 20–30	Budgetary information is entered into the computer.
January 1	New fiscal year begins.

Revenue Estimates

A key part of the budgetary process is the determination of how much money the organization will have available for spending the following year. This amount consists of (1) the surplus or deficit (fund balance) carried forward into the budget year, and (2) the revenues expected to be collected during the budget year.

The process of determining how much money the organization will have available for spending the following year consists of the following steps:

1. Determine the probable balance in each fund at the end of the current year.
2. Project the revenues expected to be collected during the budget year:
    a. Determine the revenues or revenue bases for several prior years and the current year.
    b. Apply a trend analysis to the above data in order to obtain a preliminary estimate of the revenues or revenue bases of the budget year.
    c. Adjust the preliminary estimates of the revenues or revenue bases for factors likely to affect them, such as the condition of the local economy, special events, changes in tax rates, and changes in the level of support from outside sources.
    d. If working with revenue bases, multiply by the appropriate tax rates, license fees, and so on.
    e. Determine the transfers expected from other funds (e.g., residual equity of a Capital Projects Fund).
3. Prepare a statement of actual and estimated revenues (and transfers-in), such as the one illustrated in Table 10–5.

Current-Year Surpluses or Deficits

A surplus can reduce the amount of revenue that must be raised in order to finance a given level of expenditures. A deficit, however, is likely to increase the amount of revenue that must be raised, since most state and local governmental units and not-for-profit organizations are either reluctant or unable to carry deficits forward from year to year.

To determine the amount of surplus or deficit to be carried forward, a projection must be made of the total revenues and expenditures that will be incurred during the current year. A separate projection should be made for each fund used (e.g., General Fund, Special Revenue Funds, and so on).

Current-year revenues are projected by

1. Comparing collections to date with budgeted and prior-year collections
2. Determining the causes of any significant differences found in step 1
3. Determining any factors that might affect the revenues of the remainder of the year (e.g., the effect that the closing of a major department store will have on sales tax collections during the year)
4. Projecting the revenue collections for the remainder of the year on the basis of the information gathered in the preceding steps (this can be done by means of a combination of trend analysis, economic projections, and intuition)

TABLE 10–5 Statement of Actual and Estimated Revenues (and Transfers-in)

Fund: General
Date: September 15, 1989

Prepared by ___PNW___
Approved by ___LVT___

Acct. No.	Source	1988 Actual	Jan.–Aug. 1989 Actual	Sept.–Dec. 1989 Est. Act.	Total 1989 Est. Act.	1989 Budget	1990 Estimated	Remarks
1110	Property tax	$3,246,575	$1,384,300	$1,940,700	$3,325,000	$3,325,000	$3,550,000	Reassessment of property
1112	Liquor tax	355,240	235,650	124,350	360,000	354,000	480,000	International Exposition
1114	Sales tax	1,864,680	1,252,840	857,160	2,110,000	2,200,000	2,650,000	Same as above
1116	Royalty payments	385,000	245,000	120,000	365,000	375,000	300,000	Decline in gas production
1119	Fines & penalties	84,610	63,450	30,000	93,450	92,000	100,000	International Exposition
1121	Rental charges	8,500	6,500	3,500	10,000	9,600	11,000	Same as above
	Subtotal	$5,944,605	$3,187,740	$3,075,710	$6,263,450	$6,355,500	$7,091,000	
2010	Transfer from Expendable Trust Fund	122,000	—	145,000	145,000	145,000	150,000	Higher interest rates
	Total	$6,066,605	$3,187,740	$3,220,710	$6,408,450	$6,500,500	$7,241,000	

Projecting current-year revenues becomes easier as the year passes. As a result, many organizations delay this process as long as possible. Such delays, however, increase the difficulty of realistically budgeting the following year's expenditures, since the persons preparing such estimates have no solid information on how much money will be available.

One solution to this problem is the preparation of tentative revenue estimates early in the budgetary process, deliberately erring on the side of conservatism. As better information becomes available, the current-year revenue estimates can be updated. Another approach is to use three levels of estimates—optimistic, probable, and pessimistic—and to ask the subunits to prepare three levels of expenditure requests. This approach, while providing flexibility, requires significantly more effort on the part of all concerned and can lead to misunderstandings and credibility gaps.

The methods used to project revenues vary from source to source. Property taxes are generally easy to project for the remainder of the year because they have already been levied and are secured by the property being taxed. In addition, most governmental units set up an allowance for uncollectibles early in the year, and patterns of collection usually remain constant from year to year. Unless some major event has taken place (or is expected to), property tax collections can be assumed to follow prior-year patterns of activity.

Collections of other taxes, license fees, fines, and fees for services are more difficult to project. The best approach to predicting these sources of revenue is to apply a trend analysis to the prior-year collections and to temper the result with knowledge of current and future events (such as the closing of a large factory, a change in tax rates, or an increase in the legal drinking age).

Federal grants and state revenue-sharing monies can usually be predicted for the current year with a degree of certainty, since commitments for these items are made early in the year. Even in this area, however, problems can arise if the organization's fiscal year differs from that of the grantor agency or if the grantor agency cuts back on its outlays due to its own financial problems.

The best way to project total current-year expenditures is to determine, on an item-by-item basis, whether the expenditures incurred to date are above or below the budgeted level and at what rate the various subunits will continue to spend. Since budgets usually show only annual dollar amounts, it is often necessary to assume a constant rate of spending and to project the year-to-date expenditures forward at this rate. The budget officer should also discuss the current year's spending with the director or manager of each subunit in order to determine the existence of any factors that might increase or decrease the rate of spending for the remainder of the year. This task can be simplified if each subunit produces periodic reports comparing budgeted and actual expenditures, such as the ones described at the end of this chapter.

The process of projecting annual expenditures is simplified in organizations that have rules against, or operate in jurisdictions that have laws against, overspending their budgets. In these organizations, the budget officer can usually assume that the amount budgeted is the amount that will be spent.

Once the current year's projected revenues and expenditures have been determined, the surplus or deficit to be carried to the next year can be calculated as follows:

	Prior-year surplus (deficit)
Plus:	Estimated current-year revenues
Less:	Estimated current-year expenditures

To illustrate, assume that at the end of the prior year the General Fund of a city had a surplus of $500,000. The budget officer of this city determines that the total revenues of the current year, recorded in this fund, will amount to $8 million and that the total expenditures will amount to $8.2 million. The projected surplus in this fund for the current year is calculated as follows:

	Prior-year surplus	$ 500,000
Plus:	Projected revenues	8,000,000
Less:	Projected expenditures	(8,200,000)
	Projected surplus	$ 300,000

The handling of surpluses varies among organizations. Some organizations feel free to spend their surpluses the following year. Others follow a policy of building them up and saving them for emergencies. The policy to be followed in the treatment of surpluses should be made clear by law and by the legislative body of the organization.

Budget-Year Revenue Projections

When projecting the revenues of the budget year, each source should be considered separately. Revenue sources consist of two components:

1. A **revenue base**—The entity on which the revenues are based (e.g., property values, retail sales, number of parking tickets, number of admissions to municipal swimming pool, number of memberships, and so on).
2. A **revenue rate**—The percentage of the value of the revenue base that, by law or prior agreement, is transferred to the organization or the revenue per unit of service (e.g., New Orleans has a 4 percent city sales tax; therefore, an amount equivalent to 4 percent of the retail sales that take place there will eventually be transferred to the city).

The amount of revenue collected is the product of the revenue base and the revenue rate:

Revenues Collected = Revenue Base × Revenue Rate

To illustrate: Assume that the budget officer of a city estimates that the retail sales of the following year will amount to $10 million and that the city taxes retail sales at the rate of 3 percent. The *estimated* revenues from sales taxes will be:

$$\$10,000,000 \times .03 = \underline{\underline{\$300,000}}$$

This analysis should be performed on all taxes, fees, and other revenues. For some types of revenues, the analysis can be fairly simple. For example, the tax assessor can generally supply information on the assessed value of all real property in the jurisdiction. The estimated property taxes can then be determined by multiplying the valuation provided by the assessor's office by the estimated millage (tax) rate.

Other revenues are more difficult to predict, as they are controlled by such factors as the national economy and the fortunes of a local industry. For example, a source of revenue for one tourist-oriented city is a hotel occupancy tax. Many of the people who visit this city are from the Midwest, a region whose economy is heavily dependent on the automotive and steel industries. A downturn in the level of activity of these industries results in fewer people visiting the city, fewer hotel bookings, and lower revenues from the hotel occupancy tax (as well as from the sales and amusement taxes). Thus, when forecasting revenues from "tourist-oriented" sources, the budget officer of this city must consider the condition of the economies of the various regions (and nations) from which visitors are drawn. The following factors must also be considered when projecting revenues:

1. **Local economic conditions** can be influenced by the projected activity of local industries as well as national and, in many cases, worldwide economic conditions. Measures of these conditions are found in the various business and commodity-price indices and in locally generated statistics, such as housing starts, school enrollments, sales tax collections, population trends, and trends in building permits.
2. **Special events** that will take place in a particular year. For example, a city might host an international exhibition. Such an event would attract an unusually large number of tourists—which would significantly increase revenues from various tourist-oriented sources.
3. **Legal factors** such as changes in tax rates, the addition or deletion of fees and taxes, possible reassessments of real property, and changes in taxes and fees mandated by the courts or higher governmental units.
4. **Internal or administrative factors** such as the opening of a self-financing facility or the receipt of federal funds, the amount of which is based on the level of a particular activity.

When gathering information, outside sources should be used extensively but not exclusively. Groups such as the League of Women Voters and the various chambers of commerce devote a great deal of time and effort to gathering information relevant to the operation of governmental and other not-for-profit organizations. This information can prove very useful. It should be remembered, however, that the preparers of this information are often lobbying organizations. Persons using this information should therefore be alert for possible biases.

Certain types of revenues, such as fines and sales taxes, may be projected by using past trends. A tool commonly used to make such projections is **trend analysis**. Trend analysis can be used to estimate future revenues from any source that increases (or decreases) at a reasonably steady pace. To perform a trend analysis, data for the past five or more years should be assembled, along with an estimate for the current year. The revenue base rather than the level of collections should be measured, since tax rates, the levels of fines, and so forth, tend to rise over a period of time, adding an extra variable. Determining the following year's revenue base and multiplying by the expected rates provides more accurate projections.

Once the data have been assembled, the analysis involves the following steps:

1. Determine the year-to-year changes in the revenue base for each of the prior years
2. Determine the average rate of change over the period
3. Multiply the average rate of change (plus 100 percent) by the estimated revenue base of the current year, to obtain the *unadjusted* projected revenue base
4. Adjust the unadjusted projected revenue base for known factors that may cause a deviation from past patterns of behavior, to obtain the *adjusted* projected revenue base.
5. Multiply the adjusted projected revenue base by the appropriate tax rate, license fee, level of average fine, and so on, to obtain the projected revenues

To illustrate, assume that a city wishes to project revenues from a tax on hotel occupancy. The tax rate for the budget year 1990 is expected to be 5 percent of the price paid for each room. The number of people visiting the city has been growing at a fairly steady rate, as have the room rates. Hotel occupancy rates have averaged around 80 percent. In the budget year, however, the city will host an international exposition. The local chamber of commerce estimates that hotel occupancy rates will average 96 percent that year. Due to the construction of several new hotels, the number of rooms available will rise by 10 percent, all of which will be available at the beginning of the year. Room rates, however, will only rise at about the same rate that they have in the past, due to the increased competition brought about by the new hotels.

Room occupancy revenues reported by the hotels in this city over the past five years have been as follows (in millions of dollars)

1984	$1.2
1985	1.4
1986	1.7
1987	2.1
1988	2.5
1989	3.0 (est.)

To project the revenues from the hotel occupancy tax for the budget year, the following steps are performed:

1. Determine the year-to-year changes in the revenue base for each of the prior years:

$$
\begin{array}{llllllllll}
1985/1984 & = & 1.4/1.2 & = & 1.167 & - & 1.000 & = & \underline{16.7\%} \\
1986/1985 & = & 1.7/1.4 & = & 1.214 & - & 1.000 & = & \underline{21.4\%} \\
1987/1986 & = & 2.1/1.7 & = & 1.235 & - & 1.000 & = & \underline{23.5\%} \\
1988/1987 & = & 2.5/2.1 & = & 1.190 & - & 1.000 & = & \underline{19.0\%} \\
1989/1988 & = & 3.0/2.5 & = & 1.200 & - & 1.000 & = & \underline{20.0\%}
\end{array}
$$

2. Determine the average rate of change over the period. Since we are working with estimates, a simple arithmetic average will suffice:

$$
\begin{array}{l}
16.7\% \\
21.4 \\
23.5 \\
19.0 \\
\underline{20.0} \\
5\,|\,100.6\% \\
\underline{20.1\%} = \text{Average rate of change over period}
\end{array}
$$

3. Multiply the average rate of change (plus 100 percent) by the estimated revenue base of the current year:

120.1% × $3.0 = $3,603,000 (rounded) = unadjusted projected 1990 revenue base

4. Adjust the unadjusted projected revenue base for known factors that may cause a deviation from past patterns of behavior. In this problem, the occupancy rate is expected to rise from 80 to 96 percent during the budget year because of the international exposition. In addition, the number of available hotel rooms is expected to increase by 10 percent, all of which will be available at the beginning of the year:
   a. Percentage increase in occupancy rate = 96%/80% = 1.20 − 1.00 = $\underline{20\%}$
   b. Percentage increase in hotel rooms = $\underline{\underline{10\%}}$

$3,603,000 × 120% × 110% = $\underline{\underline{\$4,755,960}}$ = adjusted projected 1990 revenue base

Do not try to multiply the unadjusted projected 1990 revenue base by 130 percent, as each of the above factors is independent of the other. For example, even if no new rooms were added, the base would rise by 20 percent due to the increase in the occupancy rate. If the occupancy rate were to remain constant, the base would rise by 10 percent because of the new rooms.

5. Multiply the adjusted projected 1990 revenue base by the projected tax rate (5%):

$$\$4,755,960 \times 5\% = \underline{\underline{\$237,800}} \text{ (rounded)} = \text{projected 1990 revenue}$$

Thus the revenue from the hotel occupancy tax for 1990 can be budgeted at $237,800.

When dealing with estimates it is best to use simple, rounded figures in order to avoid falling into the GIGO (garbage in–garbage out) trap. This happens when rough estimates are multiplied by various factors and odd numbers result. Regrettably, many people tend to assume that if a number is carried out to pennies or to several decimal places it must be correct, regardless of its source.

Revenues that must be handled separately are grants, entitlements, and shared revenues. These revenues are usually received from other governmental units and are known collectively as **intergovernmental revenues**. According to the National Council on Governmental Accounting (NCGA), **grants** are contributions or gifts of cash or other assets that must be used or expended for specified purposes, activities, or facilities. **Entitlements** are payments to which state or local governmental units are entitled, pursuant to an allocation formula determined by the organization providing the monies (usually the federal government, but some states also have entitlement programs). **Shared revenues** are revenues that are received by one governmental unit (e.g., a state) and are shared, on a predetermined basis, with another governmental unit or class of governmental units.[3]

The difficulty of projecting intergovernmental revenues varies by type of revenue. Revenues based on formula distributions of state revenues, such as sales taxes, are fairly easy to predict. Revenues from federal grants, however, are more difficult to predict, although the distributing agencies are often able to provide tentative information on the probable distributions from continuing sources, on which grants are likely to be approved, and on the levels of payments likely to be made on existing and approved grants.

Once the projected revenues have been determined, they should be recorded on a **statement of actual and estimated revenues** (also known as a revenue summary). This statement is used to present the estimated revenues of the budget year and to compare these estimated revenues with the actual revenues of prior years and, as far as possible, the current year. It can also be used to present transfers expected to be received from other funds, such as residual equity and operating transfers. When preparing a statement of actual and esti-

---

[3]National Council on Governmental Accounting, *Statement 2*, "Grant, Entitlement and Shared Revenue Accounting and Reporting by State and Local Governments" (Chicago: Municipal Finance Officers Association of the United States and Canada, 1980), p. 1.

mated revenues, it is advisable to include an explanation of the assumptions made and the methods used to derive the estimates shown. Such a statement is shown in Table 10–5. This particular summary is a simplified one and is applicable to a small city. The statements of large organizations, however, are similar. They just contain more detailed information.

Departmental Expenditure Requests

Expenditure requests should be prepared by each department, program, or other subunit of the organization. These documents should show the expenditures of the prior year, the total estimated expenditures of the current year, and the proposed level of expenditures of the budget year. They should be accompanied by detailed supporting statements for each major object of expenditure. Such work sheets can be used to answer questions that may be raised by the budget officer, the CEO, or the legislative body. They can also be used to justify both new and continuing expenditures.

Expenditure requests serve a number of purposes. First, they enable the CEO and the legislative body to evaluate the performance of each subunit (this same function, of course, can also be performed by quarterly or monthly budget comparisons, which will be discussed later). They also enable persons making budgetary decisions to determine the propriety of each request in terms of the goals of the *entire* organization as opposed to the individual subunits; and when resources are limited, they enable these persons to allocate resources to those activities of each subunit that best serve the organization as a *whole*.

Finally, expenditure requests force department heads and other managers, at least once a year, to take a close look at the objectives and the current levels of activity of their subunits and to determine whether more efficient methods can be developed to meet these objectives. If these persons wish to expand the scope of the activities of their subunits, they must be able to justify the additional expenditures necessary and to disclose the impact on the organization, as a whole, of disallowing the additional expenditures.

The following series of steps should be applied to each expenditure when preparing departmental expenditure requests:

1. Determine the level of the expenditure for the past year and project the level of the expenditure for the current year.
2. Apply inflation and cost-of-living factors and other allowances for "uncontrollable" factors to each current-year expenditure. This will result in a "standstill" expenditure request.
3. Determine what activities should be expanded, contracted, or discontinued. Identify any new activities that, if funded, will commence the following year.
4. Adjust each proposed expenditure for the changes in the type and level of activities determined and identified in step 3.
5. Prepare a justification for each new activity or each increase in the level of an existing activity. Include, in this justification, the effect that *not* adopting or increasing the level of the activity will have on the organization. For this step, a PPB or ZBB type of analysis can be helpful.

6. Prepare a **budgetary work sheet** for each type of expenditure. The formats of the work sheets will vary with the type of expenditure being projected, although each work sheet should show the prior-year, current-year, and projected budget-year level of expenditures for each line item (object-of-expenditure).

7. Summarize the information from each work sheet on the expenditure request.

Departmental or program expenditures are generally broken into three categories: personal services, operating expenses, and equipment.

Personal Services

The heart of a personal services budget is the **position classification plan**. This document lists all the position titles and their corresponding salaries. From it, past and current personnel costs can be identified. The positions expected to be occupied during the budget year should be recorded on the budgetary work sheet, along with the past, current, and projected rate or salary attached to each position.

Employee (fringe) benefits should be treated as a separate item, although they can be combined with salaries and wages on the budgetary work sheet. The best approach to the handling of this item of cost is to determine the total expenditures for the prior year or the current year to date, and to divide this amount by the total payroll, to obtain the **employee benefit cost per payroll dollar**. This ratio can then be used when determining the full cost of new positions or existing positions at new salary levels.

Since employee benefits (Social Security, vacation pay, sick pay, and so on) are generally a function of salaries, the above method usually provides accurate data. However, the cost of certain benefits, such as paid hospitalization, may be fixed. That is, it may be the same for all employees regardless of salary level. Generally speaking, however, the cost of such benefits is a relatively small part of the total employee benefit cost. In addition, it tends to average out, and since the budget is based on estimates, the cost of "fixed" benefits does not usually create any serious problems.

One final note: When budgeting employee benefits, be sure to apply the budget year's rates. Unemployment insurance and FICA (Social Security) rates, in particular, tend to change very frequently.

Other personal service costs that must be considered are overtime, shift differentials, and requests for temporary help. For example, on certain holidays it is sometimes necessary to ask police officers to work overtime in order to handle the crowds of parade watchers. In addition, some cities hire students to perform special tasks, such as street repairs, during the summer. These costs are usually known well in advance and, by multiplying the projected hours by the appropriate pay and fringe benefit rates, they can easily be determined.

Compensation for members of the legislative body must also be included in the personal services section of the budget request. These people are paid either a fixed salary per year or a certain stipend for each meeting attended. In the latter case, their compensation can be estimated by multiplying the number of meetings expected to be held (a number often set by law) by a fixed rate per meeting.

In many organizations, a **salary-vacancy factor (SVF)** is used to fine-tune the expected cost of personal services. A SVF represents the portion of the budgeted salaries that is not expected to be spent because of a delay in hiring personnel or because vacancies will be filled at lower-than-budgeted salaries. This factor can be estimated by looking at past experience and future hiring policies. If a hiring freeze is expected to be in effect during the budget year, the SVF can be significant.

A personal services (budgetary) work sheet is shown in Table 10–6. Note that it includes prior- and current-year data, as well as the adjustments for cost-of-living and changes in fringe benefit rates. Note also that it gives a brief justification for the expansion of the level of service. The total of the personal services expenditures is transferred to the departmental expenditure request shown in Table 10–12. To assist in the preparation of their personal services work sheets, many governmental units prepare a salary work sheet, one of which is shown in Table 10–7.

Operating Expenses

Operating expenses are those outlays necessary in carrying out the organization's routine operations. Examples of such expenses are postage, office supplies, utilities, printing, reproduction, professional services, employee travel, fuel, and vehicle maintenance. If the scope of the organization's operations does not change, the level of these expenses can be estimated by using the current-year's level plus an inflation factor.

When budgeting operating expenses, each item should be questioned in order to determine whether it is necessary and, if so, whether its usage can be reduced. For example, can fuel be saved by replacing the existing police cruisers with more fuel-efficient models?

In the budgetary work sheet, the prior- and current-year outlays should be listed for each object of expenditure, along with the budget request. As with personal services, the inflation factor used should be shown. In addition, a justification should be made for any new items or any item whose usage is expected to increase significantly. All employee travel should be shown on a separate work sheet that lists the name of the person traveling and the date, destination, purpose, and estimated cost of each trip. Many organizations also show employee travel as a separate item on their departmental expenditure requests. A sample operating expense work sheet is shown in Table 10–8 and a sample travel work sheet is shown in Table 10–9.

Equipment

The **equipment** category includes items that normally last more than one year and cost more than a predetermined dollar amount (e.g., $50). Items not

TABLE 10—6 Personal Services Work Sheet

Fund: General
Function: Public Safety
Department: Police

Prepared by PÉ
Approved by PRT
Date: September 15, 1989

CODE	POSITION TITLE	PRIOR-YEAR ACTUAL			CURRENT-YEAR EST. ACTUAL			BUDGET REQUESTS†			REMARKS
		NO.	RATE*	AMOUNT	NO.	RATE*	AMOUNT	NO.	RATE*	AMOUNT	
101	Chief	1	$30,300	$30,300	1	$31,500	$ 31,500	1	$34,504	$ 34,504	
102	Captain	2	26,000	52,000	2	27,000	54,000	2	29,737	59,474	
104	Lieutenant	4	22,500	90,000	4	23,500	94,000	4	24,896	99,584	
105	Detective	2	17,200	34,400	2	18,000	36,000	2	19,068	38,136	
106	Sergeant	5	18,000	90,000	5	18,500	92,500	5	19,598	97,990	
180	Police Officer	12	16,000	192,000	12	17,000	204,000	14	18,007	252,098	Two new positions‡
	Total	26		$488,700	26		$512,000	28		$581,786	

* Includes employee benefits, which are budgeted at 13.5% of salaries and wages. This rate is 1% higher than the current rate (12.5%) because of an expected increase in the FICA rate (.6%) and the state unemployment rate (.4%). The prior-year rate is 11.1% of salaries and wages.

† Includes a cost-of-living factor of 5.0% plus an additional merit increase of $1,000 each for the Chief and Captains.

‡ *Justification and new positions:* In the latter part of the current year, an area of four square miles was annexed. To provide an adequate level of protection to this area and the original parts of the city, an additional patrol unit is necessary. If this additional unit is denied, the annexed area containing 562 residents will receive inadequate police protection or the entire city will receive a lower level of protection due to the overextending of available personnel and equipment. In either case the level of crime can be expected to rise significantly if the additional unit is not approved.

TABLE 10–7 Budget Year Salary Work Sheet

Fund: General
Function: Public Safety
Department: Police

Prepared by _____ PE
Approved by _____ PRT
Date: September 10, 1989

CODE	POSITION TITLE	1989 BASE	COST-OF-LIVING ADJ.*	MERIT	1990 BASE	FRINGE BENEFITS†	BUDGET REQUEST
101	Chief	$28,000	$1,400	$ 1,000	$30,400	$4,104	$34,504
102	Captain	24,000	1,200	1,000	26,200	3,537	29,737
104	Lieutenant	20,890	1,045	—	21,935	2,961	24,896
105	Detective	16,000	800	—	16,800	2,268	19,068
106	Sergeant	16,445	822	—	17,267	2,331	19,598
180	Police Officer	15,110	755	—	15,865	2,142	18,007

* 5.0% of 1989 base.

† 13.5% of salaries and wages.

TABLE 10–8 Operating Expense Work Sheet*

Fund: General
Function: Public Safety
Department: Police

Prepared by: WPE
Approved by: PRT
Date: September 15, 1989

CODE	OBJECT	PRIOR-YEAR ACTUAL	CURRENT-YEAR BUDGET	CURRENT-YEAR EST. ACTUAL	BUDGET REQUEST†	AMOUNT APPROPRIATED	REMARKS
	Contractual Services						
301	Advertising	$ 110	$ 100	$ 85	$ 100		
310	Printing	1,500	1,600	1,650	1,800		
320	Vehicle maintenance	7,500	8,000	8,000	8,400		Improved radio system
330	Communication	6,000	5,600	6,000	6,200		
350	Dues and subscriptions	180	200	200	200		
360	Postage	280	300	325	350		
370	Telephone	580	600	750	600		
380	Professional services	425	400	450	500		Staff training, medical
	Subtotal	$16,575	$16,800	$17,460	$18,150		
	Supplies and Materials						
401	Office supplies	$ 1,200	$ 1,100	$ 1,150	$ 1,200		
410	Building maintenance	4,500	4,700	4,800	5,000		Extra patrol unit
420	Fuel	10,135	10,500	10,250	12,000		
430	Ground maintenance	975	1,000	950	1,000		
440	Reproduction	1,250	1,400	1,420	1,500		
450	Uniform allowances	175	400	250	800		New personnel
460	Security supplies	1,010	1,200	1,235	1,300		New personnel
490	Miscellaneous	450	400	350	500		
	Grand total	$60,500	$61,600	$61,450	$62,350		

* Employee travel is reported separately.
† An inflation factor of 4.5% is used where applicable.

TABLE 10-9 Travel Work Sheet

Fund: General
Function: Public Safety
Department: Police

Prepared by _____ BNE
Approved by _____ PRT
Date: September 15, 1989

NAME AND/OR POSITION TITLE	DATES OF TRAVEL	DESTINATION	PURPOSE OF TRAVEL	BUDGET REQUEST*	AMOUNT APPROPRIATED
K. Lacho, Chief	3/1–3/3	Houston	Supervisory training	$ 500	
S. Spade, Detective	4/11–4/12	Seattle	Technical training	1,200	
B. Miller, Captain	7/22	Local	Sensitivity training	100	
R. Harris, Detective	8/15	Local	Report-writing training	50	
R. Columbo, Lieutenant	9/18	San Jose	Technical training	1,100	
K. Lacho, Chief	11/15–11/18	Tampa	Professional meetings	800	
B. Miller, Captain	11/15–11/18	Tampa	Professional meetings	800	
R. Lugar, Captain	11/15–11/18	Tampa	Professional meetings	800	
Total requested travel				$5,350	

* Includes conference fees or tuition, air fare, lodging, and a per diem allowance at locally authorized rates.

meeting both criteria should be classified as operating expenses. Typical items of equipment are furniture, typewriters, police cruisers, and lawn mowers.

Many organizations include the purchase of equipment in their capital budget. Other organizations use their capital budgets to record only the construction of buildings, streets, bridges, and so forth.

The work sheet used when budgeting expenditures for equipment should contain a description of each item of equipment requested and should state whether each item is an addition to or a replacement for an existing item. The work sheet should also indicate the number of items of each type requested and the cost per item. Finally, the work sheet should contain a justification for all the additional items of equipment requested. An equipment work sheet is shown in Table 10–10.

Capital Outlays

The term **capital outlays** is used to describe the cost of major building and renovation projects undertaken by the organization. These activities include new construction as well as the repair, alteration, and expansion of various facilities, such as buildings, roads, parks, bridges, airports, and levees. Capital projects can be performed by outside contractors or by organizational personnel. In may cases these projects are partially funded by state and federal grants. They can also be funded by the proceeds of bond issues.

Many organizations prepare capital budgets, which are approved separately from their operating budgets. Other organizations include capital projects in their operating budgets, treating their capital outlays in the same manner as other expenditures. In this text we will assume the latter approach and will include capital outlay requests in the operating budget.

A **capital outlay request summary** is shown in Table 10–11. In this illustration, the city has been given a plantation house, which it intends to restore and turn into a museum. In addition, the city is planning to build a new police station, work on a stadium (a three-year project), and rebuild several bridges. The capital outlay request summary contains information describing each project, the dollar amounts requested, and the amount of the cost allocated to the various departments (when more than one department or program benefits from a particular project). Supplementary schedules (not shown) can be used when many like items are requested for one project, such as pieces of antique furniture for the plantation house.

Some organizations prepare narrative explanations of the various projects under construction. Such explanations usually contain detailed descriptions of the projects, as well as discussions of the cost of finishing the projects and maintaining them when they are complete. The narrative explanations can also contain information on the sources of financing, the completion dates, and the justifications for the projects.

Many governmental units supplement their capital outlay request summaries with **long-run capital programs**. A long-run capital program presents in-

TABLE 10–10 Equipment Work Sheet

Fund: General
Function: Public Safety
Department: Police

Prepared by TE
Approved by PRT
Date: September 15, 1989

CODE	ITEM	ADDITION OR REPLACEMENT	NUMBER REQUESTED	NET COST PER UNIT*	BUDGET REQUEST	AMOUNT APPROPRIATED	REMARKS
504	Motor scooter	R	1	$ 1,800	$ 1,800		
505	Police cruiser	R	2	12,000	24,000		Necessary because of the annexation of four square miles of outlying area.
505	Police cruiser	A	1	12,500	12,500		
506	.38-caliber pistol	A	3	150	450		Same as above.
510	Typewriter	R	2	800	1,600		
515	Desk	R	2	350	700		Necessary because of increased number of records that must be maintained due to federal grant
518	File cabinet, 3-drawer	A	4	100	400		
522	Radio transmitter (used)	A	1	7,600	7,600		Necessary to improve communication between police patrol and dispatcher.
	Total				$49,050		

*Cost of new item less trade-in or resale value of item being replaced.

TABLE 10–11 Capital Outlay Request Summary

Date: September 15, 1989   Prepared by___ **BER**___

PROJECT DESCRIPTION	BUDGET REQUEST	DEPARTMENT CHARGED	REMARKS
Restore Ellett plantation house	$100,000	Parks	Purchase of furniture
Police station	300,000	Police	Darby and Manoa Roads
Rebuild bridges	800,000	Streets	Marple Canal and Darby Creek
C.S. "Doc" Watson Stadium	300,000	Parks	1/3 of estimated cost
Total requested	$1,500,000		

formation on the capital improvements desired over a long period of time (e.g., five years). It lists the projects planned, the estimated cost of each project, and the proposed source or sources of funding for each project. Generally it is prepared on a "continuous" basis, with a future year added, a past year dropped, and the other years "fine-tuned."

Although some people may regard long-run capital programs as "wish lists" and many projects may never be started, long-run capital programs are good organizing, planning, and communicating tools. They enable users to see at a glance what is needed, what is wanted, and what the organization can afford. Such information is particularly valuable to legislators who must balance the needs of one organization against the needs of others in order to allocate limited resources.

One question that often arises is whether costly items, such as fire engines and road machinery, should be placed in the capital budget or in the operating budget. The authors of this book believe that items of a routine nature, such as police cruisers, should be included in the operating budget regardless of cost, and that the capital budget should be used exclusively for nonroutine items, such as buildings, bridges, and the *initial* paving of streets. This is not, however, a unanimously held view.

Departmental Expenditure Request Document

When the work sheets for personal services, operating expenses, and equipment and the capital outlay request summaries are finished, certain information is transferred from these forms to the **departmental expenditure request document**. This schedule contains, at a minimum, the title of each object-of-expenditure, the level of prior- and current-year expenditures, and the requested level of expenditures for the budget year. It can also contain a column in which the amount actually appropriated by the legislative body is recorded.

Some organizations summarize the requested level of expenditures by activity (e.g., vice squad, juvenile control, traffic control, and so on) and include this summary in a supplementary schedule. Such information can help the CEO and the members of the legislative body to make judgments on the costs and benefits of specific activities. A departmental expenditure request is shown in Table 10–12.

Nondepartmental Expenditure Requests

Nondepartmental expenditures are expenditures that do not relate to any one specific department or activity. Instead, they benefit the organization as a whole. Examples of nondepartmental expenditures include interest on bonds, utilities and maintenance costs of buildings used by different departments or programs (such as a city hall), certain pension costs, and liability insurance premiums for city-owned vehicles. In addition, many organizations set up a reserve, or "slush fund," to cover emergencies or contingencies (such as cleaning up after a flood).

The work sheet used to budget nondepartmental expenditures is similar to the one used to budget departmental operating expenses. However, since nondepartmental operating expenditures are usually of a fixed nature (e.g., interest on a bond issue), and since their planned level is usually determined by the budget officer or the CEO, the work sheet used to budget them is prepared by the budget officer. A nondepartmental expenditure request is shown in Table 10–13.

Work Programs

Many organizations supplement their budget requests with **work programs** which are schedules of specific activities to be performed by the organization in carrying out its assigned functions. They may be in narrative or tabular form, although the latter is preferable because it is easier to read. Regardless of their form, work programs should indicate the following:

1. The purpose of the subunit of the organization (e.g., public safety)
2. Each activity to be performed, along with a description of the activity when its nature is not obvious
3. The units used to measure the activity
4. The value of the work performed, expressed in the units described in number 3
5. The cost of each unit of work performed
6. The total cost of each activity

Data should also be provided on the personnel, materials, supplies, and equipment needed to carry out each activity.

A work program should, at a minimum, cover the past year, the current year, and the budget year. It can be enhanced by comparisons between the three years, narrative descriptions of existing and proposed activities, and the reasons for changes in the level or scope of the various activities.

TABLE 10–12 Departmental Expenditure Request

Fund: General
Function: Public Safety
Department: Police

Prepared by _____ BER
Approved by _____ PRT
Date: September 15, 1989

CODE	OBJECT	PRIOR-YEAR ACTUAL	CURRENT-YEAR BUDGET	CURRENT-YEAR EST. ACTUAL	BUDGET REQUEST	AMOUNT APPROPRIATED
100	Personal services	$488,700	$515,600	$512,000	$581,786	
200	Travel	4,600	4,800	4,800	5,350	
3–600	Operating expenses	60,500	61,600	61,450	62,350	
700	Equipment	42,470	46,500	45,800	49,050	
800	Capital outlays	236,000	100,000	110,000	300,000	
	Total	$832,270	$728,500	$734,050	$998,536	

Narrative: The police department maintains law and order in the community. Major departmental expenditures are for personnel, operating expenses, and equipment. Because of the increased area of the city, the department must add two police officers and an additional police cruiser. In addition, it must replace three police cruisers that have reached the end of their useful lives. The department also plans to build a substation at Darby and Manoa Roads to service the area that was recently annexed by the city. Finally, the department must upgrade its communication system because of a recently passed law requiring that police departments throughout the state maintain comprehensive communication networks that are integrated into the state system.

TABLE 10–13 Nondepartmental Expenditure Request

Fund: General
Date: September 15, 1989

Prepared by ___CCW___
Approved by ___LVT___

CODE	OBJECT	PRIOR-YEAR ACTUAL	CURRENT-YEAR BUDGET	CURRENT-YEAR EST. ACTUAL	BUDGET REQUEST	AMOUNT APPROPR.	REMARKS
710	Redemption of bonds*	$500,000	$500,000	$500,000	$1,300,000		6.0% debentures of 1990
725	Interest on bonds*	205,000	180,000	180,000	165,000		Extra costs of redeeming bonds
730	Fiscal agent fees*	1,000	1,000	1,000	1,500		
810	Repairs	—	—	3,000	20,000		Damage to City Hall from dust storm
850	Legal settlements	150,000	120,000	210,000	200,000		Uninsured portion of damage claims
925	Audit fees	12,000	15,000	15,500	18,000		Inflation
930	Legal services	35,000	35,000	40,000	40,000		Inflation
950	Advertising	2,000	2,500	2,450	8,000		Promote international exposition
	Total	$905,000	$853,500	$951,950	$1,752,500		

*Transfer to Debt Service Fund.

Budgetary Review

The departmental expenditure request documents are submitted to the budget officer, along with the work sheets, work programs (if any), and any other supporting materials. The budget officer, or a member of his or her staff, determines whether each expenditure request document has been properly prepared and whether each requested item is justified and realistic, as well as appropriate. If the budget officer believes that the expenditure request documents have been property prepared and that each item is justified, realistic, and appropriate, he or she summarizes the information received and transmits it, along with the backup materials and revenue estimates, to the CEO. The CEO reviews the information and prepares recommendations for the legislative body. A budget summary is shown in Table 10–14.

Determining whether the expenditure request documents have been properly prepared is a relatively simple procedure. It consists primarily of ascertaining that all the requested information has been provided, that the arithmetic on each form is correct, and that no errors have been made when transferring information from one form to another.

TABLE 10-14 Budget Summary

City of Hope
General Fund
Budget Summary
Fiscal Year 1990

Revenues		
Property tax		$3,550,000
Liquor tax		480,000
Sales tax		2,650,000
Royalty payments		300,000
Fines and penalties		100,000
Rental charges		11,000 $7,091,000
Appropriations		
Administration:		
Personal services	$435,000	
Travel	22,400	
Operating expenses	85,800	
Equipment	24,600	$ 567,800
Fire:		
Personal services	$715,000	
Travel	12,500	
Operating expenses	335,000	
Equipment	146,250	1,208,750
Parks:		
Personal services	$246,350	
Travel	1,850	
Operating expenses	82,350	
Equipment	72,300	
Capital outlays	400,000	802,850

TABLE 10-14   (cont.)

Police:			
Personal services	$581,786		
Travel	5,350		
Operating expenses	62,350		
Equipment	49,050		
Capital outlays	300,000	998,536	
Streets:			
Personal services	$364,750		
Travel	1,150		
Operating expenses	103,360		
Equipment	246,000		
Capital outlays	800,000	1,515,260	
Nondepartmental:			
Repairs	$ 20,000		
Legal settlements	200,000		
Audit fees	18,000		
Legal services	40,000		
Advertising	8,000	286,000	5,379,196
Excess of revenues over appropriations			$1,711,804
Other Financing Sources (Uses)			
Transfer from Expendible Trust Fund		$ 150,000	
Transfer to Debt Service Fund		(1,466,500)	(1,316,500)
Excess of revenues and other sources over expenditures and other uses			$ 395,304

Determining whether each requested item is justified, realistic, and appropriate is more difficult. The budget officer must determine the need for each activity and level of service, the validity of the assumptions underlying each budgetary calculation, and whether each requested item falls within the budgetary guidelines. If a requested item exceeds these guidelines, the budget officer must determine why this is so and whether the additional request is justified.

For example, in the personal services work sheet in Table 10–6, two additional police officers are requested, along with additional equipment, because of the annexation of an unincorporated area into the city. If the budgetary guidelines specify no new positions or if the revenue picture is not optimistic, the budget officer must determine whether the same level of services can be delivered with existing resources or whether a lower level of services will suffice.

If the CEO and the legislative body are to make *informed* decisions, supplementary data must be included with the expenditure requests. This information can come from

1. *Performance reports*—work plans, personnel reports, productivity studies, and so on.
2. *Independent research*—cost-benefit analyses, program audits, feasibility studies, and so on.

3. *Reports and studies from outside sources*—press releases, program status reports prepared for funding agencies, reports prepared by citizens' groups, and so on.

At all times, the budget officer should be in close contact with the department heads, program directors, and other persons responsible for preparing expenditure requests. A budget officer who feels that a request is questionable should meet with the person who prepared the request, in order to resolve the matter. If the matter cannot be resolved at this level, the person preparing the request should have the right to appeal to the CEO.

The budget officer is also responsible, in most organizations, for ensuring that the total proposed expenditures do not exceed the estimated revenues plus any surplus likely to be on hand at the end of the current year. Since the total expenditure requests of most organizations usually exceed the projected revenues of those organizations, even after the screening process discussed above, and since most organizations are required, by law or charter, to operate within a balanced budget, the budget director is usually forced to decide which requests should be included in the budget document and which requests should be reduced or eliminated.

When balancing the budget, the budget officer should first determine whether a perceived need for more resources can be met by shifting existing resources from another area. For example, the budget officer may agree with the need for an additional police officer position. Upon reviewing the budget of another department, the budget officer might discover that that department employs a security guard. In this case the budget officer might arrange a meeting between the police chief and the head of that department to determine whether the job performed by the security guard can be performed by extending the police patrols to include that department's facility. If the outcome of this meeting is positive, a transfer can be made from the budget of the department employing the security guard to the police department's budget at very little cost to the organization. (The authors realize that not all trade-offs are this easy.)

The budget officer must also determine whether each activity should expand or reduce the level of its objectives and whether the objectives of each activity can be achieved just as effectively with fewer resources. To assist the budget officer in making such decisions (and to defend their subunits from the consequences of such decisions), persons preparing expenditure requests should include sound justifications and detailed backup data with each request.

The final review of the expenditure requests is made by the CEO. The data from the various subunits should be presented to this executive in summary form, with backup information readily available. Both subunit and organization-wide requests should be presented.

The purposes of the final review are (1) to obtain the input of the CEO into the budgetary process, (2) to act as a court of last resort for disputes between the budget officer and the persons preparing the expenditure requests, and (3) to enable the CEO to prepare specific budget recommendations before submitting them to the legislative body.

The best approach to the final review is to have each person responsible for preparing expenditure requests brief the CEO on those requests and provide "ammunition" that the CEO can use when presenting the budget to the legislative body. If the CEO has been involved in the budgetary process from its inception, and if all differences between the budget officer and the persons responsible for preparing the expenditure requests have been resolved, this final review can be a positive experience.

The Budget Document

After the final review has been completed, the budget officer assembles the budget requests, the revenue projections, and the CEO's recommendations into a comprehensive **budget document**, which is presented to the legislative body. The magnitude of a budget document can range from one to several volumes, depending on the organization's size and complexity. At a minimum, a budget document should contain

1. A *budget message*—which, in general terms, discusses
   a. The fiscal experience of the current year
   b. The present financial position of the organization
   c. The major financial issues faced during the past year and the ones that are expected to be faced during the budget year
   d. Major assumptions used when preparing the budget requests (e.g., the expected rate of inflation)
   e. Significant changes from the current year's budget
   f. The CEO's recommendations for action on the budget year's programs and financial policies
   g. Major personnel changes
   h. The future economic outlook of the organization
2. A *budget summary*—which lists the total budgeted revenues by source, and lists the total budgeted expenditures by program or department and for the organization as a whole. This part of the budget document can be enhanced by including comparisons between the budgeted revenues and expenditures and the actual revenues and expenditures of the current and past year. It can also be made more effective by highlighting significant changes in the levels of specific sources of revenue and specific expenditures.
3. *Detailed supporting schedules*—among which should be schedules of
   a. Estimated revenues by source
   b. Departmental and nondepartmental expenditure requests
   c. Budgeted fixed charges such as the repayment of debt
4. A *capital projects schedule*
5. *Detailed justifications of the budgetary recommendations*
6. *Supplementary information*—such as
   a. Departmental budget request work sheets
   b. Departmental work programs
   c. Pro forma balance sheets for each fund, as of the beginning and the end of the budget year
   d. A cash budget
   e. A schedule of interest payments, sinking fund contributions, and bond issues and retirements
7. *Drafts of appropriation and tax levy ordinances or acts*

Legislative Consideration and
Adoption of the Budget

The completed budget document is sent to the legislative body, which reviews, modifies, approves, and adopts it. Before approving the budget document, the legislative body usually conducts both formal and informal private hearings, as well as formal public hearings. In some cases the budget document is turned over to a legislative finance or ways-and-means committee for recommendations. Such recommendations, however, are just that—recommendations. They are not binding on the entire legislative body.

Private hearings can be in the form of informal briefings, such as workshop sessions conducted by the CEO, the budget officer, or the persons responsible for preparing budgetary requests. They can also take the form of lists of questions to be answered in writing by officials of the organization, and of meetings between individual legislators and the CEO or budget officer. During these hearings, items of concern to the members of the legislative body can be discussed, as can the impact of programs in which the legislators are particularly interested. As a result, many issues and questions can be resolved by the time the budget is formally presented.

At a designated meeting, the CEO formally presents the budget document to the legislative body. This presentation should include a general overview of the contents of the budget document, a discussion of the assumptions made when preparing the budget document, and a discussion of the major financial difficulties that the organization will face during the budget year. The revenue estimates and budget requests should also be reviewed, as should the justification for each new or nonroutine request.

Many organizations are required by law (or political expediency) to hold public hearings on the budget. Citizen input to budgetary decisions is obtained by allowing interested parties to comment to the legislative body on their own concerns. The process of budgetary approval is expedited if copies of the budget document (or a summary) are disseminated, in advance of the public hearings and the formal presentation, to the members of the legislative body and to the public. If the users of the budget document are allowed a reasonable amount of time to "digest" its contents, issues of concern can more readily be identified and the public hearings and deliberations of the legislative body will proceed more smoothly.

When the budget hearings are finished, the legislative body completes its deliberations, makes any modifications to the budget document it feels are necessary, and enacts a final **appropriation ordinance** or, in the case of a state, **appropriation act**. The purpose of this ordinance or act is to establish a spending ceiling for the budget year and to authorize the organization to make the expenditures listed in the budget.

Once the appropriation ordinance or act has been passed, the budget document is returned to the organization, where the budgeted amounts are entered into the accounts—as we mentioned in Chapter 4. Many organizations also publish their approved budget.

Property Tax Levy

Once the budget has been approved, the legislative body must take action to raise the revenues necessary to finance the budgeted expenditures. The collection of many types of revenue does not require frequent action on the part of the legislative body. These revenues are usually the result of past actions (e.g., license fees, sales taxes, income from investments, and so on). Other revenue measures, however, require legal action more frequently, the most common example being property taxes.

Two different approaches can be used to determine the taxes to be assessed on each piece of property. Under the first approach the assessed value of the property (less any exemptions) is multiplied by a flat rate, which is "permanently" fixed by law. Under the second, and more common, approach the property taxes are treated as a residual source of revenue.

Before an organization using the second approach can send tax bills to the property owners, it must determine a tax (millage) rate that, when applied to the assessed valuation of the property, will provide the desired amount of revenue. Although simple in concept, this approach can become complicated because of (1) uncollectible or delinquent taxes and (2) property exempt from taxation (such as land belonging to religious organizations) and exemptions due to the military service, age, physical condition, and economic status of the owner and the use of the property as a homestead. This last exemption can be particularly costly to taxing organizations. In Louisiana, for example, the homestead exemption is applied to the first $75,000 of the current market value of any piece of property used as the principal residence of its owner.

Using the residual approach, the tax (millage) rate is computed as follows:

Amount to be collected	$ 100,000	
Allowance for uncollectible property taxes	4%	
Required tax levy	$ 104,166 ($100,000/.96)	
Total assessed value of property	$10,000,000	
Less: Property not taxable	(2,000,000)	$8,000,000
Less: exemptions:		
Homestead	$ 1,000,000	
Veterans	500,000	
Old age, blindness, etc.	900,000	2,400,000
Net assessed value of property		$5,600,000

$$\text{Tax (Millage) Rate} = \frac{\text{Required Tax Levy}}{\text{Net Assessed Value of Property}}$$

$$= \frac{104,166}{5,600,000} = .0186$$

In this example, the property tax will be levied at the rate of $1.86 per $100 of net assessed valuation. If the tax rate is expressed in mills (thousandths of a dollar), it will be 18.60 mills. Thus the owner of a piece of property with a net (after exemptions) assessed value of $80,000 will be required to pay property taxes of $1,488 ($80,000 x .0186).

SELECTED REFERENCES

HATRY, HARRY P., AND JOHN F. COTTON. *Program Planning for State, County, City.* Washington, D.C.: George Washington University, 1967.

HYDE, ALBERT C., AND JAY M. SHAFRITZ, eds. *Government Budgeting: Theory, Process, Politics.* Oak Park, Ill.: Moore Publishing Company, 1978.

MOAK, LENNOX L., AND KATHRYN W. KILLIAN. *A Manual of Techniques for the Preparation, Consideration, Adoption and Administration of Operating Budgets.* Chicago: Municipal Finance Officers Association, 1963.

MUNICIPAL FINANCE OFFICERS ASSOCIATION. *An Operating Budget Handbook for Small Cities and Other Governmental Units.* Chicago, 1978.

POWELL RAY M. *Budgetary Control Procedures for Institutions.* Notre Dame, Ind.: University of Notre Dame Press, 1980.

PHYRR, PETER A. "Zero-Based Budgeting," *Harvard Business Review* (November-December 1970), pp. 111–21.

RAZEK, JOSEPH R., AND DANIEL PEARL. "Zero-Based Budgeting: An Idea Whose Time Has Come," *Louisiana Business Survey,* 9 (2) (Winter 1978): 2–3.

SECKLER-HUDSON, CATHERYN. "Performance Budgeting in Government," *Advanced Management* (March 1953), pp. 5–9, 30–32.

SMITH, ELTON C., AND ANDREA E. JACKSON. *Alabama County Finance Manual.* Auburn, Ala.: Auburn University, 1980.

STALLINGS, WAYNE. "Improving Budget Communications in Smaller Local Governments," *Government Finance,* 7 (3) (August 1978): 18–25.

REVIEW QUESTIONS

Q10–1   What is a budget? What purpose(s) does it serve?

Q10–2   List the steps involved in preparing a budget.

Q10–3   Why should revenue estimates be prepared before expenditure requests? What steps are taken when preparing revenue estimates?

Q10–4   What information should be contained in a set of budgetary instructions?

Q10–5   What is the purpose of a budget calendar?

Q10–6   How can the current year's surplus or deficit be calculated?

Q10–7   What factors should be considered when projecting (1) sales taxes, (2) property taxes, and (3) hotel occupancy taxes?

Q10–8   What are the three categories of departmental, or program, expenditures?

Q10–9   What are fringe benefits? How should they be handled in the budget?

Q10–10   What is a salary-vacancy factor? How can it be estimated?

Q10–11   What is a capital program? Why should it be prepared for several years beyond the budget year?

Q10–12   Name three sources of supplementary information that should be included with budget requests.

Q10–13   What is the purpose of a budgetary review? By whom should it be performed?

Q10–14   What is a millage rate? How is it determined?

Q10–15   What is the purpose of a cash budget? How can it assist in the smooth functioning of an organization?

EXERCISES

E10–1   (Discussion of uses of budgeting)

Rex, a budget officer, conducted a class for nonaccounting managers and program directors on the subject of budgets. Rex began the class discussion by asking, "What are some of the uses of a budget?"

One manager replied, "Planning." Another said, "Evaluating performance." Still another suggested, "Coordinating activities." "What about implementing plans?" inquired another. "Or communicating them?" added still another. "Don't forget motivation," one manager warned from the rear of the room. "I'm on the school board," commented another, "and we use it to authorize actions."

Finally, one manager asked, "Can budgets do all that?"

"Yes," Rex responded, "all that *and more.*"

REQUIRED: 1.   Define the term *budget*.
2.   Select any *four* of the uses suggested by the managers and explain how a budget might accomplish each of the four uses selected.

(IIA adapted)

E10–2   (Budgeting cash disbursements)

The City of Argus is preparing its cash budget for the month of July. The following information is available with respect to its proposed disbursements:

Items vouchered in July	$650,000
Estimated payments in July for items vouchered in July	50%
Items vouchered in June	$400,000
Estimated payments in July for all items vouchered in June	70%
Estimated payments in July for items vouchered prior to June	$ 50,000
Items purchased and vouchered in June but returned in July before payment was made	$ 20,000

REQUIRED: What are the estimated cash disbursements for July?

E10–3   (Budgeting cash receipts)

The City of Comus is preparing a cash budget for the month of May. The following information is available with respect to its sales tax collections:

Sales tax rate	5%
Estimated retail sales in May	$2,000,000
Actual retail sales in April	1,500,000
Estimated payments by merchants to city in May of sales taxes collected in May	20%
Estimated payments by merchants to city in May of sales taxes collected in April	70%
Estimated payments by merchants to city in May of sales taxes collected prior to April	$ 10,000

REQUIRED: Compute the estimated cash receipts from sales tax collections in May.

E10–4   (Determination of property tax rate)

The legislative body of Pandorra County has just approved the 1989-1990 fiscal year budget. Revenues from property taxes are budgeted at $800,000. According to the County assessor, the assessed valuation of all of the property in the County is $50 million. Of this amount, however, property worth $10 million belongs to either the federal government or to religious organizations and, therefore, is not subject to property taxes. In addition, certificates for the following exemptions have been filed:

Homestead	$2,500,000
Veterans	1,000,000
Old age, blindness, etc.	500,000

In the past, uncollectible property taxes have averaged around 2 percent of the levy. This rate is not expected to change in the foreseeable future.

REQUIRED: a. Determine the property tax rate that must be used in order to collect the desired revenue from property taxes.

b. How much would the levy be on a piece of property that was assessed for $100,000 (after exemptions)?

E10–5   (Estimating the fund balance at the end of the year)

At the end of the preceding year, the General Fund of the Atlas Township School Board had a surplus of $800,000. Revenues and expenditures of the current year are expected to be as follows:

	YEAR-TO-DATE ACTUAL	REMAINDER OF YEAR ESTIMATED
Revenues:		
Property taxes	$1,250,000	$500,000
Out-of-township tuition	50,000	20,000
Share of lottery receipts	100,000	50,000
State grants	500,000	—

	YEAR-TO-DATE ACTUAL	REMAINDER OF YEAR ESTIMATED
Expenditures:		
Salaries	$875,000	$450,000
Fringe benefits	90,000	40,000
Operating expenses	588,000	240,000
Equipment	110,000	50,000
Transportation	15,000	10,000
Repayment of debt	100,000	100,000

REQUIRED: Determine the projected year-end fund balance for this fund.

E10–6   (Trend analysis)

The City of Endymion levies a tax of 5 percent on all retail sales throughout the city. Retail sales for the current year and the past five years are
as follows (rounded and in millions):

1984	$12.1
1985	15.4
1986	17.3
1987	20.8
1988	23.4
1989 (est.)	27.3

In 1990, a new retail complex will be opened that should attract shop-
pers from nearby cities. As a result, retail sales are expected to be 10
percent higher than they would be if the complex had not been erected.

REQUIRED: Determine how much the city should budget for revenue from sales taxes
in 1990.

E10–7   (Multiple choice—budgeting)
1.   A key difference between budgets prepared by governmental units
and by commercial organizations is
a. Budgets prepared by commercial organizations must be approved by a governing body, while those prepared by governmental units need no approvals
b. Budgets prepared by governmental units are legal documents,
while those prepared by commercial organizations are not
c. Operating, capital, and cash budgets are prepared by governmental units, but only operating budgets are prepared by commercial organizations
d. Budgets prepared by commercial organizations are formally recorded in the organizations operating accóunts, while those prepared by governmental units are not
2.   Which of the following expenditures is *not* included in a cash budget?
a. Personal services
b. Redemption of bonds

    c. Utilities

    d. Depreciation

3. The nondepartmental expenditures request is prepared by

    a. The department heads as a group

    b. The auditor

    c. The city council

    d. The CEO or the budget director.

4. An objection to the object-of-expenditure approach to budgeting is

    a. Budgets prepared under this approach are complicated and difficult to prepare

    b. Information presented in this type of budget is difficult to incorporate into the accounting system

    c. Legislative bodies are given more detail than they can handle; therefore, they tend to focus on individual items rather than on the overall goals and programs of the organization

    d. Detailed comparisons between budgeted and actual revenues and expenditures are difficult to make

5. A tool commonly used to project certain types of revenues is

    a. Trend analysis

    b. PERT

    c. Queuing theory

    d. Cost-volume-profit analysis

6. Which of the following is *not* a basic rule to follow when using budgets?

    a. The budget must be presented in a positive manner

    b. The budget must have the support of top management

    c. Managers must only be held responsible for revenues and costs over which they have a degree of control

    d. The budget must be prepared by top management

7. A continuous budget

    a. Is used only by commercial organizations

    b. Covers a specific period but is continuously updated

    c. Is also known as a line-item budget

    d. Is valid over a range of activity, rather than just one level

8. The approach to budgeting that forces managers to assess the value and justify the continuation of each activity under their supervision is the

    a. Zero-based budgeting approach

    b. Planning-programming-budgeting approach

    c. Flexible budgeting approach

    d. Object-of-expenditure approach

E10–8 (Behavioral aspects of budgeting)

The operating budget is a very common instrument used by many organizations. While it usually is thought to be an important and necessary tool for management, it has been subject to some criticism from managers and researchers studying organization and human behavior.

REQUIRED: a. Describe and discuss some benefits of budgeting from the behavioral point of view.
                 b. Describe and discuss some criticisms leveled at the budgetary process from the behavioral point of view.
                 c. What solutions do you recommend to overcome the criticisms described in part b?

(CMA adapted)

PROBLEMS

P10–1 (Budgeting revenues)

The following information relates to the prior- and current-year revenues of the General Fund of the Bacchus City Levee Board.

	1988 ACTUAL	JAN.–SEPT. 1989 ACTUAL	OCT.–DEC. 1989 EST. ACT.	1989 BUDGET
Property taxes	$3,436,720	$2,334,000	$1,150,000	$3,504,000
Interest and penalties	38,486	22,800	15,000	38,000
Sales taxes	272,680	154,500	145,000	300,000
Fines and penalties	64,842	39,240	30,000	70,000
Share of lottery receipts	—	54,250	175,750	225,000
License fees	9,650	7,540	2,460	10,000

Additional information:

1. Because of a reassessment of commercial property, property taxes are expected to increase by $400,000 in 1990.

2. Interest and penalties and license fees are expected to remain constant over the next several years.

3. Because of an increase in the sales tax from 4 to 6 percent and the expectation of several large conventions in 1990, sales tax revenues are expected to increase by 60 percent.

4. Because of the conventions, fines and penalties should rise by 10 percent in 1990.

5. The lottery has been very successful in its first few months of operation. Levee Board officials expect the board's share of the lottery receipts to double in 1990.

REQUIRED: Prepare a statement of actual and estimated revenues for 1990. Assume that you are preparing it on October 15, 1989, and that the changes given above are with respect to the 1989 budget.

P10–2 (Personal services and travel work sheets)

The director of the Maintenance Department of the Bacchus City Levee Board has prepared the following position classification plan:

	1988		1989	
Position	No.	Rate	No.	Rate
Director	1	$28,000	1	$30,000
Assistant director	1	24,000	1	26,000
Foreman	4	17,500	4	19,000
Equipment operator II	8	14,250	7	16,000
Equipment operator I	12	12,100	13	13,800
Laborer, utility	30	9,200	26	10,300
Secretary	1	9,500	1	10,600

Additional information:

1. Fringe benefits are not included in the above rates. In 1988, they averaged 12.2 percent of wages and salaries. In 1989, they are averaging 12.8 percent. In 1990, they should average 13.6 percent.

2. Permission has been obtained from the legislative body to budget an 8 percent cost-of-living increase for 1990. In addition, the president of the board has recommended that the director and the assistant director each be given a $1,000 merit increase, in addition to their cost-of-living increases.

3. Due to the building of several miles of new levees in 1989, the management of the Levee Board believes that an additional maintenance crew, consisting of one foreman, one equipment operator II, and two laborers, should be hired.

4. From March 3 to March 7, the director of the Maintenance Department plans to attend a professional conference in Milwaukee, at a cost of $750. In addition, the director and the assistant director plan to attend a technical workshop in Tampa from April 21 through April 25, at a cost of $500 each. Finally, the five foremen are expected to attend a supervisory workshop, given at a nearby city, on August 18. The cost of this travel for all five foremen is expected to be $100. In 1988, travel costs amounted to $1,425. In 1989, they were budgeted at $1,500. A total of $1,600 is expected to be spent this year.

5. Assume that in 1989 the budgeted salaries are the same as the actual salaries. Assume also that the Maintenance Department's activities are recorded in the General Fund and that this department's function falls under the heading of Public Safety.

REQUIRED: For the fiscal year 1990, prepare
a. A personal services work sheet
b. A travel work sheet

P10–3 (Equipment work sheet)

During 1990, the Maintenance Department of the Bacchus City Levee

Board plans to make the following purchases of equipment. Since these items each cost more than $200, they are budgeted under the category of "Equipment." The items are:

1. Two three-quarter ton pickup trucks. These will be replacements for existing trucks and will have a net cost (after trade-in) of $9,500 each.

2. One two-ton flatbed truck. This is a new item that will be necessary because of the new work crew expected to be hired and the additional levees to be maintained. The estimated cost of the truck is $22,500.

3. Other new items to be purchased for the use of the new work crew are:
    a. One chipper $3,750
    b. Two 24" lawn mowers   700 each
    c. Two lawn vacuum cleaners   650 each
    d. One hedge trimmer   240
    e. One 5' by 8' trailer   500

4. Other items, which are replacements for existing items, to be purchased are:
    a. Three 22" lawn mowers $ 300 each
    b. Two grass trimmers   2,200 each
    c. One welding machine (used)   3,000

In 1988, the Maintenance Department spent $36,450 on equipment. For 1989, $30,000 has been budgeted, but only $18,360 of this amount has been spent to date. The director of this department estimates that by the end of fiscal year 1989, another $8,000 will be spent or encumbered for equipment.

REQUIRED: Prepare an equipment work sheet for the Maintenance Department.

P10–4   (Operating expense work sheet)
From the following data, prepared as of August 30, 1989, prepare an operating expense work sheet to be used in the fiscal year 1990 budget of the Maintenance Department of the Bacchus City Levee Board.

CODE	OBJECT OF EXPENDITURE	PRIOR-YEAR ACTUAL	CURRENT-YEAR BUDGET	YEAR-TO-DATE ACTUAL	REST OF YEAR EST. ACTUAL
	Contractual Services				
320	Vehicle and equipment maintenance	$18,450	$20,000	$15,000	$6,000
330	Communication	1,200	1,200	800	400
340	Rentals	648	800	400	200
365	Utilities	1,146	1,200	952	300
370	Telephone	240	240	180	80
380	Professional services	300	500	350	—

CODE	OBJECT OF EXPENDITURE	PRIOR-YEAR ACTUAL	CURRENT-YEAR BUDGET	YEAR-TO-DATE ACTUAL	REST OF YEAR EST. ACTUAL
	Supplies and Materials				
410	Office supplies	214	200	158	42
415	Auto and truck	286	300	200	100
418	Equipment supplies	1,614	1,500	1,250	400
420	Fuel	3,847	4,000	3,000	1,500
425	Gardening materials	1,206	1,200	860	300
430	Emergency supplies	152	200	50	100
440	Tools	876	1,000	800	200
450	Miscellaneous	136	100	75	—

Additional information:

1. Because of the crew expected to be added in 1990, the budgeted vehicle and equipment maintenance, equipment supplies, tools, and gardening materials expenditures are to be increased by 15 percent in 1990.

2. The budgets for communications, professional services, and miscellaneous supplies and materials should remain at their present levels.

3. An inflation factor of 8 percent should be applied to the fiscal year 1989 budget for the remaining items.

4. For this department, professional services consist largely of tree surgery and medical expenses for minor injuries of work crews.

P10–5   (Capital outlay requests)

The management of the Bacchus City Levee Board wishes to start or continue the following capital projects in fiscal year 1990:

1. Raise the height of the lakefront levee from 12 feet to 18 feet. This will decrease the probability of flooding in a hurricane from 25 to 5 percent. The estimated cost of this project is $450,000. The entire cost will be charged to the Facilities Department.

2. Continue construction of the Taos Avenue Bridge. The estimated cost to be incurred in fiscal year 1990 is $750,000, which is to be charged to the Facilities Department. This cost represents approximately one-half of the total cost of the project.

3. Build a new equipment storage facility. This is necessary because of the additional equipment that is expected to be purchased by the Maintenance Department. The estimated cost of this project is $50,000, all of which will be charged to the Maintenance Department.

4. Build a new office building to house the various administrative functions. The building is expected to cost $800,000. Of this amount 10 percent will be charged to the Maintenance Department. The remaining 90 percent will be charged to the Department of Administration.

REQUIRED: Prepare a capital outlay request summary for the Bacchus City Levee Board.

P10–6   (Departmental expenditure request)

Using the information given in Problems 10–2 through 10–5 and the information below, prepare a departmental expenditure request for the Maintenance Department of the Bacchus City Levee Board.

1.   The function of the department is to assist in guarding the public's safety by maintaining the levees around Bacchus City. This consists primarily of caring for the grass and trees on the levees, filling in eroded spots, and maintaining the floodgates and supply of sandbags. Because of the growth of the city, new levees have been built in outlying areas and certain levees have been raised. The care of these new levees has put a severe strain on the existing work crews' ability to maintain all of the levee system adequately.

2.   In fiscal year 1988, no capital expenditures were charged to the Maintenance Department. For fiscal year 1989, $100,000 has been budgeted. It is expected that the actual capital expenditures charged to this department in fiscal year 1989 will amount to $95,000.

P10–7   (Budgeting nondepartmental expenditures)

From the following data, prepare a nondepartmental expenditures request for the Bacchus City Levee Board for the fiscal year 1990.

CODE	OBJECT OF EXPENDITURE	PRIOR-YEAR ACTUAL	CURRENT-YEAR BUDGET	JAN.–SEPT. ACTUAL	OCT.–DEC. EST. ACT.
710	Redemption of bonds	$715,000	$890,000	$445,000	$445,000
725	Interest on bonds	52,000	60,000	30,000	30,000
730	Fiscal agent fees	554	600	450	200
810	Liability insurance	15,436	16,000	12,315	4,000
925	Audit fees	5,000	6,000	—	6,200
930	Legal services	10,000	10,000	8,500	2,000

Additional information:

1.   In 1990, bond redemptions should amount to $1 million, and interest on the bonds should be approximately $50,000. Fiscal agent fees for 1990 should amount to $600.

2.   Because of the planned increase in maintenance personnel, the new levees, and inflation, the board is increasing the amount of its insurance coverage. The 1990 premium is expected to amount to $20,000.

3.   The cost of legal services and the annual audit are expected to be 10 percent higher than the amount budgeted for 1989. The 1990 budget should be adjusted accordingly.

4.   Bond redemptions, interest, and fiscal agent fees are paid by the Debt Service Fund. During the year, the amounts budgeted (Codes 710, 725, and 730) will be transferred to that fund.

P10–8   (Budget summary)

Using the information given in P10–1 through P10–7 and the information below, prepare a budget summary for the General Fund of the Bacchus City Levee Board for fiscal year 1990.

1. The Bacchus City Levee Board has three departments: Maintenance, Facilities, and Administration.

2. Budgeted data pertaining to the Facilities and Administration departments for fiscal year 1990 are as follows:

Facilities:	
Personal services	$115,000
Travel	5,000
Equipment	65,000
Operating expenses	15,000
Capital outlays	?
Administration:	
Personal services	$500,000
Travel	10,000
Equipment	40,000
Operating expenses	30,000
Capital outlays	?

11

THE PROCESS OF CONTROL

LEARNING OBJECTIVES

After completion of this chapter, you should be able to:

1. Explain the difference between planning and control
2. Discuss the use of flexible budgets
3. Calculate material price and usage variances
4. Calculate labor rate and efficiency variances
5. Prepare a budgetary control report
6. Discuss the importance of sound internal control
7. List seven characteristics of an effective system of internal control
8. Explain why it is important that the duties involved in handling and accounting for money be split among several people

In the preceding chapter we discussed the collection and presentation of budgetary information. Such information can be very helpful in the successful management of an organization. In this chapter we will discuss how budgetary information can be used to "control" the activities of an organization and to highlight areas of overspending or underspending and their causes. We will also discuss certain measures that should be taken to minimize the problems of employee theft and poor management, commonly known as *internal controls*.

USING BUDGETARY INFORMATION

One purpose of budgets is to provide a measure or "standard" against which actual results can be measured. If the actual expenditures are equal to the budget, the activity is *under control*. If the actual expenditures are greater than or less than the budget, the activity is *out of control*. Thus, by comparing actual expenditures with budgeted expenditures, the managers, legislators, and other decision makers can judge the organization's performance and can take corrective action when necessary.

Budgetary comparisons can take several forms. For example, the GASB recommends that the operating statements of many funds show the budgeted and actual revenues and expenditures of each period[1] (see Chapter 4).

Some organizations also produce monthly statements that detail budgeted and actual expenditures, by object, and the amount of remaining budget for each item. This latter piece of information is particularly important to organizations that are subject to **antideficiency laws** (laws that make the overspending of one's budget an act subject to civil or/and criminal penalties), as well as to those managers and program directors whose performance is judged, in some measure, by whether they meet their budgets. In addition, knowledge of this amount is helpful to organizational personnel when they plan the activities of their work unit for the remainder of the fiscal year. If the amount of the remaining budget is lower than originally planned, their unit must curtail its activities or ask for more money from the legislative body. If the amount of remaining budget is higher than originally planned, their unit can expand its activities.

A well-designed **budgetary control report** (budget comparison) is illustrated in Table 11–1. In addition to showing the budget for the current month and the year to date, it shows (1) the actual expenditures incurred for these periods; (2) the differences between budgeted and actual expenditures (called **variances**), in both absolute numbers and as a percentage of budget; and (3) the amount that can be spent for the remainder of the year without exceeding the budget. If the amount spent is less than the amount budgeted, a *favorable* (F) variance is shown. If the amount spent is more than the amount budgeted, an *unfavorable* (U) variance is shown.

The budgetary control report in Table 11–1 is presented in one of several possible formats. For example, some organizations show amounts that have been encumbered, as well as spent. Other organizations include the following month's budget in this report. Regardless of the format used, the report should meet the organization's needs, all the users should be able to understand the report, and the report's use should be strongly encouraged by the upper levels of management and the legislative body of the organization.

Analyzing Variances

One problem with the performance report in Table 11–1 is that only the total variances are shown for each object of expenditure. From the data given, it is not easy to determine the *causes* of the variances. Without knowing the causes of the variances, it is difficult to take corrective action or make informed judgments.

---

[1]GASB Cod. Sec. 1100.109.

TABLE 11-1 Budgetary Control Report

Fund: General
Function: Public Safety
Department: Fire

Prepared by _RAM_

Date: September 30, 1989

| YEAR TO DATE | | | | CODE | OBJECT OF EXPENDITURE | CURRENT MONTH | | | | BUDGET REMAINING |
BUDGET	ACTUAL	VARIANCE	% BUDGET			BUDGET	ACTUAL	VARIANCE	% BUDGET	
					Contractual Services					
$ 75	$ 60	$ 15(F)	20	301	Advertising	$ 8	$ 10	$ 2(U)	25	$ 25
1,200	1,300	100(U)	8	310	Printing	133	120	13(F)	10	400
6,000	6,200	200(U)	3	320	Vehicle maintenance	667	645	22(F)	3	2,000
4,200	3,900	300(F)	7	330	Communication	467	378	89(F)	19	1,400
150	180	30(U)	20	350	Dues and subscriptions	17	21	4(U)	24	50
225	200	25(F)	11	360	Postage	25	30	5(U)	20	75
450	550	100(U)	22	370	Telephone	50	35	15(F)	30	150
300	300	—	—	380	Professional services	33	0	33(F)	100	100
$ 12,600	$ 12,690	$ 90(U)	1		Subtotal	$ 1,400	$ 1,239	$ 161(F)	12	$ 4,200
					Supplies and Materials					
$ 825	$ 850	$ 25(U)	3	401	Office supplies	$ 92	$ 97	$ 5(U)	5	$ 275
3,525	3,595	70(U)	2	410	Building maintenance	392	370	22(F)	6	1,175
7,875	7,750	125(F)	2	420	Fuel	875	825	50(F)	6	2,625
$595,875	$613,430	$17,555(U)	3		Grand total	$66,208	$68,836	$2,628(U)	4	$198,625

Certain types of expenditures cannot be controlled by department heads or program directors (e.g., the portion of the building rent allocated to that subunit of the organization). Responsibility for the control of these expenditures should rest with the CEO or the chief financial officer (CFO).

Other types of expenditures are controllable by department heads or program directors. These expenditures fall into one of the two categories: those that vary with the level of activity and those that do not. Expenditures that *do not* vary with the level of activity are said to be *fixed*. Examples of **fixed expenditures** are administrative salaries, travel, and insurance. The causes of variances in fixed expenditures are determined by looking at each individual expenditure and determining the reason for the different-than-budgeted dollar outlay for that item. Usually it is fairly obvious (e.g., an unexpected increase in insurance premiums or unauthorized travel).

Expenditures that *do* vary with the level of activity are said to be variable. **Variable expenditures** are caused by specific, identifiable activities (e.g., street cleaning). Examples of variable expenditures include the fuel used to operate street-cleaning machines and the hourly wages of the operators of these machines. The causes of variances in these expenditures can be determined by means of an analytical technique, which will be demonstrated shortly.

If expenditures can be traced to specific units of activity, they are said to be **direct**. If they cannot be traced to specific units of activity (e.g., the cleaning of a particular street), they are said to be **indirect**.

Expenditures incurred in the course of the normal operations of most organizations (i.e., expenses) are for direct materials, direct labor, and overhead. The terms *direct materials* and *direct labor* are self-explanatory. **Overhead** is a catchall term that refers to expenditures (expenses) that are not incurred for direct materials or direct labor. Expenditures classified as overhead include administrative salaries, utilities, insurance, and operating supplies.

Variable expenditures (costs) should be budgeted (for control purposes) on the basis of the actual level of activity. That is, a cost rate-per-unit-of-activity should be determined and the "budget" for the period should be this rate times the units of activity actually performed during the period. For example, assume that the overhauling of the engine of a bus owned by a transit district should take ten hours and that the average mechanic working for this district is paid $15 per-hour-worked. Thus the labor cost of an overhaul should be $150. If six engines are overhauled during a given period, the "budget" should be $900 for this item. (This type of budget is known as a **flexible budget**. It is based on the actual, or after-the-fact, level of activity.)

Variable expenditure (cost) variances fall into one of two categories:

1. Those caused by **payment** of higher- or lower-than-budgeted prices for the inputs used (e.g., direct materials or direct labor), know as (material) **price** or (labor or overhead) **rate variances**.
2. Those caused by the *use* of a higher- or lower-than-budgeted level of inputs (e.g., taking twelve hours to overhaul an engine rather than the ten hours

budgeted), known as (material) **usage** or (labor or overhead) **efficiency vari-ances**.

Each of the above variances can be calculated by using one of two simple formulas:

1. **Price (rate) variance** = (Actual Price − Budgeted Price) x Actual Usage.

2. **Usage (efficiency) variance** = (Actual Usage − Budgeted Usage) x Budgeted Price.

To continue with the above example, assume that during a given period six engines are overhauled, at a total labor cost of $952. Since the budgeted cost of overhauling six engines is $900 (6 engines x 10 hours/engine x $15/hour), a *total* variance of $52 (unfavorable) results. Assume also that the "average" mechanic who normally works on these engines becomes ill at the very beginning of the period and is replaced by a senior mechanic who earns $17 per hour, but is able to overhaul the six engines in 56 hours. The labor rate and efficiency variances are calculated as follows:

1. **Labor rate variance**   = ($17 − $15) x 56 hrs.   = $112 (unfavorable)
2. **Labor efficiency variance** = (56 hrs. − 60 hrs.) x $15 = $ 60 (favorable)

Total labor variance = $ 52 (unfavorable)

The above analysis, which can also be applied to expenditures for direct materials and overhead, requires a flexible budgeting approach. The annual budgets of most governmental and not-for-profit organizations, however, are prepared by using a "static" approach. Under this approach, expenditures are budgeted for *one* level of activity. As a result, it is necessary to assume a given level of activity when preparing these budgets.

The above-mentioned assumption, however, does not create an insurmountable problem, since budgetary control (performance) reports use information *derived* from the budget. The organization can prepare monthly budgetary control reports based on the *actual* level of activity and a final report based on the *planned* level of activity, accompanied by a statement reconciling the two levels of activity.

The above discussion of budgetary variances demonstrates one way in which budgetary information can be used to improve the efficiency with which an organization operates: by alerting managers, program directors, and other decision makers to instances of overspending or underspending and their causes so that these persons can take corrective action before the problems become more serious. Other analytical and reporting techniques, which accomplish the same purpose, are also available. They are discussed in any textbook on cost or managerial accounting.

INTERNAL CONTROL

Internal control can be defined as

> . . . the plan of organization and all of the coordinate methods and measures adopted . . . to (1) safeguard the assets, (2) check the accuracy and reliability of accounting data, (3) promote operational efficiency and (4) encourage adherence to managerial policies.[2]

This definition is very broad. It implies, correctly, that a system of internal control covers *all* the functions of an organization.

For operational purposes, internal controls are classified as either accounting or administrative. **Accounting controls** are those controls that deal with matters that have a *direct* impact on the organization's financial statements. They are the ones that (1) safeguard the assets, (2) ensure reliable accounting data, and (3) enable the management of the organization to ascertain that expenditures are properly authorized and made in accordance with appropriate laws and regulations. Specific accounting controls will be discussed later in this chapter.

Administrative controls are those controls that deal with matters that have an *indirect* impact on the financial statements. They are the ones that (1) promote operational efficiency and (2) encourage adherence to prescribed managerial policies. Specific operational controls include time-and-motion studies, energy usage controls, statistical analyses, quality controls, employee training programs, and operational audits.

In other words, accounting controls are those controls that relate to management's responsibility for maintaining the assets entrusted to it and for providing information on the financial condition and results of the organization's operations. Administrative controls are those controls that relate to management's responsibility for running the organization in a smooth, efficient manner. The controls discussed in the previous section, budgetary controls, are administrative controls. Both accounting and administrative controls are necessary if an organization is to function smoothly. For the remainder of this chapter, however, we will confine our discussion to accounting controls. Full coverage of administrative controls can be found in many textbooks on general management, cost analysis, and production control.

Internal control can be compared to the preventive maintenance a motorist gives his or her automobile. That person, for example, checks the automobile's oil in order to *prevent* a breakdown, not because of a breakdown. Similarly, the management of an organization installs a system of controls in order to *prevent* defalcations and bad management, not to catch thieves or poor managers. The system operates on the premise that people are basically honest and want to do

---

[2]Committee on Auditing Procedure, *Internal Control—Elements of a Coordinated System and Its Importance to Management and the Independent Public Accountant* (New York: American Institute of Certified Public Accountants, 1949), p. 6.

their jobs effectively. Employees, however, often face financial or other pressures and, if not restrained, might be tempted to perform acts that would be unthinkable under ordinary circumstances. If they do succumb to temptation and either steal or engage in sloppy managerial practices, everyone loses—the people served by the organization, the management of the organization, and, eventually, the dishonest or careless employees.

A good system of internal controls can act as a strong deterrent to crime and poor management by removing the temptation to steal or engage in lax practices. If an employee knows, for example, that the probability of being caught stealing is very high, that person will probably not even consider such an act. And if an employee knows that laxness on his or her part will soon be discovered or, even better, if the nature of the working environment is such that it is impossible to be lax on the job, that person will probably perform with much greater care.

Characteristics of Effective Internal Control Systems

To be effective, a system of internal controls must possess certain characteristics. These characteristics (elements) include

1. Honest, capable employees
2. A clearly defined, formal plan of organization
3. A separation of duties
4. A system of authorizations
5. Sound accounting practices
6. Adequate physical control over assets and records
7. Independent checks on performance

Honest, Capable Employees

There is an old saying that "The people who work for an organization will make it or break it." This truism applies as much to not-for-profit organizations as it does to commercial firms.

It is impossible to control the activities of all employees. Thus, if the organization is to survive, a certain amount of self-motivation and honesty must be present. Employees who are motivated, honest, and capable not only are necessary if internal controls are to work but, in the event that such controls are absent, can often manage the organization in a satisfactory manner.

Before they are hired, prospective employees should be carefully screened to make certain that they are qualified for the position being filled and that they have no previous record of questionable activities. In addition, all employees should be promoted or given greater responsibilities on the basis of performance, rather than exclusively on the basis of seniority or length of service.

Employees performing accounting or treasury functions and employees who handle cash or other negotiable assets should always be bonded. Bonding not only protects the organization from loss but acts as a psychological deterrent to potential thieves because, even though the organization might not prosecute them, the bonding companies will. In addition, the bonding companies perform a screening function for their client organizations because they generally make thorough background checks of any employees they bond.

Employees should be required to take annual vacations so that other employees can fill in for them, and their duties should be rotated every two to three years. Both of these controls reduce the likelihood of fraud. Vacations have a "rejuvenating" effect on the employees, and the job rotation reduces the monotony of routine tasks. Job rotation also enables employees to become familiar with all aspects of the organization's operations.

Once people have been hired they should be trained, not only for their current position but for future positions to which they are likely to advance. They should be given in-house and on-the-job training and should be encouraged to take courses offered by local colleges, accounting societies, and other professional organizations.

Employees should also be supervised adequately and provided with frequent feedback, both positive and negative, on the quality of their performance. When negative feedback is necessary, it should be direct and to the point and the comments should be supported by specific examples. Concrete suggestions for improvement should always be offered.

A practice that should be avoided is that of gathering "evidence" against employees all year in order to provide some sort of negative feedback at the annual review. Another bad practice is the playing of "games" with employees' performance reviews. Both of these are devastating to the morale of any organization.

Finally, the organization should develop and enforce a publicly stated conflict-of-interest policy. Knowledge of such a policy will prevent many employees from engaging, deliberately or inadvertently, in such activities.

Plan of Organization

To maintain good internal control, it is necessary to have a clearly defined, formal plan of organization. Such a plan must include definite lines of responsibility and specify who is responsible for each activity. It must also provide for the delegation of tasks and responsibilities throughout the organization while making it clear where the ultimate responsibility for each activity lies.

Every organization should maintain an up-to-date, carefully prepared **organization chart**. Each position listed on the chart should report directly to a higher position. In addition, the tasks should be arranged in such a manner as to provide for the separation of operating, custodial, and accounting responsibilities. Specific individuals should be assigned the responsibility for particular assets and for the performance of each task.

No one individual should be given the responsibility for handling all phases of a transaction. Nor should one individual be given custody of the assets, or be directly involved in the operating functions, resulting from transactions that the individual initiates. For example, a police officer who writes a ticket should not also be responsible for collecting the fine; nor should the person who orders supplies be the custodian of those supplies.

Every employee should be provided with instructions regarding the organization chart. The employee should know to whom he or she is accountable and who is accountable to him or to her. In addition, employees should be provided with a description of their own position and the positions of persons with whom they must work.

A **job** or **position description** serves several purposes:

1. It enables the employee to know what is expected from that position.
2. It enables the employee to understand the responsibilities of his or her co-workers. This is particularly important if the employee must coordinate with or fill in for someone else.
3. It helps management to organize the work flow and to provide for an equitable distribution of duties.

Written **standards of performance** should be prepared for each position in the organization. Such standards can provide a "goal" for each employee to meet, as well as an objective means of evaluating performance. Written standards enable each employee to monitor his or her own performance and take corrective action before variances from the standards warrant the attention of management. In addition, performance reviews can be conducted on an objective, factual basis. Finally, the use of standards can be a means of justifying promotions and salary increases.

The standards themselves should be attainable with a reasonable degree of effort. Standards that do not require employees to put forth such a degree of effort can lead to inefficiencies and a low level of productivity. Standards that are too difficult or impossible to achieve, however, will soon be regarded as such by the employees, with a consequent loss of morale and efficiency. Under the ideal system, employees should *occasionally* be able to achieve (or exceed) the standards.

In many organizations employees participate, individually or as a group, in the setting of standards. This approach offers the organization a number of advantages. First, the employees generally feel that the standards are "their" standards, not those of management. As a result, they are usually more willing to put forth the effort necessary to meet their standards. Second, the employees often have a deeper knowledge of operating details and problems than their managers. Such knowledge can be helpful in setting more realistic standards.

One highly successful means of getting employees to participate in the standard-setting process is through the use of **Management by Objectives (MBO).** Under a typical MBO system, each employee sets his or her own goals and objectives for the next year, subject to the management's approval. The employee's performance is then appraised on the basis of how well his or her own predetermined goals and objectives are being met.

Finally, the organization should maintain an up-to-date procedures manual. A **procedures manual** is a document that lists each task and the manner in which it should be performed. A procedures manual is useful for

1. Establishing uniform methods of performing routine tasks
2. Training new employees
3. Providing guidance for persons filling in for others
4. Assisting the managers, internal auditors, and external auditors in their review of the soundness of the organization's system of internal controls

The best plan of organization cannot be effective unless everyone involved is familiar with it and follows it. Periodic review of and training on the organization chart, job descriptions, and procedures manual will ensure that the plan of organization is current and that the employees are aware of the overall plan, their places in the plan, and the best way to perform their respective duties.

Separation of Duties

When the various steps of the accounting process are performed by a number of people rather than by one person, it is considerably more difficult to perpetuate a fraud, since many of the people involved in the process will be aware of the irregularity. For example, if one person prepares and records tax bills, receives and records payment of the tax bills, and prepares the bank deposit and delinquency notices, there is nothing to stop this person from "stealing" a portion of the collections.

If, on the other hand, one person prepares and records the tax bills, another person receives the payments and prepares the bank deposit, and a third person records the payments and prepares the delinquency notices, it will require at least two, and possibly three, persons to perpetuate a fraud. Since few people trust their co-workers to such an extent, a defalcation is unlikely and the controls have done their job—*preventing* fraud.

Specific controls falling under the category of **separation of duties** include the following:

1. One person should not handle a transaction from its inception to its final recording.
2. The accounting system should be structured in a manner that provides independent cross-checking of each employee's work.
3. Custody of assets should be separated from the record keeping for those assets.
4. Operational responsibilities should be separated from record-keeping responsibilities.

5. Responsibility for the authorization of transactions should be separated from record keeping and, in the case of purchases, custodial responsibility.
6. Mail should be opened by someone other than the cashier or the bookkeeper.
7. The purchasing function should be separated from the receiving function.

In smaller organizations it is sometimes impossible to divide accounting responsibilities. Here, nonaccountants often perform certain tasks on an "occasional" basis. For example, the city manager might be required to perform the monthly bank reconciliation; or one secretary might reconcile the cash receipts with the tax collections while another secretary prepares delinquency notices at the end of each month.

When accounting systems are computerized, the problem becomes one of separating the programming, operating, and data storage functions. The person who programs the computer should not prepare the input data or operate the machine. Nor should the person who maintains the transaction and data files perform programming or operating functions. In addition, the computer's output should be reviewed and reconciled with its input by an independent party and the computer should be "off limits" to unauthorized personnel.

Although the separation of duties is a powerful tool, it cannot be effective in the absence of other controls, nor can it be totally relied upon.[3] Nevertheless it can go a long way toward the prevention of fraud and errors.

System of Authorizations

Every transaction should be authorized by a person who (1) has no personal interest in the transaction; (2) possesses sufficient knowledge of the transaction, its purpose, and its legal ramifications; and (3) is at an appropriate level in the organization (e.g., a supervisor should not approve the purchase of a large computer). In addition, the number of persons who are permitted to authorize transactions should be limited and their authorizations should be in writing.

Authorizations can be either general or specific. In the case of general authorizations, operating personnel may approve transactions that fall within the limits set by law, regulation, or policy of the governing bodies. These authorizations include the establishment of tax rates, wage rates, authority to purchase operating supplies, and so forth. The primary vehicle for general authorizations in governmental units is the budget, under which most transactions are processed.

Authorizations should not be confused with approvals. **Approval** merely means that someone in authority believes that the transaction meets the conditions of authorization. It cannot always be assumed that because a transaction has been approved, it has been properly authorized. For example, a department

---

[3]In the **Equity Funding Case**, over one hundred persons were in collusion at one time. Like most frauds, however, this one eventually collapsed when someone became disenchanted.

head may unknowingly approve a transaction that is not in compliance with the city charter. This transaction, although approved, has not been properly authorized.

Certain transactions require specific authorizations. These are nonroutine and generally require the specific attention of the governing body (e.g., the city council) or a high-level manager. Examples include the purchase of capital assets and the issuance of bonds.

Individuals who approve or authorize such transactions should be those specified by law or those who hold appropriate positions in the organization. For example, even though the city charter may grant specific authority to department heads for certain levels of expenditures, the city council may reserve for itself the right to authorize expenditures for certain "sensitive" capital items, such as new police cars.

Sound Accounting Practices

Since much of the information used for operational and decision-making purposes originates in the financial area, it stands to reason that sound accounting practices are crucial to the well-being of any organization. Without them, the other controls become meaningless or difficult to implement.

The most basic accounting practice, the use of **double-entry accounting**, provides a key control in that the requirements that debits equal credits will reveal many errors. It seldom happens that an error on the debit side of an entry is precisely equal to an equivalent error on the credit side, or vice versa. The procedure of preparing and balancing a **trial balance** is a means of detecting errors, although it should be remembered that a balanced trial balance is not necessarily an error-free trial balance. Nevertheless, if it does not balance, you *know* that an error exists.

Other sound accounting practices are as follows:

1. Documents should be simple and well-designed. They should, if possible, be multiple purpose in order to keep the number to a minimum. They should also be designed to ensure that they will be filled out properly, by providing blocks for necessary signatures and approvals, by making the instructions *simple,* and so on.

2. All disbursements except small ones made from petty cash should be made by check.

3. A responsible official should approve certain accounting transactions. Among these are the issuing of purchase orders, the approving of invoices and payrolls for payment, the writing off of accounts receivable, the signing of checks, and the recording of important and nonroutine journal entries.

4. Transactions should be processed in a timely and efficient manner. Entries should be made in the books as soon as the transactions take place and should be made directly from the properly approved documents in order to avoid errors.

5. Cash receipts should be prelisted, by someone other than their custodian or the person who accounts for them, before being deposited in the bank; and

the deposit slip should be compared with the prelisting, as soon as it is returned, by someone other than the person recording the receipts. This is done to ensure that the amount recorded by the bank agrees with the amount recorded by the organization. Such a step will save countless hours when preparing the bank reconciliation.

6. Subsidiary and control accounts should be used whenever possible for cash, receivables, payables, and other items requiring many transactions. The subsidiary records should periodically be reconciled with the control accounts by a person not responsible for recording transactions, and the differences should be investigated and resolved.

7. Prenumbered documents, especially checks and receipts, should be used. Numbers should be assigned in a specific sequence and an accounting made for all missing or voided documents.

8. A bank reconciliation should be prepared, at least once a month, by someone not responsible for collecting cash or recording cash transactions. The monthly bank statements and canceled checks should be received, unopened, by this person.

9. Checks should not be signed without proper supporting documentation. Those for large amounts should require two signatures. Advance signing of checks should be forbidden.

10. Uncollectible accounts should periodically be reviewed to make certain that they have been properly handled and that they are really uncollectible.

11. Payroll disbursements should be backed up by employee time cards or time sheets in order to avoid erroneous payments or payments to persons not on the payroll. A separate bank account should be used for payrolls.

12. Fixed asset records should be maintained and kept up-to-date by someone other than the custodian of the fixed assets.

13. Clearly defined accounting procedures should be employed in order to prevent inconsistencies and misunderstandings. These procedures should be covered in detail in a procedures manual.

14. An up-to-date chart of accounts should be in use and readily available to all accounting personnel. A **chart of accounts** lists each account used by the organization, its number, and when it should be employed. It provides guidance to the personnel who make account classification decisions and enables them to record transactions in a uniform manner.

Adequate Physical Control Over Assets and Records

Physical controls are concerned with the actual safeguarding of the assets. If these controls are not present, the assets of the organization will be misused or will disappear. Some of these controls were discussed in the preceding section. Other controls over assets and records include the following:

1. Making a periodic inventory of physical assets and reconciling the results of this inventory with the ledger. This procedure, which should be performed by someone other than the custodian of the assets or the person who maintains the asset records, will reveal missing assets and ensure that the records are kept up-to-date.

2. Retaining records (including voided checks and other documents) in a safe place for a sufficient length of time. While specific guidelines on record re-

tention are available, a good rule of thumb is to keep routine documents, such as deposit slips and purchase orders, for seven years and important documents, such as minutes of meetings of the governing body, indefinitely.

3. Using adequate physical safeguards, such as
   a. Fireproof safes and locking fireproof file cabinets.
   b. Check protectors. These machines, which should be locked when not in use, stamp dollar amounts on checks in a manner that is difficult to duplicate or change.
   c. Cancellation machines. These machines punch "void," "paid," or some other appropriate word onto several layers of documents, making it impossible to accidentally reuse the voided, canceled, or paid documents.

4. Allowing only authorized persons access to assets. Materials, tools, and supplies should be kept in a locked storeroom to which only specific persons have access. Authorization to use certain assets (especially motor vehicles and data-processing equipment) should be in writing.

5. Depositing cash receipts intact on a daily basis. Leaving cash overnight creates temptation and often leads to thefts. The deposit should be made by someone other than the cashier or the accounts receivable bookkeeper.

Independent Checks on Performance

A system of **checks and balances** should be built into any accounting system. That is, the work of each person should be checked by some independent means. As we mentioned earlier, the double-entry accounting system provides a natural set of checks and balances. Another means of checking performance is to compare actual results (e.g., expenditures) with those budgeted.

Many organizations employ specific persons to review the various systems and activities and to report on weaknesses and deviations from prescribed procedures. This is necessary in even the best-managed organizations because those organizations change over time and employees have a tendency to forget or ignore the required way of doing things. In addition, procedures that were satisfactory at one time may no longer be adequate.

Those persons who perform reviews that are primarily nonfinancial in nature are called **operational auditors**. They are concerned with managerial practices and the efficient use of resources. Those persons who concentrate on the financial aspects of the organization's operations are called **internal auditors**. Although not "independent" in the sense that external auditors (CPAs) are, operational and internal auditors generally work apart from other accounting and operating personnel and report to top-level management. Thus they are in a position to look at the systems of accounting and internal controls objectively and to help solve any problems that may arise.

Costs vs. Benefits

Ideally, an organization will utilize all the controls discussed above. In reality, however, many organizations cannot afford the work force or the investment necessary for such controls. Other organizations need certain specialized controls. Although basic controls, such as prenumbered checks and locked storage areas, are inexpensive and should be used by every organization, other controls, such as the separation of duties and fireproof vaults, require more resources than many organizations can provide.

Before installing each control, a **cost-benefit analysis** should be performed. In such an analysis the probable loss prevented (the benefit) is compared with the cost of installing and maintaining the control. If the cost exceeds the value of the estimated benefit, the control should not be installed. For example, an organization employing only three people should not hire a fourth merely to create a separation of duties, especially if the salary of the fourth person would exceed any loss that might be incurred. On the other hand, the cost of a control like the bonding of employees is likely to be much less than the cost of a defalcation.

This section has described the rudiments of internal control and has emphasized the importance of internal control to any organization. One advantage of a good system of internal control is that audits are less likely to be unpleasant because when good internal controls are in place and in use, auditors will rely more heavily on the accounting records and will perform fewer tests.

SELECTED REFERENCES

AMERICAN INSTITUTE OF CERTIFIED PUBLIC ACCOUNTANTS. *Audits of State and Local Governmental Units*. New York, 1987.

DAVID, IRWIN T., C. EUGENE STURGEON, AND EULA L. ADAMS. *How to Evaluate and Improve Internal Controls in Governmental Units*. Chicago: Municipal Finance Officers Association, 1981.

FREEMAN, ROBERT J., HAROLD H. HENSOLD, JR., AND WILLIAM W. HOLDER. "Cost Accounting and Analysis in State and Local Governments," in *The Managerial and Cost Accountants Handbook*, ed. Homer A. Black and James Don Edwards. Homewood, Ill: Dow Jones–Irwin, 1979.

GOVERNMENT FINANCE RESEARCH CENTER. *Costing Government Services: A Guide for Decision Making*. Chicago: GFOA, 1984.

HORNGREN, CHARLES T., AND GEORGE FOSTER. *Cost Accounting: A Managerial Emphasis*. Englewood Cliffs, N.J.: Prentice Hall, 1987.

MUNICIPAL FINANCE OFFICERS ASSOCIATION. *An Operating Budget Handbook for Small Cities and Other Governmental Units*. Chicago, 1978.

PAGE, JOHN R., AND H. PAUL HOOPER. *Accounting and Information Systems*. Englewood Cliffs, N.J.: Prentice Hall, 1987, Ch. 3.

REVIEW QUESTIONS

Q11–1   What are the elements (characteristics) of internal control?

Q11–2   Distinguish between *accounting controls* and *administrative controls*.

Q11–3   Why is an organization chart important to a good system of internal control?

Q11–4   List five specific accounting controls.

Q11–5   Why should prenumbered checks always be used?

Q11–6   What is the difference between an *internal auditor* and an *external auditor*? An *internal auditor* and an *operational auditor*?

Q11–7   What advantages does an organization gain when it bonds key employees? Is it necessary to bond all employees?

Q11–8   Is it a good practice for an organization to save money by paying the lowest possible wages? Why or why not?

Q11–9   Why should an organization maintain a clearly-defined formal plan or system?

Q11–10   What is the basic premise of controls relating to the separation of duties?

Q11–11   What is a system of authorizations? Why should every organization have such a system?

Q11–12   Why should uncollectible tax bills be periodically reviewed? By whom should they be reviewed?

Q11–13   Is it a good idea to discard voided checks immediately because they just take up space and cannot be used?

Q11–14   What is a cost-benefit analysis? When should it be used?

Q11–15   What does the term *control* mean? Who should be responsible for controlling the amount of fuel used by police cars? The utilities used by a city hall?

Q11–16   Distinguish between the following terms:
1.   Fixed versus variable expenditures
2.   Direct versus indirect expenditures
3.   Flexible versus static budgets

Q11–17   The fire chief of a certain city discovered, late in the fiscal year, that the expenditures for salaries in his department were over budget by $8,000, but that the expenditures for supplies were $16,000 under budget. Rather than cut back on the size of his department, he persuaded a clerk in the finance department to "transfer" $10,000 of his supplies budget to his personnel budget so that both his salary and his supplies expenditures would be under budget for the year. Is this legal in your state? Would you like to be in the fire chief's boots?

EXERCISES

E11–1   (Discussion of accounting controls)
List *five* specific internal accounting controls you would expect to find in a well-controlled section that prepares property tax bills.
Example: A specific procedure for notifying this section of all changes in assessments.

(IIA adapted)

E11–2   (Performance reporting and flexible budgeting for a street repair department)

The Street Repair Department of Granite City uses a flexible budget to monitor its monthly performance. Since the primary function of this department is to fill potholes, the number of potholes filled is the unit of measure of activity. (Assume that the potholes are uniformly located throughout the city.) The average time required to fill a pothole (including travel to the pothole) is one-half hour. A typical pothole requires five pounds of a material that should cost $.25 per pound. Each road crew is budgeted at $15 per hour (including fringes). The variable overhead, consisting largely of fuel for the truck, is budgeted at $2 per direct labor hour. Fixed overhead is budgeted at $2,000 per month.

During the month of May, the road crew filled 800 potholes. Actual costs incurred were as follows:

Direct materials	$ 1,200
Direct labor	6,405
Variable overhead	745
Fixed overhead	1,700
Total	$10,050

REQUIRED: Prepare a performance report for the month of May showing (1) budgeted amounts; (2) actual amounts; and (3) variances for direct materials, direct labor, variable overhead, and fixed overhead.

E11–3   (Material and labor variances)

Referring to Exercise 11–2, assume that the actual materials used to fill 800 potholes cost $.20 per pound but that it took 6,000 pounds of this cheaper material to fill them. Assume also that it took the crew 420 hours to fill these potholes and that the crew was actually paid $15.25 per hour.

REQUIRED: Determine the causes of the difference between the budgeted and actual expenditures for direct materials and direct labor for the street repair crew in the month of May.

E11–4   (Multiple choice on internal control)

Select the *best* answer for each of the following multiple-choice questions.

   1. Internal accounting controls are *not* designed to provide reasonable assurance that
      a. Transactions are executed in accordance with management's authorization
      b. Irregularities will be eliminated
      c. Access to assets is permitted only in accordance with management's authorization

    d. The recorded accountability for assets is compared with the existing assets at reasonable intervals

2. For internal control purposes, which of the following individuals should preferably be responsible for the distribution of payroll checks?
   a. Bookkeeper
   b. Payroll clerk
   c. Cashier
   d. Receptionist

3. It is important that an external auditor consider the competence of the audit clients' employees because their competence bears directly and importantly on the
   a. Cost-benefit relationship of the system of internal control
   b. Achievement of the objectives of the system of internal control
   c. Comparison of recorded accountability with assets
   d. Timing of the audit tests to be performed

4. Proper segregation of functional responsibilities calls for separation of the
   a. Authorization, approval, and execution functions
   b. Authorization, execution, and payment functions
   c. Receiving, shipping, and custodial functions
   d. Authorization, recording, and custodial functions

5. Proper internal control over the cash payroll function should mandate which of the following?
   a. The payroll clerk should fill the envelopes with cash and a computation of net wages
   b. Unclaimed pay envelopes should be retained by the paymaster
   c. Each employee should be asked to sign a receipt
   d. A separate checking account for payrolls should be maintained

6. The primary purpose of the auditor's study and evaluation of internal control is to provide a basis for
   a. Determining whether procedures and records that are concerned with the safeguarding of assets are reliable
   b. Making constructive suggestions to clients concerning improvements in internal control
   c. Determining the nature, extent, and timing of audit tests to be applied
   d. Expressing an opinion

7. Internal control is a function of management, and effective control is based on the concept of charge and discharge of responsibility and duty. Which of the following is one of the overriding principles of internal control?
   a. Responsibility for accounting and financial duties should be assigned to one responsible officer
   b. Responsibility for the performance of each duty must be fixed

    c. Responsibility for the accounting duties must be borne by the members of the city council

    d. Responsibility for accounting activities and duties must be assigned only to employees who are bonded

8. When considering the effectiveness of a system of internal accounting control, the auditor should recognize that inherent limitations do exist. Which of the following is an example of an inherent limitation in a system of internal accounting control?

    a. The effectiveness of procedures depends on the segregation of employee duties

    b. Procedures are designed to ensure the execution and recording of transactions in accordance with management's authorization

    c. In the performance of most control procedures, there are possibilities of errors arising from mistakes in judgment

    d. Procedures for handling large numbers of transactions are processed by electronic data-processing equipment

9. Which of the following is an effective internal accounting control over cash payments?

    a. Signed checks should be mailed under the supervision of the check signer

    b. Spoiled checks that have been voided should be disposed of immediately

    c. Checks should be prepared only by persons responsible for cash receipts and cash disbursements

    d. A check-signing machine with two signatures should be utilized

10. The system of internal control would be *weakened* if the payroll supervisor were to be assigned the responsibility for

    a. Reviewing and approving time reports for subordinate employees

    b. Distributing payroll checks to employees

    c. Hiring subordinate employees

    d. Initiating requests for salary adjustments for subordinate employees

11. Which of the following is an effective internal accounting control measure that encourages receiving department personnel to count and inspect all materials received?

    a. Quantities ordered are excluded from the receiving department copy of the purchase order

    b. Vouchers are prepared by accounts payable department personnel only after they match item counts on the receiving report with the purchase order

    c. Receiving department personnel are expected to match and reconcile the receiving report with the purchase order

    d. Internal auditors periodically examine, on a surprise basis, the receiving department copies of receiving reports

12. Effective internal control over the payroll function should include procedures that segregate the duties of making salary payments to employees and
    a. Controlling unemployment insurance claims
    b. Maintaining employee personnel records
    c. Approving employee fringe benefits
    d. Hiring new employees

    (AICPA adapted)

13. The purpose of segregating the duties of distributing payroll checks and hiring personnel is to
    a. Separate the custody of assets from the accounting for those assets
    b. Establish clear lines of authority and responsibility
    c. Separate duties within the accounting function
    d. Separate the authorization of transactions from the custody of related assets

14. Which of the following is an internal control for disbursement by check?
    a. Checks are signed by the controller
    b. Checks are prenumbered and independently accounted for
    c. Supporting documents are marked "Paid" immediately after the canceled checks have been returned by the bank
    d. Checks are mailed by the employee who prepares the documents that authorize the check preparation

15. An example of an internal accounting control is
    a. Long-range planning
    b. A system of authorization and approvals
    c. A statement of functions and responsibilities
    d. Operational audits

    (IIA adapted)

PROBLEMS

P11–1   (Internal control over payroll records)
The Internal Audit Department was told that two employees had been terminated for falsifying their time records. The two employees had altered overtime hours on their time cards after their supervisors had approved the hours actually worked.

Several years ago the organization discontinued the use of time clocks. Since then, the various supervisors have been responsible for manually posting the time cards and approving the hours for which their subordinates should be paid. The postings are usually entered in pencil by the supervisors or their secretaries. After the postings for the week are complete, the time cards are approved and placed in the mail racks outside the supervisors' offices for pickup by the timekeepers. Sometimes the timekeepers do not pick up the time cards promptly.

REQUIRED: Assuming the organization does not wish to return to the use of time clocks, give *three* recommendations to prevent recurrence of the situation described above. For each recommendation, indicate how it will deter fraudulent reporting of hours worked.

(IIA adapted)

P11–2 (Internal control weaknesses—cash receipts)

The Art Appreciation Society operates a museum for the benefit and enjoyment of the community. During hours that the museum is open to the public, two clerks, who are positioned at the entrance, collect a five-dollar admission fee from each nonmember patron. Members of the Art Appreciation Society are permitted to enter free of charge upon presentation of their membership cards.

At the end of each day, one of the clerks delivers the proceeds to the treasurer. The treasurer counts the cash in the presence of the clerk and places it in a safe. Each Friday afternoon the treasurer and one of the clerks deliver all cash held in the safe to the bank and receive an authenticated deposit slip, which provides the basis for the weekly entry in the cash receipts journal.

The board of directors of the Art Appreciation Society has identified a need to improve the system of internal control over cash admission fees. The board has determined that the cost of installing turnstiles, sales booths, or otherwise altering the physical layout of the museum will greatly exceed any benefits that may be derived. However, the board has agreed that the sale of admission tickets must be an integral part of its improvement efforts.

You have been asked by the board of directors of the Art Appreciation Society to review the internal control over cash admission fees and offer suggestions for improvement.

REQUIRED: Indicate weaknesses in the existing system of internal control over cash admission fees and recommend one improvement for each of the weaknesses identified. Organize your answer as indicated in the following example.

WEAKNESS	RECOMMENDATION
1. There is no basis for establishing the documentation of the number of paying patrons.	1. Prenumbered admission tickets should be issued upon payment of the admission fee.

(AICPA)

Case on internal control

You are the director of an agency that, among other activities, runs a hot-lunch program which is supported by a federal grant. Your employees, of whom you have ten, buy the food, prepare it, and serve it. Each person, upon receiving a lunch, pays $.75 cash to a cashier. Cleanup, serving, and so forth, is done by volunteer workers.

Mrs. Pierce, who has been with the program since its inception, purchases food every day at the H & S Market. Each day, the cashier gives her $100 in cash from the collections of the previous day. As a practical matter, the cashier often gives her the $100 directly before making the bank deposit. Mrs. Pierce purchases the food the next morning and gives the change to Miss Roper, the cashier. Mrs. Pierce is supposed to give the cash register tapes to Mr. Hebert, the bookkeeper, but she often just tells him how much the food cost. As long as the amount seems "reasonable," nothing is ever said.

The cashier, Miss Roper, is a volunteer. In the morning she helps to prepare food. After lunch she is supposed to give you, the director, the money collected. Unfortunately, you are sometimes busy and tell her to go ahead and prepare the deposit slip and make the deposit. On other occasions you have her prepare the deposit and give it to you. Unfortunately, sometimes you forget to go to the bank, which is why you found one of last week's deposits on your dresser this morning.

After preparing and serving the food, the workers put away the remaining food and clean up, under the supervision of Mrs. Pierce. You are not usually around, as you have work to do on other projects or paperwork to finish.

You, the director, write and sign all checks. Mr. Hebert, the bookkeeper, puts the invoices on your desk or tells you about them, and you write the checks. To save service charges, you use one bank account for all activities of your agency, which is supported by several different grants. Mr. Hebert does a bank reconciliation at the end of each fiscal year.

You also write paychecks to all workers, including yourself. The payroll is based on a time sheet which each worker fills out when he or she reports for and leaves work. You look at it for "reasonableness" before writing the checks. If anything looks odd, you ask Mrs. Pierce.

Supplies and food are kept in a room in the local high school, which is also used by the school's orchestra to store its instruments.

The agency has a van that is used to carry food and transport children to and from the lunchroom. It is maintained and driven by Mr. Turner. He buys gas at the local gas station where his brother works, and he carries a credit card that was issued to your agency. Because of the early morning purchases of food, Mr. Turner keeps the van at home each night. You have told him not to use it for personal business.

REQUIRED: Can you find *at least* five weaknesses in the system of internal control? What would you do to correct them?

12

ACCOUNTING FOR COLLEGES AND UNIVERSITIES

LEARNING OBJECTIVES

After you complete this chapter, you should be able to:

1. Name four ways in which accounting for colleges and universities differs from accounting for state and local governmental units
2. List the sources of authority for the accounting principles followed by colleges and universities
3. Name the financial statements used by colleges and universities
4. Identify the issues involved in the controversy surrounding the use of depreciation by colleges and universities
5. List the types of funds used by colleges and universities and discuss how each is used
6. Explain the difference between restricted and unrestricted current funds
7. Discuss the concept of formula funding
8. Distinguish between mandatory and nonmandatory transfers
9. Prepare the journal entries necessary to record the activities of colleges and universities

The preceding chapters of this text have focused on governmental units. Although such entities are very numerous, they represent only a portion of the not-for-profit organizations in existence. Other not-for-profit organizations are colleges and universities, hospitals, voluntary health and welfare organizations, and "other" not-for-profit organizations such as country clubs, labor unions, private schools, and religious organizations.[1] In this chapter we will discuss the

---

[1] A detailed listing of "other" not-for-profit organizations can be found in the AICPA's *Statement of Position (SOP) 78-10*. These organizations are discussed in Chapter 14.

funds and accounting procedures used by colleges and universities. Since the accounting systems of private and parochial primary and secondary schools are more similar to the systems used by colleges and universities than to the ones used by governmental units, the material covered in this chapter is also applicable to those institutions.[2] The main focus of this chapter, however, is on colleges and universities.

The accounting methods and procedures used by colleges and universities are similar to those used by state and local governmental units in that both use fund accounting and, in many cases, budgetary and encumbrance accounts. The types of funds used, however, are different, with more emphasis being placed on the recording of revenues and fiduciary activities. In addition, account groups are not used to record fixed assets and long-term debt.

Colleges and universities are not as highly regulated by law as are governmental units. Therefore there is less need to use the accounting system as a means for ensuring legal compliance. As a result, the accounting methods and procedures used by these institutions allow a greater degree of flexibility and adaptability to individual conditions than those used by governmental units. Finally, colleges and universities generally use the full accrual basis of accounting for all funds.

SOURCES OF AUTHORITY

The primary rule-making bodies for colleges and universities are the Financial Accounting Standards Board (FASB), which is responsible for nongovernmental colleges and universities, and the Governmental Accounting Standards Board (GASB), which is responsible for governmental colleges and universities (those that are part of a state or a local governmental unit). The FASB has officially stated, in its *Statement No. 32*, that the AICPA's industry audit guide, *Audits of Colleges and Universities*, and the AICPA's *Statement of Position (SOP) 74–8* contain "preferable accounting principles for purposes of justifying a change in accounting principles." Until recently, the GASB was silent on the subject of colleges and universities.

In 1987, however, the FASB issued its *Statement No. 93*, "Recognition of Depreciation by Not-for-Profit Organizations," which requires that nongovernment colleges and universities depreciate their plant and equipment. The GASB countered with its own statement, which proposed that governmental colleges and universities *not* change their accounting practices because of FASB *Statement No. 93*.[3] Once this controversy is resolved, both the FASB and the GASB might take a more active part in setting standards for colleges and universities. In the

---

[2] The funds and accounting procedures used by private schools are specifically covered by AICPA, *Statement of Position (SOP) 78-10*.

[3] Governmental Accounting Standards Board, *Statement No. 8*, "Applicability of FASB *Statement No. 93*, 'Recognition of Depreciation by Not-for-Profit Organizations' to Certain State and Local Governmental Entities" (Stamford Conn: GASB, Jan. 1988).

meantime, however, the three sources listed below are still the most authorative. Accordingly, this chapter is based upon their recommendations.

The first source of generally accepted principles (GAAP) for colleges and universities is *College and University Business Administration*, published by the National Association of College and University Business Officers (NACUBO). This reference book is used primarily by college and university administrators.

Another source of generally accepted accounting principles for colleges and universities is the AICPA's industry audit guide, *Audit of Colleges and Universities*. This guide, which is largely based on the NACUBO publication, is used primarily by the certified public accountants who audit these institutions. It has been amended by the AICPA's *Statement of Position (SOP) 74–8*, which updates and clarifies many of the items covered in the industry audit guide.

The third source of generally accepted accounting principles for colleges and universities is the *Higher Education Finance Manual*, published by the U.S. Department of Education. This publication provides information on the accounting systems necessary to meet the requirements of the National Center for Educational Statistics, a federal agency that monitors the activities of educational institutions. All three of the above publications were developed in a coordinated manner. As a result, they usually agree on the accounting methods and procedures that should be used by colleges and universities.

FINANCIAL STATEMENTS OF COLLEGES AND UNIVERSITIES

Three basic financial statements are generally used by colleges and universities: a balance sheet; a statement of changes in fund balances; and a statement of current funds revenues, expenditures, and other changes.

An example of a **balance sheet** is shown in Exhibit 12–1. Note that all the funds and fund groups used by the Sample Educational Institution are presented on the same report in a **"pancake" format**[4]. This format, which is the one most commonly used, has the advantage of saving space. In addition, it enables the user to see the "big picture" at one glance. This, of course, is the same reason used to justify the use of combined financial statements by municipalities. Unlike the accounts shown in the combined balance sheets of municipalities, however, the accounts of the various funds shown in the balance sheet of a college or university are not totaled, even in memorandum form.

To provide adequate disclosure all separately incorporated, but related, units or self-supporting auxiliary enterprises for which the institution is responsible (e.g., university presses, research organizations, agricultural units, and so on) "should be (1) included in the financial statements, (2) adequately disclosed by notes, or (3) presented in separate financial statements accompanied by and cross-referenced in the basic financial statements of the institution."[5]

---

[4] A columnar format, with a column for each major fund, is also acceptable.

[5] AICPA, *Audits of Colleges and Universities*, p. 57.

EXHIBIT 12–1

Sample Educational Institution
Balance Sheet
June 3, 19X1
with Comparative Figures at June 30, 19X0

ASSETS	Current Year	Prior Year
CURRENT FUNDS		
Unrestricted		
Cash	$ 210,000	$ 110,000
Investments	450,000	360,000
Accounts receivable, less allowance of $18,000 both years	228,000	175,000
Inventories, at lower of cost (first-in, first-out basis) or market	90,000	80,000
Prepaid expenses and deferred charges	28,000	20,000
Total unrestricted	1,006,000	745,000
Restricted		
Cash	145,000	101,000
Investments	175,000	165,000
Accounts receivable, less allowance of $8,000 both years	68,000	160,000
Unbilled charges	72,000	—
Total restricted	460,000	426,000
Total current funds	1,466,000	1,171,000
LOAN FUNDS		
Cash	30,000	20,000
Investments	100,000	100,000
Loans to students, faculty, and staff less allowance of $10,000 current year and $9,000 prior year	550,000	382,000
Due from unrestricted funds	3,000	—
Total loan funds	683,000	502,000

LIABILITIES AND FUND BALANCES	Current Year	Prior Year
CURRENT FUNDS		
Unrestricted		
Accounts payable	$ 125,000	$ 100,000
Accrued liabilities	20,000	15,000
Students' deposits	30,000	35,000
Due to other funds	158,000	120,000
Deferred credits	30,000	20,000
Fund balance	643,000	455,000
Total unrestricted	1,006,000	745,000
Restricted		
Accounts payable	14,000	5,000
Fund balances	446,000	421,000
Total restricted	460,000	426,000
Total current funds	1,466,000	1,171,000
LOAN FUNDS		
Fund balances		
U.S. government grants refundable	50,000	33,000
University funds		
Restricted	483,000	369,000
Unrestricted	150,000	100,000
Total loan funds	683,000	502,000

(continued)

EXHIBIT 12–1 (cont.)

ASSETS

	Current Year	Prior Year
ENDOWMENT AND SIMILAR FUNDS		
Cash	100,000	101,000
Investments	13,900,000	11,800,000
Total endowment and similar funds	14,000,000	11,901,000
ANNUITY AND LIFE INCOME FUNDS		
Annuity funds		
Cash	$ 55,000	$ 45,000
Investments	3,260,000	3,010,000
Total annuity funds	3,315,000	3,055,000
Life income funds		
Cash	15,000	15,000
Investments	2,045,000	1,740,000
Total life income funds	2,060,000	1,755,000
Total annuity and life income funds	5,375,000	4,810,000
PLANT FUNDS		
Unexpended		
Cash	275,000	410,000
Investments	1,285,000	1,590,000
Due from unrestricted current funds	150,000	120,000
Total unexpended	1,710,000	2,120,000

LIABILITIES AND FUND BALANCES

	Current Year	Prior Year
ENDOWMENT AND SIMILAR FUNDS		
Fund balances		
Endowment	7,800,000	6,740,000
Term endowment	3,840,000	3,420,000
Quasi-endowment—unrestricted	1,000,000	800,000
Quasi-endowment—restricted	1,360,000	941,000
Total endowment and similar funds	14,000,000	11,901,000
ANNUITY AND LIFE INCOME FUNDS		
Annuity funds		
Annuities payable	$ 2,150,000	$ 2,300,000
Fund balances	1,165,000	755,000
Total annuity funds	3,315,000	3,055,000
Life income funds		
Income payable	5,000	5,000
Fund balances	2,055,000	1,750,000
Total life income funds	2,060,000	1,755,000
Total annuity and life income funds	5,375,000	4,810,000
PLANT FUNDS		
Unexpended		
Accounts payable	10,000	—
Notes payable	100,000	—
Bonds payable	400,000	—
Fund balances		
Restricted	1,000,000	1,860,000
Unrestricted	200,000	260,000
Total unexpended	1,710,000	2,120,000

(continued)

453

EXHIBIT 12–1 (cont.)

ASSETS

	Current Year	Prior Year
Renewals and replacements		
Cash	5,000	4,000
Investments	150,000	286,000
Deposits with trustees	100,000	90,000
Due from unrestricted current funds	5,000	—
Total renewals and replacements	260,000	380,000
Retirement of indebtedness		
Cash	50,000	40,000
Deposits with trustees	250,000	253,000
Total retirement of indebtedness	300,000	293,000
Investment in plant		
Land	500,000	500,000
Improvements other than buildings (net of accumulated depreciation of $77,500 and $52,500)	975,000	1,110,000
Buildings (net of accumulated depreciation of $15,300,000 and $13,300,000)	24,000,000	24,060,000
Equipment (net of accumulated depreciation of $7,450,000 and $6,450,000)	14,000,000	14,200,000
Library books	100,000	80,000
Total investment in plant	39,575,000	39,950,000
Total plant funds	41,845,000	42,743,000
Agency Funds		
Cash	50,000	70,000
Investments	60,000	20,000
Total agency funds	110,000	90,000

LIABILITIES AND FUND BALANCES

	Current Year	Prior Year
Renewals and replacements		
Fund balances		
Restricted	25,000	180,000
Unrestricted	235,000	200,000
Total renewals and replacements	260,000	380,000
Retirement of indebtedness		
Fund balances		
Restricted	185,000	125,000
Unrestricted	115,000	168,000
Total retirement of indebtedness	300,000	293,000
Investment in plant		
Notes payable	790,000	810,000
Bonds payable	2,200,000	2,400,000
Mortgages payable	400,000	200,000
Net investment in plant	36,185,000	36,540,000
Total investment in plant	39,575,000	39,950,000
Total plant funds	41,845,000	42,743,000
Agency Funds		
Deposits held in custody for others	110,000	90,000
Total agency funds	110,000	90,000

Accompanying Summary of Significant Accounting Policies and Notes to Financial Statements not included.

Source: College and University Business Administration, 4th ed., pp. 456–57, by permission of the National Association of College and University Business Officers.

The second statement, the **statement of changes in fund balances**, informs the users of the activities that caused the balances of each fund to change. It shows all additions to, deductions from, and transfers between the various funds. All funds used by the institution are shown on this statement except for one type: Agency Funds. The Agency Funds used by colleges and universities, like the ones used in municipal accounting, have no fund balances. Their assets must always equal their liabilities. Therefore they would be out of place on a statement of changes in fund balances. An example of a statement of changes in fund balances is shown in Exhibit 12–2. While this information is generally presented in columnar fashion in a single statement, separate statements are permissible for each fund group. As was true of the balance sheet, the columns of the statement of changes in fund balances should not be cross-footed (added), as the totals are likely to be misleading.

The **statement of current funds revenues, expenditures, and other changes** is one that is unique to colleges and universities. It reports on the activities of the **Current Funds**. It presents the revenues, by source, and the expenditures, by function, of the Current Funds. It also presents all the other changes that take place within these funds. While similar in form and content to an income or operating statement, it does not purport to show the net income or results of operations of the Current Funds. Rather, its purpose is to "provide the reader with adequate information concerning the details of the sources and uses of Current Funds"[6] and to "enable the institution to report the total of **unrestricted** and **restricted** Current Funds expended for each of the functional categories so that the total level of financial activity for each such function is disclosed."[7]

The net changes in fund balances represented on the statement of current funds revenues, expenditures, and other changes should be the same as the changes in the Current Funds shown on the statement of changes in fund balances. An example of a statement of current funds revenues, expenditures, and other changes is shown in Exhibit 12–3. Note that only the activities of Current Funds are reported on this statement. This is because these funds are the only **operational-type** funds used by colleges and universities. The other funds used by these institutions are generally fiduciary in nature or are used to record the activities surrounding the purchase, financing, and disposition of plant assets and the endowment and loan-type activities of the institutions.

ACCOUNTING PROBLEMS OF COLLEGES AND UNIVERSITIES

The accounts of colleges and universities are usually maintained on the accrual basis—that is, revenues are recognized (reported) when earned and expenditures are recognized when materials or services are received. As with municipalities, expenditures of colleges and universities include operating expenses (except for depreciation, which will be covered later) and "the acquisition cost of

[6] Ibid., p. 56.
[7] Ibid.

EXHIBIT 12–2

Sample Educational Institution
Statement of Changes in Fund Balances
Year Ended June 30, 19X1

	CURRENT FUNDS		Loan Funds	Endowment and Similar Funds	Annuity and Life Income Funds	PLANT FUNDS			
	Unrestricted	Restricted				Unexpended	Renewals and Replacements	Retirement of Indebtedness	Investment in Plant
Revenues and other additions									
Unrestricted current fund revenues	$7,540,000								
Expired term endowment—restricted						50,000			
State appropriations—restricted						50,000			
Federal grants and contracts—restricted		500,000							
Private gifts, grants, and contracts—restricted		370,000	100,000	1,500,000	800,000	115,000	5,000	65,000	15,000
Investment income—restricted		224,000	12,000	10,000		5,000		5,000	
Realized gains on investments—unrestricted				109,000					
Realized gains on investments—restricted			4,000	50,000		10,000	5,000	5,000	
Interest on loans receivable			7,000						
U.S. government advances			18,000						
Expended for plant facilities (including $100,000 charged to current funds expenditures)									2,550,000
Retirement of indebtedness									220,000
Accrued interest on sale of bonds								3,000	
Matured annuity and life income restricted to endowment				10,000					
Total revenues and other additions	7,540,000	1,094,000	141,000	1,679,000	800,000	230,000	10,000	78,000	2,785,000
Expenditures and other deductions									
Educational and general expenditures	4,400,000	1,014,000							
Auxiliary enterprises expenditures	1,830,000								
Indirect costs recovered		35,000							
Refunded to grantors		20,000	10,000						
Loan cancellations and write-offs			1,000						
Administrative and collection costs			1,000						

(continued)

EXHIBIT 12–2 (cont.)

	CURRENT FUNDS		Loan Funds	Endowment and Similar Funds	Annuity and Life Income Funds	PLANT FUNDS			
	Unrestricted	Restricted				Unexpended	Renewals and Replacements	Retirement of Indebtedness	Investment in Plant
Adjustment of actuarial liability for annuities payable					75,000				
Expended for plant facilities (including noncapitalized expenditures of $50,000)						1,200,000	300,000		
Retirement of indebtedness								220,000	
Interest of indebtedness								190,000	
Disposal of plant facilities									115,000
Provision for depreciation									3,025,000
Expired term endowments ($40,000 unrestricted, $50,000 restricted to plant)				90,000					
Matured annuity and life income funds restricted to endowment					10,000				
Total expenditures and other deductions	6,230,000	1,069,000	12,000	90,000	85,000	1,200,000	300,000	411,000	3,140,000
Transfers among funds—additions (deductions)									
Mandatory:									
Principle and interest	(340,000)							340,000	
Renewals and replacements	(170,000)						170,000		
Loan fund matching grant	(2,000)		2,000						
Unrestricted gifts allocated	(650,000)		50,000	550,000		50,000			
Portion of unrestricted quasi-endowment funds investment gains appropriated	40,000			(40,000)					
Total transfers	(1,122,000)		52,000	510,000		50,000	170,000	340,000	
Net increase/(decrease) for the year	188,000	25,000	181,000	2,099,000	715,000	(920,000)	(120,000)	7,000	(355,000)
Fund balance at beginning of year	455,000	421,000	502,000	11,901,000	2,505,000	2,120,000	380,000	293,000	36,540,000
Fund balance at end of year	643,000	446,000	683,000	14,000,000	3,220,000	1,200,000	260,000	300,000	36,185,000

Accompanying Summary of Significant Accounting Policies and Notes to Financial Statements not included.

Source: *College and University Business Administration,* 4th ed., pp. 458–59, by permission of the National Association of College and University Business Officers.

EXHIBIT 12-3

Sample Educational Institution
Statement of Current Funds Revenues, Expenditures, and Other Changes
Year Ended June 30, 19X1

	CURRENT YEAR			Prior Year Total
	Unrestricted	Restricted	Total	
Revenues				
Tuition and fees	$2,600,000		$2,600,000	$2,300,000
Federal appropriations	500,000		500,000	500,000
State appropriations	700,000		700,000	700,000
Local appropriations	100,000		100,000	100,000
Federal grants and contracts	20,000	$ 375,000	395,000	350,000
State grants and contracts	10,000	25,000	35,000	200,000
Local grants and contracts	5,000	25,000	30,000	45,000
Private gifts, grants, and contracts	850,000	380,000	1,230,000	1,190,000
Endowment income	325,000	209,000	534,000	500,000
Sales and services of educational activities	190,000		190,000	195,000
Sales and services of auxiliary enterprises	2,200,000		2,200,000	2,100,000
Expired term endowment	40,000		40,000	
Other sources (if any)				
Total current revenues	7,540,000	1,014,000	8,554,000	8,180,000
Expenditures and Mandatory Transfers				
Educational and general				
Instruction	2,960,000	489,000	3,449,000	3,300,000
Research	100,000	400,000	500,000	650,000
Public service	130,000	25,000	155,000	175,000
Academic support	250,000		250,000	225,000
Student services	200,000		200,000	195,000
Institutional support	450,000		450,000	445,000
Operation and maintenance of plant	220,000		220,000	200,000
Scholarships and fellowships	90,000	100,000	190,000	180,000
Educational and general expenditures	4,400,000	1,014,000	5,414,000	5,370,000
Mandatory transfers for:				
Principal and interest	90,000		90,000	50,000
Renewals and replacements	100,000		100,000	80,000
Loan fund matching grant	2,000		2,000	
Total educational and general	4,592,000	1,014,000	5,606,000	5,500,000

(continued)

EXHIBIT 12-3 (cont.)

	CURRENT YEAR			Prior Year Total
	Unrestricted	Restricted	Total	
Auxiliary enterprises				
Expenditures	1,830,000		1,830,000	1,730,000
Mandatory transfers for:				
Principal and interest	250,000		250,000	250,000
Renewals and replace-				
ments	70,000		70,000	70,000
Total auxiliary				
enterprises	2,150,000		2,150,000	2,050,000
Total expenditures and				
mandatory transfers	6,742,000	1,014,000	7,756,000	7,550,000
Other transfers and additions/(deductions)				
Excess of restricted receipts				
over transfers to revenues		45,000	45,000	40,000
Refunded to grantors		(20,000)	(20,000)	
Unrestricted gifts allocated to				
other funds	(650,000)		(650,000)	(510,000)
Portion of quasi-endowment				
gains appropriated	40,000		40,000	
Net increase in fund				
balances	188,000	25,000	213,000	160,000

Accompanying Summary of Significant Accounting Policies and Notes to Financial Statements not included.

Source: College and University Business Administration, 4th ed., pp. 460–61, by permission of the National Association of College and University Business Officers.

capital assets, such as equipment and library books, to the extent Current Funds are budgeted for and used by operating departments for such purposes."[8] Expenses applicable to the current period but not recorded on that date should be accrued, while those applicable to future periods should be deferred (recognized in a future period).

One problem that is unique to educational institutions occurs when an academic term encompasses parts of two fiscal years (e.g., the summer terms at some institutions run from early June through early August; the fiscal years of many of these institutions, however, end on June 30). When this happens, all the revenues and expenditures of the academic term in question "should be reported totally within the fiscal year in which the program is predominately conducted."[9]

Like municipalities, colleges and universities often use encumbrance ac-

[8] NACUBO, *College and University Business Administration,* 4th ed., p. 402.
[9] Ibid., p. 390.

counting in order to maintain control over expenditures and to prevent over-spending. The methods of handling encumbrances used by colleges and universities are often the same as those used by governmental units (see Chapter 5), although simpler methods are permissible. For example, many small institutions use informal memorandum records. Any method, however, is acceptable as long as it involves proper control, provide useful information, and is flexible and cost effective.

Colleges and universities should use budgetary accounting. The procedures and accounts used under such systems are similar to those found in municipal accounting. The account titles, however, are somewhat different. For example, the following entry is prepared after the governing body approves the budget:

Estimated (or unrealized) revenues	XXXXXX	
Estimated expenditures (or budget		
allocations for expenditures)		XXXXXX
Unallocated budget balance		XXXXXX
To record the approval of the budget by the		
governing body.		

Any revisions to the budget are recorded by appropriate debits and credits to the accounts shown above. At the end of the fiscal year, the budgetary accounts are reversed out, just as they are in municipal accounting.

As with other organizations, sound cash management is critical to the survival of colleges and universities. When these organizations have excess cash (e.g., at the beginning of a semester or after receiving a sizable donation), they usually invest it in interest-bearing securities.

Colleges and universities often find it advantageous to pool the investments of various funds. In addition to permitting administrative economies, the use of an investment pool makes possible a broad variety of investments. Such diversification provides a greater degree of safety and stability of revenue than is possible with a series of smaller, unrelated investments. When assets are placed in a pool, however, the identity of each fund must be maintained. This is accomplished through the use of individual accounts for the principal of each fund participating in the pool.

When investments are received as gifts, they are usually reported at their fair market (or appraised) value at the date of the gift. Alternatively, the investments may be reported at their current market value, as long as this basis is used for all of the institution's investments. If this latter method is used, unrealized gains and losses should be reported in the same manner that realized gains and losses are reported under the cost basis.[10] Any differences between the carrying value and the fair market or appraised value should be shown by the "selling" fund as realized (already incurred) gains or losses.[11]

[10] Ibid., p. 392.
[11] Ibid.

DEPRECIATION

As with the governmental-type funds used by municipalities, depreciation is not reported as an operating expense by colleges and universities. The reasoning behind this policy is that users should not, through the tuition and fees they pay, be required to finance the recovery of an investment in plant and equipment, which is usually acquired by means of gifts and governmental appropriations. When capital asset acquisitions are financed from Current Funds, they are reported as expenditures of those funds in the year of acquisition.[12]

To provide more information to statement users, however, many institutions report an allowance for depreciation on their balance sheets and a provision for depreciation on their statements of changes in the "investment in plant" subgroups of their Plant Fund groups.[13] They also record depreciation on fixed assets held as investments by their Endowment and Similar Funds groups, in order to maintain the distinction between income from and principal of these investments—a treatment similar to that given to the Nonexpendable Trust Funds used by governmental units.

Recently, the Financial Accounting Standards Board (FASB) issued *Statement of Financial Accounting Standards (SFAS) No. 93*, "Recognition of Depreciation by Not-for-Profit Organizations," which requires most not-for-profit organizations, including colleges and universities, to recognize depreciation on most long-lived, tangible assets. The reasoning behind this requirement is that these assets eventually wear out and organizations need to know at what rate their assets are wearing out. This reasoning assumes, of course, that depreciation is a true measure of wear and tear, an assumption not universally shared by accountants.

Many college and university officials and officials of governmental organizations do not believe depreciation should be reported, for the reasons stated at the beginning of this section. As a result, the Governmental Accounting Standards Board (GASB) has suggested that governmental entities—such as colleges and universities and other organizations with counterparts in the private sector—ignore *SFAS No. 93* and wait until it issues its own statements on issues that relate to depreciation. The difference of opinion between the two primary rule-making bodies creates significant reporting differences between private and public institutions and creates much confusion for users of the financial statements issued by these organizations. Hopefully, this jurisdictional dispute will soon be resolved. For its part, the FASB has delayed the implementation of *SFAS No. 93*. In this chapter, we will assume that depreciation is recorded by colleges and uiversities.

INSTITUTIONS OPERATED BY RELIGIOUS GROUPS

It is quite common for a religious group to operate an educational institution. When this happens, the records of the educational institution should be segre-

[12] Ibid.
[13] Ibid.

gated from those of the religious group, and the educational institution should be treated as a separate entity. When services are contributed by members of the religious group, they should be recorded in the accounts and on the financial statements at fair market value. These amounts can be determined by relating them to the compensation (including fringe benefits) provided to lay personnel performing similar duties. The value of the services performed by members of the religious groups should be recorded as both a gift revenue and an expenditure. Any living costs, personal allowances, and so forth, that are unique to this relationship and are not provided to lay personnel should be deducted from the gift revenue.

FUNDS USED BY COLLEGES AND UNIVERSITIES

The following types of funds are ordinarily used by colleges and universities:

1. Current Funds
2. Loan Funds
3. Endowment and Similar Funds (Term Endowment and Quasi-Endowment)
4. Annuity and Life Income Funds
5. Agency Funds
6. Plant Funds[14]

Current, Loan, Endowment, Term Endowment, and Plant Funds can be restricted or unrestricted. Annuity and Life Income and Agency Funds *must* be restricted, while Quasi-Endowment Funds *must* remain unrestricted. To be classified as **restricted**, a fund must have restrictions placed on its use by persons or organizations *outside* the institution. Otherwise it must be classified as **unrestricted**. Restricted funds should be reported separately from unrestricted funds. Within each fund, the restricted accounts should be reported separately from the unrestricted accounts.

Current Funds

Current Funds are used to account for those resources used to carry out the general operations of the institution, operations that are "directly related" to the institution's primary objectives. These objectives usually consist of teaching, research, and public service. However, such auxiliary enterprises as residence halls, food services, and intercollegiate athletics are also considered to be directly related. The term *current* refers to the fact that these resources will be expended in a short period of time.

[14]Ibid., pp. 388–89.

Current Funds serve many of the functions of the general funds used by governmental units. The scope of these funds, however, is wider, since many of the activities recorded in these funds (e.g., bookstores) are self-supporting. By contrast, similar activities are usually recorded in Enterprise Funds when conducted by governmental units.

Unrestricted Current Funds

As we mentioned earlier, Current Funds can be unrestricted or restricted. The activities of **Unrestricted Current Funds** tend to be similar to those of General or Special Revenue Funds. The revenues of these funds are usually recorded by source. Among the more common sources of revenue are tuition and fees; federal, state, and local appropriations; gifts and grants; endowment income; the sales and services of educational activities; and the sales and services of auxiliary enterprises.

Another common (and important) source of revenues for many institutions, especially those operated by state governments, is "formula" funding. **Formula funding** was developed as a means of "depoliticalizing" the allocation of resources between the various educational institutions within a state. Under the formula, which is usually based on the cost of running a "typical" institution in a given region (e.g., the Southeast), a college or university is allowed a certain dollar amount for each type of student-credit-hour (SCH) earned by that institution.[15] For example, in Louisiana (as of this writing) the formula is as follows:

Student's Academic Level	Cost Category*	Dollars Per SCH
Doctoral	Higher cost	$1,751
Doctoral	Lower cost	1,121
Master's	Higher cost	298
Master's	Lower cost	184
Upper undergraduate	Higher cost	106
Upper undergraduate	Lower cost	88
Lower undergraduate	Higher cost	81
Lower undergraduate	Lower cost	65

* Since certain areas of study, such as science and engineering, require more resources than other areas, such as liberal arts and business, they are allowed more dollars under the formula.

[15] A student-credit-hour (SCH) is a measure of the number of students and the number of credit hours being taken at an institution. Its purpose is to provide a common denominator between part-time and full-time students. A student taking one three-credit-hour course is worth 3 SCHs. A student taking five three-credit-hour courses is worth 15 SCHs, and so on.

Thus a public institution in Louisiana with the following enrollment (as of the tenth day of classes) will receive $22,795,200 in formula funding:

Student's Academic Level	Cost Category	No. of Students	Average Credit Hours per Student*	Student Credit Hours	Dollars per SCH	Dollars Funded
Doctoral	Higher cost	40	12	480	$ 1,751	$ 840,480
Doctoral	Lower cost	60	12	720	1,121	807,120
Master's	Higher cost	1,200	12	14,400	298	4,291,200
Master's	Lower cost	800	12	9,600	184	1,766,400
Upper undergraduate	Higher cost	3,000	15	45,000	106	4,770,000
Upper undergraduate	Lower cost	1,000	15	15,000	88	1,320,000
Lower undergraduate	Higher cost	5,000	15	75,000	81	6,075,000
Lower undergraduate	Lower cost	3,000	15	45,000	65	2,925,000
Total formula funding						$22,795,200

*The number of hours taken by most students ranges from six hours for part-time students to eighteen hours for full-time students. It is assumed that the majority of students at this institution are full-time students.

From the preceding discussion, it should be easy to see why certain institutions discourage the dropping of courses until after "enrollment day." It should also be obvious that "senior" institutions (those granting the largest number of advanced degrees) receive the lion's share of the available resources.

The expenditures of Unrestricted Current Funds should be classified by function. For internal operating purposes, they should also be classified by department and object (e.g., salaries). The major functional categories used by colleges and universities are (1) educational and general, (2) student aid, and (3) auxiliary enterprises. Functional subcategories include instruction, research, academic support, institutional support, operation and maintenance of plant, and scholarships, as well as those subcategories unique to the particular auxiliary enterprises operated by the institution.

Restricted Current Funds

Restricted funds pose some special problems not encountered by unrestricted funds. First, a fund cannot be designated as "restricted" by the governing board or operating management of the institution. If these parties could make such a designation, they would also have the power to "unrestrict" the fund. Thus the fund would not be a true restricted fund. Restricted funds are only used to reflect limitations placed on the use of certain resources by parties *outside* the organization.

The revenues of restricted funds are not considered to be "earned" until they have been expended in the manner set forth by the donor or the party placing the restriction. When these monies are first received, they are reported as *additions* in the statement of changes in fund balances. They are recognized as *revenues* when the required expenditures are made. Thus the total revenues reported for these funds, on the statement of current funds revenues, expenditures, and other changes, will equal the total expenditures reported for these funds on that statement. Any amounts not spent on refunds to grantors will be shown as "other transfers and additions."

The transactions usually recorded in Restricted Current Funds consist largely of the receipt of cash (or other assets), the making of expenditures, and the earning of revenues. As with other funds, revenue and expenditure accounts are closed at the end of the period. Since the revenues of the period must equal the expenditures of the period, there is no need for a debit or a credit to a fund balance account when preparing closing entries.

Interfund Transfers

Transfers from the Current (restricted and unrestricted) Funds to other types of funds of a college or university can be mandatory or nonmandatory. **Mandatory transfers** are those transfers "arising out of (1) binding legal agreements related to the financing of educational plant, such as amounts for debt, retirement, interest, and required provisions for renewals and replacements of plant, not financed from other sources; and (2) grant agreements with agencies of the federal government, donors, and other organizations to match gifts and grants to loan and other funds."[16] They may be made from either Restricted or Unrestricted Current Funds. **Nonmandatory transfers** are transfers made to other fund groups "at the discretion of the governing board to serve a variety of objectives, such as additions to loan funds, additions to quasi-endowment funds, general or specific plant additions, voluntary renewals and replacements of plant, and prepayments on debt principal."[17]

Transfers from the Current Funds to other funds are recorded and reported separately from the expenditures of those funds. They are shown in the statement of current funds revenues, expenditures, and other changes only when the governing board of the institution designates current-year revenues as the sources by which such transfers are to be funded. If the transfers are of prior-year revenues, they are shown only in the statement of changes in fund balances. When such transfers are presented in the statement of current funds revenues, expenditures, and other changes, they appear under the heading "Expenditures and Mandatory Transfers" if mandatory, and under the heading "Other Transfers and Additions/(Deductions)" if nonmandatory. Both mandatory and nonmandatory transfers are shown in the statement of changes in fund balances under the heading "Transfers among Funds—Additions/(Deductions)." Transfers to the Plant Funds (for *required* renewals, replacements, and debt service), which are financed by revenues from auxiliary enterprises, are reported on both statements as mandatory transfers for renewals and replacements.

[16] NACUBO, *College and University Business Administration*, 4th ed., p. 413.
[17] Ibid.

Account Classifications

The asset and liability accounts used by the Current Funds are usually current in nature, just like the ones used by the General Funds of municipalities. Because of the use of accrual accounting, however, these funds include prepaid expenses and deferred charges (expenses paid, but applicable to future periods) among their assets and deferred credits (monies collected in advance) among their liabilities. The Current Funds can also show long-term debt among their liabilities, as long as the debt is not related to fixed asset acquisitions. Such cases, however, are rare.

Fund balances are segregated into two categories: allocated and unallocated. The **allocated fund balance** shows the portion of the fund balance that represents the institution's equity in its auxiliary enterprises, its hospitals, and so forth, and the portion reserved for outstanding encumbrances. In addition, any other allocations established by the operating management or the governing board of the institution or by external parties should be disclosed. The **unallocated fund balance** is a residual figure, representing the fund's "free" balance.

Recording Transactions

The transactions recorded in the Unrestricted Current Fund of a college or university consist primarily of revenues, expenditures, and transfers to other funds. Since these transactions are recorded on the (full) accrual basis, inventoriable items such as supplies are recorded as assets when purchased and as expenditures when used. Illustrated below are sample transactions for typical Unrestricted Current Fund transactions:

1. Revenues of $1 million are received from tuition and fees. Of this amount, $900,000 is received in cash and $100,000 is still to be received:

Cash	900,000	
Accounts receivable	100,000	
Revenues—educational and general		1,000,000

To record revenues from tuition and fees.

Note: If it is expected that not all the receivables will be collected, it is appropriate to set up an allowance for uncollectible accounts. This is done by means of a debit to an expenditure account and a credit to an allowance account for the amount expected to remain uncollected.

2. Tuition scholarships worth $30,000 are awarded to deserving students.

Expenditures—educational and general	30,000	
Revenues—educational and general		30,000

To record the revenues and corresponding expenditures relating to tuition scholarships.

Note: Even though no resources are actually received or expended, it is customary to show the tuition that would have been received as a revenue, offset by a corresponding expenditure representing the "cost" of the scholarship.

3. Revenues from auxiliary enterprises amount to $150,000.

Cash	150,000	
Revenues—auxiliary enterprises		150,000

To record the revenues from the various auxiliary enterprises.

4. Materials and supplies purchased during the year amount to $300,000. Invoices amounting to $50,000 are outstanding at year-end.

Inventory—materials and supplies	300,000	
Cash		250,000
Accounts payable		50,000

To record the purchase of materials and supplies.

5. Materials and supplies used during the year amount to $220,000. Of this amount, $180,000 is used for educational activities and $40,000 is used by the auxiliary enterprises.

Expenditures—educational and general	180,000	
Expenditures—auxiliary enterprises	40,000	
Inventory—materials and supplies		220,000

To record the cost of materials and supplies used during the year.

6. Wages, salaries, and other operating expenses (such as utilities and insurance) amount to $810,000. Of this amount, $760,000 is chargeable to educational and general operations and $50,000 is chargeable to auxiliary enterprises.

Expenditures—educational and general	760,000	
Expenditures—auxiliary enterprises	50,000	
Cash		810,000

To record the wages, salaries, and other operating expenditures incurred during the year.

7. Grants-in-aid to students total $50,000.

Expenditures—student aid	50,000	
Cash		50,000

To record grants-in-aid awarded to students during the year.

8. In accordance with the loan agreement, a transfer of $50,000 is made to the Fund for Retirement of Indebtedness to pay interest and principal currently due on the mortgage on the new security building (see p. 476).

Mandatory transfers to the Fund for Retirement of Indebtedness	50,000	
Cash		50,000

To record the payment on the mortgage carried on the new security building.

9. A "voluntary" transfer of $10,000 is made to the Unexpended Plant Fund for the purchase of library books.

Nonmandatory transfers to the Unexpended Plant Fund	10,000	
Cash		10,000

To record the cost of library books financed by the Unrestricted Current Fund.

10. A grant of $10,000 is received from the Kezar Foundation to be used in the general operations of the university.

Cash	10,000	
Revenues—gifts and grants		10,000

To record the receipt of a general operating grant from the Kezar Foundation.

11. The revenue, expenditure, and transfer accounts are closed out at year-end.

Revenues—educational and general	1,030,000	
Revenues—auxiliary enterprises	150,000	
Revenues—gifts and grants	10,000	
Expenditures—educational and general		970,000
Expenditures—auxiliary enterprises		90,000
Expenditures—student aid		50,000
Mandatory transfers to the Fund for Retirement of Indebtedness		50,000
Nonmandatory transfers to the Unexpended Plant Fund		10,000
Fund balance—unallocated		20,000

To close out the revenue, expenditure, and transfer accounts.

As we mentioned earlier, monies received by the Restricted Current Funds are not considered "earned" until they have been expended in the manner stipulated by the donor or the party placing the restriction. When these monies are first received, they are recorded as additions to the fund balance. They are recognized as revenues when the required expenditures are made.

To illustrate, assume that a donation of $100,000 is given to the university. Of this amount, $60,000 is to be spent for library operations and $40,000 is to be used for special payments to faculty who write outstanding textbooks:

Cash	100,000	
Fund balance—library operations		60,000
Fund balance—special faculty salary		
supplements		40,000
To record the receipt of cash designated for		
library operations and for special payments to		
faculty who write outstanding textbooks.		

Since some of the cash will not be spent right away, $20,000 is invested in government securities.

Investments	20,000	
Cash		20,000
To record the purchase of government		
securities.		

When the expenditures of Restricted Current Funds, which are required by the donors or the parties placing the restrictions, are made, expenditure accounts are debited and Cash and/or payable accounts are credited. In this case, assume that $50,000 is spent on library operations, and $30,000 is spent for faculty salary supplements:

Expenditures—library operations	50,000	
Expenditures—special faculty salary		
supplements	30,000	
Cash		80,000
To record the expenditures for library opera-		
tions and special faculty salary supplements.		

Revenues of Restricted Current Funds are recognized to the extent that the expenditures have taken place for the designated purposes. In this example, the revenues of the period will equal the amounts expended in the previous example (assume that of this amount, $1,000 represent interest on the government securities and the remainder is from the gift itself):

Fund balance—library operations	50,000	
Fund balance—special faculty salary		
supplements	30,000	
Revenues—restricted gifts		79,000
Revenues—investment income		1,000
To recognize the revenues of the period.		

At the end of the fiscal year, the revenue and expenditure accounts of the Restricted Current Funds are closed out as follows:

Revenues—restricted gifts	79,000	
Revenues—investment income	1,000	
Expenditures—library operations		50,000
Expenditures—special faculty salary supplements		30,000
To close out the revenue and expenditure accounts.		

Loan Funds

Loan Funds are used to account for monies that will be lent to students, faculty, and other personnel of the college or university. The monies are received from governmental units, foundations, and individual donors, as well as the borrowers (which is why Loan Funds are called "revolving" funds). Interest received from borrowers and temporary investments is usually used to "cover" operating expenses and bad debts, as well as additional loans. As with commercial accounting, an allowance for uncollectible accounts should be established. The activities of Loan Funds, which can be likened to those of trust funds, are recorded in the statement of changes in fund balances.

Endowment and Similar Funds

Endowment and Similar Funds are those funds whose principal is nonexpendable and is invested in order to produce income. According to NACUBO, **Endowment Funds** are those funds for which donors or other external parties have stipulated that the principal must be maintained intact "and is to be invested for the purpose of producing present and future income, which may be expended or added to principal," in accordance with the terms of the donation.[18]

The designation "similar funds" is given to Term Endowment and Quasi-Endowment Funds. **Term Endowment Funds** are similar to Endowment Funds. However, all or a part of the principal of these funds may be expended after a given period of time or when a specific event occurs.

Quasi-Endowment Funds are those funds that the governing board of the institution, rather than an external party, has decided to set aside. The principal and income of these funds may be utilized at the discretion of the governing board. As a result, they are unrestricted.

Generally speaking, the income earned on the principal (dividends, interest, rents, and so on) of Endowment and Similar Funds is used for institutional purposes. Capital gains are usually reinvested and treated as additional principal on which additional income will be earned.

[18] Ibid., p. 420.

The investment income of Endowment and Similar Funds is reported as either restricted or unrestricted. If it is reported as restricted, it should be treated as an "addition" to either the appropriate unexpended endowment income account in the Restricted Current Fund or to the fund balance of the Loan, Endowment, or Plant Funds, depending on the terms of the restrictions. If it is reported as unrestricted, it should be treated as an addition to the Unrestricted Current Fund revenues.

The assets of Endowment and Similar Funds consist primarily of cash and investments. They may also include accounts receivable, prepaid items, and amounts due from other fund groups. Investments can consist of stocks and bonds, as well as real estate, patents, copyrights, royalties, and participations in oil-drilling ventures. The liabilities of these funds consist primarily of amounts due to other fund groups. There can, however, be claims or other forms of indebtedness against the assets representing investments (e.g., mortgages).

The fund balances of the Endowment and Similar Funds are increased by means of gifts, bequests, income, and capital gains required by the gift instrument to be added to the principal of the funds, and transfers to Quasi-Endowment Funds from other fund groups. The fund balances of these funds are reduced by withdrawals and transfers to other fund groups and by losses on investment transactions.

Endowment and Similar Funds should be reported in a separate section of the balance sheet and of the statement of changes in fund balances. The identity of each type of fund should be clearly differentiated in the fund balance section of the balance sheet.

Annuity and Life Income Funds

The Annuity and Life Income Funds group is made up of two subgroups: Annuity Funds and Life Income Funds. **Annuity Funds** are those funds used to account for resources given to the institution with the stipulation that a *specified dollar amount* be paid to the donor or other parties for a particular period of time. At the end of that period, the principal of the fund is transferred to the fund category specified in the agreement or, in the absence of any mention of this point in the agreement, to the Unrestricted Current Fund. **Life Income Funds** are those funds used to account for resources given to the institution with the stipulation that *all* of the *income earned* by these resources be paid to the donor or other parties for a specified period of time, usually the lifetime of the person receiving the income.

The assets of Annuity and Life Income Funds include cash, securities, and other types of investments. They may be handled separately or they may be pooled with the assets of other funds. If they are pooled, detailed records that specifically identify the annuity, life income, and other (e.g., endowment) portions of the pool and the income attributable to each, and ensure that the various regulatory provisions are being followed, must be maintained.

The liabilities of Annuity and Life Income Funds include claims against any of the assets held by the funds (e.g., a mortgage against rental property), the annuity or life income payments currently due, and amounts due to other fund groups. In addition, Annuity Funds must show, as a liability, the present value of future annuity payments. This amount is determined by actuarial calculations, which are periodically updated.

Increases in the fund balances of Annuity and Life Income Funds are caused by new gifts and income from (and gains on) investments. Gifts made to Annuity Funds must be offset by a liability equal to the actuarial value of the future payments to the donors.

Decreases in the fund balances of Annuity and Life Income Funds are caused by transfers to other fund groups, upon termination of the annuity or life income agreements, and losses on investments. In addition, changes must periodically be made to Annuity Funds when adjustments are made to their liability and fund balance accounts to reflect changes in the life expectancies of their recipients and in their anticipated return on investments.

Upon termination of an annuity or life income agreement, the principal of the fund is transferred to the fund group specified in the agreement or, in the absence of such a stipulation, "to unrestricted current funds revenues clearly identified and disclosed, so that no inference is drawn that a new gift has been received."[19] If few in number and small in amount, Annuity Funds may be recorded in the Endowment and Similar Funds group.

Agency Funds

Agency Funds are used to account for resources that the institution holds as custodian or fiscal agent for students, faculty, members of the staff, and various institution-related organizations. These funds are similar to the Agency Funds used by governmental units.

The assets of Agency Funds include cash, receivables, temporary investments, and amounts due from other fund groups. The liabilities of Agency Funds include accounts payable, amounts due to other fund groups, and the balances of the persons or organizations for which the institution is acting as a fiscal agent, custodian, or depository. Since assets must always equal liabilities, there are no fund balances in this fund group. The only basic financial statement prepared for an Agency Fund is a balance sheet, showing assets and liabilities by major type.

Plant Funds

The Plant Funds group is used to record the various transactions related to the acquisition, replacement, existence, and financing of long-lived assets, including those of auxiliary enterprises. It consists of four self-balancing subgroups:

[19] Ibid., p. 425.

1. **Unexpended Plant Funds**. This subgroup is used to account for the resources that will "finance the acquisition of long-lived plant assets and the associated liabilities."[20]

2. **Funds for Renewals and Replacements**. This subgroup is used to account for the resources that will finance the renewal or replacement (as opposed to the acquisition) of long-lived plant assets.

3. **Funds for Retirement of Indebtedness**. This subgroup is used to account for the resources set aside to pay interest charges on and to retire any long-term debt associated with plant assets. Funds for the Retirement of Indebtedness are similar to the Debt Service Funds used by governmental units.

4. **Investment in Plant**. This subgroup is used to account for the cost (or fair market value at the time of donation) of long-lived plant assets (other than those of Endowment and Similar Funds) and the sources from which the assets are funded, including any associated liabilities.

The assets of Unexpended Plant Funds, Funds for Renewals and Replacements, and Funds for Retirement of Indebtedness are derived from the following sources:

1. Funds from external agencies
2. Student fees and assessments for debt service or other plant purposes, which create an obligation equivalent to an externally imposed restriction and which are not subject to the discretionary right of the governing board to use for other purposes
3. Transfers, both mandatory and nonmandatory, from other fund groups
4. Borrowings from external sources for plant purposes
5. Borrowings by advances from other fund groups
6. Income and net gains from investments in the unrestricted and restricted elements of each of the subgroups[21]

These assets consist of cash, investments, amounts due from other fund groups, accounts and notes receivable, and deposits with others. In addition, the Unexpended Plant Funds and the Funds for Retirement of Indebtedness are often used to record construction in progress.

Liabilities of the Unexpended Plant Funds and the Funds for Renewals and Replacements usually consist of accounts, notes, mortgages, and bonds payable, as well as amounts due to other fund groups. Liabilities of the Funds for Retirement of Indebtedness usually consist of amounts due to fiscal agents, other debt service charges, and amounts due to other fund groups.

The fund balances of the Unexpended Plant Funds, the Funds for Renewals and Replacements, and the Funds for Retirement of Indebtedness represent the unexpended resources of these subgroups. They should be maintained so that unexpended resources originating from board-designated, unrestricted monies are distinguished from unexpended resources originating from monies whose use is restricted by legal provisions or by external parties. This can be

---

[20] Ibid., p. 429.
[21] Ibid., pp. 428-29.

accomplished by maintaining separate project accounts for each type of fund and separate accounts for each debt.

Additions to the fund balances of all three subgroups are the same as the sources of assets listed above, except for borrowings. Deductions from the fund balances of the Unexpended Plant Funds and the Funds for Renewals and Replacements include expenditures for new plant or for renewals and replacements of plant, losses on investments, return of unrestricted monies back to Unrestricted Current Funds, and other appropriate charges, such as certain fund-raising expenses.

Deductions from the fund balances of the Funds for Retirement of Indebtedness include expenditures for interest and repayment of principal, trustees' expenses, and fees and losses on investments. Encumbrances, in any of the Plant Funds, that are outstanding as of the reporting date should be reported by means of a footnote or as allocations of the fund balances.

The primary purpose of the Investment in Plant subgroup is to maintain a listing of those fixed assets used by the institution and of any construction in progress that is not listed in the Unexpended Plant Funds or the Funds for Renewals and Replacements subgroups. The liabilities associated with these assets are also recorded in the Investment in Plant subgroup. The assets of this subgroup usually include land, buildings, fixtures, equipment, and library books, as well as construction in progress. An allowance for depreciation on many of these assets should be shown on the balance sheet of this subgroup. In addition, a provision for depreciation should be shown for this subgroup on the statement of changes in fund balances.

The sources of assets of the Investment in Plant subgroup include the following:

1. Capitalized completion costs of projects transferred from the Unexpended Plant Funds and Funds for Renewals and Replacements subgroups
2. Capitalized costs of construction in progress transferred from the Unexpended Plant Funds and the Funds for Renewals and Replacements subgroups at the reporting date, unless held in those subgroups until completion of the project
3. Donations (at fair market value on date of gift) of plant assets
4. The cost of long-lived assets financed by expenditures of Current and other funds, except for Endowment and Similar Funds[22]

Liabilities of the Investment in Plant subgroup can include amounts owed on accounts, notes, leaseholds, bonds, and mortgages, as well as amounts due to other fund groups, which are associated with the renewal, replacement, or acquisition of fixed (plant) assets.

The fund balance of this subgroup is called **Net Investment in Plant**. It represents the carrying value of assets over liabilities and is increased by means of the acquisition of plant assets, less their associated liabilities, and through the retirement of debt incurred to acquire, renew, or replace those assets. The fund

[22] Ibid., pp. 431-32.

balance is decreased when the disposition of plant assets takes place and when depreciation is recorded.

The actual recording of transactions in the Plant Funds is relatively easy. It differs from the recording of transactions in the Current Funds in that no revenues or expenses are recorded. Only changes in assets, liabilities, and the fund balance are recorded. Even depreciation, an expense in most other organizations, is treated as a direct reduction of Net Investment in Plant.

To illustrate, assume that someone donates $100,000 to the institution to build a new security building and a mortgage of $500,000 is taken out to provide the remainder of the monies necessary to complete the project. The entries in the Unexpended Plant Fund are:

1. Cash   100,000
        Fund balance   100,000
    To record the receipt of cash to be used to
    build a new security building.

2. Cash   500,000
        Mortgage payable   500,000
    To record the receipt of cash from a
    mortgage on the new security building

If the building is one-half complete at the end of the year (and the costs are as budgeted), the entry in the Unexpended Plant Fund is:

    Construction in progress   300,000
        Cash   300,000
    To record the cost of construction completed
    to date on the new security building.

If library books are purchased for $10,000 and are "expensed" upon purchase, the entry in the Unexpended Plant Fund is:

    Fund balance   10,000
        Cash   10,000
    To record the purchase of library books.

If the previously mentioned building is completed and transferred to the Investment in Plant subgroup, the entry in the Unexpended Plant Fund is:

    Mortgage payable   500,000
    Fund balance   100,000
        Construction in progress   300,000
        Cash   300,000
    To record the completion of the security build-
    ing and the transfer of this building (and the
    accompanying mortgage) to the Investment
    in Plant subgroup.

The entry in the Investment in Plant subgroup is:

Building	600,000	
Mortgage payable		500,000
Net investment in plant		100,000

To record the transfer of the completed security building to the Investment in Plant subgroup.

If depreciation amounting to $15,000 is taken on the building, the following entry is made in the Investment in Plant subgroup:

Net investment in plant	15,000	
Accumulated depreciation		15,000

To record depreciation on the security building for the year.

When a piece of equipment is retired or a building is sold or demolished, the following entry is made in the Investment in Plant subgroup:

Net investment in plant	2,000	
Equipment		2,000

To record the sale of a motor vehicle used by campus security.

The entries in the Funds for Retirement of Indebtedness consist largely of those used to record the receipt of monies to service debt and to record the actual payments made for interest and the repayment of principal.

For example, assume that $50,000 is received from the Unrestricted Current Fund for the payment of interest and principal on the mortgage on the security building, which is recorded in the Investment in Plant subgroup. The entries in the Fund for Retirement of Indebtedness to record the receipt of the monies and the payment of interest ($10,000) and principal on the mortgages are:

1.	Cash	50,000	
	Fund balance		50,000

To record the receipt of monies to pay the interest and principal currently due on the mortgage on the security buidling.

2.	Fund balance	50,000	
	Cash		50,000

To record the payment of interest ($10,000) and principal ($40,000) currently due on the mortgage on the security building.

The entry in the Investment in Plant subgroup is:

Mortgage payable	40,000	
Net investment in plant		40,000

To record the payment of a portion of the
mortgage on the security building by the
Fund for the Retirement of Indebtedness.

SELECTED REFERENCES

AMERICAN INSTITUTE OF CERTIFIED PUBLIC ACCOUNTANTS. *Audits of Colleges and Universities.* New York, 1973.

_____. *Statement of Position 74–8.* New York, 1974

NATIONAL ASSOCIATION OF COLLEGE AND UNIVERSITY BUSINESS OFFICERS. *College and University Business Administration,* 4th ed. Washington, D.C., 1982.

NATIONAL CENTER FOR EDUCATIONAL STATISTICS. *Higher Education Finance Manual.* Washington, D.C.: U.S. Government Printing Office, 1975.

SCHEPS, CLARENCE, AND E. E. DAVIDSON. *Accounting for Colleges and Universities,* 3rd ed. Baton Rouge: Louisiana State University Press, 1978.

REVIEW QUESTIONS

Q12–1   Name four ways in which accounting for colleges and universities is different from accounting for state and local governmental units.

Q12–2   List the types of funds used by colleges and universities and describe the purpose of each.

Q12–3   What determines whether a fund is restricted or unrestricted?

Q12–4   Why are the Current Funds the only funds used by colleges and universities to record expenses?

Q12–5   When should contributions to Restricted Current Funds be recognized as revenues?

Q12–6   Why is depreciation on fixed assets not shown by the Current Operating Funds? Why is it shown by the fixed assets of the Endowment Funds?

Q12–7   How should the services performed by religious personnel of church-related schools be valued?

Q12–8   What is the difference between *restricted* and *unrestricted* assets?

Q12–9   How does the budgetary accounting used by colleges and universities differ from that used by state and local governmental units?

Q12–10   What is the most authoritative source of information on the accounting methods and procedures that should be used by colleges and universities?

Q12–11   Describe the controversy surrounding depreciation for colleges and universities. Do you think these institutions should be required to depreciate their fixed assets? Why?

EXERCISES

E12–1   (Unrestricted Current Funds)
During the year, the following transactions were recorded in the Unrestricted Current Fund of Shorthorn University:

1. Revenues from tuition and fees amounted to $1.5 million, all of which had been collected by year-end.
2. Revenues of the auxiliary enterprises amounted to $500,000 cash.
3. Materials and supplied used during the year amounted to $700,000, of which $400,000 was chargeable to educational activities and $300,000 was chargeable to the auxiliary enterprises.
4. Salaries and wages amounted to $1 million. Of this amount, $800,000 was chargeable to educational activities and $200,000 was chargeable to auxiliary activities.
5. A transfer of $100,000 was made to the Fund for the Retirement of Indebtedness to pay part of the principal and interest due on certain outstanding mortgages.

REQUIRED: 1. Prepare journal entries to record the above transactions in the Unrestricted Current Fund.
          2. Prepare the journal entry or entries necessary to close out the revenue, expenditure, and transfer accounts at year-end.

E12–2   (Loan Funds)
In 19X1, the J. Urbington Banks Foundation donated $300,000 to Friendly University to be used exclusively for student loans. During the year, loans amounting to $200,000 were made. The remaining monies in the fund were invested and, at the end of the year, $10,000 in interest (cash) had been received. In addition, $50,000 was repaid by the students, along with $3,000 in interest. At the end of the year, the Student Loan Fund issued a check for $1,000 to the Unrestricted Current Fund to cover certain administrative costs of processing loans.

REQUIRED: Prepare the appropriate journal entries in the Student Loan Fund necessary to record the above transactions.

E12–3   (Plant Funds)
In 19X1, Sunshine University received a donation of $5 million to be used to build a new library. During the year, construction of the library was started; by the end of the year, it was one-third complete. Costs incurred up to this point amounted to $2 million, all paid in cash. In September 19X2, the library was completed. The actual cost of the structure was $4.8 million. The remainder of the donation was transferred to the Unrestricted Current Fund. Depreciation on the library in 19X2 amounted to $30,000.

REQUIRED: Prepare the journal entries in the Plant Funds and in the Unrestricted Current Fund necessary to record the above events.

E12–4   (Multiple choice)

1. Which of the following should be used in accounting for not-for-profit colleges and universities?
   a. Fund accounting and accrual accounting
   b. Fund accounting but *not* accrual accounting
   c. Accrual accounting but *not* fund accounting
   d. Neither accrual accounting nor fund accounting

2. Which of the following receipts is properly recorded as Restricted Current Funds on a university's books?
   a. Tuition
   b. Student laboratory fees
   c. Housing fees
   d. Research grants

3. In the Loan Fund of a college or university, each of the following types of loans would be found except
   a. Student
   b. Staff
   c. Building
   d. Faculty

4. Which of the following is utilized for current expenditures by a not-for-profit university?

	Unrestricted Current Funds	Restricted Current Funds
a.	No	No
b.	No	Yes
c.	Yes	No
d.	Yes	Yes

5. During the years ended June 30, 19X1 and 19X2, Sonata University conducted a cancer research project financed by a $2 million gift from an alumnus. This entire amount was pledged by the donor on July 10, 19X0, although he paid only $500,000 at that date. The gift was restricted to the financing of this particular research project. During the two-year research period, Sonata's related gift receipts and research expenditures were as follows:

	YEAR ENDED JUNE 30	
	19X0	19X1
Gift receipts	$1,200,000	$ 800,000
Cancer research expenditures	900,000	1,100,000

How much gift revenue should Sonata report in the restricted column of its statement of current funds revenues, expenditures, and other changes for the year ended June 30, 19X1?
   a. $0
   b. $800,000

c. $1,100,000
d. $2,000,000

(AICPA adapted)

6. For the summer session of 19X1, Cajun University assessed its students $1,700,000 (net of refunds), covering tuition and fees for educational and general purposes. However, only $1,500,000 was expected to be realized because scholarships totaling $150,000 were granted to students, and tuition remissions of $50,000 were allowed to faculty members' children attending Cajun. What amount should Cajun include in its Unrestricted Current Funds as revenues from student tuition and fees?
   a. $1,500,000
   b. $1,550,000
   c. $1,650,000
   d. $1,700,000

(AICPA adapted)

7. On January 2, 19X1, John Reynolds established a $500,000 trust, the income from which is to be paid to Mansfield University for general operating purposes. The Wyndham National Bank was appointed by Reynolds as trustee of the fund. What journal entry is required on Mansfield's books?

		DR	CR
a.	Memorandum entry only		
b.	Cash	$500,000	
	Endowment Fund balance		$500,000
c.	Nonexpendable Endowment Fund	$500,000	
	Endowment Fund balance		$500,000
d.	Expendable Funds	$500,000	
	Endowment Fund balance		$500,000

(AICPA adapted)

8. Beehive College is sponsored by a religious group. Volunteers from this religious group regularly contribute their services to Beehive and are paid nominal amounts to cover their commuting costs. During 19X1, the total amount paid to these volunteers aggregated $12,000. The gross value of services performed by them, determined by reference to lay-equivalent salaries, amounted to $300,000. What amount should Beehive record as expenditures in 19X1 for these volunteers' services?

   a. $312,000
   b. $300,000
   c. $12,000
   d. $ -0-

(AICPA adapted)

9. Tuition waivers for which there is no intention of collection from students should be classified by a not-for-profit university as

	Revenue	Expenditures
a.	No	No
b.	No	Yes
c.	Yes	Yes
d.	Yes	No

(AICPA adapted)

10. The following expenditures were among those incurred by Alum University during 19X1:

Administrative data processing	$ 50,000
Scholarships and fellowships	100,000
Operationandmaintenanceofphysicalplant	200,000

The amount to be included in the functional classification "Institutional Support" expenditures account is
a. $50,000
b. $150,000
c. $250,000
d. $350,000

(AICPA adapted)

11. The Plant Funds group of a not-for-profit private university includes which of the following subgroups?

	Investment In Plant Funds	Unexpended Plant Funds
a.	No	Yes
b.	No	No
c.	Yes	No
d.	Yes	Yes

(AICPA adapted)

12. The following receipts were among those recorded by Glen Mills College during 19X1:

Unrestricted gifts	$500,000
Restricted Current Funds (expended for current operating purposes)	200,000
Restricted Current Funds (not yet expended)	100,000

The amount that should be included in Current Funds revenues is
a. $800,000
b. $700,000
c. $600,000
d. $500,000

E12–5   (Plant renovations)

The board of trustees of Bayou College approved plans to renovate the library. The following transactions relate to this project:

1. To help finance the project, a mortgage of $1 million was secured.
2. A transfer of $200,000 was made from the Restricted Current Fund to cover the remaining costs of the project.
3. The project was completed, before the end of the year, at a total cost of $1.1 million. Upon completion, the project was transferred to the Investment in Plant Fund, along with the accompanying mortgage.
4. The unspent monies were transferred to the Unrestricted Current Fund.
5. Before the close of the year, $75,000 was donated by a group of alumni to assist in the repayment of the mortgage and in the payment of interest on that debt.
6. The current installment of the mortgage, $50,000, was paid before the close of the year.

REQUIRED: Prepare the journal entries necessary to record the above transactions in the appropriate Plant Funds. In the margin of each entry, state which fund is being used to record that particular transaction.

PROBLEMS

P12–1   (Current Funds)

In 19X1 the legislature of the state of Transylvania granted a charter to Count Dracula Junior College, along with the right to use a sizable piece of land "in perpetuity." During the year, the following transactions took place:

1. Unrestricted revenues received were as follows:

Student tuition and fees	$2,800,000
Unrestricted gifts and grants	500,000
Governmental appropriations	1,000,000
Revenues from auxiliary enterprises	300,000
Other revenues	200,000
	$4,800,000

2. The Association of Anonymous Vampires contributed $100,000 to the college, with the stipulation that these monies be used to equip a laboratory to study blood diseases.
3. Of the student tuition and fees assessed, $2,750,000 was collected. It was estimated that $30,000 would never be collected.
4. Materials costing $1 million were purchased on account and placed in inventory during the year.

5. Expenditures recorded in the Unrestricted Current Fund were:

Educational:		
Materials	200,000	
Salaries	1,500,000	
Other expenses	200,000	1,900,000
Administrative and Student Services:		
Materials	100,000	
Salaries	200,000	
Other	50,000	350,000
Library:		
Books	500,000	
Materials	100,000	
Salaries	70,000	
Other	30,000	700,000
Plant Operations:		
Rental of temporary buildings	200,000	
Wages and salaries	100,000	
Materials	400,000	
Other	100,000	800,000
Auxiliary Enterprises:		
Wages and salaries	50,000	
Operating supplies	30,000	
Other	20,000	100,000
Total unrestricted expenditures		3,850,000

6. During the year, $900,000 was paid to the vendors who supplied materials.

7. A mandatory transfer of $500,000 was made to the Plant Fund to start construction of a classroom building.

8. Grants of $50,000 and $30,000 were awarded to Dr. Igor Mrsnk and Dr. Jan Martink, respectively, to assist with their research into causes of impure blood. Both awards were used up by the end of the year.

9. At the end of the year, a transfer of $47,000 was received from the Endowment Fund. The original donor of these monies requested they be used for faculty travel.

REQUIRED: 1. Prepare journal entries to record the above transactions in the appropriate Current Fund.
2. Prepare a balance sheet, a statement of changes in fund balances, and a statement of current funds revenues, expenditures, and other changes.

P12–2 (Loan, Endowment, and Annuity Funds)
During its first year of operations, Count Dracula Junior College had the following transactions, which should be recorded in its Loan Funds,

Endowment and Similar Funds, and/or its Annuity and Life Income Funds.

1. Dr. Frank N. Stein donated $100,000 to the college to be used for student loans. Of this amount, $50,000 was invested in preferred stock.

2. The descendants of Count Dracula donated $500,000 to the college to establish an Endowment Fund. The earnings of the fund were to be used for faculty travel. The money was invested in government securities, purchased at par value.

3. Securities worth $100,000 were donated to the Endowment Fund by the Wolf Mann family.

4. The Moriarity family donated $200,000 to the college to be used to set up an Annuity Fund. These monies were promptly invested. Any earnings on these monies, up to $10,000, were to be sent to Mr. S. Holmes at the end of each year. Any excess earnings were to be transferred to the Unrestricted Current Fund.

5. During the year, loans amounting to $45,000 were made to needy students. All loans were expected to be repaid.

6. During the year, the Endowment Fund earned $50,000 of interest on its investments. Of this amount, $45,000 was received in cash. The remaining amount will be received shortly after the end of the fiscal year.

7. While flying through the air, one student had an unfortunate accident. His loan, amounting to $2,000, was written off as uncollectible.

8. Some securities were sold by the Endowment Fund at a profit of $2,000. This amount was transferred to a Restricted Current Fund, along with the $45,000 of interest received in number 6.

9. Earnings on investments of the Annuity Fund amounted to $15,000. Of this amount, all of which had been received in cash by year-end, $10,000 was paid to Mr. S. Holmes and $5,000 was transferred to the Unrestricted Current Fund.

10. During the year, student loans amounting to $10,000 were repaid, along with accrued interest of $500. As of the end of the year, interest accrued on loans still outstanding was $2,000. This amount will be collected when the loans are repaid. In addition, on the last day of the fiscal year, the college received a check for $3,000, representing the annual dividend on the preferred stock.

REQUIRED: 1. Prepare journal entries to record the transactions listed above. Indicate which fund or funds are affected by each transaction.

2. Prepare a balance sheet and a statement of changes in fund balances for the Loan Fund, the Endowment and Similar Funds, and the Annuity Fund.

P12–3   (Plant Funds)

During the fiscal year 19X1, the following activities took place on the campus of Count Dracula Junior College; a new institution located somewhere in Transylvania:

1. The citizens of Transylvania donated $200,000 to the college, to be used for a classroom building and a laboratory building.
2. A mortgage of $3 million was taken out on the classroom building.
3. Construction of the classroom building was completed during the year at a cost of $3.5 million. The building and its accompanying mortgage were transferred to the appropriate subgroup.
4. Dr. Frank N. Burger donated $500,000 to the college, to be used to pay the interest on and principal of the mortgage. The money was immediately invested in government securities.
5. At the end of the year, the laboratory building was one-half complete. Costs incurred to date were $100,000.
6. A gift of $100,000 was presented to the Plant Fund by Jack W. Mann. Mr. Mann expressly stated that the monies should be used for the purchase of equipment. His wish was immediately carried out by means of an $80,000 purchase of classroom equipment.
7. Government securities, purchased for $200,000 with part of Dr. Frank N. Burger's donation, were sold for $220,000. In addition, interest of $40,000 was earned and collected on these *and* the unsold securities. The entire amount was paid to the First National Bank of Cluj, the holder of the mortgage. Of this amount, $60,000 was for interest and $200,000 was for the repayment of principal.
8. An uninsured piece of laboratory equipment, costing $1,000 and financed by the Plant Fund, was destroyed.
9. Depreciation on the classroom building amounted to $250,000 in 19X1.

REQUIRED: 1.   Prepare appropriate journal entries to record the above transactions.
2.   Prepare a combined balance sheet and a statement of changes in fund balances for the Plant Funds, as of the end of the fiscal year.

P12–4   (Problem from Uniform Certified Public Accountant Examination on journal entries for Current Funds)

A partial balance sheet of Rapapo State University as of the end of its fiscal year ended July 31, 19X1, is presented below:

Rapapo State University
Current Funds Balance Sheet
July 31, 19X1

ASSETS:	
Unrestricted:	$200,000
Cash	
Accounts receivable—	
tuition and fees, less allowance	
for doubtful accounts of $15,000	360,000
Prepaid expenses	40,000
Total unrestricted	600,000
Restricted:	
Cash	10,000
Investments	210,000
Total restricted	220,000
Total current funds	$820,000
LIABILITIES AND FUND BALANCES:	
Unrestricted:	
Accounts payable	$100,000
Due to other funds	40,000
Deferred revenue—tuition	
and fees	25,000
Fund balance	435,000
Total unrestricted	600,000
Restricted:	
Accounts payable	5,000
Fund balance	215,000
Total restricted	220,000
Total current funds	$820,000

The following information pertains to the year ended July 31, 19X1:

1. Cash collected from students' tuition totaled $3,000,000. Of this amount, $362,000 represented accounts receivable outstanding at July 31, 19X0; $2,500,000 was for current-year tuition; and $138,000 was for tuition applicable to the semester beginning in August 19X1.

2. Deferred revenue at July 31, 19X0, was earned during the year ended July 31, 19X1.

3. Accounts receivable at July 31, 19X0, which were not collected during the year ended July 31, 19X1, were determined to be uncollectible and were written off against the allowance account. At July 31, 19X1, the allowance account was estimated at $10,000.

4. During the year, an unrestricted appropriation of $60,000 was made by the state. This state appropriation was to be paid to Rapapo sometime in August 19X1.

5. During the year, unrestricted cash gifts of $80,000 were received from alumni. Rapapo's board of trustees allocated $30,000 of these gifts to the student loan fund.

6. During the year, investments costing $25,000 were sold for $31,000. Restricted fund investments were purchased at a cost of $40,000. Investment income of $18,000 was earned and collected during the year.

7. Unrestricted general expenses of $2,500,000 were recorded in the voucher system. At July 31, 19X1, the unrestricted accounts payable balance was $75,000.

8. The restricted accounts payable balance at July 31, 19X0, was paid.

9. The $40,000, due to other funds at July 31, 19X0, was paid to the Plant Fund as required.

10. One-quarter of the prepaid expenses at July 31, 19X0, expired during the current year and pertained to general educational expenses. There was no addition to prepaid expenses during the year.

REQUIRED: a. Prepare journal entries in summary form to record the foregoing transactions for the year ended July 31, 19X1. Number each entry to correspond with the number indicated in the description of its respective transaction. Your answer sheet should be organized as follows:

		CURRENT FUNDS			
Entry		UNRESTRICTED		RESTRICTED	
no.	Accounts	Debit	Credit	Debit	Credit

b. Prepare a statement of changes in fund balances for the year ended July 31, 19X1.

(AICPA adapted)

13

ACCOUNTING FOR HOSPITALS

LEARNING OBJECTIVES

After completion of this chapter, you should be able to:

1. Identify the sources of generally accepted accounting principles for hospitals
2. Identify the types of resources accounted for in the General Fund
3. Differentiate between restricted and unrestricted resources
4. Identify the types of funds included in the Donor-Restricted Funds for hospitals
5. Prepare financial statements for a hospital
6. Prepare the journal entries normally used in the General Fund to record the operating activities of hospitals
7. Prepare the journal entries normally used in the Donor-Restricted Funds to record the use of restricted assets
8. Define a "DRG"
9. Explain the concept of the DRG reimbursement system used by Medicare
10. Contrast the DRG reimbursement system used by Medicare with the traditional cost-reimbursed system used by Blue Cross

For many years hospital accounting existed in almost a vacuum. Recently, however, a tremendous amount of attention has been directed toward the operating activities of these institutions and all the other organizations offering health care. This interest has resulted from the growth of **third-party health-care insurers** and rising costs. The third parties involved in financing the cost of health care are the federal and state governments and private insurance companies. The public programs that receive the most attention are Medicare and Medicaid. Medicare is primarily financed by the federal government through the Social Security program; Medicaid is a welfare-type program financed by both the federal and state governments.

The interest of these third-party insurers, together with rising costs, has caused great emphasis to be placed on the accounting and reporting systems of hospitals and related health-care institutions. Health-care accounting is important because health-care insurers base their payments to an institution on allowable costs or some form of fixed rate reimbursement. Thus the measurement and control of costs are critical. (The subject of reimbursement is examined later in this chapter.)

There is no separate set of generally accepted accounting principles that is applicable only to hospitals. Instead, these institutions follow the same general rules and procedures for external reporting as do other organizations—pronouncements of the Financial Accounting Standards Board (FASB). Those hospitals operated by state and local governments, however, are subject to pronouncements of the Governmental Accounting Standards Board (GASB). If a particular type of transaction encountered by a public hospital is not covered by a GASB statement, any relevant FASB statements should be followed. In addition, guidance on accounting matters can be found in the *Hospital Audit Guide*[1] and the *Chart of Accounts*.[2]

The GASB has clearly stated its position regarding the accounting treatment to be followed by hospitals operated by governmental units:

> Hospitals that are operated by governmental units should follow the requirements of the AICPA's *Hospital Audit Guide*, as amended and interpreted. Because the accounting recommended in that guide can best be accommodated in the enterprise funds, such funds should be used in accounting for governmental hospitals.[3]

Both the *Hospital Audit Guide* and the *Chart of Accounts* generally are consistent with respect to recommended accounting procedures. The two major differences between these two publications are that:

1. The AHA feels that property, plant, and equipment should be reported at current replacement cost and the depreciation associated with these assets should be calculated based on the replacement cost. The AICPA, on the other hand, contends that original cost should be used for financial statement purposes and any reference to replacement cost should be limited to supplemental disclosures.

2. The AHA feels that long-term security investments should be reported at their current market values. In general the AICPA contends that the lower of cost or market method is appropriate.[4]

Since the *Hospital Audit Guide* governs the accountability of external auditors and we are concentrating on the external financial reporting practices of hospitals, we will generally follow the AICPA's recommendations.

---

[1]American Institute of Certified Public Accountants, *Hospital Audit Guide*, 6th ed. (New York, 1987) (The AICPA has issued an exposure draft of the seventh edition.)

[2]American Hospital Association, *Chart of Accounts* (Chicago, 1976).

[3]GASB Cod. Sec. H50.101.

[4]Detailed discussion of these topics can be found in the *Hospital Audit Guide* and the *Chart of Accounts*.

Although accounting rules followed by business organizations form the basis for hospital GAAP, in those situations where a particular accounting principle is not applicable to hospital operations, it should be ignored. This is the same situation found in proprietary-type funds in governmental accounting: *all* the elements of business GAAP are applied to governmental units unless they are not appropriate.

SECTION I—AN OVERVIEW OF HOSPITAL ACCOUNTING

The accounting literature generally separates the funds used in hospital accounting into two broad groups: the General Fund and the Donor-Restricted Funds. The **General Fund** is used to account for (1) current, or operating, resources, (2) assets whose use is limited, and (3) plant resources. The operating resources are those assets and liabilities associated with the normal operations of a hospital. Assets whose use is limited are resources (and related liabilities) that arise from a bond agreement or a third-party reimbursement agreement, or set aside by the governing board, and that the hospital is holding for a future use. The restriction on the use of these assets can be internal or external. The **plant resources** are the property, plant, and equipment used by the hospital and any related liabilities. In summary, the General Fund is used to account for *all* assets and liabilities not included in the Donor-Restricted Funds.

The **Donor-Restricted Funds** are used to account for the resources that must be used in compliance with the terms of a gift, grant, and so forth. Notice that a restricted fund is used only when an *external* limitation is placed on the use of the resources and the resources are not related to a bond agreement or third-party reimbursement.

The General Fund

As previously mentioned, the General Fund is used to account for the current or operating resources, assets whose use is limited, and plant resources. The **current,** or **operating, resources** are those resources used in the daily operations of a hospital. Thus we find that the current assets used, together with the current liabilities incurred in the regular operations of the hospital, are reported in this fund. The current assets include items such as cash, receivables, inventories, and prepaid expenses; and the current liabilities include items such as accounts payable, notes payable, and accrued expenses.

Assets whose use is limited include:

(a) assets set aside by the governing board for identified purposes and over which the board retains control and may, at its discretion, subsequently use for other purposes;

(b) proceeds of debt issues and funds of the health-care entity deposited with a trustee and limited to use in accordance with the requirements of an indenture or similar document; and

(c) other assets limited to use for identified purposes through an agreement between the health-care entity and an outside party other than a donor or grantor.[5]

These assets usually consist of liquid resources (usually cash and marketable securities) that are invested until they are used for their designated purpose.

Plant resources include the property and equipment used in the operations of the hospital and any related liabilities. These items are reported net of accumulated depreciation.

Exhibit 13–1 is a balance sheet for Sample Hospital. Study it carefully, and identify those items previously mentioned. Notice the "pancake" presentation of the funds. This format is used as an alternative to the columnar format generally followed in governmental accounting. In addition, note that the difference between the total assets and the total liabilities is labeled "Fund balance."

The operating statement of a hospital is called a **statement of revenues and expenses of General Funds** (see Exhibit 13–2). In general, the full accrual basis of accounting is used. Therefore we are measuring expenses and not expenditures. Thus we find depreciation included in the measurement of income. Review Exhibit 13–2. Notice that *patient service revenue* is the main source of revenue for the operations of the hospital. *Net patient service revenue* is the excess of the *gross* billings for services less provisions for uncollectible accounts and other items. These other items will be examined later in this chapter.

Other operating revenue is revenue generated by the operations of the hospital that are not involved in patient care. These include parking fees, cafeteria revenues, and so forth.

Operating expenses are *all* the expenses incurred in the daily operations of the hospital. These include nursing, general and administrative services, depreciation, and so forth. The excess of operating revenues over the operating expenses is called *income from operations*.

Nonoperating revenue is the revenue generated by the hospital that is *not* related to patient care, patient services, or the sale of hospital-related goods. This includes unrestricted gifts, donated services, and so forth. The final figure on the operating statement is labeled *excess of revenues over expenses* (or expenses over revenues) and is comparable with the net income of an Enterprise Fund for a governmental unit.

Donor-Restricted Funds

Donor-Restricted Funds are used to account for the resources available to the hospital that have limitations placed on their use by outside third parties and the restricted resources that are not related to a bond agreement or a third-party reimbursement agreement. These are generally Endowment Funds, Plant Replacement and Expansion Funds, and Specific Purpose Funds.

---

[5]American Institute of Certified Public Accountants, *Statement of Position 85-1* (New York, 1985) par. 7.

EXHIBIT 13–1

Sample Hospital
Balance Sheets
December 31, 19X7 and 19X6

GENERAL FUNDS

Assets	19X7	19X6	Liabilities and Fund Balances	19X7	19X6
Current assets:			Current liabilities:		
Cash and short-term investments, at cost which approximates market (notes 4, 6, and 7)	$ 1,703,000	$ 3,875,000	Current installments of long-term debt (note 6)	$ 1,470,000	$ 1,750,000
Assets whose use is limited and are required for current liabilities	970,000	1,300,000	Accounts payable	2,217,000	2,085,000
Patient accounts receivable, net of estimated uncollectibles of $2,500,000 in 19X7 and $2,400,000 in 19X6	15,100,000	14,194,000	Accrued expenses	3,396,000	3,225,000
			Retainage and construction accounts payable	955,000	722,000
Estimated third-party payer settlements—Medicare (note 2)	441,000	600,000	Estimated third-party payer settlements—Medicaid (note 2)	2,143,000	1,942,000
Inventory of supplies at lower of cost (first-in, first-out) or market	1,163,000	938,000	Deferred third-party reimbursement	200,000	210,000
Other current assets (note 3)	406,000	438,000	Advances from third-party payers	122,000	632,000
Due from Donor-Restricted Funds, net	—	500,000	Due to Donor-Restricted Funds, net	300,000	—
Total current assets	19,783,000	21,845,000	Total current liabilities	10,803,000	10,616,000
Assets whose use is limited (notes 4, 6, and 7):					
By board for capital improvements	11,000,000	10,000,000	Deferred third-party reimbursement	746,000	984,000
By agreements with third-party payers for funded depreciation	9,234,000	6,151,000			
Under malpractice funding arrangement—held by trustee	3,007,000	2,682,000	Estimated malpractice costs (note 7)	3,807,000	2,682,000
Under indenture agreement—held by trustee	11,708,000	11,008,000			
Total assets whose use is limited	34,949,000	29,841,000	Long-term debt, excluding current installments (note 6)	23,144,000	24,014,000

(continued)

EXHIBIT 13–1 (cont.)

Assets	19X7	19X6	Liabilities and Fund Balances	19X7	19X6
			GENERAL FUNDS		
Less assets whose use is limited and that are required for current liabilities	970,000	1,300,000			
Noncurrent assets whose use is limited	33,979,000	28,541,000			
Property and equipment, net (notes 5 and 6)	51,038,000	50,492,000	Fund balance	67,910,000	63,917,000
Other assets:					
Deferred financing costs	693,000	759,000			
Investment in affiliated company (note 3)	917,000	576,000			
			Commitments and contingent liabilities (notes 2, 5, 7, 11, 12, and 13)		
Total other assets	1,610,000	1,335,000			
	$106,410,000	$102,213,000		$106,410,000	$102,213,000
			DONOR-RESTRICTED FUNDS		
Specific Purpose Funds:			Specific Purpose Funds:		
Cash	$ 48,000	$ 75,000	Accounts payable	$ 205,000	$ 63,000
Investments, at cost which			Deferred grant revenue	50,000	—
approximates market	728,000	455,000	Due to general funds	—	255,000
Grants receivable	100,000	67,000	Fund balance	621,000	279,000
	$ 876,000	$ 597,000		$ 876,000	$ 597,000
Plant Replacement and Expansion Funds:			Plant Replacement and Expansion Funds:		
Cash	$ 24,000	$ 321,000	Due to general funds	$ —	$ 345,000
Investments, at cost which			Fund balance	558,000	521,000
approximates market	252,000	165,000			
Pledges receivable, net of estimated uncollectibles of $60,000 in 19X7 and $120,000 in 19X6	132,000	380,000			
Due from General Funds	150,000	—			
	$ 558,000	$ 866,000		$ 558,000	$ 866,000

(continued)

EXHIBIT 13–1 (cont.)

DONOR-RESTRICTED FUNDS

Assets	19X7	19X6	Liabilities and Fund Balances	19X7	19X6
Endowment Funds:			**Endowment Funds:**		
Cash	$1,253,000	$1,303,000	Fund balance	$6,659,000	$6,723,000
Investments, net of $175,000 valuation allowance in 19X7 , market value $5,198,000 in 19X7, and $5,013,000 in 19X6 (note 8)	5,256,000	5,320,000			
Due from General Funds	150,000	100,000			
	$6,659,000	$6,723,000		$6,659,000	$6,723,000
Student Loan Funds:			**Student Loan Funds:**		
Cash	$ 330,000	$ 303,000	Accounts payable	–	$ 9,000
			Advance from U.S. Government	42,000	–
Loans receivable, net of estimated uncollectibles of $90,000 in 19X7 and 19X6	513,000	468,000	Fund balance	801,000	762,000
	$ 843,000	$ 771,000		$ 843,000	$ 771,0000

Notes to financial statements not included.

Source: Adapted from Exposure Draft: Proposed Audit and Accounting Guide, Audits of Providers of Health-Care Services (New York: AICPA, March 15, 1988), pp. 87–88.

EXHIBIT 13-2

Sample Hospital
Statement of Revenues and Expenses of General Funds
Year Ended December 31, 19X7 and 19X6

	19X7	19X6
Net patient service revenue (note 2)	$91,646,000	$87,839,000
Other operating revenue	5,680,000	4,994,000
Total operating revenues	97,326,000	92,833,000
Operating expenses (notes 6, 7, 11, and 12):		
Wages, salaries, and benefits	65,891,000	60,091,000
Supplies and other	15,112,000	13,573,000
Purchased services	8,383,000	8,218,000
Medical malpractice costs	1,125,000	200,000
Depreciation and amortization	4,782,000	4,280,000
Interest expense	1,422,000	1,439,000
Total operating expenses	96,715,000	87,801,000
Income from operations	611,000	5,032,000
Nonoperating revenue (expense):		
Unrestricted gifts and bequests (note 10)	1,122,000	1,136,000
Loss on investment in affiliated company (note 3)	(53,000)	—
Income on investments:		
Whose use is limited by board for capital improvements	1,120,000	1,050,000
Whose use is limited under indenture agreement	100,000	90,000
Whose use is limited by agreements with third-party payors for funded depreciation	850,000	675,000
Nonoperating revenue, net	3,139,000	2,951,000
Excess of revenues over expenses	$ 3,750,000	$ 7,983,000

Notes to financial statements not included.

Source: Adapted from *Exposure Draft: Proposed Audit and Accounting Guide, Audits of Providers of Health-Care Services* (New York: American Institute of Certified Public Accountants, March 15, 1988), p. 89.

Endowment Funds are used when resources are donated to the hospital and the terms of the agreement require that the principal be maintained intact. The income from these funds can be either restricted or unrestricted. Thus an Endowment Fund is like a Nonexpendable Trust Fund. The financial reporting of the fund's income depends on whether it is restricted or unrestricted. If the income is restricted, it is usually reported in a Specific Purpose Fund, Plant Fund, or as other operating revenue in the General Fund; if it is unrestricted, it should be reported in the General Fund as nonoperating revenue. In either case it is *not* reported as revenue in the Endowment Fund.

An Endowment Fund may be "permanent" or "term." These captions refer to the period of time during which the hospital must keep the principal intact. The principal of a **permanent endowment** must remain intact forever, whereas **term endowments** will "expire" some time in the future, after which the management of the hospital can use the resources as it desires or as prescribed in the endowment contract.

Plant Replacement and Expansion Funds are used to accumulate resources contributed by outsiders that can only be used to replace existing plant assets or to expand the existing plant. When the expenditures are made to acquire the assets, the necessary resources are transferred to the General Fund.

Specific Purpose Funds consist of resources that are donor restricted other than those classified as endowment or plant. These resources are generally used for specific operating purposes. For example, assume that an individual donates funds to a hospital for cancer research. As the research expenses are incurred, they are recorded in the General Fund. Periodically an amount equal to the research expenses is transferred from the Specific Purpose Fund to the General Fund in order to "cover" the expenses. This transfer is generally recorded as "other operating revenue" in the General Fund and a reduction of the fund balance of the Specific Purpose Fund.

Refer again to Exhibit 13–1—the balance sheet of Sample Hospital. Notice that the assets of the restricted funds consist of cash, investments, and receivables. Due to the nature of the limitations on the use of the assets, they are usually invested until the hospital has incurred expenses or purchased assets that comply with the donor restrictions. The equity side of the balance sheet usually consists of amounts due to other funds and some form of fund balance. Exhibit 13–1 also includes an additional Donor-Restricted Fund—a Student Loan Fund. Since this is a Donor-Restricted Fund, these resources were provided by outside third-parties for the purpose of making loans to medical students.

Operating statements are **not** prepared for the Donor-Restricted Funds. Instead a statement of changes in fund balances, such as that in Exhibit 13–3, is presented. Notice that a summary of the changes in the balance of the General Fund also is included. The most important feature of this statement, however, is that the changes in the restricted funds are **never** reported as income or loss but rather as changes in fund balance. An operating statement is only prepared for the daily operations of the hospital accounted for in the General Fund. Examine the particular types of changes included in the fund balance for the restricted funds and relate them to the above discussion.

To provide the information necessary to prepare the statement of changes in fund balances, the source of each change is needed. Therefore we will identify these items as *Fund balance*, followed by an identification of the event that caused fund balance to change. For example, earnings from investments would be credited to Fund balance—investment income. Remember that these items are *not* considered to be revenues.

When discussing financial reporting for governmental units, we indicated that whenever the full accrual basis of accounting is used and a balance sheet and income statement are presented, a statement of cash flows also should be provided (see discussion regarding the GASB exposure draft in Chapters 3 and 9). The same rules apply to hospital reporting. Exhibit 13–4 is an adaptation of the illustration used in the health-care exposure draft. The data in the exposure draft are adapted to the format proposed by the GASB.

EXHIBIT 13-3

Sample Hospital
Statements of Charges in Fund Balances
Years Ended December 31, 19X7 and 19X6

| | 19X7 | | | | | 19X6 | | | | |
| | | DONOR-RESTRICTED FUNDS | | | | | DONOR-RESTRICTED FUNDS | | | |
	General Funds	Specific Purpose Funds	Plant Replacement and Expansion Funds	Endowment Funds	Student Loan Funds	General Funds	Specific Purpose Funds	Plant Replacement and Expansion Funds	Endowment Funds	Student Loan Funds
Balances at beginning of year	$63,917,000	$279,000	$521,000	$6,723,000	$762,000	$56,679,000	$221,000	$501,000	$5,973,000	$712,000
Additions:										
Excess of revenues over expenses	3,750,000	—	—	—	—	7,983,000	—	—	—	—
Gifts, grants, and bequests (notes 9 and 10)	—	842,000	220,000	—	27,000	—	518,000	290,000	—	40,000
Investment income	—	50,000	20,000	750,000	12,000	—	40,000	15,000	650,000	10,000
Gain on sale of investments	—	—	100,000	20,000	—	—	—	20,000	100,000	—
Transfer to finance property and equipment additions	243,000	—	(243,000)	—	—	255,000	—	(255,000)	—	—
	3,993,000	892,000	97,000	770,000	39,000	8,238,000	558,000	70,000	750,000	50,000
Deductions:										
Provision for uncollectible pledges	—	—	(60,000)	—	—	—	—	(50,000)	—	—
Transfer to Sample Health Systems (note 10)	—	—	—	—	—	(1,000,000)	—	—	—	—
Realized loss on sale of investments	—	—	—	(659,000)	—	—	—	—	—	—
Unrealized loss on marketable equity securities (note 8)	—	—	—	(175,000)	—	—	—	—	—	—
Transfer to other operating revenue	—	(550,000)	—	—	—	—	(500,000)	—	—	—
	—	(550,000)	(60,000)	(834,000)	—	(1,000,000)	(500,000)	(50,000)	—	—
Balances at end of year	$67,910,000	$621,000	$558,000	$6,659,000	$801,000	$63,917,000	$279,000	$521,000	$6,723,000	$762,000

Notes to financial statement not included.

Source: Adapted from Exposure Draft: Proposed Audit and Accounting Guide. Audits of Providers of Health-Care Services (New York: American Institute of Certified Public Accountants, March 15, 1988), p. 90.

497

EXHIBIT 13-4

Sample Hospital
Cash Flow Statement
Year Ended December 31, 19X7

	19X7
Cash flows from operating activities:	
Net operating income	$ 611,000
Items not requiring cash currently:	
Depreciation and amortization	4,782,000
Deferred third-party reimbursement	(238,000)
Amortization of deferred financing costs	66,000
Increase in estimated malpractice costs	1,125,000
Increase in patient accounts receivable	(906,000)
Decrease in estimated third-party payer settlements—Medicare	159,000
Increase in inventory	(225,000)
Decrease in other current assets	32,000
Increase in accounts payable	132,000
Increase in accrued expenses	171,000
Increase in estimated third-party payer settlements—Medicaid	201,000
Decrease in deferred third-party reimbursement	(10,000)
Decrease in advances from third-party payers	(510,000)
Net cash provided by operating activities	5,390,000
Cash flows from noncapital financing activities:	
Decrease in due from donor-restricted funds	500,000
Increase in due to donor-restricted funds	300,000
Unrestricted gifts and bequests	1,122,000
Net cash provided by noncapital financing activities	1,922,000
Cash flows from capital and related financing activities:	
Acquisition of property and equipment	(5,328,000)
Less: Capital lease obligations incurred	600,000
Increase in retainage and construction accounts payable	183,000
Property and equipment financed by donor-restricted assets	243,000
Increase in assets whose use is limited	(5,108,000)
Repayment of long-term debt	(1,750,000)
Net cash used for capital and related financing activities	(11,160,000)
Cash flows from investing activities:	
Income from investments	2,070,000
Increase in investment in affiliated company	(394,000)
Net cash provided from investment activities	1,676,000
Net decrease in cash and cash equivalents	(2,172,000)
Cash and cash equivalents at beginning of year	3,875,000
Cash and cash equivalents at end of year	$ 1,703,000

Source: Adapted from *Exposure Draft: Proposed Audit and Accounting Guide, Audits of Providers of Health-Care Services* (New York: American Institute of Certified Public Accountants, March 15, 1988), pp. 91–92.

Now that you have an overall conceptual view of the funds and the financial statements involved in hospital accounting, you should be able to understand the operating transactions generally incurred by these funds.

SECTION II—ACCOUNTING PROCEDURES FOR THE GENERAL FUND

The General Fund is used to account for (1) current, or operating, resources, (2) assets whose use is limited, and (3) plant resources. The major source of operating revenue is from nursing services and other professional services. These items are recorded at the *gross* (established) rate. Assume that the regular charges for nursing services are $735,000 and the charges for other professional services are $300,000. Based upon this information, the following entry is made:[6]

Patient accounts receivable	1,035,000	
Nursing services revenue		735,000
Other professional services revenue		300,000
To record the patient service revenue.		

Although we have used one account for each type of revenue, remember that these are *control* accounts and they are used in the same manner as control accounts in governmental accounting. **Subsidiary records** are used to accumulate the revenues for the unit to which the patient was admitted—e.g., surgery, pediatrics, obstetrics, and so on. Other professional service revenues are subdivided by the department rendering the service—e.g., physical therapy, radiology, EKG, and so on. While other methods of classification can be used, this type of subsidiary data enables the hospital management to evaluate the operations of each department.

In the health-care industry, it is common for third parties to pay for medical costs. These third parties usually place limits on the amount that they will reimburse the hospital. Whether the reimbursement is based on allowable costs or some form of a fixed rate, the amount "allowed" by the third-party payer is often less than the established rates. The difference between these two amounts is referred to as **a contractual adjustment**. Usually the hospital will not collect these amounts. In such instances the uncollectible amounts are written off. If the hospital can collect the difference between the amount billed and the amount reimbursed by third-party payers from the patients, these amounts are not included in the contractual adjustments. Instead they are billed to the patients. (The subject of reimbursement is examined later in this chapter.)

Other types of adjustments to gross patient revenues are made for bad debts, charity work, and "discounts" granted to the clergy, volunteers, and employees. In these cases the adjustments represent the amount of the established billing rates that the hospital will not collect. The only difference lies in the reason for the uncollectibility.

---

[6]Assume that the hospital used in this illustration has been in operation for several years.

The deduction for bad debts is an estimate of the uncollectible accounts. This estimate is usually made by the allowance method. Since the allowance method for accounting for bad debts has already been discussed in relation to governmental accounting, it will not be reexamined here.

If the hospital encounters contractual adjustments of $90,000 and charity services of $50,000, and its management estimates uncollectible accounts to be $65,000, the following entry is made:

Provision for contractual adjustments	90,000	
Provision for charity services	50,000	
Provision for uncollectible accounts	65,000	
Allowance for contractual adjustments		5,000
Allowance for uncollectible accounts		65,000
Patient accounts receivable		135,000

To record deductions from patient revenues.

Since we are using entries that summarize a hospital's activities over a full year, it is important to remember that some of the revenue deductions are realized during the year, but others will not be realized until some time in the future. For example, some contractual adjustments have been determined during the year and can be applied directly against the patient's account, whereas in other cases the amount must be estimated. In the above journal entry, it was assumed that $85,000 of contractual adjustments were realized during the year and that an amount of only $5,000 had to be estimated at the end of the year.

In case of charity services, however, a hospital should classify a patient as a "charity patient" as soon as possible. Therefore the entire amount of the provision for charity services ($50,000) is deducted directly from Patient accounts receivable. Like the realized contractual adjustments, these amounts are known and the specific receivables to which they apply are also known. The net result of these two situations is a credit to Patient accounts receivable for $135,000 ($85,000 for contractual adjustments plus $50,000 for charity services).

In addition, you will recall from previous discussions that the uncollectible account allowance is used because we do not specifically know which patients will turn out to be "bad debts." As a result, the entire amount of the estimated bad debts must be debited to the *Provision for uncollectible accounts* and credited to the *Allowance for uncollectible accounts*. Thus each element in the entry to record the deductions from revenue must be carefully analyzed.

During the year, collections of $1 million of receivables are recorded as follows:

Cash	1,000,000	
Patient accounts receivable		1,000,000

To record collection of receivables.

The expenses related to the general operation of a hospital consist of nursing and other professional services, general services, fiscal services, and administrative services. The entry used to record some of these is (amounts assumed):

Nursing services expense	400,000	
Other professional services expense	250,000	
General services expense	200,000	
Fiscal services expense	155,000	
Administrative services expense	145,000	
Cash		1,000,000
Accounts payable, salaries payable, etc.		150,000
To record some of the operating expenses.		

For simplicity, we have combined the recording and payment of expenses in the above entry and we have combined several liability items. Since we are dealing with summary journal entries that cover an entire year, this will have no effect on the results of our illustrations.

During the year, the acquisition and use of inventory items are recorded as follows (amounts assumed):

Inventories	125,000	
Accounts payable		125,000
To record the purchase of inventory.		
Nursing services expense	75,000	
Other professional services expense	40,000	
General services expense	5,000	
Inventories		120,000
To record the use of inventory.		

Since full accrual accounting is used for hospitals, the items of property, plant, and equipment are recorded as assets when acquired and are depreciated over their useful lives. The entry to record this expense is as follows (amounts assumed):

Depreciation expense	200,000	
Accumulated depreciation—plant and		
equipment		200,000
To record depreciation for the year.		

Revenues received from parking fees, the cafeteria, and so forth, are recorded as follows (amounts assumed):

Cash	245,000	
Other receivables	5,000	
Other operating revenues		250,000
To record other operating revenues.		

Individuals such as nurses and doctors will often donate their services to a hospital. This situation is prevalent in those hospitals operated by a religious group. These services are recorded as an expense at their fair value and an

offsetting credit is made to a nonoperating revenue account. If $34,000 of such services is received during the year, the following entry is made:

Nursing services expense	25,000	
Other professional services expense	9,000	
Nonoperating revenue		34,000
To record the value of donated professional services.		

The receipt of $50,000 of unrestricted cash gifts is recorded as follows:

Cash	50,000	
Nonoperating revenue		50,000
To record the receipt of unrestricted gifts.		

During the year, the hospital repays $15,000 of short-term loans and pays $3,000 in interest. In addition, $1,000 of interest is accrued at the end of the year. The entry to record these events is:

Notes payable	15,000	
Interest expense	4,000	
Cash		18,000
Interest payable		1,000
To record the payment made on the principal of notes outstanding and the interest expense for the year.		

As previously mentioned, the segregation of funds by the managing board does *not* create a restricted fund. Instead such funds are treated as unrestricted because the board has the authority to change any previous actions. In our example we will assume that the managing board of the hospital has a fund that is used to provide resources for modernizing the plant and equipment. During the year, the board transfers an additional $5,000 to the fund and the investments earn $3,000, of which $2,500 is received in cash. The entries to record these events are:

Cash—board-designated for plant and equipment	5,000	
Cash		5,000
To record board designation of resources for plant and equipment replacement.		
Cash—board-designated for plant and equipment	2,500	
Interest receivable—board-designated investments	500	
Nonoperating revenue		3,000
To record income from board-designated investments.		

During the year, the hospital issued $5 million of twenty-year bonds to provide funds for the acquisition of new X-ray equipment. These resources were deposited directly with the First National Bank as prescribed in the bond indenture. (Thus they are classified as assets whose use is limited.) The following entry should be made when the bonds are issued:

Cash—acquisition of equipment	5,000,000	
Bonds payable		5,000,000

To record the issuance of bonds and the deposit of the proceeds.

Later in the year, the hospital used some of the bond proceeds to acquire new equipment for the operating rooms. The following entry is necessary to record the acquisition:

Equipment	1,060,000	
Cash—acquisition of equipment		1,060,000

To record the purchase of operating room equipment.

During the year, the hospital incurred several interfund transactions. We will attempt to conserve space and provide an adequate explanation of these events by deferring their discussion until a later section of this chapter. Since these and other entries will be recorded in the General Fund, closing entries will also be discussed in a later section of this chapter.

SECTION III—ACCOUNTING PROCEDURES FOR DONOR-RESTRICTED FUNDS

Hospital accounting uses the classification Donor-Restricted Funds to identify the funds that have resources that are limited in use by external, third-party donors or grantors. The restricted funds generally used by hospitals are (1) Endowment Funds, (2) Plant Replacement and Expansion Funds, and (3) Specific Purpose Funds. The activities recorded in these funds are the subject of this section.

Endowment Funds

Endowment Funds are used when a donor gives a hospital a principal sum that must be maintained intact. The income from the investment of the assets can be either restricted or unrestricted in use. To illustrate, assume that an individual, John Pie, gives a hospital marketable securities with a fair market value of $300,000. The receipt of the gift is recorded as follows:

Marketable securities	300,000	
Fund balance—Pie Endowment		300,000

To record the receipt of Endowment Fund securities.

If the use of the income from the endowment is restricted—e.g., to finance the cost of cancer research—it is recorded as an increase in fund balance in Specific Purpose Fund. If this income totals $30,000 during the year and $25,000 of that amount is received in cash, the following entries are made:

Entry in the books of the Endow- ment Fund	Cash	25,000	
	Interest receivable	5,000	
	Due to Specific Purpose Fund		30,000
	To record investment income due to a Specific Purpose Fund.		

Entry in the books of the Specific Purpose Fund	Due from Endowment Fund	30,000	
	Fund balance—investment income		30,000
	To record investment income from the Pie Endowment Fund.		

Remember that revenues and expenses are *not* reported in the restricted funds. Instead, these items are classified as increases or decreases in fund balance. Therefore the above credit to Fund balance—investment income is a credit to the Fund balance account. The investment income designation is used in order to identify the source of the change in fund balance (see Exhibit 13–3).

The use of the resources by the Specific Purpose Fund is similar to the accounting for the Walters and Joneson grant illustrated later in this chapter.

If the income is not restricted in its use, it is recorded as a nonoperating revenue in the General Fund as follows:

Entry in the books of the Endow- ment Fund	Cash	25,000	
	Interest receivable	5,000	
	Due to General Fund		30,000
	To record investment income due to the General Fund.		

Entry in the books of the General Fund	Due from Endowment Fund	30,000	
	Nonoperating revenue		30,000
	To record unrestricted endowment revenue.		

Note that under both of the assumptions the original recording of the assets earned was in the Endowment Fund and a "due to" account was used. The purpose of this sequence is to provide information for controlling the use of income from Endowment Funds.

Plant Replacement and Expansion Funds

Plant Replacement and Expansion Funds are used to accumulate resources contributed by third-party donors that can only be used to replace existing plant assets or to expand the existing plant. Since the plant items are part of the General Fund, the acquisition of these assets results in a transfer from the Plant Replacement and Expansion Fund to the General Fund. Assume that Mrs. John T. Kitty donates $100,000 cash to a hospital and that this money must be used to replace existing assets. The receipt of this donation is recorded in the Plant Replacement and Expansion Fund as follows:

Cash	100,000	
Fund balance—Kitty		100,000
To record gift from Mrs. Kitty.		

The acquisition of equipment using the Kitty gift is recorded as follows (amount assumed):

Entry in the books of the Plant Replacement and Expansion Fund

Transfer to General Fund	80,000	
Cash		80,000
To record acquisition of equipment from the Kitty Fund.		

Entry in the books of the General Fund

Equipment	80,000	
Transfer from Plant Replacement and Expansion Fund		80,000
To record acquisition of equipment from restricted funds.		

If the resources of the fund are invested in marketable securities, the recording of investment income is determined by the restrictions, if any, placed on that income. The same restrictions that apply to the gift or grant usually apply to any income earned by investing the resources. Therefore the investment income is recorded in the Plant Replacement and Expansion Fund as follows (amounts assumed):

Cash	1,500	
Interest receivable	500	
Fund balance—investment income		2,000
To record investment income.		

If there are no restrictions on the use of the investment income, it is recorded in the General Fund as nonoperating revenue (see discussion of Endowment Funds).

Specific Purpose Funds

Specific Purpose Funds consist of resources that usually are donor restricted for specific operating purposes. To illustrate, assume that a hospital receives a $500,000 grant from the Walters and Joneson Drug Company that is intended to provide funds for research into methods of providing care and counseling for individuals who have become addicted to drugs. The entry to record the receipt of the grant is:

Cash	500,000	
Fund balance—Walters and Joneson grant		500,000
To record receipt of research grant.		

If the managing board immediately invests $480,000 of the grant in marketable securities, the following entry is made:

Marketable securities	480,000	
Cash		480,000
To record the investment of grant proceeds.		

The expenses associated with the research program are recorded in the General Fund, and an appropriate amount of cash is transferred from the Specific Purpose Fund to the General Fund to "cover" the expenses. If the hospital pays $15,000 for the research program's expenses, the following entries are made:

Entries in the books of the General Fund

Research expenses	15,000	
Cash		15,000
To record research expenses.		
Due from Walters and Joneson Fund	15,000	
Other operating revenue		15,000
To record amount due from Walters and Joneson Fund.		
Cash	15,000	
Due from Walters and Joneson Fund		15,000
To record receipt of cash from Walters and Joneson Fund.		

Entries in the books of the Specific Purpose Fund

Transfer to General Fund	15,000	
Due to General Fund		15,000
To record transfer to General Fund.		
Due to General Fund	15,000	
Cash		15,000
To record payment of cash to General Fund.		

Note that in the above entries the expense is recorded in the books of the General Fund and is offset by the other operating revenue. The effect of these transactions on the Specific Purpose Fund is reported in the statement of changes in fund balance.

If we assume that the income from the investment activity of the Specific Purpose Fund has the same restriction as the original grant, the following entry is made to record it (amounts assumed):

Cash	45,000	
Interest receivable	3,000	
Fund balance—investment income		48,000

To record investment income for the year.

If the investment income is not restricted, it is recorded in the same way as unrestricted endowment income.

SECTION IV—THE CLOSING PROCESS

The closing process for hospitals is similar to that used by other institutions. All the temporary accounts that were used during the period must be closed and their balances transferred to the Fund balance account for each fund.

In several instances we presented alternative solutions to situations involving the use of income in the restricted funds. To illustrate the closing entries, we will assume that

1. The earnings of the Pie Endowment Fund are not restricted—i.e., they are recorded as nonoperating revenues in the General Fund.
2. The $48,000 of investment earnings in the Walters and Joneson Fund and the $2,000 of investment earnings in the Plant Replacement and Expansion Fund are restricted—i.e., they remain in each fund.

Given these assumptions, the following closing entries are appropriate:

Entries in	Nursing services revenue	735,000	
the books	Other professional services revenue	300,000	
of the	Other operating revenues	265,000	
General	Nonoperating revenue	120,000	
Fund	Fund balance	308,000	
	Provision for contractual adjustments		90,000
	Provision for charity services		50,000
	Provision for uncollectible accounts		65,000
	Nursing services expense		500,000
	Other professional services expense		299,000
	General services expense		205,000
	Fiscal services expense		155,000
	Administrative services expense		145,000
	Depreciation expense		200,000
	Interest expense		4,000
	Research expenses		15,000

To close the revenue and expense accounts into Fund balance.

Transfer from Plant Replacement and Expansion Fund	80,000	
Fund balance		80,000
To close the transfer accounts into Fund balance.		

Entry in the books of the Plant Replacement and Expansion Fund

Fund balance—investment income	2,000	
Fund balance	78,000	
Transfer to General Fund		80,000
To close the temporary accounts into Fund balance.		

Entry in the books of the Specific Purpose Fund

Fund balance—investment income	48,000	
Transfer to General Fund		15,000
Fund balance—Walters and Joneson grant		33,000
To close the temporary accounts into Fund balance.		

Note that the only fund that has revenue and expense accounts is the General Fund. All the other hospital funds reflect the changes resulting from equity-type transactions by using Fund balance accounts. A review of Exhibits 13–2 and 13–3 will indicate how these items are reported in the financial statements.

SECTION V—REIMBURSEMENT PROGRAMS

One of the unique features of the health-care industry is the role played by third-party insurers. Health-care insurance programs have been established by the federal and state governments and by private insurance companies. The most popular programs are Medicare, Medicaid, and Blue Cross/Blue Shield. **Medicare** is a federal program that generally provides medical insurance for individuals who (1) qualify for Social Security and have attained age 65, (2) are permanently disabled, or (3) elect coverage of physicians' services at age 65 and agree to pay insurance premiums for this coverage. **Medicaid** is a program that is funded by both the federal and the various state governments and provides medical insurance for individuals who cannot afford to pay for health-care services. **Blue Cross/Blue Shield** is one of the largest insurance companies that furnish prepaid health insurance.

Prospective Medicare Plan

The Tax Equity and Fiscal Responsibility Act (TEFRA) required the Department of Health and Human Services to develop a **prospective reimbursement plan** for Medicare cases to replace the previously used cost-reimbursement plan.

The problems with the cost-reimbursement plan were directly related to the *cost-based* nature of the reimbursement procedures. These problems can be summarized as follows:

1. There was little incentive for a hospital to be run efficiently, since reimbursement was generally based on costs incurred.
2. The same services may be reimbursed at different amounts for different hospitals.
3. The reimbursement process has created an excessively burdensome reporting process.[7]

The prospective reimbursement plan stipulates that payments to hospitals are based on the type of treatments provided the patient. For this purpose, types of illnesses and treatments have been categorized into **Diagnosis-Related Groups (DRGs)**. The actual amount reimbursed depends on the payment amount determined in advance by the government. While there may be some differences in reimbursement amount in different areas of the country, each hospital in a given geographic area receives the same amount for each DRG, depending on its classification as urban or rural. Thus an uncomplicated appendectomy results in the same reimbursement to all hospitals in a given urban or rural area. This was *not* the case under the previously used cost-reimbursed system.

TEFRA also provided for separate consideration for several types of hospitals, such as pediatric and psychiatric hospitals. This initial exemption results from the fact that DRGs have not yet been developed for these institutions. Therefore the cost-based reimbursement system will still be used in certain instances.

Efficient hospitals benefit from the prospective reimbursement plan because they are allowed to retain any reimbursement in excess of their cost. Inefficient hospitals, however, have to absorb any costs in excess of the reimbursement.

Efficiently operated hospitals benefit from this plan because they receive a reimbursement amount based upon the *average* cost of the DRG in the census division (region) in which they are located. Therefore this plan has several operating strategy implications for hospital management. Among these are:

1. Careful review of the staffing mix of the hospital
2. More efficient budgetary control through the use of a cost accounting system
3. Increased control over the use of supplies
4. Careful review of underutilized capital equipment
5. Establishment and monitoring of patient discharge planning systems, with the intent of minimizing the patient's stay in the hospital

---

[7]"Executive Summary of 'The Report to Congress on Hospital Prospective Payment for Medicare,'" *Healthcare Financial Management*, 37, No. 3 (March 1983), pp. 67–68.

6. More efficient policies relative to standard admission procedures, tests, and so on

7. Improved internal review of existing procedures [8]

Other Reimbursement Plans

Reimbursement under Medicaid usually follows the rules established for Medicare because of the federal matching funds provision of the Medicaid program and because Medicaid reimbursement is limited to the amount that would have been paid under Medicare for like services. Thus we can probably expect many states to adopt the new Medicare prospective reimbursement plan for Medicaid cases.

Private health-care insurance programs are not directly related to either Medicare or Medicaid. Therefore changes in either of these systems will not necessarily produce changes in the reimbursement methods followed by companies such as Blue Cross. Blue Cross reimburses hospitals based on the terms of the contract in force in the state in which the hospital is located. These reimbursement plans generally vary from a cost-plus basis to reimbursement based on the charges made by the hospital for the services performed. A hospital that participates in the Blue Cross program usually agrees not to bill the patients for amounts in excess of the types of charges *covered* by Blue Cross. Examples of *noncovered* charges, which may be billed to the patients, include the difference between the charges for a private room and those for a semiprivate room and television rentals. Other examples of third-party payers include systems such as preferred-provider organizations and health-maintenance organizations. While these have accounting implications, a discussion of their effects is beyond the scope of this text.

SELECTED REFERENCES

AMERICAN HOSPITAL ASSOCIATION. *Chart of Accounts for Hospitals.* Chicago, 1976.

AMERICAN INSTITUTE OF CERTIFIED PUBLIC ACCOUNTANTS. *Hospital Audit Guide.* New York, 1987.

_____ . *Proposal Audit and Accounting Guide, Audits of Providers of Health-Care Services.* New York, 1988.

AVERILL, RICHARD F., AND MICHAEL JAY KALISON, J.D. "A Positive First Step: Prospective Payment by DRG," *Healthcare Financial Management*, 37, No. 2 (February 1983): 12, 14, 18, 20, and 22.

BAINBRIDGE, MARK A., AND DOUGLAS G. GEIB II. "Capitalized Interest: Statement 62 Changes Accounting for Tax-Exempt Borrowings," *Healthcare Financial Management*, 37, No. 4 (April 1983): 34, 36, 38, 40, 42–44, 49, 52, and 53.

CLEVERLEY, WILLIAM O., ed. *Handbook of Health-Care Accounting and Finance.* 2 vols. Rockville, Md.: Aspen Systems Corporation, 1982.

DELOITTE HASKINS & SELLS. *Health-Care Review*, New York. Monthly publication.

[8]American Hospital Association, "Medicare Prospective Pricing: Legislative Summary and Management Implications," *Medicare Payment: Cost-Per-Case Management, Special Report 3*, April 1983, p. 6.

GROSS, MALVERN J., JR., AND WILLIAM WARSHAUER, JR. *Financial and Accounting Guide for Non-profit Organizations*, 3rd ed. New York: Ronald Press, 1979.

KOVERNER, R. R. "Business/Nonbusiness: Why Should We Care?" *Healthcare Financial Management*, 37, No. 2 (February 1983): 26, 28, 32, and 33.

REVIEW QUESTIONS

Section I

Q13–1 Which major publications deal specifically with the application of generally accepted accounting principles to hospital accounting?

Q13–2 Identify two areas of hospital accounting that are treated differently in the publications of the AICPA and the AHA.

Q13–3 Which fund or funds used in hospital accounting provide operating data in the form of revenues and expenses?

Q13–4 What is a "pancake" form of balance sheet?

Section II

Q13–5 What is the difference between the *operating resources* and *board-designated resources*?

Q13–6 Hospital charges are recorded at the gross or established rate. How does the accounting system allow for a situation where an insurance company pays only a portion of the established rate?

Q13–7 Distinguish between *other operating revenue* and *nonoperating revenue* and give three examples of each.

Q13–8 How are *assets whose use is limited* reported?

Section III

Q13–9 What is the difference between *restricted* and *unrestricted funds*?

Q13–10 What is the difference between *Endowment Funds* and *Specific Purpose Funds*?

Q13–11 How is the income of restricted funds reported in hospital financial statements?

Q13–12 How are assets purchased by a Plant Replacement and Expansion Fund reported in hospital financial statements?

Section IV

Q13–13 Is it necessary to have a separate closing entry (or entries) for each fund?

Q13–14 What types of accounts are closed each period?

Q13–15 Are closing entries for hospitals different from those used for other fund accounting systems?

Section V

Q13–16 Distinguish between *Medicare, Medicaid,* and *Blue Cross.*

Q13–17 How will the Medicare prospective reimbursement plan solve the major problems of the Medicare system for hospital reimbursement?

Q13–18 What basis does Blue Cross use for reimbursement of hospitals?

EXERCISES

Section I

E13–1 (Fill-in-the-blanks—general terminology)
1. The AICPA publishes the _____ as a source of information on hospital accounting.
2. There (is or is not) _____ a separate set of generally accepted accounting principles for hospitals.
3. Operating resources and the board-designated resources are subdivisions of the _____.
4. The Endowment Funds, the Plant Replacement and Expansion Funds, and the Specific Purpose Funds are included in the

    _____.

5. The daily operations of a hospital are accounted for in the _____ Fund.
6. Parking fees, cafeteria revenues, and pharmacy revenues are reported on the _____ as _____.
7. Hospitals use the _____ basis of accounting.

E13–2 (Multiple choice—use of funds)
The Brite-Hope Hospital uses the following types of funds:
A. General Fund
B. Endowment Funds
C. Plant Replacement and Expansion Funds
D. Specific Purpose Funds
Using the letters given above, identify which fund or funds would be used to account for the following events:
1. The operations of the cafeteria.
2. A gift received from an individual for medical research (at this time consider only the receipt of the gift).
3. Income is earned on investments of money donated by the Manybucks Corporation (the original gift and all income earned must be used to provide up-to-date equipment for the hospital).
4. The hospital received $1 million in securities from an individual. The principal of the gift must be maintained intact. (Consider only the receipt of the gift).

5. The managing board of the hospital decided to start a fund for cancer research. It transferred $30,000 into the fund. Which fund would be used to record the receipt of the money?
6. The payment of salaries to the nursing staff.
7. Depreciation is recorded on the equipment in use.
8. The purchase of additional hospital equipment.

E13–3   (Identification of financial statements for hospital funds)
The following codes are available for some of the various types of financial statements issued by hospitals:

BS—Balance Sheet
SRE—Statement of Revenues and Expenses
SFB—Statement of Changes in Fund Balance

Using these codes, identify which statement or statements would be prepared for each of the following funds:
1. General Fund _____
2. Endowment Funds _____
3. Plant Replacement and Expansion Funds _____
4. Specific Purpose Funds _____

Section II

E13–4   (Accounting for uncollectible patient accounts)
The Metro County Hospital could not collect the amount billed to a patient. The patient declared bankruptcy and had no assets with which to pay his debts. Assuming the patient owed the hospital $3,000, prepare the entry or entries necessary to record the uncollectible account if the hospital uses the "allowance method." After preparing the necessary entry or entries, indicate what effect the write-off will have on the balance sheet.

E13–5   (Recognition of depreciation for governmental units, colleges and universities, and hospitals)
Compare and contrast the method or methods of accounting recognition of depreciation for governmental units, colleges and universities, and hospitals.

E13–6   (General Fund transactions)
The managing board of the H Memorial Hospital established an Emergency Fund in order to provide for emergency repairs to hospital assets. During 19X1, $12,000 was used to repair the electrical system of the emergency rooms. Prepare the journal entry or entries necessary to record the use of the $12,000 of Emergency Fund assets. If more than one fund is involved, identify the funds used.

Section III

E13–7 (Description of the receipt and use of a gift)

Α wealthy individual gave $500,000 to the City Hospital for the construction of a new surgery wing. *Explain* how the gift would be recorded and how the use of the funds would affect the financial statements of the hospital. Do not use journal entries.

E13–8 (Journal entries for the receipt and use of a gift)

Using the same information given in Exercise 13–7, prepare the journal entries that would be used to record the data. In addition, identify the fund or funds in which the entries would be recorded.

E13–9 (Use of funds)

The following transactions relate to the Tableaux Hospital. Indicate which fund or funds would be used to record the data.
1.   Collected $2,345 from a patient.
2.   Received a grant from Toosuups Drug Company for a study of the effects of morphine on female patients.
3.   Received unrestricted gifts of $50,000.
4.   Purchased equipment by using resources previously accumulated in the Plant Replacement and Expansion Fund.
5.   Research expenses totaling $12,000 were incurred in studying the effects of morphine on female patients.
6.   The board decided to begin a fund for nursing education. Initially $10,000 of general hospital resources was transferred to the fund.
7.   A local firm acquired a new computer. Its old computer was donated to the hospital.
8.   Marketable securities were donated by a business in order to help the hospital acquire new equipment.
9.   The securities in number 8 produced income of $5,000. Assume that the investment income is restricted in the same way as the original gift.

Section IV

E13–10 (Explanation of the closing process)

Explain the dual purpose of closing entries and relate the procedure to the financial statement reporting of fund balance.

E13–11 (Closing entries from data created by students)

Make up a trial balance for each type of fund that hospitals generally use. Use your imagination and knowledge regarding the type of transactions incurred by each type of fund. After you have completed the trial balances, prepare the necessary closing entries for each fund. As a practical suggestion, limit the number of temporary accounts in each trial balance to four or five.

Section V

E13–12 (Discussion of the prospective Medicare reimbursement plan and federal expenditures)

Explain how the prospective reimbursement system for Medicare should help reduce federal expenditures for health care.

E13–13 (Explanation of the Medicare prospective reimbursement plan)

Assume that you have been hired as a consultant for the Faith Memorial Hospital. Your first task is to explain the Medicare prospective reimbursement plan to the controller. Outline the points you would make in your presentation.

PROBLEMS

Section I

P13–1 (Use of funds in hospital accounting)

Four different types of funds are generally used in hospital accounting. Identify at least three types of situations that would require the use of each fund.

P13–2 (Analysis of the operations of a hospital)

You have been hired as a consultant to the managing board of Sample Hospital. Review the information presented in the statement of revenues and expenses contained in Exhibit 13–2 and comment on the operations of the hospital.

P13–3 (Preparation of a statement of revenues and expenses)

The following selected information was taken from the books and records of Glendora Hospital (a voluntary hospital) as of and for the year ended June 30, 19X1:

1. Patient service revenue totaled $16,000,000, with allowances and uncollectible accounts amounting to $3,400,000. Other operating revenue aggregated $346,000 and included $160,000 from Specific Purpose Funds. Revenue of $6,000,000 recognized under cost-reimbursement agreements is subject to audit and retroactive adjustment by third-party payers. Estimated retroactive adjustments under these agreements have been included in allowances.

2. Unrestricted gifts and bequests of $410,000 were received.

3. Unrestricted income from endowment funds totaled $160,000. Income from assets whose use is limited by the board totaled $82,000.

4. Operating expenses totaled $13,370,000 and included $500,000 for depreciation computed on the straight-line basis. However, accelerated depreciation is used to determine reimbursable costs under certain third-party reimbursement agreements. Net cost reimbursement revenue amounting to $220,000, resulting from the difference in depreciation methods, was deferred to future years.

5. Also included in operating expenses are pension costs of $100,000, in connection with a noncontributory pension plan covering substantially all of Glendora's employees. Accrued pension costs are funded currently. Prior service cost is being amortized over a period of 20 years. The actuarially computed value of vested and nonvested benefits at year-end amounted to $3,000,000 and $350,000 respectively. The assumed rate of return used in determining the actuarial present value of accumulated plan benefits was 8 percent. The plan's net assets available for benefits at year-end was $3,050,000.
6. Gifts and bequests are recorded at fair market values when received.
7. Patient service revenue is accounted for at established rates on the accrual basis.

REQUIRED: 1. Prepare a formal statement of revenues and expenses for Glendora Hospital for the year ended June 30, 19X1.
2. Draft the appropriated disclosures in separate notes accompanying the statement of revenues and expenses, referencing each note to its respective item in the statement.

(AICPA adapted)

Section II

P13–4 (Journal entries and financial statements—General Fund)
Following is a trial balance for the Hope Hospital:

Hope Hospital
General Fund
Trial Balance
December 31, 19X1

Cash	$ 6,000	
Patient accounts receivable	20,000	
Allowance for uncollectible receivables		$ 3,000
Inventories	5,000	
Land	300,000	
Building	1,000,000	
Accumulated depreciation—building		34,000
Equipment	1,500,000	
Accumulated depreciation—equipment		55,000
Accounts payable		8,000
Bonds payable		2,000,000
Fund balance		731,000
	$2,831,000	$2,831,000

During 19X2, the following transactions took place:
1. Patients were billed for $1.2 million. Of this amount, $1 million was nursing services revenue and the remainder was other professional services revenue.

2. Inventories of $56,000 were purchased on credit.
3. Operating expenses were incurred as follows:

Nursing services expense	$375,000
Other professional services expense	265,000
General services expense	200,000
Fiscal services expense	100,000
Administrative services expense	90,000

   Assume that all the expenses were incurred on credit.
4. The board decided to establish a fund whose income would be used for the continuing education of young doctors. An initial amount of $2,000 was used to establish the fund.
5. The full amount transferred in number 4 was invested in marketable securities.
6. Collections of patient receivables totaled $1,195,000. In addition, $3,000 of patient receivables was written off as uncollectible.
7. Payments on accounts payable totaled $1,032,000.
8. The use of inventories was recorded as follows:

Nursing services	$30,000
Other professional services	20,000

9. The provision for estimated uncollectible accounts for the year was $2,000.
10. Income from board-designated investments was $300. The entire amount was collected in cash. Assume that the cash remained in the General Fund.
11. Depreciation was recorded as follows: building, $10,000; equipment, $12,000.
12. Interest of $100,000 was paid in cash.

REQUIRED:
1. Prepare all the journal entries necessary to record the above transactions and identify the fund or funds involved.
2. Prepare a balance sheet for the General Fund at December 31, 19X2.
3. Prepare a statement of revenues and expenses for the General Fund for 19X2.
4. Prepare a statement of changes in fund balance for the General Fund for 19X2.

P13–5 (Journal entries and financial statements—General Fund)
The Medical Foundation of America was established in 19X1. This nonprofit hospital began operations in January of that year. The following transactions occurred during the year:
1. In order to supply cash to begin operations, long-term revenue bonds were issued. The proceeds were $1,750,000. The bonds were issued for their face value.
2. The physical assets of the hospital were purchased for $1,498,000 cash. The appraised value of the land, building, and equipment was $300,000, $700,000, and $498,000 respectively.

3. Patients were billed a total of $2.5 million. The entire amount was for nursing services.
4. Inventory was purchased for $7,000 cash.
5. Patients were billed separately for professional services other than nursing care. The amount of the billing was $75,000.
6. The managing board decided to set up a fund for the replacement of the used equipment it had purchased in number 2. An initial contribution of $10,000 was made to the fund.
7. The entire amount transferred to the fund in number 6 was invested in marketable securities.
8. Inventories were used as follows:

Nursing care	$5,000
Other professional services	1,000

9. Patient receivables of $2,490,000 were collected.
10. Additional equipment was acquired, using general resources, $1,400.
11. Securities purchased by the board-designated resources were sold for $8,300. The original cost was $7,800. The difference represents investment revenue.
12. Operating expenses of the hospital were $1.7 million. Included in this amount were outstanding debts at the end of the year, $34,000; the remainder were paid during the year. The expenses should be charged as follows:

Nursing care	$1,000,000
Other professional services	200,000
General services	150,000
Fiscal services	150,000
Administrative services	200,000

13. Interest on the bonds for the year was $175,000. Of this amount, $87,500 was paid in cash.
14. The board-designated resources were used to pay $8,300 for new equipment.
15. Depreciation was recorded as follows: building $70,000; equipment, $51,000.

REQUIRED: 1. Prepare all the journal entries necessary to record the above transactions and identify the fund or funds involved.
2. Prepare a balance sheet for the General Fund at December 31, 19X1.
3. Prepare a statement of revenues and expenses for the General Fund for 19X1.
4. Prepare a statement of changes in fund balance for the General Fund for 19X1.

Section III

P13–6   (Journal entries and financial statements for restricted funds)
The Gremillion Memorial Hospital had the following transactions during 19X1.

1. A gift of $75,000 was received from T. J. Wealthy. The terms of the gift specified that the principal amount must be maintained intact permanently. The income could be spent for any purpose that would help the hospital. The total amount of the gift was immediately invested in marketable securities.

2. Keith-Kyle Company gave the hospital a grant of $355,000 for cancer research. The proceeds from the grant were invested in marketable securities.

3. Paigekat Company donated $500,000 to the hospital for the construction of a building addition that would be devoted to dealing with mental patients.

4. Architectural fees for the building addition for the mental unit were paid in cash, $30,000. The remainder of the Paigekat gift was invested in marketable securities.

5. During the year, the hospital began a fund-raising drive for the mental unit. Pledges totaling $200,000 and cash donations totaling $30,000 were received. (*Hint*: Record the pledges as receivables.)

6. Investment income of $30,000 was received in cash on the Keith-Kyle Company Fund investments. In addition, $20,000 of investments matured. The hospital paid face value upon purchasing these securities. Assume that the investment income is restricted in the same way as the original grant.

7. Cancer research costs of $45,000 were incurred and paid by the General Fund. The Keith-Kyle Company Fund reimbursed the General Fund for these expenditures.

8. Income of $8,000 was earned by the T. J. Wealthy Fund investments. Of this amount, $7,000 was received in cash.

9. Collections of pledges during the year totaled $25,000.

10. The General Fund paid $20,000 for part of the cost of the construction of the mental unit.

REQUIRED: 1. Prepare all the journal entries necessary to record the above transactions in the restricted funds of the Gremillion Memorial Hospital and identify each fund used. If an entry would not be recorded in a restricted fund, write "No entry" next to the transaction number.

2. Prepare a balance sheet for each restricted fund as of December 31, 19X1.

3. Prepare a statement of changes in fund balances for the restricted funds for 19X1.

P13–7   (Journal entries and selected financial statements for hospitals)
Following is a trial balance for the United Memorial Hospital:

United Memorial Hospital
General Fund
Trial Balance
July 1, 19X1

Cash	$ 12,000	
Patient accounts receivable	30,000	
Allowance for uncollectible patient accounts		$ 4,000
Land	600,000	
Buildings	2,345,000	
Accumulated depreciation—building		650,000
Equipment	1,700,000	
Accumulated depreciation—equipment		400,000
Accounts payable		15,000
Notes payable		100,000
Bonds payable		2,000,000
Fund balance		1,518,000
	$4,687,000	$4,687,000

During the 19X1–X2 fiscal year, the following selected transactions took
place:

1. Patients were billed a total of $2 million. Of this amount, $1.3
million was for nursing services and the remainder was for other
professional services.
2. Several patient accounts were classified as uncollectible and written off. These accounts totaled $2,800.
3. The Telerand Corporation gave the hospital a grant for research
into the use of a verbally operated microscope. The grant was for
$500,000. The entire amount was immediately invested in market-
able securities.
4. Operating expenses were incurred as follows:

Nursing services	$600,000
Other professional services	300,000
General services	200,000
Administrative services	175,000
Fiscal services	100,000

Assume that all expenses were incurred on credit.
5. Patient receivables of $2,010,000 were collected.
6. Accounts payable of $1,370,000 were paid.
7. Several individuals in the community contributed a total of $1 mil-
lion for the expansion of the burn unit of the hospital. This money
was invested in marketable securities until the plans for the unit
were completed. The fund was titled the Burn Unit Fund.

8. Interest expense on the outstanding debt was $210,000. Of this amount, $105,000 was paid in cash.
9. The managing board decided to establish a fund for the development of its professional staff. The amount transferred from general hospital resources was $25,000. The new fund was called the Professional Improvement Fund.
10. The construction and planning costs incurred on the new burn unit totaled $200,000. This amount was paid from the Burn Unit Fund Cash account. To make these payments, investments that originally cost $190,000 were sold for $205,000. In addition, $10,000 cash income was received on the investments. Assume that the income from the investments has the same restrictions as the original donation.
11. During the year, the hospital received $50,000 cash income from the investment of the Telerand grant money. Assume that the investment income is restricted in the same way as the original grant.
12. Research costs associated with the Telerand grant were $45,000. These costs were paid with cash generated by the investment of the original grant.
13. John Q. Citizen gave the hospital $15,000, which must be maintained intact. The income from the gift can be used in any way the managing board feels is helpful to the hospital. The money was immediately invested in marketable securities.
14. Investments in the John Q. Citizen Fund earned $2,000 during the year. Of this amount $1,900 was received in cash.

REQUIRED: 1. Prepare all the journal entries necessary to record the above transactions and identify the fund or funds involved.
2. Prepare a balance sheet for each of the restricted funds at June 30, 19X2.
3. Prepare a statement of changes in fund balance for each of the restricted funds for the fiscal year 19X1–X2.

Section IV

P13–8 (Closing entries—General Fund)
Using the data given in Problem 13–4, prepare the closing entry or entries necessary for the General Fund.

P13–9 (Closing entries—General Fund)
Using the data given in Problem 13–5, prepare the closing entry or entries necessary for the General Fund.

P13–10 (Closing entries—restricted funds)
Using the data given in Problem 13–6, prepare the closing entry or entries necessary for the restricted funds.

P13–11 (Closing entries—all hospital funds)
Using the data given in Problem 13–7, prepare the closing entry or entries necessary for all the funds used by the hospital.

P13–12   (Work sheet and adjustment/corrections)

Esperanza Hospital's postclosing trial balance and blank work papers at December 31, 19X2, appear on pages 524 and 525. Esperanza, which is a nonprofit hospital, did *not* maintain its books in conformity with the principles of hospital fund accounting. Effective January 1, 19X3, Esperanza's board of trustees voted to adjust the December 31, 19X2, general ledger balances, and to establish separate funds for the General (unrestricted) Funds, the Endowment Fund, and the Plant Replacement and Expansion Fund.

Additional account information:

1.   "Investment in corporate bonds" pertains to the amount required to be accumulated under an agreement with a private foundation to provide cash donations equal to accumulated depreciation until the funds are needed for asset replacement. The $500,000 balance at December 31, 19X2, is less than the full amount required because of errors in computation of building depreciation for past years. Included in the allowance for depreciation is a correctly computed amount of $90,000, applicable to equipment.

2.   "Endowment Fund Balance" has been credited with the following:

Donor's bequest of cash	$300,000
Gains on sales of securities	100,000
Interest and dividends earned in 19X0, 19X1, and 19X2	120,000
Total	$520,000

The terms of the bequest specify that the principal, plus all gains on sales of investments, are to remain fully invested in U.S. government or corporate securities. At December 31, 19X2, $400,000 was invested in U.S. Treasury bills. The bequest further specifies that interest and dividends earned on investments are to be used for payment of current operating expenses.

3.   "Land" comprises the following:

Donation of land several years ago, at appraised value	$ 40,000
Appreciation in fair value of land as determined by independent appraiser 4 years ago	60,000
Total	$100,000

4.   "Building" comprises the following:

Hospital building completed in January 40 years ago, when operations were started (estimated useful life 50 years), at cost	$720,000
Installation of elevator in January 20 years ago (estimated useful life 20 years), at cost	80,000
Total	$800,000

REQUIRED: Complete the work sheet on the following pages, and enter the adjustments necessary to restate the general ledger account balances properly. Distribute the adjusted balances to establish the separate fund accounts. Formal journal entries are not required, but supporting computations should be referenced to the work sheet adjustments.

(AICPA adapted)

Section V

P13–13   (Analysis of the effects of the Medicare prospective reimbursement plan)

Contact a hospital administrator in your area and discuss the changes that the prospective Medicare reimbursement plan caused in his or her hospital operations. Did the overall results benefit the hospital?

P13-14   (Analysis of a DRG schedule)

Contact the Medicare office in your region and obtain a DRG reimbursement schedule. Discuss this schedule with a local hospital administrator. Identify those areas that are not realistic for his or her hospital.

Esperanza Hospital
Work Sheet to Adjust General Ledger Balances
and to Establish Separate Funds
January 1, 19X3

ACCOUNT	TRIAL BALANCE DECEMBER 1, 19X2		ADJUSTMENTS		GENERAL (UNRESTRICTED) FUNDS		ENDOWMENT FUND		PLANT REPLACEMENT AND EXPANSION FUND	
	Debit	Credit	Debit	Credit	Debit	Credit	Debit	Credit	Debit	Credit
Cash	60,000									
Investment in U.S. Treasury bills	400,000									
Investment in corporate bonds	500,000									
Interest receivable	10,000									
Accounts receivable	50,000									
Inventory	30,000									
Land	100,000									
Building	800,000									
Equipment	170,000									
Allowance for depreciation		410,000								
Accounts payable		20,000								
Notes payable		70,000								
Endowment Fund balance		520,000								
Other fund balances		1,100,000								

Esperanza Hospital
Work Sheet to Adjust General Ledger Balances
and to Establish Separate Funds
January 1, 19X3

ACCOUNT	TRIAL BALANCE DECEMBER 1, 19X2		ADJUSTMENTS		GENERAL (UNRESTRICTED) FUNDS		ENDOWMENT FUND		PLANT REPLACEMENT AND EXPANSION FUND	
	Debit	Credit	Debit	Credit	Debit	Credit	Debit	Credit	Debit	Credit
Totals	2,120,000	2,120,000								

14

Accounting for Voluntary Health and Welfare and Other Not-for-Profit Organizations

---

LEARNING OBJECTIVES

After you complete this chapter, you should be able to:

1. Distinguish between a voluntary health and welfare organization and an "other" not-for-profit organization
2. Explain what a 78–10 organization is
3. List at least ten types of 78–10 organizations
4. Identify the sources of authority for the accounting procedures used by voluntary health and welfare and 78–10 organizations
5. List the funds used by voluntary health and welfare and 78–10 organizations
6. Name the financial statements used by voluntary health and welfare and 78–10 organizations
7. Compare and contrast the financial statements used by voluntary health and welfare and 78–10 organizations
8. Discuss the treatment of depreciation by voluntary health and welfare and 78–10 organizations
9. Explain how grants and payments to affiliated organizations are handled by 78–10 organizations
10. Prepare the journal entries necessary to record the activities of a voluntary health and welfare organization

Voluntary health and welfare organizations (VHWOs) are nongovernmental organizations that receive voluntary contributions from the general public that are used for health, welfare, or community services. These organizations, which are also known as human service organizations, are operated on a not-for-profit basis and are exempt from many taxes.[1] Examples of VHWOs include the American Cancer Society, the Boy Scouts of America, the National Urban League, and the Young Women's Christian Association of the U.S.A. Accounting principles specifically related to these organizations are prescribed in *Audits of Voluntary Health and Welfare Organizations*, which is published by the American Institute of Certified Public Accountants.[2]

Other not-for-profit organizations (ONPOs) are those not-for-profit organizations which, until 1978, were not covered by existing audit guides. They include the following:

Cemetery organizations
Civic organizations
Fraternal organizations
Labor unions
Libraries
Museums
Other cultural institutions
Performing arts organizations
Political parties
Private and community foundations
Private elementary and secondary schools
Professional associations
Public broadcasting stations
Religious organizations
Research and scientific organizations
Social and country clubs
Trade associations
Zoological and botanical societies[3]

In 1978, the Accounting Standards Division of the American Institute of Certified Public Accountants (AICPA) issued *Statement of Position 78–10*, titled "Accounting Principles and Reporting Practices for Certain Nonprofit Organizations" (SOP 78–10). The purpose of this statement was to ". . . . recommend financial accounting principles and reporting practices for nonprofit organiza-

[1] AICPA, *Audits of Voluntary Health and Welfare Organizations* (New York: AICPA, 1974), p. v.

[2] Other sources that are based on the audit guide and provide more detailed coverage are *Accounting & Financial Reporting: A Guide for United Ways and Not-for-Profit Human Service Organizations* published by the United Way of America; and *Standards of Accounting and Financial Reporting for Voluntary Health and Welfare Organizations* published by the National Health Council.

[3] AICPA, *Audits of Certain Nonprofit Organizations* (New York: AICPA, 1981), pp. 1–2. The *Audit Guide* indicates that this listing is not intended to be all-inclusive.

tions not covered by existing guides. . . ."[4] In 1981, the AICPA issued an audit and accounting guide, *Audits of Certain Nonprofit Organizations*. Together these two publications form the basis of those generally accepted accounting principles that are unique to not-for-profit organizations and for which there was previously no specific audit guide. These organizations are collectively referred to as **78–10 organizations** as well as ONPOs.

Since the types of organizations included in SOP 78–10 are rather diverse, the Accounting Standards Division has recommended general rules for external financial reporting that are applicable to most 78–10 organizations. In addition, the division has included special rules for those organizations or situations that are sufficiently different from the general model to necessitate special consideration.

It should be noted that the Financial Accounting Standards Board has the final authority for determining the accounting procedures used by the organizations discussed in this chapter. The audit guides for voluntary health and welfare organizations, "other" nonprofit organizations, and SOP 78–10 have been formally adopted by the FASB.

FUNDS USED

Fund accounting is followed by voluntary health and welfare organizations and 78–10 organizations[5] because they normally have resources whose use is restricted as well as resources whose use is unrestricted. The funds generally used are the following:

1. The **Current Unrestricted Fund** (or its equivalent). Included in this fund are the unrestricted resources that are available for the general operations of the organization. The distinction between *restricted* and *unrestricted* is the same as that used for colleges and universities and hospitals; i.e., restricted resources are those whose use is limited by outside third parties. Therefore, resources restricted in use by the governing board of an organization are included in the organization's Current Unrestricted Fund. Since land, buildings, and equipment are usually accounted for in a separate fund, the Current Unrestricted Fund is generally used to account for current assets that can be used in the operations of the organization at the discretion of its management.

2. **Current Restricted Funds** (or their equivalents). Included in these funds are those resources that are available for use in the operations of an organization, as specified by a donor, grantor, and so forth. The typical sources of these resources are restricted gifts and grants, restricted endowment income, and so on.

---

[4] AICPA, *Statements of Position of the Accounting Standards Division as of January 1, 1980* (New York: AICPA), par 10,250.002.

[5] To simplify future references to voluntary health and welfare organizations and 78-10 organizations, they will collectively be referred to as "other not-for-profit organizations" (ONPOs).

3. **Land, Building, and Equipment Fund** (or its equivalent). This fund is used to account for the land, buildings, and equipment currently in use in the operations of the organization, together with any associated depreciation and long-term debt. In addition, it is used to account for the resources whose use is restricted to the acquisition of land, buildings, or equipment.

While the funds identified above are generally used by all ONPOs, some of these organizations need "special" funds to allow for the unique characteristics of their operating environment. Examples of such funds are Endowment Funds, Custodian (Agency) Funds, Loan Funds, Annuity Funds, and Strike Funds. Since these funds either have been discussed in previous chapters or have self-explanatory titles, we will not discuss them here.

FINANCIAL STATEMENTS

Due to the intangible nature of many of the services offered by ONPOs, it is practically impossible to place a monetary value on them. Thus it is impossible to prepare financial statements that can measure the results of operations in the same sense as those used for business enterprises. The basic functions of the financial reporting process for ONPOs are therefore limited to (1) providing information on how the resources of the organization were obtained and used during the period, (2) presenting the resources available for future use at the end of the period, and (3) reporting on the organization's ability to continue to supply services in the future.

The financial statements for ONPOs are prepared for four general types of users of financial information: (1) the management group of the organization (e.g., directors and other individuals who have the responsibility for carrying out the day-to-day operations of the organization); (2) the government officials who have the oversight responsibility for such organizations; (3) the individuals who contribute resources to the organization; and (4) the constituents of the organization.[6]

To provide financial information to this diverse group, three basic financial statements are generally prepared by ONPOs: (1) a balance sheet, (2) an operating (activity) statement, and (3) a statement of changes in financial position. (The statement of changes in financial position is not required for voluntary health and welfare organizations; however, a statement of functional expenses is required.)[7]

---

[6] An in-depth discussion of these objectives and users is included in *Statement of Financial Accounting Concepts No. 4*, "Objectives of Financial Reporting by Nonbusiness Organizations" (Stamford, Conn.: Financial Accounting Standards Board, 1980).

[7] AICPA, *Audits of Voluntary Health and Welfare Organizations* (1974), p. 33.

Balance Sheet

The following balance sheets are illustrated in this chapter:[8]

Exhibit	Organization
14–1	Voluntary Health and Welfare Organization
14–4	Country Club
14–6	Museum
14–8	Religious Organization
14–11	Union

Carefully review the balance sheets illustrated, studying the particular funds used by each type of organization and the particular assets, liabilities, and fund balance (equity) normally associated with those organizations. (All exhibits can be found at the end of the chapter, beginning on p. 544.)

Note that there are two key differences between voluntary health and welfare organizations and 78–10 organizations. The first difference is the use of the "pancake" presentation of multiple funds for a voluntary health and welfare organization and the use of the separate columns for each fund by 78–10 organizations (see Exhibits 14–1, 14–6, 14–8, and 14–11). This particular difference is one of appearance, rather than fact, because the choice of format is optional.

The second difference is that the *Audit Guide* for voluntary health and welfare organizations does not recommend the classified format, whereas the *Audit Guide* for the 78–10 organizations does recommend such a format.

The assets usually found on a balance sheet for ONPOs include cash, investments, receivables (usually pledges), inventories, and various accruals. The liabilities are generally those debts associated with the operations of the organization (accounts payable, other payables, deferred revenues, and so on) in the unrestricted funds; and notes, mortgages, and deposits in the restricted funds.

Contrast the country club's balance sheet (Exhibit 14–4) with the others presented. The country club's balance sheet closely resembles that of a profit-oriented business. Such a resemblance is to be expected because country clubs are essentially businesses that are owned by their members. On the other hand, the balance sheets used by the other organizations illustrated more closely resemble the typical fund accounting format used throughout this text.

Note that the treatment of the land, buildings, and equipment-type assets by country clubs and unions is the same. That is, both types of organizations usually include these items in their Operating Fund, as opposed to a separate Plant or Building Fund that is used by voluntary health and welfare organizations, museums, and religious organizations. The specific reporting requirements for these types of assets is discussed later in this chapter.

[8] The format of this chapter is different from that of previous chapters of this text. Since we are discussing many different types of organizations that are classified as ONPOs, the financial statements are grouped at the end of this chapter. This enables us to put all the financial statements of a particular type of organization together to see the entire picture of the financial reporting process for each type of organization discussed.

The general accounting principles that have been discussed in previous chapters are also applicable to ONPOs. Thus the full accrual basis of accounting is used, and the assets of these organizations are reported, using the applicable form of original cost—e.g., estimated collectible amount for receivables; and cost, less accumulated depreciation, for assets such as buildings.

A particular organization may occasionally encounter situations that differ from those illustrated. In such cases the general principles discussed in this chapter should be applied. An example of such a situation would be a country club that has received resources whose use is restricted by outside parties. In such a case, a restricted fund could be used. The reader of the financial statements should be aware of any restrictions that are placed on the use of the organization's resources.

Land, buildings, and equipment

Notice that there is some variation in the treatment of these types of assets among ONPOs. Voluntary health and welfare organizations generally use a separate fund to record these assets, whereas the 78–10 organizations have the option of using a separate fund or reporting these assets in an unrestricted or a restricted fund, as appropriate.

In Exhibit 14–1 notice that the fund balance is separated into "expended" and "unexpended—restricted" portions. The expended portion ($484,000 in 19X2) is the excess of the land, buildings, and equipment ($516,000) over the mortgage payable ($32,000). The remainder ($212,000 in 19X2) represents the amount of the resources whose use is restricted to the acquisition of land, buildings, and equipment (Cash, Investments, and Pledges receivable).

In extreme situations it may be impossible for the recipient organization to value assets such as rare books and art. Under these circumstances, such assets should not appear on the financial statements. Instead, a note to the financial statements describing the situation should be included in the annual report (see Note 11 of the Sample Museum statement—Exhibit 14–7).

Since it is impossible to describe all the balance-sheet-related reporting issues of each ONPO, we have limited our discussion to several of the more important of these issues. This should clarify the manner in which the assets, liabilities, and fund balance of these organizations are treated. This same approach is followed for the operating statements discussed below.

Operating Statement (Activity Statement)

The **operating** or **activity statement** has a rather broad function in not-for-profit accounting. As already mentioned in previous chapters of this text, it usually includes not only revenues and expenses but also capital transactions, transfers between funds, and other changes in an organization's fund balance. Exhibits 14–2, 14–5, 14–7, 14–9, and 14–12 contain operating statements for the ONPOs discussed in this chapter.

Due to the many different types of organizations covered by the ONPO classification, there are several permissible variations in reporting format. However, the format used must disclose any third-party donor or grantor restrictions placed on the resources received in order to distinguish between those funds that are available for current operating purposes and those whose use is limited. This is usually done by the fund accounting/reporting format.

The operating statements for some of the ONPOs are different from any statements previously discussed in this text (see Exhibits 14–2, 14–7, and 14–9). Note the presence of "public support" and "revenues" for each of the funds used. **Public support** is differentiated from revenues in terms of the *source* of the resources. If resources are received with no direct benefit to the provider, they are classified as public support. These include contributions, legacies, and the *net* resources (contributions less direct costs) received from special events, such as dinners and parties. On the other hand, if the resources are earned by providing goods or services, the classification **revenues** is used. Typical revenues include membership dues and investment income.

Generally accepted accounting principles for ONPOs require the use of the full accrual basis of accounting. As a result, revenues and public support items are reported when earned, not when collected.

One of the required items of the operating statement is an **excess line** caption (see Exhibits 14–2, 14–5, 14–7, 14–9, and 14–12). This is used to identify an excess of revenues and support over expenses (or vice versa). Due to the nonprofit nature of the operations of these organizations, it is *not* referred to as net income. However, it is a matter of economic fact that such organizations cannot continue to exist if the resources received in the form of revenue or support do not at least equal the cost of providing the services for which the organization was established.

The expenses associated with the operations of ONPOs are classified as program expenses and supporting expenses. **Program expenses** are those expenses incurred in rendering the services for which the organization was established. As indicated in Exhibits 14–2, 14–7, 14–9, and 14–12, these include research, public health and education, fellowships, and strike assistance to local unions.

Supporting expenses are those expenses incurred in fund raising and in managing the organization. They represent expenses that are *not* directly involved in achieving the purpose for which the organization was established. Therefore ONPOs generally attempt to keep these expenses to a minimum.

The proper classification of expenses is important because it enables the user of the financial statements to identify the cost of providing the services or activities of the organization apart from the costs incurred in "running" it.

Supporting expenses are usually charged against the Current Unrestricted Fund (or its equivalent). However, some of these expenses may occasionally be directly involved with the activities of one or more of the restricted funds. In that case they are reported as an expense in the particular restricted fund.

A problem often arises when a particular cost incurred can be associated with both program expenses and supporting expenses. An example of such a cost is the cost of materials related to the distribution of pamphlets and other literature that provide information regarding a particular program offered by an organization *and* general information about the organization. Such costs must be allocated to program expenses and to supporting expenses.

Note the difference between the reporting method described above and that used for a country club (see Exhibit 14–5). As previously mentioned, the operations of a country club are very close to those of a commercial business. Therefore there is usually no concept of program expenses and supporting expenses.

The bottom portion of the operating statement is used to calculate the ending fund balance. This consists of the beginning fund balance, the excess of public support and revenues over expenses (or vice versa), transfers, and miscellaneous items.

SPECIAL ITEMS

Depreciation

Voluntary health and welfare organizations and 78–10 organizations must record depreciation, on their financial statements, on all long-lived, exhaustible tangible assets—except for certain works of art and historical treasures "whose economic benefit or service potential is used up so slowly that their estimated useful lives are extraordinarily long."[9] These organizations do not need to depreciate inexhaustible long-lived assets (such as gem collections in museums). They must, however, catalog and control such assets. They must also disclose information on all long-lived assets, and the depreciation methods used, in the notes to their financial statements.

Restricted Gifts, Grants, Bequests, and Other Income

Gifts, grants, bequests, and other income whose use is restricted to specific operating programs can present additional reporting problems. Voluntary health and welfare organizations report the receipt of such resources as revenue in the Current Restricted Fund (unless it specifically relates to a future period).[10] For 78–10 organizations, however, the rules are somewhat different. Restricted current receipts are recognized as revenue (of a given period) only to the extent that "allowable" expenses have been incurred during that period. Any excess receipts are reported as **deferred revenue** or **deferred support** on the balance sheet until those resources are used in accordance with the restrictions placed on them.[11]

---

[9] FASB, *Statement of Financial Accounting Standards No. 93*, "Recognition of Depreciation by Not-for-Profit Organizations" (Stamford, Conn: FASB, August 1987), par. 6.

[10] AICPA, *Statements of Position of the Accounting Standards Division as of January 1, 1980*, par. 10,250.055.

[11] Ibid., par. 10,250.062.

Unrestricted Gifts and Grants

Unrestricted gifts, grants, and so forth, should be reported on the operating statement of the Unrestricted Current Fund (or its equivalent) (see Exhibits 14–7 and 14–9). These revenues also include pledges that can legally be enforced (net of estimated uncollectible pledges).[12]

Revenue from Investment Activities

The reporting of investment income and gains and losses incurred when disposing of investments is similar to that of the items previously discussed. Those amounts that are unrestricted are reported on the activity statement of the unrestricted fund in the period earned. The 78–10 organizations report restricted amounts as deferred items on the balance sheet until they are "used." Voluntary health and welfare organizations report restricted investment revenue as revenue of the particular restricted fund.

In some instances the investment income and gains and losses from investment activities must be added to the principal, in accordance with the terms of the endowment. Such items should be reported as capital additions or deductions.

Subscription and Membership Income

For many 78–10 organizations, subscription and membership income are the primary basis of support for their operating activities. In general, these items are recognized as revenue in the period or periods in which they can be used to "cover" services rendered by the organization. For example, membership dues that are collected in September of each year, but apply to calendar-year memberships, are recognized as revenue during the period in which the individual receives membership privileges—in this case the calendar year (e.g., see Exhibits 14–4 and 14–5).

Items such as nonrefundable initiation fees and life membership fees can cause some measurement problems. Like membership dues, the key factor for revenue recognition lies in the period over which these fees "cover" services rendered by the organization. Thus these items should be recognized as revenue on a basis that reflects the services available to the members during this period of time. If, in fact, the items are not related to services rendered but are actually contributions, they should be recognized as revenue in the period or periods in which the organization is entitled to them.

Donated Materials, Facilities, and Services

If donated materials and facilities of a significant amount are used by an organization, a **contribution** should be recorded, along with an **offsetting expense**, based on the fair market value of the items contributed. If, however, the

---

[12] The *Audit Guide* for voluntary health and welfare organizations does not mention the concept of legal enforcement of pledges.

items contributed are merely passed through the organization to individuals receiving services of the organization, they should not be recorded as contributions.

While the same logic is applied to the donated services, the problem is much more complex. However, in those situations in which the value of the services is significant, they should be recorded if

1. The services performed are a normal part of the program or supporting services and would otherwise be performed by salaried personnel
2. The organization exercises control over the employment and duties of the donors of the services
3. The organization has a clearly measurable basis for the amount
4. The services of the reporting organization are not principally intended for the benefit of its members[13]

When these conditions are met, a contribution should be recorded for the value of the services donated, along with an offsetting expense (see Exhibits 14–7 and 14–9).

Grants and Payments to Affiliated Organizations

Those ONPOs that make grants to other organizations or individuals should report the expense and associated liability, if any, in the period in which the recipient is entitled to receive the grant. In those instances in which a grant may be revoked in future years, at the discretion of the grantor institution, the unpaid amount should be recorded only when the grant is renewed. However, if only routine performance is required, the entire amount of the grant should be expensed in the initial period.

Payments to an affiliated state or national organization by a local organization should be reported on the activity statement as an expense or a deduction from revenues, depending on the arrangement (contract) between the two institutions.

Transfers

Transfers between funds should be reported separately in the fund balance section of the activity statement. These movements of resources do not constitute revenues, support, or expenses.

Functional Reporting

The expenses incurred by 78–10 organizations may be reported on a functional basis or on an object basis. Using the **functional basis**, the individual expenses are reported by function or program. Thus such items as the salaries and supplies used by each program are reported as an expense of that activity.

---

[13] These requirements have been compiled from *Audits of Voluntary Health and Welfare Organizations* (p. 21) and *Statements of Position of the Accounting Standards Division as of January 1, 1980*, par. 10,250.067.

Using the **object basis**, expenses are reported by type. Therefore the activity statement reflects the *total* salaries expense, *total* supplies used, and so forth, as individual items. The functional basis is generally recognized as being preferable in most instances, especially those in which the organization receives a significant amount of support from the general public. Such a classification enables the reader to determine the cost of the various programs offered by the organization. No matter which basis is chosen, however, the organization's programs should, at a minimum, be described in the notes to the financial statements.[14]

Voluntary health and welfare organizations should provide a separate statement of functional expenses (see Exhibit 14–3). This statement identifies each program and support service and the amount of each expense incurred on an object basis.

For financial reporting purposes, a **program** is considered to be an activity that is directly related to the purpose for which the organization was established. While most organizations are involved in many programs, it is possible that an organization may have only one such activity.

The expenses identified as **management and general** are those associated with the overall direction and management of the organization, in addition to those associated with record keeping, the annual report, and so forth.

Fund raising and other supporting services expenses are expenses associated with the solicitation of money, materials, and so forth, for which the individual or organization making the contribution receives no direct economic benefit. They include such items as printing, personnel, and the cost of maintaining a mailing list. In addition, the cost of any "gifts" that are sent to prospective contributors should be disclosed.

Statement of Changes in Financial Position

The statement of changes in financial position provides the user of the financial statements with information regarding the financing, investing, and operating activities of the organization.[15] Due to its complexity, it is not discussed in this text. However, such a statement is shown in Exhibit 14–10. As previously indicated, voluntary health and welfare organizations do not have to prepare a statement of changes in financial position for external reporting purposes.

---

[14] AICPA, *Statements of Position of the Accounting Standards Division as of January 1, 1980*, par. 10,250.085.

[15] The concept of resource flows for not-for-profit-organizations is currently under study by the Financial Accounting Standards Board. Since the FASB had not issued a statement or an exposure draft at the time this book went to press, we have used existing rules for the disclosures presented in this chapter.

ILLUSTRATIVE TRANSACTIONS
OF NOT-FOR-PROFIT ORGANIZATIONS

Voluntary Health and Welfare Organizations

Assume that the Society for the Rehabilitation of Addled Professors of Accounting (SRAPA) is formed at the beginning of 19X1. It receives its support from the public-at-large, as well as through the United Way. SRAPA owns a building and various pieces of equipment, which are used to carry out its services—counseling and education programs. It uses the following funds:

1. Current Unrestricted Fund
2. Current Restricted Fund
3. Land, Buildings, and Equipment Fund

The transactions for each fund, for 19X1, are as follows:

Current unrestricted fund

1. Unrestricted pledges of $130,000, which apply to the current period, are made by various people. Of this amount, $15,000 is not expected to be collectible.

Pledges receivable	130,000	
Allowance for uncollectible pledges		15,000
Support—contributions		115,000

To record pledges received and estimated uncollectibles.

2. Joe Breaux makes a contribution of $18,000 but stipulates that this money not be used until the following year. As a result, this contribution must be recorded as a deferred revenue.

Cash	18,000	
Deferred support—contributions		18,000

To record cash gift, which is to be used in 19X2.

3. Pledges receivable of $110,000 are collected, and pledges of $12,000 are written off.

Cash	110,000	
Allowance for uncollectible pledges	12,000	
Pledges receivable		122,000

To record collection and write-off of certain pledges.

4. Of the above amount, $20,000 is invested in government securities.

Investments	20,000	
Cash		20,000

To record the purchase of government
securities.

5. The society's allocation from the United Way amounts to $65,000. From this
amount a share of the United Way's fund-raising costs—$5,000—is deducted.

Cash	60,000	
United Way fund-raising costs	5,000	
Received from United Way		65,000

To record 19X1 allocation from United Way.

6. A fund-raising book sale is held. The event raises $12,000. Out of this amount,
however, $3,000 of related direct costs are incurred and paid. (As a general
rule, support from fund-raising events is recorded *net* of the direct costs of the
events.)

Cash	12,000	
Support—special events		12,000
To record support from book sale.		

Support—special events	3,000	
Cash		3,000

To record direct costs of book sale.

7. Investment income of $2,000 is earned during the year. Of this amount, $1,500
is received by year-end.

Cash	1,500	
Accrued interest receivable	500	
Revenue—investment income		2,000

To record 19X1 investment income.

8. Membership dues of $2,500 are collected during the year.

Cash	2,500	
Revenues—membership dues		2,500

To record receipt of membership dues.

9. Services donated to the society are as follows:
   a. A psychologist provides counseling to a number of accounting professors
      at no cost. The services are valued at $3,000.
   b. An attorney performs certain legal work for free. The services are valued
      at $600.

Expenses—counseling services	3,000	
Expenses—administration	600	
Support—donated services		3,600

To record receipt of donated services.

10. Supplies, with a market value of $800, are donated to the society by a local accounting firm. They are used in the general operation of the organization.

Expenses—administration	800	
Support—donated supplies		800

To record receipt of donated supplies.

11. Salaries and wages incurred during the year (including fringe benefits) are allocated as follows:

Administration	$25,000
Counseling services	60,000
Education	50,000
Fund raising	5,000

By year-end all salaries, wages, and fringe benefits have been paid.

Expenses—administration	25,000	
Expenses—counseling services	60,000	
Expenses—education	50,000	
Expenses—fund raising	5,000	
Cash		140,000

To record salaries, wages, and fringe benefits for 19X1.

12. Other expenses are allocated as follows:

Contractual services:		
Counseling services	$10,000	
Education	5,000	$15,000
Supplies (all education)		10,000
Miscellaneous expenses:		
Administration	$ 5,000	
Counseling services	2,000	
Education	3,000	
Fund raising	1,000	11,000
Total		$36,000

Of this amount, all but $4,000 has been paid by year-end.

Expenses—administration	5,000	
Expenses—counseling services	12,000	
Expenses—education	18,000	
Expenses—fund raising	1,000	
Accounts payable		4,000
Cash		32,000

To record expenses incurred in 19X1 and payment of vouchers.

13. The closing entry for 19X1 is:

Support—contributions	115,000	
Support—special events	9,000	
Support—donated services	3,600	
Support—donated materials	800	
Revenues—investment income	2,000	
Revenues—membership dues	2,500	
Received from United Way	65,000	
Expenses—administration		31,400
Expenses—counseling services		75,000
Expenses—education		68,000
Expenses—fund raising		6,000
United Way fund-raising costs		5,000
Fund balance—unrestricted		12,500

To close revenue, support, expense, and fund-raising cost accounts.

Current restricted fund

1. Pledges of $20,000 and cash gifts of $10,000 are received, with the stipulation that they be used only for special educational programs. Twenty percent of the pledges are estimated to be uncollectible.

Cash	10,000	
Pledges receivable	20,000	
Allowance for uncollectible pledges		4,000
Support—contributions		26,000

To record restricted gifts and pledges.

2. Restricted-purpose pledges of $15,000 are collected and another $2,000 are written off.

Cash	15,000	
Allowance for uncollected pledges	2,000	
Pledges receivable		17,000

To record collection and write-off of restricted pledges.

3. Special educational expenses of $21,000 are paid by this fund in 19X1.

Expenses—special education	21,000	
Cash		21,000

To record expenses of special education program.

4. The closing entry is:

Support—contributions	26,000	
Expenses—special education		21,000
Fund balance—restricted		5,000

To close support and expense accounts.

Land, buildings, and equipment fund

1. The society received a grant of $250,000 from the Kezar Foundation, to be used for the purchase of a building and equipment.

| Cash | 250,000 | |
| Support—contributions | | 250,000 |

To record contribution for purchase of building and equipment.

2. An investment of $100,000 is made in government securities.

| Investments | 100,000 | |
| Cash | | 100,000 |

To record investment in government securities.

3. Equipment costing $50,000 is purchased, using the resources donated by the Kezar Foundation.

| Equipment | 50,000 | |
| Cash | | 50,000 |

To record purchase of equipment with monies restricted for that purpose.

4. A building is purchased for $400,000. A down payment of $80,000 is made and a mortgage is taken out for the remainder.

Building	400,000	
Mortgage payable		320,000
Cash		80,000

To record purchase of building with restricted monies and mortgage.

5. Interest of $8,000 is received on the investment in government securities.

| Cash | 8,000 | |
| Revenue—investment income | | 8,000 |

To record earnings on investments.

6. Payments of $10,000 are made on the mortgage during the year. Of this amount, $8,000 is for interest.

Mortgage payable	2,000	
Expenses—interest	8,000	
Cash		10,000

To record payments on mortgage.

7. Depreciation for the year amounts to $20,000 on the building and $10,000 on the equipment. It is allocated as follows:

Administration	$ 3,000
Counseling services	10,000
Educational services	16,000
Fund raising	1,000

Depreciation expense—administration	3,000	
Depreciation expense—counseling services	10,000	
Depreciation expense—educational services	16,000	
Depreciation expense—fund raising	1,000	
Accumulated depreciation—building		20,000
Accumulated depreciation—equipment		10,000

To record depreciation on buildings and equipment for 19X1.

8. The closing entry is as follows:

Support—contributions	250,000	
Revenue—investment income	8,000	
Expenses—interest		8,000
Depreciation expense—administration		3,000
Depreciation expense—counseling services		10,000
Depreciation expense—educational		
services		16,000
Depreciation expense—fund raising		1,000
Fund balance—unexpended		220,000

To close support, revenue, and expense accounts.

The fund balance of the Land, Building, and Equipment Fund is generally separated into "unexpended" and "expended" portions. The **unexpended portion** equals the total of the balances in the Cash, Investment, and, in some cases, the net amount in the Pledges receivable accounts. The **expended portion** equals the net book value of the fixed assets (original cost less accumulated depreciation), less the amounts outstanding on any associated mortgages. At the end of each reporting period, it is necessary to adjust the unexpended fund balance to reflect the expended portion. The adjustment at the end of 19X1 is $102,000 ($50,000 + $400,000 - $320,000 + $2,000 - $30,000 = $102,000). The entry to make this adjustment is:

Fund balance—unexpended	102,000	
Fund balance—expended		102,000

To adjust fund balance—expended to reflect
the change in net investment in fixed assets.

Other Not-for-Profit Organizations

If the organization in the above illustration had been an ONPO, certain fund titles would have been different. The Current Unrestricted Fund and the Current Restricted Fund would have been called the Operating Fund—Unrestricted and the Operating Fund—Restricted, respectively. The Land, Buildings, and Equipment Fund would most likely have been called the Plant Fund.

Except for the different fund names, the entries shown for the Current Unrestricted Fund would have been similar for both types of organizations. The entries for the Current Restricted Fund and the Land, Buildings, and Equipment Fund, however, would have been somewhat different. These differences would have been due to the fact that ONPOs recognize restricted sources of support and revenues only when they incur qualifying expenses, whereas VHWOs recognize these sources of support and revenues when received. In addition, ONPOs make a distinction between public support and capital additions, whereas VHWOs treat both as public support.

If the society had been an ONPO, the entries in the Current Restricted Fund (Operating Fund—Restricted) and the Land, Buildings, and Equipment (Plant) Fund would have been the ones shown below. (Compare these entries with the ones beginning on page 537.)

Current restricted fund (Operating Fund—Restricted)

1.	Cash	10,000	
	Pledges receivable	20,000	
	Allowance for uncollectible pledges		4,000
	Deferred support—contributions		26,000
2.	Same as VHWO		
3a.	Expense—special education	21,000	
	Cash		21,000
3b.	Deferred support—contributions	21,000	
	Support—contributions		21,000
4.	Support—contributions	21,000	
	Expenses—special education		21,000

Notice that the support is deferred until the resources are actually spent. The remaining balance in the Deferred support account will appear in the liability section of the balance sheet.

Land, buildings, and equipment fund (Plant Fund)

1.	Cash	250,000	
	Deferred capital additions—contributions		250,000
2.	Same as VHWO		
3a.	Equipment	50,000	
	Cash		50,000
3b.	Deferred capital additions—contributions	50,000	
	Capital additions—contributions		50,000
4a.	Building	400,000	
	Mortgage payable		320,000
	Cash		80,000
4b.	Deferred capital additions—contributions	80,000	
	Capital additions—contributions		80,000
5.	Cash	8,000	
	Deferred revenues—investment income		8,000
6a.	Mortgage payable	2,000	
	Expenses—interest	8,000	
	Cash		10,000
6b.	Deferred revenues—investment Income	8,000	
	Deferred capital additions—contributions	2,000	
	Revenue—investment income		8,000
	Capital additions—contributions		2,000

(Assume that income from investments is used to pay interest on the mortgage.)

7.   Same as VHWO

The closing entries would simply reflect the differences shown above and, because of space limitations, are not shown.

EXHIBIT 14–1

Voluntary Health and Welfare Service
Balance Sheets
December 31, 19X2 and 19X1

ASSETS	19X2	19X1
	Current Funds Unrestricted	
Cash	$2,207,000	$2,530,000
Investments (Note 2):		
For long-term purposes	2,727,000	2,245,000
Other	1,075,000	950,000
Pledges receivable less allowance for uncollectibles of $105,000 and $92,000	475,000	363,000
Inventories of educational materials, at cost	70,000	61,000
Accrued interest, other receivables, and prepaid expenses	286,000	186,000
Total	$6,840,000	$6,335,000

LIABILITIES AND FUND BALANCES	19X2	19X1
Accounts payable	$ 148,000	$ 139,000
Research grants payable	596,000	616,000
Contributions designated for future periods	245,000	219,000
Total liabilities and deferred revenues	989,000	974,000
Fund balances:		
Designated by the governing board for:		
Long-term investments	2,800,000	2,300,000
Purchases of new equipment	100,000	–
Research purposes (Note 3)	1,152,000	1,748,000
Undesignated, available for general activities (Note 4)	1,799,000	1,313,000
Total fund balance	5,851,000	5,361,000
Total	$6,840,000	$6,335,000

Exhibit 14—1 (cont.)

Restricted

ASSETS	19X2	19X1	LIABILITIES AND FUND BALANCES	19X2	19X1
Cash	$ 3,000	$ 5,000	Fund balances:		
Investments (Note 2)	71,000	72,000	Professional education	$ 84,000	$ —
Grants receivable	58,000	46,000	Research grants	48,000	123,000
Total	$ 132,000	$ 123,000	Total	$ 132,000	$ 123,000

Land, Building and Equipment Fund

ASSETS	19X2	19X1	LIABILITIES AND FUND BALANCES	19X2	19X1
Cash	$ 3,000	$ 2,000	Mortgage payable, 8% due 19XX	$ 32,000	$ 36,000
Investments (Note 2)	177,000	145,000			
Pledges receivable less allowance for uncollectibles of $7,500 and $5,000	32,000	25,000	Fund balances:		
			Expended	484,000	477,000
Land, building, and equipment, at cost less accumulated depreciation of $296,000 and $262,000 (Note 5)	516,000	513,000	Unexpended—restricted	212,000	172,000
			Total fund balance	696,000	649,000
Total	$ 728,000	$ 685,000	Total	$ 728,000	$ 685,000

Endowment Funds

ASSETS	19X2	19X1	LIABILITIES AND FUND BALANCES	19X2	19X1
Cash	$ 4,000	$ 10,000	Fund balance	$1,948,000	$2,017,000
Investments (Note 2)	1,944,000	2,007,000			
Total	$1,948,000	$2,017,000	Total	$1,948,000	$2,017,000

Accompanying notes to financial statements not included.

Source: AICPA, *Audits of Voluntary Health and Welfare Organizations*, pp. 46-47.

EXHIBIT 14–2

Voluntary Health and Welfare Service
Statement of Support, Revenue, Expenses
and Changes in Fund Balances
Year Ended December 31, 19X2
(with comparative totals for 19X1)

| | 19X2 | | | | TOTAL ALL FUNDS | |
| | CURRENT FUNDS | | Land, Building and Equipment Fund | Endowment Fund | | |
	Unrestricted	Restricted			19X2	19X1
Public support and revenue:						
Public support:						
Contribution (net of estimated uncollectible pledges of $195,000 in 19X2 and $150,000 in 19X1)	$3,764,000	$162,000	$ –	$ 2,000	$3,928,000	$3,976,000
Contributions to Building Fund	–	–	72,000	–	72,000	150,000
Special events (net of direct costs of $181,000 in 19X2 and $163,000 in 19X1)	104,000	–	–	–	104,000	92,000
Legacies and bequests	92,000	–	–	4,000	96,000	129,000
Received from federated and nonfederated campaigns (which incurred related fund-raising expenses of $38,000 in 19X2 and $29,000 in 19X1)	275,000	–	–	–	275,000	308,000
Total public support	4,235,000	162,000	72,000	6,000	4,475,000	4,655,000
Revenue:						
Membership dues	17,000	–	–	–	17,000	12,000
Investment income	98,000	10,000	–	–	108,000	94,000
Realized gain on investment transactions	200,000	–	–	25,000	225,000	275,000
Miscellaneous	42,000	–	–	–	42,000	47,000
Total revenue	357,000	10,000	–	25,000	392,000	428,000
Total support and revenue	4,592,000	172,000	72,000	31,000	$4,867,000	$5,083,000

EXHIBIT 14–2 (cont.)

| | 19X2 | | | | TOTAL ALL FUNDS | |
| | CURRENT FUNDS | | Land, Build-ing, and Equipment Fund | Endowment Fund | 19X2 | 19X1 |
	Unrestricted	Restricted				
Expenses:						
Program services:						
Research	1,257,000	155,000	2,000	—	$1,414,000	$1,365,000
Public health education	539,000	—	5,000	—	544,000	485,000
Professional education and training	612,000	—	6,000	—	618,000	516,000
Community services	568,000	—	10,000	—	578,000	486,000
Total program services	2,976,000	155,000	23,000	—	3,154,000	2,852,000
Supporting services:						
Management and general	567,000	—	7,000	—	574,000	638,000
Fund raising	642,000	—	12,000	—	654,000	546,000
Total supporting services	1,209,000	—	19,000	—	1,228,000	1,184,000
Total expenses	4,185,000	155,000	42,000	—	$4,382,000	$4,036,000
Excess (deficiency) of public support and revenue over expenses	407,000	17,000	30,000	31,000		
Other changes in fund balances:						
Property and equipment acquisitions from unrestricted funds	(17,000)	—	17,000	—		
Transfer of realized Endowment Fund appreciation	100,000	—	—	(100,000)		
Returned to donor	—	(8,000)	—	—		
Fund balances, beginning of year	5,361,000	123,000	649,000	2,017,000		
Fund balances, end of year	$5,851,000	$132,000	$696,000	$1,948,000		

Accompanying notes to financial statements not included.

Source: AICPA, *Audits of Voluntary Health and Welfare Organizations*, pp. 42–43.

EXHIBIT 14—3

Voluntary Health and Welfare Service
Statement of Functional Expenses
Year Ended December 31, 19X2
(with comparative totals for 19X1)

	19X2									
	PROGRAM SERVICES					SUPPORTING SERVICES			TOTAL EXPENSES	
	Research	Public Health Education	Professional Education and Training	Community Services	Total	Management and General	Fund Raising	Total	19X2	19X1
Salaries	$ 45,000	$291,000	$251,000	$269,000	$ 856,000	$331,000	$368,000	$ 699,000	$1,555,000	$1,433,000
Employee health and retirement benefits	4,000	14,000	14,000	14,000	46,000	22,000	15,000	37,000	83,000	75,000
Payroll taxes, etc.	2,000	16,000	13,000	14,000	45,000	18,000	18,000	36,000	81,000	75,000
Total salaries and related expenses	51,000	321,000	278,000	297,000	947,000	371,000	401,000	772,000	1,719,000	1,583,000
Professional fees and contract service payments	1,000	10,000	3,000	8,000	22,000	26,000	8,000	34,000	56,000	53,000
Supplies	2,000	13,000	13,000	13,000	41,000	18,000	17,000	35,000	76,000	71,000
Telephone and telegraph	2,000	13,000	10,000	11,000	36,000	15,000	23,000	38,000	74,000	68,000
Postage and shipping	2,000	17,000	13,000	9,000	41,000	13,000	30,000	43,000	84,000	80,000
Occupancy	5,000	26,000	22,000	25,000	78,000	30,000	27,000	57,000	135,000	126,000
Rental of equipment	1,000	24,000	14,000	4,000	43,000	3,000	16,000	19,000	62,000	58,000
Local transportation	3,000	22,000	20,000	22,000	67,000	23,000	30,000	53,000	120,000	113,000
Conferences, conventions, meetings	8,000	19,000	71,000	20,000	118,000	38,000	13,000	51,000	169,000	156,000
Printing and publications	4,000	56,000	43,000	11,000	114,000	14,000	64,000	78,000	192,000	184,000
Awards and grants	1,332,000	14,000	119,000	144,000	1,609,000	—	—	—	1,609,000	1,448,000
Miscellaneous	1,000	4,000	6,000	4,000	15,000	16,000	21,000	37,000	52,000	64,000
Total expenses before depreciation	1,412,000	539,000	612,000	568,000	3,131,000	567,000	650,000	1,217,000	4,348,000	4,004,000
Depreciation of buildings and equipment	2,000	5,000	6,000	10,000	23,000	7,000	4,000	11,000	34,000	32,000
Total expenses	$1,414,000	$544,000	$618,000	$578,000	$3,154,000	$574,000	$654,000	$1,228,000	$4,382,000	$4,036,000

Accompanying notes to financial statements not included.

Source: AICPA, Audits of Voluntary Health and Welfare Organizations, pp. 44–45.

EXHIBIT 14-4

Sample Country Club
Balance Sheet
March 31, 19X1 and 19X0

	19X1	19X0
ASSETS		
Current assets		
Cash	$ 44,413	$ 37,812
Investments (Note 2)	289,554	388,007
Accounts receivable, less allowances of $5,000		
in 19X1, and $6,000 in 19X0	71,831	45,898
Inventories, at lower of cost (FIFO) or market	27,930	28,137
Prepaid expenses	19,154	13,948
Total current assets	452,882	513,802
Property and equipment, at cost (Note 3)		
Land and land improvements	1,085,319	1,098,828
Buildings	1,331,590	1,200,585
Furniture, fixtures, and equipment	274,761	254,540
	2,691,670	2,553,953
Less accumulated depreciation	864,564	824,088
	1,827,106	1,729,865
Other assets		
Deferred charges	15,077	16,524
Beverage license	10,500	10,500
	25,577	27,024
	$2,305,565	$2,270,691
LIABILITIES AND MEMBERSHIP EQUITY		
Current liabilities		
Accounts payable and accrued expenses	$ 61,426	$ 63,600
Deferred revenues—initiation fees (Note 1)	15,677	7,755
Due to resigned members	16,400	12,900
Taxes	20,330	23,668
Total current liabilities	113,833	107,923
Membership equity		
Proprietary certificates, 500 at $1,500 each—		
no change during the years	750,000	750,000
Cumulative excess of revenue over expenses	1,441,732	1,412,768
	2,191,732	2,162,768
	$2,305,565	$2,270,691

Source: AICPA, *Audits of Certain Nonprofit Organizations,* p. 114 (SOP 78-10).

EXHIBIT 14-5

Sample Country Club
Statement of Revenue, Expenses, and Changes in
Cumulative Excess of Revenue over Expenses
Years Ended March 31, 19X1 and 19X0

	19X1	19X0
Revenue		
Dues	$ 590,000	$ 600,000
Restaurant and bar charges	270,412	265,042
Greens fees	171,509	163,200
Tennis and swimming fees	83,829	67,675
Initiation fees	61,475	95,220
Locker and room rentals	49,759	49,954
Interest and discounts	28,860	28,831
Golf cart rentals	26,584	24,999
Other—net	4,011	3,893
Total revenue	1,286,439	1,298,814
Expenses		
Greens	241,867	244,823
House	212,880	210,952
Restaurant and bar	153,035	136,707
Tennis and swimming	67,402	48,726
General and administrative	533,838	690,551
Net (gains) losses on investments	98,453	(98,813)
Total expenses	1,307,475	1,232,946
Expenses (deficiency) of revenue over expenses before capital additions	(21,036)	65,868
Capital additions		
Assessments for capital improvements	50,000	—
Excess (deficiency) of revenue over expenses after capital additions	28,964	65,868
Cumulative excess of revenue over expenses— beginning of year	1,412,768	1,346,900
Cumulative excess of revenue over expenses—end of year	$1,441,732,	$1,412,768

Source: AICPA, *Audits of Certain Nonprofit Organizations*, p. 115 (SOP 78-10).

EXHIBIT 14–6

Sample Museum
Balance Sheet
June 30, 19X1
(with comparative totals for 19X0)

	Operating Fund	Plant Fund	Endowment Fund	Total	June 30, 19X0 Total
ASSETS					
Current assets					
Cash	$ 19,800	—	—	$ 19,800	$ 23,700
Receivables, less reserve of $7,700	145,500	—	—	145,500	125,800
Investments (Note 2)	210,000	—	—	210,000	—
Inventories, at lower of cost (FIFO) or market	121,100	—	—	121,100	120,600
Prepayments	26,600	—	—	26,600	12,700
Total current assets	523,000	—	—	523,000	282,800
Fixed assets, net of depreciation (Note 3)	—	$1,964,000	—	1,964,000	1,866,800
Art collection (Note 11)					
Cash held for investment	—	—	$ 6,000	6,000	3,800
Investments (Note 2)	4,044,500	—	7,688,400	11,732,900	11,709,300
Total	$4,567,500	$1,964,000	$7,694,400	14,225,900	$13,862,700
LIABILITIES AND FUND BALANCES					
Current liabilities					
Accounts payable and accrued expenses	$ 256,900	—	—	$ 256,900	$ 252,900
Deferred revenue and restricted gifts, current portion (Note 5)	242,100	—	—	242,100	208,100
Total current liabilities	499,000	—	—	499,000	461,000
Deferred revenue and restricted gifts, noncurrent portion (Note 5)	409,900	—	—	409,900	167,300
Fund balances					
Endowment	—	—	$7,694,400	7,694,400	7,621,800
Land, buildings, and equipment	—	$1,964,000	—	1,964,000	1,866,800
Unrestricted					
Designated for investment	3,490,000	—	—	3,490,000	3,490,000
Designated for plant expansion	150,000	—	—	150,000	—
Unappropriated	18,600	—	—	18,600	255,800
Total fund balances	3,658,600	1,964,000	7,694,400	13,317,000	13,234,400
Total	$4,567,500	$1,964,000	$7,694,400	$14,225,900	$13,862,700

Source: AICPA, *Audits of Certain Nonprofit Organizations*, pp. 126–27 (SOP 78-10).

551

EXHIBIT 14–7

Sample Museum
Statement of Activity
Year Ended June 30, 19X1
(with comparative totals for 19X0)

	Operating Fund	Plant Fund	Endowment Fund	Total	Year Ended June 30, 19X0 Total
Support and revenue					
Admissions	$ 131,100	—	—	$ 131,100	$ 123,400
Government appropriations	110,700	—	—	110,700	104,000
Gifts and grants (Note 5 and 8)	130,000	—	—	130,000	124,700
Memberships	48,400	—	—	48,400	39,900
Investment income	828,800	—	—	828,800	841,700
Net realized investment gains (losses)	6,300	—	—	6,300	(2,600)
Revenue, auxiliary activities	483,100	—	—	483,100	417,200
Total	1,738,400	—	—	1,738,400	1,648,300
Expenses					
Program					
Curatorial and conservation	578,600	$27,400	—	606,000	602,000
Exhibits	108,600	—	—	108,600	109,100
Education	133,400	4,800	—	138,200	131,600
Fellowships	68,200	—	—	68,200	52,800
Public information	66,400	2,700	—	69,100	67,700
Accession of art for collection, net of deaccessions (Note 11)	200,000	—	—	200,000	170,000
Supporting services					
Management and general	67,400	10,800	—	78,200	77,300
Fund raising	10,300	—	—	10,300	9,600
Cost of sales and expense of auxiliary activities	441,100	8,700	—	449,800	384,600
Total	1,674,000	54,400	—	1,728,400	1,604,700
Excess (deficiency) of support and revenue over expenses before capital additions	64,400	(54,400)	—	10,000	43,600

EXHIBIT 14–7 (cont.)

	Operating Fund	Plant Fund	Endowment Fund	Total	June 30, 19X0 Total
Capital additions					
Gifts and grants (Note 8)	—	—	$ 76,400	$ 76,400	18,200
Net investment income	—	—	4,700	4,700	1,800
Net realized investment gains (losses)	—	—	(8,500)	(8,500)	(2,000)
Total	—	—	72,600	72,600	18,000
Excess (deficiency) of support and revenue over expenses after capital additions	64,400	(54,400)	72,600	82,600	61,600
Fund balances, beginning of period	3,745,800	1,866,800	7,621,800	13,234,400	13,172,800
Add (deduct) transfers (Note 9)	(151,600)	151,600	—	—	—
Fund balances, end of period	$3,658,600	$1,964,000	$7,694,400	$13,317,000	13,234,400

Notes to Financial Statement

Note 10—Contributed Services

A substantial number of unpaid volunteers have made significant contributions of their time to develop the Museum's programs, principally in membership development and educational programs. The value of this contributed time is not reflected in these statements since it is not susceptible to objective measurement or valuation.

Note 11—Art Collection

In conformity with the practice followed by many museums, art objects purchased and donated are not included in the balance sheet.

The value of the objects acquired by gift for which the Museum can make a reasonable estimate is reported as gifts in the Statement of Activity ($28,000 in the year ended June 30, 19X1).

The cost of all objects purchased, together with the value of objects acquired by gift as indicated in the preceding paragraph, less the proceeds from deaccessions of objects, is reported as a separate program expense. During the year ended June 30, 19X1, purchase of art objects amounted to $185,000 and the proceeds from deaccessions was $13,000.

Gifts of cash or other property restricted by donors for the purchase of items for the collection are classified as deferred revenue until acquisitions are made in accordance with the terms of the gifts.

Source: AICPA, Audits of Certain Nonprofit Organizations, pp. 128–29, 131 (SOP 78-10).

EXHIBIT 14–8

Sample Religious Organization
Balance Sheet
December 31, 19X1

	EXPENDABLE FUNDS				NONEXPENDABLE FUNDS		Total
	Operating	Deposit and Loan	Total	Plant Fund	Endowment	Annuity and Life Income	All Funds
ASSETS							
Cash	$1,750,000	$ 10,000	$ 1,760,000	$ 408,000	$ 20,000	$ 2,000	$ 2,190,000
Accounts receivable, less allowance for doubtful receivables of $12,000	520,000	—	520,000	—	—	—	520,000
Pledges receivable, less allowance for doubtful pledges of $25,000	500,000	—	500,000	80,000	—	—	580,000
Investments (Note 2)	3,800,000	300,000	4,100,000	260,000	1,300,000	178,000	5,838,000
Loans receivable, less allowance for doubtful loans of $350,000	—	2,600,000	2,600,000	—	—	—	2,600,000
Advances to plant funds	—	3,500,000	3,500,000	—	—	—	—*
Land, buildings, and equipment at cost, less accumulated depreciation of $23,500,000 (Note 3)	—	—	—	44,800,000	—	—	44,800,000
Other assets	150,000	—	150,000	—	—	—	150,000
Total assets	$6,720,000	$6,410,000	$13,130,000	$45,548,000	$1,320,000	$180,000	$56,678,000

EXHIBIT 14—8 (cont.)

	EXPENDABLE FUNDS				NONEXPENDABLE FUNDS		
	Operating	Deposit and Loan	Total	Plant Fund	Endowment	Annuity and Life Income	Total All Funds
LIABILITIES AND FUND BALANCES							
Accounts payable and accrued expenses	$ 600,000	—	$ 600,000	$ 20,000	—	$120,000	$ 740,000
Deferred amounts (Note 6)							
Unrestricted	160,000	—	160,000	—	—	—	160,000
Restricted	870,000	—	870,000	328,000	—	60,000	1,258,000
Advances from expendable funds	—	—	—	3,500,000	—	—	—*
Deposits payable	—	$7,310,000	7,310,000	—	—	—	7,310,000
Long-term debt (Note 4)	—	—	—	2,800,000	—	—	2,800,000
Total liabilities	1,630,000	7,310,000	8,940,000	6,648,000	—	180,000	12,268,000
Fund balances (deficit)							
Unrestricted							
Designated for long-term investment	3,800,000	—	3,800,000	—	—	—	3,800,000
Undesignated	1,290,000	(900,000)	390,000	—	—	—	390,000
	5,090,000	(900,000)	4,190,000	—	—	—	4,190,000
Restricted	—	—	—	—	$1,320,000	—	1,320,000
Net investment in plant	—	—	—	38,900,000	—	—	38,900,000
Total fund balances (deficit)	5,090,000	(900,000)	4,190,000	38,900,000	1,320,000	—	44,410,000
Total liabilities and fund balances	$6,720,000	$6,410,000	$13,130,000	$45,548,000	$1,320,000	$180,000	$56,678,000

* Interfund borrowings eliminated in combination.

Source: AICPA, *Audits of Certain Nonprofit Organizations,* pp. 146–47 (SOP 78-10).

EXHIBIT 14-9

Sample Religious Organization
Statement of Support and Revenue, Expenses,
Capital Additions, and Changes in Fund Balances
Year Ended December 31, 19X1

	EXPENDABLE FUNDS				Plant Fund	Nonexpendable Endowment Funds	Total All Funds
	OPERATING		Deposit and Loan	Total			
	Unrestricted	Restricted					
Support and revenue							
Contributions and bequests	$ 6,800,000	$180,000	—	$ 6,980,000	—	—	$ 6,980,000
Fees for services	4,000,000	—	—	4,000,000	—	—	4,000,000
Endowment and other investment income	200,000	40,000	—	240,000	—	—	240,000
Net gain on investment transactions	250,000	—	—	250,000	—	—	250,000
Contributed services	950,000	—	—	950,000	—	—	950,000
Auxiliary activities	205,000	—	$535,000	740,000	—	—	740,000
Total support and revenue	12,405,000	220,000	535,000	13,160,000	—	—	13,160,000
Expenses							
Program services							
Pastoral	3,300,000	45,000	—	3,345,000	$ 300,000	—	3,645,000
Education	4,000,000	80,000	—	4,080,000	460,000	—	4,540,000
Health care	2,800,000	25,000	—	2,825,000	250,000	—	3,075,000
Social services	900,000	50,000	—	950,000	85,000	—	1,035,000
Cemeteries	220,000	20,000	—	240,000	20,000	—	260,000
Religious personnel development	600,000	—	—	600,000	55,000	—	655,000
Auxiliary activities	160,000	—	685,000	845,000	5,000	—	850,000
Total program services	11,980,000	220,000	685,000	12,885,000	1,175,000	—	14,060,000

EXHIBIT 14–9 (cont.)

| | EXPENDABLE FUNDS | | | | Plant Fund | Nonexpendable Endowment Funds | Total All Funds |
| | OPERATING | | Deposit and Loan | Total | | | |
	Unrestricted	Restricted					
Supporting services							
General administration	180,000	—	—	180,000	15,000	—	195,000
Fund raising	120,000	—	—	120,000	10,000	—	130,000
Total supporting services	300,000	—	—	300,000	25,000	—	325,000
Total expenses	12,280,000	220,000	685,000	13,185,000	1,200,000	—	14,385,000
Excess (deficiency) of support and revenue over expenses before capital additions	125,000	—	(150,000)	(25,000)	(1,200,000)	—	(1,225,000)
Capital additions							
Contributions and bequests	—	—	—	—	310,000	$ 200,000	510,000
Investment income	—	—	—	—	15,000	—	15,000
Net gain on investment transactions	—	—	—	—	—	80,000	80,000
Total capital additions	—	—	—	—	325,000	280,000	605,000
Excess (deficiency) of support and revenue over expenses after capital additions	125,000	—	(150,000)	(25,000)	(875,000)	280,000	(620,000)
Fund balance (deficit) at beginning of year	5,315,000	—	(750,000)	4,565,000	39,425,000	1,040,000	45,030,000
Transfers to plant funds for plant acquisitions and principal debt service payments financed from operating funds	(350,000)	—	—	(350,000)	350,000	—	—
Fund balances (deficit) at end of year	$ 5,090,000	—	$(900,000)	$ 4,190,000	$38,900,000	$1,320,000	$44,410,000

Source: AICPA, Audits of Certain Nonprofit Organizations, pp. 148–49 (SOP 78-10).

EXHIBIT 14-10

558

Sample Religious Organization
Statement of Changes in Financial Position
Year Ended December 31, 19X1

	EXPENDABLE FUNDS			Plant Fund	NONEXPENDABLE FUNDS		Total All Funds
	Operating	Deposit and Loan	Total		Endowment	Annuity and Life Income	
Resources provided							
Excess (deficiency) of support and revenue over expenses before capital additions	$125,000	$(150,000)	$(25,000)	$(1,200,000)	—	—	$(1,225,000)
Capital additions							
Contributions and bequests	—	—	—	310,000	$200,000	—	510,000
Investment income	—	—	—	15,000	—	—	15,000
Net gain on investment transactions	—	—	—	—	80,000	—	80,000
Excess (deficiency) of support and revenue over expenses after capital additions	125,000	(150,000)	(25,000)	(875,000)	280,000	—	(620,000)
Items that do not use (provide) resources							
Provision for depreciation	—	—	—	1,200,000	—	—	1,200,000
Net gain on investment transactions	(250,000)	(15,000)	(265,000)	—	(80,000)	$(12,000)	(357,000)
Issuance of long-term debt	—	—	—	400,000	—	—	400,000
Increase in deferred amounts	650,000	—	650,000	3,000	—	2,000	655,000
Proceeds from sale of investments	1,800,000	210,000	2,010,000	332,000	590,000	49,000	2,981,000
Total resources provided	2,325,000	45,000	2,370,000	1,060,000	790,000	39,000	4,259,000
Resources used							
Purchases of building and equipment	—	—	—	755,000	—	—	755,000
Reduction of long-term debt	—	—	—	320,000	—	—	320,000
Purchases of investments	1,830,000	70,000	1,900,000	—	784,000	36,000	2,720,000
Increase in accounts and pledges receivable	400,000	—	400,000	5,000	—	—	405,000
Increase in loans receivable	—	45,000	45,000	—	—	—	45,000
Decrease in accounts payable and accrued expenses	70,000	—	70,000	10,000	—	2,000	82,000
Decrease in deposits payable	—	10,000	10,000	—	—	—	10,000
Total resources used	2,300,000	125,000	2,425,000	1,090,000	784,000	38,000	4,337,000
Transfers to plant funds for plant acquisitions and principal debt service payments financed from operating funds	(350,000)	—	(350,000)	350,000	—	—	—
Increase (decrease) in cash	$(325,000)	$(80,000)	$(405,000)	$320,000	$6,000	$1,000	$(78,000)

Source: AICPA, *Audits of Certain Nonprofit Organizations*, pp. 150–51 (SOP 78-10).

EXHIBIT 14–11

Sample Union
Balance Sheet
December 31, 19X1
(with comparative totals for 19X0)

	General Fund (Undesignated)	Strike Insurance Fund (Designated)	December 31, 19X1 Total	December 31, 19X0 Total
ASSETS				
Current assets				
Cash (including savings accounts of $2,100,000 and $1,050,000) (Note 3)	$ 650,800	$ 1,710,000	$ 2,360,800	$ 1,238,100
Investments at market	491,800	9,054,200	9,546,000	9,640,400
Per capita dues receivable	51,800	133,200	185,000	189,500
Accrued interest receivable	1,800	210,700	212,500	214,600
Loans to affiliated organizations (Note 4)	21,400	—	21,400	27,300
Accounts receivable (less allowance for doubtful accounts of $2,300 and $2,500)	67,900	—	67,900	68,900
Prepaid expenses	74,900	—	74,900	71,500
Total current assets	1,360,400	11,108,100	12,468,500	11,450,300
Property, furniture, and equipment at cost (Note 1)				
Land	678,400	—	678,400	678,400
Buildings (net of accumulated depreciation of $743,500 and $675,600)	1,973,400	—	1,973,400	1,515,500
Furniture and equipment (net of accumulated depreciation of $314,800 and $278,200)	50,800	—	50,800	87,400
Total property, furniture, and equipment	2,702,600	—	2,702,600	2,281,300
Total assets	$4,063,000	$11,108,100	$15,171,100	$$13,731,600

(continued)

EXHIBIT 14–11 (cont.)

	General Fund (Undesignated)	Strike Insurance Fund (Designated)	December 31, 19X1 Total	December 31, 19X0 Total
LIABILITIES AND FUND BALANCES				
Current liabilities				
Accounts payable	$ 337,600	—	$ 337,600	$ 423,100
Notes payable	13,100	—	13,100	19,600
Affiliation dues payable	48,800	—	48,800	49,600
Accrued salaries	31,500	—	31,500	33,000
Payroll taxes and employee deductions payable	89,300	—	89,300	90,400
Total current liabilities	520,300	—	520,300	615,700
Fund balances	3,542,700	11,108,100	14,650,800	13,115,900
Total liabilities and fund balances	$4,063,000	$11,108,100	$15,171,100	$13,731,600

Source: AICPA, *Audits of Certain Nonprofit Organizations*, pp. 160–61 (SOP 78-10).

EXHIBIT 14–12

Sample Union
Statement of Revenue, Expenses,
and Changes in Fund Balances
Year Ended December 31, 19X1
(with comparative totals for 19X0)

	General Fund (Undesignated)	Strike Insurance Fund (Designated)	December 31, 19X1 Total	December 31, 19X0 Total
Revenue				
Per capita dues (Note 2)	$9,385,500	$3,532,300	$12,917,800	$13,219,800
Initiation fees	24,100	—	24,100	22,800
Sales of organizational supplies	26,700	—	26,700	17,900
Rental income	216,300	—	216,300	216,100
Administration fees—apprentice training	11,800	—	11,800	12,100
Interest income	28,100	609,000	637,100	644,100
Total revenue	9,692,500	4,141,300	13,833,800	14,132,800
Expense (Note 6)				
Program services				
Strike assistance to local unions	877,900	2,630,500	3,508,400	3,345,600
Constitutional convention	154,600	—	154,600	132,800
Field office services				
Organization	2,054,000	—	2,054,000	2,106,500
Negotiation	2,156,700	—	2,156,700	2,212,000
Grievance	924,300	—	924,300	947,900
Total program services	6,167,500	2,630,500	8,798,000	8,744,800
Administrative and general	3,537,700	57,600	3,595,300	1,425,200
Net (gains) losses on investments	(94,400)	—	(94,400)	2,062,800
Total expense	9,610,800	2,688,100	12,298,900	12,232,800
Excess of revenue over expense	81,700	1,453,200	1,534,900	1,900,000
Fund balances, beginning of year	3,461,000	9,654,900	13,115,900	11,215,900
Fund balances, end of year	$3,542,700	$11,108,100	$14,650,800	$13,115,900

Source: AICPA, *Audits of Certain Nonprofit Organizations*, pp. 162–63 (SOP 78-10).

SELECTED REFERENCES

American Institute of Certified Public Accountants. *Audits of Certain Nonprofit Organizations.* New York, 1981.

Anthony, Robert N. *Financial Accounting in Nonbusiness Organizations.* Stamford, Conn.: Financial Accounting Standards Board, 1978.

Ellis, Loudell O. *Church Treasurer's Handbook.* Valley Forge, Pa.: Judson Press, 1978.

Gross, Malvern J., Jr., and William Warshauer, Jr. *Financial and Accounting Guide for Nonprofit Organizations,* 3rd ed. New York: Ronald Press, 1979.

United Way of America. *Accounting & Financial Reporting.* Alexandria, Va., 1974.

REVIEW QUESTIONS

Q14–1 What is the difference between a *voluntary health and welfare organization* and an *"other" not-for-profit organization*?

Q14–2 Identify several organizations that would be classified in the "voluntary health and welfare" category.

Q14–3 What is the purpose of *SOP 78–10*?

Q14–4 What body has the final authority for determining the accounting procedures used by voluntary health and welfare organizations and 78–10 organizations?

Q14–5 Identify and briefly describe the funds generally used by voluntary health and welfare organizations.

Q14–6 Which fund or funds are recommended for use by 78–10 organizations?

Q14–7 Which three basic financial statements are used by voluntary health and welfare organizations?

Q14–8 Comment on the following statement: 78–10 organizations must prepare the same financial statements as voluntary health and welfare organizations.

Q14–9 How are uncollected pledges reported in the financial statements of voluntary health and welfare organizations?

Q14–10 The illustration of a balance sheet for a country club does not contain a restricted fund. Does this mean that such organizations cannot use restricted funds? Explain your answer.

Q14–11 What is *deferred revenue*?

Q14–12 What is the *functional basis* for reporting expenses?

Q14–13 How do *program expenses* differ from *supporting expenses*?

Q14–14 What is the purpose of the statement of functional expenses for a voluntary health and welfare organization?

EXERCISES

E14–1 (Funds used by voluntary health and welfare organizations)
Using the coding system below, indicate which fund or funds would be used to record each of the transactions described.

CUF—Currnet Unrestricted Fund
CRF—Current Restricted Fund
LBEF—Land, Building, and Equipment Fund
EF—Endowment Fund
CF—Custodian Fund
LlAF—Loan and Annuity Fund

1. The organization received unrestricted pledges of $400,000. Of this amount, $390,000 is expected to be collected.
2. Jane Public gave the organization securities with a market value of $1.2 million. The gift provided that the principal must be maintained intact; however, the income could be spent for any purpose that had the governing board's approval.
3. Unrestricted contributions that were designated for use in the following year were received. These contributions totaled $50,000.
4. Salaries of employees inolved in rendering services to the public totaled $75,000.

E14-2   (Recording journal entries for voluntary health and welfare organizations)
Prepare the journal entries necessary to record the data given in Exercise 14–1. In addition, indicate which fund is used for each entry.

E14–3   (Multiple choice)
1. A voluntary health and welfare organization received several pledges during 19X0. Two of these pledges were specifically intended for use in 19X2. The individuals making the pledges paid the organization $10,000 cash in 19X1. These events would be recognized as:
   a. A deferred credit in the balance sheet at the end of 19X0 and as support in 19X1
   b. A deferred credit in the balance sheet at the end of 19X0 and 19X1, and as support in 19X2
   c. Support in 19X1
   d. Support in 19X1, and no deferred credit in the balance sheet at the end of 19X0

   (AICPA adapted)
2. Why do voluntary health and welfare organizations, unlike some not-for-profit organizations, record depreciation of fixed assets?
   a. Fixed assets are more likely to be material in amount in a voluntary health and welfare organization than in other not-for-profit organizations
   b. Voluntary health and welfare organizations purchase their fixed assets, and therefore have a historical cost basis from which to determine amounts to be depreciated

c. A fixed asset used by a voluntary health and welfare organization has alternative uses in private industry and this opportunity cost should be reflected in the organization's financial statements

d. Contributors look for the most efficient use of funds; and since depreciation represents a cost of employing fixed assets, it is appropriate that a voluntary health and welfare organization reflect it as a cost of providing services

(AICPA)

3. Which of the following funds of a voluntary health and welfare organization does not have a counterpart fund in governmental accounting?
   a. Current Unrestricted
   b. Land, Building, and Equipment
   c. Custodian
   d. Endowment

(AICPA)

4. Which of the following financial statements is required for a voluntary health and welfare organization, but not for governmental units?
   a. Balance sheet
   b. Activity statement
   c. Statement of functional expenses
   d. Statement of changes in financial position

5. Endowment income that is restricted in use to finance the operations of a voluntary health and welfare organization should be recorded in
   a. The Current Unrestricted Fund
   b. A Current Restricted Fund
   c. An Endowment Fund
   d. An Annuity Fund

6. A mortgage on the land and buildings owned by a voluntary health and welfare organization should be reported in
   a. The Current Unrestricted Fund
   b. A Current Restricted Fund
   c. The Land, Building, and Equipment Fund
   d. A Loan Fund

7. Which of the following funds may have one or more items of public support or revenue?
   a. The Current Unrestricted Fund
   b. The Land, Building, and Equipment Fund
   c. An Endowment Fund
   d. All of the above could have one or more items of public support or revenue

8. The Prevent Cancer Organization incurred several expenses during 19X1. Which of the following would *not* be classified as program support?

a. Instruction for cancer prevention to the general public
b. Pamphlets mailed to the general public regarding the "danger signals of cancer"
c. Postage announcing the 19X1 Kickoff Dinner
d. Salaries of personnel who perform cancer research

9. Aviary Haven, a voluntary health and welfare organization funded by contributions from the general public, received unrestricted pledges of $500,000 during 19X1. It was estimated that 12 percent of these pledges would be uncollectible. By the end of 19X1, $400,000 of the pledges had been collected; and it was expected that $40,000 more would be collected in 19X2, with the balance of $60,000 to be written off as uncollectible. Donors did not specify any periods during which the donations were to be used. What amount should Aviary include under public support in 19X1 for net contributions?

a. $500,000
b. $452,000
c. $440,000
d. $400,000

(AICPA adapted)

10. The following expenditures were among those incurred by a non-profit botanical society during 19X1:

Printing of annual report	$10,000
Unsolicited merchandise sent to encourage contributions	20,000

What amount should be classified as fund-raising costs in the society's activity statement?

a. $0
b. $10,000
c. $20,000
d. $30,000

(AICPA adapted)

E14–4 (Description of financial reporting treatment of different items)

a. Explain the financial reporting of restricted current receipts for 78–10 organizations. Does this approach differ from that of voluntary health and welfare organizations?

b. Describe the method of reporting fund-raising expenses for 78–10 organizations. Why are these expenses reported in this manner?

E14–5 (Statement of revenues, expenses, and changes in cumulative excess of revenues over expenses for a country club)

The following information was taken from the records of the John O'Groats Country Club. All account balances are as of the end of the accounting year, June 30, 19X1.

Cash	$ 12,000
Dues	631,000
Locker room rentals to members	20,000
Expenses associated with the golf course	255,000
Expenses associated with the tennis courts	105,000
Initiation fees	78,000
Prepaid expenses	8,000
Administration expenses	65,000
Fees: Golf course	87,000
Swimming pool	44,000
Tennis courts	12,000
Expenses associated with the swimming pool	31,000
Land, buildings, and equipment	800,987
Investments	56,000
19X1 assessments against members for capital improvements	200,000
Balance in cumulative excess of revenue over expenses at 6/30/X0	
(after closing entries were posted)	97,000

REQUIRED: Prepare a statement of revenues, expenses, and changes in cumulative excess of revenues over expenses for the John O'Groats Country Club.

E14–6 (Financial statement reporting of plant-type assets of 78–10 organizations)

When discussing 78–10 organizations with several of your colleagues, you discovered that one friend feels that plant-type assets should be recorded in a separate fund while another feels that they should be reported as part of the Unrestricted Current Fund. Which position is correct? Why?

E14–7 (Journal entries for a not-for-profit organization)

The Society to Save Humankind from Its Ills, a voluntary health and welfare organization, was founded in 19X1. This organization conducts two types of programs: education and testing. During 19X1, the following events took place:

1. Pledges amounting to $200,000 were received. Of this amount, $50,000 was restricted for the use of a special research program. All of the restricted pledges and $140,000 of the unrestricted pledges is expected to be collected.

2. Les Miller made a $1,000 cash contribution, to be used as the directors of the society see fit. However, Mr. Miller stipulated that it not be used until 19X2.

3. The restricted pledges were all collected. With respect to the unrestricted pledges, $120,000 was collected and $5,000 was written off.

4. The society received a $10,000 allocation from the United Fund. Of this amount, $2,000 was deducted for fund-raising costs.
5. The society invested $10,000 of unrestricted funds in government securities. Earnings on these resources amounted to $500 in 19X1.
6. During the year, $40,000 of restricted funds is spent on research projects.
7. A grant of $500,000 was made to the society by the Allen Company. The grant was to be used to purchase equipment and for a down payment on a building. Cash donations of $10,000, for the purpose of debt service (paying interest and principal on the mortgage) were also received.
8. Equipment was purchased for $75,000, using resources donated by the Allen Company.
9. A down payment of $400,000 was made on a building costing $1,000,000. A 20-year mortgage was taken out for the remainder.
10. The following services were donated to the society, all of which should be recorded:
    a. Free accounting work by a local accounting firm—$500
    b. Free tests by a national testing laboratory—$1,000
    c. The services, at no cost, of several teachers from a local junior college. They conducted physical fitness and wellness programs—$2,000

    In addition, the accounting firm donated supplies worth $200.
11. Salaries, wages, and other operating expenses for 19X1 amounted to $135,000. They were paid with unrestricted monies and were allocated as follows:

Administration	$20,000
Education	90,000
Testing	15,000
Fund raising	10,000

12. Interest of $8,000 was paid on the mortgage during the year.
13. Depreciation amounted to $50,000 on the building and $10,000 on the equipment. It was allocated as follows:

	Building	Equipment
Administration	$ 10,000	—
Education	20,000	$3,000
Testing	20,000	7,000

14. Revenues from membership dues amounted to $18,000 in 19X1.

REQUIRED:
1. Prepare journal entries for the transactions listed above, by fund, including the appropriate closing entries.
2. Prepare those entries that would be different if the society had been an ONPO. Do not prepare closing entries.

PROBLEMS

P14–1   (Preparation of financial statements for a voluntary health and welfare organization)

You have recently been hired by the Society for the Elimination of Apathy. This organization does research into the causes of apathy. The accounting records were maintained according to GAAP during the year; however, due to a computer malfunction, the accounts have become jumbled. You should prepare in good form all the financial statements necessary for the society for 19X1.

Debits

Cash—unrestricted	$1,000,000
Investments of restricted funds	500,000
Management and general expenses—unrestricted	400,000
—depreciation	10,000
Investment of unrestricted funds	500,000
Land, buildings, and equipment at cost	4,000,000
Research expenses—unrestricted	3,000,000
—restricted	200,000
—depreciation	70,000
Community services expenses—unrestricted	800,000
—restricted	10,000
Fund-raising expenses—unrestricted	150,000
—restricted	1,000
Pledges receivable—unrestricted	400,000
Cash—land, building, and equipment	10,000
Cash—restricted	8,000
Investment—land, building, and equipment	500,000
Other receivables—unrestricted	5,000

Detailed expenses:

	Research	Community Services	Management	Fund Raising
Salaries and payroll taxes	$2,000,000	$500,000	$300,000	$30,000
Professional fees	535,000	100,000	60,000	20,000
Supplies	650,000	10,000	1,000	3,000
Postage	7,000	100,000	1,000	40,000
Printing	3,000	60,000	23,000	55,000
Miscellaneous	5,000	40,000	15,000	3,000
Depreciation	70,000	—	10,000	—

Credits

Mortgage payable—land, building, and equipment	$1,000,000
Fund balance—restricted—research grants	508,000
Accounts payable—unrestricted	300,000
Contributions—unrestricted	4,800,000
—restricted	200,000
—land, building, and equipment*	99,000
Research grants payable—unrestricted	1,000,000

* Report as 19X1 revenue.

Credits	
Fund balance—unrestricted—designated for new equipment (12/31/X1)	500,000
—undesignated (12/31/X1)	105,000
Investment income—undesignated	45,000
—restricted	49,000
—land, building, and equipment	48,000
Gain on sale of investments—unrestricted	5,000
Fund balance—land, building, and equipment—expended	1,500,000
unexpended—restricted	510,000
Accumulated depreciation	1,500,000
Miscellaneous revenue—undesignated	3,000
—restricted	2,000
—land, building, and equipment	1,000

Note: 1. Equipment costing $20,000 was acquired during the year by using unrestricted funds.

2. The beginning fund balances were:

Unrestricted	$ 122,000
Restricted	468,000
Land, building, and equipment	1,922,000

P14–2 (Journal entries for a voluntary health and welfare organization) Following are some of the transactions for the EI (Eye Institute) during 19X1.

1. Pledges were received as follows:

Unrestricted	$3,000,000
Restricted to research	1,000,000

2. During the year, 90 percent of all pledges were collected.
3. Amounts received from the United Fund totaled $1.5 million.
4. The EI paid $20,000 to the United Fund as its share of the fund-raising costs for 19X1.
5. Salaries for 19X1 totaled $500,000, and the related payroll costs were $100,000. The entire amount was paid in cash.
6. An additional parcel of land and a small building were acquired, using assets segregated for that purpose. The land was appraised for $75,000 and the building was appraised for $160,000. The institute paid $23,500 down and financed the remainder with a mortgage.
7. Depreciation for the year was $246,000.
8. The following general operating costs were paid:

Professional management fees	$ 75,000
Professional fees for research	500,000
Supplies	5,000
Printing	15,000
Utilities	100,000
Miscellaneous	15,000

9. Restricted resources were used as follows:

Research salaries	300,000
Payroll cost	30,000
Supplies	20,000
Postage	150,000

10. Unrestricted contributions received in 19X1, but designated for use in 19X2, totaled $35,000.

11. Equipment that cost $3,000 was acquired with unrestricted funds.

12. At the end of the year, management estimates that all the pledges outstanding in the Current Restricted and the Land, Building, and Equipment Funds will be collected; however, $10,000 of the pledges in the Current Unrestricted Fund will probably not be collected.

13. At the end of the year, supplies that cost $500 were still on hand (see number 8).

14. Interest paid on the mortgage on the land and building was $20,000.

15. The distribution of expenses into functional categories in the Current Unrestricted Fund was as follows:*

Fund raising	$ 12,000
Management and general	78,500
Research	850,000
Public service	359,000
	$1,299,500

16. The distribution of expenses into functional categories in the Current Restricted Fund was as follows:*

Research	$305,000
Public service	55,000
Fund raising	140,000
	$500,000

17. The distribution of depreciation and the interest on the mortgage was as follows:*

Management and general	$ 22,000
Fund raising	6,000
Research	215,000
Community service	23,000
	$266,000

*Assume journal entries are made for the distribution.

REQUIRED: Prepare the journal entries necessary to record the above data; also indicate the fund used for each entry.

P14–3   (Financial statements for a religious organization)
The following data were taken from the accounting records of the Sea
Isle Church Federation at December 31, 19X1:

Cash—operating*	$ 150,000
—loan	18,000
—plant	8,000
Land, building, and equipment—plant (at cost)	1,250,000
Fund balance—unrestricted (12/31/X1)—operating	309,000
Accounts payable—operating	75,000
—plant	40,000
Support and revenue—contributions	
—expendable, unrestricted	975,000
—plant	40,000
Support services—general and administrative	
—expendable, unrestricted	180,000
—plant	20,000
Support services—fund raising	
—expendable, unrestricted	5,000
—plant	2,000
Accounts receivable—operating	20,000
Allowance for uncollectible accounts—operating	4,000
Loans receivable—loan	400,000
Allowance for uncollectible loans—loan	10,000
Deferred contributions—plant	100,000
Restricted fund balance—loan (12/31/X1)	408,000
—plant (12/31/X1)	1,925,000
. —endowment (12/31/X1)	40,000
Support and revenue—fees for services	
—expendable, unrestricted	50,000
Support and revenue—investment income	
—plant	51,000
—endowment (not expendable)	5,000
Support and revenue—interest on loans—loan	40,000
Pledges receivable—operating	233,000
—plant	310,000
Allowance for uncollectible pledges—operating	15,000
—plant	3,000
Investments—plant	500,000
—endowment	40,000
Expenses—program services:	
Pastoral—expended, unrestricted	580,000
—plant	78,000
Education—expended, unrestricted	300,00
—plant	5,000
Cemeteries—expended, unrestricted	40,000
—plant	20,000

* All operating accounts are unrestricted.

REQUIRED: 1.   Prepare a balance sheet for the Sea Isle Church Federation as of December 31, 19X1.

   2.   Prepare a statement of support, revenue, expenses, and changes in
fund balance for the year ended December 31, 19X1.

P14–4   (Revenue recognition)
The following information relates to a hypothetical 78–10 organization

Total cash collected during the year for dues	$ 240,000
Dues owed by members as of 12/31/X0	10,000
Dues owed by members as of 12/31/X1	12,000
Collections during 19X1 that represented advance payments on 19X2 dues	6,000
Collections from members that were restricted for capital additions	154,0090
19X1 receipts restricted to use in the Public Awareness Program	141,000
Amount spent in 19X1 on the Public Awareness Program	97,000
Gain on sale of investment securities held in an unrestricted fund	14,000
Investment income earned on unrestricted investments	51,000
Income earned on investment of restricted investments (the income from the investments is subject to the same restrictions as the principal)	6,000
Unrestricted pledges made by individuals during the current year	340,000
Expected uncollectible, unrestricted pledges	20,000
Pledges made by individuals in response to a Plant Expansion Program	500,000
Expected uncollectible pledges related to the Plant Expansion Program	25,000
Value of services donated by professionals for continuing programs (the value of these services is based on similar services rendered by these professionals in their private practice)	424,000
Value of clothes donated by members of the community and distributed to hurricane victims in southwestern Louisiana (the value of these items was estimated by the project manager)	65,000
Rooms currently used by the organization are donated by a wealthy member who owns the building in which the organization is located (similar space in the building rents for $10,000 per year)	10,000

REQUIRED: Determine the amount of support or revenue that would be reported by the 78–10 organization during 19X1. In addition, label the income as to type and state whether it is restricted or unrestricted.

P14–5   (Problem from Uniform Certified Public Accountant Examination comparing treatment of certain transactions by governmental units and voluntary health and welfare organizations)
Listed below are four independent transactions or events that relate to a local government and to a voluntary health and welfare organization:
1. $25,000 was disbursed from the General Fund (or its equivalent) for the cash purchase of new equipment.
2.   An unrestricted cash gift of $100,000 was received from a donor.
3.   Listed common stocks with a total carrying value of $50,000, exclusive of any allowance, were sold by an Endowment Fund for $55,000, before any dividends were earned on these stocks. There are no restrictions on the gain.
4. $1,000,000 face amount of general obligation bonds payable were sold at par, with the proceeds required to be used solely for construction of a new building. This building was completed at a total cost of $1,000,000, and the total amount of bond issue proceeds was disbursed in connection therewith. Disregard interest capitalization.

REQUIRED: a. For each of the above-listed transactions or events, prepare journal entries, without explanations, specifying the affected funds and account groups, and showing how these transactions or events should be recorded by a local government whose debt is serviced by general tax revenues.

b. For each of the above-listed transactions or events, prepare journal entries, without explanations, specifying the affected funds, and showing how these transactions or events should be recorded by a voluntary health and welfare organization that maintains a separate plant fund.

(AICPA)

P14–6   (Preparation of financial statements for a voluntary health and welfare organization)

Following are the adjusted Current Funds trial balances of the Community Association for Handicapped Children, a voluntary health and welfare organization, at June 20, 19X1.

Community Association for Handicapped Children
Adjusted Current Funds Trial Balances
June 30, 19X1

	UNRESTRICTED		RESTRICTED	
	Dr.	Cr.	Dr.	Cr.
Cash	$ 40,000		$ 9,000	
Bequest receivable			5,000	
Pledges receivable	12,000			
Accrued interest receivable	1,000			
Investments (at cost, which				
approximates market)	100,000			
Accounts payable and accrued expenses		$ 50,000		$ 1,000
Deferred revenue		2,000		
Allowance for uncollectible pledges		3,000		
Fund balances, July 1, 19X0:				
Designated		12,000		
Undesignated		26,000		
Restricted				3,000
Transfers of endowment fund income		20,000		
Contributions		300,000		15,000
Membership dues		25,000		
Program service fees		30,000		
Investment income		10,000		
Deaf children's program	120,000			
Blind children's program	150,000			
Management and general services	45,000		4,000	
Fund-raising services	8,000		1,000	
Provision for uncollectible pledges	2,000			
	$478,000	$478,000	$19,000	$19,000

REQUIRED: a. Prepare a statement of support, revenue, and expenses and changes in fund balances, separately presenting each current fund, for the year ended June 30, 19X1.

b. Prepare a balance sheet, separately presenting each current fund as of June 30, 19X1.

(AICPA adapted)

INDEX